A COMPANION TO YOUR STUDY OF THE DOCTRINE AND COVENANTS

VOL. 1

Daniel H. Ludlow

Deseret Book Company
Salt Lake City, Utah
1978

© 1978 by Daniel H. Ludlow
All rights reserved
Printed in the United States of America
ISBN 0-87747-722-1
Library of Congress Catalog Card No. 78-64752

CONTENTS

CONTENTS OF VOLUME 2

PREFACE

A Companion to Your Study of the Doctrine and Covenants is designed to be of maximum use to the reader and student of the Doctrine and Covenants. It is arranged to provide helpful background and supplementary information on the sacred scripture as it is read page by page and section by section.

Part I provides information on the purpose and coming forth of the Doctrine and Covenants. A few of the subjects discussed are: the principles of revelation; the importance of this method of communication of God with his prophets; the relationship of prophecy to scripture; a definition of scripture—spoken, written, and canonized; why, how, when, and where the revelations recorded in the Doctrine and Covenants were received; the procedures followed in publishing *A Book of Commandments* and the 1835 edition of the Doctrine and Covenants. Several topics concerned with the historical background of the Doctrine and Covenants are also discussed in this first part.

Part II provides basic and essential information on each of the sections in the Doctrine and Covenants. The following order is used in providing this information:

1. *Background information* for each section. The superscription of each section in the Doctrine and Covenants includes some historical background on that section, but the information is often scanty and the reader is frequently referred to the appropriate material in *History of the Church.* This *Companion* provides additional historical background and generally includes essential reference materials from *History of the Church* and other sources.

2. *Definitions, explanations, and resource materials* pertaining to some of the more difficult verses and passages in each section. Illustrative materials are usually provided from the writings and sermons of General Authorities, who, in the opinion of the author, receive at the time of their setting apart a special gift to interpret and teach the scriptures.

The Appendixes will save the student of the Doctrine and

Covenants hundreds of hours of research in finding resource materials related to the Doctrine and Covenants. Appendix A includes definitions, explanations, selected quotations, and selected scriptural references on over 200 key words and terms that are used frequently throughout the Doctrine and Covenants. These key words and terms are listed alphabetically for ease in quick reference. Appendix B contains a list of all the persons who are referred to in the Doctrine and Covenants or for whom a section in the Doctrine and Covenants is given. Biographical information is also given on 50 persons, particularly those mentioned several times in the revelations.

This *Companion* does not include verbatim the text from the Doctrine and Covenants. The reader will probably want to read a particular section in the Doctrine and Covenants first; then he may wish to refer to this *Companion* for additional helps pertaining to the contents of that particular section. In the discussions of the verses of that section, references may also be included to additional information in the Appendixes concerning key words, key terms, or individuals. If this book is properly used in this manner, it should truly be a companion to your study of the Doctrine and Covenants.

ACKNOWLEDGMENTS

Two firm convictions helped the author determine the format and decide on the contents of this volume.

1. The Doctrine and Covenants is a divinely inspired scripture and thus is one of the most important books ever to be published; it represents teachings directly from God through his prophets to the people of this generation.

2. The General Authorities, at the time of their setting apart, receive a special gift of discernment that helps them understand and teach the scriptures; also, members of the First Presidency, the Council of the Twelve, and the Patriarch to the Church are prophets, seers, and revelators with a special responsibility to interpret and teach the principles of the gospel.

When the author was first asked to prepare this volume, his original intent was to write most of the material himself and to include only a few brief selected quotations from the General Authorities to supplement, reinforce, and strengthen his own explanations and commentaries. However, it soon became apparent that the General Authorities throughout the decades have thoroughly covered most of the topics he intended to cover. In addition, the special gift of discernment enjoyed by them was evident in the quality and thoroughness of the choice quotations. Some of these resource materials were difficult to find, however, as they were scattered throughout scores of volumes and publications and were often interspersed with other materials not directly related to the Doctrine and Covenants.

The challenge then became to select, compile, and arrange the numerous resource materials so they would be readily available and to organize them so they would be of most use to the student and teacher of the Doctrine and Covenants.

To help accomplish these purposes, the author read thousands of pages of material from the sermons and writings of the General Authorities in such publications as *Conference Reports,* Church magazines, *Journal of Discourses,* compilations of statements by the presidents and other leaders of the Church, and their personal books. Materials from these voluminous sources that were related to the Doctrine and Covenants and its teachings were then carefully selected and organized. More than 3,000 pages of these selections were then abridged and trimmed, maintaining the original words and meanings of the author to form these volumes.

Of necessity, this research has criss-crossed the paths of those who have published earlier materials on the Doctrine and Covenants. Because of the thorough research of these earlier writers and compilers, it was not unusual to find the same choice statement from a General Authority in several compilations and publications. This not only helped confirm the author's feeling on the significance of the statement, but verified the importance of the utterances of authorized servants who have spoken by the power or under the direction of the Holy Ghost.

Special appreciation is expressed for the following publications: *Church History and Modern Revelation,* by Joseph Fielding Smith; *Doctrine and Covenants Commentary,* by Hyrum M. Smith and Janne M. Sjodahl; *Latter-day Prophets and the Doctrine and Covenants,* by Roy W. Doxey; *Doctrine and Covenants: Institute of Religion Self-Instruction Program,* published by the Church Educational System.

Appreciation is gratefully extended to—

My wife, Luene, and our three daughters who are still at home—Kathy, Shauna, and Michelle—for their invaluable help, support, and understanding. Particular thanks to Kathy for her hundreds of hours of around-the-clock typing during the last two months of preparation of the manuscript.

Gary Gillespie for being such a perceptive and supporting associate for several years, and for his editorial skills and thoughtful, helpful comments in regard to this manuscript.

Eleanor Knowles for editorial assistance and for her astute insights and many hours of work.

Lowell M. Durham, Jr., for his stablizing influence and good common sense.

Wm. James Mortimer for his encouragement, mature judgment, refreshing good humor, and close friendship.

KEY TO ABBREVIATIONS

AF	*Articles of Faith*, James E. Talmage
AGQ	*Answers to Gospel Questions*, Joseph Fielding Smith
APPP	*Autobiography of Parley P. Pratt*
ASIF	*Address to Seminary and Institute Faculty*
BE	*Biographical Encyclopedia*, Andrew Jenson
BYUSY	*Brigham Young University Speeches of the Year*
CBM	*A Companion to Your Study of the Book of Mormon*, Daniel H. Ludlow
CHC	*A Comprehensive History of the Church*, B. H. Roberts
CHMR	*Church History and Modern Revelation*, Joseph Fielding Smith
CR	*Conference Report*
CN	*Church News*
DBY	*Discourses of Brigham Young*
DCC	*Doctrine and Covenants Commentary*, Hyrum M. Smith and Janne M. Sjodahl
DS	*Doctrines of Salvation*, Joseph Fielding Smith
ECH	*Essentials in Church History*, Joseph Fielding Smith
ER	*Evidences and Reconciliations*, John A. Widtsoe
FPM	*Faith Precedes the Miracle*, Spencer W. Kimball
GD	*Gospel Doctrine*, Joseph F. Smith
GI	*Gospel Interpretations*, John A. Widtsoe
GK	*Gospel Kingdom*, John Taylor
HC	*History of the Church*, Joseph Smith

IE	*Improvement Era*
JC	*Jesus the Christ,* James E. Talmage
JD	*Journal of Discourses*
JI	*Juvenile Instructor*
JS	*Joseph Smith,* John A. Widtsoe
KT	*Key to the Science of Theology,* Parley P. Pratt
LDPS	*Latter-day Prophets Speak,* Daniel H. Ludlow
LHCK	*Life of Heber C. Kimball,* Orson F. Whitney
LJS	*Life of Joseph Smith the Prophet,* George Q. Cannon
MA	*Mediation and Atonement,* John Taylor
MD	*Mormon Doctrine,* 1966 ed., Bruce R. McConkie
MDC	*The Message of the Doctrine and Covenants,* John A. Widtsoe
MDOP	*Masterful Discourses of Orson Pratt*
MF	*The Miracle of Forgiveness,* Spencer W. Kimball
MS	*Millennial Star*
MWW	*A Marvelous Work and a Wonder,* LeGrand Richards
NE	*New Era*
PC	*Program of The Church of Jesus Christ of Latter-day Saints*
SMJB	*Sermons and Missionary Services of Melvin J. Ballard,* Bryant S. Hinckley
SNT	*Saturday Night Thoughts,* Orson F. Whitney
TPJS	*Teachings of the Prophet Joseph Smith,* compiled by Joseph Fielding Smith
VM	*The Vitality of Mormonism,* James E. Talmage
WP	*The Way to Perfection,* Joseph Fielding Smith
YFY	*Your Faith and You,* Mark E. Petersen

PART I
INTRODUCTION
TO THE DOCTRINE
AND COVENANTS

THE PRINCIPLE OF REVELATION

First and foremost, the Doctrine and Covenants is a book of revelations. Primarily its sections consist of revelations from God to his prophet upon the earth, and because it was first assembled and published during the lifetime of Joseph Smith, most of the revelations therein are revelations from God to him.

Latter-day Saints believe in and are deeply committed to the principle of revelation. One of our Articles of Faith indicates, "We believe in the gift of tongues, prophecy, revelation" (A of F 1:7), while another one states, "We believe all that God has revealed, all that He does now reveal, and we believe that He will yet reveal many great and important things pertaining to the Kingdom of God" (A of F 1:9).

Our living prophet has declared: "Of all things, that for which we should be most grateful today is that the heavens are indeed open and that the restored church of Jesus Christ is founded upon the rock of revelation. Continuous revelation is indeed the very lifeblood of the gospel of the living Lord and Savior, Jesus Christ." (Spencer W. Kimball, *Ensign,* May 1977, p. 76.)

Revelation is one of the gifts of the Holy Ghost and is available to every worthy member of the Church. Each righteous person is entitled to revelation in his or her own personal life and in any responsibilities he or she may have. The Prophet Joseph Smith said: "It is also the privilege of any officer in this Church to obtain revelations, so far as relates to his particular calling and duty in the Church." (*HC* 2:477.) He also declared: "No man can receive the Holy Ghost without receiving revelations. The Holy Ghost is a revelator." (*TPJS,* p. 328.)

Accordingly, those who are saints indeed, those who have been born again, those who are so living as to be in tune with the Spirit—they are they who receive revelation, personal revelation, revelation which is the mind and will of God to them as individuals. They know there are apostles and prophets directing the kingdom who receive revelation for the Church and the world. But they as individuals receive personal revelation in their own affairs.

And there are no restrictions placed upon them; there are no limitations as to what they may see and know and comprehend. No eternal truths will be withheld, if they obey the laws entitling them to receive such truths.

Joseph Smith and the prophets had revelation. They saw God, viewed the visions of eternity, entertained angels, came upon Mount Zion, stood in heavenly places, and had communion with the general assembly and Church of the Firstborn.

Of these very experiences Joseph Smith said: ". . . God hath not revealed anything to Joseph, but what He will make known unto the Twelve, and even the least Saint may know all things as fast as he is able to bear them." (*TPJS*, p. 149.)

. . . Revelations are not reserved for a limited few or for those called to positions of importance in the Church. It is not position in the Church that confers spiritual gifts. It is not being a bishop, a stake president, or an apostle that makes revelation and salvation available. These are high and holy callings which open the door to the privilege of great service among men. But it is not a call to a special office that opens the windows of revelation to a truth seeker. Rather it is personal righteousness; it is keeping the commandments; it is seeking the Lord while he may be found.

God is no respecter of persons. He will give revelation to me and to you on the same terms and conditions. I can see what Joseph Smith and Sidney Rigdon saw in the vision of the degrees of glory—and so can you. I can entertain angels and see God, I can receive an outpouring of the gifts of the Spirit—and so can you.

There are goals to gain, summits to climb, revelations to receive. In the eternal scope of things we have scarcely started out on the course to glory and exaltation. The Lord wants his saints to receive line upon line, precept upon precept, truth upon truth, revelation upon revelation, until we know all things and have become like him. (Bruce R. McConkie, *IE*, December 1969, p. 85.)

God is a God of order. He recognizes the right of each person to receive revelation directly from him and from and through those in authority over that person. However, as far as revelation for the Church is concerned, the channel of communication is from the top down.

In statements of our prophets we find the following:

I will inform you that it is contrary to the economy of God for any member of the Church, or any one, to receive instruction for those in authority, higher than themselves; therefore you will see the impropriety of giving heed to them; but if any person have a vision or a visitation from a heavenly messenger, it must be for his own benefit and instruction; for the fundamental principles, government, and doctrine of the Church are vested in the keys of the kingdom. (Joseph Smith, *TPJS,* p. 21.)

God gave revelations unto this Church in exceeding great plainness, and there was one principle that was emphatically dwelt on and enforced, namely, that there was but one channel, one channel alone, through which the word of God and the commandments of God should come to this people. The word of God was not to come from the people up. It was not *vox populi, vox dei,* but it was to be *vox dei, vox populi*—that is, the voice of God and then the voice of the people—from God downward through the channel that he should appoint, by the means that he should institute. (George Q. Cannon, *JD* 24:362-63.)

When visions, dreams, tongues, prophecy, impressions or any extraordinary gift of inspiration, convey something out of harmony with accepted revelations of the Church or contrary to the decisions of its constituted authorities, Latter-day Saints may know that it is not of God, no matter how plausible it may appear. Also, they should understand that directions for the guidance of the Church will come, by revelation, through the head. All faithful members are entitled to the inspiration of the Holy Spirit for themselves, their families, and for those over whom they are appointed and ordained to preside. But anything at discord with that which comes from God through the head of the Church is not to be received as authoritative or reliable. (First Presidency, *IE,* Sept. 1913, p. 1148.)

The president of the Church stands in the Church as Moses did to the children of Israel, according to the revelations. (John Taylor, *TS* 6:22.)

Only the Prophet and President of the Church can receive revelation for the Church. Thus, every faithful Latter-day Saint should be anxious to hear and follow the inspired teachings of the living prophet so he can receive blessings in his own life and better discharge his responsibilities to his family and any responsibilities he might have in the Church. The Savior taught that we should live "by every word that proceedeth out of the mouth of God." (Matt. 4:4.) Modern-day prophets have declared:

The first thing necessary to the establishment of His [the Lord's] kingdom . . . is to raise up a prophet and have him declare the will of God; the next is to have people yield obedience to the word of the Lord through that prophet. . . .

How does faith required as the first principle in the plan of salvation or the gospel come? Let Paul answer: "So then faith cometh by hearing, and hearing by the word of God." (Rom. 10:17.) It is not the letter then that bringeth faith, but hearing the word of God dispensed by a living oracle or minister of God, clothed upon with power from on high. *It is not a recorded gospel, but a preached word which emanates with power from a man of God inspired by the Holy Ghost.* (John Taylor, *GK*, pp. 214, 332.)

Faith comes by hearing the word of God, through the testimony of the servants of God; that testimony is always attended by the Spirit of prophecy and revelation. (Joseph Smith, *HC* 3:379.)

If we talk about the living oracles and want to pay respect to them, how shall we do this? Shall we do it by never reading their words—by paying no attention to that which they say? That is a very poor way of doing. We ought to listen to their words. When we cannot hear their words, we should read them; for they are the words of the authorized servants of God. I feel that there is a great neglect among us in this respect. (George Q. Cannon, *CR,* 1897, p. 38.)

A Latter-day Saint who truly believes in the principle of continuous revelation and recognizes that the inspired words of the living prophet are the mind and will of God will want to do everything he can to learn and to live the teachings of the living prophet. President J. Reuben Clark, Jr., stated: "We do not lack a prophet; what we lack is a listening ear by the people and a determination to live as God has commanded. That is all we need. The way has been made perfectly clear." (*CR,* October 1948, p. 80.) And President Marion G. Romney declared: " 'He that receiveth my servants receiveth me.' Who are his servants? They are his representatives in the offices of the Priesthood—the General, Stake, Priesthood Quorum, and Ward officers. It behooves us to keep this in mind when we are tempted to disregard our presiding authorities, bishops, quorum and stake presidents, etc., when, within the jurisdiction of their callings, they give us counsel and advice." (*CR,* October 1960, p. 73.)

WHAT IS
SCRIPTURE?

The basic dictionary definition of scripture is "the sacred writings of a religion" or "a body of writings considered as authoritative." The definition listed first in the dictionary is "the books of the Old and New Testaments or either of them, the Bible." In this sense, a scripture might also be "a passage from the Bible." Thus, according to the standard dictionary definitions, scriptures must be written.

However, in a revelation in this dispensation, the Lord indicated that when he has authorized servants on the earth, scripture might also be spoken, and would not necessarily be written. Speaking of those who have been ordained "to proclaim the everlasting gospel, by the Spirit of the living God, from people to people, and from land to land . . . whose mission is appointed unto them to go forth" (in other words, in today's terminology, "speaking of the General Authorities"), the Lord has said: "And whatsoever they shall speak when moved upon by the Holy Ghost shall be scripture, shall be the will of the Lord, shall be the mind of the Lord, shall be the word of the Lord, shall be the voice of the Lord, and the power of God unto salvation." (D&C 68:4.)

In this more general sense, scripture today includes that which is stated or written by the General Authorities and also includes the approved *standard works* or officially recognized (canonized) scriptures.

What is the place, then, of spoken or written scripture in the Church that has never been canonized and is not part of the standard works? This is what our prophets, seers, and revelators have told us:

We believe that God is as willing today as He ever has been to reveal His mind and will to man, and that He does so through His appointed servants—prophets, seers, and revelators—invested through ordination with the authority of the Holy Priesthood. We rely therefore on the teachings of the living oracles of God as of equal validity with the doctrines of the written word. (James E. Talmage, *AF*, p. 7.)

We of the Latter-day Saints have our own Scriptures. We have the Scriptures which other Christian sects use, namely, the Bible, including the Old and New Testaments, but we also have the Book of Mormon, the Doctrine and Covenants, the Pearl of Great Price, and the Living Oracles of the Church. (J. Reuben Clark, Jr., *CN,* Dec. 17, 1960, p. 14.)

So we invite all men everywhere to be willing to listen to the living prophets that God has raised up in this dispensation so that they can be taught correct principles and not be tossed to and fro with every wind of doctrine. (LeGrand Richards, *CR,* April 1965, p. 120.)

The older I get and the closer the contact I have with the President of the Church, the more I realize that the greatest of all scriptures which we have in the world today is current scripture. What the mouthpiece of God says to His children is scripture. It is intended for all the children of God upon the earth. It is His word and His will and His law made manifest through scripture, and I love it more than all other. It applies to me today specifically, and to you all. (Henry D. Moyle, BYU Fireside, January 1963, pp.7-8.)

The very moment that we set aside the living oracles we set aside the revelations of God. Why? Because the revelations of God command us plainly that we shall hearken to the living oracles. Hence, if we undertake to follow the written word, and at the same time do not give heed to the living oracles of God, the written word will condemn us. (Orson Pratt, *JD* 7:373.)

The prophets Joseph Smith and Brigham Young also emphasized the importance of receiving living (current) scripture from the living prophet, as indicated in the following statement by Wilford Woodruff:

I will refer to a certain meeting I attended in the town of Kirtland in my early days. . . . some remarks were made . . . with regard to the living oracles and with regard to the written word of God. . . . a leading man in the church . . . talked upon the subject, and said: "You have got the word of God before you here in the Bible, Book of Mormon, and Doctrine and Covenants; you have the written word of God, and you who give revelations should give revelations according to those books, as what is written in those books is the word of God. We should confine ourselves to them."

When he concluded, Brother Joseph turned to Brother Brigham Young and said, "Brother Brigham, I want you to take the stand and tell us your views with regard to the living oracles and the written word of God." Brother Brigham took the stand, and he took the Bible, and laid it down; he took the Book of Mormon, and laid it down; and he took the Book of Doctrine and Covenants, and laid it down before him, and he said: "There is the written word of God to us, concerning the work of God from the beginning of the world, almost, to our day." "And now," said he, "when compared with the living oracles those books are nothing to me; those books do not convey the word of God direct to us now, as do the words of a Prophet or a man bearing the Holy Priesthood in our day and generation. *I would rather have the living oracles than all the writing in the books.*" That was the course he pursued. When he was through, Brother Joseph said to the congregation, "*Brother Brigham has told you the word of the Lord, and he has told you the truth.*"

. . . The Bible is all right, the Book of Mormon is all right, the Doctrine and Covenants is all right, and they proclaim the work of God and the word of God in the earth in this day and generation until the coming of the Son of Man; but the Holy Priesthood is not confined particularly to those books, that is, it did not cease when those books were made. (Wilford Woodruff, *CR,* October 1897, pp. 22-23.)

The statement of the Lord concerning scripture indicates that the words of the General Authorities must be spoken as "moved upon by the Holy Ghost" before those words can be considered scripture. The question naturally arises, how can a member of the Church know when a General Authority is speaking by the power of the Holy Ghost? Presidents J. Reuben Clark, Jr., and Harold B. Lee have provided the following answers.

I have given some thought to this question, and the answer thereto so far as I can determine, is: We can tell when the speakers are "moved upon by the Holy Ghost," only when we, ourselves, are "moved upon by the Holy Ghost." In a way, this completely shifts the responsibility from them to us to determine when they so speak. (J. Reuben Clark, Jr., *CN,* July 31, 1954, p. 9.)

We can know, or have the assurance that they are speaking under inspiration if we so live that we can have a witness that what they are speaking is the word of the Lord. There is only one safety, and that is that we shall live to have the witness to know. (Harold B. Lee, *ASIF,* July 8, 1964, p. 14.)

The importance of spoken or noncanonized written scripture cannot be overemphasized, because it is the source of all canonized scripture. The usual pattern for the development of canonized scripture is that it is first given by the Lord to his living prophet, who teaches it to the people; then the prophet either writes the teachings himself or has another write for him so the people can refer back to the exact words. The written words are then presented to the members of the Church, usually in a general conference, for their vote as to whether or not they are willing to accept the statement as part of the official scripture. Once the scripture is voted upon and accepted, it is said to be *canonized* and becomes part of the official written scripture or standard works.

Thus it is readily evident that when people refuse to accept the words of the living prophet, they in effect cut themselves off from the opportunity of receiving additional canonized scripture.

The procedure for canonizing scripture was illustrated in the April 1976 annual conference of the Church when two revelations were presented to and accepted by the membership of the Church. President N. Eldon Tanner made the following statement:

President Kimball has asked me to read a very important resolution for your sustaining vote. At a meeting of the Council of the First Presidency and Quorum of the Twelve held in the Salt Lake Temple on March 25, 1976, approval was given to add to the Pearl of Great Price the following two revelations:

First, a vision of the celestial kingdom given to Joseph Smith, the Prophet, in the Kirtland Temple, on January 21, 1836, which deals with the salvation of those who die without a knowledge of the gospel.

And second, a vision given to President Joseph F. Smith in Salt Lake City, Utah, on October 3, 1918, showing the visit of the Lord Jesus Christ in the spirit world and setting forth the doctrine of the redemption of the dead.

It is proposed that we sustain and approve this action and adopt these revelations as part of the standard works of The Church of Jesus Christ of Latter-day Saints. All in favor please manifest it. Contrary, if there be any, by the same sign. Thank you. President Kimball, the voting seems to be unanimous in the affirmative.

These revelations are now part of the official written scripture of the Church and are published as part of the Pearl of Great Price.

In answer to the question "What is scripture?" it might be said that canonized scripture is written scripture that has been formally voted upon and received by the members of the Church. Such canonized scripture becomes the *standard* by which the other teachings of the Church can be tested; hence, the books containing canonized scripture are known as the *standard works.*

In addition, the talks and writings of General Authorities when they "are moved upon by the Holy Ghost" are also scripture, and faithful members of the Church pay as much attention to these scriptures as to the standard works.

The official magazines of the Church contain many of the talks and writings of the General Authorities, and presently the *Ensign* contains copies of all the talks given at the annual and semiannual general conferences. These talks, of course, should be carefully studied.

Does canonized scripture come only to the prophet and president of the Church?

Yes. No one except the prophet and president is authorized to receive scripture for the entire church, as is explained in these statements:

The Presidents or Presidency are over the Church; and revelations of the mind and will of God to the Church, are to come through the Presidency. This is the order of heaven, and the power and privilege of this Priesthood. (Joseph Smith, *TPJS*, p. 111.)

Here we must have in mind—must know—that only the President of the Church, the presiding High Priest, is sustained as Prophet, Seer, and Revelator for the church, and he alone has the right to receive revelations for the church, either new or amendatory, or to give authoritative interpretations of scriptures that shall be binding on the Church, or change in any way the existing doctrines of the church. He is God's sole mouthpiece on earth for The Church of Jesus Christ of Latter-day Saints, the only true Church. He alone may declare the mind and will of God to his people. No officer of any other church in the world has this high right and lofty prerogative. (J. Reuben Clark, Jr., *CN*, July 31, 1954, p. 10.)

Revelations given of God through his prophets, however, are not subject to an approving or sustaining vote of the people in order to establish their validity. Members of the Church may vote to publish a particular revelation along with the other scriptures, or the people may bind themselves by covenant to follow the instructions found in the revealed word. But there is no provision in the Lord's plan for the members of the Church to pass upon the validity of revelations themselves by a vote of the Church. . . . Revelation is revelation. When the Lord speaks, he has spoken. His word is to be accepted and obeyed if men expect to receive salvation. To reject the word of the Lord is to reject the Lord himself to that extent. (Bruce R. McConkie, *MD*, p. 150.)

Are scriptures intended for the whole world or only for members of the Church?

Every person who has ever lived on this earth, who is now living on this earth, or who will yet live on this earth is either a son or daughter of God, our Heavenly Father. He is interested in the welfare of each of his children and wants to teach each one what he should know and do in order to be happy and to have joy. He has revealed his teachings to his prophets, and they are part of his scriptures. The scriptures are intended for the whole world.

Because we are all sons and daughters of God, who is our loving Father in heaven, and he is vitally concerned with our welfare, all of us should be anxious and eager to read the scriptures and then to apply the principles of the scriptures to our lives.

The adversary of God and of all righteousness—whose names and titles include Lucifer, Satan, and the devil—does not want us to read the scriptures. Therefore, either the adversary himself or one of his emissaries tries to convince us the scriptures are not important ("they are ancient history"; "they were written only for another people of another time"; "they do not apply to you today") or that we do not have time to read, study, and ponder the scriptures. In the case of the Doctrine and Covenants, the adversary would like to convince members of the Church that this volume of scripture is only for earlier members and to assure nonmembers that the teachings are false and do not pertain to them.

Unfortunately, some members have fallen into the belief that the Doctrine and Covenants is intended only for them. This belief might result because of several reasons, including the fact that only a few scriptures from the Doctrine and Covenants are included in the standard missionary discussions. It has also been noted that the opening words of the first verse in section 1 are "Hearken, O ye people of my church." Before that first verse is completed, however, the Lord addresses himself to the "people from afar" and those upon "the islands of the sea," which could, and probably does, include those who are nonmembers. The statement of the Lord in verse two definitely includes nonmembers: "For verily the voice of the Lord is unto all men, and there is none to escape." (D&C 1:2.)

The prophets of the Lord in this dispensation have also declared that the Doctrine and Covenants is intended for the entire world. President Joseph Fielding Smith has written:

It seems a strange thing that many good brethren in the Church seem to think that the Lord never intended that the Book of

Mormon, and more especially the Doctrine and Covenants, should go forth to the world. We hear the expression from time to time, that these, and especially the revelations in the Doctrine and Covenants are intended solely for members of the church, but the Lord in his instructions has counseled otherwise. They were intended to be a warning to all the world. [D&C 1:4-7.] (Joseph Fielding Smith, *CHMR* 2:41-42.)

The Lord has given so many revelations, in our own day. We have this Doctrine and Covenants full of them, all pertaining unto the Latter-day Saints and to the world. For this is not our book alone. This Doctrine and Covenants is my book and your book; but more than that, it belongs to all the world, to the Catholics, to the Presbyterians, to the Methodists, to the infidel, to the non-believer. It is his book if he will accept it, if he will receive it. The Lord has given it unto the world for their salvation. If you do not believe it, you read the first section in this book, the preface, and you will find that the Lord has sent this book and the things which it contains unto the people afar off, on the islands of the sea, in foreign lands, and his voice is unto all people, that all may hear. And so I say it belongs to all the world, not only to the Latter-day Saints, and they will be judged by it, and you will be judged by it. We will all be judged by it, by the things which this book contains and by the things which the other books contain which are holy scripture, which the Lord has given unto us; and if we fail to comprehend these things, if we will not search, if we will not study, if we will not take hold on the things which the Lord has revealed unto us, then his condemnation shall rest upon us, and we shall be removed from his presence and from his kingdom. And I say that in all soberness, because it is true. (Joseph Fielding Smith, *CR*, October 1919, p. 146.)

Why is the reading of scripture so important?

Inasmuch as scripture is the mind and will of God to man, every person should be vitally interested in searching the scriptures and studying them diligently. The Savior and his ancient and modern prophets have all emphasized the importance of studying the scriptures and of living according to the teachings contained therein.

In the New Testament the Savior counseled, "Search the scriptures; for in them ye think ye have eternal life: and they are they which testify of me." (John 5:39.)

And to the peoples of the Book of Mormon he commanded, "Search these things diligently." (3 Ne. 23:1.)

The importance of reading, pondering, and living the

truths of the scriptures has been emphasized by all the prophets, ancient and modern. President Spencer W. Kimball has indicated that "no father, no son, no mother, no daughter should get so busy that he or she does not have time to study the scriptures." (*Ensign,* May 1976, p. 47.) In a special First Presidency message prepared for the September 1976 *Ensign,* President Kimball counseled:

Brethren and sisters, my purpose in preparing this message is to encourage you to study the scriptures. As the Lord has said, "Search the scriptures; for . . . they are they which testify of me." (John 5:39.)

Perhaps you will have noticed that for many years the General Authorities have urged us all with increasing frequency and in a spirit of love to adopt a program of daily gospel study in our homes, both as individuals and as families. Also, the standard works have replaced all other materials as texts in the adult curriculum of the church, and scarcely a meeting comes to a close without an inspired admonition from priesthood leaders to read and study the scriptures. . . .

Nevertheless, we are saddened to learn, as we travel about the stakes and missions of the Church, that there are still many of the Saints who are not reading and pondering the scriptures regularly, and who have little knowledge of the Lord's instructions to the children of men. . . .

Besides the almost constant encouragement and prompting which we receive from our present-day Church leaders, the prophets of old seem to cry out to us in almost every page of the scriptures, urging us to study the word of the Lord, the holy scriptures, "which are able to make thee wise unto salvation through faith which is in Christ Jesus." (2 Tim. 3:15.) But we do not always hear, and we might well ask ourselves why.

Sometimes it seems we take the scriptures too much for granted because we do not fully appreciate how rare a thing it is to possess them, and how blessed we are because we do have them. . . .

Lest the foregoing be lightly passed over, let me pause here to point out a common error in the mind of man—that is, the tendency, when someone speaks of faithfulness or success in one thing or another, to think "me," and when someone mentions failure or neglect, to think "them." But I ask us all to honestly evaluate our performance in scripture study. It is a common thing to have a few passages of scripture at our disposal, floating in our minds, as it were, and thus to have the illusion that we know a great deal about the gospel. In this sense, having a little knowledge can be a problem indeed. I am convinced that each of us, at some time in our lives, must discover the scriptures for ourselves—and not just discover them once, but rediscover them again and again.

Other prophets have also counseled us to study the scriptures, individually and as families:

The Old and New Testaments, the Book of Mormon, and the book of Doctrine and Covenants . . . are like a lighthouse in the ocean or a finger-post which points out the road we should travel. Where do they point? To the fountain of light. . . . That is what these books are for. They are of God; they are valuable and necessary: by them we can establish the doctrine of Christ. (Brigham Young, *JD* 8:219.)

In our homes . . . it is our privilege, nay, it is our duty, to call our families together to be taught the truths of the Holy Scriptures. In every home, children should be encouraged to read the word of the Lord, as it has been revealed to us in all dispensations. We should read the Bible, the Book of Mormon, the Doctrine and Covenants, and the Pearl of Great Price; not only read it in our homes, but explain it to our children, that they may understand the hand dealings of God with the peoples of the earth. (George Albert Smith, *CR*, April 1914, p. 12.)

I cannot impress upon the . . . Church too much the importance of reading the Scriptures and of trying to learn their meaning. They are told to us in clear enough language so that we can always be reasonably certain when we are in the true paths. . . .

Read your Scriptures, read them early and read them late, read them in your youth and do not abandon them when you get older. (J. Reuben Clark, Jr., in a pamphlet prepared for the youth of the Church, December 1960, pp. 11-12, 14.)

Search the scriptures—search the revelations which we publish, and ask your Heavenly Father, in the name of His Son Jesus Christ, to manifest the truth unto you, and if you do it with an eye single to His glory nothing doubting, He will answer you by the power of His Holy Spirit. You will then know for yourselves and not for another. You will not then be dependent on man for the knowledge of God; nor will there be any room for speculation. No; for when men receive their instruction from Him that made them, they know how He will save them. Then again we say: Search the Scriptures, search the Prophets and learn what portion of them belongs to you. (Joseph Smith, *TPJS*, p. 11.)

THE DOCTRINE AND COVENANTS

From the earlier discussion of what is scripture, it is evident that when the revelations and other teachings of the prophets contained in the Doctrine and Covenants were first received from the Lord through the power of the Holy Ghost, they were scripture. When these things were taught to or published for the members of the Church, they became scripture *for the Church.* When they were formally accepted by the membership of the Church, they became part of the *canonized scripture* or *standard works* of the Church. Elder Bruce R. McConkie has written the following concerning this process:

Any message, whether written or spoken, that comes from God to man by the power of the Holy Ghost is *scripture.* If it is written and accepted by the Church, it becomes part of the *scriptures or standard works* and ever thereafter may be read and studied with profit. Much of what is in the scriptures was given orally in the first instance and was thereafter recorded either by the uttering prophet or an inspired scribe. Other portions of what is in holy writ were written by the inspired authors by way of revelation and commandment. (*MD,* p. 682.)

The Doctrine and Covenants is one of the standard works of The Church of Jesus Christ of Latter-day Saints, together with the Bible (both Old Testament and New Testament), the Book of Mormon, and the Pearl of Great Price.

The beginning of the Doctrine and Covenants story is really the First Vision of the Prophet Joseph Smith, for at that time the iron ceiling of heaven was shattered after an apostasy that had lasted for hundreds of years. The account of the First Vision is found in the Pearl of Great Price (Joseph Smith—History) and should be carefully read by every student of the Doctrine and Covenants.

The various appearances of the Angel Moroni to the Prophet Joseph Smith also provide important background to a serious study of the Doctrine and Covenants. Although the accounts of these heavenly visitations are not in the Doctrine and Covenants, they are available in the Pearl of Great Price (JS-H 1:29-60) and in the *History of the Church* (1:9-22).

Also, the words of the angel in which he paraphrased the promise of Malachi concerning the return of Elijah the prophet comprise section 2 in the Doctrine and Covenants; chronologically, this section is the earliest revelation contained in the present Doctrine and Covenants.

The next section chronologically is section 3 (July 1828), which is concerned with the loss of 116 pages of manuscript, and from that time forth the materials for the various sections are revealed rather frequently. The materials for seventeen sections were received by the end of 1829; another nineteen sections were received in 1830; and in the following two years (1831-32) the materials for fifty-three were received.

Once the Church was established and the Lord had revealed the principles, practices, and procedures that should guide his kingdom upon the earth, it is natural that the number of revelations necessary to establish and run the Church should diminish. However, the material for an additional forty-five revelations or sections was received before the death of the Prophet. The final two sections were published to announce the martyrdom of the Prophet and his brother (section 135) and to "give the Word and the Will of the Lord" through his prophet Brigham Young concerning the organization of the Saints as they were preparing for the migration to the West (section 136.)

Primarily, however, the Doctrine and Covenants is a book of revelations. Most of the sections contain direct revelations from God to his prophets (primarily Joseph Smith), but other sections contain information derived from revelations, such as answers to scriptural questions (sections 77, 113), items of instruction (sections 130, 131), letters (sections 127, 128), inspired translation of earlier scripture (section 7), and prayers, including the dedicatory prayer for the Kirtland Temple (sections 13, 65, 109).

Both the Preface (section 1) and the Appendix (section 133) were received by revelation, although they were given for a specific purpose. Other sections are almost pure prophecy (sections 87, 121), while others include the minutes of a high council meeting (section 102), a declaration of belief concerning government (section 134), historical information on the martyrdom of Joseph and Hyrum Smith (section 135), and instructions concerning the organization of the Saints for migration to the West (section 136). The

"Official Declaration" concerning the cessation of polygamy (the Manifesto) is also published with each copy of the Doctrine and Covenants.

The question might be asked, Have any sections been added to the Doctrine and Covenants since the death of the Prophet Joseph Smith except for sections 135, 136, and the Manifesto? The answer is, Yes. Sections 2, 13, 77, 85, 87, 103, 105, 108-32 were not published in the 1835 edition of the Doctrine and Covenants (some of them had not even been received at that time), but were published in later editions after being accepted by the Church as canonized scripture.

Elder John A. Widtsoe has answered the question "What does the Doctrine and Covenants contain?" in the following words:

The first thing to be remembered is that the revelations contained in the Book of Doctrine and Covenants are answers to questions. If that is kept in mind it will help to a better understanding. . . .

In the History of the Church you will find that the Prophet says, "I inquired of the Lord." The revelation follows. In each the answer to a question is a dominating part of the revelation. Sometimes it is an answer amplified and an explanation of an existing condition. That explains the somewhat disjointed nature of the Book of Doctrine and Covenants. Since each revelation is an answer to a special question, there could not be a consecutive developing treatment of any one theme. If the question is known, then this supplementary material of the revelation is better understood. As one reads carefully from the first to the last, a developing purpose and increasing thought will be found fitting the spiritual development and temporal needs of the Prophet and his associates. Another important thing should be remembered, that the very earliest revelations foreshadow everything that is found in the book. With the knowledge we have today, we can take the earliest fifteen revelations in the book and read into them practically every doctrine, principle and project that characterized the succeeding revelations. The Mind that gave the revelations possessed the whole plan. But it was given piecemeal to the Church as required. (*MDC*, pp. 4-9.)

Who is the source of the revelations contained in the Doctrine and Covenants?

All revelations come from the Lord. Concerning prophecy, the apostle Peter said that it "came not in old time by the will of man: but holy men of God spake as they were moved by the Holy Ghost." (2 Pet. 1:21.) The same might

Sections of the Doctrine and Covenants Listed by Date and Place Received

	1823–1829	1830	1831–1832	1833–1837	1838–1844	1847
PENNSYLVANIA (15)						
Harmony (15)	11[a]	4[d]				
NEW YORK (25)						
Manchester (4)	1[b]	3[e]				
Fayette (20)	5[c]	12[f]	3[g]			
Other, N.Y. (1)				1[m]		
OHIO (64)						
Kirtland (46)			24[h]	22[n]		
Hiram (15)			15[i]			
Other, Ohio (3)			3[j]			
MISSOURI (20)						
Jackson County (6)			6[k]			
Far West (and vicinity) (8)					8[q]	
Liberty Jail (3)					3[r]	
Other, Missouri (3)			2[l]	1[o]		
ILLINOIS (10)						
Nauvoo (and vicinity) (10)					10[s]	
OTHER AREAS (2)				1[p]		1[t]
TOTALS (136)	17	19	53	25	21	1

(a) sections 3–13. (b) section 2. (c) sections 14–18. (d) sections 24–27. (e) sections 19, 22, 23. (f) sections 20, 21, 28–37. (g) sections 38–40. (h) sections 41–50, 52–56, 63, 64, 70, 72, 84–88. (i) sections 1, 65, 67–69, 71, 73–74, 76–81, 133. (j) sections 51, 66, 75. (k) sections 57–60, 82–83. (l) sections 61–62. (m) section 100. (n) sections 89–99, 101–104, 106–110, 112, 134. (o) section 105. (p) section 111. (q) sections 113–120. (r) sections 121–123. (s) sections 124–132, 135. (t) section 136.

also be said of revelation. When a person reads the revelations of the Doctrine and Covenants, he is literally reading the mind and will of the Lord as given through his prophets.

The Giver of all the revelations is Jesus Christ. The God spoken of in the Doctrine and Covenants is Jesus of Nazareth. Apparently the Father does not speak in them. He speaks through his Son. It is a fundamental doctrine of Mormonism that God the Father has commissioned his Son Jesus Christ to do certain work. He is the one that looks after the affairs of this earth, and all things pertaining to the Church are done by him. God the Father has appeared very few times upon the earth, at the beginning of the dispensations. He appeared in the Garden of Eden. He spoke out of heaven at the time of the Savior's baptism. He appeared in the grove to the Prophet Joseph Smith. (John A. Widtsoe, *MDC,* pp. 4-9.)

At whose request were the revelations in the Doctrine and Covenants given?

The Prophet Joseph Smith requested the help from the Lord. Often the Prophet prayed for guidance and help for himself, in behalf of the Church, or for specific groups within the Church. Sometimes individual members (or even individuals who were still investigating the Church) would ask Joseph Smith to pose a particular question of the Lord; usually the request would be to determine the mind and will of the Lord concerning that particular person.

Either the person and/or the Lord might have one of several reasons for requesting or giving a particular revelation, including general instruction, personal guidance, scriptural enlightenment, prophecy, law, etc.

Elder Widtsoe has written the following concerning the revelations in the Doctrine and Covenants.

The language, with the exception of the words actually spoken by heavenly beings, is the language of the Prophet. The ideas were given to Joseph Smith. He wrote them in the best language at his command. He was inspired at times by the loftiness of the ideals so that his language or words are far above that ordinarily used by a backwoods boy of that day.

There are four classes of revelations: (1) those given to individuals, (2) those given to the Church for doctrinal information, (3) those given for organization purposes and (4) those dealing with miscellaneous subjects.

There are two kinds of teachings in the Doctrine and Covenants. One is "special" in its nature, pertaining, say, to the organization of the united order in Missouri, or how baptism should be performed, or what blessing to ask upon the bread and water. The second kind are of general application, dealing with the principles which are eternal, applicable at all times and under all conditions. (*MDC*, pp. 4-9.)

Where and when were the revelations in the Doctrine and Covenants received?

Most of the revelations in the Doctrine and Covenants were received between 1829 and 1832, which was the period just before the Church was organized and during its early formative years. During this time Joseph Smith was living in New York and Ohio, so most of the revelations were given in these two states.

By what means were the revelations requested and received?

The Lord has counseled all his children to request blessings and return thanks to him in prayer: "Ask, and it shall be given you; seek, and ye shall find; knock, and it shall be opened unto you: For every one that asketh receiveth; and he that seeketh findeth; and to him that knocketh it shall be opened." (Matt. 7:7-8.)

Thus it might be said in general that the only form of inquiry used by the Prophet in requesting the help that resulted in the revelations to him was prayer. However, prayer may take many different forms, as is suggested by one of the hymns of the Church, "Prayer Is the Soul's Sincere Desire" (*Hymns,* no. 220):

> *Prayer is the soul's sincere desire,*
> *Uttered or unexpressed,*
> *The motion of a hidden fire,*
> *That trembles in the breast.*
>
> *Prayer is the burden of a sigh,*
> *The falling of a tear,*
> *The upward glancing of an eye,*
> *When none but God is near.*
>
> *Prayer is the simplest form of speech,*
> *That infant lips can try,*
> *Prayer, the sublimest strains that reach*
> *The Majesty on high.*

The Lord has chosen various means of answering the prayers of his prophets and communicating with them throughout the centuries. At times, he has spoken with his prophets "face to face" or in a personal visit. (See 2 Ne. 11:2-3; Ether 3:6-16; 12:39; the First Vision of Joseph Smith in JS-H 1:14-20; D&C 76.)

At other times, he has spoken to his prophets but has not shown himself to their physical sense of sight. (Read 3 Ne. 1:12; 9:1-22; Ether 2:14; D&C 130:12-13.) At still other times, he has spoken to his prophets in the "still small voice of the Spirit," which might include the impressions of the Spirit upon the mind of the receptive prophet. (See Enos 1:10; D&C 85.)

He has also spoken to his prophets through angels or other heavenly messengers. (See 1 Ne. 3:29; 11:21; Mosiah 27:11; 3 Ne. 19:14; D&C 2; 13; 27:1-4; 110.) And sometimes he communicates to his prophets through visions and dreams. (Read 1 Ne. 1:8; 2:2; D&C 76; 107:93.)

Virtually all of these methods of communication to his prophets were employed by the Lord in the revelations contained in the Doctrine and Covenants.

We are also told that some of the revelations were received as Joseph Smith inquired "through the Urim and Thummim," and these revelations may have employed several of these methods of communication.

Were all the revelations in the Doctrine and Covenants received through the Urim and Thummim?

No. Many of the early revelations (such as those contained in sections 3, 6, 7, 11, 14-17) were received through the use of the Urim and Thummim, but probably most of the revelations were received without the use of those sacred stones. Of course, the Prophet may have received some revelations through the Urim and Thummim in addition to those that he specifically mentioned were received through that means.

We are not certain of the exact function of the Urim and Thummim in requesting or receiving revelations. The Prophet simply stated that he "inquired through the Urim and Thummim."

Elder John A. Widtsoe has suggested that the Urim and Thummim may have helped the Prophet to concentrate his spiritual powers toward the Lord during the early years until he learned how to use his faith directly in receiving answers to his requests:

When the Prophet was young and inexperienced, he had in his possession as a help the Urim and Thummim. The Urim and Thummim were stones set in a silver bowl—not spectacles, but apparently means by which he was able to concentrate, to focus attention upon the subject under consideration until he became so in harmony with the spiritual forces about him that the thing under consideration became clear to him. We do not know the process. . . . Probably the Urim and Thummim were means by which the Prophet was able to concentrate upon a subject. He says often in his journal when problems arose, "I inquired of the Lord through the Urim and Thummim."

As the Prophet became stronger spiritually, he had no need of the Urim and Thummim, and they were taken from him. He then says, "I inquired of the Lord." He acquired power over himself until he was able to concentrate sufficiently to put himself in tune with spiritual forces and then to obtain the necessary answers. A number of revelations were given by such direct inspiration. (John A. Widtsoe, *MDC*, pp. 4-9.)

What determined the order in which the revelations were printed in the Doctrine and Covenants?

In the main, Joseph Smith and others assigned to prepare the revelations for publication decided to print them in the chronological order in which they were received. However, there were several deviations from this general pattern, perhaps the most notable of which were—

—the placement of what is now section 1 at the beginning of the record, even though the particular revelation in that section was not received until November 1, 1831. However, in giving this particular revelation, the Lord indicated that it was to be a "Preface" to his other revelations that were to be printed in the same volume.

—the placement of what is now section 133 near the end of the book. This section was also given the first part of November (the 3rd) 1831, but was identified as the "Appendix" and has been part of the end of the revelations received by Joseph Smith.

Sections 10 and 134 are examples of other revelations known to be printed out of chronological sequence.

Because the revelations are usually printed in chronological order, the reader and student of the Doctrine and Covenants can more easily relate each revelation to the events in Church history that usually precipitated the question leading to that particular revelation.

What is the relationship of the Doctrine and Covenants to Church history?

Most, if not all, of the revelations and other teachings in the Doctrine and Covenants were received as answers to prayers. Naturally, the Prophet Joseph Smith was praying about those problems and situations with which he was immediately concerned in his everyday life or in the current life of the Church. The revelations of the Doctrine and Covenants were thus given by the Lord to help solve the problems of his prophet and of his growing, emerging church. Because these revelations are vitally linked with Church history, they can be best understood in the context of the particular time and/or place that prompted the questioning prayer of the Prophet and in turn resulted in the subsequent revelation.

Are all the revelations given to Joseph Smith included in the Doctrine and Covenants?

No. Joseph Smith received many revelations in addition to those included in the Doctrine and Covenants. Some of these he was specifically commanded not to include. For some others, he was commanded to include only portions of the revelation. (See D&C 76:114-19.) Other revelations were not published either because it was not necessary to publish them at that particular time or because the message of the revelation was so personal to the individual that the principles therein may not have had general application.

It is an erroneous thought to believe that the Prophet selected all of the revelations he had received and placed them in the collection which was to become the Book of Commandments. Each of the revelations selected for that volume was placed there because the Prophet considered that it had some value to the Church in regard to its teachings. There are some revelations still in possession of the Church which were not included. Some of these we can readily believe were not included because the inspiration of the Prophet was that it was not necessary, or because some of them had an application which was not intended for publication and to be sent to an unbelieving world. (Joseph Fielding Smith, *CHMR* 1:20.)

Are revelations being received by the prophets today? If so, why are they not included in the Doctrine and Covenants?

As indicated in the chapter titled "What Is Scripture?" there are two major types of scripture in the Church today: (1) the canonized scripture, which is written and contained in the standard works of the Church (Old Testament, New Testament, Book of Mormon, Doctrine and Covenants, and Pearl of Great Price) and (2) the spoken or written noncanonized scripture that comes initially as the General Authorities speak or write when "moved upon by the power of the Holy Ghost." Of course, this latter type of scripture, which is initially revealed through the mind of the General Authority, is often subsequently written down and published throughout the Church, either in conference reports, Church magazines, or other publications of the Church.

Both types of scripture are equally binding upon the membership of the Church; therefore, it is not necessary that every new revelation or inspired teaching of the Prophet or of the other General Authorities be published as part of the canonized scripture such as the Doctrine and Covenants.

When the Lord has a revelation to be placed in the Doctrine and Covenants he will indicate it. The Doctrine and Covenants does not contain all the revelations given to the Prophet Joseph Smith. It is a "selection" of revelations which contain doctrines and commandments covering every phase of salvation, which, if we will follow them, will direct us to the celestial kingdom. The Lord has given revelation to each of the presidents of the Church, but it is unnecessary that every word revealed should be added to that volume. President Wilford Woodruff said:

"I have had the administration of angels in my day and time, though I never prayed for an angel. I have had, in several instances, the administration of holy angels. . . . The Lord revealed to me by vision, by revelations, and by the Holy Spirit, many things that lay before me."

President Brigham Young had similar experiences, and the revelations of the Lord were with him in directing the pioneers across the plains. He had the revelations from the Lord in the building of colonies and cities throughout the western territory and in sending forth men and women to colonize them. The history which is written gives evidence of that inspiration. . . .

Can you tell me why some members of the Church are clamoring for more revelation to be placed in the Doctrine and Covenants, when most of those who do are not keeping the commandments of the Lord that are already revealed? What privilege does a person have to ask for more revelation, when he does not conform his life to the commandments already given? There is a very significant statement in Section 59 of the Doctrine and Covenants as follows:

"And they (the Saints who are faithful) shall also be crowned with blessings from above, yea, and with commandments not a few, and with revelations in their time—they that are faithful and diligent before me." (D&C 59:4.) . . .

Let us one and all take an inward look. Perhaps it is because we have not humbled ourselves; because we have failed to heed the commandments and to accept and abide in the revelations already given, that there is not more given to us. It is my humble opinion that we are receiving council by inspiration, or revelation, at every general conference of the Church. Would it not be wise for the members of the Church to pay more heed to these counsels and prepare ourselves for more to come? (Joseph Fielding Smith, *AGQ*, 2:202-5.)

It has been observed that the people want revelation. This is revelation; and were it written, it would then be written revelation, as truly as the revelations which are contained in the Book of Doctrine and Covenants. I could give you revelation about going to California, for I know the mind of the Lord upon that matter. I could give you revelation upon the subject of paying your tithing and building a temple to the name of the Lord; for the light is in me. I could put these revelations as straight to the line of truth in writing as any revelation you ever read. I could write the mind of the Lord, and you could put it in your pockets. But before we desire more written revelation, let us fulfil the revelations that are already written, and which we have scarcely begun to fulfil. (Brigham Young, *JD* 6:319.)

Concerning the question "Are revelations being received by the prophets today?" the answer is a definite yes. The following testimony of the living prophet is a stirring witness to the Church and to the world concerning this vital question:

Of all things, that for which we should be most grateful today is that the heavens are indeed open and that the restored church of Jesus Christ is founded upon the rock of revelation. Continuous revelation is indeed the very lifeblood of the gospel of the living Lord and Savior, Jesus Christ.

We proclaim to the world in one of our Articles of Faith, "We believe all that God has revealed, all that He does now reveal, and we believe that He will yet reveal many great and important things pertaining to the Kingdom of God." (Ninth Article of Faith.)

From the scripture of ancient time comes this ringing declaration: "Surely the Lord God will do nothing, but he revealeth his secret unto his servants the prophets." (Amos 3:7.)

If the Bible were "the end of the prophets," then it was through lack of faith and belief, and that is the reason the heavens at times were closed and locked and became as iron, and the earth as brass. When the heavens are sealed, the spiritual darkness that follows is not unlike that physical darkness in Nephite history, when "neither candles, neither torches; neither could there be fire kindled with their fine and exceedingly dry wood." (3 Ne. 8:21.)

The Lord will not force himself upon people, and if they do not believe, they will receive no revelation. If they are content to depend upon their own limited calculations and interpretations, then, of course, the Lord will leave them to their chosen fate.

Speaking of miracles and revelation, the Book of Mormon prophet Moroni states this:

"If these things have ceased, then has faith ceased also; and awful is the state of man, for they are as though there had been no redemption made." (Moro. 7:38.)

In the meridian of time, the Son of God, the Light of the World, came and opened the curtains of heaven, and earth and heaven were again in communion.

But when the light of that century went out, the darkness was again impenetrable; the heavens were sealed and the "dark ages" moved in.

I bear witness to the world today that more than a century and a half ago the iron ceiling was shattered; the heavens were once again opened, and since that time revelations have been continuous. . . .

A young lad, Joseph Smith, of incomparable faith, broke the spell, shattered the "heavens of iron" and reestablished communication. Heaven kissed the earth, light dissipated the darkness, and God again spoke to man, revealing anew "his secret unto his servants the prophets." (Amos 3:7.) A new prophet was in the land and through him God set up his kingdom, never to be destroyed nor left to another people—a kingdom that will stand forever.

The foreverness of this kingdom and the revelations which it brought into existence are absolute realities. Never again will the sun go down; never again will all men prove totally unworthy of communication with their Maker. Never again will God be hidden from his children on the earth. Revelation is here to remain. . . .

There are those who would assume that with the printing and binding of these sacred records, that would be the "end of the prophets." But again we testify to the world that revelation continues and that the vaults and files of the Church contain these revelations which come month to month and day to day. We testify also that there is, since 1830 when The Church of Jesus Christ of Latter-day Saints was organized, and will continue to be, so long as time shall last, a prophet, recognized of God and his people, who will continue to interpret the mind and will of the Lord. . . .

. . . I say, in the deepest of humility, but also by the power and force of a burning testimony in my soul, that from the prophet of the Restoration to the prophet of our own year, the communication line is unbroken, the authority is continuous, and light, brilliant and penetrating, continues to shine. The sound of the voice of the Lord is a continuous melody and a thunderous appeal. For nearly a century and a half there has been no interruption.

Man never needs to stand alone. Every faithful person may have the inspiration for his own limited kingdom. But the Lord definitely calls prophets today and reveals his secrets unto them as he did yesterday, he does today, and will do tomorrow; that is the way it is. (Spencer W. Kimball, *Ensign,* May 1977, pp. 76-78.)

The discontinuance of publishing the revelations of the living prophets in the Doctrine and Covenants should not be interpreted to mean that revelations have ceased in the Church.

A good example of modern revelation is the announcement of the First Presidency on June 9, 1978, of the revelation that "has confirmed that the long-promised day has come when every faithful, worthy man in the Church may receive the holy priesthood . . . without regard for race or color." The full printed text announcing the revelation follows:

As we have witnessed the expansion of the work of the Lord over the earth, we have been grateful that people of many nations have responded to the message of the restored gospel, and have joined the Church in ever-increasing numbers. This, in turn, has inspired us with a desire to extend to every worthy member of the Church all of the privileges and blessings which the gospel affords.

Aware of the promises made by the prophets and presidents of the Church who have preceded us that at some time, in God's eternal plan, all of our brethren who are worthy may receive the priesthood, and witnessing the faithfulness of those from whom the priesthood had been withheld, we have pleaded long and earnestly in behalf of these, our faithful brethren, spending many hours in the upper room of the temple supplicating the Lord for divine guidance.

He has heard our prayers, and by revelation has confirmed that the long-promised day has come when every faithful, worthy man in the Church may receive the holy priesthood, with power to exercise its divine authority, and enjoy with his loved ones every blessing that flows therefrom, including the blessings of the temple. Accordingly, all worthy male members of the Church may be ordained to the priesthood without regard for race or color. Priesthood leaders are instructed to follow the policy of carefully interviewing all candidates for ordination to either the Aaronic or Melchizedek Priesthood to insure that they meet the established standards for worthiness.

We declare with soberness that the Lord has now made known His will for the blessing of all His children throughout the earth who will hearken to the voice of His authorized servants, and prepare themselves to receive every blessing of the gospel.

Sincerely yours,
Spencer W. Kimball
N. Eldon Tanner
Marion G. Romney
The First Presidency

Why is a study of the Doctrine and Covenants so important?

The Doctrine and Covenants is unique among the standard works of The Church of Jesus Christ of Latter-day Saints. It was revealed in this dispensation and is intended primarily for people who will live on the earth during this dispensation.

The Old Testament was revealed to prophets in ancient times primarily to prepare the people of those days for the first coming of the Savior. Gospel principles in the Old Testament, of course, are beneficial and instructive for all people of all ages.

The New Testament was written as a witness and testimony of the divinity of Jesus Christ, and as such it is important for all people of all times. The latter part of the New Testament, however, consists of letters and other instructions concerned primarily with the branches and members of the Church in the meridian of time.

The Book of Mormon was written and compiled by prophets in ancient times, but this book is primarily intended for people of this dispensation as a second witness of the Bible and of the divinity of Jesus Christ.

The Pearl of Great Price contains some of the writings and teachings of ancient prophets as well as the history and testimony of Joseph Smith and doctrinal instructions by other prophets of this dispensation.

More than any of the other canonized scriptures, the Doctrine and Covenants has largely been revealed to and written by the prophets of this dispensation for the instruction and edification of the people of these times. Concerning the importance of the Doctrine and Covenants, President Joseph Fielding Smith has written:

In my judgment there is no book on earth yet to come to man as important as the book known as the Doctrine and Covenants, with all due respect to the Book of Mormon, and the Bible, and the Pearl of Great Price, which we say are our standards in doctrine.

The book of Doctrine and Covenants to us stands in a peculiar position above them all.

I am going to tell you why. When I say that, do not for a moment think I do not value the Book of Mormon, the Bible, and the Pearl of Great Price, just as much as any man that lives; I think I do. I do not know of anybody who has read them more, and I appreciate them; they are wonderful; they contain doctrine and revelation and commandments that we should heed; but the Bible is a history containing the doctrine and commandments given to the people anciently. That applies also to the Book of Mormon. It is doctrine and the history and the commandments of the people who dwelt upon this continent anciently.

But this Doctrine and Covenants contains the word of God to those who dwell here now. . . . More precious than gold, the Prophet says we should treasure it more than the riches of the whole earth. I wonder if we do? If we value it, understand it, and know what it contains, we will value it more than wealth; it is worth more to us than the riches of the earth. (Joseph Fielding Smith, *DS* 3:198-99.)

The preface to the *Doctrine and Covenants Commentary* also suggests that the Doctrine and Covenants is distinctly different from the other scriptures:

The Doctrine and Covenants is different from these three volumes. [Bible, Book of Mormon, Pearl of Great Price.] It is in every respect a modern book. It contains revelations given during a period extending from 1823 to 1847. It covers the rise and development of the Church, restored in our day. It enables us to follow the tender watchcare of God over the infant Church, during its days of numerical weakness and the incessant assaults of the adversary, in the form of persecution, temptations, and apostasy, and to watch the retreat of the people of God into the wilderness. It contains "doctrines," "covenants," and predictions, all of the utmost importance to every nation and every individual on earth. . . . The Doctrine and Covenants has been given to us for our instruction and salvation. We are interested in it, and should study it diligently and intelligently. (Smith and Sjodahl, *DCC,* p. xiii.)

ADDITIONAL INFORMATION

Soon after some of the revelations were received, members of the Church or other interested individuals were naturally interested in knowing exactly what the revelations said. Often the revelation was written down and circulated, even if it were given primarily for the benefit of a particular person or group of people, much the same way as patriarchal blessings might be recorded and distributed today, even though they are for the personal benefit and instruction of the person receiving the blessing.

In time, copies of several of the revelations were in circulation, and, as would be normal, some persons started to make a collection of these revelations. Missionaries traveling away from the headquarters of the Church particularly were interested in having complete and correct copies of these revelations, particularly if the revelations could assist them in their missionary efforts.

Because of growing interest in and demand for the revelations, the matter of their possible publication received special attention at a conference of the Church held during November 1831, where a specific request of the Lord was made. It was during the proceedings of this conference that sections 1 and 133 were received. After a vote by the members at the conference, it was decided to go ahead with the publication of 65 of the revelations in a book to be entitled *A Book of Commandments.*

At this special conference at Hiram, Ohio, November 1, 1831, the Lord gave the revelation to the Prophet that he said was to serve as the preface "unto the book of my commandments." (D&C 1:6.) The *History of the Church* contains the following account from the *Far West Record:*

The same afternoon, the following occurred: "Brother Joseph Smith, Jun., said that inasmuch as the Lord had bestowed a great blessing upon us in giving commandments and revelations, he asked the conference what testimony they were willing to attach to these commandments which would shortly be sent to the world. A number of the brethren arose and said that they were willing to testify to the world that they knew that they were of the Lord."

In the second day's proceedings of the conference it is recorded: "The revelation of last evening read by the moderator [this was Oliver Cowdery]. The brethren then arose in turn and bore witness to the truth of the Book of Commandments; after which Brother Joseph Smith, Jun., arose and expressed his feelings and gratitude concerning the commandments and preface received yesterday." (*HC* 1:222.)

Oliver Cowdery and John Whitmer were given the responsibility of taking the 65 revelations selected to Jackson County, Missouri, where they were to be printed by the W. W. Phelps and Company printing press. Initially ten thousand copies were to be printed; this was later changed to three thousand copies.

A number of copies of all 65 chapters had been printed— but none bound into books—when a mob destroyed the press and most of the printed contents July 20, 1833. The books were never made widely available. The title page stated: "A Book of Commandments for the Government of the Church of Christ, Organized According to Law, on the 6th of April, 1830. Zion: Published by W. W. Phelps & Co. 1833."

Why and how was the title Doctrine and Covenants selected?

Information is not provided in *History of the Church* as to why the name *A Book of Commandments* (1833) was changed to *Doctrine and Covenants* (1835). However, thirty-seven additional revelations were proposed to be included in the new publication, and the brethren may have felt it desirable to have a more comprehensive, inclusive, and descriptive title. It is also of some interest to note the following entry from Joseph Smith concerning the revelation now printed as section 133: "On the third day of November, 1831, I inquired of the Lord and received the following important revelation, which has since been added to the book of Doctrine and Covenants, and called the Appendix." (*HC* 1:229.)

The following statements discuss the meanings of *doctrine* and *covenants* and indicate the appropriateness of the title:

As the name implies, this volume of Scripture contains doctrine and covenants. "Doctrine" means "teaching," "instruction." It denotes more especially what is taught as truth, for us to believe, as distinct from precepts, by which rules, to be obeyed, are given. "Doctrine" refers to belief; precept to conduct.

In the Doctrine and Covenants our Lord teaches us what to believe concerning the Godhead, the Church, the Priesthood, the Millennium, the resurrection, the state of man after death in eternal glory, or the opposite, and many other subjects about which it is necessary to have true information.

The word "covenant" is a term by which God indicates the settled arrangement between Him and His people. . . . The nature of this covenant is revealed to us in this precious volume of the word of God. It shows us what obligations we take upon ourselves in baptism, and what blessings we secure; what covenants we renew by partaking of the Sacrament, and what promises accompany that ordinance. In one word, it teaches us how to worship God in Spirit and in truth, and reveals to us the way opened up, back to the presence of God. (Smith and Sjodahl, *DCC*, pp. xiii-xv.)

DOCTRINE: Gospel teachings or positions which have such general acceptance as to be considered settled and therefore authoritative; statements of the fundamental revealed message of salvation through Jesus Christ; gospel truths; the system of principles, rules, and laws under which the Church operates.

The instructional aspect of the gospel through which one may come to know God and eternal truths respecting the purpose of life and the means of salvation.

COVENANTS: The revealed terms and conditions upon which a person may qualify himself to receive promised blessings from God through entering into agreements to be obedient; a binding contract or mutual promise between God and man; the revealed conditional promises of the Lord.

The operational or practical side of living the gospel by those who have faith in God's promises and are willing to agree to live his way in order to achieve the promised blessings. (*Institute Self-Instruction Course*, p. 51.)

The term "covenant" signifies the settled arrangement between God and man, whereby the eternal Father undertakes to save His children. This arrangement is also called His "oath," His "counsel," and His "promise" (Ps. 89:3, 4; Heb. 6:13-20). "Commandments" are the laws, or rules man must obey as a condition of obtaining salvation. (Smith and Sjodahl, *DCC*, p. 4.)

Why is the 1835 edition of the Doctrine and Covenants considered to be so important?

First, it was the first time these revelations were published under the title "Doctrine and Covenants." Thus, in a sense, the 1835 edition might be considered the *first* edition of the Doctrine and Covenants.

Second, *A Book of Commandments* contained only sixty-five chapters; and since virtually all of the copies of this earlier publication were destroyed by the mob, it was never widely circulated in the Church. The 1835 edition of the Doctrine and Covenants contained 102 sections, and it was widely distributed.

Briefly, the history of the 1835 edition is that after most of the copies of *A Book of Commandments* were destroyed by the mob, the Church leaders decided to try to publish these revelations and include some revelations not included in the earlier publication. The Lord had designated a committee of stewards over the revelations, consisting of Joseph Smith, Sidney Rigdon, Oliver Cowdery, and Frederick G. Williams.

At a general assembly of the Saints August 17, 1835, the proposal was accepted to publish 102 sections in a volume to be named the Doctrine and Covenants.

The title page of the 1835 edition of the Doctrine and Covenants reads: "Doctrine and Covenants of The Church of Jesus Christ of Latter-day Saints: Carefully Selected from the Revelations of God, and Compiled by Joseph Smith, Junior, Oliver Cowdery, Sidney Rigdon, Frederick G. Williams, [Presiding Elders of said Church.] Proprietors. Kirtland, Ohio. Printed by F. G. Williams & Co. for the Proprietors. 1835."

This edition consisted of the following:

1. A preface, signed by Joseph Smith, Oliver Cowdery, and Sidney Rigdon.

2. The Seven Lectures on Faith (pages 6 through 74).

3. One hundred and two sections of revelations and other materials (pages 75 through 254). Section 101 was an article on marriage, which was dropped from subsequent editions after the revelation on the eternity of the marriage covenant was recorded.

4. Minutes of the meeting of the general assembly of the Church on August 17, 1835 (pp. 255-57).

5. A three-page index, which currently would probably be called a table of contents.

6. A nineteen-page section titled "Contents," which currently would probably be called an index.

7. A one-page sheet titled "Notes to the Reader," which served as an errata sheet.

Following is the text of the Preface to the 1835 edition:

To the members of the church of the Latter Day Saints—
DEAR BRETHREN:

We deem it to be unnecessary to entertain you with a lengthy preface to the following volume, but merely to say, that it contains in short, the leading items of the religion which we have professed to believe.

The first part of the book will be found to contain a series of Lectures as delivered before a Theological class in this place, and in consequence of their embracing the important doctrine of salvation, we have arranged them into the following work.

The second part contains items or principles for the regulation of the church, as taken from the revelations which have been given since its organization, as well as from former ones.

There may be an aversion in the minds of some against receiving any thing purporting to be articles of religious faith, in consequence of there being so many now extant; but if men believe a system, and profess that it was given by inspiration, certainly, the more intelligibly they can present it, the better. It does not make a principle untrue to *print* it, neither does it make it true not to print it.

The church viewing this subject to be of importance, appointed, through their servants and delegates the High Council, your servants to select and compile this work. Several reasons might be adduced in favor of this move of the Council, but we only add a few words. They knew that the church was evil spoken of in many places—its faith and belief misrepresented, and the way of truth thus subverted. By some it was represented as disbelieving the bible, by others as being an enemy to all good order and uprightness, and by others as being injurious to the peace of all governments civil and political.

We have, therefore, endeavored to present, though in few words, *our* belief, and when we say this, humbly trust, the faith and principles of this society as a body.

We do not present this little volume with any other expectation than that we are to be called to answer to every principle advanced, in that day when the secrets of all hearts will be revealed, and the reward of every man's labor be given him.

With sentiments of esteem and sincere respect, we subscribe ourselves your brethren in the bonds of the gospel of our Lord Jesus Christ.

Kirtland, Ohio, February 17, 1835.   JOSEPH SMITH jr.
                                                    OLIVER COWDERY.
                                                    SIDNEY RIGDON.
                                                    F. G. WILLIAMS.

What are the Lectures on Faith?

The seven Lectures on Faith were prepared initially for use in sessions of the School of the Prophets that were held in Kirtland, Ohio, during the winter of 1834-35. It was decided to include them in the Doctrine and Covenants in 1835 in order to make them available in printed form to the members of the Church. They were never presented to nor voted upon by the members of the Church to be included as canonized scripture, and were intended only to be theological lectures or lessons.

The footnote in *History of the Church* 2:176 indicates the following concerning the Lectures on Faith:

> They are not to be regarded as of equal authority in matters of doctrine with the revelations of God in the Doctrine and Covenants, but as stated by Elder John Smith, who, when the book of Doctrine and Covenants was submitted to the several quorums of the Priesthood for acceptance, (Aug. 17, 1835) speaking in behalf of the Kirtland High Council, "bore record that the revelations in said book were true, and that the lectures judicially were written and compiled, and were profitable for doctrine." The distinction which Elder John Smith here makes should be observed as a marking the difference between the Lectures on Faith and the revelations of God in the Doctrine and Covenants.

The Lectures on Faith were printed in subsequent editions of the Doctrine and Covenants until 1921, when it was decided to publish them separately and not include them under the same cover with the Doctrine and Covenants.

Why was the article on marriage that was published in the editions of the Doctrine and Covenants from 1835 to 1876 deleted from all subsequent editions?

This article was not a revelation and was never approved as a revelation. It was written originally by Oliver Cowdery and presented to and approved by the general assembly of the Church August 17, 1835, for publication with the revelations. Neither Joseph Smith nor Frederick G. Williams, one of the counselors in the First Presidency, was present at this assembly, as they were in Michigan. (*HC* 2:243.)

Also, it should be remembered that this article was prepared by Oliver Cowdery *before* some of the revelations were received and/or recorded concerning the eternal nature of the marriage covenant. For example, the article suggested "that all marriages in this church . . . should be solemnized in a public meeting . . . and that the solemnization should be performed by a presiding high priest, high priest, bishop, elder, or priest." (Page 251 of the 1835 edition.)

On July 12, 1843, the revelation of the Lord to his prophet was recorded, which indicated that marriage (which he identified as "a new and everlasting covenant") was intended to be eternal and should be performed only by a person who has been "appointed on the earth to hold this power" that can bind husband and wife together "both . . . for time and for all eternity." (D&C 132:7.) The members of the Church then understood that if a marriage is to be eternal, it must be performed in the proper place (today, a temple) and by the proper authority (an ordained officiator in the temple who has received the keys of sealing from the prophet and president of the Church).

Because of new revelation and procedures, the earlier instructions in the article on marriage were out-of-date, and the article was deleted from the 1876 edition and all subsequent editions of the Doctrine and Covenants. (For further information on this subject, see *DS* 3:194-98.)

What is the origin of the "Testimony of the Twelve Apostles," which has been published in each copy of the Doctrine and Covenants?

At a general assembly held in Kirtland, Ohio, in August 1835, further consideration was given to the publication of some of the revelations received by Joseph Smith. Many persons bore individual testimonies that they knew the revelations were true and represented the mind and will of the Lord. W. W. Phelps then read a written testimony of the Twelve, the wording of which is as follows:

TESTIMONY OF THE TWELVE APOSTLES TO THE TRUTH OF THE BOOK OF DOCTRINE AND COVENANTS

The Testimony of the Witnesses to the Book of the Lord's Commandments, which commandments He gave to His Church through Joseph Smith, Jun., who was appointed by the voice of the Church for this purpose:

We, therefore, feel willing to bear testimony to all the world of mankind, to every creature upon the face of the earth, that the Lord has borne record to our souls, through the Holy Ghost shed forth upon us, that these commandments were given by inspiration of God, and are profitable for all men and are verily true.

We give this testimony unto the world, the Lord being our helper; and it is through the grace of God the Father, and His Son, Jesus Christ, that we are permitted to have this privilege of bearing this testimony unto the world, in the which we rejoice exceedingly, praying the Lord always that the children of men may be profited thereby.

THOMAS B. MARSH	ORSON HYDE	WILLIAM SMITH
DAVID W. PATTEN	WM. E. M'LELLIN	ORSON PRATT
BRIGHAM YOUNG	PARLEY P. PRATT	JOHN F. BOYNTON
HEBER C. KIMBALL	LUKE S. JOHNSON	LYMAN E. JOHNSON

This testimony has been included in every copy of the Doctrine and Covenants that has been published. In the 1835 edition, the testimony was published on page 256 as part of the minutes of the general assembly of August 17, 1835, without the printed names of the individual members of the Council of the Twelve.

Subsequently it was decided to publish the testimony on a separate page near the front of the volume, and to add the names of the Twelve "in the order in which they stood in the quorum." (*HC* 2:245.)

How many major editions of the Doctrine and Covenants have been published in English?

Usually only five major editions are listed in English: 1833, 1835, 1844, 1876, and 1921. The 1879 edition is listed below because that edition used footnotes for the first time. Here is a rundown on the various English-language editions:

1. *1833 edition*—published under the title *A Book of Commandments;* consisted of 65 chapters.

2. *1835 edition*—consisted of 102 sections plus seven Lectures on Faith. The sections of the current edition that were published in the 1835 edition include sections 1, 3-12, 14-76, 78-84, 86, 88-102, 104, 106-107, 133-134.

3. *1844 edition*—consisted of 111 sections plus the Lectures on Faith.

4. *1876 edition*—consisted of 136 sections, plus the Lectures on Faith. Included was this statement: "First issued, as divided into chapters and verses, by Orson Pratt." Concerning the revelations in this edition, Elder Joseph F. Smith of the Council of the Twelve proposed the following at the October 1880 general conference: "I move that we receive and accept the revelations contained in these books as

revelations from God to The Church of Jesus Christ of Latter-day Saints and to all the world." (*MS* 42:724.) The motion was accepted unanimously.

5. *1879 edition*—consisted of 136 sections plus the Lectures on Faith. "First issued with footnotes."

6. *1921 edition*—consisted of 136 sections plus the Official Declaration ("Manifesto"), but minus the Lectures on Faith. "First published in double-column pages, with present chapter headings, revised footnote references, and index."

The 1921 edition is the same as the current (1978) edition. Thus, the current edition is essentially the same as the 1876 edition except for the omission of the Lectures on Faith and for the addition of (1) introductions (superscriptions) to the sections, (2) a double-column page format, (3) revised footnote references, and (4) an index.

Into what non-English languages has the Doctrine and Covenants been published?

Non-English languages into which the complete Doctrine and Covenants has been published, as of September 1978, include:

Armenian	1941	Korean	1968
Chinese	1975	Maori	1919
Danish	1852	Norwegian	1957
Dutch	1908	Portuguese	1950
Finnish	1955	Samoan	1963
French	1958	Spanish	1948
German	1876	Swedish	1888
Hawaiian	1914	Tahitian	1965
Italian	1965	Tongan	1959
Japanese	1957	Welsh	1851

The Doctrine and Covenants was also printed in 1948 in Braille for the use of the blind, and is presently (summer 1978) being translated into Hungarian, Icelandic, Indonesian, Thai, and Vietnamese.

PART II
A COMPANION TO
YOUR STUDY OF
THE DOCTRINE AND
COVENANTS

SECTION 1

Background information on section 1

"Section one in the Doctrine and Covenants is not the first revelation received, but it is so placed in the book because the Lord gave it as the preface to the book of his commandments. The Doctrine and Covenants is distinctively peculiar and interesting to all who believe in it that it is the only book in existence which bears the honor of a preface given by the Lord himself. This, however, is consistent and should be the case, for it is as he declares his book. It was not written by Joseph Smith, but was dictated by Jesus Christ, and contains his and his Father's word to the Church and to all the world that faith in God, repentance from sin and membership in his Church might be given to all who will believe, and that once again the New and Everlasting covenant might be established.

"This revelation known as section one, was given at the wonderful conference held in Hiram [Ohio], November 1 and 2, 1831, when the publication of the commandments was under consideration." (Joseph Fielding Smith, *CHMR* 1:251-52.)

"The conference lasted two days. In the afternoon of the first day of the conference, according to the minutes of the meeting, the preface to the Book of Commandments was 'received by inspiration.' The same afternoon, the following occurred: 'Brother Joseph Smith, Jun., said that inasmuch as the Lord had bestowed a great blessing upon us in giving commandments and revelations, he asked the conference what testimony they were willing to attach to these commandments which would shortly be sent to the world. A number of the brethren arose and said that they were willing to testify to the world that they knew that they were of the Lord.'

"In the second day's proceedings of the conference it is recorded: 'The revelation of last evening read by the moderator [this was Oliver Cowdery]. The brethren then arose in turn and bore witness to the truth of the Book of Commandments; after which Brother Joseph Smith, Jun., arose and expressed his feelings and gratitude concerning the commandments and preface received yesterday.' " (Footnote, *HC* 1:222.)

"I returned from the conference at Orange, to Hiram; and as Oliver Cowdery and John Whitmer were to start for Independence, Missouri, a special conference was appointed for the first of November, at which I received the following: [Section 1, quoted.]" (Joseph Smith, *HC* 1:221-22.)

1:2 *"the voice of the Lord is unto all men"*

The introductory salutation "O ye people of my church" should not be interpreted to mean that the Doctrine and Covenants is intended only for members of the Church. In this same verse the Lord also addresses "ye people from afar; and ye that are upon the isles of the sea."

The second verse makes it clear that these revelations are intended for all men: "For verily the voice of the Lord is unto all men, and there is none to escape; and there is no eye that shall not see, neither ear that shall not hear, neither heart that shall not be penetrated." (D&C 1:2.)

The universal application of these revelations is also indicated in verse 4 ("the voice of warning shall be unto all people"), verse 6 ("unto you, O inhabitants of the earth"), verse 11 ("the voice of the Lord is unto the ends of the earth, that all that will hear may hear"), and verse 34 ("I the Lord am willing to make these things known unto all flesh").

"It seems a strange thing that many good brethren in the Church seem to think that the Lord never intended that the Book of Mormon, and more especially the Doctrine and Covenants, should go forth to the world. We hear the expression from time to time, that these, and especially the revelations in the Doctrine and Covenants are intended solely for members of the Church, but the Lord in his instructions has counseled otherwise. They were intended to be a warning to all the world." (Joseph Fielding Smith, *CHMR* 1:271.)

"So our message is a world message. It is intended for all of our Father's children. When God the Father and his Son Jesus Christ saw fit to come here to earth and appear to a boy prophet, surely such a visitation was intended to bless all of our Father's children." (Ezra Taft Benson, *CR,* April 1961, p. 113.)

1:2 *"there is none to escape"*

"You cannot go anywhere but where God can find you out." (Joseph Smith, *HC* 6:366.)

1:3 *"the rebellious shall be pierced with much sorrow"*

"This expression [the rebellious] refers to every soul who rejects the everlasting Gospel. When the Church of Jesus Christ of Latter-day Saints was established, this position was made clear to all the world. When the light comes, they can no longer hide their errors, their iniquities, their secret acts. The light reveals these things. That is the true cause of the enmity toward the Church. They want the light extinguished. It hurts them." (Smith and Sjodahl, *DCC,* p. 5.)

"Every soul that is deprived of hearing in this mortal world, shall have the privilege of hearing in the world of spirits where the Gospel also is declared. . . . The elders shall go forth and none shall stay them until the Lord declares it is enough. We have all been witnesses to some of the terrible destructions which have been poured without measure, because men have rejected divine truth." (Joseph Fielding Smith, *CHMR* 1:253.)

1:3, 10, 12 *Reasons for publication of the Doctrine and Covenants*

The Lord indicates in numerous places throughout the Doctrine and Covenants that one of the major purposes for giving and publishing these revelations is to prepare the people of the earth for forthcoming judgments, including the final judgment. In this one revelation alone, the Lord includes the following admonitions concerning coming judgments:

1. . . . the rebellious shall be pierced with much sorrow; for their iniquities shall be spoken upon the housetops, and their secret acts shall be revealed. (Verse 3.)
2. Prepare ye, prepare ye, for that which is to come, for the Lord is nigh. (Verse 12.)
3. . . . the Lord shall come to recompense unto every man according to his work, and measure to every man according to the measure which he has measured to his fellow man. (Verse 10.)

1:6   *"preface unto the book of my commandments"*

As indicated in the background information on this section, many of the revelations now included in the Doctrine and Covenants were first published as the Book of Commandments in 1835. This revelation (section 1) served as the preface to the Book of Commandments just as it does for the Doctrine and Covenants.

1:10   *"the Lord shall . . . recompense unto every man"*

"In the first section of the Doctrine and Covenants we read: [1:10 quoted].

"This teaching deserves the most careful consideration, for on judgment day the Lord will mete out to us precisely as we have dealt with our fellowmen, unless we have fully repented. It is a staggering thought, and yet it is an integral factor in the Lord's method of judgment. Do we realize its broad significance? Do we see how we shall reap what we sow?

"This principle, showing the manner by which God will judge us, puts a new light upon the commandment to love our neighbors as ourselves, and should persuade us to take that law seriously.

"It also helps us to understand the deep meaning of the Golden Rule: 'All things whatsoever ye would that men should do to you, do ye even so to them.' This is a commandment, and to further emphasize it the Lord said: 'This is the law and the prophets.' (3 Ne. 14:12.)" (Mark E. Petersen, *Ensign*, May 1977, p. 74.)

1:12   *"prepare ye for that which is to come"*

"The coming of the Lord is nigh, and his anger is kindled against all who reject his word and his mercy. The day is soon to come when all who will not hear the voice of the Lord, or his servants, the prophets and apostles, shall be cut off from among the people. This will be a terrible thing. It has been predicted since the days of Moses. It was spoken of by Nephi (1 Ne. 22:20-22); and by our Savior to the Nephites (3 Ne. 20:23-24; 21:11); by Peter to the Jews (Acts 3:22-23); which words of Peter were quoted by Moroni to the Prophet Joseph Smith (P. of G. P., p. 51), who said it was soon to be fulfilled. We must not think that this has reference merely to those who reject the Gospel, but it is also to those who have professed the name of Christ but who are unwilling to heed the word of the servants of the Lord. They are to be cut off from among the people of the covenant. (3 Ne. 21:11.) The Savior declared that, 'The Son of man shall send forth his angels, and they shall gather out of his kingdom all things that offend, and them which do iniquity.' (Matt. 13:41.) His kingdom is the Church. Even today the cleansing process is going on, but eventually it will come with dreadful suddenness, and none who work iniquity shall escape." (Joseph Fielding Smith, *CHMR* 1:254.)

1:13   *"the anger of the Lord is kindled"*

"God is long-suffering, and infinitely patient, but His anger is now kindled, and He has unsheathed His sword. It is 'bathed in heaven.' This is a very expressive term from Isaiah 34:5, where it is used to signify the pouring out of the indignation of the Lord upon all nations and His fury upon their armies, delivering them to destruction and slaughter." (Smith and Sjodahl, *DCC*, p. 5.)

"I prophesy, in the name of the Lord God of Israel, anguish and wrath and tribulation and the withdrawing of the Spirit of God from the earth await this generation, until they are visited with utter desolation. This generation is as corrupt as the generation of the Jews that crucified Christ; and if He were here today, and should preach the same doctrine He did then they would put Him to death." (Joseph Smith, *HC* 5:68.)

1:16   *"Babylon"*

The ancient city of Babylon became a symbol for wickedness, rebellion, and depravity which has continued in the scriptures to this day. See *Babylon* in Appendix A.

1:17   *"I the Lord, knowing the calamity"*

"The law must take its course, and when men refuse the offer and tender the Lord has given by which they may be saved, they cannot blame the Lord if calamities, judgments and destructions come upon them. The Lord cannot avert it, it must take its course, and yet our Father in his kindness and mercy has offered the way and the means of escape. [Sec. 5:18-19; 133:16.] . . .

"I understand from this [Sec. 1:17-18, 22-24] that the Lord plainly knew the condition of the world, what it was in 1830, and what it would be today. . . . Knowing the calamities that were coming to his children, unless they changed their course, knowing their disposition that there would be no repentance in their hearts, and yet with a great desire to save them, he called upon his servant, Joseph Smith, to warn men, to call repentance, and others to join in this great proclamation to all men: 'Repent, for the kingdom of God is at hand.' [Sec. 33:10; 42:7.] And not only to warn men that there was peril and danger ahead, but to offer the means of escape from the perils that would come. . . ." (Melvin J. Ballard, *CR,* October 1923, pp. 30-31.)

1:19, 23, 24 *"weak things of the world"*

See *Weak things of the world* in Appendix A.

1:24 *"that they might come to understanding"*

"It is the duty of the members of this Church to make themselves familiar with the revelations as they have been given and with the commandments as they have been taught in these revelations, or have been presented in them and given to the people, that they might know the truth which makes us free. And if we will study them, if we will put them into practice, if we will keep the commandments of the Lord, we will know the truth and there shall be no weapon formed against us that shall prosper. [Sec. 71:9-11.] There shall be no false doctrines, no teaching of men that will deceive us. . . .

"If you treasure up the word of the Lord, if you study these revelations, not merely those that are in the Doctrine and Covenants, but those that are in all the standard works of the Church, and you put into practice the commandments that are here found, you will not be deceived in these perilous times, but you shall have the spirit of discernment and you will know the truth and shall know falsehood, for you shall have power to know the spirits of men and to understand the Spirit of the Lord." (Joseph Fielding Smith, *CR,* October 1931, pp. 17-18.)

1:29 *Translation of the Book of Mormon*

Joseph Smith never gave in great detail the exact procedures he followed in translating the Book of Mormon. As advised by the Lord, the Prophet simply stated, "Through the medium of the Urim and Thummim I translated the record by the gift and power of God." (*Times and Seasons,* Mar. 1, 1842.)

On October 25, 1831, a conference was held at the home of Brother Sirenes Burnett of Cuyahoga County, Ohio, and the minutes of the meeting indicate that Joseph Smith said that "it was not intended to tell the world all the particulars of the coming forth of the Book of Mormon" and also that "it was not expedient for him to relate these things." (Kirkham, *A New Witness for Christ in America* 1:194.)

1:30 *"out of obscurity and out of darkness"*

The Church of Jesus Christ has existed on the earth in previous dispensations, both on the eastern continent (as indicated in the New Testament) and on the western continent (as taught in the Book of Mormon). These churches had gone into apostasy, and for hundreds of years the peoples of the earth had gone through the era that even the historians refer to as the Dark Ages.

The Renaissance and the Reformation started the world back toward the enlightenment possible in the true gospel. In the first vision of the Prophet Joseph Smith, the iron ceiling of heaven was again shattered and the rays of revelation started to illuminate the earth. Angels from the presence of God came with messages and scriptures (Moroni) and with priesthood authority and keys (John the Baptist, Peter, James, and John), until once again men upon the earth had power and were commissioned "to lay the foundation of this church, and to bring it forth out of obscurity and out of darkness, the only true and living church upon the face of the whole earth." (D&C 1:30.)

See (1) *Church,* and (2) *Darkness* in Appendix A.

1:30 *"the only true and living church"*

The expression *the only true and living church* contains two terms that are uniquely appropriate in referring to The Church of Jesus Christ of Latter-day Saints. It is the *true* church because it was organized under the direction of God himself under the supervision of angelic messengers who restored to the earth the priesthood authority and keys necessary for the establishment of the kingdom of God upon the earth. It is the *living* church because it was founded by the "only true and living God" (D&C 20:19); because it has a living prophet at its head upon the earth; and because it is a vital, expanding, growing, developing organization.

See *Church* in Appendix A.

"The position that The Church of Jesus Christ of Latter-day Saints is the only true Church upon the face of the earth is fundamental. . . . Now to those who think us uncharitable, we say that it was not devised by us; it was declared by Him, for he gave commandments to the early brethren, and I quote: [D&C 1:30 quoted.]

"Now this is not to say that the churches, all of them, are without some truth. They have some truth—some of them very much of it. They have a form of godliness. Often the clergy and adherents are not without dedication, and many of them practice remarkably well the virtues of Christianity. They are, nonetheless, incomplete. By his declaration, '. . . they teach for doctrines the commandments of men, having a form of godliness, but they deny the power thereof.' (JS-H 1:19.)

"Now we do not say they are wrong so much as we say they are incomplete. The fullness of the gospel has been restored. The power and the authority to act for Him is present with us. The power and the authority of the priesthood rests upon this church. The Lord revealed: [D&C 84:19-21 quoted.]" (Boyd K. Packer, *CR,* October 1969, p. 37.)

"We constitute a Church that has been organized and named by the Lord Jesus Christ. . . . This Church was not formed on man's initiative, it was not called into being because of some brilliant leader who stepped forward with a new plan; and therefore we cannot, we have not the power nor the authority to make any kind of affiliation with any other church; let me say with equal earnestness, no other denomination, no sect can ever affiliate as such with this, The Church of Jesus Christ of Latter-day Saints. There have been overtures made by some religious bodies to find out the terms under which they probably could come in with us; and the answer has been: Come in as every member of this Church has come in through the door; and note that the door is just wide enough to admit you, one at a time, the door of baptism, that ye may receive the Holy Ghost by the laying on of hands. [Sec. 20:37; 22; 33:11-13.]" (James E. Talmage, *CR,* April 1920, pp. 103-4.)

1:30   *"speaking unto the church collectively and not individually"*

"Please mark his words: 'The only true and living church upon the face of the whole earth, with which I the Lord am well pleased.' But that is not the end of the sentence or paragraph: 'with which I the Lord am well pleased, *speaking unto the church collectively and not individually.'*

"There lies a vital distinction. It is expressed, but we often overlook it. It is a distinction that should be heeded in all our organizations within the Church and without; the difference between the collective status or conditions or achievements and the work of the individual. . . .

"We as individuals are not doing all that could be done, all that should be done. I have no concern for the Church as a whole; its destiny is foretold, it is going on to glorious victory. [Sec. 65.] But that does not say that each of us who are members of the Church will go on to glorious victory; we may be left behind entirely. What are we doing individually?" (James E. Talmage, *CR,* October 1928, p. 118.)

1:35   *"the devil shall have power"*

"During the last one hundred years, or since these words [D&C 1:34-36] were spoken, more light and knowledge has come into the world in the realm of science, through the laboratory, and otherwise, than in all the ages that have preceded it, and if this were all used for the alleviation of human suffering, peace and prosperity could be here, and poverty abolished.

"But when we see men and nations spending their wealth to use the gas engine, the laboratory, the airplane, as means of human destruction, surely the devil has seized the blessings and privileges the Almighty intended to use to bring about peace, and is using them to destroy that which he presently shall lose the right to rule over. If the devil is not in the character of warfare that goes over the front-line trenches, swoops down upon the poor helpless women and children, drops its deadly bombs and assassinates them, then I do not know anything that has ever happened in this world that is so like the work of the devil as that. He is ruling in the midst of them." (Melvin J. Ballard, *CR,* October 1938, pp. 105-6.)

1:36 *"the Lord shall . . . come down"*

"In our day, we have been told some similar things about the power of the Lord among his peoples. In the very first revelation, or the preface to the revelations, the Lord said: [Sec. 1:35-36, quoted.]

"One of the ways by which 'he comes down among his people' is clearly explained in the revelation in which he defines certain gifts of the Spirit. He enumerates some of the gifts of the Spirit which men might enjoy; knowledge, and faith, and discernment, and the gift of tongues, and the testimony of knowledge that Jesus is the Son of God, and then he says this: '. . . unto such as God shall appoint and ordain to watch over the church, . . . are to have it given unto them to discern all those gifts. . . .' (D&C 46:27.)" (Harold B. Lee, *CR,* October 1960, p. 16.)

1:36 *"Idumea, or the world"*

"*Idumea* or Edom, of which Bozrah was the principal city, was a nation to the south of the Salt Sea, through which the trade route (called the King's Highway) ran between Egypt and Arabia. The Idumeans or Edomites were a wicked non-Israelitish people; hence, traveling through their country symbolized to the prophetic mind the pilgrimage of men through a wicked world. Idumea therefore meant the world." (Bruce R. McConkie, *MD,* p. 374.)

1:37 *"Search these commandments"*

"All members of the Church are commanded to search and obey these commandments. This is also true of all others. If we fail to do so and remain ignorant of the doctrines, covenants and commandments the Lord has given us, we shall stand condemned before his throne in the day of judgment when the books are opened. It behooves us to search that we may know the will of the Lord and thus grow in faith, knowledge and wisdom. (Alma 12:9; D&C 76:1-10)." (Joseph Fielding Smith, *CHMR* 1:256.)

1:38 *"whether by mine own voice or by the voice of my servants, it is the same"*

In his second epistle, the apostle Peter indicated that "prophecy came not in old time by the will of man: but holy men of God spake as they were moved upon by the Holy

Ghost." (2 Pe. 1:21.) When a prophet speaks under the influence of the Holy Ghost, in actuality he is not speaking his own words, but the words of God. See *Voice of the Lord* in Appendix A.

SECTION 2

Background information on section 2

The Prophet Joseph Smith has provided the following account of the first appearance to him of the Angel Moroni on the evening of September 21, 1823:

While I was thus in the act of calling upon God, I discovered a light appearing in my room, which continued to increase until the room was lighter than at noonday, when immediately a personage appeared at my bedside, standing in the air, for his feet did not touch the floor. He had on a loose robe of most exquisite whiteness. It was a whiteness beyond anything earthly I had ever seen; nor do I believe that any earthly thing could be made to appear so exceedingly white and brilliant. His hands were naked, and his arms also, a little above the wrist; so, also, were his feet naked, as were his legs, a little above the ankles. His head and neck were also bare. I could discover that he had no other clothing on but his robe, as it was open, so that I could see into his bosom.

Not only was his robe exceedingly white, but his whole person was glorious beyond description, and his countenance truly like lightning. The room was exceedingly light, but not so very bright as immediately round his person. When I first looked upon him, I was afraid; but the fear soon left me.

He called me by name, and said unto me that he was a messenger sent from the presence of God to me, and that his name was Moroni; that God had a work for me to do. . . .

After telling me these things, he commenced quoting the prophecies of the Old Testament. He first quoted part of the third chapter of Malachi, and he quoted also the fourth or last chapter of the same prophecy, though with a little variation from the way it reads in our Bible. Instead of quoting the first verse as it reads in our books, he quoted it thus:

For behold the day cometh that shall burn as an oven, and all the proud, yea, and all that do wickedly shall burn as stubble: for they that come shall burn them, saith the Lord of hosts, that it shall leave them neither root nor branch.

And again, he quoted the fifth verse thus:

Behold I will reveal unto you the Priesthood, by the hand of Elijah the prophet, before the coming of the great and dreadful day of the Lord.

He also quoted the next verse differently:

And he shall plant in the hearts of the children the promises made to the fathers, and the hearts of the children shall turn to their fathers; if it were not so, the whole earth would be utterly wasted at his coming. (*HC* 1:9, 11-12. Also in JS-H 1:30-39.)

2:1-3 *The prophesied appearance of Elijah the prophet*

"The whole world ought to take notice of this prediction [Mal. 4:5, 6], but the world does not understand it. Surely the signs of the times point to the fact that the great and dreadful day is near, even at our doors. The fig tree, figuratively, is putting forth her leaves. The turmoil, trouble, the war and bloodshed that we have seen, and which we still see, all point to the fact that this day for the coming of the Son of God is near. Therefore, Elijah the prophet is due to appear. I am sure you agree with me that he has already appeared, for we have it so recorded by the testimony of witnesses. [See Section 110.] It was on the third day of April, 1836, when he came to the Kirtland Temple, to Joseph Smith and Oliver Cowdery, and conferred upon them the keys of his priesthood and told them that he came in fulfillment of the prophecy of Malachi, to turn the hearts of the fathers to the children and the children to their fathers, lest the whole earth be smitten with a curse." (Joseph Fielding Smith, *CR,* April 1948, p. 132.)

2:1 *"Elijah the prophet"*

"Why should he send Elijah? Because he held the keys of the authority to administer in all the ordinances of the priesthood, and without the authority that is given, the ordinances could not be administered in righteousness.

"Salvation could not come to this world without the mediation of Jesus Christ. How shall God come to the rescue of the generations? He will send Elijah the prophet. The law revealed to Moses in Horeb never was revealed to the children of Israel as a nation. Elijah shall reveal the covenants to seal the hearts of the fathers to the children and the children to the fathers. The anointing and sealing is to be called, elected, and the election made sure." (Spencer W. Kimball, *Ensign,* May 1978, p. 48.)

See also *Elijah* in Appendix A.

2:1 *"the great and dreadful day of the Lord"*

See *Great and dreadful day of the Lord* in Appendix A.

2:2 *"the hearts of the children shall turn to their fathers"*

"The greatest responsibility in this world that God has laid upon us is to seek after our dead. The Apostle says, '. . . they without us cannot be made perfect' (Heb. 11:40); for it is necessary that the sealing power should be in our hands to seal our children and our dead for the fulness of the dispensation of times—a dispensation to meet the promises made by Jesus Christ before the foundation of the world for the salvation of man. [Titus 1:2.] . . . It is necessary that those who are going before and those who come after us should have salvation in common with us; and thus hath God made it obligatory upon man. Hence, God said, 'I will send you Elijah the prophet before the coming of the great and dreadful day of the Lord; and he shall turn the heart of the fathers to the children, and the heart of the children to their fathers, lest I come and smite the earth with a curse.' (Mal. 4:5.)" (Joseph Smith, *TPJS*, p. 356.)

2:3 *"the whole earth would be utterly wasted"*

One purpose of earth life is to provide an opportunity for each family on the earth to be sealed to the preceding family, and thus back to Adam and then to our Heavenly Father. This bond will enable us to share blessings more fully.

If the priesthood keys required to perform these sealings were not restored to the earth in this dispensation, then this work for both us and our dead ancestors could not be completed. Thus, in a sense, the earth would have been utterly wasted as this great purpose in the plan of God would not have been realized.

Also, it should be remembered that when Jesus Christ comes in his glory to reign on the earth as King of kings and Lord of lords, all the wicked will be destroyed. A righteous people must be prepared to meet him, or literally the whole population of the earth at that time will be utterly wasted.

"In the days of Noah, God destroyed the world by a flood, and he has promised to destroy it by fire in the last days: but before it should take place Elijah should come first and turn the hearts of the fathers to the children, etc.

"Now comes the point. What is this office and work of Elijah? It is one of the greatest and most important subjects that God has revealed. He should send Elijah to seal the children to the fathers, and the fathers to the children.

"Now was this merely confined to the living, to settle difficulties with families on earth? By no means. It was a far greater work. Elijah! what would you do if you were here? Would you confine your work to the living alone? No, I would refer you to the Scriptures, where the subject is manifest: that is, without us, they could not be made perfect, nor we without them; the fathers without the children, nor the children without the fathers. [Heb. 11:40; D&C 128:18.]

"I wish you to understand this subject, for it is important; and if you will receive it, this is the spirit of Elijah, that we redeem our dead, and connect ourselves with our fathers which are in heaven, and seal up our dead to come forth in the first resurrection; and here we want the power of Elijah to seal those who dwell on earth to those who dwell in heaven. This is the power of Elijah and the keys of the kingdom of Jehovah." (Joseph Smith, *HC* 6:251-52.)

Supplementary readings for section 2

The prophecy concerning the coming of Elijah before "the great and dreadful day of the Lord" is one of the most carefully documented prophecies of all time. It appears in all the standard works of the Church:

1. The prophecy was revealed to Malachi and appears in the last book of the Old Testament. (See especially Malachi 4:5-6.)

2. The resurrected Jesus Christ was commanded of the Father to give these scriptures to the righteous inhabitants of the American continent. Thus, the prophecy is contained in the Book of Mormon (3 Ne. 24 and 25), where the Savior also indicated that this prophecy had been given unto Malachi by "the Father" (3 Ne. 24:1).

3. The Angel Moroni quoted and explained this prophecy of Malachi when he first appeared to the Prophet Joseph Smith September 21, 1823. This account is recorded in Joseph Smith—History (verses 36-39) in the Pearl of Great Price.

4. The Doctrine and Covenants contains Moroni's wording of the prophecy (section 2) and also an account of the fulfillment of the prophecy (section 110:13-16).

Many Christians who believe in the prophetic principle of the Old Testament have assumed that this prophecy of Malachi was fulfilled at the time Elijah appeared on the Mount of Transfiguration to Peter, James, and John. (Matt. 17:1-13.) However, Latter-day Saints know that the prophecy was fulfilled April 3, 1836, when Elijah appeared in the Kirtland Temple. In fact, Elijah specifically mentioned during the visitation that he had come in fulfillment of the prophecy "which was spoken of by the mouth of Malachi." (D&C 110:14.)

The wording of the prophecy in the Bible and the Book of Mormon is identical but differs somewhat from the accounts in the Pearl of Great Price and the Doctrine and Covenants, which are also identical. Moroni's alterations from the Bible and Book of Mormon texts were probably for emphasis and clarification rather than for correction.

SECTION 3

Background information on section 3

Section 3 of the Doctrine and Covenants was given following the loss of the 116 pages of manuscript of the Book of Mormon, which had been translated by Joseph Smith when Martin Harris was his scribe. In the *History of the Church,* the Prophet wrote the following:

Mr. Harris . . . returned again to my house about the 12th of April, 1828, and commenced writing for me while I translated from the plates, which we continued until the 14th of June following, by which time he had written one hundred and sixteen pages of manuscript on foolscap paper. Some time after Mr. Harris had begun to write for me, he began to importune me to give him liberty to carry the writings home and show them; and desired of me that I would inquire of the Lord, through the Urim and Thummim, if he might not do so. I did inquire, and the answer was that he must not. However, he was not satisfied with this answer, and desired that I should inquire again. I did so, and the answer was as before. Still he could not be contented, but insisted that I should inquire once more. After much solicitation I again inquired of the Lord, and permission was granted him to have the writings on certain conditions; which were, that he show them only to his brother, Preserved Harris, his own wife, his father and his mother, and a Mrs. Cobb, a sister to his wife. In accordance with this last answer, I required of him that he should bind himself in a covenant to me in a most solemn manner that he would not do otherwise than had been directed. He did so. He bound himself as I required of him, took the writings, and went his way. Notwithstanding, however, the great restrictions which he had been laid under, and the solemnity of the covenant which he had made with me, he did show them to others, and by stratagem they got them away from him, and they never have been recovered unto this day.

In the meantime, while Martin Harris was gone with the writings, I went to visit my father's family at Manchester. I continued there for a short season, and then returned to my place in Pennsylvania. Immediately after my return home, I was walking out a little distance, when, behold, the former heavenly messenger appeared and handed to me the Urim and Thummim again—for it had been taken from me in consequence of my having wearied the Lord in asking for the privilege of letting Martin Harris take the writings, which he lost by transgression—and I inquired of the Lord through it, and obtained the following: [Sec. 3 follows.] (*HC* 1:20-22.)

3:1   *"the purposes of God cannot be frustrated"*

The prophets declare and the scriptures clearly teach that God knoweth all things (2 Ne. 9:20); he knows the end from the beginning (1 Ne. 9:6); he is the same yesterday, today, and forever (1 Ne. 10:18); and the past, present, and future are continually before his eyes (D&C 130:7). (See *Knowledge of God* in Appendix A.)

Inasmuch as God knows the future, he can plan and prepare for every eventuality; thus, it is absolute folly for man to suppose that he can frustrate the work of God.

Hundreds of years before the birth of Christ, God knew that in the last days evil men would try to thwart his work by attempting to destroy some of the scriptures. He provided for this by commanding His prophets anciently to keep parallel records.

Both Nephi and Mormon, the ancient prophets and historians involved, were faithful to their commands. Nephi prepared the small plates of Nephi, and Mormon wrote an abridgment of the record of Lehi on his plates. Both of those parallel records were preserved, and now that the manuscript copy of one of the records (Mormon's abridgment of the book of Lehi) had fallen into the hands of wicked men, the Lord was able to replace it with the other record (Nephi's small plates).

Truly, "it is *not* the work of God that is frustrated, but the work of men." (D&C 3:3.)

3:3   *"it is not the work of God that is frustrated, but the work of men"*

"Naturally, both Martin Harris and Joseph Smith passed through very severe mental torture following the loss of the manuscript. This was especially true of the Prophet. The Lord, knowing the end from the beginning, had provided for just this emergency and in a revelation given to the Prophet before the Lord took from him his gift, he was informed that the work and designs of the Almighty cannot be frustrated by puny man or by the devil. The Prophet was taught that even though a man may receive many revelations, if he sets himself up in his own strength or follows his carnal desires he will incur the displeasures, even the vengeance, of a just God. In his infinite wisdom our Father has provided for every problem or difficulty that may arise to stop or hinder the progress of His work. No power on earth or in hell can overthrow or defeat that which God has decreed. Every plan of the adversary will fail, for the Lord knows the secret thoughts of men, and sees the future with a vision clear and perfect, even as though it were in the past. [Sec. 38:21.] Jacob, son of Lehi, in his rejoicing declared: 'O how great the holiness of our God! For he knoweth all things, and there is not anything save he knows it.' (2 Nephi 9:20.) He knew that Satan would try to frustrate the coming forth of the Book of Mormon by the stealing and changing of the manuscript, and provided for it hundreds of years before the birth of Jesus Christ. Martin Harris without a doubt fell prey to the enticings of Satan, in his constant pleading for the manuscript. Satan played upon his pride and he foolishly thought that by the showing of the manuscript his kindred could be convinced.

"There is always danger when men boast in their own strength, or when they seek to satisfy their own desires. When those desires are contrary to the will of the Lord, and are still persisted in, they will without fail return in punishment upon their heads." (Joseph Fielding Smith, *CHMR* 1:24-25.)

3:6-8 *"you should not have feared man more than God"*

In his admonition to Joseph Smith, the Lord counsels him not to go on "in the persuasions of men," but to follow "the counsels of God." (D&C 3:6-7.)

The Lord's rebuke that Joseph had "oft . . . transgressed the commandments and the laws of God" (verse 6) should not be interpreted to mean that the Prophet was guilty of a grave moral sin. The Prophet later wrote: "No one need suppose me guilty of any great or malignant sins. A disposition to commit such was never in my nature." (JS-H 2:28.)

The Prophet had, however, submitted to the importunings of Martin Harris, even after the Lord had informed him that the 116 pages of manuscript should not be given to Mr. Harris. It is for this indiscretion (following after "the persuasions of men") that the Prophet is being reprimanded here.

3:9   *"Joseph . . . thou wast chosen"*

"The Prophet Joseph was chosen to do the work of the Lord. So was Isaiah (Isa. 49:5); Jeremiah (Jer. 1:5); Paul (Acts 9:15); and many others. But although God had selected him to be His instrument, unless he kept the commandments and instructions imparted to him, he would fall and lose his gift. God does not preordain man's fate, except conditionally. If He has decreed that men shall live by food, He has also made it necessary to prepare and to eat the food in order to enjoy the gift and blessings of life. That is the condition. He chose Israel to be His people, but only on the condition that they would keep His commandments. When they rejected Him, He rejected them. There is no other predestination." (Smith and Sjodahl, *DCC,* p. 20.)

3:12-13   *Martin Harris is "a wicked man"*

Martin Harris is reprimanded by the Lord (verses 12 and 13) and is referred to as a "wicked man." The following reasons are listed for his wickedness:

1. He has set at naught the counsels of God.

2. He has broken sacred promises that were made "before God."

3. He has depended upon his own judgment and boasted in his own wisdom.

"At heart, Martin was not wicked and desired to do what was right. He had faith in the mission of Joseph Smith, and that very faith led to his undoing, for he could not stand the gibes of relatives and friends. It was because of this that he desired to obtain the manuscript that these relatives and friends might be convinced. . . . His wickedness consisted in his selfish desire to gratify his own wish contrary to the will of the Lord, after he had been denied this request before it was granted. Moreover, he was wicked in that he violated a most sacred and solemn covenant and trust which he made with the Lord through the Prophet Joseph Smith. From his wicked act, or acts, he humbly repented and again found favor with the Lord to the extent that he was privileged to stand as one of the special three witnesses of the Book of Mormon, and to behold the plates in the presence of the holy angel. He was deprived, however, from ever again acting as scribe in the translation of this sacred record of the Nephites." (Joseph Fielding Smith, *CHMR* 1:28.)

3:16-20   *Meaning of the titles "Nephites" and "Lamanites"*

The Book of Mormon teaches that the people of Lehi, early in their history, divided into groups according to the names of their forefathers; hence, they became known as Lamanites, Lemuelites, Nephites, Jacobites, Josephites, Zoramites, and Ishmaelites. (Jacob 1:13.) In his writings, however, the prophet Jacob divided the people in two groups: Lamanites and Nephites. "I shall call them Lamanites that seek to destroy the people of Nephi, and those who are friendly I shall call Nephites, or the people of Nephi." (Jacob 1:14.)

Through the centuries of Book of Mormon history, some of the blood descendants of Nephi and his followers became known as Lamanites if they joined with those who sought "to destroy the people of Nephi." In a somewhat similar manner, the blood descendants of Laman and his followers might have been called Nephites if they became friendly toward or joined with the people of Nephi.

At the resurrection of Jesus Christ all of the wicked were destroyed from among this people, and for nearly two hundred years there were no "manner of ites; but they were in one, the children of Christ, and heirs to the kingdom of God." (4 Ne. 1:17.)

In A.D. 194 a group of people broke off from the true church and took "upon them the name of Lamanites; therefore there began to be Lamanites again in the land." (4 Ne. 1:20.) Later, in A.D. 231,

there was a great division among the people.

And . . . there arose a people who were called Nephites, and they were true believers in Christ; and among them there were those who were called by the Lamanites—Jacobites, and Josephites, and Zoramites;

Therefore the true believers in Christ . . . were called Nephites, and Jacobites, and Josephites, and Zoramites.

And . . . they who rejected the gospel were called Lamanites, and Lemuelites, and Ishmaelites. (4 Ne. 1:35-38.)

There is no indication that these divisions were along lineal bloodlines; rather, the two major divisions (Nephites and Lamanites) simply indicated whether or not the people believed in Christ.

The major designations continued until the close of the Book of Mormon period when the Lamanites destroyed the

Nephites in battle (Mormon 4-6). However, it should not be assumed that all the lineal blood descendants of the Nephites (including Jacobites, Josephites, and Zoramites) were destroyed, as some of them had undoubtedly earlier joined with the unbelieving Lamanites. The prophet Moroni suggests that even in the period following the wars of A.D. 385, some of the so-called Nephites were spared if they would "deny the Christ." (Moro. 1:2.)

In this revelation the Lord clearly indicates there are still descendants of all the sons of Lehi upon the earth as well as descendants of Zoram and Ishmael. (D&C 3:16-20.) In another revelation the Lord also refers to "the Lamanites, and also all that had become Lamanites because of their dissensions." (D&C 10:48.)

3:16-20 *"these plates" are preserved for the descendants of Lehi*

"These Lamanites are heirs to the promises, and God has said, without qualification, that he will give this land to them for an everlasting inheritance [3 Ne. 20:13-14]; that they shall be, with us, the builders of the new Jerusalem [3 Ne. 21:20-25]; the powers of heaven shall be among them, and they shall know the record of their fathers which has been brought to us through the instrumentality of the Prophet Joseph Smith." (Anthony W. Ivins, *CR,* April 1915, p. 112.)

3:19-20 *Purposes of the Lord in publishing the Book of Mormon*

The Lord has listed in this one revelation several purposes for the preservation of the plates of the Book of Mormon and for the publication of that sacred record:

1. "That the promises of the Lord might be fulfilled" (verse 19; see also Enos verses 16-18; 2 Ne. 26:16-17; D&C 10:45-51)

2. "That the Lamanites might come to the knowledge of their fathers" (verse 20; see also 1 Ne. 13:34-35, 39-42; Morm. 5:12-13)

3. That the Lamanites "might know the promises of the Lord" (verse 20; see also 2 Ne. 3:6-23; 29:11-14)

4. That the Lamanites might "believe the gospel . . . and that through their repentance they might be saved" (verse 20; see also Morm. 7:2-9; 8:4-16, 25-26; the preface of the Book of Mormon)

The prophet Mormon, who was given the responsibility of

abridging the ancient records of the forefathers of the Lamanites, was also told by the Lord some of the purposes for the preservation of the record. Thus, the wording of Mormon's testimony is similar to the words used by the Lord in this revelation: "Know ye that ye are of the house of Israel. Know ye that ye must come unto repentance, or ye cannot be saved. . . . Know ye that ye must come to the knowledge of your fathers, and repent of all your sins and iniquities, and believe in Jesus Christ, that he is the Son of God. . . ." (Morm. 7:2-3, 5.)

SECTION 4

"This section [4] was given through the Prophet Joseph Smith to his father, Joseph Smith, Sen., at Harmony, Pennsylvania, February, 1829. Joseph Smith, Sr., was the first person to believe the story of the Prophet and encouraged him to continue faithful to the teachings of the angel. . . . In February, 1829, he came to his son, the youthful prophet, and asked to know by revelation the will of the Lord. This section of the Doctrine and Covenants is the result of that humble inquiry.

"This revelation is very short, only seven verses, but it contains sufficient counsel and instruction for a life-time study. No one has yet mastered it. It was not intended as a personal revelation to Joseph Smith, but to be of benefit to all who desire to embark in the service of God. It is a revelation to each member of the Church, especially to all who hold the Priesthood. Perhaps there is no other revelation in all our scriptures that embodies greater instruction pertaining to the manner of qualification of members of the Church for the service of God, and in such condensed form than this revelation. It is as broad, as high and as deep as eternity. No elder of the Church is qualified to teach in the Church, or carry the message of Salvation to the world, until he has absorbed, in part at least, this heaven-sent instruction." (Joseph Fielding Smith, *CHMR* 1:34-35.)

4:1 *"a marvelous work is about to come forth"*

"The Book of Mormon is a marvelous work, no matter from what angle it is viewed. It was marvelous because it was brought to light by immortal hands. It was marvelous that a young man, with only a limited school education, and poor as far as this world's riches go, should be called upon to translate and publish it. It is marvelous in the story it tells, the teachings it gives and the prophecies it contains. It is marvelous in the effects it has produced. . . . However, the marvelous work is not confined to the coming forth of the Book of Mormon, but has reference to all that pertains to the restoration in the Dispensation of the Fulness of Times." (Smith and Sjodahl, *DCC*, pp. 23-24.)

"More than seven hundred years before the birth of Jesus Christ the Lord spoke through Isaiah of the coming forth of the Book of Mormon and the restoration of the Gospel. Isaiah, by prophecy, spoke of the restoration of the new and everlasting covenant, and the Lord performing a 'marvelous work and a wonder.' . . . This marvelous work is the restoration of the Church and the Gospel with all the power and authority, keys and blessings which pertain to this great work for the salvation of the children of men. All who have given diligent attention to the Church and the great things it has accomplished, and is accomplishing, must feel and know that the word of the Lord is fulfilled, even though many of the marvels are yet future." (Joseph Fielding Smith, *CHMR* 1:35.)

See *Great and marvelous work* in Appendix A.

4:2 *Serve God "with all your heart, might, mind, and strength"*

"Because the Lord was about to begin a marvelous work among the children of men, he needed servants who were willing to give themselves entirely to that work—'heart, might, mind, and strength'; that is affections, will-power, reasoning faculty, and physical strength, all must be dedicated to the service of the Lord in this latter-day work." (Smith and Sjodahl, *DCC*, p. 24.)

See also *Might, mind, and strength* in Appendix A.

4:2 *"that ye may stand blameless"*

"The preaching of the Gospel should be done in the spirit of the utmost humility and perseverance. Missionaries are commanded not to idle away their time, but to give to the Lord their heart, and serve him with all their 'might, mind and strength.' Every missionary who goes forth is under the solemn obligation and pledge to bear testimony of the restoration of the Gospel, and witness of its truth. In doing this he leaves all who hear him without excuse and their sins are on their own heads. If he fails to do this then he will not 'stand blameless before God at the last day.' " (Joseph Fielding Smith, *CHMR* 1:343.)

4:3   *"if ye have desires to serve God, ye are called"*

"My understanding is that the most important mission that I have in this life is: first, to keep the commandments of God, as they have been taught to me; and next, to teach them to my Father's children who do not understand them. . . . It is not necessary for you to be called to go into the mission field in order to proclaim the truth. Begin on the man who lives next door by inspiring confidence in him, by inspiring love in him for you because of your righteousness, and your missionary work has already begun. [Sec. 4:4-7, quoted.]" (George Albert Smith, *CR,* October 1916, pp. 50-51.)

4:4   *"the field is white already to harvest"*

"After the long night of apostasy, the world was filled with tradition, false doctrine and practice which were accepted as divine truth, since they had come down for hundreds of years. Error was venerable; people worshipped, as their fathers before them, the doctrines of men, as Isaiah declared. It was no small labor to go forth to reap the field, for the wheat had to be nurtured and carefully watered that it might grow to the harvest. Yet there were many who were waiting to hear the message of the restoration—choice spirits held in reserve to come forth in this great dispensation of the Fulness of Times. The need of laborers was great, but those available were few, yet they went forth in the power the Lord gave them, and none could stay them. Woe be to the man who sets his hand to the sickle and is not diligent, or who leaves the unharvested field. The Lord says of him that he stands in danger and may perish and lose salvation to his own soul (v. 4)." (Joseph Fielding Smith, *CHMR* 1:36.)

See also *Harvest symbols* in Appendix A.

4:5-6   *Qualities for missionary service*

The Lord provides two lists of characteristics that qualify a person for missionary work. The first list (faith, hope, charity, love) appears to be general and inclusive, while the second list (faith, virtue, knowledge, temperance, patience, brotherly kindness, godliness, charity, humility, diligence) seems to be more specific, although two terms, *faith* and *charity,* are common to both groups.

"It is true, we are engaged in a warfare, and all of us should be valiant warriors in the cause in which we are engaged. Our first enemy we will find within ourselves. It is a good thing to overcome that enemy first, and bring ourselves into strict obedience to the principles of life and salvation which he has given to the world for the salvation of men. When we shall have conquered ourselves, it will be well for us to wage our war without, against false teachings, false doctrines, false customs, habits and ways, against error, unbelief. . . ." (Joseph Fielding Smith, *CR,* October 1914, p. 128.)

SECTION 5

Background information on section 5

"Having humbly repented of his folly which brought upon him the charge from the Lord of wickedness [Sec. 3:12; 10:1], Martin Harris again sought the Prophet Joseph Smith and pleaded for the privilege to become one of the three witnesses which were spoken of in the Book of Mormon (2 Nephi 27:12-14). It was in the summer of 1828 when the manuscript was lost, and in March, 1829, when Martin again pleaded with the Prophet for this great privilege of being a witness. The Lord hearkened to his request and the Lord gave the revelation known as Section 5 in the Doctrine and Covenants." (Joseph Fielding Smith, *CHMR* 1:35-36.)

5:7-10 *"this generation shall have my word through you"*

"The Lord has always sent his accredited witnesses to testify of his truth, and has declared that all who reject these witnesses shall be under condemnation. This revelation declared that this generation shall have the word of the Lord through Joseph Smith. There may be some who think that this is unreasonable, and the Lord should use some miraculous means to convert the world. Frequently when strangers . . . hear the story of the coming forth of the Book of Mormon, they ask if the plates are in some museum where they may be seen. Some of them with some scientific training, express themselves to the effect that if the scholars could see and examine the plates and learn to read them, they would bear witness to the truth of the Book of Mormon and the veracity of Joseph Smith and the whole world would then be converted. When they are informed that the angel took the plates again, they turn away in their skepticism, shaking their heads, but the Lord has said: 'For my thoughts are not your thoughts, neither are your ways my ways,' saith the Lord. 'For as the heavens are higher than the earth, so are my ways higher than your ways, and my thoughts than your thoughts.' (Isa. 55:8-9.) We have learned that people are not converted by miracles or by examining records. If the Lord had the plates where scholars could examine them, they would have scoffed at them just as much as they do today. People are converted by their hearts being penetrated by the Spirit of the Lord when they humbly hearken to the testimonies of the Lord's servants. The Jews witnessed the miracles of our Lord, but this did not prevent them from crying out against him and having him crucified. (Joseph Fielding Smith, *CHMR* 1:36-37.)

5:11 *"in addition . . . the testimony of three"*

Before the second coming of Christ when all the wicked will be destroyed, the Lord will prove to the world that this is his work. The wicked will then be left without excuse, much as the wicked were left without excuse on the American continents when the resurrected Jesus Christ appeared shortly after his resurrection.

Our Heavenly Father is primarily interested in our being *converted* to his principles rather than our being simply *convinced* of them. Thus, the generation of Joseph Smith was to receive these things (the Book of Mormon, etc.) by faith through the word of the Prophet Joseph Smith.

In this revelation, the Lord indicates that three other persons will also be shown the plates of Mormon and will testify of them. (See also D&C 17; *HC* 1:52-57, and "The Testimony of Three Witnesses," published in the front of each copy of the Book of Mormon.)

"In giving the world the testimony of three witnesses in addition to Joseph Smith, the Lord fulfilled the law. We are called upon in this life to walk by faith, not by sight, not by the proclamation of heavenly messengers with the voice of thunder, but by the proclamation of accredited witnesses whom the Lord sends and by whom every work shall be established. [John 8:17.] The Lord made the promise that the testimony of the three should go forth with his words that were given through Joseph Smith, and this should be declared to all the world. These witnesses should know that these things are true and 'from heaven will I declare it unto them,' said the Lord. The testimony which they have given and which is recorded in each copy of the Book of Mormon in the most solemn language has gone forth to the four

corners of the earth, in fulfillment of the promise made in
the Book of Mormon. (See 2 Ne. 27:12-14.)" (Joseph Fielding Smith, *CHMR* 1:40.)

5:14   *"to none else will I grant this power"*

The three special witnesses of the plates of the Book of
Mormon were shown these things by an angel sent from
God, and the voice of God declared from the heavens "that
these things are true" (D&C 5:12; 17; *HC* 1:52-57). Although eight other persons were shown the plates by Joseph
Smith the Prophet (*HC* 1:57-58), this experience was not accompanied by visual or aural heavenly manifestations. Thus,
the three witnesses were the only ones who received this
"same testimony" as indicated in D&C 5:14.

5:14   *The Church is likened to an army with banners*

The expressive term "clear as the moon, and fair as the
sun, and terrible as an army with banners" is full of beauty
and poetry, and it has the appearance of being of ancient
form. It is found only once in the Bible—the Song of
Solomon (or Canticles) 6:10. For further information on this
term, see *Banners* in Appendix A.

5:16-17   *"wait yet a little while" to be baptized*

All things must be done in correct order and sequence.
The Lord indicates here that all true believers in the Book of
Mormon should be baptized of the water and of the Spirit,
but he also indicates that this ordinance should not yet be
performed inasmuch as Joseph Smith had not yet had the
priesthood conferred upon him. When the Aaronic Priesthood was restored by John the Baptist, the "keys . . . of baptism by immersion for the remission of sins" were also restored and could then be used. (D&C 13.)

5:18-19   *"if they repent not"*

"The Lord always warns the people of a new dispensation
through prophets raised up unto them in their own day. This
he has done for this generation through the great prophet of
the restoration, Joseph Smith, Jr. Through him the Lord
repeatedly declared that the world was ripening in iniquity
and that unless men repented destruction would overtake
them. For example, in March, 1829, he said: [Sec. 5:19-20,

quoted.] You will note that this prediction, as were like predictions in the past, is conditional. 'If they repent not,' is the condition. For this generation, as for all others, the Lord has provided the means of escape. This means is now, and has always been, the Gospel of Jesus Christ." (Marion G. Romney, *CR*, April 1958, p. 128.)

5:19 *"brightness of my coming"*

The term "brightness of my coming" refers to the second coming of Jesus Christ when he will come in glory and great power to judge the nations and establish his kingdom. In a revelation given in October 1831, the Lord refers to the time when "the Son of Man shall come down in heaven, clothed in the brightness of his glory, to meet the kingdom of God which is set up on the earth." (D&C 65:5.) The term is also used by Paul in 2 Thessalonians 2:8, wherein he states that "the Lord shall consume [the wicked] . . . with the brightness of his coming."

See *Second Coming* in Appendix A.

5:21 *"yield to the persuasions of men no more"*

The counsel of the Lord to Joseph Smith to "walk more uprightly before me, and to yield to the persuasions of men no more" is similar to his earlier admonition that the Prophet should not "have gone on in the persuasions of men." (D&C 3:6.) In the earlier revelation, the Lord explained why this counsel is necessary: "For, behold, you should not have feared man more than God . . . men set at naught the counsels of God, and despise his words." (D&C 3:7.)

The youthful Prophet had naturally been inclined to place confidence and trust in his older associates who had shown interest in and concern for him. Martin Harris already had betrayed this confidence once (see background information for section 3), and the Lord is here warning Joseph Smith again to place his first trust in him rather than in Martin Harris or the arm of flesh.

5:22 *"even if you should be slain"*

The expression "even if you should be slain" appears to be a foreshadowing of the type of death that was eventually experienced by Joseph Smith.

5:23 *"concerning the man [Martin Harris] that desires the witness"*

"Martin Harris had already received a remarkable proof of the truth of the claims made by the Prophet Joseph regarding the Book of Mormon, when he carried a facsimile of the engravings to New York scientists. Professor Anthon had told him, as he himself states, that the 'hieroglyphics were true characters.' He had also, through the Prophet, received revelations (Sec. 3:12). But he was not yet satisfied." (Smith and Sjodahl, *DCC*, p. 25.)

SECTION 6

Background information on section 6

"Previous to joining the Prophet Joseph Smith, Oliver Cowdery had met David Whitmer at Palmyra, and conversed with him concerning the rumors rife in that vicinity about the finding of the Book of Mormon plates. This chance meeting resulted in a friendship between the young men, and finally when Cowdery determined to visit the Prophet in Harmony, he went via the Whitmer residence, at Fayette, which was near the town of Waterloo, at the head of Seneca Lake, Seneca county, New York; and promised his friend David Whitmer that after visiting the Prophet he would write him his impressions as to the truth or untruth of Joseph Smith's having an ancient record." (Footnote, *HC* 1:32.)

"When Oliver Cowdery went to Pennsylvania, he promised to write me what he should learn about these matters, which he did. He wrote me that Joseph had told him (Oliver's) secret thoughts, and all he had meditated about going to see him, which no man on earth knew, as he supposed, but himself, and so he stopped to write for Joseph." (David Whitmer, *Historical Record: Church Ency. Book 1,* 6:208 [May 1887].)

"On the 5th day of April, 1829, Oliver Cowdery came to my house, until which time I had never seen him. He stated to me that, having been teaching school in the neighborhood where my father resided, and my father being one of those who sent to the school, he went to board for a season at his house, and while there the family related to him the circumstances of my having received the plates, and accordingly he had come to make inquiries of me. Two days after the arrival of Mr. Cowdery (being the 7th of April) I commenced to translate the Book of Mormon, and he began to write for me, which, having continued for some time, I inquired of the Lord through the Urim and Thummim, and obtained the following: [Section 6, follows.]" (Joseph Smith, *HC* 1:32-33.)

6:1 *"A great and marvelous work"*

The Lord uses the adjectives "great and marvelous" several times to refer to different aspects of his work, including two references in this one revelation: 6:1 and 6:11. See *Great and marvelous work* in Appendix A.

6:2 *God's word is "sharper than a two-edged sword"*

For information on this descriptive term, see *Sword* in Appendix A.

"The Word of God is 'quick'; it is 'living,' and not dead. It is 'powerful'; it is a force, like compressed steam, or electricity. As a sharp, two-edged sword it pierces and cuts, and penetrates to the inmost parts of man, being a 'discerner of the thoughts and intents of the heart' (Heb. 4:12. Compare Isa. 49:2; Eph. 6:17; Rev. 2:16; 19:15)." (Smith and Sjodahl, *DCC,* p. 33.)

6:3-4 *"the field is white already to harvest"*

See *Harvest symbols* in Appendix A.

6:5 *"if you will knock it shall be opened"*

See *Prayer* in Appendix A.

"There is no reason in the world why any soul should not know where to find the truth. If he will only humble himself and seek in the spirit of humility and faith, going to the Lord just as the Prophet Joseph Smith went to the Lord to find the truth, he will find it. 'Knock, and it shall be opened unto you.' This is my testimony. I know it is true." (Joseph Fielding Smith, *CR,* April 1951, p. 59.)

6:6 *"establish the cause of Zion"*

"The question as to individual responsibility for the welfare of the Church was asked in the early days of members of the Church. Several of the men who labored with the Prophet Joseph Smith came to him in those early days and said: 'What shall we do?' They might have said: 'What shall we do to be saved?' The Lord in every instance gave an answer. We have a series of short revelations in the Doctrine and Covenants, which are answers to that question. I find in every one a significant statement, worded almost identically in all of these revelations, to Hyrum Smith, David Whitmer, Oliver Cowdery, and others of less fame in the Church: 'Keep my commandments, and seek to bring forth and establish the cause of Zion.' [Sec. 6:6; 11:6; 14:6.] That is our business, the business of the Latter-day Saints. . . .

"We are here to build Zion to Almighty God, for the blessing of all the world. In that aim we are unique and different from all other peoples. We must respect that obligation, and not be afraid of it. We cannot walk as other men, or talk as other men, or do as other men, for we have a different destiny, obligation, and responsibility placed upon us, and we must fit ourselves for that great destiny and obligation." (John A. Widtsoe, *CR,* April 1940, p. 36.)

6:7 *"Seek not for riches"*

See *Riches* in Appendix A.

"The great criterion of success in the world is that men can make money, but I want to say to you Latter-day Saints that to do this is not true success. . . . What is the matter? Why, the appetite for money grows upon a man, increases and strengthens unless he is careful, just as much as the appetite for whiskey, and it gets possession of him, and he loves the money instead of loving it only for the good that he can do with it. He does not estimate properly the value of things." (Heber J. Grant, *CR,* October 1911, p. 23.)

"It is thought by many that the possession of gold and silver will produce for them happiness, and hence, thousands hunt the mountains for the precious metals; in this they are mistaken. The possession of wealth alone does not produce happiness." (Brigham Young, *JD* 11:15.)

6:7 *"mysteries of God"*

See *Mysteries* in Appendix A.

6:7 *"eternal life"*

See *Eternal life* in Appendix A.

6:9 *"Say nothing but repentance"*

See *Repentance* in Appendix A.

"In the revelation to Oliver Cowdery, and to several others who came to ask what the Lord would have them do, the Lord said: 'Say nothing but repentance unto this generation; keep my commandments, and assist to bring forth my work.' We must not infer from this expression that those who went forth to preach were limited in their teachings so that all they could say was 'repent from your sins,' but in teaching the principles of the Gospel they should do so with the desire to teach repentance to the people and bring them in humility to a realization of the need for remission of sins. Even today in all of our preaching it should be with the desire to bring people to repentance and faith in God. That was the burden of John's message as he went forth to prepare the way for the Lord: 'Repent ye; for the kingdom of heaven is at hand,' he declared to the people, but he also taught them the necessity of baptism and officiated in that ordinance for all who repented of their sins. [Matt. 3:11.]" (Joseph Fielding Smith, *CHMR* 1:39-40.)

6:10 *"Behold thou hast a gift"*

"Oliver Cowdery's gift was the spirit of revelation (Section 8:3, 4), by which he could obtain knowledge of things divine. He also had the gift of Aaron. Aaron was the spokesman of Moses, and Oliver Cowdery became the first spokesman of the Prophet, or of the Church, when, on the 30th of April, 1830, he preached the first public discourse in this dispensation." (Smith and Sjodahl, *DCC*, p. 35.)

6:16 *"none else save God knowest thy thoughts"*

Although Lucifer has a great deal of power, which he uses to tempt, deceive, and entice men, he does not have the power to read thoughts, as "there is none else save God that knowest thy thoughts and the intents of thy heart." The writings of Moses also indicate that Satan does not know the mind of God: "And Satan . . . knew not the mind of God, therefore he sought to destroy the world." (Moses 4:6.)

6:21 *"I am Jesus Christ, the Son of God"*

See *Jesus Christ* in Appendix A.

"Jesus Christ, our Lord, is the source of these Revelations. He is the Word, as well as the Redeemer of the world. He is the Light which shineth in darkness; not which *shone* formerly, but which *now* shineth. The Darkness is that condition of the world, which is unaffected by the light of divine revelation, because of the ignorance, superstition, and enmity of men. In that condition the world does not comprehend the light of revelation. That kind of darkness remains apart, unyielding, unpenetrated, now as in the day when John wrote his Gospel (John 1:5)." (Smith and Sjodahl, *DCC*, p. 36.)

6:22-24 *"I have told you things which no man knoweth"*

Inasmuch as only the Lord knows the "thoughts and the intents" of men (D&C 6:16), the Lord truly gave unto Oliver Cowdery a witness from Him when he reminded Oliver of thoughts and feelings that could only be known by the Lord and by Oliver himself.

"After we had received this revelation [Section 6], Oliver Cowdery stated to me that after he had gone to my father's to board, and after the family had communicated to him concerning my having obtained the plates, that one night after he had retired to bed he called upon the Lord to know if these things were so, and the Lord manifested to him that they were true, but he had kept the circumstances entirely secret, and had mentioned it to no one; so that after this revelation was given he knew that the work was true, because no being living knew of the thing alluded to in the revelation, but God and himself." (Joseph Smith, *HC* 1:35.)

6:25-28 *Counsel for Oliver Cowdery*

This revelation was received during the same month that Oliver Cowdery first started to serve as scribe for Joseph Smith in the translation of the Book of Mormon. As Oliver Cowdery witnessed the gift of translation being manifested through Joseph, it would seem only natural that he would wonder about the gift and desire it for himself. Here the Lord counsels Oliver to be patient and faithful to the opportunities that had been given to him, so that additional power could be given to him later to "assist in bringing to light" those scriptures or parts of scriptures that were then not available to the peoples of the earth. This reference evidently refers both to the Book of Mormon and to Joseph Smith's inspired version of the Bible.

6:25-27 *"records which contain much of my gospel . . . have been kept back"*

"It was in the summer of the year 1830 that the Lord called on Joseph Smith to commence his correction of the Bible. In June, the word of the Lord came to him that other scripture, in addition to the Book of Mormon, was to be given. This was according to the promise made to Oliver Cowdery and Joseph Smith as given in Section 6:25-27, in April, 1829. In June, 1830, the Prophet commenced to translate the words of Moses which were given to Moses when he was caught up into a high mountain where he talked with the Lord face to face. This vision of Moses is one of the most remarkable revelations given in this dispensation. It is published in the Pearl of Great Price." (Joseph Fielding Smith, *CHMR* 1:119.)

6:28 *"in the mouth of two or three witnesses"*

"Oliver Cowdery, whose reputation for honesty has never been questioned, was with Joseph Smith when John the Baptist came to restore the authority of the Aaronic Priesthood, and when Peter, James and John appeared to restore the Melchizedek Priesthood, and also when the foundation-laying revelations from spiritual beings, given at the time of the dedication of the Kirtland Temple, were received. [Sec. 13; 27:12-13; 110.] Of all these joint experiences, Oliver Cowdery often bore testimony.

"Sidney Rigdon, who was with Joseph Smith when the revelation called the Vision was received, bore testimony in diverse places to the glimpse at that time, with Joseph Smith, of heavenly personages, including the Lord himself. [Sec. 76:19-24.]" (John A. Widtsoe, *JS*, pp. 338-39.)

6:34 *"if ye are built upon my rock"*

For information on the term *rock,* see *Rock* in Appendix A.

6:34 *"they cannot prevail"*

"I remember reading, when a boy, a helpful passage from the Doctrine and Covenants. Let me read it here. As a lad I felt fear, sometimes of men, but more often of the dark outside forces. I often wondered if this persecuted people, after all, would be able to accomplish all that was pictured in its destiny. Then I found in my reading of the Doctrine and Covenants this passage which has been a joy and a help and a strength to me all my life, for the Lord said to his people in Harmony, Pennsylvania, before the Church was organized: [Sec. 6:34-37, quoted.]

"What do we care for the slanderer or the liar; what do we care for the enemy who arises to defeat our holy purposes? We have the truth, the mightiest weapon God has given to his people, and we shall win, in the end, if we do the things that God requires us to do." (John A. Widtsoe, *CR,* October 1923, p. 27.)

6:36   *"doubt not, fear not"*

"Keep courage. Do not feel sorry for yourselves. Whatever you do, do not feel sorry for yourselves. You live in a great age of opportunity. I remember the words of one very sharp and shrewd observer who said, 'Whenever I hear someone sigh and say that life is hard, I am tempted to ask "compared to what?" ' What are the alternatives? No one ever promised us it would be easy. It is a schooling; it is an opportunity; it is a learning period, and a wonderful one. Despite all the disappointments and difficulties, the great and ultimate rewards are beyond price." (Richard L. Evans, *CR*, April 1961, p. 76.)

6:37   *Behold my wounds*

The reminder of the Savior to behold "the wounds which pierced my side, and also the prints of the nails in my hands and feet" is evidently meant here in a figurative sense only. There is no indication that the Savior actually, physically showed himself to Joseph Smith and Oliver Cowdery on this occasion. Rather, he is reminding them to be faithful in their callings, as was evident by the marks of the crucifixion.

SECTION 7

Background information on section 7

One of the most frequently misunderstood chapters in all the scriptures is John 21, which tells of the appearance of the resurrected Jesus Christ on the shore of the Sea of Galilee. Verses 20-23 are particularly difficult:

Then Peter, turning about, seeth the disciple whom Jesus loved following; which also leaned on his breast at supper, and said, Lord, which is he that betrayeth thee?

Peter seeing him saith to Jesus, Lord, and what shall this man do?

Jesus saith unto him, If I will that he tarry till I come, what is that to thee? follow thou me.

Then went this saying abroad among the brethren, that that disciple should not die: yet Jesus said not unto him, He shall not die; but, If I will that he tarry till I come, what is that to thee? (John 21:20-23.)

Instead of simply wondering about these verses, Joseph Smith and Oliver Cowdery asked the Lord concerning the exact status of John the Beloved, and they were privileged to read the words that were written by John himself concerning this incident. (D&C 7.)

Later on as they continued with the translation of the Book of Mormon, they received additional insights into the mission and condition of John. When the resurrected Jesus Christ appeared to his chosen twelve disciples among the descendants of Lehi and asked them to express their hearts' desire, he indicated to three of them, "Ye have desired the thing which John, my beloved, who was with me in my ministry, before that I was lifted up by the Jews, desired of me." (3 Ne. 28:6.)

The Savior then explained to them the promise he had made to John:

Therefore, more blessed are ye, for ye shall never taste of death; but ye shall live to behold all the doings of the Father unto the children of men, even until all things shall be fulfilled according to the will of the Father, when I shall come in my glory with the powers of heaven.

And ye shall never endure the pains of death; but when I shall come in my glory ye shall be changed in the twinkling of an eye from mortality to immortality; and then shall ye be blessed in the kingdom of my Father.

And again, ye shall not have pain while ye shall dwell in the flesh, neither sorrow save it be for the sins of the world; and all this will I do because of the thing which ye have desired of me, for ye have desired that ye might bring the souls of men unto me, while the world shall stand. (3 Ne. 28:7-9.)

Joseph Smith and Oliver Cowdery "inquired through the Urim and Thummim" as to what had happened to John, the beloved disciple. As a result of that inquiry, the truths contained in Section 7 were revealed to them. There is no indication that the actual parchment containing the writings of John was at any time physically in the hands of the Prophet. All things are possible unto God (Matt. 19:26), and surely the exact words of John's writings could have been revealed to Joseph Smith, even if the parchment no longer existed. As is indicated in a later revelation, all things "past, present, and future" are continually before the Lord. (D&C 130:7.)

"The question might be asked, whether the Prophet had actually seen the parchment written and hidden by John, or a copy of it; if so, where and when did he obtain it, and what became of it?

"The history of the Prophet does not furnish information on these subjects. But it is not necessary to suppose that the Prophet had St. John's parchment, or a copy of it, before him, when he received this Revelation. It was the contents of the document that were revealed. It was just as easy for the Spirit of the Lord to communicate the contents of that record to the Prophet, without the actual presence of it, as it would have been to enable him to understand the language in which John wrote it, whether Greek or Aramæan, which languages neither Joseph nor Oliver could have read, except by special divine interposition, even if they had had the manuscript before them. The miracle would have been practically the same. . . .

"There is, therefore, no difficulty in accepting the proposition that God could make the contents of John's parchment known to His Servants, whether the document was accessible to them or not. That John committed our Lord's last promise to him and Peter to writing is probable. It must have made a deep and lasting impression on him." (Smith and Sjodahl, *DCC*, p. 40.)

"During the month of April I continued to translate, and he (Oliver Cowdery) to write, with little cessation, during which time we received several revelations. A difference of opinion arising between us about the account of John the Apostle, mentioned in the New Testament, as to whether he died or continued to live, we mutually agreed to settle it by the Urim and Thummim and the following is the word which we received: [Section 7 follows.]" (Joseph Smith, *HC* 1:35-36.)

7:1-8   *The promise to John the Beloved*

"From this revelation the conversation between our Lord and Peter recorded in the twenty-first chapter of John (verses 18-24), is clarified, and we know that John was blessed with the privilege of remaining on the earth until the second coming of Christ. This also explains the words of the Savior regarding some remaining until he should come to his kingdom. [Matt. 16:28.]" (Joseph Fielding Smith, *CHMR* 1:44.)

7:2   *"power over death"*

Latter-day Saints use the term *translated being* to refer to those special persons who have been given "power over death." This expression does not mean that these people will not die; rather it means that death will have no power over them until the time comes for them to die and then to be resurrected in the twinkling of an eye.

"Translated bodies cannot enter into rest until they have undergone a change equivalent to death. Translated bodies are designed for future missions." (Joseph Smith, *HC* 4:425.)

"Now the doctrine of translation is a power which belongs to this Priesthood. There are many things which belong to the powers of the Priesthood and the keys thereof, that have been kept hid from before the foundation of the world; they are hid from the wise and prudent to be revealed in the last times.

"Many have supposed that the doctrine of translation was a doctrine whereby men were taken immediately into the presence of God, and into an eternal fulness, but this is a mistaken idea. Their place of habitation is that of the terrestrial order, and a place prepared for such characters he held in reserve to be ministering angels unto many planets, and who as yet have not entered into so great a fulness as those who are resurrected from the dead. 'Others were tortured, not accepting deliverance, that they might obtain a better resurrection.' (Heb. 11th chap., part of the 35th verse.)

"Now it was evident that there was a better resurrection, or else God would not have revealed it unto Paul. Wherein then, can it be said a better resurrection. This distinction is made between the doctrine of the actual resurrection and translation: translation obtains deliverance from the tortures and sufferings of the body, but their existence will prolong as to the labors and toils of the ministry, before they can enter into so great a rest and glory." (Joseph Smith, *HC* 4:425.)

"Mormon, in regarding the history of the labors of the Disciples of Christ, not only gives an excellent account of their ministry and powers, but also describes the fact that while the three who tarry will eventually have to be changed from mortality to immortality, they are not subject to pain, disease, and the ills of the flesh, and they have power over the elements. They also have the authority to minister to all the scattered tribes of Israel until Christ comes. (3 Nephi 28:8-40.)" (Joseph Fielding Smith, *CHMR* 1:48-49.)

7:3   *"until I come in my glory"*

"This expression is almost identical with that used by our Lord on another occasion, when He said, 'For the Son of man shall come in the glory of his Father. . . . Verily I say unto you, There be some standing here, which shall not taste death, till they see the Son of man coming in his kingdom' (Matt. 16:28; Mark 9:1; Luke 9:27). Peter suffered martyrdom. . . James [and] many of the other Apostles were slain. John had 'power over death.' Tradition says that on one occasion he came unharmed from a cauldron of boiling oil; and that on another occasion he was a captive among a band of robbers, whose chieftain became converted through his preaching." (Smith and Sjodahl, *DCC*, p. 41.)

7:3   *"thou shalt . . . prophesy before nations"*

"A great mission was given unto John because of his

desire, and he is even now laboring as 'a flaming fire and a ministering angel, for those who are heirs of salvation.' In the tenth chapter of Revelation we read that John was given a little book by the angel and commanded to eat it up, which he did, and he said 'it was in my mouth sweet as honey; and as soon as I had eaten it, my belly was bitter.' And the angel said by way of interpretation of this act: 'Thou must prophesy again before many peoples, and nations, and tongues, and kings.' When this mission was given, John was an old man far beyond the allotted years of three score and ten. In answer to a question as to the meaning of this vision of the book, the Prophet Joseph Smith said: It was a mission and an ordinance for John to gather the tribes of Israel. (D&C 77:14.) At a conference of the Church, held June, 1831, Joseph Smith said 'that John the Revelator was then among the ten tribes of Israel who had been led away by Shalmaneser, king of Assyria, to prepare them for their return from their long dispersion.' (*History of the Church* 1:176; *Essentials in Church History*, p. 126.)" (Joseph Fielding Smith, *CHMR* 1:48.)

"He [John the Beloved] 'prophesied before nations, kindred, tongues and people' through the Book of Revelation, in which the history of the world, as committed to the records of heaven before the foundations of the world were laid, is outlined. He prophesied more particularly about the general apostasy (Rev. 9:20, 21; 13:1-18); and the restoration of the Gospel (10:1-11; 14:1-3)." (Smith and Sjodahl, *DCC*, p. 41.)

7:5-6   *The desire of John the Beloved*

The Savior's statement to Peter that John "has desired that he might do more, or a greater work yet among men than what he has before done" compares the worth of John's future work and mission to that which John had already accomplished. It does not necessarily compare the importance of John's future mission with the importance of Peter's future mission.

7:6   *"I will make him . . . a ministering angel"*

"John received the promise that he would be a 'ministering angel' for the benefit of the heirs of salvation on earth. The bishops of the seven Asiatic churches are addressed as *angels,* and the inference is that it was a common title at that time of all bishops, in Europe and Africa, as well as Asia. The word *angel* means *messenger.* It is almost synonymous with the word *apostle,* which also means *messenger.*" (Smith and Sjodahl, *DCC,* p. 41.)

"When the Prophet Joseph [Smith] had finished the endowments of the First Presidency, the Twelve and the Presiding Bishops, the First Presidency proceeded to lay hands upon each one of them to seal and confirm the anointing; and at the close of each blessing the whole of the quorums responded to it with a loud shout of Hosanna! Hosanna! etc. [in the Kirtland Temple.] While these things were being attended to, the beloved disciple John was seen in our midst by the Prophet Joseph, Oliver Cowdery and others." (Heber C. Kimball, *LHCK,* pp. 91-92.)

7:6-7 *Peter shall minister for heirs of salvation and for James and John*

The word *minister* in verse 7 does not mean that Peter will serve "under the direction of" James and John, nor does the same word in verse 6 mean that John will be directed by those who are heirs of salvation. In both instances *minister* means "to administer to, or help to meet the needs of." That Peter was the presiding apostle under Christ is made abundantly clear in both ancient and modern scriptures. (See Matt. 16:18-19; John 21:15-19; Acts 1:15-26; 2:14, 37:42; Gal. 1:18; D&C 27:12; 49:11; 128:10, 20.)

7:7 *"unto you three I will give this power"*

The Savior in New Testament times frequently selected the same three apostles (Peter, James, and John) to accompany him on sacred occasions. They were present with the Savior on the Mount of Transfiguration (Matt. 17:1-8; Mark 9:2-8; Luke 9:28-36) and were invited to be near him during his experiences in the Garden of Gethsemane (Matt. 26:37-46; Mark 14:32-42).

In this revelation (D&C 7:7), the Savior indicates that he has given to Peter, James, and John the "keys" of his ministry until he comes. When John the Baptist later restored the Aaronic Priesthood (D&C 13), he specifically stated that he was acting under the direction of Peter, James, and John. (See *HC* 1:39 and D&C 27:7-8, 12.)

Soon after the appearance of John the Baptist, the three ancient apostles—Peter, James, and John—appeared and ordained Joseph Smith and Oliver Cowdery "to be apostles" and bestowed upon them the keys of the ministry of Christ. (See D&C 27:12; 128:20, and *HC* 1:40-43.)

SECTION 8

Background information on section 8

"Whilst continuing the work of translation, during the month of April, Oliver Cowdery became exceedingly anxious to have the power to translate bestowed upon him, and in relation to this desire the following revelations were obtained: [Sections 8 and 9, follow.]" (Joseph Smith, *HC* 1:36.)

8:1 *"you shall receive a knowledge of the engravings of old records"*

"At this time the Lord seemed perfectly willing that Oliver Cowdery as well as Joseph Smith should engage in this labor of translating the plates, and he gave in some detail what qualifications are necessary for the reception of knowledge by revelation and also the procedure necessary in translating ancient records. Oliver was informed that this power could not be received except by the exercise of faith with an honest heart, and by this faith, knowledge of the ancient records and their engravings should be made known." (Joseph Fielding Smith, *CHMR* 1:46.)

8:2, 3 *"the spirit of revelation"*

The Lord here defines for Oliver Cowdery (and for the whole world, through the publication of this revelation) the "spirit of revelation": ". . . I will tell you in your mind and in your heart, by the Holy Ghost, which shall come upon you and which shall dwell in your heart" (D&C 8:2). Thus revelation, as with prophecy, comes not by the will of men, but holy men speak as they are "moved by the Holy Ghost." (2 Pet. 1:21.)

See *Revelation* in Appendix A.

"I will read a portion of a revelation given through the Prophet Joseph Smith, previous to the organization of the Church, dated April 1829: [Sec. 8:1-3, quoted.] . . . The same Spirit of revelation that Moses had, concerning which God speaks through the Prophet Joseph Smith, has rested upon men that have held the keys of this kingdom, whether it was during President [Brigham] Young's life or at the present time—that same Spirit of revelation rests upon him who holds the presidency as senior apostle in the midst of the people of God. The apostles of this Church have all the authority, they have all the keys, and it is within the preview of their office and calling to have all the Spirit of revelation necessary to lead this people into the presence of the Lamb in the celestial kingdom of our God. . . .

"But it is the truth, that the same Spirit of revelation that rested upon Moses, and which enabled him to lead the children of Israel through the Red Sea [Ex. 14:26-31; Heb. 11:29], rests upon the servants of God in the midst of this people, and you will find it so to your entire satisfaction if you will listen to their counsels and be guided by them." (George Q. Cannon, *JD* 21:264, 271.)

8:3-5 *"the spirit of revelation . . . is thy gift"*

"The Lord placed great emphasis on the necessity of holding sacred the gifts of God. Oliver had a gift (Sec. 8:3-4), even that of revelation, but he was admonished to receive it in humility and with a contrite spirit. All who receive gifts of the Spirit should do so with a humble spirit. The gifts are sacred and we should hold them so, and 'trifle not with sacred things.' [Sec. 6:12.] . . . His gifts are holy, sacred, and all who receive them should remember from whence they come and for what they are to be used. [Sec. 46:9-10.]" (Joseph Fielding Smith, *CHMR* 1:40.)

"The gift of revelation promised to Oliver Cowdery was to be a protection to him, if he would need it, and it would deliver him out of the hands of his enemies, and protect him from the destroyer. This the Lord endeavored to impress upon him by saying: 'Oh, remember these words, and keep my commandments. Remember this is your gift.' " (Joseph Fielding Smith, *CHMR* 1:52.)

8:4 *"if it were not so, they would slay you"*

This warning by the Lord would seem to indicate that if Oliver Cowdery had not responded to the spirit of revelation, he would probably have been killed in a state of apostasy. Oliver later resisted the spirit of revelation enough that he apostatized from the faith, though he was later rebaptized and joined again with the Church. For further information on the later life of Oliver Cowdery, see *Oliver Cowdery* in Appendix B.

8:6-8 *"you have another gift . . . the gift of Aaron"*

"There was another gift bestowed upon Oliver Cowdery, and that was the gift of Aaron. Like Aaron with his rod in his hand going before Moses as a spokesman, so Oliver Cowdery was to go before Joseph Smith. Whatever he should ask the Lord by power of this gift should be granted if asked in faith and in wisdom. Oliver was blessed with the great honor of holding the keys of this dispensation with Joseph Smith, and like Aaron [Ex. 4:10-17], did become a spokesman on numerous occasions. It was Oliver who delivered the first public discourse in this dispensation." (Joseph Fielding Smith, *CHMR* 1:48.)

"Oliver Cowdery also had the 'gift of Aaron.' Aaron was the elder brother of Moses. Being prompted by the Spirit of the Lord, he met his younger brother in the wilderness and accompanied him to Egypt. He introduced him to the children of Israel in the land of Goshen. He was his spokesman before Pharaoh, and he assisted him in opening up the dispensation which Moses was commissioned to proclaim (Exodus 4:27-31). This was the gift of Aaron. In some respects Oliver Cowdery was the Aaron of the new and last dispensation." (Smith and Sjodahl, *DCC,* p. 44.)

8:12 *The Lord speaks again to Oliver Cowdery*

The statement by the Lord to Oliver Cowdery that He is "the same that spake unto you from the beginning" evidently refers to the night when Oliver Cowdery had cried unto the Lord in his heart that he might know "concerning the truth of these things." (See D&C 6:22-23 and *HC* 1:35.)

SECTION 9

Although this revelation was given for the specific benefit of Oliver Cowdery, everyone who reads it might well learn the principle and apply it to himself: each should perform well the assignment given him by the Lord and should not seek to do the work of another unless he is asked to do so.

Oliver had been called to serve as a scribe for Joseph Smith, who had been given the responsibility for translating the Book of Mormon. (D&C 1:29.) It was the Lord's desire that Oliver continue with his work as scribe until the translation of the Book of Mormon was finished (9:1); then the Lord promised Oliver that He would give him power to assist in the translation of other records (9:2-3).

Oliver became impatient and tried to translate on his own. The remainder of the revelation is the explanation of the Lord to Oliver concerning this failure.

"It seems probable that Oliver Cowdery desired to translate out of curiosity, and the Lord taught him his place by showing him that translating was not the easy thing he had thought it to be. In a subsequent revelation (Sec. 9), the explanation was made that Oliver's failure came because he did not continue as he commenced, and the task being a difficult one, his faith deserted him. The lesson he learned was very necessary, for he was shown that his place was to act as scribe for Joseph Smith and that it was the latter who was called and appointed by command of the Lord to do the translating. There must have been some impatience in having to sit and act as scribe, but when he failed to master the gift of translating, he was then willing to accept the will of the Lord." (Joseph Fielding Smith, *CHMR* 1:50-51.)

9:2 *"other records"*

"The Lord told him that he was to continue as scribe until the translation of the Book of Mormon was completed, and that there were other ancient records to come forth, and that he might have the privilege of translating these at some future day if he would remain faithful. We learn from the Book of Mormon that there are many records and that at some time when the people are prepared by faith to receive them that they shall also be translated and published for the knowledge and salvation of the faithful. (2 Ne. 27:7-8; 3 Ne. 26:6-11; Ether 3:22-28 and 4:5-7.)

"Later there came into the hands of the Prophet other records which had to be translated, such as the Book of Abraham, but these records of ancient inhabitants on this American continent were not translated. It is possible that some of them might have been translated had the people received the Book of Mormon with full purpose of heart and had been faithful to its teachings. This was the promise the Lord made through Mormon. He said he would try the faith of the people and if they were willing to accept the lesser things (i.e., the Book of Mormon), then he would make known to them the greater things. That we have failed in this is very apparent, we have not accepted the revelations in the Book of Mormon, neither in the Doctrine and Covenants with that faith and willingness to know the will of the Lord which would entitle us to receive this greater information. Oliver Cowdery was a party to this failure by turning away from the Church for a number of years when it needed his service. He therefore lost his privilege to translate through his own disobedience, and the people have lost the privilege of receiving the 'greater things' spoken of by the Lord to Mormon (3 Nephi 26:8-11) until the day shall come when they are willing to be obedient in all things and will exercise faith such as was had by the brother of Jared. It should be remembered that such faith has rarely been seen on the earth. It appears, therefore, that we must wait until the reign of unrighteousness is at an end before the Lord will give to the people these writings, containing 'a revelation from God, from the beginning of the world to the ending thereof.' [2 Ne. 27:7.]" (Joseph Fielding Smith, *CHMR* 1:48-49.)

"When Joseph got the plates, the angel instructed him to carry them back to the hill Cumorah, which he did. Oliver says that when Joseph and Oliver went there, the hill opened, and they walked into a cave, in which there was a large and spacious room. He says he did not think, at the time, whether they had the light of the sun, or artificial light; but it was just as light as day. They laid the plates on a table; it was a large table that stood in the room. Under this table there was a pile of plates as much as two feet high, and there were altogether in this room more plates than, probably, many wagon loads; they were piled up in the corners and along the walls. The first time they went there, the sword of Laban hung upon the wall; but when they went again, it had been taken down and laid upon the table across the gold plates; it was unsheathed, and on it were written these words, 'This sword will never be sheathed again until the kingdoms of this world become the kingdom of our God and His Christ.' I take the liberty of referring to those things so that they will not be forgotten and lost.

"Now, you may think I am unwise in publicly telling these things, thinking, perhaps, I should preserve them in my own breast; but such is not in my mind. I would like the people called Latter-day Saints to understand some little things with regard to the workings and dealings of the Lord with His people here upon the earth. I could relate to you a great many more, all of which are familiar to many of our brethren and sisters." (Brigham Young, *JD* 19:38.)

9:7-9 *"you must study it out in your mind"*

Spiritual effort, as well as mental and physical effort, was required in order to translate the sacred records of the Book of Mormon. Oliver Cowdery thought that all he needed to do in order to translate was to ask the Lord, but here he is told that he must also "study it out" in his mind as well as to ask the Lord whether or not it is right. The Lord also gives Oliver a key so that he will know when the translation is right: his bosom shall burn within him.

"With a glad heart Oliver took over the work of translating, and the Prophet Joseph was ready to act as scribe. The attempt was a failure; it seems that Oliver Cowdery thought that it would be an easy matter with the aid of the Urim and Thummim to understand the engravings and give their equivalent meaning in the English language, without taking thought or studying it out in his mind. He therefore failed to comprehend the instructions the Lord had given him, notwithstanding the Lord told him he should have the gift of revelation." (Joseph Fielding Smith, *CHMR* 1:49.)

9:8   *"your bosom shall burn within you"*

"A similar privilege is given to any member of the Church who seeks knowledge in the spirit of prayer and faith. The Lord will cause the feeling of security and truth to take hold of the individual and burn within the bosom, and there will be an overwhelming feeling that the thing is right. Missionaries have felt the manifestation of this gift while laboring in the field; when searching the scriptures; when speaking before congregations on the streets and in public gatherings. When you have been listening to some inspired speaker who has presented a new thought to you, have you not felt that burning within and the satisfaction in your heart that this new thought is true? On the other hand, have you experienced the feeling of stupor, gloom, or uneasiness when some thought has been presented which was in conflict with the revealed word of the Lord, and you have felt by this manifestation of the Spirit that what was said is not true? It is a great gift, which all may receive, to have this spirit of discernment, or revelation, for it is the spirit of revelation. . . . The better our understanding of the scriptures and the more diligent we are in the service of the Lord, the better will we comprehend this truth and have this gift bestowed upon us. . . . We have a sure word by which we may be guided in these matters, and that is faithful, prayerful obedience to the commandments of the Lord." (Joseph Fielding Smith, *CHMR* 1:52.)

"There is a key given in the ninth section of the book of Doctrine and Covenants, which would be very profitable for the Latter-day Saints to follow even now. [D&C 9:8-9 quoted.]

"You do not know what to do today to solve your financial problems, what to plant, whether to buy or sell cattle, sheep or other things. It is your privilege to study it out; counsel together with the best wisdom and judgment the Lord shall give you, reach your conclusions, and then go to the Lord with it, tell him what you have planned to do. If the thing you have planned to do is for your good and your blessing, and you are determined to serve the Lord, pay your tithes and your offerings and keep his commandments, I promise that he will fulfil that promise upon your head, and your bosom shall burn within by the whisperings of the Spirit that it is right. But if it is not right, you shall have no such feelings, but you shall have a stupor of thought, and your heart will be turned away from that thing.

"I know of nothing today that the Latter-day Saints need more than the guidance of the Holy Spirit in the solution of the problems of life." (Melvin J. Ballard, *CR,* April 1931, pp. 37-38.)

"It is impossible to advance in the principles of truth, to increase in heavenly knowledge, except we exercise our reasoning faculties and exert ourselves in a proper manner. We have an instance recorded in the Doctrine and Covenants of a misunderstanding on the part of Oliver Cowdery, touching this principle. . . . [D&C 9:7-8 quoted.]

"So in regard to us, respecting the things which we are undertaking, if we expect to improve, to advance in the work immediately before us, and finally to obtain possession of those gifts and glories, coming up to that condition of exaltation we anticipate, we must take thought and reflect, we must exert ourselves, and that to the utmost of our ability." (Lorenzo Snow, *JD* 18:371-72.)

9:12 *"I have given . . . Joseph sufficient strength"*

As the prophet Nephi observed many centuries before, "the Lord giveth no commandment unto the children of men, save he shall prepare a way for them that they may accomplish the thing which he commandeth them." (1 Ne. 3:7.) The application of this principle is evident in the translation of the plates of the Book of Mormon by Joseph Smith. Although the Prophet was relatively unlearned by worldly standards and had not formally studied ancient languages, yet he succeeded in translating the Book of Mormon by the gift and power of God and through the use of the Urim and Thummim.

As indicated in this revelation, the Lord had given Oliver Cowdery the right to translate part of the record. When Oliver failed in his attempts, the Lord gave unto his "servant Joseph sufficient strength, whereby it is made up." Thus, the total responsibility for translation was left with Joseph.

9:14 *"a hair of your head shall not be lost"*

This descriptive expression indicates that the Lord is aware of everything we do. It is used one time in the New Testament (Mark 21:18) and four times in the Doctrine and Covenants (9:14; 29:25; 84:8, 116).

SECTION 10

Background information on section 10

"This Revelation should be read in connection with Sec. 3.

"As soon as the 116 pages of manuscript had been lost through the carelessness of Martin Harris, the Urim and Thummim was taken from the Prophet. The sacred instrument was restored after a short time, and the Revelation in Section 3, especially rebuking Martin Harris, was received. Then both the plates and the Urim and Thummim were removed for a few days. It was necessary that the young Prophet should learn the lesson that he was entirely dependent on the Lord. When they were restored, he received the Revelation in Section 10, containing instructions to himself with regard to the lost portion of the manuscript. (See Footnote, *HC* 1:23.)" (Smith and Sjodahl, *DCC,* p. 49.)

"After I had obtained the above revelation [Section 3], both the plates and the Urim and Thummim were taken from me again; but in a few days they were returned to me, when I inquired of the Lord, and the Lord said thus unto me: [Section 10, follows.]" (Joseph Smith, *HC* 1:23.)

10:1 *"Urim and Thummim"*

For information on the Urim and Thummim, see *Urim and Thummim* in Appendix A.

10:1 *Martin Harris "a wicked man"*

Martin Harris is herein designated as a "wicked man" because he broke his covenant with the Lord that he would show the 116 pages of manuscript to only five persons. This disobedience also caused the Angel Moroni to reclaim the plates of Mormon and the Urim and Thummim from Joseph Smith, which in turn caused him to lose the gift of translation, and thus his mind became darkened. Therefore, the Lord said to Joseph Smith that Martin Harris was "a wicked man, for he has sought to take away the things wherewith you have been entrusted; and he has also sought to destroy your gift." (10:7.)

For additional information on why Martin Harris was called a "wicked man," read the material for 3:12-13. Also, read the biographical sketch of Martin Harris in Appendix B.

10:4   *"Do not run faster or labor more than you have strength"*

"The scriptural advice, 'Do not run faster or labor more than you have strength' (D&C 10:4) suggests paced progress, much as God used seven creative periods in preparing man and this earth. There is a difference, therefore, between being 'anxiously engaged' and being over-anxious and thus underengaged." (Neal A. Maxwell, *Ensign,* November 1976, pp. 12-13.)

10:5, *Satan exists*
10-33, 63

The revelations in the Doctrine and Covenants clearly and consistently teach the reality of Satan (the devil; Lucifer) and warn against his nefarious teachings and practices. (As examples, see also 19:3; 24:1; 28:11; 40:2; 50:3; 53:12, 14; 63:28; 64:17; 132:57.) Even before this revelation was received in the summer of 1828, Joseph Smith had felt the evil influence and power of Satan.

The Prophet's first recorded direct experiences with evil forces were immediately before his first vision in the spring of 1820:

After I had retired to the place where I had previously designed to go, having looked around me, and finding myself alone, I kneeled down and began to offer up the desire of my heart to God. I had scarcely done so, when immediately I was seized upon by some power which entirely overcame me, and had such an astonishing influence over me as to bind my tongue so that I could not speak. Thick darkness gathered around me, and it seemed to me for a time as if I were doomed to sudden destruction.

But, exerting all my powers to call upon God to deliver me out of the power of this enemy which had seized upon me, and at the very moment when I was ready to sink into despair and abandon myself to destruction—not to an imaginary ruin, but to the power of some actual being from the unseen world, who had such marvelous power as I had never before felt in any being—just at this moment of great alarm, I saw a pillar of light exactly over my head, above the brightness of the sun, which descended gradually until it fell upon me.

It no sooner appeared than I found myself delivered from the enemy which held me bound. (JS-H 1:15-17.)

The attacks of Satan and his followers against the Prophet, the gospel, the restored scriptures, and the baptized members of the Church have been almost constant since that time. Within a few days of the first vision, the persecution and hatred toward Joseph Smith started. His recollections of these events are recorded in the Pearl of Great Price, Joseph Smith—History 1:22-25 (also known as Joseph Smith 2).

For additional information on Satan, see *Satan* in Appendix A.

10:10-31   *"they say and think in their hearts"*

The Lord, who knows all things, including thoughts and the intents of the heart (D&C 6:16), here explains the evil designs of those who have stolen the 116 pages of manuscript. They intend to withhold their purloined copy of the translation until Joseph Smith has retranslated the same pages. Then they intend to alter the words of the earlier translation and try to convince others that Joseph Smith is a liar when he pretends to translate, for they would claim he cannot translate the same way twice. Thus, the plan of Satan was to "overpower" the testimony of the Prophet so "that the work may not come forth in this generation." (D&C 10:33.) However, the Lord truly did show unto the world that his "wisdom is greater than the cunning of the devil" (D&C 10:43) by providing for the alternate record of the small plates of Nephi to be translated. (See information for D&C 3:1 and 10:38-42.)

10:29   *"to get thee to tempt the Lord thy God"*

"To pray for a translation of 116 written pages, word for word the same as the missing portion, would be 'tempting' the Lord. It would be asking for a miracle as great as that by which Satan suggested that our Lord prove his Divine commission, which suggestion Christ declined by quoting Deut. 6:16, 'Thou shalt not tempt the Lord thy God' (Matt. 4:5-7). If we expect God to perform miracles in our behalf, when we bring trouble upon ourselves by disobedience, we 'tempt' God." (Smith and Sjodahl, *DCC,* p. 53.)

10:38-42 *"translate the engravings which are on the plates of Nephi"*

When Nephi, the son of Lehi, was first commanded by the Lord to write a record on plates, he prepared and started to write on the large plates of Nephi. (1 Ne. 19:1-4.) Later he was commanded by the Lord to make a second set of plates (which later became known as the small plates of Nephi) and to engrave on them "an account . . . of the ministry" of his people. (1 Ne. 9:3.) He was obedient to this command, even though he confessed he did not understand the purpose thereof. (1 Ne. 9:5.) It was sufficient for him to know that the Lord wanted the second record "for a wise purpose in him" and that "the Lord knoweth all things from the beginning; wherefore, he prepareth a way to accomplish all his works among the children of men." (1 Ne. 9:5-6.)

At least one of the purposes the Lord had in mind for this second record is made clear in the events leading up to this revelation.

The plates Joseph Smith received from the angel Moroni were the plates of Mormon, which contained Mormon's abridgment of the large plates of Nephi (see 3 Ne. 5:8-10; Mormon 2:17-18; 5:9), including an abridgment of Nephi's writings that were evidently included in the book of Lehi. The Prophet's translation of Mormon's abridgment of the book of Lehi, comprising 116 pages of manuscript, was subsequently lost by Martin Harris. (See *HC* 1:20-22.)

In this revelation (section 10), the Lord instructs Joseph Smith not to retranslate the abridgment of the book of Lehi, but to translate the small plates of Nephi in their stead. Thus, the earlier "wise purpose of the Lord" is at least partially made manifest.

10:45 *"translate this first part of the engravings of Nephi"*

"The Prophet Nephi kept a record of the sacred history of his people on what he was pleased to call the small plates which he had made. The historians who followed him continued that history down to the reign of King Benjamin, when the plates of this record were full. When Mormon was making his abridgment the Lord inspired him to attach these 'small plates' to his abridgment. He did not know why, only that the Spirit whispered to him to do so. [W of M 3-7.] The Lord, who knows the end from the beginning, thus prepared for the loss of the abridged record which was given to Martin Harris. Mormon therefore had a double account of the early history of his people from the time of the call of Lehi from Jerusalem down to the end of the writings of Amaleki, the last to write on the small plates of Nephi. The Lord, thus knowing that the manuscript covering this period of history would be stolen in the manner described, provided the better record to take the place of the abridgment. He denied Joseph Smith the privilege of translating the abridgment the second time, and thus prevented him from falling into the trap set by his enemies, but commanded him to translate the small plates giving the full account as kept by the early prophets and scribes." (Joseph Fielding Smith, *CHMR* 1:28-29.)

10:45-51   *Promises to the holy prophets of the Lehites*

The Lord had promised many of the prophets and leaders of the Lehite civilization (the Nephites and Lamanites of the Book of Mormon) that their records would come forth in later generations to their descendants. A partial listing of these promises include the promises to:

Lehi (and Joseph who was sold into Egypt)—2 Ne. 3:6-23.
Nephi—1 Ne. 9:1-6; 13:35-41; 19:1-6, 18; 2 Ne. 11:2-3; 25:7-8; 26:16-17; 28:1-2; 29:11; 33:10-15.
Jacob—Jacob 1:1-8; 4:1-4.
Enos—1:12-18.
Jarom—1:1-2.
Mormon—W of M 1:1-6; Morm. 5:8-13; 7:9.
Moroni—Morm. 8:14-16, 25-35; 9:36-37; Moro. 10:24, 27-29.

Note also the general promise of the Lord in 2 Nephi 29:8-14 that there will be three great scriptural witnesses of the last days which will testify of each other.

"The Lord makes known that the Nephite prophets in prayer earnestly sought that their writings should be preserved to come forth and to speak as from the dead, to bear witness to the remnant of Lehi, and also the Jews and Gentiles, that God had revealed to them the fulness of the Gospel. Their anxiety was that in these last days men might be brought to repentance and faith in God through the testimony given many centuries before to these Nephite prophets. In fact, we learn from the Book of Mormon that this is the main object of the Book of Mormon as stated in many of its passages." (Joseph Fielding Smith, *CHMR* 1:29.)

"Nephi made two records. In one he preserved an account of his father Lehi's life and genealogy, and the history of his people. This history was continued for many generations, by historians, such as Mosiah, Alma, Helaman, etc. The Prophet Mormon made an abridgment from this vast amount of historical material. The Prophet Joseph translated this abridgment, and it was the first part of that translation which was lost.

"But Nephi also made another record. In this he preserved an account of events connected with the depature of his father from Jerusalem and their landing in America. This history was continued for 400 years, down to the reign of King Benjamin. It was chiefly an ecclesiastical history.

"The Prophet Mormon found these 'smaller plates' of Nephi and attached them to his own abridgment of the 'larger plates.' And thus there was a double line of history of the Nephites for 400 years. The Prophet Mormon says he added the smaller plates to his abridgment 'for a wise purpose' (Mormon 1:7), 'for thus it whispereth me, according to the working of the Spirit of the Lord which is in me,' and Nephi says he made those smaller plates in obedience to a commandment of God, given for some reason unknown to him (1 Ne. 9:5)." (Smith and Sjodahl, *DCC*, pp. 54-55.)

10:48   *"and also all that had become Lamanites"*

Some readers of the Book of Mormon have erroneously assumed that all the blood descendants of Nephi and his followers were destroyed in the great battles of A.D. 363 to 385. (Morm. 4-6.) Thus they have wrongly believed that only the blood descendants of Laman survived this great destruction.

In his writings, Moroni suggests that those Nephites who were willing to deny Christ were spared and joined with the Lamanites. (Moro. 1:2-3.) Also, during the golden age of the people of Lehi after the appearance of the resurrected Jesus Christ, there were no people known as "Lamanites nor any manner of -ites." (4 Ne. 17.) The people who later were known as Lamanites were descendants of the group of people "who had revolted from the Church" in A.D. 194 "and taken upon them the name of Lamanites." (4 Ne. 20.) The record later states that in A.D. 231 "the true worshipers of Christ . . . were called Nephites. . . . And . . . they who rejected the gospel were called Lamanites." (4 Ne. 36-38.)

Therefore, the Lamanites of the last great battles were descendants of those who revolted against the true church of Christ between about A.D. 194 and 231. They might be actual blood descendants of Nephi, Jacob, Joseph, or Sam, as well as Laman, Lemuel, or the sons of Ishamel.

In this revelation the Lord thus refers to "the Lamanites, and also all that had become Lamanites because of their dissensions." (10:48.) (For further information on this subject, see the material listed after D&C 3:16-20.)

10:59   *"Other sheep I have which are not of this fold"*

The reference that Jesus made to his disciples concerning his "other sheep" is recorded in John 10:16. Concerning this scripture, Elder LeGrand Richards has written:

"A writer on the life of Christ has indicated that he would find no excuse for this passage of scripture, since he knew of no other sheep except those to whom Jesus ministered. Some have explained that it must have been the Gentiles, but Jesus indicated: '. . . I am not sent but unto the lost sheep of the house of Israel.' (Matt. 15:24.)

"It should be noted that Jesus did not minister unto the Gentiles, although he did send his Apostles unto them after his crucifixion. [Matt. 28:19-20.]

"After Jesus had been crucified and had ascended unto his Father, he visited his 'other sheep' in America, known as the Nephites, and there chose twelve disciples and organized his Church, as he had done among the Jews, an account of which is given in some detail in Third Nephi of the Book of Mormon. [3 Ne. 15:11-24.]" (LeGrand Richards, *MWW*, pp. 51-52.)

"The words of the Lord to his disciples as written in the tenth chapter of John, verse sixteen, is one of the passages, with a hidden meaning to the teachers in the sectarian world. Some commentators, like the Jewish disciples, think the Lord was speaking of the Gentiles, but they fail to understand that the Lord said he was not sent to the Gentiles, but to the lost sheep of the house of Israel. It was not until after his resurrection that he commissioned his disciples to go into all the world and preach the Gospel. While he was with them and when he sent them forth into the cities and villages where he intended later to go, he expressly commanded them that they were not to go 'into the way of the Gentiles, and into any city of the Samaritans . . . but rather to the lost sheep of the house of Israel.' He also told the woman of Canaan who came to him seeking a blessing, 'I am not sent but unto the lost sheep of the house of Israel.'

"When Jesus appeared to the Nephites he told them that they were the other sheep of whom he had spoken to his disciples in Palestine, but because of their unbelief he was forbidden by his Father to tell them more. To the Nephites he made it very plain that not only were they of the 'other sheep,' but there were still others, including the ten lost tribes, who would also hear his voice, and eventually, when the gathering of Israel is complete, these other members of the house of Israel who were scattered would be gathered and bring their records with them. In that day the records of the Jews and of the Nephites and also the other tribes of the house of Israel, which he had led away, should join their records, and these scattered and punished people would be gathered home unto the lands of their possessions and then he would remember his covenant with Abraham and once again they would be his people and forever. (See 2 Ne. 29; 3 Ne. 15 and 16.)" (Joseph Fielding Smith, *CHMR* 1:32.)

10:62-63   *The Book of Mormon to restore true doctrines*

The Lord indicates here another purpose for the publication of the Book of Mormon: "to bring to light the true points of my doctrine."

The essentials of the gospel of Jesus Christ were taught by the Savior to the Jews and were contained in records that are now known as the New Testament. The prophet Nephi, the first writer in the present Book of Mormon, saw in a vision nearly 600 B.C. that many of the "plain and . . . precious" parts of the gospel were to be taken out of the Jewish scriptures—the Bible. (1 Ne. 13:2-26.) The Lord told Nephi that he would be "merciful unto the Gentiles" in that he would "bring forth unto them, in mine own power, much of my gospel, which shall be plain and precious, saith the Lamb." (1 Ne. 13:34.)

In this revelation (D&C 10:46-49, 62-63), the Lord indicates that he is fulfilling his promise to the ancient prophets by including in the Book of Mormon "all those parts of my gospel which my holy prophets, yea, and also my disciples, desired in their prayers should come forth unto this people." (D&C 10:46.)

10:63 *"they do wrest the scriptures"*

One meaning of the word *wrest* is "to direct to an unnatural or improper use"; another meaning is "to deflect or change from a true or normal bearing, significance, or interpretation." Thus, persons who "wrest" the scriptures place a meaning upon the words that was not intended by the Lord who gave the scriptures. As Peter has indicated, "No prophecy of the scripture is of any private interpretation." (2 Pet. 1:20.)

"One of the reasons people apostatize from this Church is that they have failed to heed the warning of the scriptures against listening to false teachers who raise their voices in our midst. [Sec. 45:5-6; 2 Nephi 28:20-31.] In spite of the fact that these warnings of the scriptures are crystal clear, many of our people fail to heed them.

"How do these false teachers lead people astray? They do so by attacking the fundamental doctrines of the Church. [Sec. 52:9, 14-20, 36.) They attack the teachings of the Authorities. They seek to develop doctrinal disputes among the people to undermine their faith, and they lead people to apostasy when they do such things as that. Very often false teachers who have come among us endeavor to justify their position by claiming to have received some revelation or dream directing them, they say, in the paths which they tread. . . .

"Remember, too, the Savior told the Prophet Joseph Smith that it is Satan who 'doth stir up the hearts of the people to contention concerning the points of doctrine,' and that when individuals put themselves in the hands of Satan in doing these things 'they do err, for they do wrest the scriptures and do not understand them.' " (Mark E. Petersen, *CR,* October 1945, pp. 88, 92.)

10:65 *"as a hen gathereth chickens under her wings"*

This descriptive expression reflects the great love and concern of the Lord for his people. It is found in three sections of the Doctrine and Covenants: 10:65, 29:2, and 43:24.

"Remember that powerful truth found in Matthew 23:37:

'. . . how often would I have gathered thy children together, even as a hen gathereth her chickens under her wings, and ye would not!' With your indulgence, I would like to repeat that quotation once more and add just two words of admonition: '. . . how often would I have gathered thy children together, even as a hen gathereth her chickens under her wings, and ye would not *help me!*' How many of us are actively helping the Lord gather his flock?" (Marvin J. Ashton, *Ensign,* December 1971, p. 101.)

10:68 *"Whosoever declareth more or less than this . . . is not of me"*

"There is no need of this people being called together to change the Articles of their Faith, or their creed, for that which they have received is not of man, but from God. . . . This is a grand difference between the work of man and the work of God. [Sec. 88:66-67; 93:24-25.] That which is of man must be modified and changed to meet the demands of various ages in which mankind live, but that which is of God will endure, as the Gospel of Jesus Christ, as revealed through the Prophet Joseph Smith, has endured the scrutiny of critics, the discoveries and the light of science in our day and time." (Abraham O. Woodruff, *CR,* October 1901, p. 53.)

10:69 *"endureth to the end"*

See *Endure to the end* in Appendix A.

10:69 *"my rock"*

See *Rock* in Appendix A.

10:69 *"the gates of hell"*

See *Hell* in Appendix A.

10:70 *"life and light of the world"*

See *Light* in Appendix A.

SECTION 11

Background information on section 11

Joseph Smith recorded the following account of the events that followed shortly after he and Oliver Cowdery had received the Aaronic Priesthood and had been baptized on May 15, 1829:

Our minds being now enlightened, we began to have the Scriptures laid open to our understandings, and the true meaning and intention of their more mysterious passages revealed unto us in a manner which we never could attain to previously, nor ever before had thought of. In the meantime we were forced to keep secret the circumstances of having received the Priesthood and our having been baptized, owing to a spirit of persecution which had already manifested itself in the neighborhood....

After a few days, however, feeling it to be our duty, we commenced to reason out of the Scriptures with our acquaintances and friends, as we happened to meet with them. About this time my brother Samuel H. Smith came to visit us....

Not many days afterwards, my brother Hyrum Smith came to us to inquire concerning these things, when at his earnest request, I inquired of the Lord through the Urim and Thummim, and received for him the following: [Section 11 follows.] (Joseph Smith, *HC* 1:43-45.)

11:1-9 *Blessing for Hyrum Smith*

These introductory verses of the blessing of Hyrum Smith are virtually word-for-word the same as the blessing given the previous month to Oliver Cowdery, which is recorded in section 6.

For information concerning the terms and expressions of these first nine verses, read the materials listed for the corresponding verses in section 6. The remainder of the blessing to Hyrum varies considerably from the latter part of the blessing to Oliver.

11:10 *"thou hast a gift"*

"The Lord declared that Hyrum Smith had a gift. The

great gift which he possessed was that of a tender, sympathetic heart, a merciful spirit. The Lord on a later occasion said: 'Blessed is my servant Hyrum Smith; for I, the Lord, love him because of the integrity of his heart, and because he loveth that which is right before me, saith the Lord.' (D&C 124:15.) This great gift was manifest in his jealous watch-care over the Prophet lest some harm come to him." (Joseph Fielding Smith, *CHMR* 1:52.)

11:11 *"I am the light which shineth in darkness"*

See *Light* in Appendix A.

11:13 *"my Spirit . . . shall enlighten your mind"*

"There is a way by which persons can keep their consciences clear before God and man, and that is to preserve within them the Spirit of God, which is the spirit of revelation to every man and woman. It will reveal to them, even in the simplest of matters, what they shall do, by making suggestions to them. We should try to learn the nature of this spirit, that we may understand its suggestions, and then we will always be able to do right. This is the grand privilege of every Latter-day Saint. We know that it is our right to have the manifestations of the spirit every day of our lives. . . .

"From the time we receive the Gospel, go down into the waters of baptism, and have hands laid upon us afterwards for the gift of the Holy Ghost, we have a friend, if we do not drive it from us by doing wrong. That friend is the Holy Spirit, the Holy Ghost, which partakes of the things of God and shows them unto us. This is a grand means that the Lord has provided for us, that we may know the light, and not be groveling continually in the dark. [Sec. 88:66-68.]" (Lorenzo Snow, *CR,* April 1899, p. 52.)

11:13, *Preparing for missionary service*
16-26

The Lord here teaches Hyrum Smith several steps to be followed in preparing for a mission:

1. Desire to serve the Lord. (11:10, 17.)
2. Live worthily to receive the Spirit of the Lord so it can "enlighten your mind, which shall fill your soul with joy." (11:13.)
3. Keep the commandments of the Lord, assisting in the work of the Lord in any way that you might be asked. (11:18-20.)
4. Seek to obtain the word of the Lord through (a) studying the

word of the Lord that had already gone forth—the Bible— and (b) studying the word of the Lord that was then being translated—the Book of Mormon. (11:21-22.)

5. Build upon the gospel, denying not either the spirit of revelation nor the spirit of prophecy. (11:24-25.)

The Lord indicates further that these suggestions are for "all who have good desires" to serve. (11:27.)

1:15-17   *"you need not suppose that you are called to preach until you are called"*

God is a God of order, so even though a person might have the desire to preach the gospel, he still needs to be called of God by one having authority before he can legally and officially represent the Lord. The Lord therefore counsels Hyrum Smith to prepare to give missionary service, but not to "suppose that you are called to preach until you are called." (11:15.)

"Hyrum Smith had a desire to engage in public speaking, as a minister. It was, therefore, necessary to correct certain prevalent errors concerning preaching, for the benefit of the little circle of friends who, under divine guidance, now were laying the foundations of the Church. One of these errors was the assumption that a minister can prove that he has divine authority, by quoting the commission of our Lord to His first Apostles. The Lord therefore instructs His servant not to suppose that he is sent to preach until he is actually called, as were the Twelve." (Smith and Sjodahl, *DCC*, p. 63.)

"It is quite the common thing in the world for men to assume authority and to act in the name of the Lord when he has not called them. No man is authorized to act in the name of the Lord, or to officiate in any ordinance, unless he has been properly called. For this reason the Priesthood was restored and the Church organized. When this revelation was given the Church had not been organized. Presumably some of those who sought light and the will of the Lord felt that when the Lord spoke to them, they were authorized to go forth to act in his name. Here he informs Hyrum Smith that he was to wait (v. 15), yet he was to put his trust in the Holy Spirit and to walk humbly, to judge righteously, 'and this is my Spirit.' " (Joseph Fielding Smith, *CHMR* 1:57.)

11:21 *"you shall have my Spirit . . . unto the convincing of men"*

"Let one go forth who is careful to logically prove all he says by numerous quotations from the revelations, and let another travel with him who can say, by the power of the Holy Ghost, Thus saith the Lord, and you will invariably find that the man who testifies by the power of the Holy Ghost will convince and gather many more of the honest and upright than will the merely logical reasoner." (Brigham Young, *JD* 8:53-54.)

11:20 *"might, mind and strength"*

See *Might, mind, and strength* in Appendix A.

11:24 *"my rock, which is my gospel"*

See *Rock* in Appendix A.

11:25 *"Deny not the spirit of revelation"*

See *Revelation* in Appendix A.

"He [Hyrum Smith] was not to deny the Spirit of Revelation. This is good counsel for all of us today. There are some members of the Church who seemingly complain because the Lord is not giving revelations to be placed in the Doctrine and Covenants as in the beginning, and they ask why revelation has ceased in the Church. Usually it is the case that these critics are not faithfully keeping the commandments the Lord has already given and their eyes are blind to the fact that revelation and the guidance of the Lord is being meted out to the Church constantly. No one with the spirit of discernment can fail to see that the hand of the Lord has guided this people from the beginning and this guidance is manifest today as in other times to all who are humble and have a contrite spirit. (See Jacob 4:8.)" (Joseph Fielding Smith, *CHMR* 1:53.)

11:30 *"as many as receive me . . . I give power to become the sons of God"*

"Salvation is attainable only through compliance with the laws and ordinances of the Gospel; and all who are thus saved become sons and daughters unto God in a distinctive sense. In a revelation given through Joseph Smith the Prophet to Emma Smith, the Lord Jesus addressed the woman as 'My daughter,' and said: 'for verily I say unto you, all those who receive my gospel are sons and daughters in my kingdom.' (D&C 25:1.) In many instances the Lord had addressed men as his sons. (E.g. D&C 9:1; 34:3; 121:7.)

"That by obedience to the Gospel men may become sons of God, both as sons of Jesus Christ, and, through him, as sons of his Father, is set forth in many revelations given in the current dispensation. Thus we read in an utterance of the Lord Jesus to Hyrum Smith in 1829; [D&C 11:28-30, quoted.] [Note: see also D&C 34:1-3; 35:1-2; 39:1-4; 45:7-8.]" (First Presidency, *AF,* pp. 468-69.)

SECTION 12

Background information on section 12

"About the same time [as the revelation in section 11 was given to Hyrum Smith] an old gentleman came to visit us of whose name I wish to make honorable mention—Mr. Joseph Knight, Sen., of Colesville, Broome County, New York, who, having heard of the manner in which we were occupying our time, very kindly and considerately brought us a quantity of provisions, in order that we might not be interrupted in the work of translation (of the Book of Mormon plates) by the want of such necessities of life; and I would just mention here, as in duty bound, that he several times brought us supplies, a distance of at least thirty miles, which enabled us to continue the work when otherwise we must have relinquished it for a season. Being very anxious to know his duty as to this work, I inquired of the Lord for him, and obtained the following: [Section 12 follows.]" (Joseph Smith, *HC* 1:47-48.)

12:1-6 *Blessing for Joseph Knight, Sr.*

For biographical information on Joseph Knight, Sr., see *Joseph Knight, Sr.* in Appendix B.

The first six verses of this blessing to Joseph Knight, Sr., are virtually word-for-word the same as the earlier blessings given to Oliver Cowdery (section 6) and Hyrum Smith (section 11).

For information concerning these terms and expressions, read the materials listed for the corresponding verses in section 6. Other scriptures also have instances of such repetitions; for example, compare Isaiah 2:2-4 with Micah 5:1-3.

12:7-8 *Principles apply to all*

The Lord indicates that the counsel in the preceding verses (1 through 6) applies "to all those who have desires to bring forth and establish this work." (12:7.) Perhaps this helps to explain why the introductory statements are so similar in the blessings to Oliver Cowdery (section 6), Hyrum Smith (section 11), Joseph Knight, Sr. (section 12), and David Whitmer (section 14).

Again, love, faith, hope, charity, and temperance are listed as characteristics that help qualify a person for the work of the Lord. (Compare with section 4.)

SECTION 13

Background information on section 13

"On the 5th of April, 1829, Oliver Cowdery came to my house, until which time I had never seen him. . . . Two days after the arrival of Mr. Cowdery (being the 7th of April), I commenced to translate the Book of Mormon, and he began to write for me. . . .

"We still continued the work of translation, when in the ensuing month (May, 1829), we on a certain day went into the woods to pray and inquire of the Lord respecting baptism for the remission of sins, that we found mentioned in the translation of the plates. While we were thus employed, praying and calling upon the Lord, a messenger from heaven descended in a cloud of light, and having laid his hands upon us, he ordained us, saying: [Section 13, quoted.]

"He said this Aaronic Priesthood had not the power of laying on hands for the gift of the Holy Ghost, but that this should be conferred on us hereafter; and he commanded us to go and be baptized, and gave us instructions that I should baptize Oliver Cowdery, and afterwards that he should baptize me. Accordingly we went and were baptized. I baptized him first, and afterwards he baptized me, after which I laid my hands upon his head and ordained him to the Aaronic Priesthood, and afterwards he laid his hands on me and ordained me to the same Priesthood—for so we were commanded.

"The messenger who visited us on this occasion, and conferred this Priesthood upon us, said that his name was John, the same that is called John the Baptist in the New Testament [Lk. 3:1-17; 7:24-35], and that he acted under the direction of Peter, James and John, who held the keys of the Priesthood of Melchizedek, which Priesthood he said would in due time be conferred on us, and that I should be called the first Elder of the Church and he (Oliver Cowdery) the second. It was on the 15th day of May, 1829, that we were ordained under the hand of this messenger and baptized.

"Immediately on our coming up out of the water after we had been baptized we experienced great and glorious blessings from our Heavenly Father. No sooner had I baptized Oliver Cowdery, than the Holy Ghost fell upon us and he stood up and prophesied concerning the rise of this Church, and many other things connected with the Church, and this generation of the children of men. We were filled with the Holy Ghost, and rejoiced in the God of our salvation." (Joseph Smith, *HC* 1:32-33.)

13:1 *"until" the sons of Levi*

The use of the word *until* in this prayer of ordination does not mean that the Priesthood of Aaron will be taken from the earth once the sons of Levi "offer again an offering unto the Lord in righteousness." It is used in a continuing sense, much as in the expression "God be with you *until* we meet again." In his recording of this event, Oliver Cowdery used the word *that* rather than *until* but in either case the intent is clear. Following is his descriptive account of his reflections and feelings during the time these revelations and angelic visitations were being received:

Near this time of the setting of the sun, Sabbath evening, April 5th, 1829, my natural eyes for the first time beheld this brother [Joseph Smith]. He then resided in Harmony, Susquehanna County, Pennsylvania. On Monday, the 6th, I assisted him in arranging some business of a temporal nature, and on Tuesday, the 7th, commenced to write the Book of Mormon. These were days never to be forgotten—to sit under the sound of a voice dictated by the inspiration of heaven, awakened by the utmost gratitude of this bosom! Day after day I continued, uninterrupted, to write from his mouth, as he translated with the Urim and Thummim, or as the Nephites would have said, "Interpreters," the history or record called "The Book of Mormon." . . .

No men, in their sober senses, could translate and write the directions given to the Nephites from the mouth of the Savior, of the precise manner in which men should build up his Church, and especially when corruption had spread an uncertainty over all forms and systems practiced among men, without desiring a privilege of showing the willingness of the heart by being buried in the liquid grave, to answer a good conscience by the resurrection of Jesus Christ. . . . we only waited for the commandment to be given "Arise and be baptized."

This was not long desired before it was realized. The Lord, who is rich in mercy, and ever willing to answer the consistent prayer of the humble, after we had called upon him in a fervent manner, aside from the abodes of men, condescended to manifest to us his will. On a sudden, as from the midst of eternity, the voice of the Redeemer spake to us. While the veil was parted and the angel of God came down clothed with glory and delivered the anxiously looked-for message, and the keys of the gospel of repentance. What joy! what wonder! what amazement! While the world was racked and distracted—while millions were groping as the blind for the wall, and while all men were resting upon uncertainty, as a general mass, our eyes beheld, our ears heard, as in the "blaze of day"; yes, more—above the glitter of the May sunbeam, which shed its brilliancy over the face of nature! Then his voice, though mild, pierced to the centre, and his words, "I am thy fellow-servant," dispelled every fear. We listened, we gazed, we admired! 'Twas the voice of an angel from glory, 'twas a message from the Most High! And as we heard we rejoiced, while his love enkindled upon our souls, and we were wrapt in the vision of the Almighty! Where was room for doubt? Nowhere; uncertainty had fled, doubt had sunk no more to rise, while fiction and deception had fled forever!

But, dear brother, think further, think for a moment what joy filled our hearts and with what surprise we must have bowed, (for who would not have bowed the knee for such a blessing?) when we received under his hand the Holy Priesthood as he said, "Upon you, my fellow servants, in the name of the Messiah, I confer this Priesthood and this authority, which shall remain upon earth, that the sons of Levi may yet offer an offering unto the Lord in righteousness!" (Letter to W. W. Phelps, *MS* 3:153-54.)

13:1   *"the sons of Levi"*

"Now as to the 'sons of Levi,' spoken of by John the Baptist in his ordination of Joseph Smith and Oliver Cowdery. (D&C 13.) They are, or will be, descendants of Levi, holding the Priesthood of Aaron, who will make the offerings predicted by the prophets to be presented to the Lord in latter days in Zion and in Jerusalem. (See Malachi 3:2-4; D&C 124:38, and 128:24.) In Zion, men chosen of the Lord for the special work mentioned will be persons sanctified by the spirit unto 'the renewing of their bodies.' (D&C 84:32-34.) At Jerusalem they will be Levites by lineal descent, offering the sacrifices that will be required after the restoration spoken of in Zechariah 14:16-21, and many others of the prophets of old concerning 'the restitution of all things.' (Acts 3:19-21.)" (Charles W. Penrose, *IE,* August 1912, p. 952.)

13:1 *"an offering unto the Lord in righteousness"*

Several explanations have been given concerning the nature of the offering that is to be offered in righteousness again by the sons of Levi. Over thirteen years after this ordination by John the Baptist, Joseph Smith wrote an epistle dated September 6, 1842, in which he mentioned that the Lord would "purify the sons of Levi, and purge them as gold and silver, that they may offer unto the Lord an offering in righteousness" (D&C 128:24.) The Prophet then pled with the Saints: "Let us, therefore, as a church and a people, and as Latter-day Saints, offer unto the Lord an offering in righteousness; and let us present in his holy temple, when it is finished, a book containing the records of our dead, which shall be worthy of all acceptation." (D&C 128:24.)

"The question often arises: 'What will be the nature of the offering that will be made by the sons of Levi?' While nothing has been given by revelation definitely stating what it will be, yet the implication in all the scriptures is that it will be just what they did before in ancient Israel. The Prophet Joseph Smith has said:

" 'It is generally supposed that sacrifice was entirely done away when the Great Sacrifice was offered up, and that there will be no necessity for the ordinance of sacrifice in the future: but those who assert this are certainly not acquainted with the duties, privileges, and authority of the Priesthood, or with the prophets. . . .

" 'These sacrifices as well as every ordinance, belonging to the priesthood, will when the Temple of the Lord is built, and the sons of Levi be purified, be fully restored and attended to in all their powers, ramifications, and blessings.' (*TPJS,* p. 172.)

"In the restoration of all things, these ancient practices which were given in the beginning—not the carnal law—and which had a bearing on the coming of Jesus Christ, will be restored. That sacrifice by blood should continue to be necessary forever, we need not suppose to be the case. (3 Ne. 9:18-20.)" (Joseph Fielding Smith, *CHMR* 1:65.)

"What kind of offering will the sons of Levi make to fulfill the words of Malachi and John? Logically such a sacrifice as they were authorized to make in the days of their former ministry when they were first called. Will such a sacrifice be offered in the temple? Evidently not in any temple as they are constructed for work of salvation and exaltation today. It should be remembered that the great temple, which is yet to be built in the City Zion, will not be one edifice, but twelve. Some of these temples will be for the lesser priesthood.

"RESTORATION OF BLOOD SACRIFICES. We are living in the dispensation of the fulness of times into which all things are to be gathered, and *all things* are to be restored since the beginning. Even this earth is to be restored to the condition which prevailed before Adam's transgression. Now in the nature of things, the law of sacrifice will have to be restored, or *all things* which were decreed by the Lord would not be restored. It will be necessary, therefore, for the sons of Levi, who offered the blood sacrifices anciently in Israel, to offer such a sacrifice again to round out and complete this ordinance in this dispensation. Sacrifice by the shedding of blood was instituted in the days of Adam and of necessity will have to be restored.

"The sacrifice of animals will be done to complete the restoration when the temple spoken of is built; at the beginning of the millennium, or in the restoration, blood sacrifices will be performed long enough to complete the fulness of the restoration in this dispensation. Afterwards sacrifice will be of some other character." (Joseph Fielding Smith, *DS* 3:93-94.)

13:1 *"I [John the Baptist] confer"*

For information on John the Baptist, see *John the Baptist* in Appendix A.

13:1 *"the Priesthood of Aaron . . . holds the keys . . . of the gospel"*

See *Aaronic Priesthood* in Appendix A.

"From the visit of John the Baptist, we learn these great truths:

1. That one must be ordained to the necessary priesthood by one having authority before he can administer the ordinances of the Gospel.

2. That the Aaronic Priesthood holds the keys of:
   a. The ministering of angels.
   b. The Gospel of repentance.
   c. Baptism by immersion for the remission of sins.

3. That this Priesthood shall never be taken again from the earth until 'the sons of Levi do offer again an offering unto the Lord in righteousness.'

4. That while the Aaronic Priesthood is divine authority from God, its administration is limited; it 'had not the power of laying on hands for the gift of the Holy Ghost'; that in conferring this Priesthood upon Joseph Smith and Oliver Cowdery, John the Baptist acted under the direction of Peter, James, and John, who held the keys of the Priesthood of Melchizedek, which should thereafter be conferred upon them." (LeGrand Richards, *MWW,* p. 73.)

SECTION 14

Background information on section 14

"Shortly after commencing to translate, I became acquainted with Mr. Peter Whitmer, of Fayette, Seneca County, New York, and also with some of his family. In the beginning of the month of June, his son, David Whitmer, came to the place where we were residing, and brought with him a two-horse wagon, for the purpose of having us accompany him to his father's place, and there remain until we should finish the work. [See Sec. 6:14-24, Orson Pratt commentary.] It was arranged that we should have our board free of charge, and the assistance of one of his brothers to write for me, and also his own assistance when convenient. Having much need of such timely aid in an undertaking so arduous, and being informed that the people in the neighborhood of the Whitmers were anxiously awaiting the opportunity to inquire into these things, we accepted the invitation, and accompanied Mr. Whitmer to his father's house, and there resided until the translation was finished and the copyright secured. Upon our arrival, we found Mr. Whitmer's family very anxious concerning the work, and very friendly toward ourselves. They continued so, boarded and lodged us according to arrangements; and John Whitmer, in particular, assisted us very much in writing during the remainder of the work.

"In the meantime, David, John and Peter Whitmer, Jun., became our zealous friends and assistants in the work; and being anxious to know their respective duties, and having desired with much earnestness that I should inquire of the Lord concerning them, I did so, through the means of the Urim and Thummim, and obtained for them in succession the following revelations: [Sections 14, 15, and 16 follow.]" (Joseph Smith, HC 1:48-49.)

14:1-5 Blessing for David Whitmer

For biographical information on David Whitmer, see

David Whitmer in Appendix B. The first five verses of this blessing to David Whitmer are virtually word-for-word the same as the blessing given previously to Oliver Cowdery as recorded in section 6. For information concerning the terms and expressions of these verses, read the materials listed for the corresponding verses in section 6.

14:7   *"if you keep my commandments and endure to the end"*

"In the revelation given to David Whitmer (Sec. 14), the Lord made him the promise that if he would keep the commandments and endure to the end, he should have eternal life, moreover he was commanded to assist in bringing forth the Lord's work and that the time would come when he would be a witness 'of the things of which you shall both hear and see, and also that you may declare repentance unto this generation.' This promise was based upon his faithfulness, and David was faithful and sincerely in earnest in his devotion to the Church and Joseph Smith when that witness came and for several years afterwards." (Joseph Fielding Smith, *CHMR* 1:62.)

14:8   *"you may stand as a witness"*

In this verse, David Whitmer's blessing differs significantly from the blessings of Joseph Knight, Sr. (section 12) and Hyrum Smith (section 11), which were given only shortly before. Here David Whitmer is specifically promised that he will be a witness in a special way "of the things of which you shall both hear and see." (14:8.) As will be shown in connection with section 17, David Whitmer was called by the Lord as one of the three special witnesses of the Book of Mormon; on that occasion he *heard* the voice of the Lord and *saw* the angel and the plates of Mormon, exactly as this blessing promised.

"There was one incident of significance that occurred when the Angel Moroni presented the plates before the three witnesses. The record states: 'In his hands he held the plates which we had been praying for these to have a view of. He turned over the leaves one by one, so that we could see them, and discern the engravings thereon distinctly. He then addressed himself to David Whitmer, and said, "David, blessed is the Lord, and he that keepeth his commandments," when immediately afterwards, we heard a voice from out of the bright light above us, saying, "These plates have been revealed by the power of God, and they have been translated by the power of God." ' (*HC* 1:54.)" (Joseph Fielding Smith, *CHMR* 1:63.)

14:9   *Jesus Christ created the heavens and the earth*

See *Jesus Christ* in Appendix A. The inspired version of the Bible by Joseph Smith and the latter-day scriptures make it clear that Jesus Christ as the pre-earthly Jehovah and the Firstborn Son of God in the Spirit was the Creator of "the heavens and the earth and all things that in them are." (3 Ne. 9:15.) King Benjamin indicated that the Savior would "be called Jesus Christ, the Son of God, the Father of heaven and earth, the Creator of all things from the beginning." (Mosiah 3:8.)

The inspired version of the gospel of John teaches that the Savior "was in the beginning with God. All things were made by him; and without him was not anything made which was made." (John 1:2-3.)

14:9   *"a light which cannot be hid in darkness"*

See *Light* in Appendix A.

SECTION 15

Background information on section 15

"John [Whitmer] displayed his eagerness to be of assistance and did some writing for the Prophet at that time [June 1829]. With his brothers, he desired earnestly to know what message the Lord had for him, and due to his solicitation the Lord gave him a revelation (Sec. 15) through the Urim and Thummim." (Joseph Fielding Smith, *CHMR* 1:64.)

15:1 *"my servant John [Whitmer]"*

For biographical information on John Whitmer, see *John Whitmer* in Appendix B.

15:2 *"mine arm is over all the earth"*

See *Arm of the Lord* in Appendix A.

15:3 *"no man knoweth save me and thee alone"*

In an earlier revelation to Oliver Cowdery, the Lord had said, ". . . there is none else save God that knowest thy thoughts and the intents of thy heart." (D&C 6:16.) The Lord here tells John Whitmer essentially the same thing: "I will tell you that which no man knoweth save me and thee alone."

15:6 *"declare repentance"*

See *Repentance* in Appendix A.

In earlier revelations the Lord had counseled his servants to "say nothing but repentance unto this generation." (D&C 6:9; 11:9.) In this revelation, the Lord emphasizes again "that the thing which will be of most worth unto you will be to declare repentance unto this people."

"Cast your minds back to the early days of this Church, and there stood this man John Whitmer, recently come into the Church of Christ. Various occupations in which he might engage were before him. He had the opportunity to labor upon the farm, to engage in merchandising, to follow mining, to study the profession of medicine or law, or to adopt one of the many other occupations in which men employ themselves. The question he asked himself at that time was, What would be the most worth to him? . . . At a critical time in his life, when he must choose which way to go, that voice said unto him that which would be of most worth unto him was to declare repentance unto the people and bring souls unto Christ. The message was of such importance that it came to him with 'sharpness and with power.' It was the voice of Jesus Christ." (Rudger Clawson, *CR,* April 1902, p. 7.)

SECTION 16

Background information on section 16

"Peter Whitmer, Jr., became very friendly with the Prophet and assisted him when the Prophet was translating the Book of Mormon. He also desired the word of the Lord in relation to his responsibilities and received the revelation by Urim and Thummim known as section sixteen. [June 1829; Fayette, New York.] (Joseph Fielding Smith, *CHMR* 1:64.)

"The Doctrine and Covenants is a compilation of the revelations received by Joseph Smith to individuals and for the guidance of the Church. From the first years of the work the Prophet kept every scrap of paper pertaining to the progress of the work, in fact, this care of things that must have seemed trivial is one of the evidences of the sincerity of the man. For example, when John and Peter Whitmer asked for help, he received for each of them a revelation, substantially the same: [Sections 15 and 16, quoted.]

"This simple revelation is directed to the individual and at first sign it has no permanent value for the Church. Yet as a revelation from God it was preserved and published. An insincere man could have eliminated this and other similar revelations as of little consequence. Not so with Joseph. The Lord has spoken. The words were part of the building of the kingdom of God, and the same advice would be useful to many men then and now. [Sec. 93:49.]" (John A. Widtsoe, *JS*, pp. 251-52.)

16:1-6 *Blessing for Peter Whitmer, Jr.*

For biographical information on Peter Whitmer, Jr., see *Peter Whitmer, Jr.* in Appendix B. This blessing for Peter Whitmer, Jr., is word-for-word the same as the blessing given to John Whitmer as recorded in section 15. For information on any of these verses, refer to the materials listed for the corresponding verses of section 15.

SECTION 17

Background information on section 17

"In the course of the work of translation, we ascertained that three special witnesses were to be provided by the Lord, to whom He would grant that they should see the plates from which this work (the Book of Mormon) should be translated; and that these witnesses should bear record of the same, as will be found recorded, Book of Mormon, page 581 [Ether 5:2-4, 1920 ed.], also p. 86 [2 Ne. 11:3, 1920 ed.]. Almost immediately after we had made this discovery, it occurred to Oliver Cowdery, David Whitmer and the aforementioned Martin Harris (who had come to inquire after our progress in the work) that they would have me inquire of the Lord to know if they might not obtain of him the privilege to be these three special witnesses; and finally they became so very solicitous, and urged me so much to inquire that at length I complied; and through the Urim and Thummim, I obtained of the Lord for them the following: [D&C 17.]" (Joseph Smith, *HC* 1:52-53.)

"In March, 1829, the Lord declared to Joseph that three men should have the privilege of seeing the plates and bearing witness to their existence. (Sec. 5; *HC* 1:52.) A similar prediction was found also in the Book of Mormon itself. (2 Ne. 11:3; Ether 5:3.) Oliver Cowdery, David Whitmer, and Martin Harris were later designated as these witnesses. In full conformity with the prediction, in June 1829, when the translation of the plates was approaching the end, this promise was realized. [Sec. 17 was received by Joseph Smith at Fayette, New York, June 1829.]

"Joseph and his three friends at the Peter Whitmer, Sr., home in Fayette, Seneca County, New York, went into the nearby woods one day, and there engaged in earnest prayer that the plates might by shown to them by Moroni. (*HC* 1:52-59.) To this they testified in a written and published statement. This event is related by Joseph Smith in his history, and published while the witnesses were living." (John A. Widtsoe, *JS*, p. 46.)

17:1 *"you shall have a view of the plates . . . breastplate . . . sword . . . Urim and Thummim . . . directors"*

In this one verse, the Lord lists five sacred objects that will be shown to the three special witnesses (Oliver Cowdery, David Whitmer, and Martin Harris):

1. "The plates." Joseph Smith at different times had been translating from two sets of plates: (1) the small plates of Nephi, the translation of which comprises the first 132 pages in the present Book of Mormon, and (2) the plates of Mormon, which include an abridgment of the large plates of Nephi, some writings by Moroni, and a sealed portion. From the descriptions later provided by the Three Witnesses, it was evidently the plates of Mormon that they beheld at this time.

2. "The breastplate." When the Angel Moroni first told Joseph Smith of the sacred records in his possession, he also indicated that hid up with the plates "were two stones, in silver bows—and these stones, fastened to a breastplate, constituted what is called the Urim and Thummim." (JS-H 1:35.) When the Prophet later looked into the stone box where the records were deposited, he said that he "looked in, and there indeed did I behold the plates, the Urim and Thummim, and the breastplate." (JS-H 1:52.) The Prophet recorded that later, September 22, 1827, "the time arrived for obtaining the plates, the Urim and Thummim, and the breastplate." (JS-H 1:59.)

It is not clear as to which of the ancient prophets had originally made the breastplate, but evidently it was prepared to be used with the "two stones" or Urim and Thummim.

Lucy Mack Smith, mother of the Prophet, indicated that she was privileged to handle the breastplate. Her description follows:

He [Joseph Smith] handed me the breast-plate spoken of in his history.

It was wrapped in a thin muslin handkerchief, so thin that I could feel its proportions without any difficulty.

It was concave on one side and convex on the other, and extended from the neck downwards, as far as the center of the stomach of a man of extraordinary size. It had four straps of the same material, for the purpose of fastening it to the breast, two of which ran back to go over the shoulders, and the other two were designed to fasten to the hips. They were just the width of two of my fingers (for I measured them), and they had holes in the end of them, to be convenient in fastening. After I had examined it, Joseph placed it in the chest with the Urim and Thummim. (*History of Joseph Smith by His Mother, Lucy Mack Smith* [Bookcraft, 1958 ed.], p. 112.)

3. "The sword of Laban." This sword is first mentioned by Nephi about 600 B.C. and is described as follows: ". . . the hilt thereof was of pure gold, and the workmanship thereof was exceeding fine, and . . . the blade thereof was of the most precious steel." (1 Ne. 4:9.)

The people of Lehi brought this sword with them to the promised land, and it became a sacred object to them (Mosiah 1:16), was used in helping to preserve the freedom of the people (Jacob 1:10), and was also used as a pattern for making other swords (2 Ne. 5:14).

4. "The Urim and Thummim." These particular Urim and Thummim "were given to the brother of Jared upon the mount, when he talked with the Lord face to face." (D&C 17:1.) This incident is recounted in Ether, where the Lord said to the brother of Jared, ". . . these two stones will I give unto thee, and ye shall seal them up also with the things which ye shalt write. . . . in my own due time . . . these stones shall magnify to the eyes of men these things which ye shall write." (Ether 3:23-24.) Joseph Smith described the Urim and Thummim and their function as "two transparent stones set in the rim of a bow fastened to a breastplate. Through the medium of the Urim and Thummim I translated the record by the gift and power of God." (*HC* 4:537.)

Another similar description of these sacred stones was given by the Prophet's mother: "The Urim and Thummim consisted of two smooth three-cornered diamonds, set in glass, and the glasses were set in silver bows, which were connected with each other in much the same way as old fashioned spectacles only much larger." (Edward Stevenson, *Reminiscences of the Prophet Joseph,* p. 24.)

Joseph Fielding Smith has explained the use of the Urim and Thummim as follows:

The Urim and Thummim shown to the witnesses and which Joseph Smith received were prepared by the Lord for the purpose of translating these sacred records. They were given to the brother of Jared on the mount and he sealed them up with the writings which he made of the visions of the Lord, so that at a later day they were to be used to bring to light his record of the Jaredite people. [Ether 3:23, 28.] These "stones" were in the possession of King Mosiah and by him were used in translating the Jaredite record. [Moses 28:11-19.] They were later hidden up by Moroni with the abridgment of Nephite history, with the other articles mentioned in section seventeen. (*CHMR* 1:40-42.)

(*Note:* for other scriptural references to Urim and Thummim or "holy interpreters," as they were sometimes called, see Omni 1:20-22; Mosiah 8:13-19; 21:27-28; 28:11-20; Alma 37:21-26; Ether 4:5; Ex. 28:20; Lev. 8:8; Deut. 33:8; Ezra 2:63; Neh. 7:65. See also *Urim and Thummim* in Appendix A.)

5. "The miraculous directors." As indicated in this revelation, the miraculous directors "were given to Lehi while in the wilderness, on the borders of the Red Sea." (D&C 17:1.) A description of this sacred object was given by Nephi as "a round ball of curious workmanship; and it was of fine brass. And within the ball were two spindles; and the one pointed the way whither we should go into the wilderness." (1 Ne. 16:10.) Nephi later discovered that writings would sometimes appear on the ball (1 Ne. 16:26-27), and he observed that "the pointers which were in the ball . . . did work according to the faith and diligence and heed which we did give unto them" (1 Ne. 16:28).

Smith and Sjodahl have provided the following information on the miraculous directors:

When the time had come for Lehi to leave the Valley of Lemuel, the voice of the Lord came to him during the night, commanding him to begin the perilous journey across the desert. It was no easy undertaking. Who was to act as guide? Undoubtedly, Lehi spent the night in prayer, asking for light and guidance. Early in the morning he stood in the tent door, anxiously surveying the surroundings, and then he beheld on the ground a brass ball. On examining this, he found that it had two spindles, one of which pointed the way (I. Nephi 16:10). When Lehi perceived the wonderful qualities of this instrument, he exclaimed, in ecstasy, *Liahona!* and that became its name (Alma 37:38). Liahona is a Hebrew word with, possibly, a Nephite termination, added later. *L* means "to"; *Jah* is an abbreviated form of the sacred name, "Jehovah," and *on* means "light." The meaning, then, is, "To Jehovah is light"; that is, "God has light; light comes from God," for He had answered his prayers for light and guidance. Similarly, Hagar, after having seen the Angel of the Lord, said, *Beer-lahai-roi;* that is, "The well of the Living One who seeth me" (Gen. 16:13).

The Prophet Joseph renders the word, "compass," as the nearest modern equivalent to it, just as one might properly apply the modern term "dreadnought" to an ancient viking ship; but it was not a compass, for it pointed out only the way the travelers were to follow, and it worked according to their faith; it was not dependent on the magnetic pole. (Smith and Sjodahl, *DCC,* p. 78.)

17:3   *"you shall testify of them"*

Each copy of the Book of Mormon contains a copy of the testimony of the three special witnesses. In the first edition of the Book of Mormon, this testimony occupied a page by itself in the back; since then the testimony has been published at the front of the book together with the testimony of the eight witnesses.

17:6   *"as your Lord and your God liveth it is true"*

Sometimes when the Lord intends that his words be accepted as though they were part of a sacred covenant with the receiver, he states a fact and then reaffirms it with a strong statement that might even be considered a sacred oath. In this revelation, a good example is the strong, definite, unequivocating, declarative words: "As your Lord and your God liveth it is true."

17:4, 8-9   *"this you shall do that . . ."*

The Lord indicates in this revelation several reasons why the three special witnesses are being privileged to see the plates and other sacred objects:

1. that "Joseph Smith may not be destroyed" (v. 4);

2. that the Lord might bring about his "righteous purposes unto the children of men" (vv. 4 and 9);

3. that "the gates of hell shall not prevail" against the three witnesses (v. 8).

In an earlier revelation the Lord had promised Joseph Smith that "these things" should be shown to three others of his servants; that they "should know of a surety that these things are true," for the Lord would declare it unto them "from heaven"; that they would "behold and view these things as they are"; that "to none else" would this same testimony be given; and that they were to testify to these things or they would be condemned. (D&C 5:10-15, 26-27. See also 14:8.) Also, in an earlier revelation the Lord had declared "in the mouth of two or three witnesses shall every word be established." (D&C 6:28. See also 5:11, 15; 2 Cor. 13:1; and Deut. 19:15).

SECTION 18

Background information on section 18

"We now became anxious to have that promise realized to us, which the angel that conferred upon us the Aaronic Priesthood had given us [Sec. 13], viz., that provided we continued faithful, we should also have the Melchizedek Priesthood, which holds the authority of the laying on of hands for the gift of the Holy Ghost. We had for some time made this matter a subject of humble prayer, more particularly to seek of the Lord what we now so earnestly desired; and here, to our unspeakable satisfaction, did we realize the truth of the Savior's promise—'Ask, and it shall be given you; seek, and ye shall find; knock, and it shall be opened unto you'—for we had not long been engaged in solemn and fervent prayer, when the word of the Lord came unto us in the chamber [of old Father Whitmer in Fayette, Seneca County (Sec. 128:21)], commanding us that I should ordain Oliver Cowdery to be an Elder in the Church of Jesus Christ; and that he also should ordain me to the same office; and then to ordain others, as it should be made known unto us from time to time. We were, however, commanded to defer this our ordination until such times as it should be practicable to have our brethren, who had been and who should be baptized, assembled together, when we must have by vote whether they were willing to accept us as spiritual teachers or not; when also we were commanded to bless bread and break it with them, and to take wine, bless it, and drink it with them; afterward proceed to ordain each other according to commandment; then call out such men as the Spirit should dictate, and ordain them; and then attend to the laying of hands for the gift of the Holy Ghost, upon all those whom we had previously baptized, doing all things in the name of the Lord. The following commandment will further illustrate the nature of our calling to this Priesthood, as well as that of others who were yet to be sought after. [Section 18.]" (Joseph Smith, *HC* 1:60-62.)

"Nearly six years before the calling of the Twelve

Apostles in this dispensation, and several months before the organization of the Church, the Lord indicated by revelation that a council of twelve Apostles would be chosen, and Oliver Cowdery and David Whitmer were informed that it was to be their privilege to choose out the Twelve and instruct them in the duties of that calling. . . .

"At this early day, Oliver Cowdery and David Whitmer, who had sought the privilege of acting as two of the three witnesses of the Book of Mormon were appointed by divine revelation to seek out the Twelve. Martin Harris, who had been named as the other witness, was not named in this revelation as one who should share in this great honor. It was by sore and sincere repentance that the privilege was granted him to become a witness of the Book of Mormon, and the Lord still withheld from Martin the full exercise of his spirit when the call of the other two men came to choose out the Twelve. Before the time arrived for the choosing of the twelve special witnesses for Christ six years later, Martin had placed himself in a position where he could be recognized, and therefore the Prophet, by the revelation of the Lord, included Martin Harris with the other brethren in the choosing and ordaining of the Twelve Apostles." (Joseph Fielding Smith, *CHMR* 1:80, 82.)

"Before the Church could be organized it was essential that there be revealed such matters as pertained to the organization of the Church. This was done between the time the witnesses viewed the plates of the ancient record and the sixth of April, 1830. The first of these (D&C Sec. 18) was given to Joseph Smith, Oliver Cowdery and David Whitmer, at Fayette. It made known the calling of the Twelve Apostles who should be chosen in this dispensation, although it was about six years before they were called. It gave instructions 'relative to the building up of the Church of Christ according to the fulness of the Gospel.'" (Joseph Fielding Smith, *ECH,* pp. 84-85.)

18:2   *"the things you have written are true"*

"I told the brethren that the Book of Mormon was the most correct of any book on earth, and the keystone of our religion, and a man would get nearer to God by abiding by its precepts than by any other book." (Joseph Smith, *HC* 4:461.)

18:2 *"you [Oliver Cowdery] know that they are true"*

"In this revelation, Oliver Cowdery was informed that he had received a witness by the Spirit of Truth of the work, especially of the Book of Mormon. Many times during the translating of the record, manifestations of this kind had come to him. Not only had the Spirit made this truth manifest, but he had previous to this revelation stood in the presence of a heavenly messenger and under his hands received the Holy Aaronic Priesthood. Therefore, the Lord could say to him: 'I have manifested unto you by my Spirit in many instances, that the things which you have written (i.e., as scribe) are true; wherefore you know that they are true.' " (Joseph Fielding Smith, *CHMR* 1:81.)

18:4, *"my church, my gospel, and my rock"*
5, 17   The Lord uses the three words *church, gospel,* and *rock* several times in sequence and in close relationship to each other. Here he states that in the scriptures are all things "concerning the foundation of my church, my gospel, and my rock. Wherefore, if you shall build up my church, upon the foundation of my gospel and my rock, the gates of hell shall not prevail against you." Later in this same revelation, he states, "You have my gospel before you, and my rock, and my salvation." (18:17.)

These statements throw additional light on Matthew's account of the words of the Savior to Peter, "Upon this rock I will build my church; and the gates of hell shall not prevail against it." (Matt. 16:18.)

See (1) *Church,* (2) *Gospel,* and (3) *Rock* in Appendix A.

18:8 *"his name is Joseph"*

"Attention is called to the name, because the Scriptures predict the coming of a great deliverer in the latter days, so named. Nephi says that Joseph, the Patriarch, predicted the coming forth of the House of Israel on the American continents, of a 'righteous branch' and a Seer, whose name, he said, 'shall be called after me' (Joseph), and after the name of his father (2 Ne. 3:1-15). (Smith and Sjodahl, *DCC,* p. 83.)

18:9 *"you are called even with that same calling with which [Paul] was called"*

The priesthood of God is the power and authority to act

for and in behalf of God. Certainly God, who is unchangeable—the same yesterday, today, and forever—has the right
and the power to select whomever he will to represent him
and act for him on the earth. In New Testament times, the
Savior called and ordained twelve men whom he called both
disciples and apostles to be special witnesses for him. Later
other men, including Paul, were called and ordained as
apostles. In this revelation, the Lord announces that he is going to give some men in this dispensation the same powers
and authority he gave anciently to Paul. (18:9.)

18:15-16 *"how great shall be your joy"* if you bring souls unto
Jesus Christ

"And how are we to determine the value of souls? This
matter has been determined for us also by revelation: [Sec.
18:16, quoted.] The souls of men are so precious in the sight
of God that he gave to the world his Only Begotten Son, that
by the shedding of his blood he might draw all men unto
him. That is why the great Prophet of this dispensation, Joseph Smith, and these others, John Whitmer, Oliver
Cowdery, David Whitmer, and the rest, were called to bring
souls unto Christ. And if one of these men should labor all
his days, and bring save it be but one soul unto Christ, and
that one should be his wife, what great joy he would have
with his wife in heaven. Then if he should labor all his days
and bring unto Christ the souls of his wife and his children,
and none else perchance, how great would be his joy in
heaven with his wife and children." (Rudger Clawson, *CR,*
April 1901, pp. 7-8.)

"And now . . . let me emphasize that the noblest aim in
life is to strive to live to make other lives better and happier.
The most worthy calling in life is that in which man can
serve best his fellow man. . . .

"Such is the divine message given to the Prophet Joseph
Smith in these words: 'Remember the worth of souls is great
in the sight of God.' (D&C 18:10.) Such is the philosophy
expressed by the Redeemer in the seemingly paradoxical
statement 'Whosoever will lose his life for my sake will find
it.' (Matt. 16:25.)

"The meaning of this becomes clear in the light of another
passage which says: 'Inasmuch as ye have done it unto one
of the least of these my brethren, ye have done it unto me.'

(Matt. 25:40.)" (David O. McKay, *CR,* April 1961, p. 131.)

"There are many reasons why the worth of souls is great in the sight of God, and why he desired to have them redeemed. First, man is the offspring of God in the spirit; we are his children, and as such he has a deep love and earnest concern for us one and all. . . . Second, it is the privilege of those who are faithful to become like God. The human soul will not only become immortal through the resurrection, but may be exalted to godhood, as a joint heir with Jesus Christ. Man's possibilities as a son of God are unlimited, because he, too, like his father, will be infinite. A soul, therefore, is worth more than a world which is created for his habitation." (Joseph Fielding Smith, *CHMR* 1:83.)

18:20 *"contend against no church"*

"When we are commanded to 'contend against no church save it be the church of the devil,' we must understand that this is instruction to us to contend against all evil, that which is opposed to righteousness and truth. James declares that 'every good gift and every perfect gift is from above, and cometh down from the Father of lights, with whom is no variableness, neither shadow of turning,' and the scriptures also teach, 'for there is nothing which is good save it comes from the Lord; and that which is evil cometh from the devil.' (Omni 1:25.) All who go forth to teach should do so in wisdom and not contend with the churches or engage in profitless debates, but teach in the spirit of kindness and try to persuade people to receive the truth." (Joseph Fielding Smith, *CHMR* 1:83.)

18:20 *"the church of the devil"*

"The Devil has his church, his kingdom, 'I beheld this great and abominable church: and I saw the devil, that he was the foundation of it' (1 Ne. 13:6). 'There are two churches only; the one is the church of the Lamb of God, and the other is the church of the devil' (1 Ne. 14:10). The church of the adversary may be known by its fundamental principle of government. In the beginning he declared himself in favor of salvation by compulsion, and although he was cast out of heaven for refusing to submit to the divine Council, he has continued his agitation for that plan among the children of men ever since. His church consists of those who adopt his plan and seek to destroy the free agency of man by brute force. . . . The church of the adversary may also be known by contention and strife, by false doctrines, and by all manner of iniquity. A minister of the Lord makes war upon the domain of the adversary by the sword of the Spirit; not by persecution." (Smith and Sjodahl, *DCC,* pp. 85-86.)

"I do not understand that when the Lord states that those churches shall be overthrown—I mean the church of the devil, using his expression, and those that are making false claims, and shall be thrown into the fire, as he says [Rev. 18]—I do not understand that all members of those churches are to meet destruction, physically or otherwise. He is speaking there of the church collectively, and he is not pleased with it; but individually he may be well pleased with many of his sons and daughters who have been under an environment that has led them into those churches which are not of God." (James E. Talmage, *CR,* October 1928, p. 120.)

18:23   *"Jesus Christ is the name, . . . and there is none other name given"*

Jesus Christ is the divine Savior and Redeemer of all mankind. It is through his atonement that all mankind are saved (1) from the permanent effects of physical death through the resurrection and (2) from the effects of spiritual death through repentance of all their sins. Thus faith in the Lord Jesus Christ and in his divine atonement is absolutely essential for a man to be saved from hell. These concepts are not only clearly taught in the revelations in the Doctrine and Covenants, but they are also taught in the Book of Mormon and other scriptures. The prophet Nephi declared, "There is none other name given under heaven save it be . . . Jesus Christ . . . whereby man can be saved." (2 Ne. 25:20.) King Benjamin's words are equally definite: ". . . there shall be no other name given nor any other way nor means whereby salvation can come unto the children of men, only in and through the name of Christ, the Lord Omnipotent." (Mosiah 3:17.)

See also *Jesus Christ* in Appendix A.

"In the New Testament He has revealed Himself as Jesus, the Savior, and Christ, the Anointed One (see v. 22). 'Thou shalt call His name JESUS: for he shall save his people from their sins' (Matt. 1:21). To take upon oneself His name is, therefore, more than to become a disciple; it is to engage in His service for the salvation of men. JESUS CHRIST is the name given of the Father, and there is no other through which man can be saved. It is the name in which men shall be called at the last day—the day of judgment (Mosiah 5:9)—and those who know not the Name can have no place in the Kingdom of God (vv. 23-25)." (Smith and Sjodahl, *DCC*, p. 86.)

"I am thankful that the Church to which I belong preaches Christ and him crucified, and resurrected, the Christ that ascended into heaven, the Christ that was the offspring in the flesh, as well as in the spirit, of the very eternal Father, the Christ who is the Savior and Redeemer of mankind, beside whom there is none, beside whose name there is no name under heaven whereby mankind may be saved." (James E. Talmage, *CR,* April 1916, p. 131.)

8:26-38 *"the Twelve shall be my disciples"*

The Lord herein makes known to his prophet and to at least two of his associates (Oliver Cowdery and David Whitmer) that eventually twelve disciples will be chosen and called to be special witnesses of Jesus Christ "to go into all the world to preach my gospel unto every creature." (18:28, 31-36.) Oliver and David are given the specific commandment to "search out the Twelve," which they subsequently do. (18:37.)

When these twelve are selected, called, and ordained, the Lord indicates they "are called to be the Twelve Apostles, or special witnesses of Christ in all the world." (107:23.)

For additional responsibilities of the Twelve Apostles, see *Council of the Twelve* in Appendix A.

"After the opening of the Dispensation of the Fulness of Times the Lord made it known that the organization of the primitive Church of Jesus Christ was to be restored. As early as June, 1829, before the Church was organized, a revelation came calling the witnesses of the Book of Mormon to choose the twelve who should constitute the council of the apostles. In this revelation the Lord gave this instruction to the future twelve: [Sec. 18:26-36, quoted.]

"It was nearly six years after this revelation that the apostles were chosen. After the return of Zion's Camp from Missouri to Kirtland the Prophet Joseph Smith called together all the brethren who went forth on that journey. From these men who had been willing to risk their lives in the service of the Lord, the three witnesses, who were set apart to choose out the twelve, made the selection of the apostles. This was on the 14th day of February, 1835, and the men were chosen in the following order: (1) Lyman E. Johnson, (2) Brigham Young, (3) Heber C. Kimball, (4) Orson Hyde, (5) David W. Patten, (6) Luke S. Johnson, (7) William E. McLellin, (8) John F. Boynton, (9) Orson Pratt, (10) William Smith, (11) Thomas B. Marsh, (12) Parley P. Pratt.

"After the twelve had all been selected and ordained they were organized according to age in the council. Thomas B. Marsh, the oldest, became the senior and the first man ordained. Lyman E. Johnson, the junior." (Joseph Fielding Smith, *IE*, April 1935, p. 212.)

18:26-36   *The Twelve to preach and testify*

"All these, your brethren, who are called to the Apostleship, and to minister in the midst of the house of Israel, are endowed, or ought to be endowed richly, with the spirit of their calling. For instance, these twelve disciples of Christ are supposed to be eye and ear witnesses of the divine mission of Jesus Christ. It is not permissible for them to simply say, I believe; I have accepted it, just because I believe it. Read the Revelation. The Lord informs us that they must *know,* they must get the knowledge for themselves, it must be with them as if they had seen with their eyes and heard with their ears, and they know the truth. That is their mission, to testify of Jesus Christ and Him crucified, and risen from the dead and clothed now with almighty power at the right hand of God, the Savior of the world." (Smith and Sjodahl, *DCC,* p. 89.)

18:34-36   *"these words are . . . of me . . . you can testify that you have heard my voice"*

"In the first part of this dispensation, He [the Lord] gave a revelation directly to the Twelve in which He added to what He had previously given, when He said, 'And I, Jesus Christ, your Lord and your God, have spoken it. These words are not of men nor of man, but of me; wherefore you shall testify they are of me and not of man; for it is my voice which speaketh them unto you; for they are given by my Spirit unto you, and by my power you can read them one to another; and save it were by my power you could not have them. Wherefore you can testify that you have heard my voice, and know my words.' (D&C 18:34-36.)

"Now I ask you to think of the import of the Lord's revelation. In the scriptures are contained His words, and when one having power to teach them speaks them to you it is as though it were by His own voice, so that those who hear can testify that they have both heard His voice and that they know His words. . . .

"I wish that our faith was sufficiently simple that we could read what I have just read to you, and I shall repeat it now, and I ask you to think about it again. The words that are in these scriptures are the words of the Lord, and when one like these authorized servants read them to you by the power and authority they possess and by the Spirit, you, all of you, all of us, can say, I have now heard His words, and I have heard His voice. Because whether it be 'by His own voice or by the voice of his servants, it is the same.' " (Harold B. Lee, *CN*, Dec. 3, 1960, p. 14.)

18:42   *"the years of accountability"*

This revelation was given within two months of when John the Baptist had restored the Aaronic Priesthood and Joseph Smith and Oliver Cowdery had subsequently baptized each other (D&C 13). Earlier in this revelation (18:7), the Lord had already referred to this baptism.

In this verse the Lord provides additional information on the sacred ordinances of baptism: men, women, and children who have repented should be baptized, but children are not to be baptized unless they "have arrived at the years of accountability." This instruction was repeated in a revelation given in April 1830 at about the time the Church was organized wherein the Lord explicitly said, "No one can be received into the church of Christ unless he has arrived unto the years of accountability before God, and is capable of repentance." (D&C 20:71.)

Still later the Lord revealed the exact age when he considers children to be accountable, the age at which they should be baptized—"when eight years old." (D&C 68:25.)

For additional information as to why infants should not be baptized, read Moroni 8:5-26. See also *Children* in Appendix A.

SECTION 19

"This revelation was given some time in March, 1830 [Manchester, New York]. It would seem that Martin Harris had come to Joseph Smith seeking further assurance in relation to his standing before the Lord, being sorely troubled in his spirit because of his transgression. He had already been granted the privilege on his earnest solicitation of being one of the three witnesses, and that wonderful vision had been given. [Sections 5 and 17.] Perhaps out of this came much serious reflection and he sought further light. However, there is no indication in the *History of the Church* as to the reason why the revelation was given and the exact day is unknown when it was given. It was without question a revelation of great comfort to Martin, and it is one of the great revelations given in this dispensation; there are few of greater import than this. The doctrine of the atonement of the Lord, as directly applying to the individual, and his exposition of 'eternal punishment,' as here set forth, give to the members of the Church light which was not previously known." (Joseph Fielding Smith, *CHMR* 1:80-81.)

19:1 *Names of the Lord*

See (1) *Alpha and Omega,* and (2) *Jesus Christ* in Appendix A.

"Our Lord begins this Revelation by introducing Himself under five different names, each indicating His nature or work:

"*Alpha and Omega*] The first and the last letter of the Greek alphabet, used as symbols of the beginning and the ending. Christ is so called, because He is the Author and the Preserver of all things (Heb. 1:2, 10).

"*Christ the Lord*] 'Christ' means 'anointed.' Prophets, Priests, and Kings were anointed, and our Lord unites all these offices in Him. He is the anointed Lord. The Greek word Christ is the same as the Hebrew Messiah (Mashiac), the title used in John 1:41, and 4:25.

"*I am He*] This is equivalent to Jehovah (See notes on Sec. 18:21).

"*The Beginning and the End*] He was in the beginning and will remain throughout all eternities. He is endless (v. 4).

"*The Redeemer of the World*] Christ is our Redeemer. He delivers those who turn to Him from the bondage of sin and guilt. He has 'bought' us (1 Cor. 6:20; 7:23; 2 Pet. 2:1). And the world will in due time be delivered from the power of Satan, from sin and all its consequences, such as war, poverty, ignorance, sickness, and even death." (Smith and Sjodahl, *DCC,* p. 91.)

19:3   *"the destroying of Satan and his works at the end of the world"*

"The works of Satan cannot be destroyed until the end of the world, and the last day of judgment (v. 3), when every man shall be judged 'according to his works and the deeds which he hath done.' Paul told the Corinthian Saints that the last enemy to be destroyed is death. This of necessity must be so, for when death is destroyed mortality comes to an end. At that time all the children of God, except sons of perdition, will be redeemed from hell and the second death." (Joseph Fielding Smith, *CHMR* 1:86-87.)

19:4-12   *"endless . . . eternal"*

"The explanation given in this revelation of eternal punishment, endless punishment and eternal damnation, throws a flood of light on many passages of ancient scripture. The Lord permitted the prophets of old to speak of endless punishment, and the fire that is not quenched—even Christ did this himself—that the sinners might be impressed and brought to repentance. It was done, so the Lord reveals, in a manner 'more express than other scriptures, that it might work upon the hearts of the children of men, altogether for my name's glory.' Here the Lord explains the mystery. 'Eternal punishment' is God's punishment, since he is Eternal. All the laws of God are eternal, but in meting out punishment to men in mortality, he has not declared that there is no opportunity for forgiveness even in the life to come. The Savior said, [Matt. 12:21-32 quoted]. This shows that the Savior taught that sins—all sins, in fact, which were not unto death—could be forgiven in the world to come.

"The same punishment follows the same offense or transgression of the law. The prison remains, it has been explained, even when the prisoner goes free; also the same punishment awaits each transgressor of each particular offense, but when the law is satisfied the prisoner goes free." (Joseph Fielding Smith, *CHMR* 1:87-88.)

"During this hundred years many other great truths not known before, have been declared to the people, and one of the greatest is that to hell there is an exit as well as an entrance. [Sec. 76:81-85; Matt. 5:25-26.] Hell is no place to which a vindictive Judge sends prisoners to suffer and to be punished principally for his glory; but it is a place prepared for the teaching, the disciplining of those who failed to learn here upon the earth what they should have learned. True, we read of everlasting punishment, unending suffering, eternal damnation. [Matt. 18:8; 25:41, 46; Rev. 14:10-11.] That is a direful expression, but in his mercy the Lord has made plain what those words mean. 'Eternal punishment,' he says, 'is God's punishment,' for he is eternal; and that condition or state or possibility will ever exist for the sinner who deserves and really needs such condemnation; but this does not mean that the individual sufferer or sinner is to be kept in hell longer than is necessary to bring him to a fitness for something better. When he reaches that stage the prison doors will open and there will be rejoicing among the hosts who welcome him into a better state. The Lord has not abated in the least what he said in earlier dispensations concerning the operation of his law and his Gospel, but he had made clear unto us his goodness and mercy through it all, for it is his glory and his work to bring about the immortality and eternal life of man. [Moses 1:39.]" (James E. Talmage, *CR*, April 1930, p. 97.)

" 'Endless torment,' 'eternal damnation' are expressions which denote the punishment inflicted by the Endless One, the Eternal One. 'Eternal punishment' is contrasted with such punishment as man can inflict on man in time here on earth." (Smith and Sjodahl, *DCC*, p. 94.)

19:15-21 *"I command you to repent . . ."*

See *Repentance* in Appendix A.

It is of interest to note that the heading of this section of the Doctrine and Covenants indicates that it is "A Commandment of God" rather than referring to it only as a "revelation" as is the usual format. Section 19 might thus be referred to as a revelatory commandment, for the revelation contains not only instruction but also a definite and clear commandment—to repent: "I command you to repent" (verse 15), "I command you again to repent" (verse 20), "I command you that you preach naught but repentance" (verse 21).

When the doctrine of repentance is fully understood, then it is seen that repentance is all that ever needs to be taught, for repentance means not only to stop doing those things which are wrong but also to start doing those things which are right.

19:17   *"if they would not repent they must suffer"*

"The unrepentant are to be sorely punished. This is evident from the words of the Lord in this revelation (verses 15-19). Our Father in heaven is very merciful, long-suffering and forgiving. He has promised to forgive the repentant sinner. Never has greater love been manifest than that by our Father in sending his Son, and by that Son in coming to the earth, to die for man. But one of the immutable, or eternal laws of God is that the unrepentant sinner must suffer even as Christ suffered (verses 15-18), for the blood of Christ will not cleanse those who will not repent and in humility accept the free gift which comes from God." (Joseph Fielding Smith, *CHMR* 1:88.)

19:18   *"Which suffering caused myself, even God . . . to bleed at every pore"*

"We cannot comprehend the great suffering that the Lord had to take upon himself to bring to pass this redemption from death and from sin. . . .

"We get into the habit of thinking, that his great suffering was when he was nailed to the cross by his hands and his feet and was left there to suffer until he died. As excruciating as this pain was, that was not the greatest suffering that he had to undergo, for in some way which I cannot understand, but which I accept on faith, and which you must accept on faith, he carried on his back the burden of the sins of the whole world. It is hard enough for me to carry my own sins. How is it with you? And yet he had to carry the sins of the whole world, as our Savior and the Redeemer of a fallen world, and so great was his suffering before he went to the cross, we are informed that blood oozed from the pores of his body. . . ." (Joseph Fielding Smith, *CR*, October 1947, pp. 147-48.)

"Christ's agony in the garden is unfathomable by the finite mind, both as to intensity and cause. . . . In that hour of anguish Christ met and overcame all the horrors that Satan . . . could inflict. . . . In some manner, actual and terribly real though to man incomprehensible, the Savior took upon Himself the burden of the sins of mankind from Adam to the end of the world." (James E. Talmage, *JC*, p. 613.)

"It . . . was in the garden. That is where he bled from every pore in his body.

"Now I cannot comprehend that pain. I have suffered pain, you have suffered pain, and sometimes it has been quite severe; but I cannot comprehend pain, which is *mental anguish more than physical,* that would cause the blood, like sweat, to come out upon the body. It was something terrible, something terrific; so we can understand why he would cry unto his Father: '. . . If it be possible, let this cup pass from me: nevertheless not as I will, but as thou wilt.' [Matthew 26:39]." (Joseph Fielding Smith, *DS* 1:130.)

19:22 *"they cannot bear meat now, but milk they must receive"*

This descriptive expression teaches the necessity of "first steps." The basic principles of the gospel should be taught first; then when the truly converted person is strengthened by the reception of the Holy Ghost, he can better understand and appreciate the higher ordinances.

19:26 *"impart [of your property] freely to the printing of the Book of Mormon"*

"On February 28, 1828, Martin Harris, a prosperous farmer of Palmyra, friendly to Joseph, took one of these transcripts [copy of characters from the gold plates] to New York City. There two eminent students of ancient languages, Doctors Anthon and Mitchell, examined them. In later years both of these men acknowledged that the characters were presented to them. Martin Harris declared that the 'experts' said the characters were a mixture of ancient alphabets. However, when they learned how the characters had been obtained and that part of the 'book' or plates were sealed, they repudiated their first positive statement. Egyptology was in its early infancy at that time. The visit and the statements of the two men were sufficient, however, to induce Harris to become a scribe for the Prophet, and later, when the Book of Mormon was to be published, to mortgage his farm for $3,000 with which to pay the printer." (John A. Widtsoe, *JS*, p. 39.)

19:27 *"the Jew, of whom the Lamanites are a remnant"*

See *Jew* in Appendix A.

19:28 *"pray vocally as well as in thy heart"*

See *Prayer* in Appendix A.

The scriptures contain numerous references and statements from the Lord and his prophets concerning the purpose, power, and efficacy of prayer. Over a hundred references are listed under the topic "Prayer" in *A Topical Guide to the Scriptures of The Church of Jesus Christ of Latter-day Saints,* and these are only examples of many more that could have been listed. In this revelation the Lord counsels us not to limit our prayers either to all public prayers or to all private prayers: "I command thee," he says, to "pray vocally *as well as* in thy heart," "before the world *as well as* in secret," and "in public *as well as* in private."

"How impressive are those few simple words [19:28, 38] in regard to prayer! How far-reaching! They center into a man's life and comprehend his whole existence, at least from the years of his accountability until he passes into the grave. He must pray under all circumstances. Prayer is not reserved for the Sabbath day or for any particular occasion. It is not only to be used at the general conferences of the Church, but the spirit of prayer must be in our hearts unceasingly. We must pray in our families, we must pray in secret; we must pray in our hearts. The spirit of prayer must be with us when we retire at night and when we arise in the morning. It must be upon us when we leave our homes or in the valleys, or wherever we are. We are told in the words which I have quoted that if the spirit is upon us the Lord will bless us, and the blessings which will come in answer to prayer will be of more importance to us than treasures of earth." (Rudger Clawson, *CR*, April 1904, pp. 42-43.)

19:30   *"reviling not against revilers"*

"Some there are who think we are afraid to meet anyone
in debate. Not so. It is much harder for our young brethren
to keep from debating than it is to engage in it; for they feel
that they have the truth, and they are not afraid to meet
anyone in defense of principles in which they believe. But
we have only one object in view in going out amongst the nations, and that is to follow the Master's instructions—to go
out and teach men. That is our work. We do not go out to
win battles as debaters; but we go out to teach men that
which we have received, and which we know is true. . . .
Those who seek to debate with our Elders and thirst for the
honor of beating them in argument, do not want to be
taught; they simply want contention. Paul tells us to avoid
contention. He said: 'But if any man seem to be contentious,
we have no such custom, neither the churches of God.' [1
Cor. 11:16.] So we say, contention is not our custom, and we
advise our missionaries not to contend, but simply go out
and teach the principles of the Gospel." (Anthon H. Lund,
CR, October 1902, pp. 80-81.)

19:31-32   *"a great and the last commandment"*

The good news of the gospel of Jesus Christ might be said
to include many laws and commandments. However, a
major purpose of the gospel is to reveal and teach those principles or laws which are necessary to be obeyed in order to
be saved in the presence of our Heavenly Father.

The Prophet Joseph Smith taught, and the Church has accepted as an article of faith, "that the first principles and ordinances of the Gospel are: first, Faith in the Lord Jesus
Christ; second, Repentance; third, Baptism by immersion
for the remission of sins; fourth, Laying on of hands for the
gift of the Holy Ghost." (A of F 4.) These are the absolute
essentials, the basics, for without them it would be impossible to understand or to keep the other commandments; without them no person could be saved.

When the resurrected Jesus Christ appeared to the
righteous Lehites on the western continent, his disciples
wanted to know what the true church should be called. The
Savior answered that it should be called after his name if it
were built upon his gospel. (3 Ne. 27:3-12.) He then reviewed for his disciples the essential aspects of the gospel

and summarized in these words: "Now this is the command-ment: Repent, all ye ends of the earth, and come unto me and be baptized in my name, that ye may be sanctified by the reception of the Holy Ghost, that ye might stand spotless before me at the last day. Verily, verily I say unto you, this is my gospel." (3 Ne. 27:20-21.)

In this revelation (D&C 19) the Lord reiterates these basic teachings and indicates this is a great and last command-ment.

19:37 *"Hosanna, hosanna"*

See *Hosanna* in Appendix A.

19:39 *"canst thou read this without rejoicing"*

Frequently when we read the scriptures we read them piecemeal in a rather disjointed, unorganized manner in order to find a particular statement for a sacrament meeting talk or a reference that can be used in teaching a class.

It is the testimony of the compiler of this volume that, as members of the true and living church, we would benefit greatly by taking the time and finding the privacy to read and ponder the scriptures, placing them in the context in which they were given. It was in such privacy and spirit of meditation and contemplation that this section (19) was read in preparing these materials. When so read and pondered, the words of this revelation are so overpowering and overwhelming that it is difficult to read them all without melting into tears.

Truly the revelations in the Doctrine and Covenants are the words of "Alpha and Omega, Christ the Lord . . . the be-ginning and the end, the Redeemer of the world" (verse 1). And how can one read them "without rejoicing and lifting up thy heart for gladness" (verse 39)?

148

SECTION 20

Background information on section 20

"The Prophet states that after he and Oliver Cowdery received the Priesthood they continued to receive instructions from the Lord, and they waited for the fulfilment of the promise made by John for the organization of the Church. In the meantime they had received several revelations." (Joseph Fielding Smith, *CHMR* 1:90.)

"In this manner did the Lord continue to give us instructions from time to time, concerning the duties which now devolved upon us; and among many other things of the kind, we obtained of Him the following, by the spirit of prophecy and revelation; which not only gave us much information, but also pointed out to us the precise day upon which, according to His will and commandment, we should proceed to organize His Church once more here upon the earth: [D&C 20.]" (Joseph Smith, *HC* 1:64.)

"This revelation (Sec. 20), instructing the Prophet and his brethren to organize the Church, was given either on or a very short time before the sixth day of April, 1830." (Joseph Fielding Smith, *CHMR* 1:90.)

20:1 *"being one thousand eight hundred and thirty years since the coming of our Lord and Savior Jesus Christ in the flesh"*

"The time of Messiah's birth is a subject upon which specialists in theology and history, and those who are designated in literature 'the learned,' fail to agree. Numerous lines of investigation have been followed, only to reach divergent conclusions, both as to the year and as to the month and day within the year at which the 'Christian era' in reality began. . . .

"Without attempting to analyze the mass of calculation data relating to this subject, we accept the Dionysian basis as correct with respect to the year, which to us is B.C. 1, and, as

shall be shown, in an early month of that year. In support of
this belief we cite the inspired record known as the 'Revelation on Church Government, given through Joseph the
Prophet, in April, 1830,' which opens with these words: 'The
rise of the Church of Christ in these last days, being one
thousand eight hundred and thirty years since the coming of
our Lord and Savior Jesus Christ in the flesh.'

"Another evidence of the correctness of our commonly accepted chronology is furnished by the Book of Mormon
record. Therein we read that 'in the commencement of the
first year of the reign of Zedekiah, king of Judah,' the word
of the Lord came to Lehi at Jerusalem, directing him to take
his family and depart into the wilderness. [1 Ne. 1:4; 2:2-4.]
In the early stages of their journey toward the sea, Lehi
prophesied, as had been shown him of the Lord, concerning
the impending destruction of Jerusalem and the captivity of
the Jews. Furthermore, he predicted the eventual return of
the people of Judah from their exile in Babylon, and the
birth of the Messiah, which latter event he definitely
declared would take place six hundred years from the time
he and his people had left Jerusalem. [1 Ne. 10:4.] This
specification of time was repeated by later prophecy [1
Nephi 19:8; 2 Ne. 25:19]; and the signs of the actual
fulfilment are recorded as having been realized 'six hundred
years from the time that Lehi left Jerusalem.' [3 Ne. 1:1.]
These scriptures fix the time of the beginning of Zedekiah's
reign as six hundred years before the birth of Christ. According to the commonly accepted reckoning, Zedekiah was
made king in the year 597 B.C. This shows a discrepancy of
about three years between the commonly accepted date of
Zedekiah's inauguration as king and that given in the Book
of Mormon statement; and, as already seen, there is a
difference of between three and four years between the
Dionysian reckoning and the nearest approach to an
agreement among scholars concerning the beginning of the
current era. Book of Mormon chronology therefore sustains
in general the correctness of the common or Dionysian
system.

"As to the season of the year in which Christ was born,
there is among the learned as great a diversity of opinion as
that relating to the year itself. It is claimed by many Biblical
scholars that December 25th, the day celebrated in Chris-

tendom as Christmas, cannot be the correct date. We believe April 6th to be the birthday of Jesus Christ, as indicated in a revelation of the present dispensation already cited [Sec. 20:1; 21:3], in which that day is made without qualification the completion of the one thousand eight hundred and thirtieth year since the coming of the Lord in the flesh. This acceptance is admittedly based on faith in modern revelation, and in no wise is set forth as the result of chronological research or analysis. We believe that Jesus Christ was born in Bethlehem of Judea, April 6, B.C. 1." (James E. Talmage, *JC*, pp. 102-4.)

20:1 *"the sixth day of . . . April"*

"A wonderful day, the sixth day of April! Many notable things have occurred on it. The organization of the Church for one great and notable thing. The Prophet Joseph recites in his own story that it was early in the spring of 1820, one hundred and ten years ago, when he went into the woods to pray. I like to think of that also as being on the sixth day of April. We have no definite knowledge of it, but I believe it in my heart and in my soul. . . . I believe with all my heart and soul that the sixth day of April was the birthday of the Lord Jesus, our Savior and Redeemer. . . . More likely was it in the spring of the year than on the twenty-fifth day of December, which is celebrated as the birthday of the Savior; yet we go on celebrating that day, and it is all right to do so, inasmuch as that is the day the world generally accepts. But I repeat, it is my individual opinion, firmly fixed in my mind, that the sixth day of April is the birthday of the Savior of the world. I further like to believe that the resurrection of the Redeemer, which marked his triumph over death and the grave, also occurred on the sixth of April, though I have no definite proof.

"Another notable event that occurred on this day is part of the history of this glorious country of ours—the United States of America. The Lord says in the revelations given through the Prophet Joseph Smith that he raised up wise men for the very purpose of framing the constitution, which guarantees liberty to all. [Sec. 101:80.] It was born on the sixth of April. It had previously been adopted by the Constitutional Convention and submitted to the various States for ratification. While it was intended that the returns should all be in by the fourth of March, it was not until the sixth day of April that the electoral votes of the different States were counted by the Senate and House then in session. And on the sixth day of April, George Washington was declared to be the President of the United States. So the nation had its real birth at that time." (Charles W. Nibley, *CR*, April 1930, pp. 26-27.)

20:1 *"the fourth month . . . on the sixth day"*

The following statement by Joseph Smith indicates that he believed the Savior was crucified on April 6 in the thirty-third year of our present calendar (April 6, A.D. 33). This would mean that April 6 would have marked both the birth date and the death date of the Savior.

On the 6th of April, in the land of Zion . . . met for instruction and the service of God, at the Ferry on Big Blue River. . . .

The day was spent in a very agreeable manner, in giving and receiving knowledge which appertained to this last kingdom—it being just 1,800 years since the Savior laid down his life that men might have everlasting life, preparatory for the last dispensation. (HC 1:337.)

"Let us inquire if the day observed by the Christian world as the day of his (Christ's) birth—the 25th of December—is or is not the real Christmas day. A great many authors have found out from their researches that it is not. I think that there is scarcely an author at the present day that believes that the 25th of December was the day that Christ was born. . . . It is generally believed and conceded by the learned who have investigated the matter that Christ was born in April. . . . It is stated that according to the best of their judgment from the researches they have made, Christ was crucified on the 6th of April. That is the day on which this Church was organized. But when these learned men go back from the day of his crucifixion to the day of his birth, they are at a loss, having no certain evidence or testimony by which they can determine it." (Orson Pratt. Quoted by B. H. Roberts in *Outlines of Ecclesiastical History*, p. 17.)

20:2-3 *Use of the word "apostle"*

"In this section [section 20; see also 27:12] the Lord declares that Joseph Smith, Jr., and Oliver Cowdery 'were called of God and ordained' apostles. This is verily true;

however, attention has already been called to the fact that Peter, James and John conferred the Melchizedek Priesthood with its keys upon them, and not any office. Moreover, that by command of the angel, and later the voice of God, Joseph Smith ordained Oliver Cowdery an elder, and Oliver Cowdery ordained Joseph Smith an elder on the 6th day of April, 1830, when the Church was organized. Again, by command of the Lord, Joseph Smith was ordained a high priest in the Church, June 3, 1831, and Oliver Cowdery was ordained to the same office August 28th of that same year. Later they received other ordinations. It is very improbable that either of these men would be ordained to the office of apostle before they were ordained elders or high priests. This has been a mystery to some. It will all be clear enough if we keep in mind that these two men received under the hands of the ancient apostles the Melchizedek Priesthood, out of which, the Lord has said, all the offices come, and, as President Joseph F. Smith has said, 'the Priesthood is greater than any of its offices,' and when Joseph Smith and Oliver Cowdery stood in the presence of holy heavenly messengers and under their hands had the Priesthood conferred upon them, they became apostles, that is to say, *special witnesses* for Christ, even before any office had been conferred upon any man in this dispensation. An apostle is an especial witness for Christ, and these two men were fully prepared by testimony to officiate as such before all the world before the organization of the Church, and the office of elder had been conferred upon them." (Joseph Fielding Smith, *CHMR* 1:91-92.)

20:5 *"first elder . . . was entangled again in the vanities of the world"*

"It seems that this has reference [D&C 20:5] to Joseph Smith's early youth, between the time of his great vision of the Father and the Son and the coming of Moroni. The Prophet calls attention to this folly during that period, but also says that no one need think that he was guilty of any grievous sin, but being shunned by those who should have befriended him, he says, 'I was left to all kinds of temptations; and, mingling with all kinds of society, I frequently fell into many foolish errors, and displayed the weakness of youth, and the foibles of human nature.' (*HC* 1:1-9.)" Joseph Fielding Smith, *CHMR* 1:92.)

"Joseph had received a marvelous manifestation of divine favor, in the answer given to his first prayer, but afterwards he was 'entangled again in the vanities of the world.' In his autobiography the Prophet ascribes this, in part, to the unkind treatment accorded him by the religious people. He was young and inexperienced; they ostracized and slandered him, and, consequently, he 'was left to all kinds of temptations.' And this is placed on record for our instruction. Christians cannot be too careful in their conduct among their fellow men. It is a mark of integrity and veracity that this weakness of youth is made as prominent in the record as are the divine manifestations. In the sacred Scriptures the failings of Moses, or the difficulties between Paul and Peter, are recorded as well as their good qualities and victories over sin. A mere human history would conceal such imperfections, as far as possible. God places them on record for the instruction of others." (Smith and Sjodahl, *DCC,* pp. 99-100.)

20:6 *"God ministered unto him [Joseph Smith] by an holy angel"*

"When he repented and sought God in prayer the angel Moroni was sent to him. This was another marvelous manifestation that his repentance had been accepted and his sins forgiven." (Smith and Sjodahl, *DCC*, p. 100.)

20:9 Book of Mormon contains *"the fulness of the gospel of Jesus Christ"*

See *Gospel* in Appendix A.

"We are told that the Book of Mormon contains the fulness of the gospel, that those who like to get up a dispute, say that the Book of Mormon does not contain any reference to the work of salvation for the dead, and there are many other things pertaining to the gospel that are not developed in that book, and yet we are told that book contains 'the fulness of the everlasting gospel.' Well, what is the fulness of the gospel? You read carefully the revelation in regard to the three glories, section 76, in the Doctrine and Covenants, and you find there defined what the gospel is. [Sec. 76:40-43.] There God, the Eternal Father, and Jesus Christ, his Son, and the Holy Ghost, are held up as the three persons in the Trinity—the one God, the Father, the Word and the Holy

Ghost, all three being united and being one God. When people believe in that doctrine and obey the ordinances which are spoken of in the same list of principles [Sec. 20:17-28], you get the fulness of the gospel for this reason: if you really believe so as to have faith in our Eternal Father and in his Son, Jesus Christ, the Redeemer, and will hear him, you will learn all about what is needed to be done for the salvation of the living and the redemption of the dead." (Charles W. Penrose, *CR*, April 1922, pp. 27-28.)

"The Lord has stated a number of times that the Book of Mormon contains the fulness of the Gospel, or 'all things written concerning the foundation; of the Church and Gospel. Some people have wondered in regard to this, when in the Book of Mormon there is nothing recorded pertaining to the eternity of marriage and baptism for the dead. A careful reading will show that the Lord does not say that it contains all of the principles in their fulness, but the fulness necessary for the foundation of his Church and his Gospel. . . . Let us not forget that baptism for the dead is not a new doctrine, but merely the application of the principle of baptism *for the dead.* . . . Moreover, the meaning of the word 'fulness' as used in these scriptures is 'abundance,' or sufficient for the purposes intended. . . . (See 3 Ne. 26:8-9.)" (Joseph Fielding Smith, *CHMR* 1:81-82.)

20:11 *The Book of Mormon to prove "that the holy scriptures are true"*

See *Book of Mormon* in Appendix A.

"This book [Book of Mormon] is the strongest corroborative evidence to the divinity of the things contained in the Bible, that there is in the world. It is the strongest evidence of the divinity of the mission of the Redeemer of the world, that can be found, the Bible alone excepted. . . . Not one line in it, not one doctrine which it reaches, not one truth which it sets forth, has been found to be out of harmony with the word of the Lord, as contained in the Bible, and as it has come to us through his inspired servants—a thing which can be said of no other book in the world." (Anthony W. Ivins, *CR*, April 1921, pp. 20-21.)

20:12 *God the same "yesterday, today, and forever"*

See *God* in Appendix A.

20:14 *"crown of eternal life"*

See *Eternal life* in Appendix A.

20:17, 28 *"God in heaven . . . is infinite . . . eternal . . . unchangeable"*

See *God* in Appendix A.

20:19 *The true and living God and church*

The modifying term "only true and living" is used in the revelations in conjunction with *only two nouns*: the "only true and living *God*" (20:19) and the "only true and living *church*" (1:30).

See *Church* and *God* in Appendix A.

20:20 *"man became sensual and devilish"*

See *Carnal, sensual, and devilish* in Appendix A.

20:24 *"on the right hand of God"*

See *Right hand* in Appendix A.

20:26 *"the meridian of time"*

See *Meridian of time* in Appendix A.

20:28 *"Father, Son, and Holy Ghost are one God"*

See *Godhead* in Appendix A.

20:30 *"justification . . . is just and true"*

"Justification is true. Through the grace of God, and the promise made to us before the foundation of the world, that we could be redeemed through the blood of Jesus Christ and come back into his presence, we are justified in seeking this gift and have a claim upon this promise through obedience. We are justified, through the grace of our Lord, if we keep his commandments." (Joseph Fielding Smith, *CHMR* 1:93-94.)

"We know that justification through Christ is just and true (2 Ne. 2:5; Rom. 5:1). Justification is a judicial act, whereby God declares that the sinner who repents and by faith accepts the sacrifice of the Lamb of God, and who is baptized according to the Word of God, is acquitted and received into His Kingdom." (Smith and Sjodahl, *DCC*, p. 104.)

20:31 *"sanctification . . . is just and true"*

See *Sanctify* in Appendix A.

"Sanctification is the work of the Holy Spirit by which he who is justified is enabled to keep the Commandments of God and grow in holiness (Helaman 3:35)." (Smith and Sjodahl, *DCC*, p. 104.)

20:31   *"mights, minds and strength"*

See *Might, mind, and strength* in Appendix A.

20:31-34   *"man may fall from grace"*

"As I understand this scripture [D&C 20:31-34] it means that Jesus Christ is kind and merciful to us when we serve him with our whole hearts, but not any of us can take refuge in past righteousness or service. It also means that there is a possibility that any one of us can fall out of good standing, even those who have already achieved a certain degree of righteousness. Therefore, we need to be on our constant guard, each of us, that we not allow ourselves to fall into habits of carelessness in our faith, in our prayers, or in our various Church activities or responsibilities. It is for this reason that I am resolving again to live closer to God each day and to follow his chosen prophets and apostles more diligently than I have ever done in the past." (Theodore M. Burton, *Ensign*, June 1974, p. 116.)

"I am brought to believe that it is possible for men to repent and then to unrepent, and to fail to keep their repentance good; and I believe that the victory is in the retaining our repentance and making it good, so that the spirit of the Lord may dwell richly with us." (Francis M. Lyman, *CR*, October 1897, p. 16.)

20:35   *"neither adding to, nor diminishing from the prophecy"* of the book of John

Because this statement by John appears in the last book of the Bible (Rev. 22:18-19), it has been misinterpreted by some to mean there could not be any other scripture than the Bible itself. However, the Bible had not been canonized in its present form at the time John wrote his book of Revelation. Thus, he must have been referring to his own book only, or perhaps he was cautioning people not to "add to" (include false teachings with) the holy scriptures.

20:37   *"commandment to the church concerning baptism"*

"In this revelation [section 20] the Church about to be restored is taught in the fundamental principles so that, when that restoration comes, all things for its welfare will be in readiness. For hundreds of years man had been teaching false doctrines, and none more glaring than that in relation to the principle of baptism. Here the Lord makes it very plain, and gives instructions who shall be admitted into the Church. The question is frequently raised whether or not those who have not repented of all their sins should be admitted into the Church, in the hope that they may finish their repentance when they are full-fledged members of the Church. The Lord has been very explicit in this revelation on this point, and if it is followed there will be no mistake." (Joseph Fielding Smith, *CHMR* 1:94.)

"There are three requirements of an applicant for baptism: (1) He must be humble, so that he asks for it as a favor. He who comes with broken heart and contrite spirit is in the proper frame of mind for that ordinance; (2) He must show before the Church that he is repentant and willing to take upon him the name of Jesus Christ (Sec. 18:21). This confession is made before the Church when it is made in the presence of an Elder, or Elders, representing the Church; (3) he must manifest by his works that he has received the Spirit. An infant cannot comply with these conditions." (Smith and Sjodahl, *DCC*, p. 104.)

20:37 *"broken hearts and contrite spirits"*

"Mark you, the Lord says before a man comes into the Church he must have a desire, he must come with a broken heart and contrite spirit. What is a broken heart? One that is humble, one that is touched by the Spirit of the Lord, and which is willing to abide in all the covenants and the obligations which the Gospel entails. . . . Every baptized person who has fully repented, who comes into the Church with a broken heart and a contrite spirit, has made a covenant to continue with that broken heart, with that contrite spirit, which means a repentant spirit." (Joseph Fielding Smith, *CR*, October 1941, p. 93.)

20:37 *"truly manifest by their works that they have received of the Spirit of Christ unto the remission of their sins"*

Oliver Cowdery felt that the above statement was wrong and so notified the Prophet. Joseph Smith relates how Oliver was led to see the error of his thinking:

Whilst thus employed in the work appointed me by my Heavenly Father, I received a letter from Oliver Cowdery, the contents of which gave me both sorrow and uneasiness. Not having that letter now in my possession, I cannot of course give it here in full, but merely an extract of the most prominent parts, which I can yet, and expect long to, remember. He wrote to inform me that he had discovered an error in one of the commandments—Book of Doctrine and Covenants: "And truly manifest by their works that they have received of the Spirit of Christ unto a remission of their sins."

The above quotation, he said, was erroneous, and added: "I command you in the name of God to erase those words, that no priestcraft be amongst us!"

I immediately wrote to him in reply, in which I asked him by what authority he took upon him to command me to alter or erase, to add to or dimish from, a revelation or commandment from Almighty God.

A few days afterwards I visited him and Mr. Whitmer's family, when I found the family in general of his opinion concerning the words above quoted, and it was not without both labor and perseverance that I could prevail with any of them to reason calmly on the subject. However, Christian Whitmer at length became convinced that the sentence was reasonable, and according to Scripture; and finally, with his assistance, I succeeded in bringing, not only the Whitmer family, but also Oliver Cowdery to acknowledge that they had been in error, and that the sentence in dispute was in accordance with the rest of the commandment. And thus was this error rooted out. (*HC* 1:104-5.)

20:38-67 *"duty of elders, priests, teachers, deacons"*

See *Priesthood offices* in Appendix A.

"The Lord could not reveal to the Church in the beginning all the knowledge and organization which would be essential to the full and complete organization of the Church. Had this been done, it would have been like an overwhelming flood that would have brought destruction. The truth had to come piecemeal—line upon line, precept upon precept, just like knowledge comes to all of us. However, all that was revealed in this section was expedient for the government of the Church at the time of its organization. What the Lord revealed at this time is just as expedient and necessary today. We have had nothing, for instance, given since that day to add to or improve on the instruction concerning the duties of teachers. We learn at this time the

Lord revealed that the designation 'Elder' is one applicable to the apostles and likewise to all others who hold the Melchizedek Priesthood. The use of this designation makes it needless to use unnecessarily sacred terms as 'Apostle,' 'Patriarch,' 'High Priest,' etc. It is proper in general usage to speak of the apostles, the seventies and all others holding the Melchizedek Priesthood as 'elders.' Of course, the term President, in speaking of the First Presidency, is the proper designation." (Joseph Fielding Smith, *CHMR* 1:95.)

". . . I know that the Lord wants us to have our boys, at twelve [deacons] in groups of twelve, presided over by sweet, clean, wholesome boys of their age. I know that he wants to have our boys [teachers] in groups of twenty-four, under presidencies of their own group, watching over the Church, to see that there is no iniquity, evil-speaking, or backbiting in the Church.

"It seems so fitting to me to think that the Lord has made provision that the young men [priests] shall sit at the feet of the bishop and be instructed, with him as president; that he shall be taught, and that he shall go into the house of the saints; that he shall preach, teach, exhort, and expound the scripture; that ninety-six men, older, maturer, and receiving the Holy Melchizedek Priesthood [elders] shall stand next to the presidency of the stake and be a standing ministry of the stake. . . . So beautiful, so perfect, so complete, is the Lord's way! [Sec. 107:85-89.]" (Alonzo A. Hinckley, *CR*, April 1935, pp. 74-75.)

20:61 *"meet in conference once in three months"*

In the very early days of the Church some of these conferences were priesthood conferences. When the stakes were the major ecclesiastical units of the Church under the general authorities, these quarterly conferences were primarily stake conferences. Today, they might include ward, region, and even area conferences.

20::64 *Certificates of ordination to offices in the priesthood*

The practice of issuing certificates of ordination to those receiving the various offices of the priesthood has continued to the present time.

20:68-69 *"The duty of . . . members"*

"Now, when people come into this Church they should,

by all means, subscribe to the regulations which the Lord himself has laid down by commandment. But does that mean after we are in the Church, after we have confessed our sins and have forsaken them, that we can return to them after membership has been secured? That would not be consistent." (Joseph Fielding Smith, *CR*, October 1941, p. 93.)

20:70   *Blessing of children*

"We have nothing to say against a father blessing his children, the genius of the Priesthood being primarily patriarchal, with God himself, the great Father of us all, at the head. Indeed, we claim that every man holding the Melchizedek Priesthood is a patriarch in his own home, with the right to bless all his children and grandchildren, even all the fruits of his loins, nor do we object to the father taking his babe on the eighth day and giving it a father's blessing. But we do not think that this privilege, whether exercised or unimproved, should interfere with our obedience to that law of the Lord wherein it is stated: [new edition Doctrine and Covenants, sec. 20, verse 70, page 117, quoted.] Outside of the all-important fact that this is a direct command of Jehovah, and as such should be studiously complied with without hesitancy or objection, we think quite a number of excellent reasons can be adduced to prove that this command is attended with beneficial results to babe and to parents, who, by bringing their child before the Church, manifest their faith in the sight of their brethren and sisters, in God's word and to his promises, as well as their thankfulness to him for increasing their posterity and for the safe delivery of his handmaiden. The child is also benefited by the united faith and responsive prayers of the assembled saints, which faith seals the 'more sure word of prophecy' pronounced upon the head of the child, as it also gives more abundant power to the officiating High Priest or Elder to manifest the good pleasure of the Lord with regard to it. And again, the blessing is thus given in the presence of the Church recorder, and there is much less likelihood of the record being omitted or errors entering therein than there would be should the rite be attended to at home. In this, as in all other things, the path of revelation is the path of safety." (John Taylor, *MS* 40:235-36.)

20:71   *"the years of accountability"*

For information on *years of accountability*, read the materials for 18:42 and see *Children* in Appendix A.

20:71-74   *Instructions regarding baptism*

"The mode of baptism is here taught [20:72-74]. This is in conformity with all that is recorded in the New Testament and makes it clear that the teachings in the world called baptism by sprinkling or pouring water on the head is a false doctrine. We are taught that baptism is only by immersion and that it cannot be performed except it be by one who has divine authority. The elder or the priest shall go down into the water with the candidate, and after repeating the prayer the Lord has given for that ordinance, shall immerse the candidate in water. Another point which should be remembered is that 'no one can be received into the Church of Christ unless he has arrived unto the years of accountability before God, and is capable of repentance.' " [See Moroni 8 and D&C 29:46.] (Joseph Fielding Smith, *CHMR* 1:96.)

20:75-79   *Instructions regarding the sacrament*

See *Sacrament* in Appendix A.

"*Bread and wine*] These are the Emblems. Bread is the proper emblem of the spiritual food we receive in the Sacrament. 'Wine' is here used as a synonym for the *Cup*, the term found in Matt. 26:27; Mark 14:23; Luke 22:20; 1. Cor. 11:25 (Sec. 27:2). The essential part of the Sacrament is that those who partake of it receive broken bread and drink of the cup, in remembrance of the broken body and spilt blood of the Redeemer, for the broken bread and the cup are the emblems; both must be blessed, and both must be received by the communicants." (Smith and Sjodahl, *DCC*, p. 111.)

"The Lord has given to the Church very few forms. In the ordinance of baptism, definite words are given which must be used by the priest or elder who officiates. The blessings on the Sacrament are also set prayers." (Joseph Fielding Smith, *CHMR* 1:96.)

20:80   *"Any member . . . transgressing . . . shall be dealt with"*

See *Excommunication* in Appendix A.

"The Lord anticipated the fact that there would be transgressors in the Church. We are reminded of the parable of the net cast into the sea, which gathered of all kinds, some of which had to be thrown away. As long as the world remains in its present condition, there will be those who will not endure to the end. There will be the fault-finders, the critics of those who hold the Priesthood and of the doctrines of the Church. Therefore, it is necessary that regulations be given for treating all transgressors fairly and with justice. Where the extreme penalty is inflicted, the names of those expelled are no longer to be kept on the records, but are to be blotted out." (Joseph Fielding Smith, *CHMR* 1:97.)

20:81-84 *Record of members to be kept*

See *Records* in Appendix A.

"The matter of record keeping is one of the most important duties devolving on the Church. . . . If a man values his membership in the Church he will guard with the most jealous care his standing in the ward or branch to which he belongs. One of the most deplorable things with which we have to contend is the fact that members of the Church will move from one ward or branch to another, and fail to keep in touch with the local organization of the Church. Sometimes this is done because such members desire to hide and avoid being handled for their standing. Others do this evil thing because they are afraid they will be called upon to attend to Church duties; others out of pure neglect. Membership in the Church is our very valued possession and treasure. Why? Because without it we are deprived, not only of the fellowship of the Church but of all its blessings, and a continued course of aloofness will in time place us outside the pale of the Church entirely." (Joseph Fielding Smith, *CHMR* 1:96-97, 99.)

SECTION 21

Background information on section 21

"Whilst the Book of Mormon was in the hands of the printer, we still continued to bear testimony and give information, as far as we had opportunity; and also make known to our brethren that we had received a commandment to organize the Church; and accordingly we met together for that purpose, at the house of Mr. Peter Whitmer, Sen., (being six in number) on Tuesday, the sixth day of April, A.D. one thousand eight hundred and thirty. Having opened the meeting by solemn prayer to our Heavenly Father, we proceeded, according to previous commandment, to call on our brethren to know whether they accepted us as their teachers in the things of the Kingdom of God, and whether they were satisfied that we should proceed and be organized as a Church according to said commandment which we had received. To these several propositions they consented by a unanimous vote. I then laid my hands upon Oliver Cowdery, and ordained him an Elder of the 'Church of Jesus Christ of Latter-day Saints'; after which, he ordained me also to the office of an Elder of said Church. We then took bread, blessed it, and brake it with them; also wine, blessed it, and drank it with them. We then laid our hands on each individual member of the Church present, that they might receive the gift of the Holy Ghost, and be confirmed members of the Church of Christ. The Holy Ghost was poured out upon us to a very great degree—some prophesied, whilst we all praised the Lord, and rejoiced exceedingly. Whilst yet together, I received the following commandment: [Section 21, follows.]" (Joseph Smith, *HC* 1:74-78.)

"It was on a Tuesday morning when this little band convened in one of the most solemn meetings, and one of the greatest moments, that had been held in eighteen hundred years. The organization was made in accordance with the laws of the State of New York, which required six members to effect such an organization. All of these six members, namely, Joseph Smith, Oliver Cowdery, Hyrum Smith, Peter Whitmer Jr., David Whitmer and Samuel H. Smith, were young men." (Joseph Fielding Smith, *CHMR* 1:98.)

21:1 *"there shall be a record kept among you"*

"At the beginning of this revelation [Sec. 21] we were told that there should be a recorder in the Church, that records should be kept among the people. This important work in the Church, of keeping records, was commanded; and if we read farther we will find that John Whitmer was appointed to be Church recorder, to write the events of the Church. I mention this to show you how important this part of our Church government is, to keep history, to keep a record of what takes place." (Anthon H. Lund, *CR,* April 1913, p. 11.)

21:1 *"a seer, a translator, a prophet"*

See *Seer* in Appendix A.

The titles "prophet, seer, and revelator" are used in sustaining the general officers of the Church. The president of the Church is sustained first; then his counselors are sustained with him as the quorum of the First Presidency. The president and members of the Council of the Twelve are sustained next. Then the conducting officer makes the proposal that the members of the First Presidency, the members of the Council of the Twelve, and the Patriarch to the Church be sustained as "prophets, seers, and revelators."

"A Seer has the divine gift of 'seeing,' or having visions. Moses, Samuel, Isaiah, Ezekiel, and many others were seers, so called because they were privileged to have a nearer view of the divine glory and power than other mortals have. Joseph Smith also was a seer. (See Mosiah 8:13.). . . A translator renders the spoken, or written, word into another language. Here it means one who does so by the gift of divine inspiration. . . . A prophet is one who speaks for another. Aaron was the prophet of Moses (Ex. 7:1), when, as his brother's spokesman, he appeared before Pharaoh. Paul (Titus 1:12) quotes Epimenides, a Cretan poet, as a prophet. A Prophet of God is one who speaks for the Almighty, by divine authority. He does not always foretell future events. Sometimes he reveals the past; sometimes he speaks of the present, and sometimes he predicts things to come. Some of the Old Testament Prophets were eminent statesmen, historians, and privy councilors of kings; others occupied less prominent positions, but all were the divinely inspired instructors of the people, whose special function it was to maintain the worship of Jehovah against adverse influences.

"Originally the Hebrews called the Prophets, Seers (1 Sam. 9:9), and that designation is used by Lehi, when he blesses his sons and quotes to them the prophecies of his ancestor, Joseph (2 Ne. 3:5-22)." (Smith and Sjodahl, *DCC*, pp. 115-16.)

21:2-4 *"to lay the foundation" of the Church*

"These words [Sec. 21:1-12] were the words of Jehovah, delivered to the Prophet Joseph Smith upon the day that the Church was organized. The Church was very weak in numbers then, but strong in spirit. In this revelation the Lord intimates that he was about to move the cause of Zion in mighty power, and talked to the Prophet as if it were an accomplished fact. He desired, it seems, that his people, though few in number, should be impressed with the fact that a Prophet, Seer and Revelator stood at the head; for he instructed that a record to this effect should be kept. He also desired to impress the people with the great truth that this Church should be built up, not by the power of man, but by the power of the Holy Ghost; that no man, though he might be a Prophet or an Apostle, should take the honor unto himself of building up the Church of Christ, but that the honor and the glory must be given to God. Did not the Lord say to the Prophet Daniel that in the latter days the God of heaven would set up his kingdom, and it should be as a stone cut out of the mountain without hands, which should roll until it filled the whole earth. [Dan. 2:34-35, 44.] The God of heaven was to do this, but he would use men as his instruments." (Rudger Clawson, *CR*, October 1901, pp. 7-8.)

21:5 *"his word ye shall receive, as if from mine own mouth"*

See *Voice of the Lord* in Appendix A.

"There has been much speculation in relation to the statement of the Lord to the Prophet Joseph Smith: 'For his word ye shall receive, as if from mine own mouth, in all patience and faith.' This is the word which the Lord gave to Israel in relation to Moses. It is just as true in the case of any other person who is sustained as mouthpiece of the Almighty. Later, in speaking of his inspired servants, the Lord said: 'And whatsoever they shall speak when moved upon by the Holy Ghost shall be scripture, shall be the will of the Lord, shall be the mind of the Lord, shall be the word of the Lord, shall be the voice of the Lord, and the power of God unto salvation.' (D&C 68:4.) In this dispensation the same characteristics are shown by the people as were in ancient times. We are more inclined to accept as the word of the Lord something which was uttered in some former dispensation, but look with critical eye and unbelief upon that which the Lord delivers today through his chosen servants. Yet the word of the Lord is very clear on this matter." (Joseph Fielding Smith, *CHMR* 1:107-8.)

"Now the only safety we have as members of this church is to do exactly what the Lord said to the Church in that day when the Church was organized. We must learn to give heed to the words and commandments that the Lord shall give through his prophet, 'as he receiveth them, walking in all holiness before me; . . . as if from mine own mouth, in all patience and faith.' (D&C 21:4-5.) There will be some things that take patience and faith. You may not like what comes from the authority of the Church. It may contradict your political views. It may contradict your social views. It may interfere with some of your social life. But if you listen to these things, as if from the mouth of the Lord himself, with patience and faith, the promise is that 'the gates of hell shall not prevail against you; yea, and the Lord God will disperse the powers of darkness from before you, and cause the heavens to shake for your good, and his name's glory.' (D&C 21:6.)" (Harold B. Lee, *CR*, October 1970, p. 152.)

21:10 *"be ordained by . . . Oliver Cowdery"*

The same pattern was followed by Joseph Smith and Oliver Cowdery in this ordination as was followed in their baptism earlier. Oliver Cowdery first laid his hands upon the head of Joseph Smith and ordained him; then the Prophet laid his hands upon the head of Oliver Cowdery and ordained him.

21:11 *"you [Oliver Cowdery] are an elder. . . , he [Joseph Smith] being the first"*

The general administrative organization was kept rather simple in the early days of the restored Church. Joseph Smith was designated by the Lord as the "first elder," and Oliver Cowdery served as the "second elder."

"Joseph had informed the little flock that gathered there when the Church was organized of what the Lord commanded, and it was proposed to them that Joseph Smith be the first Elder of the Church, and Oliver the second. Then Joseph ordained Oliver and Oliver ordained Joseph to the office of an Elder. This was not bestowing the Melchizedek Priesthood on either of them. They held that before. It had been conferred upon them by Peter, James and John. [Sec. 27:12-13.]" (Anthon H. Lund, *CR*, April 1913, pp. 9-10.)

"Now the Church was organized [April 1830], but not all the officers of the Church as we have them today, for the simple reason they did not have enough members in the Church to make a complete organization. Ten months after the Church was organized, Edward Partridge was ordained a Bishop to the Church, and in June following the first High Priests were ordained. In December, 1833, Joseph Smith, Senior, was ordained a Patriarch, and two months later the first High Council was organized. The Quorum of Twelve Apostles was organized. [Feb. 1835.] All the offices in the Priesthood were now established and men were ordained to fill them." (Anthon H. Lund, *CR*, April 1917, pp. 14-15.)

21:10, 12 *"Oliver Cowdery . . . the first preacher of this church unto the church"*

"The first public meeting of the Church after the day of its organization was held at the house of Peter Whitmer in Fayette, on the 11th day of April, 1830. On that occasion, Oliver Cowdery, under Joseph's direction, proclaimed the word of God for the comfort and instruction of saints and strangers. The appointment for this meeting had gone forth through all the neighborhood; and many persons came to hear what wonderful things were to be spoken by the men who professed to be called directly of God to the ministry. This was the first public discourse delivered by an authorized servant of God in these last days. At the conclusion of the services a number of persons demanded baptism and membership among the people of God." (George Q. Cannon, *LJS*, p. 61.)

SECTION 22

Background information on section 22

"Immediately after the Church was organized, converts were made. Some of these had belonged to churches which believed in baptism by immersion. In fact, many of the early converts of the Church had previously accepted this mode believing that it was right. The question of divine authority, however, was not firmly fixed in their minds. When they desired to come into the Church, having received the testimony that Joseph Smith had told a true story, they wondered why it was necessary for them to be baptized again when they had complied with an ordinance of baptism by immersion.

"The revelation in section 22 indicates that the baptism they had received had not been made in the true spirit because it was unauthorized and performed by those not having authority, although it was done in sincerity, but in ignorance." (Joseph Fielding Smith, *CHMR* 1:109.)

In chronological sequence, this is the first revelation in the Doctrine and Covenants that is designated as being given "*to* The Church of Jesus Christ of Latter-day Saints." All the revelations given before were to individuals or for general instruction.

22:1 *"a new and an everlasting covenant"*

The term "new and everlasting covenant" is sometimes used to refer to individual ordinances as well as to the gospel in general.

See *Covenant* in Appendix A.

22:2 *"strait gate"*

See *Strait* in Appendix A.

22:4 *"enter ye in at the gate"*

"The divine command to all men is that they enter in by the door. 'He that entereth not by the door into the sheepfold, but climbeth up some other way, the same is a thief and a robber.' The scriptures are very definite in their instruction that there is but one plan of salvation, and one way by which we may be saved. Yet the notion prevails abundantly among all men that the Lord is so liberal, so kind, so loving, that he will permit every man to seek his own salvation in any organization which he desires to join, and that there are no set rules, except that a person live a clean life, in order to return into the presence of the Lord." (Joseph Fielding Smith, *CHMR* 1:111.)

22:4 *"seek not to counsel your God"*

One of the lessons to be learned in this life is to put implicit faith in our Heavenly Father, who knoweth all things, who is kind, loving, and merciful, and who wants his children to be happy and to have joy. If all mankind believed in these qualities of God and had faith in his plan, then all would seek eagerly to take counsel at his hand rather than to counsel him.

SECTION 23

"The following persons being anxious to know of the Lord what might be their respective duties in relation to this work, I inquired of the Lord, and received for them the following:

"Revelation to Oliver Cowdery, Hyrum Smith, Samuel H. Smith, Joseph Smith, Sen., and Joseph Knight, Sen. Given at Manchester, New York, April 1830. [Section 23, follows.]" (Joseph Smith, *HC* 1:80.)

For biographical information on these six brethren, check each of their names in Appendix B.

23:1-2 *"Oliver . . . beware of pride"*

In this brief blessing for Oliver Cowdery, the Lord indicates the weakness of Oliver that eventually led him out of the Church for several years. As indicated in his biographical sketch (see Appendix B), Oliver later found it hard to take direction from the Prophet Joseph Smith, set himself up as being equal or superior to the Prophet, and apostatized from the truth.

"Pride . . . was one of Oliver Cowdery's besetting sins. If he could have humbled himself in the troubled days of Kirtland he would not have lost his place and membership in the Church. That which had been bestowed upon him was exceedingly great and had he been willing to humble himself, it was his privilege to stand with the Prophet Joseph Smith through all time and eternity, holding the keys of the Dispensation of the Fulness of Times. However, at this particular time when this word was sought, he was free from condemnation." (Joseph Fielding Smith, *CHMR* 1:120-21.)

23:3 *"Hyrum . . . thy duty is unto the Church forever"*

"Hyrum Smith, the beloved brother of Joseph, successfully proclaimed the gospel, after his tongue had been loosened. On November 7th, 1837, he was appointed a counselor to the Prophet instead of Fred. G. Williams, who was rejected by the Conference at Far West. On January 19th, 1841, he was appointed Patriarch to the Church, for which office he had been blessed by his father, it being his by birthright. He was continually strengthening the Church." (Smith and Sjodahl, *DCC*, p. 120.)

"There is another thing of great significance in this brief blessing to Hyrum Smith (Sec. 23:3) which is: 'Wherefore thy duty is unto the church forever, and this because of thy family. Amen.' It is doubtful if the Prophet Joseph fully understood the meaning of this expression when this revelation was given. In later years it was made clear. Evidently it has reference to the office of Patriarch and in this office, it was his duty and that of his family forever." (Joseph Fielding Smith, *CHMR* 1:121.)

23:4 *"Samuel, thou art not as yet called to preach before the world"*

At the time of this blessing, Samuel Smith, a younger brother of the Prophet, would have been only 22 years old. He had already served as one of the eight special witnesses to the plates of the Book of Mormon. Here, however, he is notified by the Lord that he is not "as yet called to preach before the world."

"Samuel was the third person baptized in this dispensation. He was one of the first to be ordained to the office of Elder, and it was not long after this revelation when he was sent forth to teach, which he did with marked success, far beyond his own realization." (Joseph Fielding Smith, *CHMR* 1:113.)

23:5 *"Joseph [Smith Sr.] . . . this is thy duty henceforth and forever"*

As was evidently the case with Hyrum, the words "this is thy duty henceforth and forever" in regard to Joseph Smith, Sr., have reference to the office of patriarch that Father Smith received shortly thereafter (D&C 107:40; 124:91) and held to his death September 14, 1840.

23:6 *"Joseph [Knight] . . . take up your cross"*

See *Cross* in Appendix A.

23:6 *"pray vocally before the world as well as in secret"*

See *Prayer* in Appendix A.

SECTION 24

Background information on section 24

"After our departure from Colesville, after the trial, the Church there was very anxious, as might be expected, concerning our again visiting them, during which time Sister Knight, wife of Newel Knight, had a dream which enabled her to say that we would visit them that day, which really came to pass, for a few hours afterwards we arrived; and thus was our faith much strengthened concerning dreams and visions in the last days, foretold by the ancient Prophet Joel [Joel 2:28-29]; and although we this time were forced to seek safety from our enemies by flight, we did feel confident that eventually we should come off victorious, if we only continued faithful to him who had called us forth from darkness into the marvelous light of the everlasting Gospel of our Lord Jesus Christ.

"Shortly after our return home we received the following commandments: [Sections 24, 25, and 26, follow.]" (Joseph Smith, *HC* 1:101.)

"Accompanied by his wife and three of the Elders, he [Joseph Smith] went again to Colesville. Here they found many people awaiting baptism. Joseph prepared to accede to their demand. A suitable portion of a little stream in that locality was prepared for the purpose of the administration of the ordinance; but in the night sectarian priests, fearful of losing their congregations and their hire, instigated evil men to desecrate the spot and to destroy all the preparations of the Elders. . . . A few days later the ordinance was administered by Oliver Cowdery to thirteen persons at Colesville. . . .

"While the baptisms were in progress an angry mob collected, and threatened destruction to the Elders and believers. The mob surrounded the house of Joseph Knight and his son Newel and railed with devilish hatred at the inmates. The Prophet spoke to them and made an effort to calm their passions, but without avail. Wearied with their own impotent wrath, the mobs departed; but only to concoct new plots.

"That night a meeting was to be held, and when the believers and sympathizers had assembled, and Joseph was about to offer them instruction and consolation, a constable approached and arrested him on a warrant charging him with being a disorderly person, for setting the country in an uproar by circulating the Book of Mormon and by preaching a gospel of revelation. . . .

"A court was convened to consider the strange charges brought against the young man, Joseph Smith; and hateful lies, of every form which the father of falsehood could devise, were circulated to create popular dislike. . . . The bitter feeling of endangered priestcraft was visible throughout the trial; but all the accusations which were made were but lies, and none were sustained. The court declared an acquittal. The evidence in the trial was a high tribute to the character of Joseph Smith. . . .

"This paper [a warrant] was secured on the oath of a sectarian bigot; and no sooner was Joseph acquitted by the court in Chenango County than he was seized under the new warrant and dragged back to Colesville. . . .

"When the morning came, Joseph was arraigned before the magistrate's court of Colesville. Arrayed against him were some of the people who had been discomfited at the trial in Chenango County. This time they were determined to secure a conviction. By the side of the Prophet were his friends and advocates who had aided him in the former trial. Despite the vindictive effort of the mob, the court discharged the Prophet, declaring that nothing was shown to his dishonor." (George Q. Cannon, *LJS*, p. 64-67.)

24:2   *"thou art not excusable in thy transgressions"*

"Instead of being lifted up by the favor which had been shown to him, Joseph was made to feel his own weaknesses. Chosen to be a prophet and the leader of God's people, he was conscious that he was only human, subject to human temptations and human frailties. Having the honesty and courage inspired by the Spirit of the Lord, he dared to confess this openly; and, under the same inspiration, acknowledge his transgression and make his contrition known. He was not above any law which applied to his fellow-man. Of his responsibility to God and his brethren of the Church, he was required by the law revealed through himself to the

Church, to give as strict an account as any other member. They who participated with him in authority owed it not to him as an individual, but to the eternal power to which they were alike responsible." (George Q. Cannon, *LJS,* pp. 58-59.)

24:3, 9 *"magnify thine office"*

"Sometimes we speak loosely of magnifying our priesthood, but what the revelations speak of is magnifying our callings in the priesthood, as elders, seventies, high priests, patriarchs, and apostles.

"The priesthood held by man is the power and authority of God delegated to man on earth to act in all things for the salvation of mankind. Priesthood offices or callings are ministerial assignments to perform specially assigned service in the priesthood. And the way to magnify these callings is to do the work designed to be performed by those who hold the particular office involved.

"It does not matter what office we hold as long as we are true and faithful to our obligations. One office is not greater than another, although for administrative reasons one priesthood holder may be called to preside over and direct the labors of another. . . .

"We are called upon to magnify our callings in the priesthood and to do the work which goes with the office we receive. And so the Lord says, in the revelation on priesthood: 'Therefore, let every man stand in his own office, and labor in his own calling; . . . that the system may be kept perfect.' (D&C 84:109-110.)

"This is one of the great goals toward which we are working in the priesthood program of the Church, to have elders do the work of elders, seventies the work of seventies, high priests the work of high priests, and so on, so that all priesthood holders may magnify their own callings and reap the rich blessings promised from such a course." (Joseph Fielding Smith, *CR,* October 1970, pp. 90-92.)

24:9 *"in temporal labors thou shalt not have strength"*

The Prophet's strength was in spiritual guidance of the people and in establishing the Church in all its fulness. To attend to this grave responsibility required nearly all of his time, and there was no time for him to spend his strength in temporal matters. However, the dividing line between the spiritual and the temporal is very hazy. The Lord taught the

Prophet how to build cities, to make roads, to establish schools, and to build temples. However, his field was in spiritual knowledge and in imparting this knowledge to the world. (Joseph Fielding Smith, *CHMR* 1:122-23.)

24:13 *Oliver, "require not miracles"*

See *Miracles* and *Signs* in Appendix A.

"You will recollect that I have often told you that miracles would not save a person, and I say that they never should. . . . What will make me believe? What made the Twelve Apostles of Jesus Christ witnesses? What constituted them Apostles, special witnesses to the world? Was it seeing miracles? No. What was it? The visions of their minds were opened, and it was necessary that a few should receive light, knowledge, and intelligence, that all the powers of earth and hell could not gainsay or compete with. [Matt. 16:13-18; Gal. 1:11-12.]" (Brigham Young, *JD* 3:206.)

24:15 *"leave a cursing . . . by casting off the dust of your feet"*

See *Feet* in Appendix A.

"Our Lord instructed His Disciples to shake the dust off their feet, when departing from a house where they had not been received (Matt. 10:14). Paul did so when leaving Antioch, in Pisidia (Acts 13:51). Those who rejected the gospel message were to be considered as pagans, with whom Jews held no social intercourse. Even the dust of their dwellings and their cities, was to be treated as defilement, necessitating a cleansing. But this is not an act to be performed on slight provocation. A disciple of the Lord must learn of Him patience and long-suffering." (Smith and Sjodahl, *DCC*, p. 126.)

24:18 *"take no purse nor scrip"*

See *Purse or scrip* in Appendix A.

"For me to travel and preach without purse and scrip was never hard; I never saw the day, I never was in the place, nor went into a house when I was alone, or when I would take the lead and do the talking, but what I could get all I wanted. . . . I could make the acquaintance of the family, and sit and sing to them and chat with them, and they would be friendly." (Brigham Young, *JD* 4:34.)

24:19 *"prune my vineyard"*

See *Vineyard* in Appendix A.

SECTION 25

Background information on section 25

"This revelation was given to Emma Smith, wife of Joseph Smith. She was the daughter of Isaac and Elizabeth Lewis Hale, and was born July 10, 1804. She was married to the Prophet in 1827, while he was under the tutelage of the Angel Moroni. She believed in the Prophet, although her parents did not, and she was baptized by Oliver Cowdery in June, 1830. Her life from that time on was a very trying one, due to constant persecution and mobbings. She passed through these trials with her husband and shared them, as did the faithful wives of the leaders of the Church. The calling given to Emma Smith in this revelation was an important one, and was fulfilled.

"Emma Smith was human, possessing many of the characteristics which are found in most of us. Being the wife of the man whom the Almighty had blessed, she felt, as most women would have felt under like circumstances, that she was entitled to some special favors. It was difficult for her to understand why she could not view the plates, the Urim and Thummim, and other sacred things, which view had been given to special witnesses. At times this human thought caused her to murmur and ask the questions of the Prophet why she was denied this privilege. In this revelation the Lord admonishes her and tells her that it is for a wise purpose to be made known in time to come, why she and the world were deprived of this privilege." (Joseph Fielding Smith, *CHMR* 1:117.)

For biographical information on Emma Smith, see *Emma Smith* in Appendix B.

25:1 *"those who receive my gospel are sons and daughters in my kingdom"*

"The Lord has revealed that his work and his glory is to bring to pass the immortality and eternal life of man.

Moreover, he has said . . . that the greatest of all his gifts is the gift of eternal life, and all who receive this gift partake of the fulness of his kingdom. While the ancient scriptures teach that those who keep their covenants and are true to the end shall become sons of God, yet this promise became obscure to men in the great apostasy. In fact, it was not understood by the Jews in the days of our Lord's ministry, and they accused him of blasphemy because he said he was the Son of God. His answer was that in the law it is written that God called them gods unto whom his words came, and 'the scriptures cannot be broken.' In the primitive Church of Jesus Christ this doctrine was plainly taught, but later, when false teachers crept into the church, and ordinances were changed, the true value of this expression became lost, and remained so until the restoration of the Gospel. In these early revelations the Lord frequently declared to those who sought him, that if they would be true to the cause they should inherit eternal life, and become his sons and his daughters. This promised blessing is based on the redemption made through the shedding of the blood of Jesus Christ." (Joseph Fielding Smith, *CHMR* 1:124-25.)

25:3 *Emma Smith an "elect lady"*

"Emma was an elect lady. 'In the early days of this dispensation Emma Smith, the Prophet's wife, was in such complete harmony with the Lord's program that he forgave her of her sins and addressed her as an elect lady.' . . . An *elect lady* is a female member of the Church who has already received, or who through obedience is qualified to receive, the fulness of gospel blessings. This includes temple endowments, celestial marriage, and the fulness of the sealing power. She is one who has been elected or chosen by faithfulness as a daughter of God in this life, an heir of God, a member of his household. Her position is comparable to that of the elders who magnify their callings in the priesthood and thereby receive all that the Father hath. (D&C 84:38.) . . . Just as it is possible for the very elect to be deceived, and to fall from grace through disobedience, so an elect lady, by failing to endure to the end, can lose her chosen status." (Bruce R. McConkie, *MD*, p. 217.)

"I assisted in commencing the organization of 'The Female Relief Society of Nauvoo' in the Lodge Room. Sister

Emma Smith, President, and Sister Elizabeth Ann Whitney
and Sarah M. Cleveland, Counselors. I gave much instruction, read in the New Testament, and Book of Doctrine and
Covenants, concerning the Elect Lady, and showed that the
elect meant to be elected to a certain work, etc., and that the
revelation was then fulfilled by Sister Emma's election to the
Presidency of the Society, she having previously been ordained to expound the Scriptures. [Sec. 25:3, 7.]" (Joseph
Smith, *HC* 4:552-53.)

25:4   *"Murmur not because of the things which thou hast not
seen"*

"In this revelation the Lord admonishes her and tells her
that it is for a wise purpose to be made known in time to
come, why she and the world were deprived of this privilege
[of seeing the gold plates, etc.]. Her duty was to be obedient
to her husband, hearken to him in faith, and she should have
an inheritance in Zion. Even greater blessings were in store
for her, she should be a daughter of God in his kingdom,
and a crown of righteousness should she receive. Moreover,
she was told that her duty was to be a comfort with consoling
words to her husband in his afflictions, for he should have
many. (D&C 24:8.) Any man who has had afflictions knows
what a comfort a confiding wife can be." (Joseph Fielding
Smith, *CHMR* 1:125.)

25:6   *"be unto him for a scribe"*

Emma Smith had served as a scribe for her husband, Joseph Smith, during the early days of the translation of the
Book of Mormon.

25:7   *"thou shalt be ordained . . . to expound scriptures"*

"The term 'ordain' was used generally in the early days of
the Church in reference to both ordination and setting apart,
and, too, correctly according to the meaning of the word.
Men holding the Priesthood were said to have been 'ordained' to preside over branches and to perform special
work. Sisters also were said to have been 'ordained' when
they were called to some special duty or responsibility. In
later years we developed a distinction between ordain and
setting apart. Men are ordained to offices in the Priesthood
and set apart to preside over stakes, wards, branches,
missions, and auxiliary organizations. The sisters are set

apart—not ordained—as presidents of auxiliary organizations, to missions, etc. This saying that Emma Smith was 'ordained' to expound scripture, does not mean that she had conferred upon her the Priesthood, but that she was set apart to this calling, which found its fulfillment in the Relief Society of the Church." (Joseph Fielding Smith, *CHMR* 1:126.)

"I was in Nauvoo at the time the Relief Society was organized by the Prophet Joseph Smith, and I was present on the occasion. . . . At that meeting the Prophet called Sister Emma to be an elect lady. That means that she was called to a certain work; and was in fulfillment of a certain revelation concerning her. [Sec. 25:13.] She was elected to preside over the Relief Society, and she was ordained to expound the scriptures. In compliance with Brother Joseph's request, I set her apart and also ordained Sister Whitney, wife of Bishop Newel K. Whitney, and Sister Cleveland, wife of Judge Cleveland, to be her counselors. Some of the sisters have thought that these sisters mentioned were in this ordination ordained to the Priesthood. And for the information of all interested in this subject I will say, it is not the calling of these sisters to hold the Priesthood, only in connection with their husbands, they being one with their husbands." (John Taylor, *JD* 21:367-68.)

25:11 *"make a selection of sacred hymns"*

"The necessity of having a book of hymns became apparent at the time of the organization of the Church, and while Emma Smith may have felt she had been slighted in not having the privilege of viewing the plates, yet it was a signal honor to her to be called to be an 'elect lady' and . . . to have the privilege of divine appointment to expound scriptures in the Church, and also to be chosen to select hymns to be published for the use of the Church. Evidently she had talent for this work. That talent is shown in the selection which was made. With the help of Elder William W. Phelps, she went to work, and a selection of hymns was made." (Joseph Fielding Smith, *CHMR* 1:126.)

"It was not until 1835 . . . that the commission given to Emma Smith was fulfilled. In that year the first hymnbook for the Church was published in Kirtland by 'Frederick G. Williams and Co.' Following is the Preface to this hymnbook:

PREFACE

" 'In order to sing by the Spirit, and with the understanding, it is necessary that the church of the Latter-day Saints should have a collection of "Sacred Hymns," adapted to their faith and belief in the gospel, and, as far as can be, holding forth the promises made to the fathers who died in the precious faith of a glorious resurrection, and a thousand years' reign on earth with the Son of Man in his glory. Notwithstanding the church, as it were, is still in its infancy, yet, as the song of the righteous is a prayer unto God, it is sincerely hoped that the following collection, selected with an eye single to his glory, may answer every purpose till more are composed, or till we are blessed with a copious variety of the songs of Zion.'

"Twenty of the hymns in this book which are found in later editions, are by William W. Phelps; two are by Parley P. Pratt and one by Eliza R. Snow. Other hymns were selected from other publications, but with wisdom and care. There were all told 90 hymns." (Joseph Fielding Smith, *CHMR* 1:326.)

"Not only does the spoken word touch the hearts of the children of men, but our Heavenly Father, knowing the importance of appropriate singing in worship, called Emma Smith and appointed her to select the hymns that were published in the first hymn book of The Church of Jesus Christ of Latter-day Saints. They have been added to from time to time, until today the songs of Zion are sung in many lands, and the words of the Gospel of Jesus Christ have been interpreted in many lands, not only by the spoken word, but by the hymns that are sung from the hearts of those who accept the Gospel of our Lord." (George Albert Smith, *CR,* October 1938, pp. 27-28.)

25:12 *"the song of the righteous is a prayer unto me"*

"A Church without sacred singing would be cold and dead. Music is one of the most ancient of the fine arts. . . . Music is an expression of the feelings and emotions of man. Our singing in our sacred places should be done unto edifying.

". . . Matthew tells us that after the feast of the Passover, when Christ introduced the Sacrament before they went forth in the spirit of sadness from that supper table from whence Christ knew he was going to his betrayal and death, they had 'sung an hymn,' a sad hymn depicting their feelings without doubt.

"Since singing is pleasing to the Lord and a prayer unto him when it is 'sacred' and a song of the heart, Latter-day Saints should endeavor always to sing in harmony with the Spirit and with understanding. Frequently the spirit of a meeting is hampered by improper music and singing. Jazz, under no condition, can be called sacred. Light, frivolous songs are always out of place in the sacred services of the Church. . . .

"Choir leaders should endeavor to be prepared with songs which will harmonize perfectly with the theme of the meeting. Musical numbers should be made to harmonize with the spirit of such meetings." (Joseph Fielding Smith, *CHMR* 1:127-28.)

"There are many references in the scriptures, both ancient and modern, that attest to the influence of righteous music. The Lord, Himself, was prepared for His greatest test through its influence, for the scripture records: 'And when they had sung an hymn, they went out into the mount of Olives.' (Mark 14:26.)" (Boyd K. Packer, *CR,* October 1973, pp. 24-25.)

"God delights in the song of the heart; not in the mere sounds of the lips. Singing from the heart is worship; wherefore Paul says, 'I will sing with the spirit, and I will sing with the understanding also' (I Cor. 14:15). In such singing God takes delight. No music is as sweet as religious compositions; none is so majestic, so inspiring." (Smith and Sjodahl, *DCC,* p. 129.)

"I believe that we can worship in song as acceptably to him as in any other way. . . . I know of no people on earth who have written into their songs the principles of the Gospel they believe in more than have the Latter-day Saints." (Reed Smoot, *CR,* October 1912, pp. 50-51.)

25:12 *"it [song of the righteous] shall be answered with a blessing"*

"Good music is gracious praise of God. It is delightsome to the ear, and it is one of our most acceptable methods of worshipping God. And those who sing in this choir and in all the choirs of the saints should sing with the spirit and with the understanding. They should not sing merely because it is a profession, or because they have a good voice; but they should sing also because they have the spirit of it and can enter into the spirit of prayer and praise to God who gave them their sweet voices." (Joseph F. Smith, *CR,* October 1899, p. 69.)

25:14 *"beware of pride"*

"Emma Smith is admonished to beware of pride and told to let her soul delight in her husband. . . . After the death of the Prophet Joseph Smith and his brother, the Patriarch Hyrum Smith, Emma Smith refused to hearken to the counsels of the presiding authorities of the Church. President Brigham Young endeavored to treat her with kindness and offered to furnish her with teams and provisions and care for her and bring her to Salt Lake Valley, but she refused this offer, resented the counsels of the Apostles and departed from the body of the Church." (Joseph Fielding Smith, *CHMR* 1:126-27.)

SECTION 26

Background information on section 26

"In the Church of Christ where the government is that of the Kingdom of Heaven, neither autocracy nor democracy obtains, but government by *Common Consent.* That is to say, the initiative in all that pertains to the government of the Church rests with the Head of the Church, even our Lord Jesus Christ, and He exercises this sovereign function through his authorized servants, upon whom He has bestowed the Holy Priesthood: but it is the privilege of the people to accept, or reject, His laws and ordinances, for God has given every individual free agency. Obedience must be voluntary. The government of the Church has been called a *Theo-democracy.* It is the form of government that will be general during the Millennium." (Smith and Sjodahl, *DCC,* pp. 131-32.)

See also background information for section 24.

26:1 *Study the scriptures*

See *Scriptures* in Appendix A.

26:2 *"all things shall be done by common consent"*

See *Common consent* and *Sustain* in Appendix A.

"There are two forms of government. The *one-man* form does not recognize the right of the governed to a voice in the government. This is called autocracy, and is frequently referred to as 'paternalism.' Government by the 'people' means the rule of the majority, no matter by what means or methods that majority has been obtained. This is democracy. All human forms of government belong to one of these; they are either autocracies or democracies, or modifications of them. Both have merits, and also defects. In autocracies there is a tendency to disregard individual rights for the benefit of the few; in democracies the danger is that the worst element may obtain preponderance, because citizens of that class will employ means to gain their ends, which citizens with a high moral standard would never adopt. Democracies with party rule sometimes are exposed to all the evils of mob rule.

"In the Church of Christ where the government is that of the Kingdom of Heaven, neither autocracy nor democracy obtains, but government by *Common Consent.*" (Smith and Sjodahl, *DCC,* p. 131.)

SECTION 27

Background information on section 27

"Early in the month of August, Newel Knight and his wife paid us a visit at my place in Harmony, Pennsylvania; and as neither his wife nor mine had been as yet confirmed, it was proposed that we should confirm them and partake together of the sacrament, before he and his wife should leave us. In order to prepare for this I set out to procure some wine for the occasion, but had gone only a short distance when I was met by a heavenly messenger, and received the following revelation, the first four paragraphs of which were written at this time, and the remainder in September following: [Section 27.]" (Joseph Smith, *HC* 1:106.)

"This heavenly messenger told Joseph Smith that it mattered not what should be used for the Sacrament, and he was not to purchase wine or strong drink from his enemies. The reason for this is obvious, for the Prophet had many enemies. However, this reason went further than merely protection against his enemies, for it was a caution against evil and designing persons who would adulterate these things. (See Word of Wisdom, section 89.) Joseph Smith was also told that wine should not be used for the Sacrament unless it was made by the Saints, and should be had new among them. While the Church did not adopt the custom of using water exclusively in the Sacrament at that early time, yet it was from this time that water was used as a substitute for wine, which had been used principally because of its resemblance to blood. Today throughout the Church water is used in the Sacrament in remembrance of the blood of Jesus Christ which was shed for the remission of sins in behalf of all who repent and accept the Gospel." (Joseph Fielding Smith, *CHMR* 1:132.)

27:2 *"it mattereth not what ye shall eat or . . . drink when ye partake of the sacrament"*

See *Sacrament* in Appendix A.

"By some it is very well understood that in the days of ancient Israel while in the land of Palestine they were not blessed so profusely as we are with the crystal streams from the mountains. They were in the habit of drinking a great deal of wine, and among the few who have continued to inhabit that land, this habit I believe has been kept up to the present time. It is a wine country. But the Lord has said to us it mattereth not what we partake of when we administer the cup to the people, inasmuch as we do it with an eye single to the glory of God; it is then acceptable to him. Consequently we use water as though it were wine; for we are commanded to drink not of wine for this sacred purpose except it be made by our own hands." (Brigham Young, *JD* 19:92.)

27:5   *"I will drink of the fruit of the vine with you"*

The Savior includes prophets from Old Testament, New Testament, and Book of Mormon times as being among those with whom he will partake of the sacrament in his "Father's kingdom . . . on the earth." It is interesting to note that Joseph who was sold into Egypt was included (usually the Bible refers to the God of "Abraham, Isaac, and Jacob"); he is mentioned prominently in both the Bible and the Book of Mormon and, of course, is the forefather of many of the peoples of the Book of Mormon.

"The Savior informed his Apostles on the night he ate the Passover that he would not drink of the 'fruit of the vine' with them again, until he should 'drink it new with them in the kingdom of God.' [See Matt. 26:29 and Luke 22:18.] This was reiterated in the revelation to Joseph Smith, wherein the Lord promised to drink and eat with his prophets and saints, in his Father's kingdom which shall be built up on the earth." (Joseph Fielding Smith, *CHMR* 1:132-33.)

"Can a resurrected being eat food of earth? [Luke 24:39-43.] A resurrected being can function upon any lower plane. A resurrected personage can do anything that a mortal personage can do, and much besides." (James E. Talmage, *CR,* April 1928, p. 93.)

27:5   *"the record of the stick of Ephraim"*

The "stick of Ephraim" might include additional records than are included in our present Book of Mormon—for example, (1) the sealed portion of the plates of Mormon, (2) the brass plates of Laban, (3) the unabridged large plates of Nephi.

27:7 *"Elias"*

See *Elias* in Appendix A.

"It was Gabriel who appeared to Zacharias and promised him a son, and who appeared to Mary and announced the coming of the Son of God as recorded by Luke. It was also Gabriel as an Elias who is mentioned in the Doctrine and Covenants, Section 27, verse 7, and was Gabriel or Noah, who stands next to Michael or Adam in the Priesthood." (Joseph Fielding Smith, *CR,* April 1960, p. 72.)

27:13 *"dispensation of the gospel for the last times; and for the fulness of times"*

See *Dispensation* in Appendix A.

"Now the thing to be known is, what the fulness of times means, or the extent or authority thereof. It means this, that the dispensation of the fulness of times is made up of all the dispensations that have been given since the world began, until this time. Unto Adam first was given a dispensation. It is well known that God spake to him with his own voice in the garden, and gave him the promise of the Messiah. [Moses 4:14-21; 5:9.] And unto Noah also was a dispensation given; for Jesus said, 'As it was in the days of Noah, so shall it be also in the days of the Son of Man' [Matt. 24:37]; and as the righteous were saved then, and the wicked destroyed, so it will be now. And from Noah to Abraham, and from Abraham to Moses, and from Moses to Elias, and from Elias to John the Baptist, and from them to Jesus Christ, and from Jesus Christ to Peter, James and John, the Apostles—all received in their time a dispensation by revelation from God, to accomplish the great scheme of restitution spoken of by all the holy prophets since the world began; the end of which is the dispensation of the fulness of times, in the which all things shall be fulfilled that have been spoken of since the earth was made. [Sec. 128:20-21.]" (David W. Patten, *HC* 3:51-53.)

"It is called the 'dispensation of the fulness of times,' wherein God will gather together all things in one, whether they be things in the heavens or things in the earth. It is a dispensation in which all the holy prophets that ever lived upon the face of the earth are interested. They prophesied about it as the grand and great consummation in the accomplishment of the purposes of God [Acts 3:19-21]; purposes which he designed before the morning stars sang together, or the sons of God shouted for joy, or this world itself rolled into existence. It is a work in which we, our progenitors and our posterity are especially interested. . . ." (John Taylor, *JD* 24:260-61.)

27:15-18 *"take upon you my whole armor . . . breastplate . . . shield . . . helmet . . . sword"*

See *Armor of God* in Appendix A.

27:16 *"the preparation of the gospel of peace"*

" 'Preparation' is the word used in Eph. 6:15, where it means 'equipment.' He who desires victory in this conflict, must have the entire equipment of the gospel. This includes the holy Priesthood, the ordinances of the Church, continuous revelation, and all other divinely-appointed means of salvation. . . ." (Smith and Sjodahl, *DCC,* p. 138.)

If the principles of the gospel were lived by all the peoples on the earth, we would have peace; thus it is indeed the "gospel of peace."

SECTION 28

Background information on section 28

"To our great grief, however, we soon found that Satan had been lying in wait to deceive, and seeking whom he might devour. Brother Hiram Page had in his possession a certain stone, by which he had obtained certain 'revelations' concerning the upbuilding of Zion, the order of the Church, etc., all of which were entirely at variance with the order of God's house as laid down in the New Testament, as well as in our late revelations. As a conference meeting had been appointed for the 26th day of September, I thought it wisdom not to do much more than to converse with the brethren on the subject, until the conference should meet. Finding, however, that many, especially the Whitmer family and Oliver Cowdery, were believing much in the things set forth by this stone, we thought best to inquire of the Lord concerning so important a matter; and before conference convened, we received the following: [Section 28.]" (Joseph Smith, *HC* 1:109-10.)

"Hiram Page was born in Vermont in 1800. He joined the Church five days after its organization and was baptized by Oliver Cowdery in Seneca Lake. Previously he had become one of the Eight Witnesses of the Book of Mormon. Soon after his baptism he obtained a stone by means of which he received certain spurious revelations, at variance with the principles of the Gospel and the revelations received by Joseph Smith. Among other things he claimed to have received a revelation making known the place where the City of Zion would be built. In reading the Book of Mormon (Ether 13) it was discovered that Zion, or the New Jerusalem, was to be built upon this continent. This prediction caused some speculation at that early day, and Hiram Page endeavored to settle the question by means of revelation received through his stone. As it was but a few months after the organization of the Church, the members had not learned that there was but one appointed of the Lord to receive revelations for the

Church, and several others thought that Hiram Page or
Oliver Cowdery could receive revelations just as well as Jo-
seph Smith. Oliver Cowdery and the members of the
Whitmer family were deceived by these false declarations of
Hiram Page. This caused serious trouble and Oliver
Cowdery took the Prophet to task for not accepting what
Hiram Page had given. Finally the Prophet persuaded Oliver
Cowdery that these things were wrong, and later the whole
membership renounced the revelation given through this
stone, but this did not come until the Lord had given to the
Church the revelation known as section twenty-eight." (Jo-
seph Fielding Smith, *CHMR* 1:134-35.)

28:2   *"no one shall be appointed to receive commandments and
revelations in this church excepting" the head of the
Church*

"I will inform you that it is contrary to the economy of
God for any member of the Church, or any one, to receive
instructions for those in authority, higher than themselves;
therefore you will see the impropriety of giving heed to
them; but if any person have a vision or a visitation from a
heavenly messenger, it must be for his own benefit and
instruction, for the fundamental principles, government, and
doctrine of the Church are vested in the keys of the
kingdom." (Joseph Smith, *HC* 1:338.)

"Today the doctrine that revelation for the Church comes
only through the one who is duly appointed and who holds
the keys of the kingdom, and that there is but one at a time
called to that position is well understood by all faithful
members of the Church. Each member of the Church has
the right to receive inspiration and revelation for his or her
own guidance, but such revelation is not to be exploited or
made common property, but is given for the welfare of the
individual who received it." (Joseph Fielding Smith, *CHMR*
1:136.)

"It is not my business nor that of any other individual to
rise up as a revelator, as a prophet, as a seer, as an inspired
man, to give revelation for the guidance of the Church, or to
assume to dictate to the presiding authorities of the Church
in any part of the world, much less in the midst of Zion. . . .

"And the moment that individuals [Church members]

look to any other source, that moment they throw themselves open to the seductive influences of Satan, and render themselves liable to become servants of the devil; they lose sight of the true order through which the blessings of the Priesthood are to be enjoyed; they step outside of the pale of the kingdom of God, and are on dangerous ground." (Joseph F. Smith, *JD* 24:188-89.)

28:3-8 *Oliver Cowdery to write, but not by way of commandment*

"Oliver Cowdery . . . received at the same time that the Prophet Joseph did the Aaronic Priesthood. . . . He afterwards received, in common with Joseph, the administration of those who held the keys of the Apostleship in the flesh on the earth—that is, Peter, James and John. . . . He [Oliver Cowdery] became an Apostle with Joseph, being the second Apostle in The Church of Jesus Christ of Latter-day Saints. Now, it might be thought a man thus favored . . . would have stood alongside of the Prophet and been of equal authority in giving the word of God in writing unto the people. But no. God drew a distinction and plainly told Oliver Cowdery that that which he wrote to this Church should not be by way of commandments to the Church, but by wisdom. The Lord said to him [Sec. 28:4, quoted]. It was only one man's privilege, one man's authority to stand pre-eminent in the earth at one time, holding the keys and giving the commandments of God—or rather the Lord—giving his commandments through him in writing to the Church." (George Q. Cannon, *JD* 24:363-64.)

28:6 *"thou shalt not command him who is at . . . the head of the church"*

"It was very necessary that Oliver Cowdery should receive this admonition, for he was inclined to take issue with the Prophet even in regard to matters of revelation. Much good came out of this unpleasant incident, for the members were taught that there was order in the Church and only one appointed to receive commandments and revelations for their guidance, and he was the one God had called. The members at that time were largely excusable for falling into this error, because they had but recently come into the Church and had to be taught in all things pertaining to the kingdom of God and its government. They did not know that it was wrong for a man other than the Prophet to claim to be the spokesman for the Almighty, and this revelation taught them that confusion would result from such a course, and that Joseph Smith held the keys of revelation until another was appointed to succeed him." (Joseph Fielding Smith, *CHMR* 1:135-36.)

28:7   *"appoint . . . another in his stead"*

"Some of the enemies of the Church try to make a point out of the saying that Joseph Smith was to 'appoint another in his stead.' This provision was made at the time this revelation was given so that the Church would know the order even if Joseph Smith should fall. Later, after the Prophet had been tested and proved, the Lord said: [D&C 90:1-4, quoted.]

"Thus, we see, that the Lord placed upon Joseph Smith the keys of this dispensation and said that because of his faithfulness he should hold them throughout all eternity. In Nauvoo, a few months before the martyrdom, the Prophet conferred upon the heads of the Twelve Apostles all the keys and authorities which he held, and told them that henceforth they would have to bear off the kingdom, for he would be taken away." (Joseph Fielding Smith, *CHMR* 1:137.)

28:11-13   *Hiram Page deceived by Satan*

"Hiram Page was born in the year 1800, and, when a young man, traveled considerably as a physician. He joined the Church on the 11th of April, 1830, and became one of the Eight Witnesses to the Book of Mormon. In due time he removed to Independence, Mo., and later became one of the pioneers of the City of Far West. In 1838, however, he drifted away from the Church. He never rescinded his testimony. He died on the 12th of August, 1852." (Smith and Sjodahl, *DCC*, p. 143.)

28:13   *"Common consent"*

See *Common consent* in Appendix A.

SECTION 29

Background information on section 29

"In these early days of the Church the Lord revealed to the Prophet for the benefit of the members, line upon line and precept upon precept, thus unfolding to them the great truths of the Gospel. This revelation [Sec. 29] was given a few days before the conference of September 26, 1830, and in anticipation of that gathering. The Lord had commanded Oliver Cowdery to tarry [Sec. 28:10] until after this conference should be held, before departing on his mission to the Lamanites. The wonderful doctrines explained in this revelation were of such importance that it was well for Oliver and his companions to know them that they might teach the people on their way, and to the Lamanites when they arrived at their destination, with a more complete comprehension of the plan of Salvation than they otherwise would have had." (Joseph Fielding Smith, *CHMR* 1:130.)

"The Saints at Fayette were looking forward with anticipation to the conference that was to be held on the 26th of September, 1830. The first conference had been the occasion of a Pentecostal outpouring of the Holy Spirit, and there was every reason to believe that the second would be a similar spiritual feast. Some time before the September Conference this Revelation was given in the presence of six Elders." (Smith and Sjodahl, *DCC*, p. 145.)

29:1 *"Listen to the voice of Jesus Christ"*

"In giving revelations our Savior speaks at times for himself; at other times for the Father, and in the Father's name, as though he were the Father, and yet it is Jesus Christ, our Redeemer who gives the message. So, we see, in Doctrine and Covenants 29:1, that he introduces himself as 'Jesus Christ, your Redeemer,' but in the closing part of the revelation he speaks for the Father, and in the Father's name as though he were the Father, and yet it is still Jesus who is speaking, for the Father has put his name upon him for that purpose." (Joseph Fielding Smith, *DS* 1:27-28.)

29:1 *"the Great I AM"*

See *I AM* in Appendix A.

29:1 *"your Redeemer . . . hath atoned for your sins"*

See *Jesus Christ* in Appendix A.

"Again the Lord declares that through his mercy he has offered atonement for sin. As Paul said, through that atonement we were bought with a price and therefore we belong to Jesus Christ who purchased us with his blood. (See 1 Cor. 6:20; 7:23.) Man was under the bondage of sin and unable to free himself, and Jesus Christ came into the world, offering himself a ransom to pay the price of transgression through the shedding of his blood that all men might be freed from death and have remission of their sins, on condition of their repentance. Previously the Lord had made it known that his blood would not free the unrepentant sinner, who should suffer for his transgressions even as he, Christ, suffered. (Sec. 19:15-19.) Frequently in these revelations our Lord refers to himself as 'your Redeemer,' and speaks of his suffering for the remission of sin in behalf of all who will repent and obey him." (Joseph Fielding Smith, *CHMR* 1:140-41.)

29:2 *"as a hen gathereth her chickens under her wings"*

See material for D&C 10:65.

29:5 *"I am . . . your advocate with the Father"*

See *Advocate* and *Jesus Christ* in Appendix A.

29:7 *"the gathering of mine elect"*

See *Elect* in Appendix A.

"Where people are pure and chaste in their thoughts and actions, the Spirit of God has such power with them that they readily perceive and comprehend the truth. It is by this means that the best among the children of God are being gathered out from the nations. Truth cleaves to truth, light to light and purity to purity. [Section 88:40.] The Gospel gathers within its influence those who love its principles; and if any should be gathered in who cannot abide its requirements, they pass off and mingle with the elements that are congenial to the spirit they possess." (George Q. Cannon, *MS* 25:169.)

29:9-10 *"the hour is nigh"*

See *Second coming* in Appendix A.

"This Church proclaims the doctrine of the impending return of the Christ to earth in literal simplicity, without mental or other reservation in our interpretation of the scriptural predictions. He will come with the body of flesh and bones in which his Spirit was tabernacled when he ascended from Mount Olivet. One of the characteristic features of the Church concerning that great, and in the language of the scripture, both glorious and terrible event, is its nearness. It is close at hand. The mission of the Church is to prepare the earth for the coming of its Lord. Biblical prophecies are numerous [Luke 21:7-28; Mark 8:38; Acts 1:11; 1 Thess. 4:16]; the Book of Mormon prophecies are abundant, respecting the return of the Christ [1 Ne. 22:24; Mosiah 15:20; 3 Ne. 21:25; 29:2]. His own words, both before and after his crucifixion and resurrection are unambiguous, definite, convincing, and convicting unto those . . . in this day and age of the world he has spoken with his own voice unto his prophets, impressing upon them the fact that the time of his coming in judgment is near at hand. [Sec. 34:7, 8, 12; 63:34; 133:17.] Thus, within a few months after the Church was organized, in the year 1830, as recorded in the 29th section of the Doctrine and Covenants, the Lord Jesus Christ said unto his Prophet Joseph Smith: [Sec. 29:9-11, quoted.]" (James E. Talmage, *CR*, April 1916, pp. 126-27.)

29:9 *"I will burn them up"*

See *Burned* in Appendix A.

29:11 *"I will . . . dwell . . . on earth a thousand years"*

See *Millennium* in Appendix A.

"That our Lord will reign upon this Earth, and that the Saints will reign with Him for a thousand years, is clearly revealed. This truth was generally accepted among the Christians till the fourth century. From that time till the Reformation, the general opinion was against a literal Millennium. At the time of the Reformation, the so-called *Anabaptists* declared their belief in it, and that was enough to damn the doctrine in the eyes of their bigoted opponents. In England it was condemned as 'Jewish dotage.' Later, Rome declared against a literal Millennium, while Protestants took the opposite view. Some who believe in a Millennium hold that Christianity will be gradually diffused until the entire race is Christianized, and that will be the Millennium. This is an error. The world will be redeemed through the mighty arm of Jehovah; through judgments and tribulation. The general conversion will take place during the Millennium." (Smith and Sjodahl, *DCC*, p. 15.)

29:12 *"the Twelve . . . shall . . . judge"*

"We may here state that Christ is called the judge of the quick and the dead, the judge of all the earth. We further read that the Twelve Apostles who ministered in Jerusalem 'shall sit upon twelve thrones, judging the twelve tribes of Israel.' (Matt. 19:28.)

"And Nephi writes in the Book of Mormon: [1 Ne. 12:8-10, quoted.]

"This exhibits a principle of adjudication or judgment in the hands, firstly, of the Great High Priest and King, Jesus of Nazareth, the Son of God; secondly, in the hands of the Twelve Apostles on the continent of Asia, bestowed by Jesus himself; thirdly, in the Twelve Disciples on this continent, to their people, who . . . are under the presidency of the Twelve Apostles who ministered at Jerusalem; . . . and, further, the First Presidency and Twelve who have officiated in our age." (John Taylor, *MA*, pp. 152-53.)

29:13 *"a trump shall sound . . . even as upon Mount Sinai"*

See *Trump* in Appendix A.

29:14-21 *"before . . . [that] day shall come . . ."*

For information on the calamities on the earth that shall precede the second coming of Jesus Christ in power and glory, read the material listed for *Second coming* in Appendix A.

29:17 *"cup of mine indignation"*

When read in context, it is quite clear that the Lord's cup of indignation is full when the people have become so wicked that the law of justice must take effect and the prophesied punishments must come.

29:17 *"my blood shall not cleanse them if they hear me not"*

"On the cross our Savior paid the debt that made mankind free. He bought us with the price of his precious blood.

We are not our own for we are bought with a price. [Acts 20:28.] His blood atones for all our sins, through obedience to righteousness, but it shall not cleanse those who obey not his commandments." (Charles A. Callis, *CR,* October 1937, p. 122.)

29:18-20   *"flies . . . maggots . . . their flesh shall fall"*

Some of these predicted plagues were also listed by Zechariah:

" 'And this shall be the plague wherewith the Lord will smite all the people that have fought against Jerusalem; Their flesh shall consume away while they stand upon their feet, and their eyes shall consume away in their holes, and their tongues shall consume away in their mouth.' (Zech. 14:12.) There is no promise that this great plague of hail, destruction and disease shall be confined to any one section of the earth. It is a calamity which will come upon the wicked because they will not repent. We may well believe that in addition to the plague of flies there shall be included in this prediction the plague of microbes, or bacilli, new to the scientific world and with which they will not be able to cope, much of which will be the result of impure lives." (Smith and Sjodahl, *DCC,* p. 152.)

29:21   *The destruction of "the great and abominable church"*

This is the only place in the Doctrine and Covenants in which the term *great and abominable church* is used. However, it is mentioned many times in the Book of Mormon (1 Ne. 13:5-6, 26, 28, 32, 34; 14:3, 9-17), and the cross-reference in the Doctrine and Covenants suggests it is the church of the devil referred to in D&C 10:56.

29:22-25   *"there shall be a new heaven and a new earth"*

See *New heaven and a new earth* in Appendix A.

"This does not mean that this earth shall pass away and another take its place, and the heaven thereof shall pass away, and another heaven shall take its place, but that the earth and its heaven shall, after passing away, through death, be renewed again in immortality. This earth is living and must die, but since it keeps the law it shall be restored through the resurrection by which it shall become celestialized and the abode of celestial beings. . . . The Lord intends to save, not only the earth and the heavens, not only man who dwells upon the earth, but all things which he has created. The animals, the fishes of the sea, the fowls of the air, as well as man, are to be re-created, or renewed, through the resurrection, for they too are living souls." (Joseph Fielding Smith, *CR,* October 1928, pp. 99-100.)

29:25   *"not one hair, neither mote, shall be lost"*

This distinctive phrase indicates the thoroughness of God and of his judgment.

29:27   *"on my right hand"*

See *Right hand* in Appendix A.

29:28   *"Depart from me, ye cursed"*

See *Perdition* in Appendix A.

"This is the final fate of the sons of perdition (See 76:32-39). It should be noted that in Matthew those on the right side are 'blessed of my Father,' while those of the left side are 'cursed.' This curse they bring upon themselves by their disobedience, and not because it pleases the Creator to see them punished. 'For behold, justice exerciseth all his demands, and also mercy claimeth all which is her own; and thus, none but the truly penitent are saved. What, do ye suppose that mercy can rob justice? I say unto you, nay; not one whit. If so, God would cease to be God.' (Alma 42:24-25.)" (Smith and Sjodahl, *DCC,* p. 155.)

"The Lord never authorized [anyone] to say that the devil, his angels [Sec. 76:44-48] or the sons of perdition, should ever be restored; for their state of destiny was not revealed to man, is not revealed, nor ever shall be revealed, save to those who are made partakers thereof: consequently those who teach this doctrine, have not received it of the Spirit of the Lord. Truly Brother Oliver [Cowdery] declared it to be the doctrine of devils. We therefore command that this doctrine be taught no more in Zion." (Joseph Smith, *HC* 1:366.)

29:28   *"everlasting fire"*

See *Everlasting fire* in Appendix A.

29:30   *"the first shall be last, and . . . last shall be first"*

The Lord has indicated that he is no respecter of persons. (Deut. 1:17; Acts 10:34; Moro. 8:12; D&C 1:35; 38:16, 26.)

Thus the practice that the first shall be last and the last shall be first is evidently the operation of a divine principle showing the impartiality of God. Once a people has had full opportunity to accept the gospel and has refused to accept it, justice would seem to indicate that other peoples should have opportunity to hear the gospel before the first group has another chance.

In the former dispensation, the gospel was first preached to the Jews and then, after they rejected it, it was taken to the Gentiles. In the dispensation in which we live, the gospel was first taken to the Gentile nations, and scattered Israel other than the Jews were gathered out; and after being preached among the Gentile nations, it shall go to the Jews, the first being last and the last being first, as the Savior promised. (Luke 13:28-30; see also 1 Ne. 13:42.) (Joseph Fielding Smith, *DS* 3:259.)

Doctrine and Covenants references pertaining to this principle are: 29:30; 88:59; 90:9; 107:33-35, 97.

29:31-35 *All things created by the power of the Lord's Spirit— "first spiritual, secondly temporal"*

See *Spiritual* and *Temporal* in Appendix A.

"In the twenty-ninth section of the Doctrine and Covenants, God says that he made all things. He speaks there of the earth and the animals upon it, and the vegetation that grows out of the ground, and of the material things which men handle. The Lord says he created them all by the word of his power, 'firstly spiritual, and secondly temporal'; and the last of his works will be 'firstly temporal, and secondly spiritual.' But he explains further, that to him all these things are spiritual, because they are eternal. The elements are eternal, and therefore God calls them spiritual; for the things that are temporal are those that pass away, and the things that are spiritual are those that remain. . . . The elements . . . cannot be annihilated. Not one particle of matter can be annihilated; not one particle of spirit can be annihilated; for they are eternal. They always were, in their essential particles, in their primary elements, and they always will abide, though their forms may be changed by the power of the great Creator." (Charles W. Penrose, *CR,* April 1905, p. 71.)

"In our mortal, or carnal, way of thinking, many of the commandments the Lord has required seem to be temporal, but he has said that at no time has he given a temporal law. (D&C 29:34.) All things to him are spiritual, or in other words intended to be eternal. The Lord does not think in temporal terms; his plan is to bring to pass the immortality and eternal life of man. In his eyes, therefore, all the commandments that have to do with our present welfare, are considered to be but steps on the way to his eternal salvation." (Joseph Fielding Smith, *CHMR* 1:307-8.)

"Not at any time . . . law which was temporal] Man makes a distinction between temporal and spiritual laws, and some are very much concerned about keeping the two separate. To the Lord everything is both spiritual and temporal, and the laws He gives are consequently spiritual, because they concern spiritual beings. When He commanded Adam to eat bread in the sweat of his brow, or Moses to strike the rock that the people might drink, or the Prophet Joseph to erect the Nauvoo House, or the Saints in Utah to build fences and roads, such laws were for their spiritual welfare, as well as physical. To obey such laws, when given, is a spiritual duty. One who performs his daily labor 'as to the Lord, and not to men' (Eph. 6:7) derives spiritual benefit from whatever his duties are." (Smith and Sjodahl, *DCC*, p. 156.)

29:36-40 *"the devil and his angels"*

See *Satan* in Appendix A.

29:40 *"Adam . . . partook . . . transgressed . . . yielded unto temptation"*

"How did Adam and Eve sin? Did they come out in direct opposition to God and to his government? No. But they transgressed a command of the Lord, and through that transgression sin came into the world. The Lord knew they would do this, and he had designed that they should." (Brigham Young, *JD* 10:312.)

"Here let me say, that therein consisted the fall—the eating of things unfit, the taking into the body of things that made of that body a thing of earth; and I take this occasion to raise my voice against the false interpretation of scripture, which has been adopted by certain people, and is current in their minds, and is referred to in a hushed and half-secret way, that the fall of man consisted in some offense against the laws of chastity and virtue. Such a doctrine is an abomination. . . . Our first parents were pure and noble, and when we pass behind the veil we shall perhaps learn something of their high estate, more than we know now. But be it known that they were pure; they were noble. It is true that they disobeyed the law of God, in eating things they were told not to eat; but who amongst you can rise up and condemn?" (James E. Talmage, *CR,* October 1913, pp. 118-19.)

"Our first ancestor was actually tempted. This was possible, because he was endowed with free agency. There can be no free agency where there is no possibility to choose between right and wrong. . . . Hence, God gave the law concerning the fruit of the trees in the garden. Adam was tempted, but, as Paul informs us, 'he was not deceived' (1 Tim. 2:14), as was Eve. He partook of the forbidden fruit in order not to be separated from his wife, fully understanding the consequences. 'Adam fell that man might be' (2 Nephi 2:25)." (Smith and Sjodahl, *DCC,* p. 158.)

29:41-45 *The "first death" and the "last death" are both spiritual*

See *Spiritual* in Appendix A.

"When Adam transgressed in the Garden of Eden he died the spiritual death, as well as changing his nature and bringing upon himself mortality. Spiritual death is banishment from the presence of God, and Adam was shut out from the presence of the Lord. Angels were sent to him, however, to teach him the plan of salvation. The earth probation was prolonged that he might repent and accept the plan offered to him. Through his repentance, baptism and confirmation he was brought back again into the presence of God through the Holy Ghost. This same spiritual death comes upon all unrepentant and unbaptized men, and the only way they can be brought from spiritual death to spiritual life is through obedience to the Gospel. By this means all men may be redeemed, as Adam was, from the spiritual fall, but all who will not receive the Gospel 'cannot be redeemed from their spiritual fall, because they repent not.' (D&C 29:44.)" (Joseph Fielding Smith, *CHMR* 1:144.)

29:46 *"little children are redeemed"*

See *Children* in Appendix A.

"Through the atonement of Jesus Christ all little children are redeemed, for they cannot sin, and the power is not given to Satan to tempt them. The question naturally may arise as to the meaning of the words of the Lord (verse 46) that 'little children are redeemed through the Only Begotten.' This does not mean that redemption was made for them before, or at, the foundation of the world, but at that time when the plan of salvation was received provision was made for the redemption of little children and also for those who are without the law, and this was consummated in the atonement made by Jesus Christ. In a vision given to the Prophet Joseph Smith, the Lord revealed 'that all children who die before they arrive at the years of accountability, are saved in the celestial kingdom of heaven.' (*HC* 2:381.)" (Joseph Fielding Smith, *CHMR* 1:144.)

29:46 *"from the foundation of the world"*

See *Pre-earthly* existence in Appendix A.

The term *from the foundation of the world* indicates that the particular item being discussed was provided for in the pre-earthly councils before the earth was ever created in its present condition. Thus, all things related to the atonement of Jesus Christ (resurrection; possibility of sanctification and eternal life; redemption of children, etc.) were made part of the gospel plan from the very beginning, and they pertain to those who lived before the time of Christ as well as to those who lived later.

29:47 *"become accountable before me"*

See materials listed for 18:42.

SECTION 30

Background information on section 30

"At length our conference assembled. The subject of the stone previously mentioned was discussed (Section 28), and after considerable investigation Brother Page, as well as the whole Church who were present, renounced the said stone, and all things connected therewith, much to our mutual satisfaction and happiness. We now partook of the Sacrament, confirmed and ordained many, and attended to a great variety of Church business on the first of the two following days of the conference, during which time we had much of the power of God manifested amongst us; the Holy Ghost came upon us, and filled us with joy unspeakable; and peace, and faith, and hope, and charity abounded in our midst.

"Before we separated we received the following: [Sections 30 and 31, follow.]" (Joseph Smith, *HC* 1:115.)

For biographical information on David Whitmer, Peter Whitmer, Jr., and John Whitmer, see the material listed after their names in Appendix B.

30:1-4 *"David . . . your mind has been on the things of the earth . . . and you have not given heed unto my Spirit"*

"It seems a little strange that so soon after the wonderful manifestation which he [David Whitmer] had received and the witnessing of the outpouring of the Spirit at other times, that he would forget, but human nature is such that all of us need constant reminding of our responsibilities or we are likely to lapse into some indifference. The need of constant prayer and concentration of our thoughts on the things of the kingdom, and sincere attention to duty, is apparent with most of us, lest we slip. How frequently the Lord has had to caution his people against the weaknesses of the flesh!" (Joseph Fielding Smith, *CHMR* 1:146.)

30:5-8   *"Peter . . . take your journey with . . . Oliver"*

"To Peter Whitmer, Jr., the Lord gave a commandment that he should take his journey with Oliver Cowdery on a mission to the Lamanites. From the very beginning the attention of the Prophet and his brethren had been drawn to the Lamanites. This was due, of course, to the fact that great promises had been made to them in the Book of Mormon that the Gospel would be given to them in this dispensation and eventually they would be restored to full fellowship and favor before the Lord. . . . Moreover, Peter was informed that there was none appointed to be Oliver's counselor, except Joseph Smith. Thus Peter understood that it was his duty to take, not to give, counsel while on this journey. The fact that Oliver Cowdery had shared with Joseph Smith in the conferring of Priesthood and authority on all occasions naturally gave to him the authority to stand second in the Church to Joseph Smith in the government of the Church." (Joseph Fielding Smith, *CHMR* 1:136.)

30:9-11   *"John . . . proclaim my gospel"*

"John Whitmer was commanded to proclaim the Gospel. . . . He was not to fear man but devote his entire time to the cause of the Gospel. Later he was to be called to take the responsibility of keeping the history from the shoulders of Oliver Cowdery [Sec. 47:1-4]." (Joseph Fielding Smith, *CHMR* 1:136-37.)

SECTION 31

Background information on section 31

For additional biographical information on Thomas B. Marsh, who became one of the members of the initial Council of the Twelve Apostles in this dispensation, read the material after his name in Appendix B. Section 112 (verses 10-12, 14-15, 27, 34) also contains specific instructions to him.

"At [the] time Thomas B. Marsh joined the Church, he had been a member of the Methodist Church, but when comparing their doctrines with the scriptures, he failed to make them agree, so he withdrew from that sect and sought some other organization teaching the doctrines as he felt he discovered them in the Bible. He predicted that such an organization would arise. He was moved by the Spirit of the Lord to move west. His home was in Massachusetts. He met Martin Harris while the Book of Mormon was being printed and remained with him for several days and then returned to his home in Boston, but kept up correspondence with the Prophet and Oliver Cowdery, and upon learning of the organization of the Church, he moved to Palmyra in September, 1830, and was baptized by David Whitmer and a few days later was ordained an elder by Oliver Cowdery. . . .

"Thomas B. Marsh was a man of ability and could have been very useful in the Church, but he failed when persecution became strong and did not endure in his afflictions. When the opposition to the Church became severe and his feelings were disturbed, he left the Church and spoke in an evil and bitter spirit against the Prophet and the Church, thus encouraging our enemies. The falsehoods which he uttered have been used by the enemies of the Church to this day. Later in his life, however, when he was a broken man, he returned to the Church and, standing before the congregation, called upon them to look upon him as an object of apostasy, and he warned the members to avoid a course which would bring them to a similar condition." (Joseph Fielding Smith, *CHMR* 1:147-48.)

31:2   *"you have had many afflictions because of your family"*

"About the time he [Thomas B. Marsh] was preparing to
leave this Church, he received a revelation in the Printing
Office. He retired to himself, and prayed, and was humble,
and God gave him a revelation, and he wrote it. There were
from three to five pages of it; and when he came out he read
it to Brother Brigham [Young] and me. In it, God told him
what to do, and that was to sustain Brother Joseph and to
believe that what Brother Joseph had said was true. But no;
he took a course to sustain his wife and oppose the Prophet
of God, and she led him away. . . .

"Thomas B. Marsh was once the President over the
Quorum of the Twelve—over Brother Brigham, me, and
others; and God saw fit to give him a revelation to forewarn
him of the course he would take; and still he took that
course. We told him that if he would listen to that revelation
he had received, he would be saved; but he listened to his
wife, and away he went. His wife is now dead. . . . She led
him some eighteen years; and as soon as she died, he came
to Winter Quarters—now Florence—and has written to us,
pleading for mercy. We have extended it to him, and he will
probably be here this season or the next." (Heber C. Kimball, *JD* 5:28-29.)

31:1-13   *"Thomas . . . Pray always, lest you . . . lose your reward"*

"Many have said to me, 'How is it that a man like you,
who understood so much of the revelations of God as
recorded in the Book of Doctrine and Covenants, should fall
away?' I told them not to feel too secure, but to take heed
lest they also should fall, for I had no scruples in my mind as
to the possibility of men falling away. [Sec. 20:32-34.]

"I can say, in reference to the Quorum of the Twelve, to
which I belonged, that I did not consider myself a whit behind any of them, and I suppose that others had the same
opinion; but, let no one feel too secure; for, before you think
of it, your steps will slide. You will not then think nor feel
for a moment as you did before you lost the Spirit of Christ;
for when men apostatize, they are left to grovel in the dark.
. . . Had I known as much of the Church of Jesus Christ and
its doctrines before I apostatized as I now know, I think I
could not have back-slidden." (Thomas B. Marsh, *JD* 5:206,
208-9.)

SECTION 32

Background information on section 32

"During this conference [at Fayette, New York], which continued three days, the utmost harmony prevailed, and all things were settled satisfactorily to all present, and a desire was manifested by all the saints to go forward and labor with all their powers to spread the great and glorious principles of truth, which had been revealed by our Heavenly Father. A number were baptized during the conference, and the word of the Lord spread and prevailed.

"At this time a great desire was manifested by several of the Elders respecting the remnants of the house of Joseph, the Lamanites, residing in the west—knowing that the purposes of God were great respecting that people, and hoping that the time had come when the promises of the Almighty in regard to them were about to be accomplished, and that they would receive the Gospel, and enjoy its blessings. The desire being so great, it was agreed that we should inquire of the Lord respecting the propriety of sending some of the Elders among them, which we accordingly did, and received the following: [D&C 32]." (Joseph Smith, *HC* 1:118.)

For biographical information on Parley P. Pratt and Ziba Peterson, see the materials listed after each of their names in Appendix B.

32:1 *"Parley P. Pratt . . . be meek and lowly of heart"*

"Parley P. Pratt was admonished to be meek and lowly of heart. In the year 1837, there were 'jarrings and discord' in the Church at Kirtland, and he was overcome with that spirit. He even tried to turn John Taylor from the Prophet by pointing out to him what he regarded as Joseph's error. Elder Taylor rebuked him as a brother, and Parley P. Pratt went to the Prophet in tears and confessed his sin, whereupon the Prophet frankly forgave him, prayed with him, and blessed him. This was meekness. It was also manliness. Only a really strong character can possess true humility." (Smith and Sjodahl, *DCC*, p. 171.)

32:1-2   *"declare my gospel . . . among the Lamanites"*

"The revelation formerly given through the Prophet to Oliver Cowdery [Sec. 28:14-16], enunciating the divine decree concerning the Lamanites and the work to be accomplished among them, created great interest in the minds of the Elders of the Church. . . . Joseph and his brethren realized the purposes of God toward the Indians of this land were great and far-reaching, and that the time would come when they must receive the Gospel and enjoy its blessings. Many of the Elders expressed a desire to take up the work of the ministry among their brethren . . . but before appointing anyone to aid Oliver and Peter Whitmer in this mission, Joseph inquired of the Lord. [Oct. 1830.]" (George Q. Cannon, *LJS*, pp. 78-79.)

"These missionaries [Oliver Cowdery, Parley P. Pratt, Peter Whitmer, Jr., Ziba Peterson], left in the fall of 1830. On the way they stopped at Kirtland, Ohio, and the neighboring villages. There they preached the newly restored gospel with astonishing results. . . . There Parley P. Pratt presented to Sidney Rigdon, his old friend and teacher, a copy of the Book of Mormon.

"Before long several persons applied for baptism. Sidney Rigdon, a Campbellite writer and eloquent preacher, entered the waters of baptism. Branches were organized. The field there seemed fertile for the preaching of the restored gospel. The missionaries spent several weeks in the Kirtland territory to expound the gospel to interested listeners.

"However, the missionaries had been called to go to the Indian territory. Winter was coming, so about November 1st, they left the congenial Kirtland area and moved westward. On the way they proselyted and left copies of the Book of Mormon here and there.

"Then the winter of 1830-31, the severest in the memories of men, descended upon them. . . . Despite the weather, and under great suffering, they walked through snow and over ice for three hundred miles. At last they reached Independence, Missouri. Since they had disposed of all their copies of the Book of Mormon, Parley P. Pratt was selected to return for a new supply.

"Meanwhile, under restrictions set up by the Indian agents, the missionaries had little access to the Indians. But they preached long and loud to the Missouri settlers. To support themselves they did such work as was available. They set up a tailor shop in Independence; some of their patrons became defenders of the Latter-day Saints later when persecution raged.

"All in all, this mission bore rich fruit." (John A. Widtsoe, *JS*, pp. 136-37.)

Oliver Cowdery also went on this mission to the Lamanites. Following are excerpts from a letter he wrote on May 7, 1831, from Kaw Township, Missouri, concerning this trip:

"Brother Ziba Peterson and myself went into the county east, and in the name of Jesus, we called on the people to repent, many of whom are, I believe, earnestly searching for truth, and if sincerely, I pray they may find that precious treasure, for it seems to be wholly fallen in the streets; and equity cannot enter. The letter we received from you, informed us that the opposition was great against you. Now, our beloved brethren, we verily believe that we also can rejoice that we are counted worthy to suffer shame for His name; for almost the whole country, . . . with all the devils from the eternal pit, are united and foaming out their shame [against us]. God forbid that I should bring a railing accusation against them, for vengeance belongeth to Him who is able to repay." (Joseph Smith, *HC* 1:182.)

SECTION 33

Background information on section 33

"The Lord,who is ever ready to instruct such as diligently seek in faith, gave the following revelation at Fayette, New York; [Section 33, follows.]" (Joseph Smith, *HC* 1:126.)

"Ezra Thayre and Northrop Sweet came in the Church at the time of the preaching of the Lamanite missionaries. In October, 1830, they were called by revelation to enter the ministry and hearken to the voice of the Lord, 'whose word is quick and powerful, sharper than a two-edged sword, to the dividing asunder of the joints and marrow.' It was not long after this that Northrop Sweet left the Church and, with some others, formed what they called 'The Pure Church of Christ,' an organization that soon came to its end." (Joseph Fielding Smith, *CHMR* 1:152.)

For biographical information on Ezra Thayre, see the material listed after his name in Appendix B.

33:1 *The Lord's "word is . . . sharper than a two-edged sword"*

See *Sword* and *Armor of God* in Appendix A.

33:1 *"the Lord . . . is a discerner of the thoughts and intents of the heart"*

See *Thoughts* in Appendix A.

33:2 *"sound of a trump"*

See *Trump in Appendix A.*

33:3 *"it is the eleventh hour"*

"This is 'the eleventh hour.' The time in which we live is compared to the eleventh hour, and so it is in the Lord's reckoning, for we are in the closing scenes of the present world. Elder Orson F. Whitney referred to our dispensation as the 'Saturday night' of time. And, according to the parable of the men employed in the vineyard, we who labor in this hour will be rewarded if we are faithful, with equal compensation with those who labored in the previous hours, or dispensations, in the history of mankind." (Joseph Fielding Smith, *CHMR* 1:153.)

"This expression is from Matt. 20:6. Our Lord had taught the Twelve that it was almost impossible for a rich man to enter the Kingdom of Heaven. Then the disciples said, in substance, 'We, at any rate, left all and followed Thee; what shall our reward be?' Christ's answer was the parable of the Laborers in the Vineyard, in which He taught them that all His servants should have a great reward, but that those who are called last will receive just as much as the first. The time in which we live is the eleventh hour, and those who obey the call now will receive just as much as the laborers of former dispensations. The reward which God gives is not on the same basis as that which obtains in the world of industry among men. It is, after all, a gift. 'The *wages* of sin is death; but the *gift* of God is eternal life through Jesus Christ our Lord' (Rom. 6:23). 'The wage at best is a free gift; for on the basis of strict accounting who of us is not in debt to God?' (Talmage, *Jesus the Christ*, p. 482)." (Smith and Sjodahl, *DCC*, p. 172.)

See also *Parables* in Appendix A.

33:3 *"the last time"*

"By the 'last time' the Lord meant the Dispensation of the Fulness of Times." (Joseph Fielding Smith, *CR*, April 1946, p. 155.)

33:4 *"my vineyard has become corrupted"*

See *Vineyard* in Appendix A.

"This is equivalent to the expression of our Lord to the Prophet Joseph Smith in the year 1820. Because of false doctrines, theories and practices, not only in the religious world, but in the world of philosophy, and science, it became necessary for the Lord to open the heavens and make his will known. The time is not far from the condition in Noah's day when the Lord declared that 'all flesh had corrupted his way upon the earth.' (Gen. 6:12.)" (Joseph Fielding Smith, *CHMR* 1:153.)

33:4 *"all having corrupt minds"*

"Let me explain, when I use the term 'corrupt' with reference to these ministers of the gospel, that I use it in the same sense that I believe the Lord used it when he made that declaration to Joseph Smith, the Prophet, in answer to the Prophet's prayer. He did not mean, nor do I mean, that the ministers of religion are personally unvirtuous or impure. I believe as a class they, perhaps in personal purity, stand a little above the average order of men. When I use the term 'corrupt' I mean, as I believe the Lord meant, that they had turned away from the truth, and have turned to that which is false. A false doctrine is a corrupt doctrine; a false religion is a corrupt religion; a false teacher is a corrupt teacher. Any man who teaches a false doctrine, who believes in and practices and teaches a false religion is a corrupt professor, because he teaches that which is impure and not true." (Hyrum M. Smith, *CR*, October 1916, p. 43.)

33:5 *"called forth out of the wilderness"*

"In the book of Revelation, Chap. 12, we have a very vivid symbolical description of the Church being driven into the wilderness by the great dragon. 'And to the woman (Church) were given two wings of a great eagle, that she might fly into the wilderness, into her place, where she is nourished for a time, and times, and half a time, from the face of the serpent.' The Lord calls attention to this in the revelation on 'the wheat and the tares.' (Sec. 86.) 'And after they had fallen asleep, the great persecutor of the church . . . behold he soweth the tares; wherefore, the tares choke the wheat and drive the church into the wilderness.' Now in the Dispensation of the Fulness of Times, the Church is again called forth from the wilderness, and her man-child (the Priesthood) is restored to her again." (Joseph Fielding Smith, *CHMR* 1:153-54.)

33:6 *"I will gather mine elect from the four quarters of the earth"*

See *Elect* and *Earth* in Appendix A.

33:7 *"the field is white . . . thrust in your sickles, and reap"*

See *Harvest symbols* in Appendix A.

33:7 *"might, mind, and strength"*

See *Might, mind, and strength* in Appendix A.

33:9 *"you shall be laden with sheaves"*

See *Harvest symbols* in Appendix A.

33:13 *"gates of hell shall not prevail against you"*

See *Hell* and *Revelation* in Appendix A.

33:15 *"I will bestow the gift of the Holy Ghost"*

"The great promise the Lord has given to all who humbly repent, is that they shall receive the guidance of the Holy Ghost. Of course, this cannot come to them unless they are confirmed by the laying on of hands by one in authority. The world does not have the guidance of the Holy Ghost, but are blessed with the light of Christ as a guide, which, if they are humble and seek the light, will lead them to the light." (Joseph Fielding Smith, *CHMR* 1:154.)

33:17 *"praying always, having your lamps trimmed and burning"*

See *Prayer, Bridegroom,* and *Virgins* in Appendix A.

"The Lord requires his people to bow the knee before him every night and morning, and to remember him in their secret prayers. Every Latter-day Saint who neglects this requirement has not that supply of oil which is necessary to prepare him for the coming of the Son of Man. The Lord requires us to be obedient to the counsels of the Priesthood, and to look to them for counsel. Every Latter-day Saint who is obdurate in his feelings and will not listen to the counsels of the servants of the Lord shows a lack of oil. The Lord requires that we shall meet together on the fast day, fasting, praying, and remembering our offerings for the relief of the poor. Every Latter-day Saint who follows his daily avocation and neglects this duty shows a lack of oil. The Lord requires us to love our wives, our husbands, our children, and to love our neighbors. The Latter-day Saint who does not do this shows a dearth of that oil that is necessary to enable him to stand and be prepared for the coming of the Son of Man. The Lord requires us to preach the Gospel to all the world, and for this reason above all others has endowed us with his divine authority. If we neglect to honor and magnify the Priesthood, as we ought to do every day of our lives, we evidence a lack of oil." (Francis M. Lyman, *CR*, April 1901, p. 46.)

SECTION 34

Background information on section 34

"In the fore part of November, Orson Pratt, a young man nineteen years of age, who had been baptized at the first preaching of his brother Parley P. Pratt, September 19th (his birthday), about six weeks previous, in Canaan, New York, came to inquire of the Lord what his duty was and received the following answer: [Section 34, follows.]" (Joseph Smith, *HC* 1:127-28.)

For additional biographical information on Orson Pratt, see the material listed after his name in Appendix B.

34:1 *"Jesus Christ your Redeemer"*

See *Jesus Christ* in Appendix A.

"Christ is our Redeemer. Redemption means deliverance by means of ransom. There is a deliverance from *guilt* (Eph. 1:7; Col. 1:14); from the power and dominance of *sin,* through the sanctifying influence of the Holy Spirit (1 Peter 1:18); and from *death* through the resurrection (Rom. 8:23). There is, finally, a deliverance from all evil (Eph. 1:14; 4:30; 1 Cor. 1:30; Titus 2:14). All this is the work of Christ, through obedience to the gospel." (Smith and Sjodahl, *DCC,* p. 177.)

34:2 *"a light which shineth in darkness and the darkness comprehendeth it not"*

See *Light* in Appendix A.

34:3-4 *"you are my son . . . you have believed"*

"The Gospel has been preached to us, and we have essayed to obey it, that we might become the sons and daughters of God—heirs of God and joint-heirs with his Son." (Joseph F. Smith, *CR,* April 1900, p. 40.)

"I remained therefore, apart from all of them [churches], praying continually in my heart that the Lord would show me the right way.

"I continued this for about one year; after which, two Elders of this Church came into the neighborhood. I heard their doctrine, and believed it to be the ancient Gospel; and as soon as the sound penetrated my ears, I knew that if the Bible was true, their doctrine was true. They taught not only the ordinances, but the gifts and blessings promised the believers, and the authority necessary in the Church in order to administer the ordinances. All these things I received with gladness. . . .

"I called upon the Lord with more faith than before, for I had then received the first principles of the Gospel. The gift of the Holy Ghost was given to me; and when it was shed forth upon me, it gave me a testimony concerning the truth of this work that no man can ever take from me. It is impossible for me, so long as I have my reasoning faculties and powers of mind, to doubt the testimony I then received as among the first evidences that were given, and that, too, by the gift and power of the Holy Ghost." (Orson Pratt, *JD* 7:177-78.)

34:6 *"cry repentance, preparing the way of the Lord for his second coming"*

See *Repentance* and *Second coming* in Appendix A.

34:7-9 *Events associated with the second coming of Jesus Christ*

See *Second coming* in Appendix A.

34:10 *"lift up your voice . . . prophesy"*

"He [Joseph Smith] inquired of the Lord, and obtained a revelation for your humble servant. He retired into the chamber of old Father Whitmer, in the house where this Church was organized in 1830. John Whitmer acted as his scribe, and I accompanied him into the chamber, for he had told me that it was my privilege to have the word of the Lord; and the Lord in that revelation, which is published here in the Book of Doctrine and Covenants, made a promise which to me, when I was in my youth, seemed to be almost too great for a person of as humble origin as myself ever to attain to. After telling in the revelation that the great day of the Lord was at hand, and calling upon me to lift up my voice among the people, to call upon them to repent and prepare the way of the Lord, and that the time was near when the heavens should be shaken, when the earth should tremble, when the stars should refuse their shining, and when great destructions awaited the wicked, the Lord said to your humble servant: 'Lift up your voice and prophesy, and it shall be given by the power of the Holy Ghost.' This was a particular point in the revelation that seemed to me too great for me ever to attain to, and yet there was a positive command that I should do it. I have often reflected upon this revelation, and have oftentimes inquired in my heart—'Have I fulfilled the commandment as I ought to have done? Have I sought as earnestly as I ought to obtain the gift of prophecy, so as to fulfill the requirement of heaven?' And I have felt sometimes to condemn myself because of my slothfulness and because of the little progress that I have made in relation to this great heavenly and divine gift. I certainly have had no inclination to prophesy to the people unless it should be given to me by the inspiration and power of the Holy Ghost; to prophesy out of my own heart is something perfectly disagreeable to my feelings, even to think of, and hence I have oftentimes, in my public discourses, avoided, when a thing would come before my mind pretty plain, uttering or declaring it for fear that I might get something out before the people in relation to the future that was wrong." (Orson Pratt, *JD* 17:290-91.)

34:11 *"If you are faithful"*

"Orson Pratt was faithful. In the obituary the Editor of the *Deseret News* said:

" 'Orson Pratt was a true Apostle of the Lord. Full of integrity, firm as a rock to his convictions, true to his brethren and his God, earnest and zealous in defense and the proclamation of the truth, ever ready to bear testimony to the Latter-day work, he had a mind stored with Scripture, ancient and modern, was an eloquent speaker, a powerful minister, a logical and convincing writer, an honest man and a great soul who reached out after eternal things, grasped them with the gift of inspiration, and brought them down to the level and comprehension of the common mind. Thousands have been brought into the Church through his preaching in many lands, thousands more by his writings. He set but little store on the wealth of this world, but he has laid up treasures in heaven which will make him eternally rich.' " (Smith and Sjodahl, *DCC,* p. 179.)

34:12 *"I come quickly"*

See *Quickly* in Appendix A.

SECTION 35

Background information on section 35

"In December, 1830, two men came from Kirtland, Ohio, to visit the Prophet at Fayette. They were Sidney Rigdon and Edward Partridge. Both had accepted the gospel, as declared to them by the western missionaries, and Sidney Rigdon had been baptized. After reaching Fayette, Edward Partridge demanded and received baptism under the Prophet's hands. These two men offered to Joseph, for the work of the Lord, their time, their talents, and all they possessed. Like all the early members of the Church, having not yet gained full understanding of the purposes of God, having not yet gained confidence in their own ability to rightly determine their conduct, they desired that the Lord should give them his special commands. Joseph prayed for revelation on their behalf, and was speedily answered." (George Q. Cannon, *LJS,* p. 83.)

35:1 *"Alpha and Omega"*

See *Alpha and Omega* in Appendix A.

35:2 *"I am one in the Father, as the Father is one in me"*

See *Godhead* in Appendix A.

35:3-4 *"Sidney . . . thou wast sent forth . . . to prepare the way"*

"The Lord told Sidney that he had looked upon him and his works, having reference to his ministry as a Baptist and later as one of the founders of the 'Disciples' with Alexander Campbell and Walter Scott. During those years the hand of the Lord was over him and directing him in the gathering of many earnest souls who could not accept the teachings of the sects of the day. His prayers in which he sought further light than the world was able to give, were not to be answered. The Lord informed him that he had been sent to prepare the way, and in the gathering of his colony and the building up of his congregation in and around Kirtland, the hand of the Lord was directing him, and the way for the reception of the fulness of truth was being prepared. . . . While Sidney was preaching and baptizing by immersion without authority, which the Lord informed him in this revelation, yet it all resulted in good when the Gospel message reached them. These men were not only convinced and ready for baptism, but were in a condition by which the Priesthood could be given them, and this was done." (Joseph Fielding Smith, *CHMR* 1:160.)

"A striking instance of divine purpose in the labors of men outside the true Church is pointed out in a revelation given in December, 1830, to Joseph Smith, Jr., and Sidney Rigdon. The Lord said: [Sec. 35:3-6, quoted.] . . .

"The labors of Sidney Rigdon, referred to in the quotation, must have alluded to his ministry in the Campbellite church, for he had been in the Church of Christ only about six weeks when this revelation was given, having embraced the Gospel at the hands of Parley P. Pratt and fellow missionaries.

"As is well understood, the followers of Alexander Campbell preach faith, repentance and baptism by immersion for the remission of sins. These views Sidney Rigdon espoused as being better than what he already had, and when the true Gospel, in its fulness, with authority from God to administer the ordinances thereof, found him, he gladly obeyed the same. In about three weeks from the time Brother Pratt and co-laborers entered Kirtland, 127 persons were baptized. Subsequently the numbers were augmented to about 1,000 souls. In the providence of the Lord, Kirtland soon became the gathering place of the Saints, the facilities there being greatly enhanced by so many people embracing the Gospel and thus making a foothold for the Prophet Joseph Smith and the Saints who should follow him from the East. There the Kirtland Temple was built." (Matthias F. Cowley, *Cowley's Talks on Doctrine*, pp. 447-48.)

35:6 *"they shall receive the Holy Ghost . . . even as the apostles of old"*

"As the people in Kirtland had been baptized by Sidney Ridgon without authority, even so they had not received the gift of the Holy Ghost. Now, with authority, he was to go forth and baptize in water and authority, and those baptized should receive the Holy Ghost." (Joseph Fielding Smith, *CHMR* 1:160.)

"A man cannot preach with effect and power to another the forgiveness of sins through faith in the Lord Jesus Christ, or baptism for the remission of sins unless he has himself been baptized for the remission of sins and has faith in the Lord Jesus Christ himself. No man can administer in the ordinances of the Gospel of Christ with effect and with power unless he has first been made partaker of them himself." (Franklin D. Richards, *CR*, October 1897, pp. 24-25.)

"The people of the world of mankind today have not that Holy Ghost that was enjoyed by those holy men of God who gave the scriptures. If they had the Holy Ghost in the same degree of power that was had by those holy men who gave us the scriptures, then they would understand the scriptures just as did men who gave the scriptures to us." (George F. Richards, *CR*, October 1944, p. 88.)

35:7 *"the Gentiles"*

See *Gentiles* in Appendix A.

35:8 *"mine arm is not shortened"*

See *Arm of the Lord* in Appendix A.

35:11 *Babylon*

See *Babylon* in Appendix A.

35:11 *"drink of the wine of the wrath of her fornication"*

This distinctive phrase appears in three sections of the Doctrine and Covenants: 35:11; 86:3; 88:94, 105. In each instance it is used in connection with Babylon (representing the apostate world and church) or with the "great church, the mother of abominations" (representing the apostate church of the devil). Those who "drink of the wine of the wrath of her fornication" participate in the worldly pleasures and sins of the apostate world and church, and thus will reap the desolations and destruction that will come upon the wicked when they are judged.

35:13 *"weak things of the world"*

See *Weak things of the world* in Appendix A.

35:13 *"Thrash the nations"*

"This expression is found in Habakkuk 3:12. Threshing, in olden times, was done by treading out the grain on a threshing-floor. The going forth of the messengers of the gospel among the nations is like trampling the wheat sheaves on the hard floor. The valuable kernels are carefully gathered up; the straw is left." (Smith and Sjodahl, *DCC*, p. 186.)

The term is used twice in the Doctrine and Covenants: 35:13 and 133:59.

35:14   *"shield and their buckler"*

See *Armor of God* in Appendix A.

35:16   *"parable of the fig-tree"*

" 'Behold the fig tree and all trees; when they now shoot forth, ye see and know of your own selves that summer is now nigh at hand.' (Luke 21:29-30.) . . . This sign of events near at hand was equally applicable to the premonitory conditions which were to herald the fall of Jerusalem and the termination of the Jewish autonomy, and to the developments by which the Lord's second advent shall be immediately preceded." (James E. Talmage, *JC*, p. 574.)

35:18   *"keys of the mystery"*

See *Mysteries* in Appendix A.

35:18   *"from the foundation of the world"*

See *Pre-earthly existence* in Appendix A.

35:18   *"the time of my coming"*

See *Second coming* in Appendix A.

35:20   *"thou shalt write for him [Joseph Smith]"*

"To Sidney he [the Lord] gave a special command that he should write for Joseph. The Lord made known to Sidney what Joseph already understood—that the Scriptures should be given, even as they were in God's own bosom, to the salvation of his elect. And soon after this time, Joseph began a new translation of the Scriptures. While he labored, many truths, buried through scores of ages, where brought forth to his understanding, and he saw in their purity and holiness all the doings of God among his children, from the days of Adam unto the birth of our Lord and Savior." (George Q. Cannon, *LJS*, pp. 83-84.)

35:24   *"I will cause the heavens to shake"*

See *Second coming* in Appendix A.

35:24 *"Satan shall tremble and Zion shall rejoice"*

See *Satan* and *Zion* in Appendix A.

35:27 *"Fear not, little flock, the kingdom is yours until I come"*

"Do you know that it is the eleventh hour of the reign of Satan on the earth? Jesus is coming to reign, and all you who fear and tremble because of your enemies, cease to fear them, and learn to fear to offend God, fear to transgress his laws, fear to do any evil to your brother, or to any being upon the earth, and do not fear Satan and his power, nor those who have only power to slay the body, for God will preserve his people." (Brigham Young, *JD* 10:250.)

SECTION 36

Background information on section 36

See background information for section 35.

"In December Sidney Rigdon came to inquire of the Lord, and with him came Edward Partridge; the latter was a pattern of piety, and one of the Lord's great men. . . . And the voice of the Lord to Edward Partridge was: [Section 36, follows.]" (Joseph Smith, *HC* 1:128, 131.)

For biographical information on Edward Partridge, see the material following his name in Appendix B.

36:1 *"voice of a trump"*

See *Trump* in Appendix A.

36:2 *"the peaceable things of the kingdom"*

The principles of the gospel are based on the love of our Heavenly Father and his Son Jesus Christ for all mankind. The living of these principles results in an inner spiritual peace, "the peace of God, which passeth all understanding." (Philip. 4:7.) Such peace is a gift of God to all the obedient. (See Ps. 37:37; 119:165; Isa. 26:3; 48:18, 22; 57:21; Rom. 8:6; 10:15; 14:17-19; 1 Cor. 14:33; Eph. 6:15.)

The "peaceable things of the kingdom" are the basic principles of the gospel, for their observance will lead to peace. If all the people on the earth would live the principles of the gospel fully, peace would be the natural and inevitable result. The gospel of Christ is truly the gospel of peace, and one of the Savior's titles is the Prince of Peace.

"The peace of Christ does not come by seeking the superficial things of life, neither does it come except as it springs from the individual's heart. Jesus said to his disciples: 'Peace I leave with you. My peace I give unto you; not as the world giveth, give I unto you.' [John 14:27.] Thus the Son of Man as the executor of his own will and testament gave to his disciples and to mankind the 'first of all human blessings.' It was a bequest conditioned upon obedience to the principles of the Gospel of Jesus Christ. It is thus be-queathed to each individual. No man is at peace with himself or his God who is untrue to his better self, who transgresses the law of right either in dealing with himself by indulging in passion, in appetite, yielding to temptations against his accusing conscience, or in dealing with his fellow men, being untrue to their trust. Peace does not come to the transgressor of law; peace comes by obedience to law, and it is that message which Jesus would have us proclaim among men." (David O. McKay, *CR,* October 1938, p. 133.)

36:3 *"Hosanna"*

See *Hosanna* in Appendix A.

36:6 *"Untoward generation"*

If a person is in favor of a particular thing or position, he is said to favor or "lean toward" it. An "untoward genera-tion" concerning the things of God is a generation that disobeys the commandments and thus proves it is not in favor of the plan of God. The characteristics of an untoward generation include disobedience, wickedness, and rebellion. This term is used once in the Bible (Acts 2:40) and twice in the Doctrine and Covenants (36:6 and 109:41). "This is an untoward generation, walking in spiritual darkness." (Joseph Fielding Smith, *CHMR* 1:150.)

36:6 *"garments spotted with the flesh"*

See *Garments* in Appendix A.

"He [Edward Partridge] was baptized by the Prophet in December 1830, while on the visit to Fayette, and was com-manded to proclaim the Gospel with a loud voice along with others who were ordained, to cry repentance saying: [Sec. 36:6, quoted.] . . . Garments spotted with flesh are garments defiled by the practices of carnal desires and disobedience to the commandments of the Lord." (Joseph Fielding Smith, *CHMR* 1:150.)

36:8 *"gird up your loins"*

See *Armor of God* in Appendix A.

36:8 *"I will suddenly come to my temple"*

"The Lord said to Edward Partridge that he would sud-denly come to his temple. There are several comings spoken of wherein the Lord will come to his temple. This promise

Edward Partridge witnessed, for he was present at the dedication of the Kirtland Temple, and the Lord came suddenly there to Joseph Smith and Oliver Cowdery and ministered unto them. He was also present at that dedication by his Spirit." (Joseph Fielding Smith, *CHMR* 1:163.)

SECTION 37

Background information on section 37

"It may be well to observe here, that the Lord greatly encouraged and strengthened the faith of His little flock, which had embraced the fulness of the everlasting Gospel, as revealed to them in the Book of Mormon, by giving some more extended information upon the Scriptures, a translation of which had already commenced. Much conjecture and conversation frequently occurred among the Saints, concerning the books mentioned, and referred to, in various places in the Old and New Testaments, which were now nowhere to be found. The common remark was, 'They are *lost books*'; but it seems the Apostolic Church had some of these writings, as Jude mentions or quotes the Prophecy of Enoch, the seventh from Adam. To the joy of the little flock, which in all, from Colesville to Canandaigua, New York, numbered about seventy members, did the Lord reveal the following doings of olden times, from the prophecy of Enoch: [Moses 7] . . .

"Soon after the words of Enoch were given, the Lord gave the following commandment: [D&C 37]." (Joseph Smith, *HC* 1:131-33, 139.)

"Section 37 is a revelation given to Joseph Smith and Sidney Rigdon in Fayette, while Sidney Rigdon was visiting the Prophet in December, 1830: It seems that, in keeping with the commandment previously given, Sidney Rigdon had commenced to write for the Prophet in his 'translation' or revision of the Scriptures. The Lord now commands them to cease for a season and prepare to go to the Ohio, because of their enemies and for their sakes.

"The call to the Ohio was for two reasons. The opposition to the Church in and around Fayette had become bitter. There had been many converts made among the followers of Sidney Rigdon in Kirtland, and the spirit there was friendly. The trend of the Church was ever westward; as persecution

arose, and it became necessary to seek protection, the
Church moved farther and farther west. The Lord had a
design in this. The place of the City of Zion was west and it
was necessary that eventually the Church be located there,
although it would not be a permanent residence until Zion is
redeemed. Not only were Joseph Smith and Sidney Rigdon
commanded to go to Ohio, but this came as a command to
the entire Church." (Joseph Fielding Smith, *CHMR* 1:163.)

For biographical information on Sidney Rigdon, see material listed after his name in Appendix B.

37:1 *"it is not expedient in me that ye should translate any
more until ye shall go to the Ohio"*

"Before the close of December 1830, after Sidney had
been aiding Joseph some little time, the Lord required the
Prophet to temporarily cease his work of translation. The
enemy of all truth was drawing his forces around about
Fayette to achieve the destruction of the Prophet, and the
downfall of the newly-founded Church. But they were to be
foiled. Fayette was not the region where the Lord designed
his people to settle. Joseph's mind had been led to look to
the western country for that purpose. Contact with Sidney
Rigdon and Edward Partridge confirmed his inclination in
that direction. The time had now arrived when it appeared
necessary for the accomplishment of God's purposes, that his
people (now increased to several score,) should have an
abiding-place. It was made known to Joseph by revelation
from the Lord, where this new resting-place should be. [V.
3.] He himself, did not expect to escape personal suffering or
persecution by this new move; nor was this in the providence
of God concerning him. But he knew that every migration
made by him under the direction of the Almighty had been
followed by prosperity and increase to the work, and he,
therefore, obeyed the command to move to the place
designated by the Lord without hesitation or doubt.

"In the revelation now referred to [Sec. 37], it was commanded that the people of God should assemble in the State
of Ohio, and there await the return of Oliver Cowdery and
his fellow-missionaries from their eventful journey into the
wilderness. Thus early in the history of the Church was the
destiny of the people outlined. Kirtland was to be a stake of

Zion: blessed by the presence of God's anointed Prophet and the Apostles of our Lord Jesus Christ: glorified by a temple built to the name of the Most High; and worthy to receive the ministrations in person of the Only Begotten Son of the Eternal Father." (George Q. Cannon, *LJS,* pp. 84-85.)

SECTION 38

Background information on section 38

"The year 1831 opened with a prospect great and glorious for the welfare of the kingdom; for on the 2nd of January, 1831, a conference was held in the town of Fayette, New York, at which the ordinary business of the Church was transacted; and in addition, the following revelation was received: [D&C 38.]" (Joseph Smith, *HC* 1:140.)

"While the Church was in New York, the Lord gave this commandment that they should move the headquarters of the Church to Kirtland, Ohio, and there he would give them his law for the government of the Church. . . . This law is embodied in Section 42, which was received shortly after the Church moved to Ohio." (Joseph Fielding Smith, *CHMR* 1:169-70.)

38:1 *Titles of the Lord*

See *I AM, Alpha and Omega, Creator,* and *Jesus Christ* in Appendix A.

38:1 *"seraphic hosts of heaven"*

"*Seraphs* are angels who reside in the presence of God. . . . It is clear that seraphs include the unembodied spirits of pre-existence, for our Lord 'looked upon the wide expanse of eternity, and *all the seraphic hosts of heaven, before the world was made.*' (D&C 38:1.) Whether the name *seraphs* also applies to perfected and resurrected angels is not clear . . . In Hebrew the plural of seraph is seraphim." (Bruce R. McConkie, *MD*, pp. 702-3.)

"In a vision of the Prophet Isaiah (6:2-3) seraphim are standing over the throne of God, in the attitude of service. They are the attendants of Jehovah, reflecting His glory and majesty, and, in His presence, they sing in chorus, 'Holy, holy, holy is the Lord of Hosts: The whole Earth is full of His glory.' Our Lord looked upon these hosts. They were standing before Him, awaiting His commands, even before the Earth had been created." (Smith and Sjodahl, *DCC*, p. 198.)

For scriptural references to seraphs or seraphim, see Isa. 6:2, 6; 2 Ne. 16:2, 6; D&C 38:1; 109:79.

38:2 *God "knoweth all things, for all things are present" before his eyes*

See *Knowledge of God* in Appendix A.

38:3 *Jesus Christ created the world and "all things" came by him*

See *Creator* in Appendix A.

38:4 *"I . . . have taken the Zion of Enoch into mine own bosom"*

See *Zion* in Appendix A.

"This city called 'Zion' because its inhabitants were all righteous and 'pure in heart' (D&C 97:21) will return when the Millennial reign is come. (Moses 7:63.)

"Enoch, the seventh from Adam (Jude 14) built a city called Zion, after the people of God, so named by the Lord, because they were united, righteous, and prosperous. This city of Enoch flourished for three hundred and sixty-five years and then the Lord, by some process not known to us, took it with all its inhabitants, 'to His bosom,' thus saving them from destruction in the flood that was to come. 'And from thence went forth the saying, Zion is fled' (Moses 7:18, 19, 68, 69). The building up of another Zion in the latter days was predicted by the prophets of old. David, for instance, says, 'When the Lord shall build up Zion, he shall appear in his glory' (Psalm 102:16). That the people of God in the latter days should be found in a mountain region, was also foretold. 'O Zion, that bringest good tidings, get thee up into a high mountain' (Isaiah 40:9, see also Ezekiel 40:2, etc.)." (Smith and Sjodahl, *DCC*, p. 199.)

"If we would carry out that which the Lord revealed, . . . it would only be a matter of a very short time until this great people would be in the same condition, absolutely, as were the people in the city of Enoch. We would be able to walk with God, we would be able to behold his face, because then faith would abound in the hearts of the people to the full extent that it would be impossible for the Lord to withhold himself, and he would reveal himself unto us as he has done in times past." (Joseph Fielding Smith, *CR,* April 1921, p. 40.)

38:9 *"gird up your loins"*

See *Armor of God* in Appendix A.

38:12 *"the angels are waiting . . . to gather the tares that they may be burned"*

See *Tares* in Appendix A.

"It certainly is time that we prepare ourselves for that which is to come. Great things await this generation—both Zion and Babylon. All these revelations concerning the fall of Babylon will have their fulfillment. Forty-five years ago, in speaking to the Church, the Lord said—[Sec. 38:10-11, quoted.] This causes silence to reign, and all eternity is pained. The angels of God are waiting to fulfill the great commandment given forty-five years ago, to go forth and reap down the earth because of the wickedness of men. How do you think eternity feels today? Why there is more wickedness, a thousand times over, in the United States now, than when that revelation was given. The whole earth is ripe in iniquity; and these inspired men, these Elders of Israel, have been commanded of the Almighty to go forth and warn the world, that their garments may be clear of the blood of all men." (Wilford Woodruff, *JD* 18:128.)

38:16-17 *"I have made the earth rich"*

"The Lord has made the earth rich. On it is to be found everything which is essential to the welfare and happiness of man. All things are placed here for the use of man, and it is pleasing to our Father in Heaven when we use them in righteousness. But beyond all the wealth and comforts of the world, the greatest riches, we are told, are those which come through obedience to the Gospel. 'He that hath eternal life is rich!' " (Joseph Fielding Smith, *CHMR* 1:169.)

38:18 *"deign"*

One basic meaning of *deign* is "to condescend to give or offer." It is evidently in this sense that the word is used here.

38:21 *"I will be your king and watch over you"*

"This will be when he descends in the clouds of heaven in power and glory. Let all people know that the parable of the fig tree is being fulfilled today. The tree puts forth its leaves and the summer is nigh. We are told that when we see these things we may know that in this generation, when these things take place, all that has been said concerning the coming Christ will be fulfilled." (Joseph Fielding Smith, *Progress of Man,* p. 490.)

38:24   *"let every man esteem his brother as himself"*

"This is made possible in the kingdom of God, because there the standard of superiority is different from that which governs in the world. It is, in fact, inverted: 'He that is greatest among you shall be your servant' (Matt. 23:11). There is no exalted position in the kingdom of God but that of service. 'I,' saith the Lord, 'am among you as he that serveth' (Luke 22:27). In this kingdom, therefore, there can be no competition for 'first' places; no envy, no agitation for offices. And it is, consequently, not impossible for every man to 'esteem his brother as himself.' " (Smith and Sjodahl, *DCC,* p. 205.)

38:27   *"if ye are not one ye are not mine"*

"If we are not united, we are not his. Here unity is the test of divine ownership as thus expressed. If we would be united in love and fellowship and harmony, this Church would convert the world, who would see in us the shining example of these qualities which evidence that divine ownership." (Harold B. Lee, *CR,* April 1950, p. 96.)

"In union there is strength, but how can a people become united while their interests are diversified? How can they become united in spiritual matters, and see eye to eye, which they can only partly understand, until they become united in regard to temporal things, which they do comprehend?" (First Presidency, *MS* 16:427, July 8, 1854.)

"The unity of the members of the Church is essential to their happiness and eternal welfare. Jesus said to his disciples, 'Why call ye me Lord, Lord, and do not the things which I say!' If we are divided and permit contention and strife to prevail among us, then we cannot receive the blessings which the Lord has for us." (Joseph Fielding Smith, *CHMR* 1:169.)

38:28 *"the enemy in the secret chambers"*

"The hatred of the wicked always has and always will follow the Priesthood and the saints. The devil will not lose sight of the power of God vested in man—the Priesthood. He fears it, he hates it, and will never cease to stir up the hearts of the debased and corrupt in anger and malice towards those who hold this power, and to persecute the saints, until he is bound." (Joseph F. Smith, *JD* 19:24.)

38:29 *"ye know not the hearts of men in your own land"*

"We cannot know the hearts of men, nor the will of God concerning nations, kingdoms and people only as it is revealed to us by the gift and power of the Holy Ghost." (Wilford Woodruff, *JD* 10:215.)

38:30 *"if ye are prepared ye shall not fear"*

"My text today is from a revelation of the Lord to Joseph Smith, the Prophet, at a conference of the Church January 2, 1831, as follows: '. . . if ye are prepared ye shall not fear.' (D&C 38:30.) [D&C 1:12, 17 also quoted.]

"What are some of the calamities for which we are to prepare? In section 29 the Lord warns us of 'a great hailstorm sent forth to destroy the crops of the earth.' (D&C 29:16.) In section 45 we read of 'an overflowing scourge; for a desolating sickness shall cover the land.' (D&C 45:31.) In section 63 the Lord declares he has 'decreed wars upon the face of the earth. . . .' (D&C 63:33.)

"In Matthew, chapter 24, we learn of 'famines, and pestilences, and earthquakes. . . .' (Matt. 24:7.) The Lord declared that these and other calamities shall occur. These particular prophecies seem not to be conditional. The Lord, with his foreknowledge, knows that they will happen. Some will come about through man's manipulations; others through the forces of nature and nature's God, but that they will come seems certain. Prophecy is but history in reverse—a divine disclosure of future events.

"Yet, through all of this, the Lord Jesus Christ has said: '. . . if ye are prepared ye shall not fear.' (D&C 38:30.)

"What, then, is the Lord's way to help us prepare for these calamities? The answer is also found in section 1 of the Doctrine and Covenants, wherein he says: [D&C 1:17-18, 37 quoted].

"Here then is the key—look to the prophets for the words of God, that will show us how to prepare for the calamities which are to come. [D&C 1:38 quoted.]" (Ezra Taft Benson, *Ensign*, January 1974, pp. 68-69.)

"No man need fear in his heart when he is conscious of having lived up to the principles of truth and righteousness as God has required it at his hands, according to his best knowledge and understanding." (Joseph F. Smith, *CR*, April 1904, p. 2.)

38:32 *"go to the Ohio"*

"While the Church was in New York, the Lord gave this commandment that they should move the headquarters of the Church to Kirtland, Ohio, and there he would give them his law for the government of the Church. He had already given them much of his law in the revelations received up to this time, but he had in store for them something more. The Church had grown in membership and it was time for other instruction to be given for the benefit of the members. This law is embodied in Section 42, which was received shortly after the Church moved to Ohio. The Elders were also promised an endowment when they were located in Ohio. This necessitated also the building of the temple at that place." (Joseph Fielding Smith, *CHMR* 1:169-70.)

38:39 *"riches of eternity"*

See *Riches of eternity* in Appendix A.

38:42 *"Be ye clean that bear the vessels of the Lord"*

See *Vessels of the Lord* in Appendix A.

234

SECTION 39

Background information on section 39

"Not long after this conference of the 2nd of January closed, there was a man came to me by the name of James Covill, who had been a Baptist minister for about forty years, and covenanted with the Lord that he would obey any command that the Lord would give to him through me, as his servant, and I received the following: [Section 39, follows.]" (Joseph Smith, *HC* 1:143.)

"We may well believe that much of this doctrine was new to James Covill. The Lord stated that he knew his works and he knew him, and that at this particular time his heart was right, and the Lord had placed great blessings upon him. He had seen great sorrow, and many times he had rejected the Lord because of his pride and the cares of the world.

"He was promised that the day of his deliverance had come, if he would hearken unto the voice of the Lord. It seems from this commandment and promise that there had been times when Mr. Covill had received a desire to join the Church, but had weakened because of his pride and the love of the world. Now, however, he had come seeking the truth, and the Lord informs him that is to him the day of deliverance from these worldly cares if he will now abide in the truth." (Joseph Fielding Smith, *CHMR* 1:158-59.)

39:1 *"eternity to all eternity, the Great I AM"*

See *Eternity to eternity, I AM,* and *Jesus Christ* in Appendix A.

39:2 *"a light which shineth in darkness"*

See *Light* in Appendix A.

39:3 *"came in the meridian of time unto mine own"*

See *Meridian of time* and *Jews* in Appendix A.

39:6 *"peaceable things of the kingdom"*

See material for D&C 36:2.

39:13 *"labor in my vineyard . . . bring forth Zion"*

      See *Vineyard* and *Zion* in Appendix A.

39:18 *"become sanctified"*

      See *Sanctify* in Appendix A.

39:19 *"Hosanna"*

      See *Hosanna* in Appendix A.

SECTION 40

See background information for section 39.

"We are led to believe that in this promised blessing, this foolish man was convinced of the truth, for it is clear that the Lord revealed to him things which he and the Lord alone knew to be the truth. However, when he withdrew from the influence of the Spirit of the Lord and had time to consider the fact that he would lose the fellowship of the world, and his place and position among his associates, he failed and rejected the promises and blessings which the Lord offered him." (Joseph Fielding Smith. *CHMR* 1:174.)

40:1-3 *Satan tempted James Covill and he rejected the gospel*

See *Satan* in Appendix A.

"When the Gospel came in its purity and plainness, and they did not receive it, then commenced their condemnation. This was the condemnation of the people in the days of Jesus. When light came into the world they were condemned because they rejected it. 'This is condemnation,' says Jesus, 'that light is come into the world and men loved darkness rather than light, because their deeds were evil.' [John 3:19.] . . . There are many instances, doubtless, in your own experience of this kind; and they have gone backward from the time they rejected the truth; they have lost the favor of man, which they rejected the truth to obtain, have been disgraced in the sight of their fellow men and have met with the very things they desired to shun. Because of the rejection of the truth by men, the anger of the Lord is kindled against them and his judgments come upon them." (George Q. Cannon, *MS* 25:118.)

"There are still others who love the truth and who recognize it, but they dare not espouse it; they are afraid of the social consequences. This whole broad land, this whole broad world, is sprinkled with such people. When the principles of the Gospel are presented to them they say, in surprise and astonishment. 'Is that Mormonism? I never dreamed it. Why, that is true—I believe it with all my heart.' And the tears spring to their eyes as they acknowledge it. But they don't come out in the open and fight for it." (Orson F. Whitney, *CR*, April 1915, p. 102.)

SECTION 41

Background information on section 41

"The latter part of January [1831], in company with Brothers Sidney Rigdon and Edward Partridge, I started with my wife for Kirtland, Ohio, where we arrived about the first of February, and were kindly received and welcomed into the house of Brother Newel K. Whitney. My wife and I lived in the family of Brother Whitney several weeks, and received every kindness and attention which could be expected, and especially from Sister Whitney.

"The branch of the Church in this part of the Lord's vineyard, which had increased to nearly one hundred members, were striving to do the will of God, so far as they knew it, though some strange notions and false spirits had crept in among them. With a little caution and some wisdom, I soon assisted the brethren and sisters to overcome them. The plan of 'common stock,' which had existed in what was called 'the family,' whose members generally had embraced the everlasting Gospel, was readily abandoned for the more perfect law of the Lord; and the false spirits were easily discerned and rejected by the light of revelation.

"The Lord gave unto the Church the following: [D&C 41.]" (Joseph Smith, *HC* 1:145-47.)

"Because there were those who had professed the name of the Lord and made covenant to serve him, like James Covill, for instance, and then they showed by their works that they did not act in sincerity, the Lord gave a revelation [section 41] for the guidance of the members and a warning to those who had professed his name who had not obeyed him. This is one of the most solemn and pointed declarations that can be found in any scripture against the hypocrite and the person who professes in sincerity, and apparently accepts in good faith, a covenant and then departs from the covenant." (Joseph Fielding Smith, *CHMR* 1:177-78.)

41:1-4 *"elders of my church . . . ye shall see that my law is kept"*

"I desire now to read a few words in relation to the duty which devolves upon the men who have been speaking during this conference. I will read a portion of the 41st Section of the Doctrine and Covenants. [Sec. 41:1-4, quoted.]

"The Lord here especially demands of the men who stand at the head of this Church and who are responsible for the guidance and direction of the people of God, that they shall see to it that the law of God is kept. It is our duty to do this. . . . The Lord requires of us that we shall see that his law is kept among the people." (Joseph F. Smith, *CR,* October 1899, p. 41.)

41:4 *"I will be your ruler"*

"In the Church of Jesus Christ, it is our Redeemer who is the ruler. Many times we have heard President Joseph F. Smith, and other Presidents, say, when they have been addressed, or spoken of, as being the head of the Church, that this was not the case. No man stands at the head of the Church but Jesus Christ, whose Church it is. This is vital to the true Church. The President of the Church on earth is the representative and 'mouthpiece' of our Lord, appointed to conduct the affairs of the Church in this mortal sphere. 'I will be your ruler when I come,' said the Lord. In the meantime his officers are to see that his law is kept." (Joseph Fielding Smith, *CHMR* 1:164.)

41:6 *"it is not meet that the things which belong to the children of the kingdom should be given to them that are not worthy"*

See *Meet* in Appendix A.

"The things of the kingdom are not for the unworthy, whether they are in or out of the Church. It is the duty of the members to hold in the most solemn and sacred manner every commandment, every covenant, every principle of truth which the Lord has revealed for their salvation. He has given to the members, if they will humbly receive them, covenants and obligations which are not for the world. Things that are most holy and sacred, which are revealed to those who have made covenant to be 'just and true,' and who have 'overcome by faith,' things which are imparted to them as a means of bringing to pass their exaltation, should not be lightly treated, ridiculed, or spoken of before the world." (Joseph Fielding Smith, *CHMR* 1:179-80.)

41:7   *"Joseph Smith, Jun., should have a house built"*

"After the Prophet arrived in Kirtland, and away from the opposition and hate that was so prevalent in and around Fayette, New York, the Lord called upon him to commence a very important work, that of revising the Bible and restoring to the words of the ancient Hebrew prophets many of the things that had been taken away. He was without a home and without any kind of office. For a time he boarded with the Whitney family. The Lord said to the members of the Church: [Sec. 41:7, quoted.] It was also necessary that Sidney Rigdon be cared for in some manner, as he was to be scribe for the Prophet in his great undertaking. Under all the conditions, some of them very unfavorable, it is remarkable what was accomplished." (Joseph Fielding Smith, *CHMR* 1:164.)

41:9   *"Edward Partridge . . . should be appointed . . . and ordained a bishop unto the church"*

For biographical information on Edward Partridge, see the material following his name in Appendix B.

"It was a magnificent tribute that the Lord paid to Edward Partridge in this revelation of February 4, 1831. He was called to be a bishop of the Church, and to be 'ordained a bishop unto the Church, and to leave his merchandise and to spend all his time in the labors of the Church.' . . . In subsequent revelations these duties were explained and the knowledge imparted that men called to this office were to be engaged in the temporal affairs of the Church particularly. There is such an inference in the fact that the Lord directed Edward Partridge to discontinue his merchandising and devote all of his time to the Church. Immediately following his appointment, he was assigned to actual duties according to the calling of a bishop and was engaged in caring for the members of the Church in relation to their lands, inheritances, and other temporal matters which were vital to the members concerned." (Joseph Fielding Smith, *CHMR* 1:180-81.)

41:11   *Edward Partridge compared to Nathanael of old*

In John 1:45-49 the Savior remarked concerning Nathanael, *"Behold an Israelite indeed, in whom is no guile!"*

SECTION 42

Background information on section 42

"In December, 1830, the Church was commanded to move its headquarters from New York state to Ohio, where the Lord promised to give his law for its government. February 9, 1831, after the Church had removed to Kirtland and had been augmented by many converts from among the Disciples, or followers of the Campbells and Sidney Rigdon, who were living in Kirtland and its vicinity, the Lord gave to the Church this revelation (Sec. 42) as a law. In this revelation many commandments given from the very beginning and reiterated in the days of Moses were again proclaimed as being in force for the government of the Church in these latter days. By grave and solemn proclamation, the members of the Church were commanded to observe all these laws and others which were yet future, but would be given for the establishment of the City of Zion—New Jerusalem—which was to be built by the law of consecration and obedience to the fulness of the Gospel." (Joseph Fielding Smith, *CHMR* 1:183-84.)

"Altogether this was a most important revelation. It threw a flood of light upon a great variety of subjects and settled many important questions. Faithful men and women were greatly delighted at being members of a Church which the Lord acknowledged as His own, and to which He communicated His word through his inspired Prophet as he did at this time." (George Q. Cannon, *LJS,* pp. 87-88.)

"This Revelation is called the Law of Christ (v. 2). In the Scriptures the Law of God is always a manifestation of His will. In nature the laws of nature are His laws. God's will determines the moral standards. It is the rule of conduct. It is necessary that God should give laws to His children. There is in every man a disposition to lord it over others. Everyone, as soon as he has formed an opinion on a subject, is inclined to force it upon others, just as Lucifer proposed to do with regard to the plan of salvation. But when God manifests *His* will, all men and women are brought to a level of equality, without which there can be no true liberty. Hence, under the divine law liberty is possible, since all are under equal obligation to obey, and have an equal chance of obtaining the reward of obedience." (Smith and Sjodahl, *DCC*, p. 238.)

42:1 *"Jesus Christ the Son of the living God"*

See *Jesus Christ* and *Living God* in Appendix A.

42:5 *"for a little season"*

See *Season* in Appendix A.

42:6 *"preaching my gospel, two by two"*

See *Missionary* in Appendix A.

"We have been and are, willing to make much sacrifice for those who have not heard the truth. . . . Why do they do this? It does not help them financially. They do it because it is a duty they owe their fellow men, and therefore, when they are called they go forth gladly. They do not ask what their salary will be nor where the money will come from. If they have the means, they are willing to make the sacrifice and spend their time in this labor of love amongst their fellow men." (Anthon H. Lund, *CR*, April 1905, p. 14.)

42:6 *"sound of a trump"*

See *Trump* in Appendix A.

42:9 *"New Jerusalem"*

"Without modern revelation we would be in complete ignorance, as is the outside religious world, concerning the New Jerusalem. Being without revelation and relying solely on what is written in the Bible, the world has erroneously interpreted the revelations and prophecies in the Bible regarding the New Jerusalem. They have confounded these prophetic sayings as having reference to the old Jerusalem. This is true also of the references to Zion. These terms, Zion and Jerusalem, are used frequently interchangeably and if the Lord had not given us light we would have been as badly confused as are other people. However, there are many references which point clearly to the fact that Zion and Jerusalem are two separate and distinct places." (Joseph Fielding Smith, *CHMR* 1:412.)

42:10   *"my servant Edward Partridge"*

For biographical information on Edward Partridge, see the information following his name in Appendix B.

42:11-14   *"preach my gospel"*

See *Missionary service* in Appendix A.

"As agents of the Lord we are not called or authorized to teach the philosophies of the world or the speculative theories of our scientific age. Our mission is to preach the doctrines of salvation in *plainness* and simplicity as they are revealed and recorded in the scriptures.

"After directing us to teach the principles of the gospel found in the standard works, as guided by the Spirit, the Lord then made that great pronouncement which governs all the teaching of his gospel by anyone in the Church: 'And the Spirit shall be given unto you by the prayer of faith; and if ye receive not the Spirit ye shall not teach.' (D&C 42:14.)" (Joseph Fielding Smith, *IE,* December 1970, p. 2.)

42:11   *"except he be ordained by some one who has authority"*

"In section 42 of the Doctrine and Covenants, the Lord sets forth the conditions for service in his kingdom. . . . [D&C 42:11 quoted.]

"This indicates that the Lord will select those who are to act for him. No one is authorized to take this authority or honor to himself; rather, an authorized servant of the Lord will ordain them or set them apart to a specific assignment, and it will be known that the authorizing agent has such authority because he will have been regularly ordained to *his* position by the heads of the Church." (Hartman Rector, Jr., *Ensign,* January 1974, p. 105.)

42:12   *"elders, priests and teachers . . . shall teach the principles of my gospel"*

"Apparently there were in the early Church those who taught for doctrines the sophistries of men. There are those today who seem to take pride in disagreeing with the orthodox teachings of the Church and who present their own opinions which are at variance with the revealed truth. Some may be partially innocent in the matter; others are feeding their own egotism; and some seem to be deliberate. Men may think as they please, but they have no right to impose upon others their unorthodox views. Such persons should realize that their own souls are in jeopardy. The Lord said to us through the Prophet Joseph Smith: [Sec. 42:12-14, quoted.]

"The great objective of all our work is to build character and increase faith in the lives of those whom we serve. If one cannot accept and teach the program of the Church in an orthodox way without reservations, he should not teach. It would be the part of honor to resign his position. Not only would he be dishonest and deceitful, but he is also actually under condemnation, for the Savior said that it were better that a millstone were hanged about his neck and he be cast into the sea than that he should lead astray doctrinally or betray the cause or give offense, destroying the faith of one of 'those little ones' who believe in him. And remember that this means not only the small children; it includes even adults who believe and trust in God. . . .

"In our own society, the murderer who kills the body is hunted, imprisoned, and executed, but the character who kills the soul by implanting doubt and shattering faith is permitted not only to go free but also is often retained in high places. The body which is killed will rise again in the resurrection with little damage to its eternal welfare, but he whose faith has been shattered may suffer long ages before complete restoration of spiritual stature can be had, if at all." (Spencer W. Kimball, *CR,* April 1948, p. 109.)

42:12 *"the Book of Mormon" contains "the fulness of the gospel"*

See *Gospel* in Appendix A.

42:14 *"the prayer of faith"*

"To continue with the revelation, now that the Lord has established the necessity for the Spirit, he proceeds to explain how to get the Spirit. The formula is apparently so simple:

"'And the Spirit shall be given unto you by the prayer of faith.' (D&C 42:14.)

"On the surface it appears that all that is necessary to receive the Spirit is to ask for it, but it is not quite so easy a question! What is the difference between just ordinary prayer and a 'prayer of faith'?

"As we consider that question, the difference is immediately apparent. The difference is *faith,* and what *is* faith? Of course, there are many definitions of faith, but one definition is 'a strong belief plus *action.*' It is not perfect knowledge (as Alma explains in Alma 32), but real faith lets a man *act* as if he knows it is true when he really doesn't.

"Therefore, faith in a real sense is power—power to act and perform without actual knowledge. The Lord's formula for receiving the Spirit, then, is to get on our knees and communicate with him. Tell him what we are going to do—make commitments with him—outline our program—and then get up off our knees and go and *do* precisely what we have told him we would do. In the *doing,* the Spirit comes." (Hartman Rector, Jr., *Ensign,* January 1974, pp. 106-7.)

42:14 *"if ye receive not the Spirit ye shall not teach"*

"All are to preach the Gospel, by the power and influence of the Holy Ghost; and no man can preach the Gospel without the Holy Ghost." (Joseph Smith, *HC* 2:477.)

"No man can teach the Word of Wisdom by the Spirit of God who does not live it. No man can proclaim this Gospel by the Spirit of the Living God unless that man is living his religion." (Heber J. Grant, *CR,* October 1937, p. 130.)

"One very important bit of instruction given to these early missionaries of the Church, which should be observed strictly today in all organizations, quorums and classes, as well as in the missions, is the commandment (verse 14) that those who received not the Spirit of the Lord should not teach. No one should be called upon to teach and no one should attempt to teach the doctrines of the Church unless he is fully converted and has an abiding testimony of their truth. This testimony can only be received through prayerful study and obedience to all the commandments of the Lord. No man or woman can teach by the Spirit what he or she does not practice. Sincerity, integrity and loyalty are essential factors, and these will be accompanied by the spirit of prayer. The Comforter, 'who knoweth all things,' we should rely on, and then our teachings shall be approved of our Father in heaven." (Joseph Fielding Smith, *CHMR* 1:184-85.)

42:17 *"the Comforter knoweth all things, and beareth record of the Father and of the Son"*

One of the major missions of the Comforter (Holy Ghost) is to testify of both the Father and the Son. The resurrected Jesus Christ taught: "I bear record of the Father, and the Father beareth record of me, and the Holy Ghost beareth record of the Father and me." (3 Ne. 11:32.)

42:18-28 *"Thou knowest my laws . . . in my scriptures"*

See *Ten Commandments* in Appendix A.

"Strange as it may seem, there are some people who believe that the Ten Commandments pertained to the law of Moses, and therefore when Christ came, these laws of the Decalogue were done away. Nothing could be farther from the truth. There is not a single commandment in the Decalogue that was not accepted by the people of God as a commandment from the very beginning. . . . In this Dispensation of the Fulness of Times, the Lord restated these fundamental laws and commanded us to observe them with the strictest obedience." (Joseph Fielding Smith, *CHMR* 1:185.)

42:18, 79 *Murderer not to be forgiven*

See *Killing* in Appendix A.

42:20 *"Thou shalt not steal"*

See *Stealing* in Appendix A.

"This commandment forbids all violations of the rights of property. But it also forbids those who have property and the power and influence that go with it, to use these in such a way as to prevent others from acquiring a just proportion of the resources of nature, or the accumulated wealth of mankind. Monopolies may be just as condemnable as anarchist plots. Dishonesty in the payment of wages, in weights and measures, in quality of commodities for which payment is exacted—all is stealing." (Smith and Sjodahl, *DCC,* p. 224.)

42:21 *"Thou shalt not lie"*

See *Lie* in Appendix A.

"This commandment forbids the violation of all obligations of truth. It should be noted that lying is a crime, not merely a fault, or a weakness. To bear false witness against a neighbor is an aggravated form of offense against this law, but to lie about him, or her, in private circles is very little better than testifying falsely in court." (Smith and Sjodahl, *DCC,* p. 255.)

42:22   *"love thy wife . . . cleave unto her and none else"*

"There are those married people who permit their eyes to wander and their hearts to become vagrant, who think it is not improper to flirt a little, to share their hearts, and have desire for someone other than the wife or the husband, the Lord says in no uncertain terms: [Sec. 42:22, quoted.]

"And, when the Lord says *all* thy heart, it allows for no sharing nor dividing nor depriving. And, to the woman it is paraphrased: 'Thou shalt love thy husband with *all* thy heart and shalt cleave unto him and none else.' The words *none else* eliminate everyone and everything. The spouse then becomes pre-eminent in the life of the husband or wife, and neither social life nor occupational life nor political life nor any other interest nor person nor thing shall ever take precedence over the companion spouse." (Spencer W. Kimball, *IE*, December 1962, p. 928.)

42:24-26   *"Thou shalt not commit adultery"*

See *Adultery* and *Sex sins* in Appendix A.

"Unlawful associations of the sexes have been designated by the Lord as among the most heinous of the sins; and the Church today regards individual purity in the sexual relation as an indispensable condition of membership. . . . Moreover, the Lord regards any approach to sexual sin as inconsistent with the professions of those who have received the Holy Spirit, for He has declared that 'he that looketh on a woman to lust after her, or if any shall commit adultery in their hearts, they shall not have the spirit, but shall deny the faith.' [See Sec. 63:16.]" (James E. Talmage, *AF*, p. 446.)

42:27   *"Thou shalt not speak evil of thy neighbor"*

"Speaking evil of one is classed as a sin against the law of the Gospel. It may be necessary when on the witness stand, or before an ecclesiastical court, to testify of one's sins, but to do so promiscuously is a sin. Even when called upon to testify, the testimony should be given in the spirit of brotherly kindness, not in the spirit of vindictiveness or gloating over the predicament of a fellow being where punishment awaits him. Speaking words that may prove harmful to another is a crime. Such words constitute the 'idle words' condemned by our Savior, for which there will come a day of judgment. (Matt 12:35-36.)" (Smith and Sjodahl, *DCC*, p. 226.)

42:29 *"If thou lovest me thou shalt serve me and keep all my commandments"*

"I believe this is the greatest lesson that can be learned—to do the right thing because you love the Lord. It is so vitally important that, I feel, if you do anything in righteousness for any other reason than you love the Lord, you are wrong—at least you are on very shaky ground. And, somewhere your reasons for acting in righteousness will not be strong enough to see you through. You will give way to expediency, or peer group pressure, or honor, or fame, or applause, or the thrill of the moment, or some other worldly reason. Unless your motives are built upon the firm foundation of love of the Lord, you will not be able to stand. . . .

"I pray that we may walk in righteousness because we love the Lord, for surely this *is* the right reason." (Hartman Rector, Jr., *Ensign,* January 1973, p. 130.)

42:30-36 *"consecrate of thy properties"*

See *Consecration* in Appendix A.

"In this revelation [section 42] the Law of Consecration is stated definitely as the law on which the New Jerusalem is to be built. This law is given for the benefit of the poor, for the building of Zion and the work of the ministry. . . . Let it be remembered that at this time (1831) the full organization of the Church had not been revealed, and some temporary arrangements were necessary until the full and complete organization should be established." (Joseph Fielding Smith, *CHMR* 1:185.)

42:35, 67 *"New Jerusalem"*

See *New Jerusalem* in Appendix A.

42:42 *"Thou shalt not be idle"*

See *Work* in Appendix A.

"There is such a thing as encouraging idleness and fostering pauperism among men. Men and women ought not to be willing to receive charity unless they are compelled to do so to keep from suffering. Every man and woman ought to possess the spirit of independence, a self-sustaining spirit, that would prompt him or her to say, when they are in need, 'I am willing to give my labor in exchange for that which you give me.' No man ought to be satisfied to receive, and to do nothing." (Joseph F. Smith, *CR,* April 1898, pp. 48-49.)

42:43-44, *"the elders . . . shall be called . . . and lay their hands upon*
48   *[the sick]"*

See *Healing* in Appendix A.

"In this revelation we get a very clear understanding of the law in relation to administration. The sick are to be nursed by members of the Church, not by enemies. The leaders are to lay hands upon the sick and if the sick have not been appointed unto death, and they and those who officiate for them have faith, they shall recover. We should remember that too frequently we lack the necessary faith, not because the Lord is not willing to give it to us, but because of our own disobedience and failure to live in accordance with the principles on which the Spirit of the Lord operates. (See Matt. 17:14-21.)" (Joseph Fielding Smith, *CHMR* 1:185-86.)

42:46   *"those that die in me shall not taste of death, for it shall*
be sweet unto them"

"Some people are confused on this subject [the doctrine of translated beings] by the following two statements by the Savior: '. . . ye shall never taste of death . . . ye shall never endure the pains of death.' (3 Nephi 28:7-8.) These statements *do not* mean the same as though the Savior had said 'Ye shall never die.' This is made clear in a revelation by the resurrected Jesus Christ to the Prophet Joseph Smith: 'And it shall come to pass that *those that die in me shall not taste of death,* for it shall be sweet unto them; And they that die not in me, wo unto them, for their death is bitter.' (D&C 42:46-47. Italics added.) In other words, death will be either a sweet or a bitter experience for people: if they are righteous, death will be a sweet experience—they will not taste of death nor feel the pains of death; if they are wicked, death will be a bitter experience. But both groups of people *must die.* As Paul stated, 'For as in Adam all die, even so in Christ shall all be made alive.' (1 Corinthians 15:22.)

"Joseph Fielding Smith has written the following concerning the present mortal condition of John the Beloved and the three Nephite disciples: '. . . translated beings are still mortal and will have to pass through the experience of death . . . although this will be instantaneous. . . . Translated beings have not passed through death; that is, they have not had the separation of the spirit and the body.' (*Answers to Gospel Questions* 1:165; 2:46.)

"And finally, the Prophet Joseph Smith has indicated that translated beings have future missions to perform: 'Translated bodies cannot enter into rest until they have undergone a change equivalent to death. Translated bodies are designed for future missions.' (*HC* 4:425.)" (*CBM*, pp. 293-94.)

"To some members of the Church the saying that those who die in the Lord shall not taste of death has been a hard saying. They have seen good faithful men and women suffer days and at times for months before they were taken. But here the Lord does not say they shall not suffer pain of body, but that they shall be free from the anguish and torment of soul which will be partaken of by the wicked, and although they may suffer in body, yet death to them will be sweet in that they will realize that they are worthy before the Lord. The Savior said to Martha: 'And whosoever liveth and believeth in me shall never die.' That is to say, they shall never die the second death and feel the torment of the wicked when they come face to face with eternity." (Joseph Fielding Smith, *CHMR* 1:186.)

42:61   *"peaceable things"*

See material for D&C 36:2.

42:64   *"secret combinations"*

The devil works through secret combinations to gain power and influence over the souls of men. Wicked people take secret oaths and vows in an attempt to protect themselves from the law and from the knowledge of other people as they murder, rob, plunder, and seek to obtain power by destroying the freedom of others.

Satan introduced these secret combinations in the days of Cain (Moses 5:16-59; 6:15), and they have been perpetuated by evil persons and secret societies since that time (Hel. 6:17-41; Ether 8:20). According to Moroni, such secret combinations led to the destruction of both the Jaredite and Nephite civilizations, and will lead to the overthrow of freedom in "all lands, nations, and countries" that allow these secret combinations to get power over the people. (Ether 8:14-26.)

"One of the most urgent, heart-stirring appeals made by Moroni as he closed the Book of Mormon was addressed to the gentile nations of the last days. He foresaw the rise of a great world-wide secret combination among the gentiles which '. . . *seeketh to overthrow the freedom of all lands, nations, and countries. . . .*' (Ether 8:25, italics added.) He warned each gentile nation of the last days to purge itself of this gigantic criminal conspiracy which would seek to rule the world. . . .

"The Prophet Moroni described how the secret combination would take over a country and then fight the work of God, persecute the righteous, and murder those who resisted. Moroni therefore proceeded to describe the working of the ancient 'secret combinations' so that modern man could recognize this great political conspiracy in the last days: . . . [Ether 8:23-25 quoted.]

"The Prophet Moroni seemed greatly exercised lest in our day we might not be able to recognize the startling fact that the same secret societies which destroyed the Jaredites and decimated numerous kingdoms of both Nephites and Lamanites would be precisely the same form of criminal conspiracy which would rise up among the gentile nations in this day.

"The strategems of the leaders of these societies are amazingly familiar to anyone who has studied the tactics of modern communist leaders." (Ezra Taft Benson, *CR*, September 1961, p. 71.)

". . . Latter-day Saints should have nothing to do with secret combinations and groups antagonistic to the constitutional law of the land, which the Lord suffered to be established, and which 'should be maintained for the rights and protection of all flesh according to just and holy principles.' " (David O. McKay, *Gospel Ideals,* p. 306.)

42:65 *"mysteries of the kingdom"*

See *Mysteries* in Appendix A.

42:73 *"the bishop . . . shall receive . . . a just remuneration for all his services in the church"*

This reference pertains to the Presiding Bishop of the Church, as no wards had been established nor bishops of wards ordained and set apart at the time this revelation was given.

42:74 *"fornication"*

"This term is sometimes used for all kinds of sexual sins (See 1 Cor. 7:2; Matt. 5:32; 1 Cor. 5:1), and also, figuratively, for idolatry (2 Chron. 21:11). But generally it stands for the sin of impurity when committed between unmarried persons." (Smith and Sjodahl, *DCC,* p. 236.)

42:78   *"keep all the commandments"*

"No man can find forgiveness for one sin because he is righteous in some other direction. In other words, the payment of tithing will never compensate for the desecration of the Sabbath day. The faithful keeping of the Sabbath day will never make amends for the breaking of the Word of Wisdom. The refraining from murder, and adultery, will not satisfy the law which forbids bearing false witness against neighbors, or coveting their possession. And the doing of good to men will never blot out the sin of blaspheming the name of the living God. We must keep the commandments, all of them, every one of them, every day of our lives, and then we will prove ourselves wise and of understanding hearts." (Hyrum M. Smith, *CR,* October 1917, p. 39.)

42:84-92   *"if he or she" commits a sin*

"Note the perfect equality in responsibility of the sexes, in the Law of God. 'If he or she' is guilty, the consequences are the same. There is no sex in crime. Equal 'rights,' to use a familiar expression, presuppose equality in responsibility." (Smith and Sjodahl, *DCC,* p. 237.)

"Our standard requires a young man to be as clean and as chaste and as pure as the girl he asks to be his wife, the mother of his children . . . We have no double standard. . . . We expect our boys to be as good as our girls, and as clean." (Melvin J. Ballard, *CR,* April 1929, pp. 67-68.)

SECTION 43

Background information on section 43

"In a revelation given in September, 1830 (Sec. 28), the Lord gave a law to the Church in regard to the receiving of revelation. This was called forth because of the Hiram Page incident. . . . Now, again, it becomes necessary for the Lord to give further instruction on this matter. The incident which called for this direction and law was due to the activity of a woman, Mrs. Hubble, who followed the lead of Hiram Page and endeavored to give revelation for the Church, and there were some who were willing to follow her. . . .

"This law is given for our government for all time. It is the one who holds the keys and who stands as the Presiding High Priest and President of the Church, who is the spokesman of the Lord for the members of the Church. Individual members may receive the inspiration and revelation for their own guidance, but not for the Church. Moreover, no member of the Church will profess to receive a revelation for his own guidance that is contradictory of any revelation coming from the President of the Church." (Joseph Fielding Smith, *CHMR* 1:172.)

"This woman's name, according to the history of the church kept by John Whitmer, was Hubble. 'She professed to be a prophetess of the Lord, and professed to have many revelations, and knew the Book of Mormon was true, and that she should become a teacher in the church of Christ. She appeared to be very sanctimonious and deceived some who were not able to detect her in her hypocrisy; others, however, had the spirit of discernment and her follies and abominations were manifest. (John Whitmer's *History of the Church,* ch. iii.)" (Joseph Smith, *HC* 1:154, footnote.)

"Soon after the foregoing revelation was received [Section 41], a woman, (Hubble) came making great pretensions of revealing commandments, laws and other curious matters; and as almost every person has advocates for both theory and practice, in the various notions and projects of the age, it became necessary to inquire of the Lord, when I received the following: [Section 43, follows.]" (Joseph Smith, *HC* 1:154.)

43:3 *"there is none other appointed . . . to receive commandments" for the Church*

"It is not the business of any individual to rise up as a revelator, as a prophet, as a seer, as an inspired man, to give revelation for the guidance of the Church, or to assume to dictate to the presiding authorities of the Church in any part of the world. . . .

"And the moment that individuals look to any other source, that moment they throw themselves open to the seductive influences of Satan, and render themselves liable to become servants of the devil; they lose sight of the true order through which the blessings of the Priesthood are to be enjoyed; they step outside of the pale of the kingdom of God, and are on dangerous ground. Whenever you see a man rise up claiming to have received direct revelation from the Lord to the Church, independent of the order and channel of the Priesthood, you may set him down as an impostor." (Joseph F. Smith, *JD* 24:188-90.)

43:4 *"he shall not have power except to appoint another"*

"This clause, at first sight, may appear difficult to understand. If the Prophet should be removed through apostasy, for instance, would he, in his fallen condition, be willing, or have authority, to ordain a successor? Would he not, more probably, make an effort to retain the position for himself? On the other hand, if the Prophet should be removed by death, how could he 'appoint another in his stead?' But whatever difficulty the passage may present, has been removed by God, when He inspired His servant to appoint a Council of Twelve Apostles and to confer upon this body all the keys, power, and authority which he held himself. Thus provision was made for a successor appointed and ordained, as the Revelation says he should be, through, or by, the Prophet, before his removal, fully equipped to step into the vacant place." (Smith and Sjodahl, *DCC*, p. 241.)

43:7 *"he that is ordained of me shall come in at the gate"*

"Let the members of the Church remember that the Lord

has said that when a man is called to any position of responsibility, and especially to preside over the Church, he will 'come in at the gate and be ordained as I have told you before, to teach those revelations which you have received and shall receive through him whom I have appointed.' (D&C 43:7.) This counsel and commandment was given that the Saints should know how to be edified and instructed and how to direct the Church in all holiness before the Lord. For many years our communities have been troubled with impostors claiming to be called of God to lead the Church as the 'one mighty and strong, holding the scepter of power,' and to set in order the inheritances. Some of these impostors have passed away, but others come, and at times are able to lead away unwise members who lack the understanding and knowledge by which the Church is governed. These revelations, given in 1830 and 1831, are for our benefit and guidance in all such matters. The Lord would have us know that he does all things in order, and whenever he calls one to lead the Church, that one will come in at the gate and be ordained by those who hold authority. It has been so from the beginning and will continue so to the end." (Joseph Fielding Smith, *CHMR* 1:137-38.)

43:8   *"instruct and edify each other"*

"By study of the principles of the Gospel, and by teaching each other, we learn how to act and how the Church should be governed. Every member of the Church should so live that by study, reflection, faith and prayer, and association with his fellow members in study, he may understand the order of the Church and how it is governed. Then if we will be faithful to the principles of truth that have been given for our guidance, we will be sanctified and will act in all holiness before the Lord." (Joseph Fielding Smith, *CHMR* 1:190.)

43:9, 11   *"be sanctified"*

See *Sanctify* in Appendix A.

"This means to be made clean and pure and fit for the service of the Lord. . . . By obedience to the Law of Christ the Saints are sanctified." (Smith and Sjodahl, *DCC*, p. 243.)

43:13   *"the mysteries of the kingdom"*

See *Mysteries* in Appendix A.

43:13   *"provide for him . . . whatsoever thing he needeth"*

"The Prophet's duties were many and arduous. It was impossible for him to attend to all that the Lord required of his hands and at the same time care for himself and family. Therefore, the Lord called upon the Saints, if they desired 'the glories of the kingdom,' which he was called upon to reveal to them, to provide for him food, raiment, shelter and 'whatsoever thing he needeth to accomplish the work wherewith I have commanded him.'" (Joseph Fielding Smith, *CHMR* 1:190.)

43:15   *"Ye are not sent forth to be taught, but to teach"*

"This is a truth which all our missionaries and teachers of the Gospel should comprehend. We have been given the privilege of the guidance of the Holy Ghost. This guidance will not come to us unless we obey the commands of the Lord and seek to know his doctrines. These we are sent out to teach as they have been revealed for the benefit of mankind. Therefore, we are duty bound to seek for our inspiration and knowledge through these revelations and commandments, and not from the doctrines and philosophies and theories of uninspired men in the world. . . . Above all, let us remember that, with the light of truth, we should be the teachers of the world, and not be partakers of their false teachings." (Joseph Fielding Smith, *CHMR* 1:190.)

"We have only one object in view in going out amongst the nations, and that is to follow the Master's instructions— to go out and teach men. That is our work. We do not go out to win battles as debaters; but we go out to teach men that which we have received, which we know is true." (Anthon H. Lund, *CR*, October 1902, pp. 80-81.)

43:17, 30   *"the great day of the Lord is nigh at hand"*

See *Second coming* in Appendix A.

"This is the message that the Prophet Joseph brought to the earth. At a general conference in Nauvoo, April 6th, 1843, he said, 'There are those of the rising generation who shall not taste death till Christ comes.' At the same time he was well aware that the coming of the Lord in the clouds was not to be expected immediately. Our Savior had told him, in answer to prayer, that, 'If thou livest until thou art eighty-five years old, thou shalt see the face of the Son of Man' (Sec.

130:15); but he was left in doubt as to whether this meant that Christ would come in power and glory at the end of the year 1890, or whether he (the Prophet) at that time, should be admitted to His presence. The Prophet says, 'I took the liberty to conclude that if I did live till that time, He would make his appearance.' (HC 5:336). This conclusion does not appear improbable. The work the Lord did accomplish through the Prophet Joseph in a few years, from 1830 to 1844, was certainly wonderful. What would it have been in 60 years! At the same time, the Prophet knew that many great events were to precede the Millennium." (Smith and Sjodahl, *DCC*, p. 246.)

43:21-22 *"the thunders . . . [and] lightnings . . . shall utter forth their voices"*

"The Lord will cause the thunders to utter their voices from the ends of the earth until they sound in the ears of all that live, and these thunders shall use the very words here predicted—'Repent, O ye inhabitants of the earth, and prepare the way of the Lord, prepare yourselves for the great day of the Lord.' These words will be distinctly heard by every soul that lives, whether in America, Asia, Africa, Europe, or upon the islands of the sea. And not only the thunders, but the lightnings will utter forth their voices in the ears of all that live, saying, 'Repent, for the great day of the Lord is come.' Besides the voices of thunder and lightning, the Lord himself, before he comes in his glory, will speak by his own voice out of heaven in the ears of all that live commanding them to repent and to prepare for his coming." (Orson Pratt, *JD* 15:332-33.)

43:24 *"as a hen gathereth her chickens under her wings"*

See material for 10:65.

43:26 *"cup of . . . indignation"*

See material for 29:17.

43:30 *"the great Millennium . . . shall come"*

See *Millennium* in Appendix A.

43:31 *"then cometh the end of the earth"*

See *Earth* in Appendix A.

"This earth is a living body. It is growing old like its inhabitants. After the Millennium, and the little season when Satan will be loosed to gather his forces and wickedness is found on the earth again, then this earth shall die. It will be consumed by fire and purified and receive its celestial resurrection that the righteous may inherit it forever." (Joseph Fielding Smith, *CHMR* 1:192.)

43:31 *"Satan shall be bound"*

See *Satan* in Appendix A.

"There are many among us who teach that the binding of Satan will be merely the binding which those dwelling on the earth will place upon him by their refusal to hear his enticings. This is not so. He will not have the privilege during that period of time to tempt any man. (D&C 101:28.)" (Joseph Fielding Smith, *CHMR* 1:192.)

43:34 *"let the solemnities of eternity rest upon your minds"*

This interesting statement indicates that we should ponder or think seriously about the truths that have to do with the eternities, such as the pre-earthly existence, the purposes of our mortal earthly experience, the plan of progression our Heavenly Father has for his children, the post-earthly spirit world, the kingdoms or degrees of glory, the promised possibility of Godhood, etc.

SECTION 44

Background information on section 44

"In the latter part of February, 1831, the Lord directed that the missionaries who had gone to the various parts of the Country be summoned to Kirtland to meet in a general Conference. . . . The Conference referred to in this Revelation convened at Kirtland, June 3rd, 1831. It was the Fourth General Conference of the Church, and the first gathering of its kind in Kirtland." (Smith and Sjodahl, *DCC*, p. 249.)

44:4 *"ye shall obtain power to organize yourselves according to the laws of man"*

"When the Lord restored the Gospel the spirit of gathering came with it. The Lord commanded the people to gather together, and that they should not only be organized as a Church, but that they should be organized under the laws of the land, so that they might not be helpless and dependent and without influence or power; but that by means of united effort and faith they should become a power for the accomplishment of righteousness in the earth. (D&C 44:4-5.) . . . For the gathering of the poor, for the spreading of the Gospel to the nations of the earth, for the maintenance of those who were required to give their constant attention day in and day out, to the work of the Lord, it was necessary to make some provision. Without this law these things could not be done, neither could temples be built and maintained, nor the poor fed and clothed." (Joseph F. Smith, *CR,* April 1900, p. 47.)

SECTION 45

Background information on section 45

"At this age of the Church [i.e., early in the spring of 1831] many false reports, lies, and foolish stories, were published in the newspapers, and circulated in every direction, to prevent people from investigating the work, or embracing the faith. A great earthquake in China, which destroyed from one to two thousand inhabitants, was burlesqued in some papers, as ' "Mormonism" in China.' But to the joy of the Saints who had to struggle against every thing that prejudice and wickedness could invent, I received the following: [D&C 45.]" (Joseph Smith, *HC* 1:158.)

"This earthquake in China is a matter of some interest in connection with the history of the church, since it was the means of bringing Simonds Ryder, a somewhat noted preacher of the Campbellite faith, into the Church. According to *Hayden's History of the Disciples on the Western Reserve* (a Campbellite book), Mr. Ryder was much perplexed over 'Mormonism,' and for a time was undecided whether to join the Church or not. 'In the month of June' (1831), writes Mr. Hayden, 'he read in a newspaper an account of the destruction of Pekin in China, and he remembered that six weeks before, a young "Mormon" girl had predicted the destruction of that city.' J. H. Kennedy, in his *Early Days of Mormonism* (Scribner's & Sons, 1888), refers to the same thing, and adds: 'This appeal to the superstitious part of his nature was the final weight in the balance and he threw the whole power of his influence upon the side of "Mormonism" ' (pp. 103-4). It was doubtless this prophecy and the conversion connected with it that led the papers mentioned in the text to refer to it as ' "Mormonism" in China.' " (Joseph Smith, *HC* 1:148, footnote.)

"Brothers and sisters, this is the day the Lord is speaking of. You see the signs are here. Be ye therefore ready. The Brethren have told you in this conference how to prepare to be ready. We have never had a conference where there has been so much direct instruction, so much admonition; when the problems have been defined and also the solution to the problem has been suggested. Let us not turn a deaf ear now, but listen to these as the words that have come from the Lord, inspired of him, and we will be safe on Zion's hill, until all that the Lord has for his children shall have been accomplished." (Harold B. Lee, *CR,* October 1973, p. 170.)

45:1-10 *Titles and powers of the Lord*

See *Jesus Christ* in Appendix A.

45:2 *"the summer shall be past"*

"One of the great failings of mankind is to ignore warnings of punishment for sin. In all ages of the world it has been the peculiar belief of men that the sayings of the prophets were to be fulfilled in times still future. That is true of the people today. We have had ample warning of the nearness of the coming of the great and dreadful day of the Lord. The signs are upon us in all their power. . . . In this revelation we are given the warning that the summer is passing and if we are heedless of the warning we will find the summer past, the harvest ended and our souls not saved. While no man knows the day or the hour, yet if we are taken unawares, we will be without excuse, for the signs are ample and we now see them being fulfilled." (Joseph Fielding Smith, *CHMR* 1:195.)

45:6 *"while it is called today"*

See *Today* in Appendix A.

45:7 *"a light that shineth in darkness"*

See *Light* in Appendix A.

45:8 *"mine own received me not"*

See *Jews* in Appendix A.

45:9 *"mine everlasting covenant . . . [and] standard"*

See *Covenant* in Appendix A.

"This Church is the standard which Isaiah said the Lord would set up for the people in the latter days. [Isa. 49:22.] This church was given to be a light to the world and to be a standard for God's people and for the Gentiles to seek to. This Church is the ensign on the mountain spoken of by the

Old Testament prophets. It is the way, the truth, and the life." (Marion G. Romney, *CR*, April 1961, p. 119.)

45:9   *"Gentiles"*

See *Gentiles* in Appendix A.

45:11-14   *"Enoch, and his brethren . . . were separated from the earth"*

See *Enoch* in Appendix A.

45:16-33,   The words of Jesus Christ to his disciples on the Mount of
35-39   Olives in New Testament times

This remarkable discourse of the Savior to his disciples is recorded in three of the Gospels (Matthew 24; Mark 13; Luke 21) and was restored to Joseph Smith and included as Joseph Smith—Matthew (JS 1) in the Pearl of Great Price. This thrilling and descriptive account in the Doctrine and Covenants (vv. 16-60) should be prayerfully and carefully compared with the other accounts.

45:19   *"thief in the night"*

This term has reference to the Lord's statement: ". . . if the goodman of the house had known in what watch the thief would come, he would have watched, and would not have suffered his house to be broken up. Therefore be ye also ready: for in such an hour as ye think not the Son of man cometh." (Matt. 24:43-44.)

Thus, the statement that the Lord will come as a "thief in the night" indicates that many people will be surprised and not prepared for him at his coming. In his epistle to the Thessalonian saints, Paul uses this analogy and suggests that saints who are guided by the Spirit and who watch for the signs of the times are not in darkness; therefore that day should not overtake them as a thief. (See 1 Thes. 4:16-18; 5:1-4.)

45:19   *"this people [Jews] shall be destroyed and scattered"*

"Jewish and Roman thought were incompatible, and in A.D. 66, thirty years after the crucifixion, a general revolt against Rome occurred, and the Jews took possession of Jerusalem. Vespasian and his son Titus were sent with a Roman army to bring them back into submission, and after a siege which continued about four years, one of the most frightful and atrocious sieges of history, characterized by unspeakable horrors, the city was taken by Titus, who burned the temple, leveled the city to the ground and scattered the Jewish people to the four corners of the earth. Historians tells us that the very foundation stones were dug up by the Romans in the hope that treasure might be found buried there. . . .

"I have gone briefly over the history of the past in order to bring before you . . . the undeniable evidence that the words uttered by Christ our Lord, in which he declared the destruction of the temple at Jerusalem and the scattering of the Jews, have been literally fulfilled. [Matt. 24:1-21.]" (Anthony W. Ivins, *CR,* October 1930, pp. 120-21.)

"I have before me a quotation of Will Durrant in his book, *The Story of Civilization,* in which he states that 'no people in history fought so tenaciously for liberty as the Jews, nor any other people against such odds.' He says further, 'No other people has ever known so long an exile, or so hard a fate.'

"Then referring to the siege of Jerusalem under Titus, lasting for 134 days, during which 1,110,000 Jews perished and 97,000 were taken captive, he states that the Romans destroyed 987 towns in Palestine and slew 580,000 men, and still a larger number, we are told, perished through starvation, disease, and fire. . . . Scarcely eight thousand Jews were left in all of Palestine. And even their banishment and scattering didn't end their persecution. . . .

"Yes, the prophecies regarding the dispersion and the suffering of Judah have been fulfilled." (Ezra Taft Benson, *CR,* April 1950, pp. 74-75.)

45:25 *"until the times of the Gentiles be fulfilled"*

See *Gentiles* in Appendix A.

"The prophecy in Section 45, verses 24-29, of the Doctrine and Covenants regarding the Jews was literally fulfilled. Jerusalem, which was trodden down by the Gentiles, is no longer trodden down, but is made the home for the Jews. They are returning to Palestine, and by this we may know that the times of the Gentiles are near their close.

"The words of the prophets are rapidly being fulfilled, but it is done on such natural principles that most of us fail to see it." (Joseph Fielding Smith, *CR,* April 1966, pp. 13, 15.)

45:26 *"men's hearts shall fail them"*

"We live in an age when, as the Lord foretold, men's hearts are failing them, not only physically but in spirit. (See D&C 45:26.) Many are giving up heart for the battle of life. Suicide ranks as a major cause of the deaths to college students. As the showdown between good and evil approaches with its accompanying trials and tribulations, Satan is increasingly striving to overcome the Saints with despair, discouragement, despondency, and depression.

"Yet, of all people, we as Latter-day Saints should be the most optimistic and the least pessimistic. For while we know that 'peace shall be taken from the earth, and the devil shall have power over his own dominion,' we are also assured that 'the Lord shall have power over his saints, and shall reign in their midst.' (D&C 1:35-36.)" (Ezra Taft Benson, *Ensign*, November 1974, p. 65.)

45:27 *"the love of men shall wax cold"*

"The expression is the same as that found in Matt. 24:12, where we read (translated literally), 'And because lawlessness has abounded, the love of the many [this indicates more than a few] shall wax cold.' 'Love' here means Christian unity, harmony. Where in the Christian world does that love, that oneness, prevail? There is an abundance of co-operation based on self-interest, or family connections: but where is there genuine Christian love, true, unselfish, constant? Its absence in the majority of men is one of the signs of the end." (Smith and Sjodahl, *DCC*, p. 262.)

45:28 *"a light shall break forth . . . it shall be the fulness of my gospel"*

See *Light* in Appendix A.

The word *light* is used in the scriptures to refer to several things having to do with the Lord and his gospel. Jesus Christ is the light and life of the world (John 1:4-5; 1 John 1:5; D&C 10:70; 11:28; 12:9; 34:2; 45:7). Truth is light (D&C 84:45; 88:6). In this revelation (D&C 45:28), light is given as being representative of the fulness of the gospel.

Also, the Savior uses the word *light* many times in sections 88 and 93 in referring to himself.

45:30 *"in that generation"*

See *Generation* in Appendix A.

45:31 *"a desolating sickness shall cover the land"*

See *Second coming* in Appendix A.

One of the impending signs of the second coming of Jesus Christ is that a desolating scourge or sickness shall cover the land. (D&C 5:19; 45:31.) Elder McConkie suggests that after the times of the Gentiles are fulfilled, "new and unheard of diseases will attack the human system." (*MD,* p. 654.) The following will result from at least one of these afflictions: "their flesh shall fall from off their bones, and their eyes from their sockets." (D&C 29:18-19.)

45:34-38 *Fulfillment of the parable of the fig tree*

One characteristic of a fig tree is that it does not put forth its leaves until relatively late in the year, long after most of the trees are in full leaf. The Savior used this feature in a parable concerning his second coming. Although the world will not know the day nor the hour of his coming, we should observe the signs of the times, for when the fig tree puts forth its leaves, we know that summer is nigh. In other words, when the signs of the second coming begin to be made manifest, we know that the second coming is nigh or near at hand.

"When Jesus said to his disciples in answer to their query: 'Show us when the end of the world shall come, and the time of thy coming' [Matt. 24:3], he spoke of certain signs that would indicate the time of his coming, the very signs that the world, if they only had eyes to see, could be beholding to-day: Said he: judge the matter even as you would judge the coming of spring. When you see the fig tree putting forth its leaf, ye know that summer is near, and so when you see these signs, you may know that the coming of the Son of man is nigh at hand." (Melvin J. Ballard, *CR,* October 1923, p. 32.)

45:40-44 *Events associated with the second coming*

See *Second coming* in Appendix A.

"If the signs of the coming of our Lord were apparent in the days of the Prophet, surely we have evidence today that the great day of his coming is drawing very near, for the signs have multiplied a thousand fold. . . . Troubles, wars, pestilence, one after another, will continue until the Ancient of Days shall come. He [Joseph Smith] saw men hunting the lives of their own sons, brother murdering brother, mothers and daughters at enmity. Armies were arrayed against armies, and there shall be blood, desolation, war and fire. Satan will rage, and then, he adds: 'I know not how soon these things will take place; but with a view of them, shall I cry peace? No! I will lift up my voice and testify of them. How long you will have good crops, and the famine be kept off, I do not know; when the fig tree leaves, know then that the summer is nigh at hand.' (*HC* 3:290-301.)" (Joseph Fielding Smith, *CHMR* 2:226-27.)

45:46 *"the saints shall come forth"*

"There must come a time, for the Lord has spoken it, when by some miraculous manner, he will gather from the four ends of the earth his people in a gathering which does not have to do with that which has already taken place.

"This seems to be a time to come—near the great day of resurrection (D&C 45:46 and Moses 7:62-63) and just preceding the time when the 'arm of the Lord shall fall upon the nations.' In that day the City of Enoch—the other City of Zion—will return and men shall again exercise perfect faith and have the guidance of divine power." (Joseph Fielding Smith, *Signs of the Times,* pp. 169-70.)

45:47 *"Then shall the arm of the Lord fall"*

See *Arm of the Lord* in Appendix A.

45:48 *"then shall the Lord set his foot upon this mount"*

"Prior to the glorious coming of the Son of God, the Jews are going to be beleaguered by the nations who threaten the very existence of the Jewish race. Then, according to Zechariah, down through the gates of heaven shall come the Lord Jesus Christ, the Captain and King for whom the Jews have wept and prayed so long, and he shall set his feet upon the Mount of Olives, and the Mount shall cleave asunder, and the Jews shall escape destruction. The God of heaven shall then, with the armies of heaven, have judgment upon the wicked, and the wicked shall be destroyed. When Jesus stands before the Jews, they will see the wounds in his hands and, recognizing their Lord and God, they shall say: '. . . What are these wounds in thine hands?' And then Jesus shall break the hearts of the Jews by saying: 'Those with which I was wounded in the house of my friends.' (Zech. 13:6.) And that nation then, and not until then, shall be born in a day.

By the authorized servants of God they shall receive the baptism of repentance; they shall receive the gift of the Holy Ghost, and become the children of God their Father and the servants of the great Jehovah." (Charles A. Callis, *CR*, October 1945, p. 81.)

45:52   *"Then shall they [the Jews] know that I am the Lord"*

"Before the second coming of Jesus Christ, the remnant of the Jews will be gathered to Palestine. . . . Part of the city of Jerusalem shall fall when a great earthquake shall take place and the Mount of Olives shall cleave in twain and into the valley thus formed the persecuted Jews shall flee for safety. At this time, Christ will appear to them and show them his hands and his feet and the predictions of Zacharias will be fulfilled. Then the Jews who have only partly believed in Christ and who have not been willing to accept him as their Redeemer, will be converted and forgiven on their repentance and a nation will be born in a day." (Joseph Fielding Smith, *CHMR* 1:197.)

45:54   *"it shall be tolerable" for the heathen in the resurrection*

"The heathen nations who have not known God shall have their part in the first resurrection. The extent of their blessing, or degree of salvation is not stated, but the Lord says it will be 'tolerable' for them. Tolerable, according to the dictionary means 'passably good; commonplace.' The Lord being just to all men, we may be assured that he will give to them in justice and according to divine law." (Smith and Sjodahl, *DCC*, p. 265.)

"The statement that the heathen dead will have place in the first resurrection is sustained by the word of scripture, and by a consideration of the principles of true justice according to which humanity is to be judged. Man will be accounted blameless or guilty, according to his deeds as interpreted in the light of the law under which he is required to live. It is inconsistent with our conception of a just God, to believe Him capable of inflicting condemnation upon any one for noncompliance with a requirement of which the person has no knowledge. Nevertheless, the laws of the Church will not be suspended even in the case of those who have sinned in darkness and ignorance; but it is reasonable to believe that the plan of redemption will afford such benighted ones an opportunity of learning the laws of God;

and surely, as fast as they so learn, will obedience be required on pain of the penalty." (James E. Talmage, *AF*, p. 519.)

45:55   *"Satan shall be bound"*

See *Satan* in Appendix A.

"We read that Satan shall be bound a thousand years. How is this to be accomplished? By our becoming so impregnated with the principles of the Gospel—with the Holy Ghost—that the enemy will have no place in us or in our families. He will be chained to all intents and purposes when he can have no influence—no power—no tabernacles into which he can enter." (Daniel H. Wells, *JD* 5:43.)

45:56-59   *"the parable . . . concerning the ten virgins" shall be fulfilled*

See *Virgins* in Appendix A.

45:60-61   *"until the New Testament be translated"*

The Lord herein authorizes Joseph Smith to work on his inspired translation of the New Testament—"I give unto you that ye may now translate it." The Lord also indicates that one purpose of the new translation of the scriptures is to help the saints "be prepared for the things to come." (D&C 45:61.)

See *Inspired Version of the Bible* in Appendix A.

45:64-71   *"it shall be called the New Jerusalem"*

"From the very beginning of the Church in this dispensation there has been agitation in relation to the place of the city New Jerusalem. The first knowledge given that this city was to be built on this continent came from the record of Ether in the Book of Mormon. (Chap. 13.) Naturally the Saints were desirous to learn of the site of this city and to assist in building it. In Section 45 the Lord called upon the Saints to gather their wealth for the purchasing of lands and for the preparation for the building of the New Jerusalem, which was to be built somewhere in the western country." (Joseph Fielding Smith, *CHMR* 1:197.)

"This Church was less than one year old when that revelation [Sec. 45:62-71] was given, and but little more than a year old when an attempt was made to carry out the divine instruction. The place for the City was revealed—Jackson

County, Missouri—and the plan whereby Zion would be established was also made known." (Orson F. Whitney, *CR*, October 1917, pp. 50-51.)

45:67, 75 *"the terror of the Lord . . . shall be there"*

The Lord will be a terror unto the wicked at the time of judgment (including the time of his second coming, which is a day of judgment) in that the wicked will be terrified of him. Fear will then seize upon them, for they will know they have been wicked, have not repented, and are to receive the consequences of their evil acts.

Paul also uses the term in connection with judgment: "For we must all appear before the judgment seat of Christ; that every one may receive the things done in his body, according to that he hath done, whether it be good or bad. Knowing therefore the terror of the Lord, we persuade men; but we are made manifest unto God; and I trust also are made manifest in your consciences." (2 Cor. 5:10-11.)

45:72-75 *"keep these things from going abroad unto the world until it is expedient in me"*

Evidently "these things" mentioned here refer to the contents of verses 64-71 wherein the Lord commands the Saints to leave the eastern countries, assemble in the western countries, build up churches unto him, and prepare to build Zion.

SECTION 46

Background information on section 46

"The next day after the above was received [Section 45], I also received the following revelation, relative to the gifts of the Holy Ghost: [Section 46, follows.]" (Joseph Smith, *HC* 1:163.)

46:2 *"conduct all meetings as . . . directed and guided by the Holy Spirit"*

"Speaking to the members of the Church in March, 1831, the Lord said: [Sec. 46:22, quoted.] This is one of the marks of the Church of Jesus Christ. In this manner the apostles and elders of old conducted their meetings, but as time passed and false philosophy and pagan practices crept into the Church, this method was changed. . . . We are commanded in this revelation to conduct such meetings as we are led and guided by the Holy Ghost. Meetings which partake of the inspiration of the hour are filled with interest and instruction.

"John Whitmer records in his history that 'in the beginning of the Church, while yet in her infancy, the disciples used to exclude unbelievers which caused some to marvel and converse on this matter because of the things written in the Book of Mormon. (3 Nephi 18:22-24.) Therefore, the Lord deigned to speak on this subject, that his people might come to an understanding, and he said that he had always given to his elders to conduct all meetings as they were led by the Spirit.' [*HC* 1:163-64.] " (Joseph Fielding Smith, *CHMR* 1:182-83.)

46:3-5 *Instructions regarding sacrament meetings*

See *Sacrament* in Appendix A.

"After the Lord gave this revelation this practice of forbidding non-members to attend sacrament services ceased. The word of the Lord to the Nephites is very clear and positive on this point, he said: '. . . . ye shall not suffer any one knowingly to partake of my flesh and blood unworthily, when ye shall minister it.' [3 Ne. 18:28.]" (Joseph Fielding Smith, *CHMR* 1:182-83.)

46:4 *"if any have trespassed, let him not partake" of the sacrament*

"To partake of the Sacrament unworthily is to take a step toward spiritual death. No man can be dishonest within himself without deadening the susceptibility of his spirit. Sin can stun the conscience as a blow on the head can stun the physical senses. He who promises one thing and deliberately fails to keep his word, adds sin to sin. On natural principles such a man 'eats and drinks condemnation to his soul.'" (David O. McKay, *CR*, October 1929, pp. 14-15.)

46:7-10 *"beware lest ye are deceived" by evil spirits*

"We may look for angels and receive their ministrations, but we are to try the spirits and prove them, for it is often the case that men make a mistake in regard to these things. God has so ordained that when he has communicated, no vision is to be taken but what you see by the seeing of the eye, or what you hear by the hearing of the ear. When you see a vision, pray for the interpretation; if you get not this, shut it up; there must be certainty in this matter. An open vision will manifest that which is more important." (Joseph Smith, *HC* 3:391.)

"In order to have the power to distinguish between truth and error and to interpret properly a dream or vision, one must have a pure heart and a contrite spirit and be living a righteous life. Satan's mission is to deceive, and he can, and does, give revelation to those who permit themselves to fall into his power. 'Lying spirits are going forth in the earth. There will be great manifestations of spirits, both false and true.' (*HC* 3:391-92.)

"The Lord has given us sound counsel in relation to all such matters in Section 46, verses 7-10. Men are often deceived by the revelations from lying spirits. This is a danger confronting all those who yield to temptation; who violate covenants, speak evil of authorities, etc. When a man does any of these things he becomes subject to deception and inspiration from an evil source." (Joseph Fielding Smith, *CHMR* 2:228.)

46:8-33   *"seek ye earnestly the best gifts"*

See *Gifts of the Spirit* in Appendix A. Also check in Appendix A the materials for each specific gift such as *Discernment, Faith, Healing, Miracles, Prophecy, Revelation, Teaching, Tongues,* and *Visions.*

"That the Saints might not be deceived, the Lord pointed out to them the proper gifts of the Spirit (Sec. 46) which are distributed among the members as the Lord sees good to bestow. Yet more than one gift may be received by any person who diligently seeks for these things. All members of the Church should seek for the gift of prophecy, for their own guidance, which is the spirit by which the word of the Lord is understood and his purposes made known. (See 1 Cor. 14:1.) Men who are called to positions of responsibility in the government of the Church are entitled to have many gifts, and the President all of them. . . ." (Joseph Fielding Smith, *CHMR* 1:201.)

46:13   *"to know that Jesus Christ is the Son of God"*

"This knowledge is placed first among the special gifts, because it is obtained only by revelation. To *believe* that Jesus of Nazareth was the Anointed One, the Messiah, and that He was crucified for the sins of the world, is not to *know* it. Knowledge is a special gift." (Smith and Sjodahl, *DCC*, p. 274.)

46:15   *"to know the differences of administration"*

"This is another special gift. The term, as used by Paul (1 Cor. 12:5) means the different divisions or courses of the priests and Levites engaged in the temple service, and in this Revelation it may refer to the different duties and responsibilities of the Priesthood in its two divisions, the Melchizedek and Aaronic. To know this is a gift of the Spirit." (Smith and Sjodahl, *DCC*, p. 274.)

46:16   *"to know the diversities of operations"*

"This refers to various spiritual influences at work, for instance such as are manifested in Spiritism, anarchism, and the numerous other 'isms.' To know whether an influence with a professedly moral, or reformatory, aim is from the Holy Spirit, or from another source, is a special gift." (Smith and Sjodahl, *DCC*, p. 274.)

46:17   *"the word of wisdom"*

"The . . . gift of the gospel which I present is that of wisdom. Wisdom cannot be disassociated from discernment, but it involves some other factors, and its applications are rather more specific. Wisdom is sometimes defined as sound judgment and a high degree of knowledge. I define wisdom as being the beneficent application of knowledge in decision. I think of wisdom not in the abstract but as functional. Life is largely made up of choices and determinations, and I can think of no wisdom that does not contemplate the good of man and society. Wisdom is true understanding. . . . [Prov. 3:15-17, 13 quoted.]

"I do not believe that true wisdom can be acquired or exercised in living without a sound fundamental knowledge of the truth about life and living. The cry of the world is for wisdom and wise men. . . . The fundamental knowledge which the Church brings you will bring you understanding. Your testimony, your spirit, and your service will direct the application of your knowledge; that is wisdom." (Stephen L Richards, *CR,* April 1950, pp. 163-64.)

46:18   *"the word of knowledge"*

"Refers to the gift to instruct others. There is a difference between wisdom, knowledge, and ability to instruct. According to Coleridge, 'common sense in an uncommon degree' is what men call *wisdom.* It is almost a direct operation of intuition. *Knowledge* is a carefully-stored-up supply of facts, generally slowly acquired. The *ability* to *instruct* is the gift to impart of this supply to others. Each is a gift of God." (Smith and Sjodahl, *DCC,* p. 274.)

46:21   *"working of miracles"*

"A special divine power is needed for the working of miracles. The Prophet Joseph had this power in a very high degree. It was one of the evidences that he had the authority of the holy Priesthood. One of the numerous miracles God performed through him was the healing of one Mrs. Johnson, who, in company with others, visited his home in Kirtland, 1831. She had, for some time, been afflicted with a lame arm. She could not raise it to her head. The conversation turned on supernatural power, and someone in the company asked if there was anybody on Earth that could heal Mrs. Johnson for instance. The Prophet arose, walked over to Mrs. Johnson, took her by the hand and said, 'Woman, in the name of the Lord Jesus Christ, I command thee to be whole,' whereupon he left the room. Mrs. Johnson at once lifted up her arm, and the next day was able to do her washing (*History of the Church,* Vol. I, p. 215)." (Smith and Sjodahl, *DCC,* p. 275.)

46:22   *"to prophesy"*

"That is, to speak in the name of the Lord, whether of things present, past, or future. This is a special gift. The Prophet Joseph had it in the highest degree. Heber C. Kimball also had the gift highly developed. At times he could see into the future as if it were an open book. During the time of famine in Salt Lake valley in 1847, when many subsisted on roots and hides of animals, and knew not where to obtain bread or clothing necessary, owing to the devastation by crickets, President Kimball declared in a public meeting that, within a short time, 'state goods' would be sold in the streets of Salt Lake City cheaper than in New York, and that the people should be abundantly supplied with food and clothing. Many who heard him refused to believe. He himself said he was afraid he had missed it. But the prophecy came true. Very soon the California gold-hunters came through the Valley. Salt Lake City became their resting-place, and they were glad to exchange their goods for whatever they could get. Many of them threw goods away, or sold them for a song, in order to lighten their wagons and be able to make better progress. (Whitney's *Life of Heber C. Kimball,* p. 401-2)." (Smith and Sjodahl, *DCC,* p. 275.)

46:31   *"all things must be done in the name of Christ"*

"Everything in this Church is to be done in the name of Jesus Christ; so we have been commanded. This Church is called 'The Church of Jesus Christ of Latter-day Saints.' That was given by revelation and commandment. [Sec. 115:3-4.] It is not merely the Church of man: and though men are called of God to work in it and to occupy prominent places in it, and use great influence in building it up, we are building it up to him who is our living Head, even Jesus Christ. We are to do all things in his name. . . .

"So, my brethren, in administering in any of the ordinances of the house of God, it is to be done in the name of Jesus Christ." (Charles W. Penrose, *CR,* April 1920, pp. 28-29.)

SECTION 47

Background information section 47

"Previous to this Oliver Cowdery had acted as historian and recorder. John Whitmer, according to his own representations, said he would rather not keep the Church history, but observed—'The will of the Lord be done, and if He desires it, I wish that He would manifest it through Joseph the Seer.'—John Whitmer's *History of the Church,* ch. vi—Accordingly the revelation was given." (*HC* 1:166, footnote.)

"John Whitmer was now appointed custodian of the records of the Church. When he was excommunicated, March 10, 1838, at Far West, he refused to deliver up the documents in his possession, and at his death they were taken charge of by his nephew, John C. Whitmer, of Richmond, Mo." (Smith and Sjodahl, *DCC,* p. 279.)

47:1-4 *"my servant John should write and keep a regular history"*

For biographical information on John Whitmer, see Appendix B.

Roy W. Doxey has indicated the extent of John Whitmer's efforts as a historian and what subsequently happened to his record:

"The history of the Church written by John Whitmer was only 'a mere sketch of the things that transpired.' His total work consisted of eighty-five pages which included many of the revelations given while he was in office. During the period when many brethren became disaffected, he was in the Presidency of the Church in Missouri. The members of the Church in that area did not sustain him and his associates in the Presidency. Although the presiding brethren demanded that he deliver the history of the Church to them he refused. Years after his death, a copy of the history was obtained by the Church." (*Doctrine and Covenants Speaks* 1:327.)

"Oliver Cowdery was the first historian of the Church. Afterwards the Lord, in revelation, appointed John Whitmer as the historian. John Whitmer was one of the eight witnesses of the Book of Mormon. He was very zealous in helping the prophet. In the later days of the translation of the Book of Mormon he acted as scribe, and afterwards he helped the prophet in preparing the revelations to be printed, and he went to Missouri for that purpose. He felt how important the work was that the Lord had commenced, and if he had only kept the spirit with him he would not have met the fate he did, that of being excommunicated from the Church. But love of worldly things took possession of him and he left the Church. But I want to say this to his credit, he never denied the testimony which he subscribed to when the Book of Mormon was printed." (Anthon H. Lund, *CR,* October 1917, pp. 10-12.)

278

SECTION 48

Background information on section 48

"In former Revelations (Secs 37:3; 38:32; 39:15) our Lord had commanded the Saints in the East to gather in Ohio, where they would be 'endowed with power from on high.' The spirit of gathering was poured out upon them, and in the spring of 1831, shortly after the arrival of the Prophet Joseph in Kirtland, many Saints began the westward move from the State of New York. The Saints in Kirtland then began to make inquiries as to how the newcomers could obtain land to settle upon, and where they should make a permanent location. This Revelation was given in answer to their inquiries." (Smith and Sjodahl, *DCC,* p. 28.)

48:4 *"obtain all that ye can in righteousness, that in time ye may be enabled to purchase land for an inheritance"*

See *Consecration, Sacrifice,* and *United Order* in Appendix A.

SECTION 49

Background information on section 49

"At about this time [March 1831] came Leman Copley, one of the sect called Shaking Quakers, and embraced the fulness of the everlasting Gospel, apparently honest-hearted, but still retaining the idea that the Shakers were right in some particulars of their faith. In order to have more perfect understanding on the subject, I inquired of the Lord, and received the following: [D&C 49.]" (Joseph Smith, *HC* 1:167.)

" 'This sect of Christians [the Shaking Quakers] arose in England, and Ann Lee has the credit of being its founder. They derive their name from their manner of worship, which is performed by singing and dancing, and clapping their hands in regular time, to a novel but rather pleasant kind of music. This sect was persecuted in England, and came to America in 1774. They first settled in Watervliet, near Albany, New York. They have, or think they have, revelations from heaven, or gifts from the Holy Spirit, which direct them in the choice of their leaders, and in other important concerns. Their dress and manners are similar to those of the society of Friends (Quakers): hence they are often called Shaking Quakers.'—Hayward's *Book of All Religions,* pp. 84-85. 'They assert, with the Quakers, that all external ordinances, especially baptism and the Lord's supper, ceased in the apostolic age; and that God had sent no one to preach since that time till they were raised up, to call in the elect in a new dispensation. They deny the doctrine of the Trinity and a vicarious atonement, as also the resurrection of the body.'—Burder's *History of All Religions,* p. 502.)" (*HC* 1:167, footnote.)

"The Shakers, or 'The United Society of Believers in Christ's Second Appearing,' had their origin in England in a Quaker revival in 1747, of which Jane and James Wardley were the leaders, but it is due to the activity of Ann Lee that the Society has been perpetuated. This organization is a celibate and communistic sect, which did not prohibit marriage but refused to accept it as a Christian principle. The Shakers believed in 'a life of innocence and purity, according to the example of Jesus Christ and his first true followers, implying entire abstinence from all sensual and carnal gratifications. . . .'

"Under the leadership of 'Mother' Ann Lee a band of six men and two women came to America, August 6, 1774. 'A group of Shakers came out of the Kentucky revival in 1800-02, and from this the branches in Kentucky and Ohio were formed. The Shakers held that God was both male and female, that Adam, having been created in the image of God, had in him the nature of both sexes, that even angels and spirits are both male and female. Christ, they believe, was one of the superior spirits and appeared in Jesus, the son of a Jewish carpenter, representing the male principle. In Mother Ann, daughter of an English blacksmith, the female principle in Christ was manifested, and in her the promise of the second coming was fulfilled. Christ's kingdom on earth began with the establishment of the Shaker communities.' (*Encyc. Brit.,* Art. Shakers.)" (Joseph Fielding Smith, *CHMR* 1:191-92.)

49:1 *"Sidney . . . Parley . . . Leman . . . preach my gospel . . . unto the Shakers"*

"Leman Copley had been a Shaker. When he embraced the gospel he was anxious to impart the truth to his former associates. He was, therefore, by revelation, chosen to accompany Sidney Rigdon and Parley P. Pratt on a mission to them." (Smith and Sjodahl, *DCC,* p. 282.)

"Elders Rigdon and Pratt fulfilled the mission appointed to them by this revelation. In company with Leman Copley, who at his own earnest request had been ordained to the Priesthood (John Whitmer's *History of the Church,* p. 20), they visited the settlement of the Shakers, near Cleveland, Ohio, and preached the Gospel to them; 'but,' writes Elder Pratt, 'they utterly refused to hear or obey the gospel.'—*Autobiography of Parley P. Pratt,* p. 65 (first ed.). John Whitmer also remarks upon this incident: 'The above-named brethren went and proclaimed [the Gospel] according to the revelation given them, but the Shakers hearkened not to their words and received not the Gospel at that time, for they are bound in tradition and priestcraft; and thus they are led away with foolish and vain imaginations.' —John Whitmer's *History of the Church.* Ms. p. 20." (*HC* 1:169, footnote.)

49:6   *"Son of Man"*

See *Son of Man* in Appendix A.

49:7   *"the hour and the day no man knoweth"*

See *Second coming* in Appendix A.

49:8   *"I have reserved unto myself, holy men that ye know not of"*

"The reference to the need of repentance by all men, except those which I have reserved unto myself, holy men that we know not of, may require some explanation. The Shakers felt that they were living lives approaching perfection, or at least, free from sin in their celibacy, etc. The Lord informs us that all men in their mortal state are subject to sin and all who have not repented and received the remission of their sins in baptism are subject to repentance and baptism for the remission of sin. The Shakers did not believe in baptism. 'Holy men that ye know not of,' who were without sin, and reserved unto the Lord, are translated persons such as John the Revelator [Sec. 7] and the Three Nephites [3 Nephi ch. 28], who do not belong to this generation and yet are in the flesh in the earth performing a special ministry until the coming of Jesus Christ." (Joseph Fielding Smith, *CHMR* 1:191.)

49:9   *"mine everlasting covenant"*

See *Covenant* in Appendix A.

49:15-17   *"marriage is ordained of God"*

See *Marriage* in Appendix A.

"The statement in relation to marriage in Section 49, was given to the Church several years before the revelation known as Section 132 [plural marriage] was revealed. Hence it is worded, as we find it here, according to the law of the Church in 1831. This statement in relation to marriage was given to correct the false doctrine of the Shakers that marriage was impure and that a true follower of Jesus Christ must remain in the condition of celibacy to be free from sin and in full fellowship with Christ." (Joseph Fielding Smith, *CHMR* 1:192.)

49:16   *"that the earth might answer the end of its creation"*

"The people who inhabit this earth were all living in the spirit life before they came to this earth. The Lord informs us that this earth was designed, before its foundations were formed, for the abode of the spirits who kept their first estate, and all such must come here and receive their tabernacles of flesh and bones, and this is according to the number, or measure, of man according to his creation before the world was made. (Compare 32:8-9.) It is the duty of mankind, in lawful and holy wedlock, to multiply according to the commandments given to Adam and Eve and later to Noah, until every spirit appointed to receive a body in this world has had that privilege. Those who teach celibacy and look upon marriage as sinful are in opposition to the word and commandment of the Lord. Such a doctrine is from an evil source and is intended to defeat the plan of redemption and the bringing into the world the spirits who kept their first estate. Satan, in every way that he can and with all his power, endeavors to defeat the work of the Lord. It is his purpose to destroy the souls of men and if he can prevent them from having bodies by teaching men and women that marriage is unrighteous and sinful, or that they should not after they are married bring children into the world, he thinks he will accomplish his purpose. All who hearken to these evil whisperings and practice this evil will stand condemned before the throne of God." (Joseph Fielding Smith, *CHMR* 1:209-10.)

49:18   *"whoso forbiddeth to abstain from meats . . . is not ordained of God"*

See material listed for D&C 89:12-13.

49:18-21   *"wo be unto man that . . . wasteth flesh"*

"After Noah came out of the Ark the Lord gave him a commandment, saying: 'Every moving thing that liveth shall be meat for you; even as the green herb have I given you all things.' Since blood is the life of mortal bodies, the commandment was also given that the blood should be shed, not eaten, when animal flesh is used for food. Moreover, the killing of animals just for sport is a sin. In the revelation under consideration the Lord pronounced a woe on whosoever wasteth flesh and hath no need and who needlessly shed the blood of his creatures. In the word of the Lord to Noah as it is interpreted in revelation to Joseph Smith, the following is found: 'And surely, blood shall not be shed, only for meat, to save your lives; and the blood of every beast will I require at your hands.'

"It is a grievous sin in the sight of God to kill merely for sport. Such a thing shows a weakness in the spiritual character of the individual. We cannot restore life when it is taken, and all creatures have the right to enjoy life and happiness on the earth where the Lord has placed them. Only for food, and then sparingly, should flesh be eaten, for all life is from God and is eternal." (Joseph Fielding Smith, *CHMR* 1:210.)

"But although God has ordained animals for the use of man, He has not sanctioned the order of things under which some have an abundance of food and clothing, while others are destitute; for that very reason 'the world lieth in sin' (v. 20). Nor must man waste animal life. To kill, when not necessary, is a sin akin to murder. 'A righteous man regardeth the life of his beast' (Prov. 12:10). Man has been entrusted with sovereignty over the animal kingdom (Gen. 1:21), that he may learn to govern, as God rules, by the power of love and justice, and become fit for his eternal destiny as a ruler of worlds." (Smith and Sjodahl, *DCC*, p. 286.)

49:20 *"it is not given that one man should possess that which is above another"*

"Every individual should be in a position to add something to the wealth of the whole. Everyone should be increasing, improving, and advancing in some way, and accomplishing something for his or her good and for the good of the whole.

"Then again, it is written that 'It is not given that one man should possess that which is above another.' Of course, there is some allowance to be made for this expression. A man who has ability superior to another man, and who is able to manage and control larger affairs than another, may possess far more than another who is not able to control and manage as much as he. But if they each had what they were capable of managing and of using wisely and prudently, they would each have alike." (Joseph F. Smith, *CR*, October 1898, pp. 23-24.)

49:22 *"the Son of Man cometh not in the form of a woman"*

"The Shakers taught that 'in this Christ-order there is neither male nor female, in the fleshly generative sense.' This originated the notion that our Savior might come as a woman just as well as a man. The idea that the Son of God, our elder Brother, is without sex, is contrary to the Word of God." (Smith and Sjodahl, *DCC*, p. 286.)

"Since the Shakers held that God was both male and female, it was easy for them to believe in 'Mother' Ann Lee as 'the female principle in Christ,' and to believe that in her Christ had made his second appearance. The Lord corrects this foolish idea and says that the Son of Man cometh not in the form of a woman, neither of a man traveling on the earth, but when he shall appear it shall be as the Only Begotten Son of God, full of power, might and dominion, who will put all enemies under his feet." (Joseph Fielding Smith, *CHMR* 1:210.)

49:24 *"the Lamanites shall blossom"*

See material for 32:2.

"The Lamanites must rise in majesty and power. We must look forward to the day when they will be 'white and delightsome' [2 Ne. 30:6], sharing the freedoms and blessings which we enjoy; when they shall have economic security, culture, refinement, and education; when they shall be operating farms and businesses and industries and shall be occupied in the professions and in teaching; when they shall be organized into wards and stakes of Zion, furnishing much of their own leadership; when they shall build and occupy and fill the temples, and serve in them." (Spencer W. Kimball, *CR*, October 1947, p. 22.)

49:25 *"Zion shall flourish upon the hills and rejoice upon the mountains"*

"On Sunday night the Prophet called on all who held the Priesthood to gather into the little log school house they had there. It was a small house, perhaps 14 feet square. But it held the whole of the Priesthood of The Church of Jesus Christ of Latter-day Saints who were then in the town of Kirtland, and who had gathered together to go off in Zion's camp. . . .

"When we got together the Prophet called upon the Elders of Israel with him to bear testimony of this work. When they got through the Prophet said, 'Brethren, I have been very much edified and instructed in your testimonies here tonight, but I want to say to you before the Lord, that you know no more concerning the destinies of this Church and kingdom than a babe upon its mother's lap. You don't comprehend it.' I was rather surprised. He said, 'It is only a little handful of Priesthood you see here tonight, but this Church will fill North and South America—it will fill the world.' Among other things he said, 'It will fill the Rocky Mountains. There will be tens of thousands of Latter-day Saints who will be gathered in the Rocky Mountains, and there they will open the door for the establishing of the Gospel among the Lamanites, who will receive the Gospel and their endowments and the blessings of God. This people will go into the Rocky Mountains; they will there build temples to the Most High. They will raise up a posterity there, and the Latter-day Saints who dwell in these mountains will stand in the flesh until the coming of the Son of Man. The Son of Man will come to them while in the Rocky Mountains.'

"I name these things because I want to bear testimony before God, angels and men that mine eyes behold the day, and have beheld for the last fifty years of my life, the fulfillment of that prophecy." (Wilford Woodruff, *CR*, April 1898, p. 57.)

49:27 *"I will go before you and be your rearward"*

In this revelation the Lord promises his faithful saints that he will be with them wherever they go. He will "go before" them, will follow after them ("be your rearward"), and will "be in [their] midst."

SECTION 50

Background information on section 50

"As I went forth among the different branches some very strange spiritual operations were manifested, which were disgusting rather than edifying. Some persons would seem to swoon away, and make unseemly gestures, and be drawn or disfigured in their countenances. Others would fall into ecstasies, and be drawn into contortions, cramps, fits, etc. Others would seem to have visions and revelations, which were not edifying, and which were not congenial to the doctrine and the spirit of the gospel. In short, a false and lying spirit seemed to be creeping into the Church.

"All these things were new and strange to me, and had originated in the Church during our absence, and previous to the arrival of Joseph Smith from New York.

"Feeling our weakness and inexperience, and lest we should err in judgment concerning these spiritual phenomena, myself, John Murdock, and several other Elders, went to Joseph Smith, and asked him to inquire of the Lord concerning these spirits or manifestations." (Parley P. Pratt, *APPP*, pp. 61-62.)

Parley P. Pratt has given us the following information concerning Joseph Smith receiving the revelation now in section 50:

After we had joined in prayer in his translating room, he dictated in our presence the following revelation: [section 50]— Each sentence was uttered slowly and very distinctly, and with a pause between each, sufficiently long for it to be recorded, by an ordinary writer, in long hand.

This was the manner in which all his written revelations were dictated and written. There was never any hesitation, reviewing, or reading back, in order to keep the run of the subject; neither did any of these communications undergo revisions, interlinings, or corrections. As he dictated them so they stood, so far as I have witnessed; and I was present to witness the dictation of several communications of several pages each. . . . (Parley P. Pratt, *APPP*, p. 62.)

Following is a footnote from the *History of the Church* concerning this matter:

This statement of Elder Pratt's is true in a general way, and valuable as a description of the manner in which revelations were dictated by the Prophet; and needs modifying only to the extent of saying that some of the early revelations first published in the "Book of Commandments," in 1833, were revised by the Prophet himself in the way of correcting errors made by the scribes and publishers; and some additional clauses were inserted to throw increased light upon the subjects treated in the revelations, and paragraphs added, to make the principles or instructions apply to officers not in the Church at the time some of the earlier revelations were given. (*HC* 1:173.)

50:2-36 *"there are many . . . false spirits"*

"In the early history of the Church, because the elders did not understand the manifestations of different spirits abroad which were disturbing the members, the Lord, in answer to prayerful inquiry, warned: [Sec. 50:2, quoted.]

"What was true then is true now, and ever will be until Satan and his evil hosts are forever bound and shorn of their power to deceive and destroy. The Prophet Joseph Smith taught, '. . . Nothing is a greater injury to the children of men than to be under the influence of a false spirit when they think they have the Spirit of God.' (*Teachings of the Prophet Joseph Smith,* page 205.) How true this statement is, and how important to know correct Church doctrine and procedures to prevent stumbling along life's way. It is a great blessing and gift to be able to discern and choose rightly between truth and error." (Delbert L. Stapley, *CR*, October 1959, p. 71.)

"I want to bear you my solemn witness that I know there are such forces [Satan's] in the world today. . . . Latter-day Saints, the prince of darkness which is of this world cometh among us today. He is knocking without the door of every one of us, of you and me and all who bear the names within themselves of the gospel of Jesus Christ, of our Lord and Savior Jesus Christ, and I pray God that he may find nothing in us, and will go away and let us alone.

"I bear you my testimony that I know these powers are in the world and I know the powers of the gospel of Jesus Christ are sufficient to thwart these powers of darkness." (Harold B. Lee, *CR*, September 1949, pp. 58-59.)

50:5   *"eternal life"*

See *Eternal life* in Appendix A.

50:14-24   *"preach my gospel by the Spirit . . . [be] edified and rejoice together"*

"The Lord's rebuke and instruction to the Elders who went forth to teach (Sec. 50:10-26) should be thoroughly studied and taken to heart by all the brethren in the Church holding the Priesthood. How necessary it is that we should be in possession of the Spirit of God that we may teach. If we do not have that spirit we should not attempt to teach until, in the spirit of repentance, prayer and faith we may obtain the guidance of the Holy Ghost. There is no saying of greater truth than 'that which doth not edify is not of God.' And that which is not of God is darkness, it matters not whether it comes in the guise of religion, ethics, philosophy or revelation. No revelation from God will fail to edify and it is a wonderful promise which is here given that [Sec. 50:24, quoted]. There have been some foolish persons who have concluded that they have become so wise that they have outgrown the Church and the revelations of the Lord. No truth is in conflict with the revealed word of the Lord, and that which our Heavenly Father has given through his prophets shall stand for it is truth, eternal truth; while that which may appear as truth in the commandments of men and devils shall cease when the fulness of truth is come." (Joseph Fielding Smith, *CHMR* 1:184-85.)

"The Lord here [Sec. 50:17-24] makes it plain that, in bringing converts into the Church, the teacher must have the Spirit of the Comforter, the Spirit of truth, the light of truth. And the one that receives that testimony must also partake of that same Spirit. Both then are edified; both are enlightened by the power of the Spirit of the Lord, the one that teaches and the one that receives.

"Now, I want to say . . . that the presidency of this Church, the Twelve Apostles, the Seventies, the leading brethren in the stakes and wards and missions, can build up this Church only by the Spirit about which I have read to you. In no other way can it be built up; assuredly not by the spirit of man. Churches may be established. Lodges may be organized, many organizations formed for the help and benefit of man—and many of them do much good too, and are praiseworthy; but they have not this distinctive feature that this Church has, which was revealed in the beginning and is emphasized, iterated and reiterated all through the revelations, namely, that without that Spirit of light and truth, that Spirit of the Lord, that Spirit of the Comforter, that power of the Holy Ghost, His Church cannot be built up. [Secs. 20:45; 21:1-2; 46:13-26; 68:3-4; 121:26-27.] If it be attempted by any other way than the Lord speaks of here in the passages which I have read [Sec. 93:19-20, also], then it is not of God. So . . . let us take it to heart; all of us who labor for Zion must know and understand that we must keep that influence and that power which comes from God in our hearts, the light of His Spirit burning in our souls." (Charles W. Nibley, *CR,* April 1929, pp. 90-92.)

50:22   *"he that preacheth and he that receiveth . . . are edified"*

"The speaker and hearer together must be guided by the voice that comes from God's presence. Then there is mutual understanding and comprehension. That principle was beautifully told to the Prophet Joseph Smith at the very beginning of the Church. The doctrine is set forth in section 50, of the book of Doctrine and Covenants, in which is explained that when both the hearer and the speaker are moved upon by the same power and spirit the greatest joy is attained. . . . [Sec. 50:22-23, quoted.]

"When apostasy comes, it is because the spirit of revelation departs from us. The wire is broken between us and the source of truth. We cannot understand, though truth be spoken, since we are not possessed of the spirit of truth. We misunderstand and misinterpret.

"There is only one way . . . to obtain and possess this mighty spirit . . . which guides the Church today and enlightens every soul, and that is by obeying strictly, with all our might, as far as we poor mortal beings are able, the laws of the Gospel. If we obey, if we practice in our lives the truths given us, then as certainly as we do that, the enlivening spirit of light, of revelation, of understanding will come to us, comprehension will enter our minds and hearts and we shall know the true joy of being Latter-day Saints." (John A. Widtsoe, *CR,* October 1934, p. 11.)

50:37   *"Joseph Wakefield"*

See material for 52:35.

50:37 *"Parley P. Pratt"*

For biographical information on Parley P. Pratt, see material following his name in Appendix B.

50:38 *"John Corrill"*

"John Corrill was also appointed to labor in the Church. He took a prominent part in the affairs of the Church for some time. In 1832 he baptized Emily Dow Partridge, a daughter of Edward Partridge, at Independence, Jackson Co., Mo. About that time he was one of seven High Priests appointed to preside over the Saints of Zion. The others were, Oliver Cowdery, W. W. Phelps, John Whitmer, Sidney Gilbert, Edward Partridge, and Isaac Morley. In 1837 he was made keeper of the Lord's storehouse, by the same Conference that sustained David Whitmer as president of the Church in Missouri, and John Whitmer and W. W. Phelps as his counselors. But notwithstanding the trust placed in him, when the fires of persecution raged with terrifying fury, he faltered, and signified his intention of publishing a booklet called, *Mormonism Fairly Delineated,* the appearance of which the mob looked forward to with hopeful anticipation (*Historical Record,* p. 458). At a special conference at Quincy, Ill., March 17, 1839, he was excommunicated for acting against the interests of the Saints. Among others who were similarly dealt with at that time were Geo. M. Hinckle, Sampson Avard, W. W. Phelps, Frederick G. Williams, and Thomas B. Marsh—all of whom were, at one time, prominent in the Church." (Smith and Sjodahl, *DCC,* p. 294.)

50:39 *"Edward Partridge"*

For biographical information on Edward Partridge, see material following his name in Appendix B.

50:43 *"the Father and I are one"*

See *Godhead* in Appendix A.

50:44 *"I am . . . the stone of Israel"*

See *Rock* in Appendix A.

SECTION 51

Background information on section 51

"Shortly after the Revelation recorded in Section 50 had been received, the Saints from Colesville, N. Y., began to arrive in Ohio. They had been directed to gather in that locality (Sec. 37:3) and they had been promised that there they would receive The Law (Sec. 38:32). The Saints in Ohio had been instructed to divide their land with their Eastern brethren (Sec. 48:2), and it was the duty of Edward Partridge, who had been appointed Bishop (Sec. 41) to take care of the newcomers, as far as possible. Under the circumstances, Bishop Partridge asked for divine guidance. The Prophet inquired of the Lord for him, and received this answer to his prayers.

"In this Revelation our Lord gives instructions concerning the temporal organizations of His people. We learn from it that it was the special duty of the Bishopric to have charge of the temporal affairs of the Church, under the direction of the Prophet." (Smith and Sjodahl, *DCC*, p. 296.)

"In this manner the Lord endeavored to teach these members, in part, at least, and train them in the great principle of consecration as a preparatory step before they should be permitted to journey to Zion, for it was in keeping with this law upon which the City of Zion was to be built. Thus these saints from the East were to be organized according to the law of God. (Sec. 51:4-6.) This land in Ohio was in this manner to be consecrated unto them 'for a little season,' until the Lord should provide for them otherwise, and command them to go hence. (Sec. 51:15-16.)" (Joseph Fielding Smith, *CHMR* 1:204.)

51:1 *"I . . . speak unto . . . Edward Partridge"*

See Appendix B for biographical information on Edward Partridge.

51:2 *"it must needs be that they be organized according to my laws"*

"In May, 1831, the Saints from New York began to arrive in Ohio and the Lord appointed Bishop Edward Partridge to assign to them their lands. They were to be made equal according to their families and their needs. The head of each family was to receive a certificate insuring for him his portion and inheritance. Should a man transgress after receiving his portion, he was not to have power to claim that portion which had been consecrated to the Bishop for the use of the poor and needy, but could retain the portion which had been deeded unto him. A storehouse was provided where the substance needful for the people in want could be kept by the Bishop. In this manner the Lord endeavored to teach these members in part, at least, and train them in the great principle of consecration as a preparatory step before they should be permitted to journey to Zion, for it was in keeping with this law upon which the City of Zion was to be built. Thus these Saints from the East were to be organized according to the Law of God. (Sec. 51:4-6.) This land in Ohio was in this manner to be consecrated unto them 'for a little season,' until the Lord should provide for them otherwise, and command them to go hence. (Sec. 51:15-16.)" (Joseph Fielding Smith, *CHMR* 1:187.)

51:13 *"let the bishop appoint a storehouse"*

See *Storehouse* in Appendix A.

"And also, in this revelation [Sec. 51], he told Edward Partridge that he should have the privilege of organizing, for this was an example unto him, in all other places, in all other churches. So it was not confined to any particular locality, to Kirtland, nor Thompson, nor to Jackson County; but in that revelation it was told the Bishop that this should be an example unto him in organizing all Churches [branches]. So that wherever Edward Partridge should find a Church, he would have the privilege of organizing them according to the United Order, the Celestial Law, or the Order of Enoch." (Lorenzo Snow, *JD* 19:344.)

51:17-18 *"let them act upon this land as for years"*

Even though the Lord has just notified the Saints that they will be on this particular land "for a little season," yet he still asks them to act in regard to the land as though they were going to stay "for years." He also indicated that this should

be "an example . . . in other places." (51:18.) The Lord
promised further that all this should "turn unto them for
their good." (51:17.) The Saints would have occasion to remember and follow this advice not only in Ohio, but also in
Missouri, in Illinois, and when they emigrated to the Great
Basin.

294

SECTION 52

Background information on section 52

"On the 3rd of June [1831], the Elders from the various parts of the country where they were laboring, came in; and the conference before appointed, convened in Kirtland; and the Lord displayed His power to the most perfect satisfaction of the Saints. The man of sin was revealed, and the authority of the Melchizedek Priesthood was manifested and conferred for the first time upon several of the Elders. It was clearly evident that the Lord gave us power in proportion to the work to be done, and strength according to the race set before us, and grace and help as our needs required. Great harmony prevailed; several were ordained; faith was strengthened; and humility, so necessary for the blessing of God to follow prayer, characterized the Saints.

"The next day, as a kind continuation of this great work of the last days, I received the following: [D&C 52.]" (Joseph Smith, *HC* 1:175-77.)

52:2, 42 *The land of Missouri designated as the "land of your inheritance"*

"In the midst of the congregation [June 1831] the Lord made known, through Joseph, that their next conference should be held far away, in the State of Missouri, upon the spot consecrated by God unto the children of Jacob, the heirs of His covenant. In the same revelation the Lord directed the Prophet and Sidney Rigdon to prepare for their journey into the land of Zion; promising to them that through their faith they should know the land which was to be forever the inheritance of the Saints of the Most High." (George Q. Cannon, *LJS*, p. 95.)

52:2 *"heirs according to the covenant"*

See material for 86:8-11.

52:3 *Joseph Smith, Sidney Rigdon, etc.*

For information on the persons mentioned by name in section 52, see Appendix B.

52:10 *"the laying on of the hands by the water's side"*

See *Laying on of hands* in Appendix A.

52:14 *"Satan is abroad in the land"*

See *Satan* in Appendix A.

52:27 *"Solomon Hancock and Simeon Carter"*

"Solomon Hancock] He was among a party of fifteen brethren who were called to go from Clay County to Kirtland, on June 23, 1834, to receive their endowments, because 'they had proved themselves faithful and true during the late persecutions.' A month afterwards he was appointed a member of the High Council in Clay County.

"Simeon Carter] The same note may refer to him. Parley P. Pratt, while on his mission to the Lamanites, stayed at the house of Simeon Carter, fifty miles west of Kirtland. They were in the act of reading the Book of Mormon, when an officer entered and arrested Elder Pratt. The book was left in the house. Pratt managed to escape, and Carter read the Book of Mormon with great interest. He was baptized and ordained an Elder, and soon organized a Branch of sixty members." (Smith and Sjodahl, *DCC*, p. 308.)

52:29 *"Levi W. Hancock and Zebedee Coltrin"*

"Levi Hancock] He was one of the First Council of Seventies, organized in Kirtland, in 1835.

"Zebedee Coltrin] He was another member of the Council." (Smith and Sjodahl, *DCC*, p. 308.)

52:30 *"Reynolds Cahoon and Samuel H. Smith"*

For additional biographical information on each of these brethren, see entries for individual names in Appendix B.

"Reynolds Cahoon and Samuel Smith] While on this journey, they preached the gospel to William E. McLellin, and so much impressed was he, that he wound up his business and followed them to Jackson County. In 1838 Cahoon was appointed first counselor to John Smith, who was made president of a Stake of Zion organized at Adam-ondi-Ahman. Lyman Wight was the second counselor. The following year, these three presided over the Saints in Iowa.

In 1848, when President Brigham Young led a company of 1,229 souls across the plains to the Mountain valleys, Isaac Morley was appointed president, with Reynolds Cahoon and William W. Major as counselors." (Smith and Sjodahl, *DCC*, p. 308.)

52:31 *"William Carter"*

"*William Carter*] One of the Utah Pioneers who put the first ploughs into the ground and planted the first potatoes in Salt Lake Valley. George W. Brown and Shadrach Roundy were the others (Whitney's *History of Utah*, Vol. I., p. 331)." (Smith and Sjodahl, *DCC*, p. 308.)

52:33 *"one man shall not build upon another's foundation, neither journey in another's track"*

"Special instructions were also given to others of the Elders, commanding them to go forth two by two in the proclamation of the word of God by the way, to every congregation where they could get a hearing. Though the western frontier of Missouri was their destination, they were commanded to take different routes and not build on each other's foundation or travel in each other's track." (George Q. Cannon, *LJS*, p. 95.)

52:35 *"Joseph Wakefield and Solomon Humphrey"*

"During the fall of 1830, a gentleman who lived in our neighborhood went to Western New York and saw the Prophet, got baptized and ordained an Elder; and that was Elder Solomon Humphrey. Very few knew the old gentleman: he died in Missouri in 1835. He was a very faithful man. Previous to joining the Church he was a Baptist exhorter. He came back to our place of residence in company with a man named Joseph Wakefield, who is named in the book of Doctrine and Covenants. They came and preached and baptized for the remission of sins." (George A. Smith, *JD* 5:104.)

52:37 *"Simonds Ryder"*

"Shortly after this, Ryder joined Ezra Booth and the Johnson boys in inflicting the outrage upon the Prophet Joseph and Sidney Rigdon, at Hiram, on the 25th of March, 1832 (Andrew Jenson, *Hist Rec.*, p. 112.)" (Smith and Sjodahl, *DCC*, p. 309.)

"Some people apostatize for very trivial reasons. Simonds Ryder furnishes an illustration of this. He received a letter at one time, in which the Prophet Joseph Smith and Sidney Rigdon informed him that it was the will of the Lord that he should preach the gospel. In this letter, as in the Revelation (Sec. 52:37), his surname was spelled with an 'i' instead of 'y,' and that was his pretext for apostatizing (*Hist. of the Church,* Vol. I., p. 261)." (Smith and Sjodahl, *DCC,* p. 487.)

52:39 *"watch over the churches"*

"Brethren—you to whom these words of admonition apply, for your own sakes, if not for the sake of those whose welfare is your charge—beware of indolence and neglect. The adversary is only too eager to take advantage of your apathy, and you may lose the very testimony of which you have been sent to bear record before the world." (Joseph F. Smith, *GD,* p. 363.)

52:39 *"let them labor with their own hands"*

"*Labor with their own hands*] It is an excellent rule in the Kingdom of God that those who labor in the ministry be independent. For the word of God does not always suit those who are rebuked by it, and if these hold the purse-strings, they are liable to draw them tight and strangle truth. Paul, in his farewell address to the Elders at Ephesus (Acts 20:34, 35), charged them to follow his example in this respect. 'Ye yourselves know,' he said, 'that these hands have ministered unto my necessities, and to them that were with me.' . . . It is not displeasing to God if the Saints share temporal blessings with those who minister to them in spiritual things, as long as it is voluntary and an expression of gratitude and love, but to preach for hire is, according to the gospel, to encourage 'idolatry' and 'wickedness.' " (Smith and Sjodahl, *DCC,* p. 310.)

SECTION 53

Background information on section 53

"Elder B. H. Roberts [in *HC*] . . . makes the remark that the Lord has had few more devoted servants in this dispensation than Algernon Sidney Gilbert. Where he was born is not known, but his father's family resided in Connecticut. For some years he was a successful merchant in Painesville, Ohio, and there the gospel found him in 1830. In the persecution that came upon the Saints in Jackson County he sacrificed all his goods. He was one of the six who offered their lives for their friends. He was a man of great practical sense, as is evidenced by the correspondence he and others engaged in with Governor Dunklin, on behalf of the brethren, but, nevertheless, he shrank from speaking publicly, and it appears that, when called to go on a mission to preach the gospel, he said he would rather die. Not long afterwards he was attacked by cholera, and the disease proved fatal." (Smith and Sjodahl, *DCC*, p. 312.)

53:1-7 *"Sidney Gilbert . . . be an agent unto this church"*

For biographical information on Sidney Gilbert, see Appendix B.

53:5 *"take your journey with . . . Joseph Smith . . . and Sidney Rigdon"*

"It was on the 19th day of June, 1831, that Joseph Smith departed from Kirtland, Ohio, to go up into Missouri, the place promised as an inheritance for the Saints and at which the New Jerusalem should sometime be established. The Prophet was accompanied by Sidney Rigdon, Martin Harris, Edward Partridge, W. W. Phelps, Joseph Coe and A. S. Gilbert and wife." (George Q. Cannon, *LJS*, p. 96.)

53:7 *"he only is saved who endureth unto the end"*

See *Endure to the end* in Appendix A.

SECTION 54

Background information on section 54

"It is difficult to determine with exactness in what the transgressions of the Saints at Thompson consisted; but it is evident that selfishness and rebellion were at the bottom of their trouble, and that Leman Copley and Ezra Thayre were immediately concerned in it. The Saints comprising the Colesville branch, when they arrived at the gathering place, in Ohio, were advised to remain together and were settled at Thompson, a place in the vicinity of Kirtland. On their arrival Bishop Edward Partridge urged the Prophet Joseph to inquire of the Lord concerning the manner of settling them, and providing for them. Whereupon the Prophet inquired of the Lord and received the revelation found on page 173. [Section 51.] It will be seen from that revelation that the Saints of the Colesville branch were to be organized under the law of consecration and stewardship. That is, in brief, the Saints were to make a consecration of whatsoever things they possessed unto the Bishop, and then each man receive from the Bishop a stewardship. Every man was to be equal in his stewardship, according to his family, his circumstances, and his needs. For details in the matter the reader is referred to the revelation itself. It is evident that some of the brethren already living at Thompson, had agreed to enter into the law of consecration and stewardship with the Saints from Colesville; and that afterwards they broke this covenant. Among these were Leman Copley and Ezra Thayre. 'A man by the name of Copley,' says Newel Knight in his journal, 'had a considerable tract of land there [in Thompson] which he offered to let the Saints occupy. Consequently a contract was agreed upon, and we commenced work in good faith. But in a short time Copley broke the engagement, and I went to Kirtland to see Brother Joseph,' etc." (*HC* 1:180, footnote.)

54:1-10 *"Newel Knight . . . stand fast in the office whereunto I have appointed you"*

For biographical information on Newel Knight, see Appendix B.

54:1-9 *"take your journey into the regions westward . . . seek ye a living like unto men"*

"The Saints from New York, principally the Colesville Branch, on their arrival in Ohio were located at a place called Thompson, about sixteen miles from Kirtland, where they were organized according to the law of the Lord. [See Sec. 51:1-15.] Leman Copley, recently converted and formerly a Shaker, owned a tract of land which he agreed to turn over to the Colesville Branch to occupy in the manner of stewardship, which was to be held for a 'little season,' or until the time should come for these people to move to Missouri. The leading Elders had been commanded to go to Missouri (Sec. 52:1-2), where the next conference of the Church was to be held. This was to prepare the way for the gathering of the Saints after the preliminary plans were arranged. It was not intended that any of the branches in Ohio should go to Missouri at that early date, but it appears that Copley, who had not been fully converted, and some others in Thompson violated their covenants, which caused confusion among the Colesville Saints and placed them at the mercy of their enemies. In their distress they sent Newel Knight, who was in charge of this branch, to the Prophet to learn what they should do. The Lord spoke to them by revelation (Sec. 54). . . . Because of this broken covenant the Saints were released from the commandment to live according to the Lord's law, of having things in common, they were to take their journey to the borders of the Lamanites, and therefore, the Lord said, 'seek a living like unto men, until I prepare a place for you.' In other words they were to seek a living as other men and not attempt to live in the united order until the Lord should command them. Almost immediately because of the word of the Lord and the pressure brought against them by enemies, they took up their journey to the 'borders of the Lamanites.' " (Joseph Fielding Smith, *CHMR* 1:187-88.)

54:10 *"they who have sought me early shall find rest to their souls"*

"The ancient prophets speak of 'entering into God's rest'

[Isa. 14:3, Heb. 4:3, 11]; what does it mean? To my mind, it means entering into the knowledge and love of God, having faith in His purposes and in his plans to such an extent that we know we are right, and that we are not hunting for something else; we are not disturbed by every wind of doctrine or by the cunning and craftiness of men who lay in wait to deceive." (Joseph F. Smith, *CR,* October 1919, p. 8.)

SECTION 55

Background information on section 55

"About the middle of June, while we were preparing for our journey to Missouri, William W. Phelps and his family arrived among us—'to do the will of the Lord,' he said: so I inquired of the Lord concerning him and received the following: [D&C 55]." (Joseph Smith, *HC* 1:184-85.)

55:1 *"William . . . after thou hast been baptized"*

For biographical information on William W. Phelps, see the material following his name in Appendix B.

"He [William W. Phelps] had not yet been baptized, but he was promised the remission of his sins and the gift of the Holy Ghost by the laying on of hands, if he would submit to the ordinances with the proper feeling, and he was to be ordained to do the work of printing for the Church; and for this cause was required to take his journey with Joseph and Sidney Rigdon to the west." (George Q. Cannon, *LJS*, p. 96.)

55:1-5 *"do the work of printing, and of selecting and writing books for schools in this church"*

"William W. Phelps, one of the most competent of the early converts, was an editor, writer, and politician. His hymns are favorites among the Latter-day Saints." (John A. Widtsoe, *JS*, p. 143.)

"Scarcely had the Church been organized before he [Joseph Smith] began to provide for common schools for children. At that time public schools were few on the frontier. In June, 1831, a year after the organization of the Church, Oliver Cowdery and W. W. Phelps were appointed a committee to select and write books for the schools." (John A. Widtsoe, *JS*, p. 223.)

"The Latter-day Saints have always been far in advance of the majority of their neighbors in regard to education of their children. Even in the earliest days they had schools that made real men and women; not schools that produced weaklings and sycophants. The old schools made for character and real worth; they took the raw material, and moulded it into beings of personality and culture." (Levi Edgar Young, quoted in Smith and Sjodahl, *DCC,* p. 319.)

SECTION 56

Background information on section 56

"Soon after I received the foregoing [Section 55], Elder Thomas B. Marsh came to inquire what he should do; as Elder Ezra Thayre, his yoke-fellow in the ministry, could not get ready to start on his mission as soon as he (Marsh) would; and I inquired of the Lord, and received the following: [D&C 56]." (Joseph Smith, *HC* 1:186.)

56:1 *"mine arm"*

See *Arm of the Lord* in Appendix A.

56:2 *"he that will not take up his cross"*

See *Cross* in Appendix A.

56:4 *"I, the Lord, command and revoke"*

This earth is the Lord's and the fulness thereof. Also, it is his gospel and his plan of life and salvation. In his love and concern for us, he is free to give us those commandments that he knows we can keep and thus receive those blessings that are predicated upon those commandments. In his mercy, however, he often revokes his commandments when his children cannot or will not obey them; otherwise, he brings his children under even more severe condemnation.

56:8 *"Ezra Thayre must repent of his pride"*

For biographical information on Ezra Thayre, see the material following his name in Appendix B.

56:14 *"you have many things to do and to repent of"*

See *Repentance* in Appendix A.

56:14 *"your sins have come up unto me"*

"This refers to the sin of not organizing under the law of consecration. Those who were responsible for the failure to do so had not been pardoned, because they preferred their own counsel to that of God." (Smith and Sjodahl, *DCC*, p. 324.)

56:16   *"Wo unto you rich men, that will not give your substance to the poor"*

"In this and the following verse the Lord indicates the main reasons why the United Order cannot be practiced on Earth at present. The rich are not willing to serve the poor with their substance. They love mammon, not their fellowmen." (Smith and Sjodahl, *DCC*, p. 325.)

"I would say to you rich men, bring in your treasures to assist in building up God's kingdom. . . . I suppose the reason why so few of the wealthy embrace the Truth is, because they are too much choked up with pride, prejudice and the things of this life, so that there is scarcely room for anything else. 'The earth is the Lord's and the fulness thereof' [1 Cor. 10:26], and if the Lord gives a man means, he gives him an increase of power to do good, and he will consequently have more to account for." (Daniel H. Wells, *MS* 26:787.)

"The rich are as dependent upon God for the light of His Spirit to guide them, and for the blessings and ordinances of the Holy Priesthood as are the poorest of the poor. The Lord, in this regard is 'no respecter of person.' [Acts 10:34.]" (Joseph F. Smith, *JD* 24:173-74.)

"The revelation of the Lord does not indicate that he has taken up either the side of the rich or the poor, and certainly he is opposed to selfishness and to class distinctions and to groups interested only in themselves. Let me read, from the fifty-sixth section, what the Lord has to say concerning both groups: [Sec. 56:16, quoted.] But on the other hand: [Sec. 56:17, quoted.] I am sure that in perfect harmony with this revelation I could add 'and blessed are the rich, too, who are pure in heart, whose hearts are broken, whose spirits are contrite, for they shall see the kingdom of God coming in power and great glory unto their deliverance.' This indicates an obligation upon both groups toward each other, the rich and the poor." (Melvin J. Ballard, *CR*, April 1937, pp. 89-90.)

56:17   *"Wo unto you poor men . . . whose eyes are full of greediness"*

"But not only the rich are to blame. The poor are also responsible, for many of them are not humble, nor honest. Many of them are dishonest; many are as greedy as any miser, and many are lazy, or given to violence on the slightest provocation. A United Order cannot be built up of mammon-slaves and belly-worshipers, be they rich or poor. Both classes must repent, and enter upon a new life before the highest ideal of a human society can be realized." (Smith and Sjodahl, *DCC,* p. 325.)

56:18   *"blessed are the poor who are pure in heart"*

"It is the state of the heart, not outward circumstances, that makes us 'blessed' or happy. 'Pure in heart' means pure in affections, unselfish in one's love of fellowmen. Purity of doctrine is not sufficient; nor the most faithful observance of ceremonies. It is the 'pure in heart' that shall see God (Matt. 5:8)." (Smith and Sjodahl, *DCC,* p. 325.)

56:19-20   *"the Lord shall come, and his recompense shall be with him"*

"He [God] holds the reins of judgment in His hands; He is a wise Lawgiver and will judge all men, not according to the narrow, contracted notions of men, but, 'according to the deeds done in the body whether they be good or evil,' or whether these deeds were done in England, America, Spain, Turkey, or India. He will judge them, 'not according to what they have not, but according to what they have,' those who have lived without law will be judged without law, and those who have a law will be judged by that law. We need not doubt the wisdom and intelligence of the Great Jehovah; He will award judgment or mercy to all nations according to their several deserts, their means of obtaining intelligence, the laws by which they are governed, the facilities afforded them of obtaining correct information, and His inscrutable designs in relation to the human family; and when the designs of God shall be made manifest, and the curtain of futurity be withdrawn, we shall all of us eventually have to confess that the Judge of all the earth has done right." (Joseph Smith, *HC* 4:595-96.)

SECTION 57

Background information on section 57

"The meeting of our brethren, who had long awaited our arrival [in Missouri], was a glorious one, and moistened with many tears. It seemed good and pleasant for brethren to meet together in unity. But our reflections were many, coming as we had from a highly cultivated state of society in the east, and standing now upon the confines or western limits of the United States, and looking into the vast wilderness of those that sat in darkness; how natural it was to observe the degradation, leanness of intellect, ferocity, and jealousy of a people that were nearly a century behind the times, and to feel for those who roamed about without the benefit of civilization, refinement, or religion; yea, and exclaim in the language of the Prophets: 'When will the wilderness blossom as the rose? When will Zion be built up in her glory, and where will Thy temple stand, unto which all nations shall come in the last days?' [Isa. 35:1; Ps. 87:1-3; Isa. 2:2-3.] Our anxiety was soon relieved by receiving the following: [Section 57, follows.]" (Joseph Smith, *HC* 1:189.)

"In the Book of Mormon the Saints were told (Ether 13:1-12), that the new Jerusalem and Holy Sanctuary of the Lord should be located in America (Comp. 3 Nephi 20:22; 21:23), and they were anxious to know where the site for the City was. In September, 1830, the Lord gave them to understand that the City should be erected 'on the borders by the Lamanites' (Sec. 28:9). In February, 1831, they were promised that a Revelation should be given on that subject, if they would pray for it (Sec. 42:62). On the 7th of March, the same year, they were given to understand that the gathering from the eastern States and the sending out of Elders on the mission to the West were preparatory steps to the establishment of that City, wherefore the Saints should gather up their riches and purchase an inheritance in the place to be indicated, which should be a place of refuge for the Saints of the most High God (Sec. 45:64-66). The time had now come for the fulfillment of the promise referred to (Sec. 42:62), and this Revelation was received. [D&C 57.]" (Smith and Sjodahl, *DCC*, pp. 327-28.)

"As rapidly as possible they [the Prophet and his party] journeyed by wagon and stage and occasionally by canal boat to Cincinnati, Ohio. From the latter point they went to Louisville, Kentucky, by steamer, . . . they reached St. Louis by steamer, and there made a brief pause. From this city on the Mississippi, the Prophet of God walked across the entire state of Missouri to Independence, Jackson County, a distance of nearly three hundred miles as traveled. This journey through the blazing heat of June and July [1831] was sweet to Joseph. There was a charm about it which lightened toil. The pains and burdens were unworthy of notice in the delightful anticipation of seeing the land for which the Lord, as had been shown to him by vision and prophecy [Sec. 57:1-3], had reserved so glorious a future. It was about the middle of July when the Prophet and his party reached Independence. During the month of their journey Joseph had taught the gospel, in the cities, the villages and the country places, in vigor and simplicity." (George Q. Cannon, *LJS*, pp. 96-97.)

57:3 *"Independence is the center place"*

"The city of Independence is situated in one of the most attractive and healthful parts of Missouri, 338 feet above the level of the Missouri River, and 1,075 feet above sea level. It is an old town. It was laid out in 1827, but in 1831 it was only a village. It is now a suburb of Kansas City." (Smith and Sjodahl, *DCC*, p. 331.)

"That temple [Independence, Mo.] will be built, as well as other things that have been projected by the inspired servants of God, for the Lord knows how to work it out. All we need to do . . . is to keep on the Lord's side and make him our friend, stand in his favor, keep his commandments, and he will work out the salvation of Zion and her redemption." (Melvin J. Ballard, *CR*, April 1921, p. 101.)

57:4 *"the line running directly between Jew and Gentile"*

"This expression—'lying westward, even unto the line running between Jew and Gentile,' has reference to the line separating the Lamanites from the settlers in Jackson County. At this time the United States Government had given to the Indians the lands west of the Missouri, only later to take them away again. The Lamanites, who are Israelites, were referred to as Jews, and the Gentiles were the people, many of whom were the lawless element, living east of the river." (Joseph Fielding Smith, *CHMR* 1:188.)

57:1-5 *"the land of Missouri . . . is . . . the place for the city of Zion"*

"I removed from Seneca County, New York, to Geauga County, Ohio, in February, 1831.

"I received, by a heavenly vision, a commandment in June following, to take my journey to the western boundaries of the State of Missouri, and there designate the very spot which was to be the central place for the commencement of the gathering together of those who embrace the fullness of the everlasting Gospel. . . . After viewing the country, seeking diligently at the hand of God, He manifested Himself unto us, and designated, to me and others, the very spot upon which He designed to commence the work of the gathering, and the upbuilding of an 'holy city,' which should be called Zion—Zion, because it is a place of righteousness, and all who build thereon are to worship the true and living God, and all believe in one doctrine, even the doctrine of our Lord and Savior Jesus Christ. 'Thy watchmen shall lift up the voice; with the voice together shall they sing: for they shall see eye to eye, when the Lord shall bring again Zion.' [Isa. 52:8.]" (Joseph Smith, *HC* 2:254.)

57:6-7, 11, 13 *Sidney Gilbert, Edward Partridge, William W. Phelps, Oliver Cowdery*

For biographical information on those mentioned in these verses, see the material following their names in Appendix B.

SECTION 58

Background information on section 58

"The first Sabbath after our arrival in Jackson county, Brother W. W. Phelps preached to a western audience over the boundary of the United States, wherein were present specimens of all the families of the earth; Shem, Ham and Japheth; several of the Lamanites or Indians—representative of Shem; quite a respectable number of negroes—descendants of Ham; and the balance was made up of citizens of the surrounding country, and fully represented themselves as pioneers of the West. At this meeting two were baptized, who had previously believed in the fulness of the Gospel.

"During this week the Colesville branch, referred to in the latter part of the last revelation, and Sidney Rigdon, Sidney Gilbert and wife and Elders Morley and Booth, arrived. I received the following: [D&C 58.]" (Joseph Smith, *HC* 1:190-91.

58:2 *"he that is faithful in tribulation, the reward . . . is greater"*

See *Adversity* in Appendix A.

58:4 *"after much tribulation come the blessings"*

"The Saints should always remember that God sees not as man sees; that he does not willingly afflict his children, and that if he requires them to endure present privation and trial it is that they may escape greater tribulations which would otherwise inevitably overtake them. If He deprives them of any present blessing it is that he may bestow upon them greater and more glorious ones by and by." (George Q. Cannon, *MS* 25:634.)

58:4 *"the hour [of the redemption of Zion] is not yet, but is nigh at hand"*

"That Zion was to be established and the city built at once was evidently the idea possessed by some of the Saints. . . .

That the city was not to be built at that time is indicated in his word: [Sec. 58:3-7, quoted.] From this we see that the glory and greatness of the city Zion was reserved for the future; although in the scriptural sense, the time 'is nigh at hand.' " (Joseph Fielding Smith, *ECH*, p. 131.)

58:7 *"that you might be honored in laying the foundation"*

"These early settlers were to lay the foundation, and prepare the way for the Saints, who were yet to come, after the preaching of the Gospel 'to the uttermost parts of the earth,' for the elders were to 'push the people together from the ends of the earth.' It was a great honor conferred upon the first laborers in the vineyard, if they would be faithful to every commandment." (Joseph Fielding Smith, *ECH*, pp. 130-31.)

58:8 *"that a feast of fat things might be prepared for the poor"*

"The Lord also promised to prepare a feast of fat things, even a supper of the house of the Lord, unto which all nations shall be invited. This invitation is to be given first to the rich and the learned, the wise and noble—classes who do not readily embrace the Gospel, and then in the day of his power, the poor, the lame, and the blind, and the deaf, should come in unto the marriage of the Lamb. In this manner the parable of the great supper (Luke 14) will be fulfilled." (Joseph Fielding Smith, *CHMR* 1:195.)

58:11 *"marriage of the Lamb"*

See *Bridegroom* and *Lamb* in Appendix A.

58:15 *"sins . . . are unbelief and blindness of heart"*

" 'Blindness of heart' means affections not guided by the light of the Spirit. Those who place their affection upon wrong objects, such as belong to the world, in preference to those that pertain to the Kingdom of God, are blind at heart, no matter how clear the physical or mental vision may be. He that loveth his own kindred more than the Lord, is blind at heart, for he is not worthy of the Lord and, consequently, not of His household (Matt. 10:37).

" 'Unbelief,' in this case means 'weak faith' (as in Mark 9:24), and it was, perhaps, the cause of the blindness of heart.

"Unbelief and blindness are sins. They must be repented

of. Some teach that we are not responsible for our beliefs. This is not the Lord's view. If we are weak in faith and blind in affections, we need to go to this Great Physician, who can heal us, and if we neglect to do this, we are guilty." (Smith and Sjodahl, *DCC*, pp. 338-39.)

58:19-22 *"my law shall be kept on this land"*

"Very strict was the command to the Saints that the law of God should be kept on the land of Zion. . . . The covenants given then were pertaining to the fulness of the Gospel upon which the City of Zion was to be built. Into this city none were to come except the pure in heart, who were willing to pledge themselves to keep the 'law of God.' At the same time they were to be subject to 'the powers that be,' and not break the law of the land, for they were to consider themselves as a part of the United States, and to this power—the Saints were to be obedient until the time should come when Christ shall take control and assert his right as the Divine ruler of the earth.

"Many of the members of the Church forgot the covenant they had made to 'keep the law of God' upon the land, which was mandatory, and this brought them into trouble. Persecutions came and eventually they were driven from their inheritances. The tribulation in part, but not all, which the Lord had promised they should suffer, came upon them because of their disobedience." (Joseph Fielding Smith, *CHMR* 1:213.)

58:21 *"he that keepeth the laws of God hath no need to break the laws of the land"*

"We believe in being subject to kings, presidents, rulers, and magistrates, in obeying, honoring, and sustaining the law." (Joseph Smith, A of F 12.)

58:26 *"a slothful . . . servant"*

"One day in South America we had the interesting experience of seeing in a hot jungle area a small brownish gray animal hanging upside down in a tree. It had rather long front paws and short back legs. Its movements were so slow that it was hard to know whether it was alive or dead. We were told that it was a sloth. I was intrigued because reference to the sloth appears in scripture. The Lord used it with disdain, referring to those who were slow to act. The word *sloth* or *slothfulness* appears in scripture twenty-five times, generally to condemn those who were slow to act. As we watched that sloth hanging in the tree, it reached out ever so slowly to pull off a leaf, then slower still brought it back and put it into its mouth. As we watched it we could understand the words *impatient, irritated, exasperated.* The Savior's reference to the sloth and slothfulness illustrates His displeasure and impatience with the person who is slow to act, who is slothful." (A. Theodore Tuttle, *Ensign,* May 1978, pp. 87-88.)

58:28   *"inasmuch as men do good they shall in nowise lose their reward"*

"If any man or any woman does good in this world, they shall not lose their reward, whether they be Latter-day Saints or not. But, if they would have all the good, all that the Lord has to bestow upon them, it is necessary for them to have faith in Him, repent of their sins, humble themselves before God and enter into covenant with Him, as the Latter-day Saints have done, and then endure in the faith to the end of their lives." (Francis M. Lyman, *CR,* October 1912, p. 44.)

58:29-33   *"he that doeth not anything until . . . commanded . . . is damned"*

See *Damned* in Appendix A.

"The word 'damned,' which occurs in this Revelation (v. 29), and elsewhere, means to be deprived of the highest glory. It does not mean 'lost.' " (Smith and Sjodahl, *DCC,* p. 347.)

"Today, as in the day when this revelation was given for the government of Zion, men are expected to bring to pass much righteousness without being commanded in all things. The Lord has given us the great gift of agency, but he expects us to use this gift in his service. If we do good, we shall receive the reward; if we obey the covenants we make, the promised blessings are assured. If, however, we break these covenants and do not abide in the law of God, then we have no promise and the blessings shall be withdrawn. The fact that covenants are sealed upon our heads does not entitle us to the blessings except we abide by the law upon which these blessings are based. (D&C 130:20-21.) There may be many disappointments to those who have not, in faithfulness, kept the law." (Joseph Fielding Smith, *CHMR* 1:213-14.)

58:42-43   *The Lord does not remember the sins of those who confess, repent, and are forgiven*

See *Forgiveness* in Appendix A.

58:43   *"he will confess [his sins]"*

See *Confess* in Appendix A.

"This does not mean that the person who has sinned is under obligation to make public his transgression, and proclaim it from the housetops, but that he will make confession in the proper place and way before those who are appointed to hear the case, according to the law given to the Church. (Sec. 42.)" (Joseph Fielding Smith, *CHMR* 1:214.)

58:50   *"Sidney Rigdon" to write "a description of the land of Zion"*

"As we had received a commandment for Elder Rigdon to write a description of the land of Zion, we sought for all the information necessary to accomplish so desirable an object. The country is unlike the timbered states of the East. . . .

"The soil is rich and fertile. . . . [It] bids fair—when the curse is taken from the land—to become one of the most blessed places on the globe. . . . The disadvantages here, as in all new countries, are self-evident—lack of mills and schools; together with the natural privations and inconveniences which the hand of industry, the refinement of society, and the polish of science, overcome.

"But all these impediments vanish when it is recollected what the Prophets have said concerning Zion in the last days; how the glory of Lebanon is to come upon her; the fir tree, the pine tree, and the box tree together, to beautify the place of His sanctuary, that He may make the place of His feet glorious. Where for brass, He will bring gold; and for iron, He will bring silver; and for wood, brass; and for stones, iron; and where the feast of fat things will be given to the just; yea, when the splendor of the Lord is brought to our consideration for the good of His people, the calculations of men and the vain glory of the world vanish, and we exclaim, 'Out of Zion the perfection of beauty, God hath shined.' [Isa. 60; Ps. 50:2.]" (Joseph Smith, *HC* 1:197-98.)

58:53   *"lest they receive none inheritance"*

"The Saints were instructed to be patient and not overzealous in their desires to gather to Zion, but to prepare their way and not come in haste. The Elders of the Church were to give counsel in these matters and none were to go up to Zion until they had received the approval of those who presided. In the course of the next few months many members of the Church located in Jackson County, but they were not permitted to enjoy their inheritances. The work of the Lord was interfered with by enemies of the Saints, and the building of Zion was postponed until some future day when the Lord shall take matters into his own hands and then all opposition shall vanish away. When that day comes, all who are deemed worthy of inheritances shall have earned the right through faithful obedience to the laws of God." (Joseph Fielding Smith, *CHMR* 1:214.)

58:57   *"consecrate and dedicate this . . . spot for the temple"*

"It was also the duty of Sidney Rigdon to consecrate and dedicate the land and the Temple lot unto the Lord.

"The land was dedicated the day after that on which this Revelation was received. Sidney Rigdon asked the Saints present:

" 'Do you receive this land for the land of your inheritance with thankful hearts, from the Lord?'

"Answer from all:—'We do.'

" 'Do you pledge yourselves to keep the law of God in this land, which you never have kept in your own lands?'

" 'We do.'

" 'Do you pledge yourselves to see that others of your brethren who shall come hither do keep the laws of God?'

" 'We do.'

"After prayer Elder Rigdon said, 'I now pronounce this land consecrated and dedicated unto the Lord for a possession and inheritance for the Saints, and for all the faithful servants of the Lord to the remotest ages of time. In the name of Jesus Christ, having authority from Him. Amen.' (*HC* 1:196.)

"The Temple lot was dedicated on August 3rd. Joseph Smith the Prophet, Edward Partridge, William W. Phelps, Oliver Cowdery, Martin Harris, and Joseph Coe were present. 'The scene,' says the Prophet, 'was solemn and impressive.' " (Smith and Sjodahl, *DCC*, p. 345.)

"On the second day of August, 1831, I assisted the Colesville Branch of the Church to lay the first log, for a house, as a foundation of Zion in Kaw township, twelve miles west of Independence. The log was carried and placed by twelve men, in honor of the twelve tribes of Israel. At the same time, through prayer, the land of Zion was consecrated and dedicated by Elder Sidney Rigdon for the gathering of the Saints. It was a season of joy to those present, and afforded a glimpse of the future, which time will yet unfold to the satisfaction of the faithful." (Joseph Smith, *HC* 1:196.)

58:65 *"the Son of Man cometh"*

See *Son of Man* and *Second coming* in Appendix A.

SECTION 59

Background information on section 59

"On the 7th, I attended the funeral of Sister Polly Knight, the wife of Joseph Knight, Sen. This was the first death in the church in this land, and I can say, a worthy member sleeps in Jesus till the resurrection.

"I also received the following: [D&C 59.]

"Polly Knight's health had been failing for some time, according to a statement made by her son, Newel. She was very ill during her journey from Kirtland to Missouri, 'Yet,' says her son, 'she would not consent to stop traveling; her only, or her greatest desire was to set her feet upon the land of Zion, and to have her body interred in that land. I went on shore and bought lumber to make a coffin in case she should die before we arrived at our place of destination—so fast did she fail. But the Lord gave her the desire of her heart, and she lived to stand upon that land.'—*Scraps of Biography,* p. 70." (*HC* 1:199, footnote.)

59:2 *"those that live shall inherit the earth"*

"The Lord said, in the greatest sermon of which we have any record: 'Blessed are the meek: for they shall inherit the earth.' This saying has been made the butt for jokes by the vulgar and ignorant who do not comprehend the sayings of our Lord. One man recently said that if the earth were given to the meek today, the 'unmeek' would take it from them tomorrow. Nevertheless, the meek shall inherit the earth, when the time comes for the Lord to give it unto them. Today, with the earth subject to Satan's rule, it is quite generally the selfish, self-centered, proud and haughty people of the earth who apparently inherit it. This is in harmony with the spirit of unrighteousness which has prevailed on the earth since the fall of man. When Christ comes to take possession of the earth and rule in his right as King of kings, he will keep his promise and the meek shall come into their own. If they die, even then their inheritance shall stand, for the earth is to be the eternal abode of those who inherit the celestial kingdom. The Lord said to Abraham: 'For all the land which thou seest, to thee will I give it, and to thy seed.' (Gen. 13:15.) This expression 'forever' in some texts has reference to this mortal existence, but in the case of this promise to Abraham, it had no such meaning, and when the Lord said he would multiply him and make his seed as numerous 'as the stars of heaven, and as the sand which is upon the sea shore,' that also was a promise extending beyond the bounds of mortality and time, for his blessing of increase was to extend forever. This earth eventually will be prepared for the righteous, or the meek, and it is their everlasting inheritance." (Joseph Fielding Smith, *CHMR* 1:215-16.)

59:2 *"their works shall follow them"*

"Suppose, then, that a man is evil in his heart—wholly given up to wickedness, and in that condition dies; his spirit will enter the spirit world intent upon evil. On the other hand, if we are striving with all the powers and faculties God has given us to improve upon our talents, to prepare ourselves to dwell in eternal life, and the grave receives our bodies while we are thus engaged, with what disposition will our spirits enter their next state? They will be still striving to do the things of God, only in a much greater degree—learning, increasing, growing in grace and in the knowledge of the truth." (Brigham Young, *JD* 7:333.)

59:4 *Revelations to be given "in their time"*

"Revelation continues in the Church: the prophet receiving it for the Church; the president for his stake, his mission, or his quorum; the bishop for his ward; the father for his family; the individual for himself.

"Many revelations have been received and are found in evidence in the onrolling work of the Lord. Perhaps one day other revelations which have been received and have been recorded will be published, and we stand in expectation that '. . . . He will yet reveal many great and important things pertaining to the Kingdom of God.' (Ninth Article of Faith.)" (Boyd K. Packer, *CR*, April 1974, p. 139.)

"There are many revelations to be made known . . . when

we are worthy and willing to receive them. These revelations and commandments cannot be made known now because of our lack of faith and unworthiness before the Lord. (See 2 Nephi 27:7-10; 3 Nephi 26:6-10; Ether 4:6-8.) We have not, after one hundred years of instruction, shown ourselves willing as a united people to receive the 'lesser things' which have been revealed to us and, therefore, are not worthy to receive these greater things which are withheld from us to our condemnation." (Joseph Fielding Smith, *CHMR* 1:216.)

59:5-6 *The Lord's reiteration of the first and second great commandments*

"In answering the question of the lawyer, 'Master, which is the great commandment in the law?' Jesus said unto him: 'Thou shalt love the Lord thy God with all thy heart, and with all thy soul, and with all thy mind. This is the first and great commandment. And the second is like unto it. Thou shalt love thy neighbor as thyself. On these two commandments hang all the law and the prophets.' (Matt. 22:36-40.) This commandment which was given to Israel before they entered into their inheritances in the Promised Land, has again, in this dispensation, been commanded of all members of the Church, and particularly of all who receive inheritances in Zion. So important is this commandment that the Latter-day Saints have had their attention called to it in a number of revelations. It is plain to be seen that on these commandments hang all the law and the prophets. If a person observes these commandments as they are given in verses 5 and 6 of this section (59) he will keep the full law of God. We cannot love our Heavenly Father, and worship him in the name of his Only Begotten Son, our Redeemer, with all our 'heart, might, mind, and strength' without keeping all other commandments. It naturally follows that we will love our neighbor as ourselves and have sympathy and love for all men who are the children of God. There would be no occasion for us to be constantly reminded that we should keep the Sabbath holy, or pay our honest tithes, or keep our bodies clean by observing the Word of Wisdom, or that we should not neglect our prayers, secret and in the family circle, we would observe all of these things and all else that we are instructed to do, IF we loved the Lord our God with all our heart, might, mind, and strength. To the extent that members of the Church observe the laws of the Lord may their love for him be measured." (Joseph Fielding Smith, *CHMR* 1:215-16.)

59:5 *"with all thy might, mind, and strength"*

See *Might, mind, and strength* in Appendix A.

"Our Lord has declared that these are the greatest commandments in the Law, because upon them 'hang' all the Law and the Prophets. The Word of God presupposes and depends on love of God and fellowmen. If there is no such love, laws and instructions are of but little avail.

" 'Heart' stands for 'emotions,' 'sentiment.' 'Might' here stands for 'soul,' the term used in Matthew 22:37, and means the spiritual faculties. 'Mind' refers to the intellect, and 'strength' to the physical attributes. This commandment enjoins on us to love our heavenly Father so that our entire beings—our emotions, our spiritual faculties, our mental and physical activities are all devoted to Him and His service." (Smith and Sjodahl, *DCC,* pp. 349-50.)

59:6 *"Thou shalt not steal . . . commit adultery . . . kill"*

See (1) *Ten Commandments,* (2) *Adultery,* (3) *Killing,* and (4) *Stealing* in Appendix A.

59:9 *"offer up thy sacraments upon my holy day"*

See *Sabbath* and *Sacrament* in Appendix A.

"God has given His children the Law of the Sabbath, in order that they may manifest their love for Him by observing that day.

"On the Sabbath, the Saints should be in the house of prayer and offer up their 'sacraments'; that is, present their devotions before the Lord, in the form of songs of praise, prayer and thanksgiving, testimonies, partaking of the Sacrament, and contemplation of the Word of God. All this is meant by the word 'sacrament,' which, in its widest range, stands for any sacred rite or ceremony whereby we affirm our allegiance to our divine Lord." (Smith and Sjodahl, *DCC,* p. 351.)

59:10 *"to rest from your labors"*

"Instead of suffering our labors to occupy the Sabbath— instead of planning our business to infringe upon the first day of the week, we should do as little as possible; if it is necessary to cook food, do so; but even if that could be dispensed with, it would be better. . . . Under the new covenant, we should remember to preserve holy one day in the week as a day of rest—as a memorial of the rest of the Lord and the rest of the Saints; also for our temporal advantage, for it is instituted for the express purpose of benefiting man." (Brigham Young, *JD* 6:277.)

59:11 *"on all days and at all times"*

"We do not believe in worshiping God, or being religious on the Sabbath day only; but we believe it is as necessary to be religious on Monday, Tuesday and every day of the week, as it is on the Sabbath day; we believe that it is as necessary to do unto our neighbors as we would they should do unto us, during the week as it is on the Sabbath. In short, we believe it is necessary to live our religion every day in the week, every hour in the day, and every moment. Believing and acting thus, we become strengthened in our faith, the Spirit of God increases within us, we advance in knowledge, and we are better able to defend the cause we are engaged in." (Joseph F. Smith, *JD* 12:329.)

59:12 *"the Lord's day"*

"The Church of Jesus Christ teaches that Sunday is the acceptable day for Sabbath observance, on the authority of direct revelation specifying the Lord's day as such. . . . The law of the Sabbath has been reaffirmed unto the Church. It is to be noted that the revelation . . . was given to the Church on a Sunday. (August 7, 1831.)" (James E. Talmage, *VM,* p. 332.)

59:12 *"thou shalt offer thine oblations"*

"In the Mosaic dispensation, an oblation, or offering, was anything presented to God to atone for sins, to merit favors, or to express gratitude for favors received. The firstlings of the flock, first fruits, tithes, incense, the shewbread, all these were oblations or offerings; some prescribed by law, some entirely voluntary. In the New and Everlasting Covenant the Lord graciously accepts tithes and offerings, donations and gifts; and the Lord's day is a very proper day upon which to remember such oblations, as well as to confess sins, publicly among the brethren, if necessary; privately before the Lord, which is always necessary." (Smith and Sjodahl, *DCC,* p. 352.)

59:13   *"let thy food be prepared with singleness of heart"*

"Upon the Sabbath, even the food should be prepared 'with singleness of heart'; that is to say, in simplicity. Our hearts, our desires, on that day should not be elaborate feasts, whereby some are prevented from having a Sabbath. A simple meal should suffice. To that extent every Sabbath should be a fast day, one bringing perfect joy.

"Our Lord, on one occasion, entered the house of Martha and Mary. Martha was cumbered about much serving, desirous of giving the Master many courses, and all in grand style. Mary was anxious to listen to the Master. To Martha's rebuke of her younger sister, our Lord gently replied, 'But one thing is needful.' This might well be always remembered on our Lord's day." (Smith and Sjodahl, *DCC*, p. 352.)

59:13   *"that thy fasting may be perfect"*

See *Fasting* in Appendix A.

59:16-24   *Bounties of the earth intended to be for a blessing to mankind*

"The intentions and purposes of the Lord towards his children have always been to make them happy. This is the very purpose for existence. Lehi has well expressed the thought in these words: 'Adam fell that men might be; and men are that they might have joy.' The Lord does not find happiness in the misery, unhappiness and suffering of men. Men have to pay the price of sin if they will not repent, but that punishment does not come because our Father, who is loving, kind and merciful, delights in giving it. He made the world good (Genesis 1:31) and placed in and upon it every needful thing to bring to its inhabitants happiness, peace and contentment, while they remain here in mortality. True, we would, under mortal conditions, have to come in contact with some sorrow, pain and restriction, no matter how well we kept the commandments of the Lord, for all of this was intended to give us experience, broaden our natures and prepare us to be like our Eternal Father; but the pain, sorrow and distress would be of such a nature that even in it we could find joy, if we were true to the will of the Lord. This would be true, because we would understand the purpose of all the vicissitudes of life and know that they are given for our knowledge and education, and that we may have this necessary experience. . . .

"This world, even in its fallen state, is beautiful with its many gifts and beneficent blessings all arranged for use of man. Our misery, poverty and jealousy come because of selfishness and greed and in the failure to heed the word of the Lord. There is no peace, no happiness, no real prosperity, except through obedience to the will of our Heavenly Father. He has reason to expect us to acknowledge his hand in all things and to keep his commandments." (Joseph Fielding Smith, *CHMR* 1:218-19.)

59:20 *"neither by extortion"*

" 'Extortion' is the act of taking something by violence, by threats, by overcharge, etc., unlawfully. It is lawful to procure, by honest labor, the means whereby the good things of the Earth may be obtained, but it is not lawful to wrest anything from another by methods contrary to this great law: 'Thou shalt love thy neighbor as thyself.' " (Smith and Sjodahl, *DCC*, p. 354.)

59:23 *"peace in this world, and eternal life in the world to come"*

See *Eternal life* in Appendix A, and the material for 36:2.

"Peace is the gift of God. Do you want peace? Go to God. Do you want peace in your families? Go to God. Do you want peace to brood over your families? If you do, live your religion, and the very peace of God will dwell and abide with you, for that is where peace comes from, and it doesn't dwell anywhere else. . . ." (John Taylor, *JD* 10:56-58.)

SECTION 60

"On the 8th day of August, 1831, at the close of the first conference held in Missouri, the elders inquired what they were to do. The Prophet inquired of the Lord and received a revelation giving them direction in relation to their return journey." (Joseph Fielding Smith, *CHMR* 1:220.)

60:2 *"they will not open their mouths . . . they hide the talent"*

See *Missionary service* in Appendix A.

"It is true that not every man is a natural missionary, and there are those who shrink from the responsibility of raising their voices in proclamation of the Gospel, and yet this is an obligation that we owe to this fallen world. The elders in the very beginning had been commanded to serve the Lord with all their 'heart, might, mind and strength' [Sec. 4:2], for the field is white and ready for the harvest. A penalty was to be inflicted upon those who failed and they were not to stand blameless at the last day. The preaching of the Gospel was to be a means to them by which they were not to perish, but bring salvation to their souls. There are many who have been sent forth who have had a fear of man, yet the Lord has promised to support them in their labors if they will trust in him." (Joseph Fielding Smith, *CHMR* 1:203-4.)

60:4 *"I shall make up my jewels"*

Jewels are precious things. Thus the jewels of the Lord are the things which are precious to him—his righteous (obedient) sons and daughters.

"This is an expression found in Malachi 3:17, where 'jewels' refers to the people of God, and where the meaning seems to be that when God segregates His people from the world, His power, as that of a monarch wearing a crown of jewels, will be made manifest to all men." (Smith and Sjodahl, *DCC*, p. 358.)

60:6   *For biographical information on the persons mentioned, see Appendix B.*

60:7   *"I am able to make you holy, and your sins are forgiven you"*

See *Jesus Christ* and *Forgiveness* in Appendix A.

In the final sense, only Jesus Christ is able to forgive, as the law of mercy and thus the principle of forgiveness are effective in our lives because of his atonement. The Savior is able to make us holy (sanctify us) when we receive the gift of the Holy Ghost and repent of all our sins.

60:8, 13-14   *"congregations of the wicked"*

Wicked people are those who disobey the commandments of God and rebel against his teachings. A *congregation* is "an assembly of people." The term *congregations of the wicked* refers to those groups or clusters of people who disobey the commandments of God and fight against him. President Joseph Fielding Smith has indicated that *wicked* in this term refers in a sense to "all who had not repented and received the Gospel." (*CHMR* 1:258.)

"Frequently the Lord refers to the people scattered abroad as 'congregations of the wicked.' We have good reason to believe that wickedness prevailed among the congregations. The elders were to seek out from among the people the honest in heart and leave their warning testimony with all others, thus they would become clean from their blood." (Joseph Fielding Smith, *CHMR* 1:223.)

60:15-16   *"shake off the dust of thy feet"*

See *Feet* in Appendix A.

SECTION 61

Background information on section 61

"On the 9th [of August, 1831], in company with ten
Elders, I left Independence landing for Kirtland. We started
down the river in canoes, and went the first day as far as Fort
Osage, where we had an excellent wild turkey for supper.
Nothing very important occurred till the third day, when
many of the dangers so common upon the western waters,
manifested themselves; and after we had encamped upon
the bank of the river, at McIlwaine's Bend, Brother Phelps,
in open vision by daylight, saw the destroyer in his most horrible power, ride upon the face of the waters; others heard
the noise, but saw not the vision.

"The next morning after prayer, I received the following:
[D&C 61.]" (Joseph Smith, *HC* 1:202-3.)

61:1 *"from everlasting to everlasting"*

See *Eternity to eternity* in Appendix A.

61:1 *"Alpha and Omega"*

See *Alpha and Omega* in Appendix A.

61:2 *"I, the Lord, forgive sins"*

See *Forgiveness* in Appendix A.

61:5 *"I . . . have decreed . . . many destructions upon the
waters"*

"The next morning, after prayer the Prophet received a
revelation in which the elders received counsel in regard to
their travels on the waters. . . . It was stated that it was not
needful for the entire company to travel by water while
people on both sides of the river were perishing for want of
the Gospel. Then the Lord points out that there are many
dangers upon the waters, and more especially upon these
waters many of which were to come hereafter." (Joseph
Fielding Smith, *CHMR* 1:206.)

61:14, 17 *"I, the Lord, in the beginning blessed the waters; but in the last days . . . I cursed the waters"*
"I, the Lord, in the beginning cursed the land, even so in the last days have I blessed it, in its time"

"In the beginning the Lord blessed the waters and cursed the land, but in these last days this was reversed, the land was to be blessed and the waters to be cursed. A little reflection will bear witness to the truth of this declaration. In the early millenniums of this earth's history, men did not understand the composition of the soils, and how they needed building up when crops were taken from them. The facilities at the command of the people were primitive and limited, acreage under cultivation was limited, famines were prevalent, and the luxuries which we have today were not obtainable. Some one may rise up and say that the soil in those days was just as productive as now, and this may be the case. It is not a matter of dispute, but the manner of cultivation did not lend itself to the abundant production which we are receiving today. . . . In those early periods we have every reason to believe that the torrents, floods, and the dangers upon the waters were not as great as they are today, and by no means as great as what the Lord has promised us. . . . In regard to the Missouri-Mississippi waters, we have seen year by year great destruction upon them, and coming from them. Millions upon millions of dollars, almost annually are lost by this great stream overflowing its banks. Many have lost their lives in the sea floods as they sweep over the land, and even upon this apparently tranquil, or sluggish stream there can arise storms that bring destruction. Verily the word of the Lord has been, and is being, fulfilled in relation to those waters. While the Lord has spoken of the sea heaving itself beyond its bounds, and the waves roaring, yet we must include the great destruction upon the waters by means of war, and especially by submarine warfare as we have learned of it in recent years." (Joseph Fielding Smith, *CHMR* 1:206-7.)

61:19 *"the destroyer rideth upon the face"* of the waters

"These brethren while encamped at McIlwaine's Bend on the Missouri, beheld the power of the destroyer as he rode upon the storm. One of that number saw him in all his fearful majesty, and the Lord revealed to the entire group something of the power of this evil personage. It may seem strange to us, but it is the fact that Satan exercises dominion and has some control over the elements. . . . Paul speaks of Satan as the 'prince of the power of the air.' (Eph. 2:2.) The Lord revealed to these brethren some of the power of the adversary of mankind and how he rides upon the storm, as a means of affording them protection. They were commanded to use judgment as they traveled upon these waters, and the saints coming to Zion were instructed to travel by land on their way up to Zion. Moreover, notwithstanding the great power of Satan upon the waters, the Lord still held command and he could protect his people whether on land or by water as they journeyed." (Joseph Fielding Smith, *CHMR* 1:224-25.)

"On the 8th of August, 1831, the Lord in a Revelation (Sec. 60) directed the Prophet Joseph and his companions to return to Kirtland by way of St. Louis. The following day the Prophet, in company with ten Elders, left Independence in canoes and proceeded down the river. The journey was uneventful, until the third day, when the dangers of river-navigation became manifest. The travelers had landed at McIlwair's, or McIlwaine's, Bend, where they encamped on the bank of the river. While here William W. Phelps had a vision in which he saw 'the destroyer' riding upon the face of the waters. Some of the Elders heard a noise, though they did not see anything. The 'destroyer' seen by William W. Phelps in a vision, was, in all probability, the Evil One himself." (Smith and Sjodahl, *DCC*, p. 361.)

61:30 *"congregations of the wicked . . . at Cincinnati"*

See material for 60:8, 13-14.

"Joseph Smith and Sidney Rigdon were commanded that they were not to preach among the people on their return journey until they came to the city of Cincinnati, and there they were to raise their voices 'among the congregations of the wicked,' for the anger of the Lord was kindled against their wickedness, 'a people who are well-nigh ripened for destruction.' At the time of this revelation Cincinnati was only a village, yet it was like other western towns, such as Independence, the gathering place of many who had been forced to flee from the larger cities because of the violation of the law. In all the border towns in that day wickedness to a very great extent prevailed." (Joseph Fielding Smith, *CHMR* 1:207-8.)

61:35 *"let them journey together ... two by two"*

"Our Lord sent His disciples out in pairs. It is not good for men to be alone; nor to travel alone. In congenial companionship there is spiritual strength. It is, moreover, desirable that baptisms and other ordinances be performed in the presence of witnesses. For these reasons the Lord sends His messengers forth in pairs or companies. Elders traveling two by two became a protection to each other against false accusers." (Smith and Sjodahl, *DCC,* p. 368.)

"The Lord called upon these brethren to travel two by two. This is how he sent his disciples out in the days of his ministry. [Mark 6:7.] When they traveled two by two they had protection. They were not as likely to fall into sin, and they were not as likely to be attacked. We ask our missionaries today to travel two by two among the 'congregations of the wicked,' as a matter of protection. Many would have been saved from temptation and sin had they adhered to this regulation and were overcome because they fell into traps set for them which never could have been sprung had they not been alone. Although they were to travel in pairs, yet the Lord cautioned them against temptation while on the way." (Joseph Fielding Smith, *CHMR* 1:208.)

61:38 *"Gird up your loins"*

See *Armor of God* in Appendix A.

61:39 *Be prepared for the second coming, "whether in life or in death"*

See *Second coming* in Appendix A.

SECTION 62

Background information on section 62

"On the 13th [of August 1831] I met several of the Elders on their way to the land of Zion, and after the joyful salutations with which brethren meet each other, who are actually 'contending for the faith once delivered to the Saints,' I received the following: [D&C 62.]" (Joseph Smith, *HC* 1:205.)

"Section 62 is a revelation of instructions to those who were on their way to Zion. They were instructed to assemble themselves upon the land of Zion, and the faithful were promised that they would be preserved and rejoice together in the land of Missouri. There was a great desire on the part of many to go to Missouri, because that was indeed to be the land of Zion, the holy city which had been spoken of by ancient prophets." (Joseph Fielding Smith, *CHMR* 1:226.)

62:1 *The Lord knows how to "succor them who are tempted"*

See *Jesus Christ* in Appendix A.

Succor means "to go to the aid of one in want or distress" or "to relieve." Fortunately, the Savior succors those "who are tempted" so they will not commit sin, and if they should sin, he will succor them if they repent.

62:3 *"the testimony which ye have borne is recorded in heaven"*

See *Book of life* in Appendix A.

62:5 *"two by two"*

See the material for 61:35.

62:5 *"congregations of the wicked"*

See material for 60:8, 13-14.

SECTION 63

Background information on section 63

"In these infant days of the Church, there was a great anxiety to obtain the word of the Lord upon every subject that in any way concerned our salvation; and as the land of Zion was now the most important temporal object in view, I inquired of the Lord for further information upon the gathering of the Saints, and the purchase of the land, and other matters, and received the following: [D&C 63.]" (Joseph Smith, *HC* 1:207.)

"When the report spread among the members of the Church that the Lord had revealed definitely where the city New Jerusalem was to be built, naturally there was rejoicing and many expressed the desire to know what they were to do in order to obtain inheritances. The Lord has given instruction repeatedly that all who go to Zion shall obey His law—the celestial law on which Zion was to be built. Those who were weak in the faith, or indifferent to the commandments, were warned that they would not be made welcome in that land unless they repented. 'Hearken, O ye people, and open your hearts and give ear from afar; and listen, you that call yourselves the people of the Lord, and hear the word of the Lord and his will concerning you.' These are the words by which this revelation is introduced." (Joseph Fielding Smith, *CHMR* 1:229.)

63:7-12 *"he that seeketh signs shall see signs, but not unto salvation"*

See *Signs* in Appendix A.

"Signs shall be given, but not unto salvation, and those who have come into the Church seeking signs and not for the glory of God, shall be punished. We have learned that signs are for the believer and are to follow faith, not to precede it, or to bring to pass conversion to the Gospel. It is a contrite spirit and a broken heart which bring the blessings of the

Father. It is the duty of man, through obedience to the Gospel principles, humility and prayer, to worship God, and these bring faith. Without faith it is impossible for man to please God, and faith is not given to those who are rebellious or unbelieving." (Joseph Fielding Smith, *CHMR* 1:230.)

63:14-16 *"adulterers . . . shall not have the Spirit"*

See *Adultery* and *Sex sins* in Appendix A.

"One of the outstanding evidences of the truth of this latter-day work is the fact that those who are unclean and guilty of immoral conduct will, if they repent not, in time deny the faith. It is this class also which seeks after signs. The Lord said to the Jews who sought a sign: 'An evil and adulterous generation seeketh after a sign. . . .' (Matt. 12:39; see also 1 Cor. 6:9.) This sin stands in the sight of God second only to murder (Alma 39:5) and denying the Holy Ghost. Those who are guilty and do not repent in a short time become fault-finders, criticizing their brethren, then the principles of the Gospel, and finally become bitter in their souls against the work and those who are engaged in it. The most bitter opponents of the Church and the Gospel many times have been proved to be immoral and leading unclean lives. The Prophet Joseph Smith has said: 'Whenever you see a man seeking after a sign you may set it down that he is an adulterous man.' (*HC* 3:385.)" (Joseph Fielding Smith, *CHMR* 1:230.)

63:14-16 *"if any shall commit adultery in their hearts"*

"Immorality was made manifest among some who had joined the Church. Evidently these thought they could hide their sins from the leaders of the Church, but some of them were discovered. Others were to be discovered, for they were known unto the Lord and their evil practices could not be hid. Of these the Lord said, 'Let such beware and repent, lest judgment shall come upon them as a snare, and their folly shall follow them in the eyes of the people.' Not only are men to be judged because of their evil deeds, but for the evil thoughts of their minds. Therefore the Lord repeated the warning which he gave in his sermon on the mount. 'And verily I say unto you, as I have said before, he that looketh upon a woman to lust after her, or if any shall commit adultery in their hearts, they shall not have the Spirit, but shall deny the faith and shall fear.'" (Joseph Fielding Smith, (*CHMR* 1:230.)

63:17   *"fire and brimstone"*

One of the most excruciating physical pains known to man is the burning of the flesh. Brimstone is a very flammable sulfur compound that burns with blue flame and emits a strong odor. The mental pain of the sinner in anguish has been compared to the severity of the physical pain caused by the burning of brimstone on the flesh; hence, the mental and spiritual pain of the sinner is "as a lake of fire and brimstone." (2 Ne. 9:16; Alma 12:17.)

"The nature of burning brimstone is such that it perfectly symbolized to the prophetic mind the eternal torment of the damned. Accordingly we read that the wicked are 'tormented with *fire and brimstone*' (Rev. 14:9-11; 19:20; 20:10), or in other words that 'their torment is *as* a lake of fire and brimstone, whose flame ascendeth up forever and ever and has no end.' (2 Ne. 9:16; Alma 12:17.) This burning scene, a horrifying 'lake of fire and brimstone,' symbolizes 'endless torment' (2 Ne. 9:19, 26; 28:23; Jacob 6:10; Alma 14:14; D&C 76:36); those who find place therein are subject to the second death. (Jacob 3:11; D&C 63:17.) They suffer the vengeance of eternal fire. (D&C 29:28; 43:33; 76:44, 105.) When the sons of perdition come forth in the resurrection, they 'rise to that resurrection which is as the lake of fire and brimstone.' (*TPJS*, p. 361.)" (Bruce R. McConkie, *MD*, pp. 280-81.)

63:17   *"second death"*

See *Second death* in Appendix A.

63:18   *"first resurrection"*

See *Resurrection* in Appendix A.

63:20-21   *"the earth shall be transfigured"*

See *Earth* in Appendix A.

"We have taught that we are living in the day of restoration, in which all things are to be brought back to a similar condition to that which was in the beginning. . . . Moreover in the Articles of Faith the Prophet declares that there will be such a restoration in which the earth shall be 'renewed and receive its paradisiacal glory.' (A of F 10.) All of this is to take place in the Dispensation of the Fulness of times, in which we live. When this is accomplished this earth will again appear as it did in the beginning. The sea will be driven back to the north; the islands will be joined to the main land and the lands will be brought together as they were before the earth was divided. (D&C 133:22-24.)

"We know that when Adam was placed on the earth it was pronounced 'good,' and he, as well as the earth, was not subject to death. There was no 'curse' on the earth. . . . The fall of Adam brought the change upon the earth, and all things upon its face partook of the conditions imposed upon Adam in the fall. (2 Ne. 22:22.)

"The transfigured earth, seen in vision, evidently was this earth in its renewed condition as described by the Prophet Isaiah (ch. 65:17 to end) as it will appear when it is prepared for the millennial reign." (Joseph Fielding Smith, *CHMR* 2:4-5.)

63:24   *"not in haste"*

"It [the gathering] was not to be undertaken in haste, but after due preparation, 'lest there should be confusion, which bringeth pestilence' (v. 24). If they went on the long journey without the necessary preparations, proper food and suitable clothing, the consequence would be sickness." (Smith and Sjodahl, *DCC*, p. 379.)

"Those who had the privilege of assembling there should not go up to Zion in haste, but gradually. The reason for this advice is apparent, for haste would lead to confusion, unsatisfactory conditions and pestilence, and then, also, it creates consternation and fear in the hearts of their enemies and arouses greater opposition. Satan desired to destroy them and in his anger endeavored to stir them up to strife and contention as well as the older settlers in Missouri." (Joseph Fielding Smith, *CHMR* 1:232.)

63:26   *"I . . . render unto Caesar the things which are Caesar's"*

This terminology is almost identical to the answer given by the Savior to the Herodians of New Testament times when they asked him whether or not it was lawful to give tribute unto Caesar. The Savior's answer was "Render therefore unto Caesar the things which are Caesar's; and unto God the things that are God's." (Matt. 22:21; see also Mark 12:16-17 and Luke 20:24-25.)

The Savior has power over all the earth and over all the governments and administrative powers on the earth. Yet he counseled his saints to purchase the lands of their inheritance. In other words, the Saints should recognize the political power by which these lands were sold and administered.

63:28 *"Satan putteth it into their hearts to anger against you, and to the shedding of blood"*

"Towards the last of August [1831] he [Joseph Smith] received another revelation in Kirtland, Ohio, on the great importance of speedily gathering up money to purchase the land in Jackson County. We take the following extract: [Sec. 63:24-31, quoted.]

"This remarkable prophecy in conjunction with those to which we have before referred [Sec. 58:6-12, 44-53], was given . . . at a time when no human sagacity could have foreseen such events. No man, unless he were a prophet, could have so clearly portrayed the subsequent history of the Church. . . . No one would for a moment have supposed, that the people of that boasted land of freedom would shed the blood of the Saints, and drive them from the lands which they had purchased, and persecute them from city to city, and from synagogue to synagogue. All other denominations had been tolerated for many years, and no such scenes of persecution had been known in the United States since their Constitution was formed. Religious freedom was the boast of the whole nation. Yet in the midst of such universal freedom and religious liberty, the voice of a great prophet is heard, declaring the word of the Lord, and predicting events that none looked for—events, that to all human appearance, were very unlikely to come to pass—events that have since been fulfilled to the letter." (Orson Pratt, *MDOP*, pp. 97-98.)

63:29-31 *"the land of Zion shall not be obtained but by purchase or by blood"*

"We learn from these verses [Sec. 63:25-31] that the Lord determined that the Latter-day Saints could secure the land of Zion only by two ways: One by purchase, the other by the shedding of blood. The Lord also determined that possession of that country should not be gained except by the purchase of the land. It should be bought and paid for by the means furnished by the Latter-day Saints, whether rich or poor. It should be bought as other people buy land. The Lord would not permit them to take possession of the land by force, or by antagonizing the people's interests. . . .

"The Lord provided a way whereby they could secure the means to purchase that country, namely by the law of consecration. . . . The Lord sent Elders throughout the States, where there were Latter-day Saints to collect means for this purpose, and the people in Jackson County were required to observe the law of consecration. [Sec. 105:28-29.] But they failed to do it, and therefore the lands were not secured. The Lord could have sustained the people against the encroachments of their enemies had they placed themselves in a condition where he would have been justified in doing so. But inasmuch as they would not comply with His requirements, the Lord could not sustain them against their enemies. So it will be with us, or with any people whom the Lord calls to comply with His requirements." (Lorenzo Snow, *CR*, October 1899, pp. 23-24.)

63:34 *"the saints also shall hardly escape"*

"There is one principle I would like to have the Latter-day Saints perfectly understand—that is, of blessings and cursings. For instance, we read that war, pestilence, plagues, famine, etc., will be visited upon the inhabitants of the earth; but if distress through the judgments of God comes upon this people, it will be because the majority have turned away from the Lord. Let the majority of the people turn away from the Holy Commandments which the Lord has delivered to us, and cease to hold the balance of power in the Church, and we may expect the judgments of God to come upon us." (Brigham Young, *JD* 10:335-36.)

63:34 *"unquenchable fire"*

See *Everlasting fire* in Appendix A.

"This unquenchable fire is, of course, the torment which comes to the wicked who do not repent and who have failed to keep the covenants and commandments. It will be the torment of the mind and soul." (Joseph Fielding Smith, *CHMR* 1:232.)

63:36 *"I, the Lord, have decreed all these things"*

"The Lord has told us that these wars would come. We have not been ignorant that they were pending, and that they were likely to burst out upon the nations of the earth at any time. We have been looking for the fulfillment of the words of the Lord that they would come. Why? Because the Lord wanted it? No; not by any means. Was it because the Lord predestined it, or designed it, in any degree? No, not at all. Why? It was for the reason that men did not hearken unto the Lord God, and he foreknew the results that would follow, because of men, and because of the nations of the earth; and therefore he was able to predict what would befall them, and came upon them in consequence of their own acts, and not because he has willed it upon them, for they are but suffering and reaping the results of their own actions." (Joseph F. Smith, *Relief Society Magazine* 2:13.)

63:39 *"Titus Billings"*

"In the month of April, 1832, he led a company of Saints from Kirtland to Jackson County. He is said to have been the second person baptized in Kirtland, having joined the Church in Kirtland in November, 1830. In 1837, at Far West, he was appointed second counselor to Bishop Partridge, Isaac Morley being the first counselor, and in 1849 he became a member of the Salt Lake Stake High Council." (Smith and Sjodahl, *DCC*, p. 382.)

63:49 *"blessed are the dead that die in the Lord"*

"God, in his eternal decrees, has ordained that all men must die, but as to the mode and manner of our exit, it matters very little. As part of the household and family of God, as beings associated with eternity as well as time, it behooves us to reflect, and that calmly and deliberately, upon our present position, and our relationship and standing before God our heavenly Father. These are important questions for us to solve, and if we can solve them satisfactorily, then all is right." (John Taylor, *JD* 17:131.)

63:50 *"when the Lord shall come"*

See *Millennium* in Appendix A.

63:51 *"old men shall die; but they shall not sleep in the dust, but they shall be changed in the twinkling of an eye"*

See *Twinkling of an eye* in Appendix A.

63:53-54 *"there will be foolish virgins among the wise"*

See *Virgins* in Appendix A.

63:55 *"I . . . am not pleased with . . . Sidney Rigdon"*

For biographical information on Sidney Rigdon, see material following his name in Appendix B.

63:60 *"I am Alpha and Omega"*

See *Alpha and Omega* in Appendix A.

63:61 *"let all men beware how they take my name in their lips"*

See *Swearing* and *Ten Commandments* in Appendix A.

SECTION 64

Background information on section 64

"The early part of September was spent in making preparations to remove to the town of Hiram [Ohio], and renew our work on the translation of the Bible. The brethren who were commanded to go up to Zion were earnestly engaged in getting ready to start in the coming October. On the 11th of September I received the following: [Sec. 64, quoted.]" (Joseph Smith, *HC* 1:211.)

"Because of interference and because he needed a quiet place in which to work, the Prophet on September 12, 1831, moved to the home of John Johnson in the township of Hiram. This was in Portage County, Ohio, about thirty miles southeast of Kirtland. From the time he moved until early in October, the Prophet spent most of his spare time preparing for the continuation of the translation of the Bible. By translation is meant a revision of the Bible by inspiration or revelation as the Lord had commanded him, and which was commenced as early as June 1830. (*HC* 1:215.) Sidney Rigdon continued to write for the Prophet in the work of revision. The day before the Prophet moved from Kirtland he received an important revelation, Section 64, as it now appears in the Doctrine and Covenants. This revelation contained a wealth of information, counsel and warning, for the guidance of the members of the Church." (Joseph Fielding Smith, *CHMR* 1:234-35.)

64:2 *"ye should overcome the world"*

"John, in his First Epistle, says: 'Whatever is born of God overcometh the world,' (5:4); and 'who is he that overcometh the world, but he that believeth that Jesus is the Son of God' (v. 5)? What he wants to say is that as long as we follow our desires to conform to the habits and customs of the world, the commandments of God are hard; but when we overcome that desire and do not conform to the spirit of the world, then His commandments are not difficult, and, if we really believe that Jesus is the Son of God, we shall not take any notice of the world, which is in rebellion against Him. . . . The Elders of the Church . . . should not conform to the world in their worship, in their life, in their amusements." (Smith and Sjodahl, *DCC,* p. 389.)

64:5 *"the keys of the mysteries of the kingdom"*

See *Mysteries* and *Keys of the priesthood* in Appendix A.

"The keys of the mysteries of the kingdom were to remain with Joseph Smith while he lived inasmuch as he should obey the Lord's ordinances. We learned in an earlier revelation that this same promise was made to him [D&C 28:7, 43:3-6], with the warning that if he should fail he would still have power to appoint or ordain his successor, and the Church was instructed that no other was appointed or would be, to give revelations for the Church and this was to be a law unto the Church. This might have saved some ambitious individuals from the pitfalls laid by the adversary, and some who were foolish enough to follow them, if they had been properly impressed with this plain and logical doctrine." (Joseph Fielding Smith, *CHMR* 2:8.)

64:7 *"I . . . forgive sins unto those who confess"*

See *Confess* and *Forgiveness* in Appendix A.

64:7 *"who have not sinned unto death"*

See *Perdition* in Appendix A.

64:9 *"he that forgiveth not his brother . . . there remaineth in him the greater sin"*

" 'Forgive as we forgive,' that is the prayer of the followers of Christ, and our Savior comments as follows:

" 'For if ye forgive men their trespasses your Heavenly Father will forgive you; but if ye forgive not men their trespasses, neither will your Father forgive your trespasses.' Read also His denunciation of those who treat their brethren with taunts and sneers and contempt (Matt. 5:22). Some people who call themselves Christians are bitter and arrogant. The religion of Christ is humanity and love.

"One of the worst traits of human nature is that exhibited by the debtor who said to his fellow-servant, 'Pay me what thou owest.' But we are all apt to feel that way. We flame into anger at the smallest provocation. We brood over injuries and magnify them. We often hear the coarse threat, 'I'll get even.'

" 'When thou sayest "I will not forgive," and standest before God with thy precious *pater noster,* and mumblest with thy mouth "Forgive us our debts, as we forgive our debtors," what is it but saying: "I do not forgive him, so do not Thou, God, forgive me" '—Luther." (Smith and Sjodahl, *DCC,* p. 391.)

64:10   *"of you it is required to forgive all men"*

"The Lord declared that when he was in his ministry his disciples sought occasion against one another and failed at times to forgive in their hearts. It was this condition which prompted Peter to ask the Lord how many times he should forgive his brother, 'till seven times?' The Lord answered him, 'I say not unto thee, until seven times, but until seventy times seven.' (Matt. 18:21-22.) As the disciples of old brought upon themselves affliction and chastening, so we, when we do not have in our hearts the spirit of forgiveness, bring upon ourselves affliction and chastening from the Lord." (Joseph Fielding Smith, *CHMR* 2:8.)

"Now . . . what the Savior meant [Matt. 7:1-2] was that you and I in our capacity as individuals as members outside of any official duty imposed upon us, should not sit in judgment upon one another. . . . It is not our province as members of the Church, to sit in judgment upon one another and call bad names when we reflect upon the acts of people. . . . The bishop's courts and the high councils have the right to sit in judgment, but it must be reached by testimony, not through any feelings or thoughts we may have in regard to the iniquity of some individual." (Charles W. Penrose, *CR,* October 1916, pp. 22-23.)

"In the ancient days, men made sacrifice that they might be forgiven. [Ex. 29:10-14; Lev. 8:14-17.] Today we are told that we must bring to the Lord for our forgiveness a humble heart and a contrite spirit. [Sec. 59:8.] As to forgiveness, the Lord has said [Sec. 64:10, quoted], which means . . . that where there is repentance, we shall forgive and receive into fellowship the repentant transgressor, leaving to God the final disposition of the sin." (J. Reuben Clark, Jr., *CR,* April 1950, pp. 166-67.)

"If we would have peace as individuals, we must supplant enmity with forbearance, which means to refrain or abstain from finding fault or from condemning others. . . . Christ . . . said:

" 'If thou bring thy gift to the altar, and there rememberest that thy brother hath ought against thee; Leave there thy gift before the altar, and go thy way; first be reconciled to thy brother, and then come and offer thy gift.' (Matt. 5:23-24.)

"Note the Savior did not say if you have ought against him, but if you find that another has ought against you. . . . Many of us, instead of following this admonition, nurse our ill-will until it grows to hatred, then this hatred expresses itself in fault-finding and even slander. . . ." (David O. McKay, *CR,* October 1938, pp. 133-34.)

"But suppose one should injure me in person, or estate, and I should overlook it, and show mercy to the individual, it would cause him to reflect upon his conduct, and show him the true bearings of his unjust act, and make him ashamed of it much better than if I retaliated. If I were to pay him back in his own coin, I should render myself worthy of what I have received. If I bear an insult with meek patience, and do not return the injury, I have a decided advantage over my adversary." (Brigham Young, *JD* 2:93.)

64:15-17 *"I . . . was angry . . . with . . . Ezra Booth . . . Isaac Morley . . . Edward Partridge"*

For additional information on each of these brethren, see Appendix B.

"Among the brethren who received the rebuke from the Lord because they 'sought evil in their hearts,' were Isaac Morley and Bishop Edward Partridge, but they speedily repented. It was not so with Ezra Booth. Before he joined the Church he was a Methodist priest. He had visited the home of the Prophet in company with Mr. John Johnson and his wife and a few other citizens of Hiram. Mrs. Johnson had been afflicted for some time with a lame arm, and was not able to lift her hand. During this visit the conversation turned on the subject of spiritual gifts such as those known in the days of the Savior and his apostles. Some one said, 'Here is Mrs. Johnson with a lame arm; has God given any power now on the earth to cure her?' A few moments later, when the conversation had turned in another direction, Joseph Smith arose, walked over to Mrs. Johnson, took her by the hand, and in a solemn manner said: 'Woman, in the name of the Lord Jesus Christ, I command thee to be whole.' Immediately he left the room. The record states that the company 'was awe-stricken at the infinite presumption of the man, and the calm assurance with which he spoke. The sudden mental and moral shock—I know not how better to explain the well-attested fact—electrified the rheumatic arm. Mrs. Johnson at once lifted it up with ease, and on her return home the next day she was able to do her washing without difficulty or pain.' This testimony is taken from *Hayden's History of the Disciples,* pp. 250, 251, and is the testimony of one who did not believe in Joseph Smith. This incident was the means of bringing Ezra Booth into the Church. Having been brought into the Church by the witness of a miracle, he wanted to have power to smite men and make them believe. When he found that this was not the way of the Lord in making converts he was disappointed and turned away, and became a pronounced apostate. He became instrumental in bringing into existence one of the earliest publications against Joseph Smith and the Church. Ezra Booth had accompanied Elder Isaac Morley to Missouri when the elders were appointed to go to that land, but his conduct at that time was not approved. It was not long after his return that he turned away and commenced to fight the Church." (Joseph Smith, *HC* 1:215-16.)

64:18 *"Sidney Gilbert"*

See Appendix B for information on this man.

64:21 *"Frederick G. Williams"*

See Appendix B for information on this man.

64:21 *"retain a strong hold in . . . Kirtland for . . . five years"*

"There were very significant reasons why the Lord desired to retain a strong hold upon Kirtland and its vicinity for five years. It was in that land where the first temple in this dispensation was to be built. In that Temple the essential keys of restoration were to be revealed. It seems apparent that had all the people moved to Zion in Missouri at that time, the building of a temple would have been frustrated by the enemies of the people. Opposition against them in Missouri was made known as soon as members of the Church began to arrive there. In 1833, they were driven from their homes, and the persecution against them raged until, in 1838, it had reached such a stage that the members of the Church, who had been driven first from Jackson County, and then from Ray and Clay counties, and finally from Caldwell where they endeavored to build up their own community, had to flee from the borders of the State. The revelation in which the Lord called upon the Saints to keep a strong hold in Kirtland, was given Sept. 11, 1831. It was in March, 1836, that the house of the Lord was dedicated and the following April when these holy keys were bestowed. After this glorious event, the members of the Church were at liberty to remove to Zion. In fact there followed a few months later an apostasy, and many turned away from the Church, but some were saved, and they were under the necessity of fleeing from the place. However, the Spirit of the Lord prevailed until his work in that place was accomplished and the appointed time had passed." (Joseph Fielding Smith, *CHMR* 1:237.)

64:23 *"It is called today until the coming of the Son of Man"*

See *Today* in Appendix A.

" 'To-day' is the time before the coming of the Lord. The expression is found in Ps. 95:7, and Heb. 3:13. The Psalm referred to was sung at the dedication of the second temple, and it means, *now,* that we had this manifestation of the goodness of God, 'harden not your heart.' The introduction of this phrase here is a prophetic allusion to the building of the Kirtland Temple and the manifestations there to be given, if the Saints would not harden their hearts." (Smith and Sjodahl, *DCC,* pp. 393-94.)

64:23 *"it is a day of sacrifice . . . for the tithing of my people"*

" 'Sacrifice' and 'tithing' seem to be used as synonymous terms here, for the law of tithing had not yet been introduced. The law of consecration was still in force. The law of tithing was first given as the standing law of the Church on the 8th of July, 1838, at Far West.

" 'This event signalized the discontinuance of the United Order, which had practically been dissolved some time before. . . . The law of tithing . . . bears about the same relation to the order of Enoch as the Mosaic law to the gospel of

Christ.' (Whitney's *Hist. of Utah,* 1:141.) The mention of tithing here is prophetic, indicating a restoration of that lesser law, instead of the greater." (Smith and Sjodahl, *DCC,* p. 394.)

"The people of the Lord have always been called upon to sacrifice. This is an essential principle of the Gospel. Likewise they are instructed to pay their tithes and offerings. It is a very strange thing that there are those in the Church who seem to feel that it will be a happy day when the law of consecration is established, yet they do not keep the law of tithing. They seem to think that it will be much simpler and more easy to obey the law of consecration than it will be to observe the law of tithing. We may say, however, that it is extremely doubtful if any person who could pay tithes honestly and does not do so, will ever have the privilege of partaking of the law of consecration. How can we live the higher law, if we cannot live the lesser law?" (Joseph Fielding Smith, CHMR 1:238.)

64:23-24 *"he that is tithed shall not be burned at his coming"*

See *Burned* in Appendix A.

"What does that mean? Does it mean that if man will not pay his tithing, that the Lord is going to send a ball of fire down from heaven and burn him up? No; the Lord does not do that way. The Lord works on natural principles. This is what it means, if I read correctly: a man who ignores the express command of the Lord, by failing to pay his tithing, it means that the Spirit of the Lord will withdraw from him; it means that the power of the priesthood will withdraw from that man, if he continues in the spirit of neglect to do his duty. He will drift away into darkness, gradually but surely, until finally (mark you) he will lift up his eyes among the wicked. That is where he will finally land; and then when the destruction comes and when the burning comes, he will be among the wicked, and will be destroyed; while those who observe the law will be found among the righteous, and they will be preserved. There is a God in heaven, and He has promised to shield and protect them. I tell you there is a day of burning, a day of destruction coming upon the wicked. And where will we be? Will we be with the wicked, or with the righteous?" (Rudger Clawson, *CR,* October 1913, p. 59.)

"The importance of the law of tithing is here shown. In

the day of the Lord the proud and the evil-doers will be destroyed, as completely as straw in a furnace (Mal. 4:1, 2). Those who obey this law will not be counted as 'straw' on that day (v. 24)." (Smith and Sjodahl, *DCC,* p. 394.)

64:24 *"tomorrow"*

> Tomorrow, referring to the second coming of Jesus Christ.
> See *Second coming* in Appendix A.

64:24 *"Babylon"*

> See *Babylon* in Appendix A.

64:27 *"it is . . . forbidden to get in debt to thine enemies"*

> "The members of the Church were commanded not to get into debt to their enemies. Whenever this is done we weaken our hands. At the time this revelation was given such a condition as debt to the enemies of the Church would have proved to be fatal to the cause." (Joseph Fielding Smith, *CHMR* 1:238.)

> "I heard day before yesterday from an eminent financier, a remark that struck me with considerable force. He was telling me how to get out of debt. . . .

> "I listened with a good deal of attention, because I thought it was worth something, and something that all of us ought to know, for a great many of us don't know and have it yet to learn. It was simply this: 'Stop immediately from going into debt. Don't go into another dollar until you get out and are free.' " (Marriner W. Merrill, *CR,* April 1899, p. 15.)

64:29 *"ye are on the Lord's errand"*

> Those who are doing the official business of the Lord in his Church are on his errand; that is, they are (or should be) doing his work as he would if he were here.

> "The Lord always blesses us when we manifest a living faith in Him, and are not afraid that we cannot accomplish some task that He requires at our hands because it looks so large and hard to perform. When we are sent out to preach the Gospel, if we could only remember all the time that we are upon the Lord's errand and that His purposes are not frustrated, how much more strength would the Elders have than they do have now in some cases. If they would only remember that the Lord commands His people to do nothing save He prepares a way whereby they can accomplish it,

what hope and courage it would afford them in their labors."
(Abraham O. Woodruff, *CR,* October 1901, p. 13.)

64:32 *"all things . . . come . . . in their time"*

"A great many members of the Church are disturbed because the redemption of Zion has not come. Some have lost
their faith because it has not come, and they have about concluded that there is not to come such a day. The Lord informs us that his words are sure and shall not fail, 'but all
things must come to pass in their time.' (Vs. 31, 32, Sec. 64.)
Again the Lord said: 'And, now, verily, I say concerning the
residue of the elders of my Church, the time has not yet
come, for many years, for them to receive their inheritance
in this land, except they desire it through the prayer of faith,
only as it shall be appointed unto them of the Lord.' (Sec.
58:44.)" (Joseph Fielding Smith, *CHMR* 1:238-39.)

64:33 *"be not weary in well-doing"*

"In the early days of tribulation in the Church the Lord
encouraged the brethren by telling them that they were laying the deliberate foundation of a great and mighty work. I
recollect how it used to cheer us up in the midst of our
persecutions." (Franklin D. Richards, *MS* 56:404.)

"Very shortly after the organization of the Church, less
than a year and a half, the Lord speaking to the elders of the
Church said: [Sec. 64:33, quoted.]

"According to the law that God had revealed, and in
keeping with the law of the land, this Church was established
with only six members. Yet the early rise of the Church from
that humble beginning was great and marvelous, the Lord
was pleased, and the brethren engaged in the work of the
ministry had been very diligent and devoted. The Lord
assuredly didn't want them to be weary in well-doing because they were laying the foundations of a great work."
(Delbert L. Stapley, *CR,* April 1951, pp. 117-18.)

64:33 *"out of small things proceedeth that which is great"*

"The Lord, in a revelation to the people, known as the
64th Section of the Doctrine and Covenants, says this: [Sec.
64:33, quoted.]

"Daniel's interpretation of Nebuchadnezzar's dream, as
the Lord gave it to him, was that in the last days—that
expression is used—in the days of certain kings also should

the God of heaven set up a kingdom that should never be thrown down or be given to another people. It was likened unto a stone cut out of the mountain without hands, that should roll forth until it should fill the whole earth.

"This Church and the Gospel constitute Mormonism, the biggest thing in this world, yet it has a very small beginning." (George F. Richards, *CR,* October 1932, p. 46.)

"In seeking a testimony of the truth of the Gospel of the Lord Jesus Christ, the Gospel restored in our day, we need chiefly to give attention to the little things of life. The little things are really the great things of life; and the things we call great in life are the little things. Life is made up of little things, our daily duties. We are too prone to say that that which is clear and understandable is of little consequence; while that which is complex and difficult to understand we sometimes hold to be great. Let us remember that the little things of life, the simple things are the ones that lead us into the greater truths." (John A. Widtsoe, *CR,* October 1938, pp. 129-30.)

64:34-36 *"the rebellious are not of the blood of Ephraim"*

"He has said unto us in His revelations that 'the willing and obedient shall eat the good of the land of Zion in these last days.' The obedient are numbered among the children of Ephraim, and the Lord says that 'the rebellious are not of the blood of Ephraim.' He further says that 'they shall be plucked out.' They 'shall be cut off and out of the land of Zion, and shall be sent away, and shall not inherit the land.'

"From the beginning of this Church until the present the men and women who have been obedient to the counsel of God's servants have always been the most favored. . . . There is an order in the Church of Christ which all must observe, and no one can be disobedient without bringing the displeasure of the Lord upon him. This is a principle which all should learn." (George Q. Cannon, *JI,* 10:222.)

SECTION 65

Background information on section 65

"The Prophet Joseph was now living at Hiram, about thirty miles south-east of Kirtland. He had gone there, on invitation of Father Johnson, in order to devote himself to his work on the Bible revision. From Sept. 12, 1831, until the first of October, he did little more than prepare to recommence the translation of the Bible. (*HC* 1:215.) What the preparations consisted in is not stated, but this Revelation, which is an inspired prayer, indicates that an important part of such preparation was communion with God in prayer.

"At Hiram, several important conferences were held. There thirteen Revelations were received, including the memorable vision recorded in Section 76. There a mob, excited by the agitation of Ezra Booth, who had denied the faith and become an enemy, tried to take the life of the Prophet and Sidney Rigdon. No doubt, this Revelation came to strengthen them for the work and experiences before them." (Smith and Sjodahl, *DCC*, p. 397.)

65:2 *"the stone which is cut out of the mountain without hands"*

"The ancient prophets declared that in the last days the God of heaven should set up a kingdom which should never be destroyed [Dan. 2:44], nor left to other people; and the very time that was calculated on, this people were struggling to bring it out. . . . I calculate to be one of the instruments of setting up the kingdom of Daniel by the word of the Lord, and I intend to lay a foundation that will revolutionize the whole world. . . . It will not be by sword or gun that this kingdom will roll on: the power of truth is such that all nations will be under the necessity of obeying the Gospel." (Joseph Smith, *HC* 6:364-65.)

"Our revelations are filled, revelations ancient and modern, with the statement that this work of the Lord is to roll forth as the stone cut out of the mountain without hands,

and fill the whole earth. [Dan. 2:35, 44-45; D&C 109:72-73.]
This Gospel of ours . . . is not merely for us. It is, said the
Lord, in his time for every creature in the world. . . . This is
The Church of Jesus Christ of Latter-day Saints, and its
destiny as well as its mission is to fill the earth and to bring
home to every man, woman and child in the world the truths
of the Gospel of which I have spoken." (J. Reuben Clark, Jr.,
CR, October 1937, p. 107.)

65:5-6 *"the kingdom of God . . . is set up on the earth . . . that the
kingdom of heaven may come"*

See *Kingdom* in Appendix A.

"In this Revelation (65) the two expressions, the kingdom
of God, and the kingdom of heaven, occur. The Prophet Joseph tells us that the kingdom of heaven is the Church. 'The
kingdom of heaven,' he says, 'is like unto a mustard seed.
Behold, then, is not this the kingdom of heaven that is raising its head in the last days in the majesty of its God, even
the Church of Latter-day Saints?' (*HC* 2:268.) He also states
that, 'Where there is a prophet, a priest, or a righteous man
unto whom God gives His oracles, there is the kingdom of
God' (*HC* 5:268). The Church, then, is also the Kingdom of
God. The two terms seem to be used as synonyms, but there
may be this distinction between them, if a distinction it be,
that the domain of God on the other side of the veil is referred to in a particular sense as the Kingdom of Heaven,
while that on this side is the Church or Kingdom of God.
The two constitute the Kingdom of God. One is God's
Kingdom in heaven; the other is His Kingdom on Earth."
(Smith and Sjodahl, *DCC,* p. 399.)

"The expression 'Kingdom of God' is used synonymously
with the term 'Church of Christ' but the Lord had made
plain that He sometimes used the term 'Kingdom of Heaven'
in a distinctive sense. In 1832 He called attention to that in
these words, addressing Himself to the elders of the Church:
[Sec. 65:1-6, quoted.]

"Such was the prayer, such is the prayer prescribed for
this people to pray, not to utter in words only, not to say
only, but to pray—that the Kingdom of God may roll forth
in the earth to prepare the earth for the coming of the
Kingdom of Heaven. That provision in the Lord's prayer,
'Thy kingdom come, thy will be done on earth as it is in

heaven' has not been abrogated. We are praying for the Kingdom of Heaven to come, and are endeavoring to prepare the earth for its coming. The Kingdom of God, already set up upon the earth, does not aspire to temporal domination among the nations. It seeks not to overthrow any existing forms of government; it does not profess to exercise control in matters that pertain to the governments of the earth, except by teaching correct principles of true government, before the Kingdom of Heaven shall come and be established upon the earth with a King at the head. But when He comes, He shall rule and reign, for it is His right." (James E. Talmage, *CR,* April 1916, pp. 128-29.)

65:5 *brightness of the coming of Jesus Christ*

See *Second coming* in Appendix A.

SECTION 66

Background information on section 66

"[On] October 11th and 25th [1831] an important conference of the Church was held. It commenced on the 11th and was adjourned until the 25th, after much business had been transacted. . . . William E. M'Lellin on the first day of the conference held October 25, 1831, sought for a blessing by revelation from the Lord. He accepted the Gospel in the spirit of faith but he had many weaknesses. In seeking this blessing he did so with full desire to know the will of the Lord concerning himself." (Joseph Fielding Smith, *CHMR* 1:244.)

66:1-13   *"William E. M'Lellin . . . you are clean, but not all; repent"*

"Through his repentance and the sincere desire to do right, the Lord declared that he was clean, 'but not all.' There had come to him forgiveness, but still there lingered on in some manner, evidently in his mind and thoughts, something from which he had not cleansed himself by full repentance. The Lord read his soul." (Joseph Fielding Smith, *CHMR* 2:17.)

66:2   *"mine everlasting covenant . . . the fulness of my gospel"*

See *Covenant* and *Gospel* in Appendix A.

66:9   *"Lay your hands upon the sick"*

See *Healing* in Appendix A.

66:10   *"Commit not adultery"*

See *Adultery* in Appendix A.

"This was a wonderful revelation to William E. M'Lellin [Sec. 66] and should have been a great blessing and incentive to him to remain faithful. One besetting sin, so the Lord revealed, was the temptation of sexual sin. He was not accused of committing such a sin, but the dangers because of his failings, which lay in this direction." (Joseph Fielding Smith, *CHMR* 2:17.)

SECTION 67

Background information on section 67

"For some months before the Prophet moved to Hiram he was inspired by the Lord to prepare the important revelations from the beginning for publication. This selection was well under way at the close of the conference of October 25th. As Oliver Cowdery and John Whitmer were making preparations to go to Missouri to attend to the duties assigned them at an earlier date, a conference was called to assemble November 1, 1831, to consider matters as might need attention before their departure. The most important matter to be considered was the publishing of 'The Book of Commandments,' as it had been decided that the compilation of revelations should be called. On the first day of the conference (November 1st) the Lord gave his endorsement to the publication by giving one of the greatest revelations ever received by man as his Preface to the Book of his Commandments.

"On the second day of the conference, the Prophet said that 'inasmuch as the Lord had bestowed a great blessing upon us in giving commandments and revelations,' he asked the conference what testimony they were willing to attach to these commandments which would shortly be sent to the world. A number of the brethren arose and said that they were willing to testify to the world that they knew that they (the commandments) 'were of the Lord.' . . .

"However there were a few of the brethren present who felt because of their superior education that there should be some improvement in the language of the revelations. Considerable time was spent in discussion concerning the language as it had been given, whereupon the Prophet through prayer received a revelation in which the Lord submitted a challenge to these learned brethren. It appears that this revelation silenced the critics, all except one. William E. M'Lellin who was given to some boasting in his own strength, and evidently who had forgotten the word of the Lord given to him at his request at the conference of October 25th accepted the challenge.

"In this revelation (Sec. 67) the Lord acknowledged the prayers that had been offered, and he declared that he knew the hearts of those who were there assembled." (Joseph Fielding Smith, *CHMR* 1:246-47.)

67:5-9 *"appoint him that is the most wise among you" to write a revelation equal to the least of these*

"After the foregoing was received [Section 67], William E. M'Lellin, as the wisest man, in his own estimation, having more learning than sense, endeavored to write a commandment like unto one of the least of the Lord's, but failed; it was an awful responsibility to write in the name of the Lord. The Elders and all present that witnessed this vain attempt of a man to imitate the language of Christ, renewed their faith in the fulness of the Gospel, and in the truth of the commandments and revelations which the Lord had given to the Church through my instrumentality; and the Elders signified a willingness to bear testimony of their truth to all the world. Accordingly I received the following:

" 'This testimony of the witnesses to the book of the Lord's commandments, which He gave to His Church through Joseph Smith, Jun., who was appointed by the voice of the Church for this purpose; we therefore feel willing to bear testimony to all the world of mankind, to every creature upon the face of all the earth and upon the islands of the sea, that the Lord has borne record to our souls, through the Holy Ghost, shed forth upon us, that these commandments were given by inspiration of God, and are profitable for all men, and are verily true. We give this testimony unto the world, the Lord being our helper; and it is through the grace of God, the Father, and His Son, Jesus Christ, that we are permitted to have this privilege of bearing this testimony unto the world, that the children of men may be profited thereby.' " (Joseph Smith, *HC* 1:226.)

"Wm. E. McLellin accepted the offer and, in a spirit of presumption, undertook to imitate the Revelations of the Lord. His effort to produce a Revelation was witnessed with great interest by the Elders, and when they became aware of his complete failure, all doubt concerning the Revelations of God vanished, and they signified their willingness to testify of their truth. Accordingly, a document containing their testimony was drawn up and given to the world." (Smith and Sjodahl, *DCC,* p. 406.)

67:10 *"you shall see me and know that I am"*

"This is a promise which no man could have given with the hope of fulfilling it. But it was fulfilled. On the evening of the first day of the dedication of the Kirtland Temple, there was a gathering of Elders, numbering over four hundred, and many of them testified that they had visions. They heard a sound of a mighty wind. 'Almost every man in the house,' one report says, 'arose, and hundreds of them were speaking in tongues, prophesying and declaring visions, almost with one voice' (JD 40:10). Frederick G. Williams testified that he saw the Savior on that occasion." (Smith and Sjodahl, *DCC,* p. 406.)

67:10 *"not with the carnal neither natural mind, but with the spiritual"*

See *Carnal* and *Spiritual* in Appendix A.

"Visions of our Lord are not perceived with the outward eye, or reflected in the natural mind, but with the spiritual eye. There is a spirit within, whose range of vision is limited by the capacity of physical organs, so that it can neither see nor hear that which lies beyond the boundaries of what we call 'matter,' but when the veil is lifted, the spirit can perceive the spiritual world." (Smith and Sjodahl, *DCC,* p. 407.)

67:11-13 *"no man has seen God at any time in the flesh, except quickened by the Spirit of God"*

This statement helps to clarify the puzzling statement in John 1:18: "No man hath seen God at any time; the only begotten Son, which is in the bosom of the Father, he hath declared him."

The Joseph Smith Translation of the Bible also clarifies the statement as found in the King James Version: "And no man hath seen God at any time, except he hath borne record of the Son; for except it is through him no man can be saved." (John 1:19.)

God is a Holy Person; no unclean thing can enter into his presence. Therefore, a mortal, sinful man must be quickened by the Spirit (the Holy Ghost) before he can endure the presence of God.

67:14 *"continue in patience until ye are perfected"*

"Paul tells us that the Church organization was given to us, among other reasons, for the perfecting of the Saints. [Eph. 4:11-12.] In spite of this commandment, and in spite of this statement of Paul, there are some people who believe that it is impossible for us to become perfect. Perfection is not for this life, they say, and so why try?

"I would like to say that I believe with all my heart that if the Lord had any idea that we could not begin in mortality on the march toward perfection, he would never have given us that commandment [Matt. 5:48]; neither would he have given us a Church organization for the perfecting of the Saints.

"I believe that in many ways, here and now in mortality, we can begin to perfect ourselves. A certain degree of perfection is attainable in this life. I believe that we can be one hundred percent perfect, for instance, in abstaining from the use of tea and coffee. We can be one hundred percent perfect in abstaining from liquor and tobacco. We can be one hundred percent perfect in abstaining from eating two meals on fast day and giving to the bishop as fast offering the value of those two meals from which we abstain.

"We can be one hundred percent perfect in keeping the commandment which says that we shall not profane the name of God. We can be perfect in keeping the commandment which says, 'Thou shalt not commit adultery. (Ex. 20:14.) We can be perfect in keeping the commandment which says, 'Thou shalt not steal.' (*Ibid.,* 15.) We can become perfect in keeping various others of the commandments that the Lord has given us.

"I am confident that one of the great desires of the Lord our God is that we shall keep that great commandment which says, 'Be ye therefore perfect.' (Matt. 5:48.)" (Mark E. Petersen, *CR,* April 1950, pp. 152-53.)

67:13 *"in mine own due time, ye shall see and know"*

"When I was about ten years of age, I began to pray for a special blessing. But I did not get an answer. Why? Father had taught us that there are three factors that must characterize every prayer that the Lord will answer: We must pray for real needs . . . we must pray worthily, and we must pray with faith.

"In answer to my first prayer, no answer came. The faith was there, I felt, to the extent that I could exert it. The need was there, I felt certainly no doubt about that, but was the worthiness? I could as always think of something, as I prayed night after night without an answer, that I had done that I should not have done, and so I continued to pray, feeling that when I could make myself worthy of an answer, I would get it. . . .

"In the latter part of the month of August, 1887, in my nineteenth year, after I had been praying nightly for nine long years with all the earnestness of my soul for this special blessing, I was alone in the bedroom, and I said, half aloud, 'O Father, wilt thou not hear me?' I was beginning to get discouraged. . . .

"Then something happened. The most glorious experience that I have received, came. In answer to my question I heard as distinctly as anything I have ever heard in my life the short, simple word: 'Yes.' Simultaneously my whole being, from the crown of my head to the soles of my feet, was filled with the most joyous feeling of elation, of peace and certainty that I could imagine a human being could experience. I sprang from my knees and jumped as high as I could, and shouted: 'O Father, I thank thee.' At last an answer had come. I knew it.

"Why did it not come before? I have thanked the Lord many times since, that He withheld the answer. . . . Since which time never has a day passed that I have forgotten to pray. And as long as memory lasts I cannot forget the thrilling experience of that night." (Joseph F. Merrill, *CR,* April 1944, pp. 151-52.)

SECTION 68

Background information on section 68

"At the close of the conference of November 1-2, 1831, Elders Orson Hyde, Luke Johnson, Lyman E. Johnson and William E. M'Lellin, came to the Prophet and sought the will of the Lord concerning themselves, and their ministry. The Prophet made inquiry and received the revelation which appears as Section sixty-eight. Surely the Lord in his wisdom poured out knowledge, line upon line, precept upon precept as the members of the Church were prepared to receive it. While this revelation was given at the request of these brethren it was not intended for them alone, but for the guidance of all officers and members of the Church. There had been bishops ordained some months before this time, but their duties and authority were not clearly defined." (Joseph Fielding Smith, *CHMR* 1:257-58.)

68:1 *"Orson Hyde"*

See Appendix B for information on Orson Hyde.

"The prophecy in this verse was literally fulfilled. Orson Hyde proclaimed the gospel 'from people to people, from land to land.' In 1832, he and Samuel H. Smith traveled in the States of New York, Massachusetts, Maine, and Rhode Island—two thousand miles—on foot. In 1835 he was ordained an Apostle, and in 1837 he went on a mission to England. In 1840 he was sent on a mission to Jerusalem. He crossed the Ocean, traveled through England and Germany, visited Constantinople, Cairo, and Alexandria, and, finally, reached the Holy City. On October 24th, 1841, he went up on the Mount of Olives and offered a prayer, dedicating Palestine for the gathering of the Jews." (Smith and Sjodahl, *DCC*, p. 409.)

68:1 *"everlasting gospel"*

See *Gospel* in Appendix A.

68:1 *"congregations of the wicked"*

See same title, Appendix A, and material for 60:8, 13-14.

68:4 *"whatsoever they shall speak when moved upon by the Holy Ghost shall be scripture"*

"Peter said that 'prophecy came not in old time by the will of man: but holy men of God spake as they were moved by the Holy Ghost.' (2 Peter 1:21.) That which they spoke under this influence we have accepted as scripture. Paul in writing to Timothy said: 'And that from a child thou hast known the holy scriptures, which are able to make thee wise unto salvation through faith which is in Christ Jesus. All scripture given by inspiration of God, is profitable for doctrine, for reproof, for correction, for instruction in righteousness.' (JST, 2 Tim. 3:16.) That which we accept as scripture today is the utterance of prophets who spoke by inspiration and in the spirit of prophecy in olden times. Age has made it venerable to many because it is ancient. The word of the Lord delivered by the power of the Holy Ghost to the servants of the Lord today is also scripture, just as much as it was in ancient times.

"This is logical and therefore reasonable, and there is no truth in the prevalent doctrine that the word of the Lord came in times of old, but that since the days of the apostles there has been no scripture and cannot be, for the canon of scripture is completed. However, we, the elders of Israel, do not always speak as 'moved upon by the Holy Ghost.' There is danger that we may permit our own inclinations and desires to influence us and we may be stubborn enough to lack the essential humility, so that the Holy Ghost cannot break through the shell with which we surround ourselves. Therefore, we should seek for humility in the spirit of prayer and obedience so that we may always be subject to the teachings of the Spirit of the Lord." (Joseph Fielding Smith, *CHMR* 1:258-59.)

"What is scripture? When one of the brethren stands before a congregation of the people today, and the inspiration of the Lord is upon him, he speaks that which the Lord would have him speak. It is just as much scripture as anything you will find written in any of these records, and yet we call these the standard works of the Church. We depend, of course, upon the

guidance of the brethren who are entitled to inspiration.

"There is only one man in the Church at a time who has the right to give revelation for the Church, and that is the President of the Church. But that does not bar any other member in this Church from speaking the word of the Lord, as indicated here in this revelation, section 68, but a revelation that is to be given as these revelations are given in this book, to the Church, will come through the presiding officer of the church; yet, the word of the Lord, as spoken by other servants at the general conferences and stake conferences, or wherever they may be when they speak that which the Lord has put into their mouths, is *just as much the words of the Lord as the writings and the words of other prophets in other dispensations."* (Joseph Fielding Smith, *DS* 1:186.)

"It is not to be thought that every word spoken by the General Authorities is inspired, or that they are moved upon by the Holy Ghost in everything they read and write. Now you keep that in mind. I don't care what his position is, if he writes something or speaks something that goes beyond anything that you can find in the standard church works, unless that one be the prophet, seer, and revelator—please note that one exception—you may immediately say, 'Well, that is his own idea.' And if he says something that contradicts what is found in the standard church works (I think that is why we call them 'standard'—it is the standard measure of all that men teach), you may know by that same token that it is false, regardless of the position of the man who says it." (Harold B. Lee, *ASIF,* July 8, 1964, p. 11.)

"The question is, how shall we know when the things they have spoken were said as they were 'moved upon by the Holy Ghost?' I have given some thought to this question, and the answer thereto so far as I can determine, is: We can tell when the speakers are 'moved upon by the Holy Ghost,' only when we, ourselves, are 'moved upon by the Holy Ghost.' In a way, this completely shifts the responsibility from them to us to determine when they so speak.

"In considering the problem involved here, it should be in mind that some of the General Authorities have had assigned to them a special calling; they possess a special gift; they are sustained as prophets, seers, and revelators, which gives them a special spiritual endowment in connection with their teaching of the people. They have the right, the power, and authority to declare the mind and will of God to his people, subject to the overall power and authority of the President of the Church. . . . Furthermore, as just indicated, the President of the Church has a further and special spiritual endowment in this respect, for he is *the* Prophet, Seer, and Revelator for the whole Church. . . .

"He alone has the right to receive revelations for the Church, either new or amendatory, or to give authoritative interpretations of scriptures that shall be binding on the Church, or change in any way the existing doctrines of the Church." (J. Reuben Clark, Jr., *ASIF,* July 7, 1954.)

68:6 *"living God"*

See *Living God* in Appendix A.

68:7 *See Appendix B for biographical information on the brethren mentioned.*

68:10-11 *"signs"*

See *Signs* and *Second coming* in Appendix A.

68:13-24 *"other bishops . . . shall be high priests . . . except they be literal descendants of Aaron"*

"In these paragraphs the Lord gives instructions regarding the appointment of Bishops. Edward Partridge was the first Bishop appointed (Sec. 41:9). Other Bishops were to be called in due time (v. 14). It was, therefore, necessary to have instructions concerning their appointment. Isaac Morley and John Corrill, who had been Bishop Partridge's counselors, were selected as second and third Bishops respectively. Morley was to select Christian Whitmer and Newel Knight for his counselors; and Corrill, Daniel Stanton and Hezekiah Peck (*HC* 1:363).

"Bishops must be High Priests, and they must be *worthy;* they must be appointed by the First Presidency of the Melchizedek Priesthood, unless they are literal descendants of Aaron (v. 15); in which case, if they are firstborn, they have a right to the Bishopric, as heirs; but even a lineal descendant of Aaron must be designated, found worthy, anointed, and ordained by the First Presidency (v. 20); any High Priest of the Melchizedek Priesthood may officiate in the Bishopric, if he is called, ordained, and set apart by the First Presidency.

"The Bishop, with his counselors, is the head of the *Ward,* under the direction of the President of the *Stake,* of which the Ward is an ecclesiastical division. He presides over the Aaronic Priesthood." (Smith and Sjodahl, *DCC,* p. 413.)

"The office of Presiding Bishop of the Church is the same as the office which was held by Aaron. It is the highest office, holding the presidency in the Aaronic Priesthood. It was this office which came to John the Baptist, and it was by virtue of the fact that he held the keys of this power and ministry that he was sent to Joseph Smith and Oliver Cowdery to restore that Priesthood, May 15, 1829. The person who has the legal right to this presiding office has not been discovered; perhaps is not in the Church, but should it be shown by revelation that there is one who is the 'firstborn among the sons of Aaron,' and thus entitled by birthright to this presidency, he could 'claim' his 'anointing' and the right to that office in the Church. The Lord has spoken it in these words: 'But, by virtue of the decree concerning their right of the priesthood descending from a father to son, they may claim their anointing if at any time they can prove their lineage, or do ascertain it by revelation from the Lord, under the hands of the above named Presidency.' [68:21.] That is to say, if the rightful heir to this office could prove the same he could claim his anointing under the hands of the Presidency of the Church. Today we are under the necessity of having high priests act as bishops in the Church, in all local offices as well as in the presiding office in this Priesthood. The direct descendants of Aaron could act without counselors, but unless they were also high priests, they could not serve as bishops in the same capacity and authority as do the bishops of the present order, who are high priests." (Joseph Fielding Smith, *CHMR* 1:259.)

68:22-24   *The Presiding Bishop to be tried by the First Presidency*

"In case of the transgression of the Presiding Bishop of the Church, he could not be tried by a high council in the stake in which he lives, but he would have to be tried by the First Presidency of the Church. The reason for this is that he holds the keys of presidency of the Aaronic Priesthood and is not under the jurisdiction of any ward or stake in this capacity. This order given for the trial of the presiding bishop does not apply to a local bishop in a ward, who is under the jurisdiction of the presidency of the stake." (Joseph Fielding Smith, *CHMR* 2:30-31.)

68:25-28 *Parents are to teach the gospel to their children*

"Every soul is precious in the sight of God. We are all his children and he desires our salvation. Free agency is given to each individual, but still the Lord has placed the responsibility upon all parents in the Church to teach their children in light and truth. He has placed the obligation upon all parents that they must teach the first principles of the gospel to their children, teach them to pray, and see that they are baptized when they are eight years of age. Parents cannot shirk or neglect this great responsibility without incurring the displeasure of a righteous God. He has not relinquished his claim upon his children when they are born into this world and therefore commands parents to teach their offspring so that they may be brought up in the truth of the everlasting Gospel. For parents to fail to do this places them in condemnation and the sin of such neglect will have to be answered with punishment on their own heads. This is a law unto Zion and all of her stakes." (Joseph Fielding Smith, *CHMR* 1:260.)

"And in that same inspired declaration by revelation [Sec. 68:25-28], the Lord gave us what we might style as a five-point program by which parents could teach faith. First, he said, their children were to be baptized when they had reached the age of accountability at eight years; second, they were to be taught to pray; third, they were to be taught to walk uprightly before the Lord; fourth, they were to be taught to keep the Sabbath day holy; and fifth, they were to be schooled not to be idle, either in the church or in their private lives.

"All parents who have followed that formula and have so taught their children have reaped the reward of an increased faith in their family, which has stood and will yet stand the test of the difficulties into which their children would yet go." (Harold B. Lee, *CR*, October 1952, p. 17.)

"Parents, if we are to teach our children to keep the commandments and walk uprightly before God, we must be their living example. We cannot break any law with impunity and expect our children to honor and obey us or the law. We cannot question the teachings and commandments of the Lord without causing great doubts in the minds of our children as to why they should keep the commandments. We cannot be hypocrites. We cannot teach or profess a belief in one thing and live another, and expect our children to obey the commandment: 'Honour thy father and thy mother: that thy days may be long upon the land which the Lord thy God giveth thee.' (Exod. 20:12.)

"Children who are taught obedience, to honor and obey the law, to have faith in God and to keep his commandments, will, as they grow up, honor their parents and be a credit to them; and they will be able to meet and solve their problems, find greater success and joy in life, and contribute greatly to the solution of the problems now causing the world such great concern. It is up to the parents to see to it that their children are prepared through obedience to law for the positions of leadership they will occupy in the future, where their responsibility will be to bring peace and righteousness to the world." (N. Eldon Tanner, *IE,* June 1970, p. 32.)

"I believe we start to fail in the home when we give up on each other. We have not failed until we have quit trying. As long as we are working diligently with love, patience, and long-suffering, despite the odds or the apparent lack of progress, we are not classified as failures in the home. We only start to fail when we give up on a son, daughter, mother, or father." (Marvin J. Ashton, *Ensign,* June 1971, pp. 31-32.)

"I have sometimes seen children of good families rebel, resist, stray, sin, and even actually fight God. In this they bring sorrow to their parents, who have done their best to set in movement a current and to teach and live as examples. But I have repeatedly seen many of these same children, after years of wandering, mellow, realize what they have been missing, repent, and make great contribution to the spiritual life of their community. The reason I believe this can take place is that, despite all the adverse winds to which these people have been subjected, they have been influenced still more, and much more than they realized, by the current of life in the homes in which they were reared. When, in later years, they feel a longing to recreate in their own families the same atmosphere they enjoyed as children, they are likely to turn to the faith that gave meaning to their parents' lives.

"There is no guarantee, of course, that righteous parents will succeed always in holding their children, and certainly they may lose them if they do not do all in their power. The children have their free agency.

"But if we as parents fail to influence our families and set them on the 'strait and narrow way,' then certainly the waves, the winds of temptation and evil will carry the posterity away from the path.

" 'Train up a child in the way he should go; and when he is old, he will not depart from it.' (Prov. 22:6.) What we do know is that righteous parents who strive to develop wholesome influences for their children will be held blameless at the last day, and that they will succeed in saving most of their children, if not all." (Spencer W. Kimball, *Ensign,* November 1974, pp. 111-12.)

68:27   *"children shall be baptized . . . when eight years old"*

"Have you a child who is eight years of age or older, who has not been baptized into the Church? . . .

"The Lord has told us several things about this matter: First, he says that little children are redeemed from before the foundations of the world. In other words, if a little child dies, he or she receives the blessings of the redemption of Christ. The child is saved in the kingdom of heaven.

"Then he tells us that little children living upon the earth in mortality are not subject to temptation by the devil. 'Wherefore,' he says, 'they cannot sin, for power is not given unto Satan to tempt little children until they begin to be accountable before me.' (D&C 29:46-47.)

"And next he tells us that children become accountable before him at eight years of age, and that is the time when they shall be baptized. (D&C 18:42; 20:71; 68:25-28.)

"If they are not thus baptized, he explains, the parents will be held responsible. . . .

"There are two main purposes in baptism: to obtain admission to the Church, and to receive remission of sins. For the adult convert both of these blessings come. For the child at the age of eight, who has been in the fold as one of those little ones spoken of by the Savior, again both blessings are conferred. He is perpetuated in his place in the kingdom of God, holding full membership; also he receives the blessing of remission for his sins, as he is now accountable for them.

"Children over eight are held responsible for their sins, according to the law of the Lord, and yet, without repentance and baptism there is no remission of those sins. No unclean thing can come into God's presence. Sin takes us away from the Lord, and places us in the power of Satan. Children who sin, and are not taught the gospel, and therefore do not obey it, are in a precarious position. Their very soul's salvation is in jeopardy." (Mark E. Petersen, *YFY,* pp. 161-163.)

68:29 *"observe the Sabbath day"*

See *Sabbath* in Appendix A.

68:31 *"riches of eternity"*

See same title in Appendix A.

68:33 *"prayers . . . in the season thereof"*

"The season of prayer is in the morning before the family separates. A good time for prayer is when you assemble at the table before you partake of the morning meal, and let the members of the family take turns in the praying. That is the season of prayer. The season of prayer for the merchant is in the morning when he goes to his place of business and before he begins his day's work, over his merchandise. The time of prayer for the shepherd is when he is out with his flocks watching over them. The time for the farmer to pray is when he goes with his plow into the field, when he goes to sow his grain, and when he goes to gather his harvest. And if a man will pray as he is commanded to do in the passage of scripture which I have read [Sec. 68:33], then he more than likely will be found in all things righteously keeping the commandments of the Lord. He will not be found scheming to take advantage of his neighbor in some trade or bargain, but in all things dealing justly, because he has prayed in the morning and has in his heart the spirit of prayer throughout the day, that the Lord will bless him in the increase of his goods, of his fields, of his flocks, or whatever it may be he is engaged in. So that is the season of prayer." (Joseph Fielding Smith, *CR,* October 1919, p. 143.)

68:33 *"the judge of my people"*

"The common judge in Israel is the ward bishop. It is his duty to watch over his flock. To aid him he has the force of the Aaronic Priesthood and all of the brethren holding the Melchizedek Priesthood who are at liberty and who may be called to serve as acting teachers and priests in his ward." (Joseph Fielding Smith, *CHMR* 1:261.)

68:35 *"I am Alpha and Omega . . . I come quickly"*

See *Alpha and Omega* and *Quickly* in Appendix A.

SECTION 69

Background information on section 69

See background information for section 67.

"At the Conference held at Hiram. November 1st and 2nd, 1831, it had been decided that Oliver Cowdery should take the *Commandments and Revelations, in manuscript,* to Independence, Mo., and publish them there; also that the Prophet should dedicate the work to God. After the dedicatory prayer, he received this Revelation, in which he was instructed to send John Whitmer with Oliver Cowdery, and charge him (Whitmer) to continue his labors as Church Historian." (Smith and Sjodahl, *DCC,* p. 417.)

69:1-2 *Oliver Cowdery to take John Whitmer with him in going "unto the land of Zion"*

For biographical information on Oliver Cowdery, see Appendix B.

"In this commandment the Lord declared that it was not wisdom that Oliver Cowdery should make the journey alone. The journey was about one thousand miles and through a sparsely settled country. There were many dangers on the way. The revelations were considered to be priceless and then, besides, Oliver carried with him sums of money to assist in the work in Missouri. John Whitmer was therefore appointed to accompany Oliver. This was not to relieve him, however, of his duty to write history, for he had been called to keep the historical record of the Church. He was to observe and make a record of all the important things which he should observe and know concerning the Church. John Whitmer was also to receive counsel from Oliver Cowdery and others." (Joseph Fielding Smith, *CHMR* 1:249.)

"It must not be understood from the first paragraph of this revelation that Oliver Cowdery was untrustworthy, and therefore it was necessary that a companion be provided for him. The fact was that much of the journey between Kirtland and Independence, or Zion, was through a sparsely settled country, the western portion of it through frontier country where there is always a gathering, more or less, of lawless people; and it was at considerable risk that a person traveled through such a country, especially when alone and carrying money with him. It was wisdom then, for the sake of Oliver Cowdery, and to insure the safety of the money and the sacred things he was to carry with him, that one should go with him that would be a true and faithful companion, hence the appointment of John Whitmer." (Joseph Smith, *HC* 1:234.)

SECTION 70

Background information on Section 70

"My time [wrote Joseph Smith] was occupied closely in reviewing the commandments and sitting in conference, for nearly two weeks; for from the first to the twelfth of November we held four special conferences. In the last which was held at Brother Johnson's, in Hiram, after deliberate consideration, in consequence of the book of revelations, now to be printed, being the foundation of the Church in these last days, and a benefit to the world, showing that the keys of the mysteries of the kingdom of our Savior are again entrusted to man; and the riches of eternity within the compass of those who are willing to live by every word that proceedeth out of the mouth of God—therefore the conference voted that they prize the revelations to be worth to the Church the riches of the whole earth, speaking temporally. The great benefits to the world which result from the Book of Mormon and the revelations which the Lord has seen fit in His infinite wisdom to grant unto us for our salvation, and for the salvation of all that will believe, were duly appreciated; and in answer to an inquiry, I received the following: [Section 70 follows.]" (Joseph Smith, *HC* 1:235-36.)

70:1-4 *Stewards appointed over the revelations and commandments*

For biographical information on all the persons mentioned in this section, see Appendix B.

"The Lord guarded these revelations with the greatest care. After the Prophet Joseph Smith had made copies and had compiled them for publication, he and Oliver Cowdery, John Whitmer, Sidney Rigdon and William W. Phelps were called by revelation to be 'stewards' over the revelations and commandments, and the Lord said that 'an account of this stewardship will I require of them in the day of judgment.'

(Sec. 70:3-4.) This indicates the importance with which the Lord held his divine word. Precautions were taken in forwarding these revelations to Zion, which was the 'seat and a place to receive and do all these things.' (i.e. publish the revelations and do the printing for the Church. See Sec. 69:6.)

"The reason for such jealous care is due to the fact that the heavens had been sealed for ages by man's rebellion and rejection of the Gospel as it was delivered by the apostles in the Meridian of Time. Again, the Lord was prepared to make known his covenants and commandments." (Joseph Fielding Smith, *CHMR* 1:253.)

70:10 *"none are exempt from this law"* of consecration

See *Consecration* in Appendix A.

70:12 *"He who is appointed to administer spiritual"* or temporal things *"is worthy of his hire"*

The Lord herein indicated that all those who were required to spend full time in the service of the Church, whether in administering spiritual things or temporal things, were worthy to receive their support from the funds of the Church. This would indicate that other service in the Church would be on an unpaid or "Church-service" basis.

"Official service in the church is unpaid. Therefore it is necessarily part-time service. The officer must earn his living while he serves the church. For the government of the church . . . very few persons are called to give their full time to the church. . . . The work of the church may be said correctly to be done by an unpaid ministry. Nevertheless, those who serve the church in this manner of sacrifice unanimously declare that the spiritual reward from the service is far greater than any material reward that might be offered. And, besides, it has been found that active participation in church affairs gives experience which is of real value in the world of affairs outside of the Church." (John A. Widtsoe, *GI*, pp. 104-5.)

70:14 *"in your temporal things you shall be equal"*

See material for 78:5-7.

"To be equal did not mean that all should have the same amount of food, but each should have according to his needs. For instance, a man would receive in proportion to the number in the family, not according to the nature of his work. He was to have, 'for food and for raiment; for an inheritance; for houses and for lands, in whatsoever circumstances I, the Lord, shall place them.' " (Joseph Fielding Smith, *CHMR* 2:39-40.)

SECTION 71

Background information on section 71

"After Oliver Cowdery and John Whitmer had departed for Jackson county Missouri, I resumed the translation of the Scriptures, and continued to labor in this branch of my calling with Elder Sidney Rigdon as my scribe, until I received the following: [section 71]." (Joseph Smith, *HC* 2:238.)

"Ezra Booth, who apostatized after his return from Missouri, did all in his power to injure the Church. He was responsible for the publication of the earliest attacks against the Church. He also caused articles to be published in the press among which were some scandalous letters published in the Ravenna *Ohio Star,* which created a bitter spirit on the part of many people. December 1, 1831, the Lord gave a revelation to Joseph Smith and Sidney Rigdon (Sec. 71) in which the Lord said: 'Behold, thus saith the Lord unto you . . . that the time has verily come that it is necessary and expedient in me that you should open your mouths in proclaiming my gospel, the things of the kingdom, expounding the mysteries thereof out of the scriptures, according to that portion of spirit and power which shall be given unto you, even as I will.' They were, therefore, released for the time of this mission from translating the scriptures, that they might go forth to confound their enemies." (Joseph Fielding Smith, *CHMR* 1:269.)

71:1 *"the mysteries"*

See *Mysteries* in Appendix A.

"The Prophet, by this time, had learned many great and glorious truths, partly by the direct Revelations he had received, and partly by close study of the Scriptures. To the world, many of these truths were 'mysteries.' The time had come to reveal them, and when they were revealed, or unveiled, they would be mysteries no longer. When the gospel of Christ was first preached by Peter, Paul, and the other

Apostles of their day, the doctrine of the Incarnation was a mystery (1 Cor. 2:7; 1 Tim. 3:16); the doctrine of the resurrection (1 Cor. 15:51), and the gathering of the Gentiles into the Church (Col. 1:26, 27) were mysteries. In our dispensation, the doctrines of the gathering and of the building of temples and the City of Zion are as great mysteries, until they are explained by the Holy Spirit of Promise. The Prophet Joseph and Sidney Rigdon were now to go forth and proclaim these and other truths to the Church and the world, for a season." (Smith and Sjodahl, *DCC*, pp. 422-23.)

71:7 *"confound your enemies; call upon them to meet you . . . in public"*

"In obedience to this call Joseph Smith and Sidney Rigdon left Kirtland December 3, 1831, and went forth in Kirtland, Shalersville, Ravenna and other places preaching boldly the truth and calling on their traducers to meet them and face their falsehoods. This was rather an unusual condition. Quite generally the Lord counsels his servants not to engage in debates and arguments, but to preach in power the fundamental principles of the Gospel. This was a condition that required some action of this kind, and the Spirit of the Lord directed these brethren to go forth and confound their enemies which they proceeded immediately to do, as their enemies were unable to substantiate their falsehoods and were surprised by this sudden challenge so boldly given. Much of the prejudice was allayed and some friends made through this action." (Joseph Fielding Smith, *CHMR* 1:269.)

SECTION 72

Background information on section 72

"Knowing now the mind of the Lord, that the time had come that the Gospel should be proclaimed in power and demonstration to the world, from the Scriptures, reasoning with men as in days of old, I took a journey to Kirtland, in company with Elder Sidney Rigdon on the 3rd day of December, to fulfill the above revelation. [Sec. 71.] On the 4th, several of the Elders and members assembled together to learn their duty, and for edification, and after some time had been spent in conversing about our temporal and spiritual welfare, I received the following: [D&C 72.]" (Joseph Smith, *HC* 1:239.)

72:3 *"it is required . . . of every steward"*

See *Steward* in Appendix A.

72:5 *"the elders . . . shall render an account of their steward-ship unto the bishop"*

"At a very early day after the organization of the Church the Lord revealed the need of a bishop to look after the temporalities and stewardships in the Church. Bishop Edward Partridge was called and sent to Zion to engage in the duties of his calling. On the 4th day of December, 1831, while the Prophet and Sidney Rigdon were engaged in their ministry refuting their enemies, a meeting of the elders was called and the Lord gave them a very important revelation. The Lord declared that it was expedient that a bishop should be called to serve in the Kirtland district. One important duty of this bishop was to look after the stewardships pertaining to the inhabitants of Kirtland and other parts of Ohio, and he was 'to render an account of his stewardship, both in time and in eternity.' " (Joseph Fielding Smith, *CHMR* 1:269.)

72:8 *"Newel K. Whitney"*

For biographical information on Newel K. Whitney, see Appendix B.

72:9-26 *"making known the duty of the bishop"*

See *Bishop* and *Priesthood offices* in Appendix A.

"The duties of the Bishop in Kirtland are here enumerated. They are, (a) to keep the Lord's storehouse and receive the funds of the Church in that part of the vineyard (v. 10); that is, to look after the needy and preside over the temporal affairs of the Church; (b) to keep an account of property consecrated for public use, as commanded (Sec. 42:31-2), and administer to the need of the Elders (v. 11), whether these were able to pay for the services rendered, or not (vv. 12-13); the Lord here makes it clear that faithful service in administering in spiritual things is also a contribution to the general funds (vv. 14-15). (c) The Bishop is, further, under obligation to furnish every Elder entitled to it, a certificate, by which the Bishop in Zion may know that the bearer has the right to receive an inheritance (vv. 16-18); he is (d) to receive an account of the labors of every Elder, in order that these might be properly recommended to the Branches they might visit (v. 19); (e) he was, finally, to aid, financially, the 'stewards' appointed to look after the literary interests of the Church (Sec. 72:20). 'This,' we read, 'shall be an ensample'—a pattern, or model for imitation—for all Branches of the Church (v. 23). All were to have Bishops with similar duties to perform." (Smith and Sjodahl, *DCC*, p. 427.)

72:12-26 *"this . . . may be consecrated"*

See *Consecration* and *United Order* in Appendix A.

"In these revelations the Lord endeavored to teach the members of the Church the law of consecration. It had been decreed that Zion (meaning at that time Jackson County) was to be built up on this divine law. All who went there were expected to consecrate their property, and then they were to receive stewardships severally according to their needs. The Lord's plan was that the poor and the needy should be assisted, and all who had substance should impart according to the Lord's divine law. [Sec. 42:30-42.]

"According to this plan the labors of those who gave their time 'in spiritual things, in administering the gospel and the things of the kingdom of the Church, and unto the world,' were to be counted worthy, but they like all others were to give an account to the bishop in Zion. It was the command—

'Every man that cometh up to Zion, must lay all things before the bishop in Zion.' Likewise, those in Kirtland and its vicinity were to give an accounting to the bishop in Kirtland, who in turn was to report to the bishop in Zion. A certificate from the judge or bishop in Kirtland was to be made and it would 'render every man acceptable and answereth all things, for an inheritance, and to be received as a wise steward, and as a faithful laborer; otherwise he shall not be accepted of the bishop in Zion.' " (Joseph Fielding Smith, *CHMR* 2:41-42.)

72:20   *"stewards over the literary concerns of my church"*

"From the very beginning of time the Lord has taken pains to see that proper records have been kept. This was one of the first commandments to the Church in 1830. The jealous care pertaining to the word of the Lord and other publications and documents, is shown forth in a number of revelations. Here (v. 20) the Lord gives instruction that his servants 'who are appointed as stewards over the literary concerns of my Church, (shall) have claim for assistance upon the bishop or bishops, in all things.' These brethren, previously named, had charge of the literary matters of the Church, the publication and care of the revelations which were to go forth unto the ends of the earth. Funds from this source were also to be obtained through the sale of the publications." (Joseph Fielding Smith, *CHMR* 1:271.)

SECTION 73

Background information on section 73

"From this time [Dec. 1831] until the 8th or 10th of January, 1832, myself and Elder Rigdon continued to preach in Shalerville, Ravenna, and other places, setting forth the truth, vindicating the cause of our Redeemer; showing that the day of vengeance was coming upon this generation like a thief in the night; that prejudice, blindness and darkness filled the minds of many, and caused them to persecute the true Church, and reject the light; by which means we did much towards allaying the exciting feelings which were growing out of the scandalous letters then being published in the Ohio *Star,* at Ravenna, by the before-mentioned apostate, Ezra Booth. [Section 64:15-16.] On the 10th of January, I received the following revelation making known the will of the Lord concerning Elders of the Church until the coming of the next conference. [Sec. 73, follows.]" (Joseph Smith, *HC* 1:241.)

73:1-6 *"translate again . . . continue the work of translation until it be finished"*

See *Inspired Version of the Bible* in Appendix A.

"While residing at Hiram, Joseph Smith was engaged in the revision of the Bible, which work was commenced in Fayette [Sec. 37], but had been delayed by command of the Lord until this time because of other duties. Sidney Rigdon, who also had located in Hiram, continued to write for him. In course of time the Prophet went through the Bible, topic by topic, revising as he was led by revelation. The work was never fully completed, for he had intended, while at Nauvoo, a number of years later, to finish the work, but was cut off by his enemies. Nevertheless, many plain and precious things were revealed which throw great light upon many subjects." (Joseph Fielding Smith, *ECH,* pp. 138-40.)

73:6 *"Gird up your loins and be sober"*

See *Armor of God* in Appendix A.

SECTION 74

Background information on section 74

"Upon the reception of the foregoing word [Sec. 73] of the Lord, I recommenced the translation of the Scriptures, and labored diligently until just before the conference, which was to convene on the 25th of January. During this period, I also received the following, as an explanation of the First Epistle to the Corinthians, 7th chapter, 14th verse: [D&C 74.]" (Joseph Smith *HC* 1:242.)

74:1-7 *An inspired explanation of 1 Corinthians 7:14*

"In the Corinthian Church, some evidently held that when the husband, or wife, had been converted, he, or she, ought to abandon the unconverted partner as unclean and contaminating. Not at all! St. Paul says, in substance, that the conversion of one of the partners has brought a sanctifying influence into the family. As Meyer puts it, 'The non-believing partner in a marriage . . . becomes partaker—as if by sacred contagion—of the higher, divinely consecrated character of his consort.' 'Else,' the Apostle argues, 'were your children unclean.' If the wife—this is the argument—must abandon a husband because he is not a Church member, she would also be obliged to abandon her children. But this is not required.

"The consecration of the believing parent includes the children. They are sanctified through the atonement of our Lord. They need no ordinance, until they arrive at the age of accountability, when they should be baptized, after proper instruction. Christians were forbidden to marry outside the Church (2 Cor. 6:14), but marriages contracted before conversion were not to be broken up, if the unconverted partner desired to continue the marriage relation." (Smith and Sjodahl, *DCC*, p. 432.)

74:2 *"among all the Jews"*

See *Jews* in Appendix A.

"Corinth was a Grecian city, the most considerable in the country of the Hellenes at the time Paul visited the place, but there were also many Jews, living there in exile, in consequence of a decree issued by Emperor Claudius (Acts 18:2), expelling the Hebrews from Rome. Some of them had joined the Church. This accounts for a controversy, in a Greek city, concerning a Mosaic rite (v. 3)." (Smith and Sjodahl, *DCC,* p. 432.)

74:5-7 *Some teachings of Paul*

"Some of these teachings, evidently, are the view of Paul the man, but when he spoke by the inspiration which the Lord placed upon him, he commanded that certain officers in the Church must by all means be married men. (1 Tim. 3:2, 12; and Tit. 1:6.) Then how truly he declared that 'nevertheless neither is the man without the woman, neither the woman without the man, in the Lord.' (1 Cor. 11:11.) It was while studying these teachings of Paul that the elders were led to inquire of the Prophet as to Paul's meanings in 1 Cor 7:14. The Prophet asked the Lord and got the answer. In this saying: [Sec. 74:1, quoted], Paul spoke not by commandment, but of himself. His intent, as explained in Section 74, being that where there were mixed families in the Church, the teachings of the Law of Moses and the doctrines which were fulfilled, should not be maintained. Male children in such families were not to be circumcised, and they would be holy. It was the doctrine of the Jews that unless this were done children were unholy. This Paul wished to correct. It was very difficult for the Jewish members of the Church to forsake all of their traditions and turn from the Law of Moses, and from circumcision which were fulfilled." (Joseph Fielding Smith, *CHMR* 2:44-45.)

74:7 *"little children are holy, being sanctified through the atonement of Jesus Christ"*

"The central thought expressed here is found in the first and last verses, and may be stated thus: Little children, sanctified through the atonement of Jesus Christ, are holy.

"Two conclusions follow from this proposition. The first, fully set forth in this Revelation, is, that little children do not need circumcision to become sanctified, as taught by the adherents of the Mosaic faith. The second is equally important, that is, little children are holy being sanctified through the atonement of Jesus Christ." (Smith and Sjodahl, *DCC,* p. 432.)

380

SECTION 75

Background information on section 75

"A few days before the conference was to commence in Amherst, Lorain county, I started with the Elders that lived in my own vicinity, and arrived in good time. At this conference much harmony prevailed, and considerable business was done to advance the kingdom, and promulgate the Gospel to the inhabitants of the surrounding country. The Elders seemed anxious for me to inquire of the Lord that they might know His will, or learn what would be most pleasing to Him for them to do, in order to bring men to a sense of their condition; for, as it was written, all men have gone out of the way, so that none doeth good, no, not one. I inquired and received the following: [D&C 75.]" (Joseph Smith, *HC* 1:242-43.)

75:1 *"Alpha and Omega"*
> See this title in Appendix A.

75:5 *"laden with many sheaves"*
> See *Harvest symbols* in Appendix A.

75:5 *"eternal life"*
> See this title in Appendix A.

75:6 *"William E. M'Lellin"*
> See Appendix B.

75:9 *"Luke Johnson"*
> See Appendix B.

75:10, 27 *"Comforter"*
> See *Holy Ghost* in Appendix A.

75:13-17, 30-36 *For information on persons mentioned in this section, see Appendix B.*

75:13 *"Orson Hyde and . . . Samuel H. Smith"*

"Soon after our return to Kirtland, I was sent on another mission in company with Brother Samuel H. Smith, a younger brother of the Prophet, who was a man slow of speech and unlearned, yet a man of good faith and extreme integrity. We journeyed early in the spring of 1832, eastward together, without 'purse or scrip,' going from house to house, teaching and preaching in families, and also in the public congregations of the people. Wherever we were received and entertained, we left our blessing; and wherever we were rejected, we washed our feet in private against those who rejected us, and bore testimony of it unto our Father in heaven, and went on our way rejoicing, according to the commandment." (Orson Hyde, *MS* 26:774-75.)

75:17 *"Burr Riggs"*

"The name appears in the minutes of the proceedings of the High Council at Kirtland, February 13th, 1833, on which occasion he was charged with neglect of duty, and especially with failure to magnify his calling as a High Priest. He admitted the charge and expressed a desire to repent, but this he evidently failed to do, for he was severed from the Church on the 26th of the same month. In all probability, his neglect of duty began by failure to perform the mission to which he was called, or by neglecting his duties as a missionary. Faithful missionaries are generally faithful members of the Priesthood and of the Church." (Smith and Sjodahl, *DCC,* p. 436.)

75:20 *"shake off the dust of your feet as a testimony"*

See *Feet* in Appendix A.

"The message and commission to these brethren is . . . of the greatest interest, in many respects similar to the commission the Savior gave his disciples when he sent them forth in their ministry throughout the land of Palestine. Whenever they entered a house and were received, they were to leave their blessing. From such houses as would not receive them and their message, they were to depart speedily shaking off the dust of their feet as a testimony against them. They were to remember also that one important duty which they were to fulfill and that was to be sure and bear testimony in every instance. If they performed their labors sincerely, humbly and diligently bearing witness of the restoration then it

would be more tolerable for the heathen in the day of judgment, than for that house which rejected the message. If no
warning had been left, however, then the judgment would be
pronounced against the servant who was expected to deliver
it. (D&C 4.)" (Joseph Fielding Smith, *CHMR* 1:276.)

75:22   *"it shall be more tolerable for the heathen"*

"This statement that it would be more tolerable for the
heathen should be considered. If the heathen are to be
judged without law and assigned to the terrestrial kingdom
(D&C 45:54; 76:72), then the chances for those who rejected
the message would imply that they may find themselves in a
lower kingdom, when the judgment comes. The elders who
delivered the message were also to be the judges in the day
of judgment against those who rejected their testimony.
Missionaries of the Church should realize this fact. They are
sent to warn the world and when they faithfully do their duty
they will stand as witnesses against those who reject them,
but if they fail to perform their duty, then those unto whom
the message should have been given, will stand up as accusers in their turn, and the unfaithful servants will be
condemned. (D&C 43:19.)" (Joseph Fielding Smith, *CHMR*
1:276.)

75:24-28   *the church should assist the families of those called to
proclaim the gospel*

"The brethren who were called to take these missionary
journeys were quite generally poor men in temporal things.
It was difficult for them to go out on the Lord's word and
leave their families without support. Yet the call was
essential, for the souls of men were at stake, and there were
those waiting to hear the message who would be a strength to
the church after they received the Gospel." (Joseph Fielding
Smith, *CHMR* 2:47-48.)

75:29   *"the idler shall not have place in the church, except he
repent"*

See *Work* in Appendix A.

"Frequently the Lord impressed upon these brethren who
were sent out the need of diligence in the service. [Sec. 75:29,
quoted.] This admonition did not apply solely to the work of
the missionary, but to all the members of the Church in their
labors, spiritually and temporally, for idleness, whether it is

in temporal things or in spiritual things, is severely condemned by the Lord. There should be none among us idle who is physically and mentally fit to labor. [Sec. 42:42.] One of the greatest blessings the Lord placed upon man is that he should labor, for it is through our labor that we progress, and without progression there can come no salvation, either in this world or in the world to come." (Joseph Fielding Smith, *CHMR* 2:47-48.)

75:33 *"Daniel Stanton"*

"When a Stake of Zion was organized at Adam-ondi-Ahman, he was made a member of the High Council, June 28th, 1838." (Smith and Sjodahl, *DCC,* p. 439.)

75:34 *"Gideon Carter"*

"He was killed in an encounter with a mob near Far West, in what is known as 'the Crooked River Battle,' Oct. 24th, 1838. At that time word had reached Far West that one Samuel Bogart, with a band of seventy-five marauders, was committing depredations. Judge Elias Higbee then ordered the military authorities to disperse the mob, and Captain David W. Patten and others volunteered for that expedition. With a company of about seventy-five men, Patten met the marauders at a point near Crooked River, and routed them completely. But in the melee David W. Patten, Gideon Carter, and Patrick O'Bannion were mortally wounded. Carter was left on the ground dead, but his body was afterwards recovered and buried." (Smith and Sjodahl, *DCC,* p. 439.)

SECTION 76

Background information on section 76

"Upon my return from Amherst [Ohio] conference, I resumed the translation of the Scriptures. From sundry revelations which had been received, it was apparent that many important points touching the salvation of man, had been taken from the Bible, or lost before it was compiled. It appeared self-evident from what truths were left, that if God rewarded every one according to the deeds done in the body the term 'Heaven,' as intended for the Saints' eternal home must include more kingdoms than one. Accordingly, on the 16th of February, 1832, while translating St. John's Gospel, myself and Elder Rigdon saw the following vision: [D&C 76.]" (Joseph Smith, *HC* 1:245.)

"Nothing could be more pleasing to the Saints upon the order of the kingdom of the Lord, than the light which burst upon the world through the foregoing vision [section 76]. Every law, every commandment, every promise, every truth, and every point touching the destiny of man, from Genesis to Revelation, where the purity of the scriptures remains unsullied by the folly of men, goes to show the perfection of the theory [of different degrees of glory in the future life] and witnesses the fact that that document is a transcript from the records of the eternal world. The sublimity of the ideas; the purity of the language; the scope for action; the continued duration for completion, in order that the heirs of salvation may confess the Lord and bow the knee; the rewards for faithfulness, and the punishments for sins, are so much beyond the narrow-mindedness of men, that every honest man is constrained to exclaim: 'It came from God.' " (Joseph Smith, *HC* 1:252-53.)

"I could explain a hundred fold more than I ever have of the glories of the kingdoms manifested to me in the vision, were I permitted, and were the people prepared to receive them." (Joseph Smith, *HC* 5:402.)

"Section 76 of the Doctrine and Covenants in its sublimity

and clearness in relation to the eternal destiny of the human family, has not been surpassed. It should be treasured by all members of the Church as a priceless heritage. It should strengthen their faith and be to them an incentive to seek the exaltation promised to all who are just and true. So plain and simple are its teachings that none should stumble or misunderstand." (Joseph Fielding Smith, *CHMR* 1:279.)

76:1 *"the Lord is God, and beside him there is no Savior"*

See *Jesus Christ* in Appendix A.

76:4 *"From eternity to eternity he is the same"*

See *Eternity to eternity* in Appendix A.

76:7 *"To them will I reveal all mysteries"*

See *Mysteries* in Appendix A.

76:7-10 *"to them will I reveal all mysteries . . . by my Spirit"*

"When the time shall come that the Spirit of the living God shall be poured out upon all flesh, in a very few moments of time the Lord could unlock the mysteries and treasures of the earth, so that we could understand not only the geographical surface of the earth, but be able, by the power of vision, to behold every particle of it inside as well as outside, and also the law that governs its elementary portions, nearly all of which is now closed from our mortal vision. We can only go about so far with our natural sight; but there is a faculty in every man and woman which is now sleeping in a dormant state; and as soon as it is touched by the Spirit of the Lord, we shall be enabled to see a new world of things as it were, mysteries will be opened up, and we will perceive naturally as if they were written, and in this way we shall be able to learn very rapidly indeed. If we want a knowledge of this world or of ourselves, when our spirits were born, or if we desire to know things that took place before the foundations of the world were laid or the nucleus was formed, when the sons of God shouted for joy, if we desired to know these things it would only be necessary for the Spirit of the Lord to touch the vision of our minds and light up our understanding, and we could gaze upon things past for thousands of generations of worlds before the earth was made, and we could see the succession of worlds that have been and were in existence long before this earth was formed; we could see the ordeals through which they had passed, see them brought into existence and passing through their several changes and finally become glorified celestial mansions in the presence of God. By this same Spirit . . . we could look forward into the distant future and behold new worlds formed and redeemed, and not only this, but see and understand the laws by which they were made, and the object and end of all these creations, being touched by the finger of the Almighty and lighted up by the Holy Ghost." (Orson Pratt, *JD* 19:178.)

76:11 *"being in the Spirit"*

"When Joseph Smith and Sidney Rigdon saw that wonderful vision of the celestial, terrestrial, and telestial glories, they said concerning it: 'Being in the Spirit, on the sixteenth day of February, in the year of our Lord, 1832, by the power of the Spirit our eyes were opened,' etc. There is the key. It was because God was with them that they were able to see the Son of God and converse with him 'in the heavenly vision.' They had eyes—spiritual eyes; they were seers. But what could they see until the Spirit came upon them and gave them the use of the seeric gift? The machinery was there, but the power had to be turned on." (Orson F. Whitney, *CR,* June 1919, p. 48.)

76:15 *"while we were doing the work of translation"*

The translation referred to here is Joseph Smith's work on the Inspired Version of the Bible. See Appendix A.

76:22 *"this is the testimony . . . which we give of him: That he lives!"*

"Joseph Smith and Sidney Rigdon also saw him, and bore testimony that they saw Him, even as Stephen saw Him [Acts 7:54-56], clothed in glory, surrounded by those inhabiting the celestial kingdom of God. They also saw God seated on His throne and Jesus Christ at His right hand, 'And they heard the voice bearing record that He is the only begotten of the Father.' So far as the Latter-day Saints are concerned, we know these things are true. There is no doubt in our minds about it. Why? Because the Spirit of Truth, the Holy Ghost, has been received by us through our obedience to the laws and ordinances of the Gospel, and He, true to His office, has testified to us of Jesus Christ, our Lord." (Hyrum M. Smith, *CR,* October 1907, pp. 34-35.)

76:23   *"the Only Begotten of the Father"*

> See *Only Begotten* and *Jesus Christ* in Appendix A.

76:24   *"the inhabitants . . . are begotten sons and daughters unto God"*

> See *Godhead* in Appendix A.
>
> "He who made the worlds, . . . controls and governs and directs them, is actually our Father, not in some mystical sense, not in some mere theory, but we were begotten of Him. In the revelation contained in the 76th Section of the Doctrine and Covenants we are told that the inhabitants of the worlds are 'begotten sons and daughters unto God.' There may be more in that than we see at the first glance . . . that the great Eternal God is our Father and we are begotten of Him or *unto* Him and to Him we owe allegiance, to Him we owe obedience, because He is our Father and our God and our King. We should obey Him because of His parentage to us: we should obey Him because we are His children and He has the right to our obedience." (Charles W. Penrose, *CR*, April 1916, pp. 15-16.)

76:24   *"by him . . . the worlds are and were created"*

> See *Creator* in Appendix A.

76:26   Lucifer (*Satan; the devil*) *"was called Perdition"*

> See *Satan* in Appendix A.
>
> "The name means 'Light-bearer' and indicates the exalted position of him who was so called, for a 'light-bearer' is a sun in the firmament. But when he was cast out, he was called *Perdition.*" (Smith and Sjodahl, *DCC*, p. 450.)

76:31-49   *"those who know . . . and . . . deny . . . and defy"*

> See *Perdition* in Appendix A.
>
> "Those who are finally lost are such as have had actual knowledge of the power of God; they have been made partakers thereof; they have not only heard of it or seen its manifestations in others, but they have received it themselves. Paul (Heb. 6:4) uses the expression, 'enlightened,' which is equivalent to 'baptized,' and is so understood by early Christian authors, because Christian baptism is followed by the reception of the Holy Ghost, who gives light and leads into all truth. He adds, 'and have tasted the heavenly gift and were made partakers of the Holy

Ghost.' In other words, they have been regenerated by the gospel and received the blessings bestowed through the ordinances thereof; and then they have 'suffered themselves to be overcome.' They have *denied* the truth and have *defied* the power of God. They have become rebels, like Lucifer. Their status is that of apostasy. . . . They have denied the Holy Spirit, after having received it; they have denied the Only Begotten Son, and by that denial crucified Him, as it were. They have been the servants of Christ but are now enlisted in the service of Lucifer, as were those who crucified the Lord; they belong in the same class.

" 'The "sons of perdition" are those who have received the gospel, those to whom the Father has revealed the Son; those who know something concerning the plan of salvation; those who have had keys placed in their hands by which they could unlock the mysteries of eternity; those who received power sufficient to overcome all things, and who, instead of using it for their own salvation, and in the interest of the salvation of others, prostituted that power and turned away from that which they knew to be true, denying the Son of God and putting Him to open shame. . . . They are governed by Satan; becoming servants to him whom they list to obey, they become the sons of perdition, doomed to suffer the wrath of God reserved for the Devil and his angels,' (Charles W. Penrose, *JD* 24:93)." (Smith and Sjodahl, *DCC,* p. 452.)

76:37   *"the second death"*

See *Death* in Appendix A.

"The end of the lost is also called the 'second death.' The first is spiritual death. When Adam was expelled from the Garden of Eden, 'he became spiritually dead, which was the first death.' But spiritual death is also the last, 'which shall be pronounced upon the wicked when I shall say: Depart, ye cursed' (Sec. 29:41). All but sons of perdition will be redeemed from Satan's power and will find some place outside of his domain. The inhabitants of this earth will be assigned to the telestial, the terrestrial or the celestial kingdom according to the law which they have kept while in mortality. Redemption does not mean exaltation, but to be released from Satan's chains. These sons of perdition have willed to go with the prince of darkness. They have reached a stage where they cannot repent, for repentance is a gift of

God, and they have placed themselves beyond its influence and power." (Smith and Sjodahl, *DCC*, p. 454.)

76: 38-39, 43   *"saves all . . . except those sons of perdition"*

"In many minds there has been a great misapprehension on the question of the resurrection. Some have had the idea, and have taught it, that the sons of perdition will not be resurrected at all. They base this idea, and draw this conclusion, from the 38th and 39th paragraphs of section 76 of the book of Doctrine and Covenants, . . .

"A careful reading of these verses, however, and especially of the preceding paragraphs, will show that the Lord does not, in this language, exclude even the sons of perdition from the resurrection. It is plain that the intention is to refer to them explicitly as the only ones on whom the second death shall have any power: '*for all the rest* shall be brought forth by the resurrection of the dead, through the triumph and the glory of the Lamb.' This excluded class are the only ones on whom the second death shall have any power, and 'the only ones who shall not be redeemed in the due time of the Lord after the sufferings of *his* wrath.'

"This is by no means to say that they are to have no resurrection. Jesus our Lord and Savior died for all, and all will be resurrected—good and bad, white and black, people of every race, whether sinners or not; and no matter how great their sins may be, the resurrection of their bodies is sure. Jesus has died for them, and they all will be redeemed from the grave through the atonement which He had made." (George Q. Cannon, *JI*, February 1900, p. 123.)

76:39   *"the Lamb, who was slain . . . before the worlds were made"*

See *Lamb of God* and *Pre-earthly existence* in Appendix A.

76:44   *"everlasting . . . endless . . . eternal punishment"*

See material for 19:6-12.

76:50   *"resurrection of the just"*

See *Resurrection* in Appendix A.

"This is also called the first resurrection, but the truth is here taught that only those who are *just* will have part in it. To be *just* is to be upright and sincere in one's actions and dealings with others. It is to be like Christ, who suffered, the just for the unjust (1 Pet. 3:18). To be just is also to be justified. That is to say, one who is just is, by God Himself, declared to be as he ought to be. Such are they who have part in the first resurrection." (Smith and Sjodahl, *DCC*, p. 459.)

76:51-70, 92 *Vision of the celestial glory*

See *Celestial* and *Degrees of glory* in Appendix A.

76:57 *"order of Enoch"*

See *Enoch* and *United Order* in Appendix A.

76:67 *"church of Enoch, and of the Firstborn"*

See *Church of the Firstborn* in Appendix A.

76:68 *"whose names are written in heaven"*

See *Book of Life* in Appendix A.

76:71-80, 91 *Vision of the terrestrial world*

See *Terrestrial* and *Degrees of glory* in Appendix A.

76:79 *"they who are not valiant in the testimony of Jesus"*

"This is a gospel of individual work. I wish our Latter-day Saints could become more valiant. As I read the seventy-sixth section of the Doctrine and Covenants, the great vision given to the Prophet Joseph Smith, I remember that the Lord says to that terrestrial degree of glory may go those who are not valiant in the testimony, which means that many of us who have received baptism by proper authority, many who have received other ordinances, even temple blessings, will not reach the celestial kingdom of glory unless we live the commandments and are valiant. What is being valiant? . . . There are many people in this Church today who think they live, but they are dead to the spiritual things. And I believe even many who are making the pretenses of being active are also spiritually dead. Their service is much of the letter and less of the spirit." (Spencer W. Kimball, *CR*, April 1951, pp. 104-5.)

76:81-90, 98-112 *Vision of the telestial world*

See *Telestial* and *Degrees of glory* in Appendix A.

76:94 *"church of the Firstborn"*

See same title in Appendix A.

76:95 *"equal in power . . . might . . . dominion"*

See material for 78:5-7.

"Those who dwell in the presence of God are faithful members of the Church of the Firstborn. They are equal. In the celestial world all the ransomed are equal in authority, in strength, in opportunities, and in possessions. Is it any wonder, then, that our Lord instituted the United Order, with equality, in the Church, as a school in which to obtain some understanding of, and training for, a place in celestial glory? Can anyone, after a life of selfishness, fill a position in a kingdom where all are equal?" (Smith and Sjodahl, *DCC*, p. 468.)

76:105 *"vengeance of eternal fire"*

See *Everlasting fire* in Appendix A, and the material for 19:6-12.

76:107 *"I . . . have trodden the wine-press alone"*

See *Wine-press* in Appendix A.

76:109 *"as innumerable as the stars"*

"There are millions and millions of kingdoms that the people have no conception of. . . . There are myriads of people pertaining to this earth who will come up and receive a glory according to their capacity." (Brigham Young, *JD* 6:347.)

76:110 *"all shall bow the knee"*

See *Knee* in Appendix A.

"The time is to come, so we read, when every knee will bow and every tongue confess that Jesus is the Lord, the Christ, to the glory of God the Father. [Phil. 2:9-11.] What a splendid prospect to have in view! What a grand goal to reach, to aid in bringing about redemption of the human family. Before that time can come, those that are wicked and corrupt and evil-minded, and who will not be obedient will have to reap the consequences of their own acts. . . . But the time is to come, away in the distant future, when the inhabitants of the earth, all who have dwelt upon it, with the exception of a few who are unredeemable, will be brought to bow the knee willingly; not by compulsion, not by coercion, not by constraint, but willingly bow the knee to King Immanuel and worship God, the true God, the Father, in Christ's holy name, and be willing, perfectly willing, to render obedience to his commandments. Of course, the condition in which they will dwell will be consequent upon their doings when they were in the flesh. They cannot all be in the same class; that is impossible." (Charles W. Penrose, *CR*, October 1913, p. 19.)

76:112 *"where God and Christ dwell they cannot come"*

"There are some people who have supposed that if we are quickened telestial bodies that eventually, throughout the ages of eternity, we will continue to progress until we will find our place in the celestial kingdom, but the scriptures and revelations of God have said that those who are quickened telestial bodies cannot come where God and Christ dwell, worlds without end." (George Albert Smith, *CR*, October 1945, p. 172.)

76:115 *"not lawful for man to utter"*

The term *not lawful* suggests they have been commanded by the Lord to say no more concerning that particular thing.

"Paul ascended into the third heaven, and he could understand the three principal rounds of Jacob's ladder—the telestial, the terrestrial, and the celestial glories or kingdoms, where Paul saw and heard things which were not lawful for him to utter. I could explain a hundred-fold more than I ever have of the glories of the kingdoms manifested to me in the vision, were I permitted, and were the people prepared to receive them. The Lord deals with this people as a tender parent with a child, communicating light and intelligence and knowledge of his sayings as they can bear it." (Joseph Smith, *HC* 5:402.)

76:116 *"they are only to be seen and understood by the power of the Holy Spirit"*

"Could we read and comprehend all that has been written from the days of Adam, on the relation of man to God and angels in a future state, we should know very little about it. Reading the experience of others, or the revelation given to *them*, can never give us a comprehensive view of our condition and true relation to God. Knowledge of these things can only be obtained by experience through the ordinances of God set forth for that purpose. Could you gaze into heaven five minutes, you would know more than you would by reading all that has ever been written on the subject." (Joseph Smith, *HC* 6:50.)

SECTION 77

Background information on section 77

"After the return of the Prophet from Amhurst, he [Joseph Smith] resumed his translation of the Scriptures. About the first of March, while engaged in this work, questions arose in regard to the meaning of some of the figurative and symbolic writings of John in the book of Revelation. There are many things therein which the brethren did not understand, therefore the Prophet inquired of the Lord and received answer to his questions." (Joseph Fielding Smith, *CHMR* 1:291.)

"This Revelation is not a complete interpretation of the book. It is a key. A key is a very small part of the house. It unlocks the door through which an entrance may be gained, but after the key has been turned, the searcher for treasure must find it for himself. It is like entering a museum in which the students must find out for themselves what they desire to know. The sources of information are there." (Smith and Sjodahl, *DCC*, p. 278.)

77:1 *"What is the sea of glass?"*

See *Earth* in Appendix A.

"While at dinner, I remarked to my family and friends present, that when the earth was sanctified and became like a sea of glass, it would be one great urim and thummim, and the Saints could look in it and see as they are seen." (Joseph Smith, *HC* 5:279.)

"This Earth will become a celestial body—be like a sea of glass, or like a Urim and Thummim; and when you wish to know anything, you can look in this Earth and see all the eternities of God. We shall make our homes here, and go on our missions as we do now." (Brigham Young, *JD* 8:200.)

"St. John, in this chapter of the Revelation, is taken up to heaven, where thrones were placed. There was the central Throne, and seated upon it One 'who was to look like a jasper and a sardine stone.' There were twenty-four thrones occupied by Elders in white raiment. There were seven lamps burning symbolizing the 'seven spirits of God,' and there was a 'sea of glass like unto crystal.' In the Temple of Solomon there was an immense basin called 'a molten sea' (1 Kings 7:23). In the Temple in heaven, of which the temples on Earth are feeble representations, there is a *glassy* sea, calm, transparent, and solid, and here we are informed that this 'sea' is 'the Earth in its sanctified, immortal, and eternal state.' The 'sea' connected with the temples of God is a baptismal font. It represents the Earth. All who desire access to the Church of Jesus Christ must come through the baptismal font, and be buried with Christ." (Smith and Sjodahl, *DCC*, p. 472.)

77:2-4   *"What are . . . the four beasts?"*

"The spirit of man is in the form of man, and the spirits of all creatures are in the likeness of their bodies. This was plainly taught by the Prophet Joseph Smith.

"By His almighty power He organized the earth, and all that it contains, from spirit and element, which exist co-eternally with Himself. He formed every plant that grows, and every animal that breathes, each after its own kind, spiritually and temporally—'that which is spiritual being in the likeness of that which is temporal, and that which is temporal in the likeness of that which is spiritual.' " (First Presidency, *IE*, January 1909, 13:75-81.)

"From this revelation (Sec. 77) we discover that every creature has a spirit, and that it existed in the spirit before it was on the earth; the spirit of every creature is in the form of its temporal, or mortal, body. Since this is true, and all forms of life partook of the effects of Adam's fall, therefore they are entitled to the resurrection and shall live again. 'And not one hair, neither mote, shall be lost, for it is the workmanship of mine hand,' said the Lord. (D&C 29:25.) Likewise the earth, which is a living body, must die, 'in like manner' as to all other mortal things, and then receive the resurrection. (Isa. 51:6.) The fact that the spirit of every animal, every fish, every fowl of the air, is in the likeness of its body, and that also it was created in the spirit in the beginning, is a contradiction of these unscientific theories which man has inflicted upon a fallen world." (Joseph Fielding Smith, *CHMR* 1:298.)

"The Revelator saw 'four beasts' or rather 'four living creatures,' 'in the midst of the throne, and round about it.' They were, possibly, supporting it, as the Cherubim in Ez. 1:4-22. Here we have an explanation of these living creatures. They represent the happiness enjoyed in that part of heaven which is called the Paradise of God, by men, by the larger animals, and by creeping things and fowls of the air. For the things on Earth are but a counterpart of things in heaven." (Smith and Sjodahl, *DCC*, p. 472.)

77:3 *"Are the four beasts limited to individual beasts, or do they represent classes or orders?"*

"We are to understand that there will be beasts of various kinds, after the resurrection, in each of the kingdoms, telestial, terrestrial and celestial. It would be a very strange thing for any of the kingdoms to be devoid of animal and plant life. These kingdoms will be very beautiful in their immortal state. Even the telestial will surpass the comprehension of mortal man. They are the creations of the Almighty and therefore they will be perfect in their own sphere, for the Lord creates no imperfections and it is his purpose, according to the divine plan, to make all of his creatures as happy as it is possible for them to be under the conditions of their immortal states." (Joseph Fielding Smith, *CHMR* 1:298-99.)

"I suppose John saw beings there of a thousand forms, that had been saved from ten thousand times ten thousand earths like this,—strange beasts of which we have no conception: all might be seen in heaven. The grand secret was to show John what there was in heaven. John learned that God glorified Himself by saving all that His hands had made, whether beasts, fowls, fishes or men; and He will glorify Himself with them.

"Says one, 'I cannot believe in the salvation of beasts.' Any man who would tell you that this could not be, would tell you that the revelations are not true. John heard the words of the beasts giving glory to God, and understood them. God who made the beasts could understand every language spoken by them. The four beasts were four of the most noble animals that had filled the measure of their creation, and had been saved from other worlds, because they were perfect; they were like angels in their sphere. We are not told where they came from, and I do not know; but they were seen and heard by John praising and glorifying God." (Joseph Smith, *HC* 5:343-44.)

"He [God] made the tadpole and the ape, the lion and the elephant; but He did not make them in His own image, nor endow them with Godlike reason and intelligence. Nevertheless, the whole animal creation will be perfected and perpetuated in the Hereafter, each class in its 'distinct order or sphere,' and will enjoy 'eternal felicity.' That fact has been made plain in this dispensation." (First Presidency, *IE*, January 1909, 13:81.)

77:4 *"What are we to understand by the eyes and wings, which the beasts had?"*

"These beasts here represented are of course symbolical; so likewise is the description of their eyes and wings. The Lord has promised those who obtain the exaltation that they shall possess great wisdom, and knowledge and power shall be given unto them. The righteous in the kingdom of God, shall be joint-heirs with Jesus Christ as sons and daughters of God, and the fulness of his kingdom will be given to them. We also learn from this revelation and the word of the Lord in other revelations that in the eternities the animals and all living creatures shall be given knowledge, and enjoy happiness, each in its own sphere, in 'their eternal felicity.' These creatures will not then be the dumb animals that we suppose them to be while in this mortal life.

"The Prophet Joseph Smith said: 'I make this broad declaration, that whenever God gives a vision of an image, or beast, or figure of any kind, he always holds himself responsible to give a revelation or interpretation of the meaning thereof, otherwise we are not responsible or accountable for our belief in it. Don't be afraid of being damned for not knowing the meaning of a vision or figure, if God has not given a revelation or interpretation of the subject.' " (Joseph Fielding Smith, *CHMR* 2:68-69.)

77:5 *"What are we to understand by the . . . elders . . . who belonged to the seven churches?"*

"It will be recalled that the forepart of John's Revelation contains a charge to the seven churches, or branches of the Church, in Asia Minor. [Rev. 1-3.] We may judge from what is written that these seven branches were all that were considered worthy of a standing in the Church at that time, indicating that the apostasy had at that day become extensive, and each of these branches received a deserved rebuke. The seven candlesticks and the seven stars also have reference to these seven branches of the Church and the seven angels spoken of had to do with these churches, or branches." (Joseph Fielding Smith, *CHMR* 2:69.)

77:6 *"What are we to understand by the book which John saw?"*

"By the seven thousand years of temporal existence is meant the time of the earth's duration from the fall of Adam to the end of time, which will come after the Millennium and 'a little season' which will follow. [D&C 29:22-23; 88:111.] The earth and all on it were in a spiritual condition before the fall, for mortality had not come bringing temporal conditions. We are now living in the second period of the earth's history, which is referred to as being a telestial condition. In other words, a condition where wickedness and all the vicissitudes of mortality endure." (Joseph Fielding Smith, *CHMR* 2:64.)

77:7 *"What are we to understand by the seven seals?"*

"The number seven denotes completeness. The plans of God are hidden completely, until they are revealed by Himself. So these seven seals signify the seven thousand years of temporal existence.

"Some ancient books consisted of parchment rolled round a piece of wood. This book contained seven skins, rolled upon one another. When the first seal was broken, the first skin was unrolled, and was found to contain a hieroglyphic painting. . . . Each skin contained some drawing. Ancient books of the East were often beautifully illustrated in this manner." (Smith and Sjodahl, *DCC*, p. 474.)

77:8 *"What are we to understand by the four angels?"*

"These angels seem to fit the description of the angels spoken of in the parable of the wheat and the tares (Matt. 13:24-43 and D&C 86:17), who pled with the Lord that they might go forth to reap down the field. They were told to let the wheat and the tares grow together to the time of the end of the harvest, which is the end of the world. (Matt. 13:38-39.) . . .

"These angels have been given power over the four parts

of the earth and they have the power of committing the everlasting Gospel to the peoples of the earth. The fulness of the
Gospel was not restored by any one messenger sent from the
presence of the Lord. All the ancient prophets who held keys
and came and restored them, had a hand in this great work
of restoration. There are, we learn from this revelation, four
angels unto whom the power has been given, to shut up the
heavens, to open them and with power unto life and also
death and destruction. These are now at work in the earth on
their sacred mission." (Joseph Fielding Smith, *CHMR* 2:70-
71.)

77:9 *"What are we to understand by the angel ascending from
the east?"*

See *Elias* in Appendix A.

"The restoration of the Gospel did not come through just
one messenger, but there are several who came and bestowed their keys of authority and power. The name Elias, is
a title. This we have been taught by the Prophet Joseph
Smith. (*Teachings*, p. 335.) It is not possible, therefore, since
so many ancient prophets had a hand in the restoration, that
in speaking of the Elias who was to come and restore all
things, do we not have a composite picture of several Eliases,
rather than one single individual? The angel with the seal directs the four angels holding the destiny of the world in their
hands, not to hurt the earth until the servants of the Lord
have been sealed. This could not be accomplished until the
Gospel was restored and proclaimed to the nations of the
earth." (Joseph Fielding Smith, *CHMR* 2:71.)

77:10 *"What time are the things . . . to be accomplished?"*

See D&C 88:92-116 for more detail concerning this time.

"In the period preceding the millennium, these things are
to be accomplished. The seals of the seven periods of time
cannot be opened by any other than the Son of God—'the
Lamb slain from the foundation of the earth.' He alone has
the power to open this book and reveal its secrets concerning
the history of the earth by each thousand years, since time
began." (Joseph Fielding Smith, *CHMR* 1:302.)

77:11 *"What are we to understand by sealing the one hundred
and forty-four thousand?"*

"It is not only necessary that you should be baptized for

your dead, but you will have to go through all the ordinances for them, the same as you have gone through to save yourselves. There will be 144,000 saviors on Mount Zion, and with them an innumerable host that no man can number." (Joseph Smith, *HC* 6:365.)

"The ten tribes will have to come forth and come to this land, to be crowned with glory in the midst of Zion by the hands of the servants of God, even the Children of Ephraim; and twelve thousand High Priests will be elected from each of these ten tribes, as well as from the scattered tribes, and sealed in their foreheads, and will be ordained and receive power to gather out of all nations, kindreds, tongues and people as many as will come unto the general assemblage of the Church of the first-born. Will not that be a great work? Imagine one hundred and forty-four thousand High Priests going forth among the nations, and gathering out as many as will come to the Church of the first-born. All that will be done, probably, in the morning of the seventh thousand years. The work is of great magnitude, Latter-day Saints, and we are living almost upon the eve of it." (Orson Pratt, *JD* 16:325-26.)

"This certainly is a great honor to be one of the 144 thousand who are especially called by the power of 'the angels to whom is given power over the nations of the earth,' to bring souls unto Christ. John the Apostle had the great desire to bring souls to Christ. [Sec. 7.] The three Nephite Disciples likewise sought this great honor and it was granted to them. [3 Nephi 28.] It is one of the noblest desires that a man can have. It will be a wonderful blessing to those who are called in this great group." (Joseph Fielding Smith, *CHMR* 2:71-72.)

77:12   *"What are we to understand by the sounding of the trumpets?"*

"In this instruction the Lord sets days against thousand years, as days, in speaking of the creation and the continuance of the earth during its mortal existence. At the close of the sixth thousand years and at the opening of the seventh, since the fall, the earth and all that remain upon its face will be changed from the telestial condition of wickedness to the terrestrial condition of peace and order. This is the day when the earth 'will be renewed and receive its paradisiacal glory,' as declared in the Tenth Article of Faith.

We are now in the great day of restoration of all things, and the renewal of the earth is the bringing of it back to a comparable condition to that which existed before the fall." (Joseph Fielding Smith, *CHMR* 1:293.)

"The symbolism of the Sabbath, and the symbolism of other days as well, is plainly indicated in the writings of Joseph Smith. In one place he says—or the Lord says through him: 'All things have their likeness, and are made to bear record of me.' (Moses 6:63.) We need not be surprised, therefore, to find among the Prophet's teachings this—I quote now from his Key to the Apocalypse: [Sec. 77:6, 12, quoted.]

"The 'days' here referred to were not ordinary days of twenty-four hours each, based upon earth's diurnal revolutions. He who 'made the world' before placing man upon it, had not then appointed unto Adam his reckoning. (Abr. 5:13.) They were not man's days, but God's days, each having a duration of a thousand years. . . .

"According to received chronology—admittedly imperfect, yet approximately correct—four thousand years, or four of the seven great days given to this planet as the period of its 'temporal existence,' had passed before Christ was crucified; while nearly two thousand years have gone by since. Consequently, Earth's long week is now drawing to a close, and we stand at the present moment in the Saturday Evening of Time, at or near the end of the sixth day of human history. Is it not a time for thought, a season for solemn meditation? Morning will break upon the millennium, the thousand years of peace, the Sabbath of the World!" (Orson F. Whitney, *SNT*, pp. 10-12.)

77:13 *"When are the things to be accomplished, which are written in the 9th chapter of Revelation?"*

"These terrible events pictured in the ninth chapter of Revelation are now being fulfilled. Part of this we have witnessed, the rest will shortly come to pass. This is, and will be, in the nature of the cleansing process to prepare the earth and its inhabitants, those who will be fortunate enough to remain, for the coming of our Savior when he shall commence his reign for a thousand years upon the earth. The reading of this chapter with the knowledge that the time of its fulfillment is at hand, should cause all men some thoughtful sober thinking." (Joseph Fielding Smith, *CHMR* 2:72.)

77:14 *"What are we to understand by the little book which was eaten by John?"*

"John as an Elias with power of restoration is yet to come. The little book is symbolical of his great mission in preparing Israel for its return in these last days. At the conference of the Church held in June 1831, the Prophet Joseph Smith said 'that John the Revelator was then among the ten tribes of Israel who had been led away by Shalmaneser, king of Assyria, to prepare them for their return from their long dispersion.' " (Joseph Fielding Smith, *CHMR* 2:72.)

"This angel had a 'little book' open, and he cried out his message with a loud voice, declaring solemnly that there would be 'time no longer,' —no more delay—but that when the seventh angel begins to sound, the mystery of God— God's plan of salvation—will be completed. This is a vision of the restoration of the Church through the instrumentality of the Prophet Joseph, who came as a messenger from God and declared that the Church was to be restored, preparatory to the second coming of Christ. The coming forth of the 'little book' was the beginning of a new prophetic era, for John was told (Rev. 10:11): 'Thou must prophesy again before many peoples, and nations, and tongues, and kings.' The establishment of the Church in our day is foretold in this chapter of the Revelation as clearly as the birth of Christ is predicted in Isaiah 9:6, 7." (Smith and Sjodahl, *DCC*, p. 477.)

77:15 *"What is to be understood by the two witnesses, in the eleventh chapter of Revelation?"*

Parley P. Pratt discusses this question very thoroughly in his booklet, *A Voice of Warning.*

"John, in his 11th chapter of Revelation, gives us many more particulars concerning this same event [the appearance of Jesus Christ to the Jews]. He informs us that, after the city and temple are rebuilt by the Jews, the Gentiles will tread it under foot forty and two months, during which time there will be two Prophets continually prophesying and working mighty miracles. And it seems that the Gentile army shall be hindered from utterly destroying and overthrowing the city, while these two Prophets continue. But, after a struggle of three years and a half, they at length succeed in destroying these two Prophets, and then overrunning much of the city,

they send gifts to each other because of the death of the two Prophets, and in the meantime will now allow their dead bodies to be put in graves, but suffer them to lie in the streets of Jerusalem three days and a half, during which the armies of the Gentiles, consisting of many kindreds, tongues and nations, passing through the city, plundering the Jews, see their dead bodies lying in the street. But after three days and a half, on a sudden, the spirit of life from God enters them, and they will arise and stand upon their feet, and great fear will fall upon them that see them. And then they shall hear a voice from heaven saying, 'Come up hither,' and they will ascend up to heaven in a cloud, and their enemies beholding them. And having described all these things, then comes the shaking, spoken of by Ezekiel [Ezek. 38:18-20], and the rending of the Mount of Olives, spoken of by Zechariah. [Zech. 14:4-5.] John says, 'The same hour was there a great earthquake, and the tenth part of the city fell, and in the earthquake were slain of men seven thousand.' [Rev. 11:13.] And then one of the next scenes that follows is the sound of voices saying, 'The kingdoms of this world are become the kingdom of our Lord, and of his Christ, and he shall reign forever and ever.' [Rev. 11:15.]" (Parley P. Pratt, *VW,* pp. 40-42.)

SECTION 78

Background information on section 78

"During the early part of the year 1832, the Prophet and Sidney Rigdon continued the work of the revision of the Scriptures. At the time the Prophet was still residing in the house of Father John Johnson, at Hiram. It was during this time [March] that this important revelation [Section 78] was given to the members of the Priesthood who were assembled imparting instructions in relation to the plan of the 'united order' or 'order of Enoch,' on which the promised Zion should be built. The Lord had revealed that it was only through obedience to his divine will, the celestial law, that Zion could be built. [D&C 63:47-49; 64:34; 105:3-5.] The members of the Church rejoiced when the Lord revealed to them the site on which the New Jerusalem, or City of Zion, should be built. [D&C 57:1-3.] Their enthusiasm, however, was not sufficient to carry them through to a conclusion in strict obedience to the divine will." (Joseph Fielding Smith, *CHMR* 2:73-74.)

Beginning with this section, some of the brethren and some of the places and things were referred to by names and titles other than their own. President Joseph Fielding Smith and Elder Orson Pratt have an explanation and some background information on this:

"The reason for the substituted names in this and some subsequent revelations was to keep from the knowledge of the enemies of the Church the true names of the brethren and some places, that they might not be known to the hurt of the Church. Some years later in the Doctrine and Covenants the correct names were inserted." (Joseph Fielding Smith, *CHMR* 1:306.)

"The names that were incorporated when it [Doctrine and Covenants] was printed, did not exist there when the manuscript revelations were given, for I saw them myself. Some of them I copied. And when the Lord was about to have the Book of Covenants given to the world it was through wisdom, in consequence of the persecutions of our enemies in Kirtland and some of the regions around, that some of the names should be changed and Joseph was called Baurak Ale, which was a Hebrew word; meaning God bless you. [D&C 103:21-22, 35; 105:16, 17.] He was also called Gazelam, being a person to whom the Lord had given the Urim and Thummim. He was also called Enoch." (Orson Pratt, *JD* 16:156.)

The following note appears in the superscription of section 78:

It was not always desirable that the individuals whom the Lord addressed in revelations should at the time be known by the world, and hence in this and in some subsequent revelations the brethren were addressed by other than their own names. The temporary necessity having passed for keeping the names of the individuals addressed unknown, their real names were subsequently given in brackets.

Following are: (a) an alphabetical list of names used to identify individuals and places without using the actual name of the person or place; (b) the real name or title listed in parentheses, and (c) the section(s) and verse(s) where these unusual names and titles are used. You will note that these names are used only in sections 78, 82, 92, 96, 103, 104, and 105.

Ahashdah (Newel K. Whitney) 78:9; 82:11; 96:2; 104:39, 40, 41.
Alam (Newel K. Whitney) 82:11.
Baneemy (mine elders) 105:27.
Baurak Ale (Joseph Smith, Jr.) 103:21, 22, 35; 105:16, 27.
Cainhannoch (New York) 104:81.
Enoch (Joseph Smith, Jr.) 78:1, 4; superscriptions to 96 and 104.
Gazelam (Joseph Smith, Jr.) 78:9; 82:11; 104:26, 43, 45, 46.
Horah (Oliver Cowdery) 82:11.
Laneshine house (printing office) 104:28, 29.
Mahalaleel (Sidney Rigdon) 82:11.
Mahemson (Martin Harris) 82:11; 104:24, 26.
Olihah (Oliver Cowdery) 82:11; 104:28, 29, 34.
Ozondah (mercantile establishment) 104:39, 40, 41.
Pelagoram (Sidney Rigdon) 78:9; 82:11; 104:20, 22.
Seth (Joseph of Egypt) 96:7.
Shalemanasseh (Martin Harris) 82:11.
Shederlaomach (Frederick G. Williams) 92:1, 2; 104:27, 29.
Shinehah (Kirtland) 82:12, 13; superscription to 96; 104:21, 40, 48.
Shinelah (print) 104:58.

Shinelane (printing) 104:63.
Shule (ashery) 104:39.
Tahhanes (the tannery) 104:20.
Talents (dollars) 104:69, 73.
Zombre (John Johnson) 96:6; 104:24, 34.

78:5-7 *"be equal in . . . earthly things"*

See *United Order* in Appendix A.

"By being equal the Lord does not mean that every man should receive the same compensation for labor performed, but that each should receive according to his needs and thus equality may be maintained. Where there is no selfishness in the hearts of the people this desirable end can be accomplished, but it is bound to fail where jealousy and selfishness are not eliminated from the soul. It is essential that we be able to keep the celestial law of equality." (Joseph Fielding Smith, *CHMR* 1:307.)

' "Equality,' as it is used in the revelation means to have an equal claim on the blessings of our Heavenly Father—on the properties of the Lord's treasury, and the influences and gifts of His Holy Spirit. This is the equality meant in the revelations, and until we attain to this equality we cannot be equal in spiritual things." (George Q. Cannon, *JD* 13:99.)

78:10 *"Satan seeketh to turn their hearts away from . . . the things . . . prepared for them"*

See *Satan* in Appendix A.

"Satan's plan is to destroy. [D&C 10:27.] Ever since his rebellion in the former estate he has determined to carry out his plan by exercising force and compulsion against mankind. All those who accepted the Lord's plan did so with an organized bond and covenant that was to be everlasting and not to be broken. The Lord's covenants are always intended to be everlasting or to have a bearing on everlasting life. The brethren were duly warned that if they broke this covenant evil consequences would follow. [D&C 78:10, quoted.] If they failed in this everlasting covenant then they were to be turned over to the buffetings of Satan until the day of redemption. We might think that the day of redemption means that they then, after their suffering, would be reinstated and receive the blessings which were first offered them. We are not justified in this conclusion. The day of redemption is the day of the resurrection. (D&C 88:16.) We should remember that the Lord has said at other times that such may not come into his presence. [D&C 64:39; 76:109-112; 88:22-31.]" (Joseph Fielding Smith, *CHMR* 2:76-77.)

78:11 *"by a bond or everlasting covenant that cannot be broken"*

"I construe the new and everlasting covenant as I could construe, in large measure, a legal contract. I believe that our Father intended that he would obligate himself as well as obligate the beneficiaries of that contract to the performance of it. I believe that no one is entitled to the full measure of its blessings unless he subjects himself to all the conditions upon which those blessings are predicated, and I construe that covenant to be broad enough to embrace every principle of the gospel." (Stephen L Richards, *CR,* October 1922, p. 67.)

78:14 *"that the church may stand independent above all other creatures beneath the celestial world"*

"By the keeping of the covenant of consecration, the Lord promised that the Church would stand independent above all other creatures beneath the celestial world. It is the will of the Lord, that eventually, the Church may take its rightful place above all other creatures upon the earth, or other spheres that are not celestial. This is the destiny of the Church, but the destiny of each of us individually depends on whether or not we will accept in faithfulness the covenants and obligations which are given us. The promise is that if we will be obedient we shall come up and be made rulers over many kingdoms. Those who receive the celestial exaltation will, without doubt, be made rulers over many kingdoms, and they will have power and authority to direct and to counsel those of lesser glories. Moreover, they will have the privilege of exaltation and of becoming creators in their own right as the sons of God." (Joseph Fielding Smith, *CHMR* 2:77.)

"The purpose of revealing the celestial order of society was to enable the Church to pass through all trials safely. God knew that persecutions and sufferings would come. He also knew that obedience to the law revealed would make the Church independent of enemies.

"The term 'creatures' is used here in its widest meaning, to signify all that is created, and refers especially to the various organizations in the world, whether ecclesiastical, political, financial, or industrial." (Smith and Sjodahl, *DCC,* p. 482.)

78:15 *"the foundations of Adam-ondi-Ahman"*

See *Adam-ondi-Ahman* in Appendix A.

78:16 *"Michael your prince"*

See *Adam* in Appendix A.

78:16 *"the Holy One, who is without beginning of days or end of life"*

See *Jesus Christ* in Appendix A.

78:18 *"riches of eternity"*

See same title in Appendix A.

78:20 *"Son Ahman"*

See *Son Ahman* in Appendix A.

78:21 *"church of the Firstborn"*

See same title in Appendix A.

SECTION 79

See first part of background information for section 78.

79:1 *"eastern countries"*

This term refers to the eastern sections (areas, states) of the United States.

79:2 *"the Comforter"*

See *Holy Ghost* in Appendix A.

SECTION 80

Background information on section 80

See first part of background information for section 78.

80:1-5 *"Stephen Burnett . . . preach the gospel to every creature that cometh under the sound of your voice"*

See *Missionary service* in Appendix A.

80:2 *"Eden Smith"*

This was a son of John Smith.

SECTION 81

See first part of background information for section 78.

81:1-7 *Frederick G. Williams called as a counselor in the First Presidency*

See *First Presidency* in Appendix A. For biographical information on Frederick G. Williams, see material following his name in Appendix B.

"In March, 1832, the Lord revealed that the First Presidency of the Church should be organized. He called by revelation Elder Frederick G. Williams to be a counselor in that body of Priesthood with Sidney Rigdon as the other counselor to Joseph Smith. The Lord said to him: [D&C 81:1-2, quoted.]

"From the time when this presidency was organized these four men were to hold these keys, for it was revealed that this authority is vested in the First Presidency of the Church. The President of the Church holds the supreme authority. They are to aid him, to sit in counsel with him and advise, but he it is, who holds the right to decision and the right of revelation for the Priesthood and for the Church. It was not until March 18, 1833, that the First Presidency was organized, although Sidney Rigdon and Frederick G. Williams had been acting in the capacity of counselors to the Prophet Joseph Smith for several months, or shortly after the call of Frederick G. Williams by revelation in March 1832." (Joseph Fielding Smith, *CHMR* 2:80.)

81:2 *"the keys of the kingdom"*

See *Keys of priesthood* in Appendix A.

"These same keys of the kingdom were held by Peter, James, and John, who served as the First Presidency of the Church in the dispensation of the Meridian of Time. Peter held the presiding power. [Matt. 16:13-19 quoted.] However, to Peter was the power of the keys of the kingdom given, and he, associated with the other members of the twelve, was to exercise them, he holding the presiding and directing power." (Joseph Fielding Smith, *CHMR* 2:81.)

81:3 *Pray "always, vocally and in thy heart, in public and in private"*

See *Prayer* in Appendix A.

81:6 *"eternal life"*

See same title in Appendix A.

81:7 *"Alpha and Omega"*

See same title in Appendix A.

SECTION 82

Background information on section 82

"On the 27th, I called a general council of the Church [Jackson county, Missouri], and was acknowledged as the President of the High Priesthood, according to a previous ordination at a conference of High Priests, Elders and members, held at Amherst, Ohio, on the 25th of January, 1832. The right hand of fellowship was given to me by the Bishop, Edward Partridge, in behalf of the Church. The scene was solemn, impressive and delightful. During the intermission, a difficulty or hardness which had existed between Bishop Partridge and Elder [Sidney] Rigdon, was amicably settled, and when we came together in the afternoon, all hearts seemed to rejoice and I received the following: [Section 82 follows.]" (Joseph Smith, *HC* 1:267.)

"The first of April 1832 the Prophet Joseph Smith with Newel K. Whitney and Jesse Gause, left for Missouri to fulfill the provisions of the revelation given in March (Sec. 78) in relation to the regulation and establishment of the storehouse for the benefit of the poor, and the consecration of properties in that land. . . .

"This revelation is one showing the 'order of Enoch' as exercised in the Church in Enoch's day." (Joseph Fielding Smith, *CHMR* 1:318-19.)

82:2 *Those in Zion are expected to "refrain from sin"*

"Repeatedly the Lord had warned the members of the Church, and especially those who had moved, or intended to move, to Zion, that his laws as given to Enoch, and as he expected them to be obeyed, were very exacting. He was starting them out with a perfect law—the law of consecration—and had notified them that on this basis only could Zion be built. There was to be no compromise with sin, and perfect unity, unselfish devotion, humility and obedience were the principles required of them, if they were to receive the blessings. Notwithstanding all the counsel that had been given by revelation, there was some deviation from these sacred principles. Some jealousies and selfishness were manifest. It was a difficult task for some to forsake living, as the Lord has said on a previous occasion, 'after the manner of men,' that is worldly men, those who had not received the truth. While the Lord was asking them to consecrate their properties, yet he was offering them far more in return than they were able to give." (Joseph Fielding Smith, *CHMR* 1:319.)

82:3-4 *"unto whom much is given much is required"*

"Jesus made it plain (Matt. 25:14-39) that each will be required to give an accounting only for the talents or gifts he has received: 'for unto whomsoever much is given, of him shall be much required.' (See Luke 12:48.) No man can say that he has received nothing. Even though it be but one talent, he will be expected to develop that talent so that when his Lord comes, he will be able to return it with profit. . . . Can you imagine any greater justification for 'weeping and gnashing of teeth,' than to learn from your Lord, when called to give an accounting for your life here upon the earth, that while you had been faithful in your spirit existence and had kept your first estate, you had failed in your second estate, and that when you were put to the test to see if you would do all things whatsoever the Lord your God had commanded you, that you had failed? Remember, the Lord said of such: 'Cast ye the unprofitable servant into outer darkness.' " (LeGrand Richards, *MWW*, pp. 259-60.)

82:4 *"inasmuch as ye keep not my sayings . . . ye become transgressors"*

"So it is; it always has been, and it always will be so: when light comes, if the people reject that light, it will condemn them, and will add to their sorrow and affliction." (Brigham Young, *JD* 6:288.)

82:5 *"darkness reigneth"*

See *Darkness* in Appendix A.

" 'Darkness' here, as in John 1:5, means the condition of the world outside divine revelation. It refers to both spiritual and moral error. Revelation from God gives light, but when divine revelation is rejected, the adversary spreads his dominion among the children of men." (Smith and Sjodahl, *DCC*, p. 490.)

82:6   *"none doeth good ... all have gone out of the way"*

"Once again there comes the warning: [D&C 82:5-6, quoted.] There are few sins more worthy of condemnation and more contemptible in the sight of our heavenly Father, than the sin of self-righteousness. He has repeatedly said that he requires of us 'a broken heart and a contrite spirit.' [D&C 20:37; 59:8.] There are individuals who, in their own opinions of themselves, never sin. The missionaries find the hardest class of people with whom to deal in the preaching of the Gospel, is that class who base their faith on belief only, and claim to be already 'saved.' Here the Lord informs us that all have sinned. This reminds us of the words of the Lord to the person who came to the Master and said: 'Good Master, what good thing shall I do, that I may have eternal life?' The Lord answered: 'Why callest thou me good? there is none good but one, that is, God.' [Matt. 19:16-17.] In the matter of perfection, this is true; man is imperfect and does transgress, therefore we all need humility, a contrite spirit, and a willingness to receive counsel and if need be correction." (Joseph Fielding Smith, *CHMR* 2:86-87.)

82:7   *"unto that soul who sinneth shall the former sins return"*

"It is present salvation and the present influence of the Holy Ghost that we need every day to keep us on saving ground. When an individual refuses to comply with the further requirements of heaven, then the sins he had formerly committed return upon his head [Ezek. 3:20]; his former righteousness departs from him, and is not accounted to him for righteousness: but if he had continued in righteousness and obedience to the requirements of heaven, he is saved all the time through baptism, the laying on of hands, and obeying the commandments of the Lord and all that is required of him by the heavens—the living oracles." (Brigham Young, *JD* 8:124.)

"Whatever the past may have been in our individual lives, it is gone. The future lies ahead, and we must face it with resolution. There is always a point from which we can begin. Even though we may have been faithful in the past, if we turn away, that faithfulness will profit us nothing. 'No man, having put his hand to the plough, and looking back, is fit for the kingdom of God.' [Luke 9:62.]" (Howard W. Hunter, *CR*, April 1961, p. 18.)

82:10 *"I, the Lord, am bound when ye do what I say; but when ye do not what I say, ye have no promise"*

" 'Mormonism' has taught me that God holds Himself accountable to law even as He expects us to do. He has set us the example in obedience to law. I know that to say this would have been heresy a few decades ago. But we have the divine word for it: [Sec. 82:10, quoted.] He operates by law and not by arbitrariness or caprice." (James E. Talmage, *CR*, April 1930, p. 96.)

"In his mercy and love for mankind, the Lord offers many covenants that will, if obeyed, bring them exaltation. Many, if not all, of these covenants are absolutely required of those who receive them. When the covenants are made that will make us sons and daughters of God, and bestow upon us the fulness of the Father's kingdom, we cannot ignore them; we cannot treat them with contempt, but we must be obedient to them in every detail, else how are we worthy of the blessings? It seems very strange that there are those who think that notwithstanding their unfaithfulness and rejection of these covenants, it is possible for them to receive them by proxy after they are dead, when they treated them with contempt and rejected them when they were living. We should be deeply impressed with this saying and realize that we are not entitled to the blessings and that the Lord is not bound to give them when we have rejected them." (Joseph Fielding Smith, *CHMR* 1:320.)

82:11-13 *For an explanation of the unusual names and titles, see background information for section 78.*

82:14 *"Zion must increase . . . ; her borders must be enlarged; her stakes must be strengthened"*

"Zion, as used here, undoubtedly had reference to the Church. At that time there was but a small body of Church members just beginning to emerge as an organization, after having experienced harsh treatment from enemies outside the Church, who had then been directed to gather together in Jackson County, Missouri, which the Lord had designated as the 'land of Zion.' As though to impress upon these early struggling members their destiny in the world, the Lord in another revelation told them this: 'Therefore, verily, thus saith the Lord, let Zion rejoice, for this is Zion—THE PURE IN

HEART; therefore, let Zion rejoice, while all the wicked shall mourn.' (D&C 97:21.)

"To be worthy of such a sacred designation as Zion, the Church must think of itself as a bride adorned for her husband, as John the Revelator recorded when he saw in vision the Holy City where the righteous dwelled, adorned as a bride for the Lamb of God as her husband. Here is portrayed the relationship the Lord desires in his people in order to be acceptable to our Lord and Master even as a wife would adorn herself in beautiful garments for her husband." (Harold B. Lee, *Ensign,* July 1973, p. 3.)

"These units [stakes] so organized are gathered together . . . for a defense against the enemies of the Lord's work, both the seen and the unseen. The apostle Paul said with reference to these enemies about which we should be concerned:

" 'For we wrestle not against flesh and blood, but against principalities, against powers, against the rulers of the darkness of this world, against spiritual wickedness in high places.' (Eph. 6:12.)

"These organizations were to be as . . . a 'refuge from the storm, and from wrath when it shall be poured out without mixture upon the whole earth.' (D&C 115:6.). . .

"I believe there has never been a time since the creation that the Lord has left the dominion of the devil to destroy his work without his power being manifest in the midst of the righteous to save the works of righteousness from being completely overthrown. . . . Today we are witnessing the demonstration of the Lord's hand even in the midst of his saints, the members of the Church. Never in this dispensation, and perhaps never before in any single period, has there been such a feeling of urgency among the members of this church as today. Her boundaries are being enlarged, her stakes are being strengthened." (Harold B. Lee, *Ensign,* July 1973, p. 4.)

82:15-24 *The order of Enoch*

See *Enoch* and *United Order* in Appendix A.

82:17 *"you are to be equal"*

See material for 78:5-7.

82:18 *"church of the living God"*

See *Church* and *Living God* in Appendix A.

82:19 *"Every man seeking the interest of his neighbor"*

"It is verily true that before we can enter into the celestial kingdom we will have to learn how to live in unity with the love of our fellows at heart, desiring their good as well as our own, and not preferring ourselves before them. Here the Lord gave to the Church the plan and the opportunity to prepare themselves by obedience to celestial law. They failed, and the privilege to practice this law of consecration had to be postponed because we were not able to esteem our neighbor as ourselves." (Joseph Fielding Smith, *CHMR* 1:322.)

82:21 *"the soul that sins against this covenant"*

"The breaking of any covenant that our Father in heaven makes with us, is a dreadful thing. We make a covenant in the waters of baptism. Many have broken it, and hence lose the promised blessings. All through our lives we are called to enter into covenants and many members of the Church seemingly fail to realize the seriousness of a violation or to understand that punishment must inevitably follow. Solemn covenants are taken by members of the Church in the Temples. These covenants are to prepare us for an exaltation. Yet there are many who receive them who utterly fail to heed them, but presumably, they think the Lord has a short memory, or that he is so extremely merciful that he will break his promises and the punishment mentioned for the violation will not be inflicted. In this manner many deceive themselves." (Joseph Fielding Smith, *CHMR* 1:322-23.)

82:21 *"buffetings of Satan"*

See *Satan* in Appendix A.

82:22 *"make unto yourselves friends with the mammon of unrighteousness"*

"The commandment of the Lord that the Saints should make themselves 'friends with the mammon of unrighteousness,' seems to be a hard saying when not properly understood. It is not intended that in making friends of the 'mammon of unrighteousness' that the brethren were to partake with them in their sins; to receive them to their bosoms, intermarry with them and otherwise come down to their level. They were to so live that peace with their enemies might be assured. They were to treat them kindly, be friendly with them as far as correct and virtuous principles would permit, but never to swear with them or drink or carouse with them. If they could allay prejudice and show a willingness to trade with and show a kindly spirit, it might help to turn them away from their bitterness. Judgment was to be left with the Lord." (Joseph Fielding Smith, *CHMR* 2:89.)

SECTION 83

Background information on section 83

"On the 27th [April 1832] we transacted considerable business for the salvation of the Saints, who were settling among a ferocious set of mobbers, like lambs among wolves. It was my endeavor to so organize the Church, that the brethren might eventually be independent of every incumbrance beneath the celestial kingdom, by bonds and covenants of mutual friendship, and mutual love.

"On the 28th and 29th, I visited the brethren above Big Blue river, in Kaw township [Missouri], a few miles west of Independence, and received a welcome only known by brethren and sisters united as one in the same faith, and by the same baptism, and supported by the same Lord. The Colesville branch, in particular, rejoiced as the ancient Saints did with Paul. ['It should be remembered that those Colesville Saints were among the first to receive the Gospel under the teachings of the Prophet, and hence his heart was naturally tender towards them, and this visit was doubtless especially delightful both to the Saints and to the Prophet.'] It is good to rejoice with the people of God. On the 30th I returned to Independence, and again sat in council with the brethren, and received the following: [Section 83, quoted.]" (Joseph Smith, *HC* 1:269.)

83:1-6 *"Laws of the Church concerning widows and orphans"*

"Here is one of the great purposes for which the law of tithing is instituted in the Church. It is intended that the widows shall be looked after when they are in need, and that the fatherless and the orphans shall be provided for from the funds of the Church; that they shall be clothed and fed, and shall have opportunity for education, the same as other children who have parents to look after them. When a child is fatherless and motherless the Church becomes the parent of that child, and it is obligatory upon the Church to take care of it, and to see that it has opportunities equal with the other children in the Church. This is a great responsibility. Have we ever seen the day since the Church was organized when we could carry out the purpose of the Lord fully and to our heart's content? We have not, because we have never had the means to do it with. But if men will obey the laws of God so that there shall be abundance in the storehouse of the Lord, we will have wherewith to feed and clothe the poor and the orphan and to look after those who are in need to the Church." (Joseph F. Smith, *CR,* October 1899, pp. 39-40.)

SECTION 84

Background information on section 84

"As soon as I could arrange my affairs, I recommenced the translation of the Scriptures, and thus I spent most of the summer. In July, we received the first number of 'The Evening and Morning Star,' which was a joyous treat to the Saints. Delightful indeed, was it to contemplate that the little band of brethren had become so large, and grown so strong, in so short a time as to be able to issue a paper of their own, which contained not only some of the revelations, but other information also,—which would gratify and enlighten the humble inquirer after truth. . . .

"The Elders during the month of September began to return from their missions to the Eastern States, and present the histories of their several stewardships in the Lord's vineyard; and while together in these seasons of joy, I inquired of the Lord, and received on the 22nd and 23rd of September, the following revelation on Priesthood: [Section 84, follows.]" (Joseph Smith, *HC* 1:273.)

84:2-3 *Location of the New Jerusalem*

See *New Jerusalem* in Appendix A.

84:4 *"which temple shall be reared in this generation"*

See *Generation* in Appendix A.

"This statement has been a stumbling block to some and there have been various interpretations of the meaning of a generation. It is held by some that a generation is one hundred years; by others that it is one hundred and twenty years; by others that a generation as expressed in this and other scriptures has reference to a period of time which is indefinite. The Savior said: 'An evil and adulterous generation seeketh after a sign.' This did not have reference to a period of years, but to a period of wickedness. A generation may mean the time of this present dispensation. Moreover, the statement is qualified in this revelation in the above quotation." (Joseph Fielding Smith, *CHMR* 1:337.)

"We understand that certain things predicted through the

Prophet Joseph Smith are to take place before this generation shall pass away, and the Lord will see to it that the
generation in which those things were predicted will not all
pass away until all shall be fulfilled, but there is no fixed period for a generation, no set time in the revelations of God,
no year or date given when these things shall take place, and
it is folly for anybody to put a date to it." (Charles W. Penrose, *CR*, April 1918, p. 20.)

84:5 *"an house shall be built"*

"There [New Jerusalem] . . . we expect to build a temple
different from all other temples in some respects. It will be
built much larger, . . . than this Tabernacle . . . according to
the revelation God gave to us forty years ago in regard to
that temple. But you may ask in what form will it be built?
Will it be built in one large room, like this Tabernacle? No;
there will be 24 different compartments in the temple that
will be built in Jackson County. The names of these compartments were given to us some 45 or 46 years ago; the
names we still have, and when we build these 24 rooms, in a
circular form and arched over the centre, we shall give the
names to all these different compartments just as the Lord
specified through Joseph Smith. . . . Perhaps you may ask for
what purpose these 24 compartments are built. I answer not
to assemble the outside world in, nor to assemble the Saints
all in one place, but these buildings will be built with a special view to the different orders, or in other words the
different quorums or councils of the two Priesthoods that
God has ordained on the earth. That is the object of having
24 rooms so that each of these different quorums, whether
they be High Priests or Seventies, or Elders, or Bishops, or
lesser Priesthood, or Teachers or Deacons, or Patriarchs, or
Apostles, or High Councils, or whatever may be the duties
that are assigned to them, they will have rooms in the temple
of the Most High God, adapted, set apart, constructed, and
dedicated for this special purpose. . . . But will there be any
other buildings excepting those 24 rooms that are all joined
together in a circular form and arched over the center—are
there any other rooms that will be built—detached from the
temple? Yes. There will be tabernacles, there will be meeting
houses for the assembling of the people on the Sabbath
day." (Orson Pratt, *JD* 25:24-25.)

84:5 *"a cloud shall rest upon it"*

"The Lord manifested Himself in ancient Israel in a cloud, shaped as a pillar, which became luminous at night. It guided the people on the journey to Canaan. It stood at the entrance to the Sanctuary, and in it God spoke to Moses. It rested on the Sanctuary and filled it, when that sacred tent was set up. It was the visible sign of God's guiding and protecting care over His people." (Smith and Sjodahl, *DCC*, p. 497.)

84:6 *"under the hand of . . . Jethro"*

"The descent of this authority, or divine power, from Adam to Moses is here given in the Lord's own words to Joseph Smith. Moses received it from Jethro, a priest of the house of Midian. The Midianites were descendants of Abraham, through the children of Keturah, wife of Abraham, therefore the Midianites, who were neighbors to the Israelites in Palestine, were related to the Israelites, and were Hebrews. As descendants of Abraham they were entitled through their faithfulness to his blessings (see Abr. 2:9-11), and in the days of Moses and preceding them, in Midian the Priesthood was found." (Joseph Fielding Smith, *CHMR* 1:338.)

"Among the scholars who are uninspired, there is doubt as to who Jethro was. In Exodus 3:1, he is called the father-in-law of Moses, but these scholars say the name may mean any male relative by marriage. In Exodus 2:18, Reuel, or Raguel, appears as the name of the father-in-law of Moses. Then it is maintained that the transaction related of Jethro in Exodus 18:12-27, is told of Hobab in Numbers 10:29. These may have been names given to Jethro by different scribes, or in different countries. We know, however, by the information given in this revelation that Jethro was the father-in-law of Moses and that Moses received the Priesthood from him. This has been a mystery to some, who have thought that only the children of Israel were blessed with the authority of Priesthood. We know that the Midianites were descendants of Abraham who had sons by his wife Keturah. . . . Evidently among the 'gifts' which Abraham gave his other sons was the authority of the Priesthood. We know that the 'Midianites' held it." (Smith and Sjodahl, *DCC*, p. 500.)

84:16   *"by the hand of . . . Adam"*

"The Lord conferred the Holy Priesthood upon Adam and said unto him: 'Now this same Priesthood which was in the beginning, shall be in the end of the world also.' (Moses 6:7)." (Joseph Fielding Smith, *CHMR* 1:337-38.)

"The Priesthood was first given to Adam; he obtained the First Presidency, and held the keys of it from generation to generation. He obtained it in the creation, before the world was formed, as in Genesis 1:26-28. He had dominion given him over every living creature. He is Michael, the archangel, spoken of in the Scriptures. Then to Noah who is Gabriel; he stands next in authority to Adam in the Priesthood; he was called of God to this office, and was the father of all living in his day, and to him was given the dominion. These men held keys first on earth, and then in heaven.

"The Priesthood is an everlasting principle, and existed with God from eternity, and will to eternity, without beginning of days or end of years. The keys have to be brought from heaven whenever the gospel is sent. When they are revealed from heaven, it is by Adam's authority." (Joseph Smith, *HC* 3:385-86.)

84:18,   *The lesser Aaronic Priesthood"*
26-30   See *Aaronic Priesthood* in Appendix A.

84:18-25,   *The greater or Melchizedek Priesthood*
29   See *Melchizedek Priesthood* in Appendix A.

84:19   *"this greater priesthood . . . holdeth the key of the mysteries of the kingdom"*

See *Mysteries* in Appendix A.

"Thus, we see, that it is impossible for men to obtain the knowledge of the mysteries of the kingdom or the knowledge of God, without the authority of the Priesthood. Secular learning, the study of the sciences, arts and history, will not reveal these vital truths to man. It is the Holy Priesthood that unlocks the door to heaven and reveals to man the mysteries of the Kingdom of God. It is this Divine Authority which makes known the knowledge of God! Is there any wonder that the world today is groping in gross darkness concerning God and the things of his kingdom? We should also remember that these great truths are not made known even to members of the Church unless they place their lives in harmony with the law on which these blessings are predicated. (D&C 130:20-21.)" (Joseph Fielding Smith, *CHMR* 1:338.)

84:19 *"this greater priesthood . . . holdeth the key . . . of the knowledge of God"*

"The Lord—speaking of the priesthood, and the power of the priesthood, and the ordinances of the Church which we received through the priesthood—had this to say: [D&C 84:19, quoted.]

"So *if there is no priesthood, there is no knowledge of God.* And that is why the world is in darkness today, because they have no priesthood. They have lost the knowledge of God. And so they have been teaching all manner of tradition, all manner of false doctrine, all manner of man-made philosophy in relation to God and the principles of truth pertaining to the salvation of men. . . .

"When we read things of this nature, it ought to make every man among us who holds the priesthood rejoice to think that we have the great authority by which *we may know God.* Not only the men holding the priesthood know that great truth, but because of that priesthood and the *ordinances thereof,* every member of the Church, men and women alike, may know God." (Joseph Fielding Smith, *DS* 3:142-43.)

84:20 *"the power of godliness"*

"What power, then, what mysterious power is it that had led and guided them [Latter-day Saints] and that still leads and guides them and holds them together as they are held? Let me tell you what it is. I will read from the book of Doctrine and Covenants, Section 84: [vs. 19-21, quoted.]

"That is what holds these people together—the power of the priesthood. And in the administration of it we have seen and do see the power of godliness; not a form of godliness, mind you, but the power of godliness. Paul said that in the latter days men would be 'having a form of godliness but denying the power thereof' [2 Tim. 3:5]; but what I refer to is the power of godliness. . . . In all the leadership of the priesthood you see that same power of godliness. . . . It is the power of godliness, of godly lives. It is the power of godly men and godly women, through the ordinances of the priesthood made manifest; and everyone shares in it." (Charles W. Nibley, *CR,* April 1927, pp. 26-27.)

84:24 *"into his rest . . . the fulness of his glory"*

"What is meant by that rest? It means fulness of everything; to enjoy a fulness of love, a fulness of light, a fulness of intelligence, a fulness of power; to sit down with Christ upon His throne, as He has overcome and sits upon the throne of the Father—the promise that was given unto the Israel of God—the promise that was given to the sons of the Most High." (George Teasdale, *CR,* April 1899, p. 32.)

84:25 *The Lord "took Moses out of their midst, and the Holy Priesthood also"*

"The Lord offered to Israel in the days of Moses the fulness of the Gospel with the Higher Priesthood and its keys, intending to give unto them the blessings of exaltation and make of them a royal Priesthood. When Moses went up into the sacred Mount Horeb and received the writings which the Lord made with his own finger, he received the fulness of the Gospel with its ordinances and covenants, but when Moses returned after his absence of forty days and found the Israelites reveling in idolatry, he broke the tablets. Later the Lord gave unto him other tablets but changed some of the commandments, and took away the Higher, or Melchizedek Priesthood, and gave to the people the carnal law." (Joseph Fielding Smith, *CHMR* 2:104.)

84:31 *"the sons of Aaron shall offer an acceptable offering"*

See material for D&C 13.

84:31-34 *"sons of Moses . . . and Aaron"*

"Who are the sons of Aaron and Levi today? They are, by virtue of the blessings of the Almighty, those who are ordained by those who hold the authority to officiate in the offices of the priesthood. It is written that those so ordained become the sons of Moses and of Aaron." (Joseph Fielding Smith, *DS* 3:93.)

" 'Sons of Moses,' and 'sons of Aaron' do not refer to their literal descendants only, for all who are faithful and obtain these Priesthoods, and magnify their calling, are sanctified by the Spirit and become the 'sons' of Moses and of Aaron, and the seed of Abraham, as well as the Church and

Kingdom, and the elect of God (v. 34). Paul expresses this thought as follows, 'Know ye therefore that they which are of faith, the same are the children of Abraham.' (Gal. 3:7)." (Smith and Sjodahl, *DCC,* p. 504.)

84:33 *"faithful . . . are sanctified . . . unto the renewing of their bodies"*

"When the Temple [in New Jerusalem] is built the sons of the two Priesthoods, that is, those who are ordained to the Priesthood of Melchizedek, that Priesthood which is after the order of the Son of God, with all its appendages; and those who have been ordained to the Priesthood of Aaron with all its appendages, the former called the sons of Moses, the latter the sons of Aaron, will enter into that Temple . . . and all of them who are pure in heart will behold the face of the Lord . . . for he will suddenly come to his Temple. . . . In doing this, he will purify not only the minds of the Priesthood in that Temple, but he will purify their bodies until they shall be quickened, renewed and strengthened, and they will be partially changed, not to immortality, but changed in part that they can be filled with the power of God, and they can stand in the presence of Jesus, and behold his face in the midst of that Temple.

"This will prepare them for further ministrations among the nations of the earth, it will prepare them to go forth in the days of tribulation and vengeance upon the nations of the wicked, when God will smite them with pestilence, plague and earthquake, such as former generations never knew. [D&C 29:14-21; 45:28-42; Rev. 9.]. . .

"When they are prepared, when they have received a renewal of their bodies in the Lord's Temple, and have been filled with the Holy Ghost and purified as gold and silver in a furnace of fire, then they will be prepared to stand before the nations of the earth and preach glad tidings of salvation in the midst of judgments that are to come like a whirlwind upon the wicked." (Orson Pratt, *JD* 15:365-66.)

84:33 *"magnifying their calling"*

"Sometimes we speak loosely of magnifying our priesthood, but what the revelations speak of is magnifying our callings in the priesthood, as elders, seventies, high priests, patriarchs, and apostles." (Joseph Fielding Smith, *CR,* October 1970, p. 91.)

"The Prophet Joseph was often asked, 'Brother Joseph, what do you mean by magnifying a calling?'

"Joseph replied: 'What does it mean to magnify a calling? It means to build it up in dignity and importance, to make it honorable and commendable in the eyes of all men, to enlarge and strengthen it, to let the light of heaven shine through it to the view of other men. And how does one magnify a calling? Simply by performing the service that pertains to it.' " (Thomas S. Monson, British Area *CR,* August 1971, p. 145.)

"In the words 'magnifying their calling,' far more seems to be implied than the mere attending of priesthood meetings, administering to the sacrament and the sick, and serving in Church work. Faithfulness to warrant the reception of the priesthood is a condition that perhaps all men do not meet. And the magnifying of their calling seems to imply a totalness which few, if any, men reach in mortality. Perfection of body and spirit seems to be included here." (Spencer W. Kimball, *MF,* p. 123.)

84:38 *"he that receiveth my Father receiveth my Father's kingdom"*

"The Latter-day Saints are promised, if they are faithful, that they shall receive the fullness, as Jesus received it; and Jesus received it as the Father received it. In the words of Paul, they become heirs of God and joint heirs with Jesus Christ. [See Romans 8:16-17.] There is nothing that the Savior has attained unto that God's faithful children are not promised. They are promised the same blessings, the same power, the same authority, the same gifts, the same graces. I know that we are apt to think that heaven is a sort of spiritual place. It is spiritual; but God our Eternal Father is a being of power. He controls the earth and the inhabitants thereof; He controls the elements of the earth; and we are promised that we shall be sharers with Him. He will give us an equal interest in all this power and authority. . . .

"The promise is that all things that He hath shall be given unto us. [See D&C 84:38.] We will be His heirs; we will be (if I may use the term without irreverence) co-partners with Him in all this power and authority. I do not know whether all the Latter-day Saints grasp this idea. It is important that we should." (George Q. Cannon, *CR,* April 1899, p. 65.)

84:39-42 *"the oath and covenant which belongeth to the priest-hood"*

See *Oath and covenant of the priesthood* in Appendix A.

"President [Joseph Fielding] Smith frequently says in prayer and in counsel that he prays for and hopes that we will be true and faithful to every covenant and responsibility that rests upon us. That the obligations of 'the oath and covenant which belongeth to the priesthood' rest upon each of us there is no doubt, because the Lord says that 'all those who receive the priesthood, receive this oath and covenant of my Father, which he cannot break, neither can it be moved.' (D&C 84:40.)

"So, we have entered into a covenant with the Lord in which he has promised us eternal life, if we keep our part of the covenant, which is, to magnify our callings in the priesthood.

"The revelation says that the Lord cannot break his part of the oath and covenant. But we can break our part of it, and many priesthood bearers do so. Of them the revelation says:

" 'But whoso breaketh this covenant after he hath received it, and altogether turneth therefrom, shall not have forgiveness of sins in this world nor in the world to come.' (Vs. 41.)

"Now, I do not think this means that all who fail to magnify their callings in the priesthood will have committed the unpardonable sin, but I do think that priesthood bearers who have entered into the covenants that we enter into—in the waters of baptism, in connection with the law of tithing, the Word of Wisdom, and the many other covenants we make—and then refuse to live up to these covenants will stand in jeopardy of losing the promise of eternal life." (Marion G. Romney, *Ensign*, July 1972, p. 99.)

84:44-47 *"the word of the Lord is truth . . . light . . . Spirit . . . "*

See *Truth, Light,* and *Holy Ghost* in Appendix A.

84:51 *"whoso cometh not unto me is under the bondage of sin"*

See *Sin* and *Darkness* in Appendix A.

84:57 *"repent and remember . . . the Book of Mormon"*

"Now, we have not been using the Book of Mormon as we should. Our homes are not as strong unless we are using it to bring our children to Christ. Our families may be corrupted by worldly trends and teachings unless we know how to use the book to expose and combat the falsehoods in socialism, organic evolution, rationalism, humanism, etc. Our missionaries are not as effective unless they are 'hissing forth' with it. Social, ethical, cultural, or educational converts will not survive under the heat of the day unless their taproots go down to the fulness of the gospel which the Book of Mormon contains. Our Church classes are not as spirit-filled unless we hold it up as a standard. And our nation will continue to degenerate unless we read and heed the words of the God of this land, Jesus Christ, and quit building up and upholding the secret combinations which the Book of Mormon tells us proved the downfall of both previous American civilizations.

"Some of the early missionaries, on returning home, were reproved by the Lord in section 84 of the Doctrine and Covenants because they had treated lightly the Book of Mormon. As a result, their minds had been darkened. The Lord said that this kind of treatment of the Book of Mormon brought the whole Church under condemnation, even all of the children of Zion. And then the Lord said, 'And they shall remain under this condemnation until they repent and remember the new covenant, even the Book of Mormon. (See D&C 84:54-57.) Are we still under that condemnation?'" (Ezra Taft Benson, *Ensign,* May 1975, p. 65.)

84:62 *"unto whatsoever place ye cannot go ye shall send"*

See *Missionary service* in Appendix A.

84:63 *"you are mine apostles"*

See *Apostles* in Appendix A.

"An apostle, the dictionary states, is 'one of the twelve chosen by Christ to proclaim His gospel; also a Christian missionary who first evangelizes a certain nation; any zealous advocate of a doctrine or cause.' . . .

"The term apostle is recognized in the Church in the sense in which it is defined in the dictionary. Men have been called apostles who have been sent forth with the gospel message when they have not been ordained to that particular office.

"This revelation was given two years and four months before the first men were ordained to the special calling as apostles in the Church, but as they were commissioned to go forth proclaiming the gospel as witnesses for Christ, he designated them as his apostles." (Joseph Fielding Smith, *IE,* April 1935, p. 208.)

84:64-73   *"these signs shall follow them that believe"*

See *Signs* and *Miracles* in Appendix A.

"These miraculous 'signs' follow belief now, the same as in days of old. I have seen devils cast out by the power of the Priesthood. I have seen and heard manifested the gift of tongues and the interpretation of tongues. I have seen the sick healed with a touch, and have been healed myself by the laying on of hands, accompanied by the prayer and power of faith." (Orson F. Whitney, *CR,* April 1930, pp. 134-35.)

84:64-73   *Gifts of the Spirit*

See *Gifts of the Spirit* in Appendix A.

"For many centuries men had been without the guidance of the Holy Ghost because there was none to lay hands on them to bestow that gift, and therefore false doctrines and traditions had found place among the nations.

"The gifts of the Spirit . . . are given to the faithful for their edification and for the edification of the Church. To one is given one gift, and to another, another gift. Some have the gift of healing, others of prophecy and vision, others to work miracles according to their faith. . . .

"These gifts and blessings are only for those who have faith and believe the Gospel. They are not for the world. Should the Lord bestow on an elder one of these great gifts and should he boast of his power, then the gift would be taken from him, for they are not for the world. 'But a commandment I gave unto them,' said the Lord to the elders, 'they shall not boast themselves of these things, neither speak them before the world; for these things are given unto you for your profit and for salvation.' (V. 73.)" (Joseph Fielding Smith, *CHMR* 1:342-43.)

84:71   *"poison shall not hurt them"*

"The Prophet Joseph relates the following, which may serve as an illustration:

" 'While at this place [Greenville, Indiana, where he stayed with Newel K. Whitney during May, 1832, the latter suffering from a fractured leg] I frequently walked out in the woods, where I saw several fresh graves; and one day, when I rose from the dinner table, I walked directly to the door and commenced vomiting most profusely. I raised large quantities of blood and poisonous matter, and so great were the muscular contortions of my system, that my jaw, in a few moments, was dislocated. This I succeeded in replacing with my own hands, and made my way to Brother Whitney (who was on the bed), as speedily as possible; he laid his hands on me and administered to me in the name of the Lord, and I was healed in an instant. . . . Thanks be to my heavenly Father for his interference in my behalf at this critical moment, in the name of Jesus Christ. Amen.' (*HC* 1:271.)

"A. Clarke observes that there is no record or tradition indicating that any of the Apostles of our Lord ever suffered death by poison, while Mohammed came to his end by that means, as did, it may be added, Socrates. The promise of immunity from poison is, therefore, very remarkable." (Smith and Sjodahl, *DCC*, pp. 515.)

84:72   *"poison of a serpent shall not have power to harm them"*

"Paul, on one occasion, shook a venomous snake from his hand, and was not injured by it (Acts 28:3-6). No less remarkable is an incident from the famous march of Zion's Camp. The members of that organization often encountered reptiles on the prairie. One day Solomon Humphrey laid himself down for a little rest, being weary. When he awoke, he saw a rattlesnake coiled up not more than a few inches from his head. Some proposed to kill it, but Brother Humphrey said, 'Let it alone; we have had a good nap together.' It was on this occasion that the Prophet Joseph instructed the brethren not to kill serpents, or any other animals, unless absolutely necessary. 'Men,' said he, 'must first become harmless themselves, before they can expect the brute creation to be so' (Andrew Jenson, *Hist. Rec.,* p. 835)." (Smith and Sjodahl, *DCC,* p. 515.)

84:73   *Do not boast of the signs that follow belief, "neither speak them before the world"*

"When a man comes in the name of the Lord healing the sick and performing mighty works, he will not come with the blare of trumpets, nor will he advertise his performance." (Joseph Fielding Smith, *IE*, December 1955, 58:894-95.)

84:76   *"they are to be upbraided"*

"The word upbraid seems to be used here in the same sense as 'reprove' in John 16:8. There it means 'convict.' It is the office of the Holy Spirit to convict the world of sin, of righteousness, and of judgment, in order to bring men and women to repentance. If those who are sent to the world with the gospel message are filled with the Holy Spirit, the result will be the conviction of sinners, and conviction will be followed by either condemnation or salvation—salvation, if the gospel is accepted; condemnation, if it is rejected." (Smith and Sjodahl, *DCC,* p. 516.)

4:78, 86   *"let no man . . . take purse or scrip"*

See *Purse or scrip* in Appendix A.

"We want the families of those who are on missions to be supplied with the necessaries and comforts of life, and we do not want the Elders to beg from the poor that are scattered among the nations. We who first went did not have this done for us, but the circumstances are different now." (Heber C. Kimball, *JD* 10:168-69.)

84:80   *"they shall not go hungry"*

"Thousands of missionaries have put this promise to the test and the Lord has kept his promise to all those who have been faithful in their calling. Surely if the Father notices when a sparrow falls, he will not forsake any who in faithful obedience to his will seek his aid. That there have been those who have gone forth and have been weary in body and mind, and who have gone hungry, there is no doubt, for there are missionaries who have not given all their heart to the Lord and they have idled away valuable time when it was needful for them to proclaim the truth." (Joseph Fielding Smith, *CHMR* 1:344.)

84:80,   *"a hair of his head shall not fall"*
116   See material for 9:14.

84:85   *"treasure up in your minds continually the words of life"*

"This advice to the members of the Church as well as to its missionaries, that they store up useful knowledge so that they will always be prepared, has, too frequently, been neglected. Every member of the Church should have a thorough knowledge of the Gospel. Such a knowledge is a protection against deception and false doctrine. Because this foundation in truth is not laid; because of lack of study of Gospel principles, many are brought into captivity to the powers of darkness. They have not been able to distinguish between truth and error. . . .

"If we would follow this advice it would not be necessary to prepare discourses beforehand, for our faith would cause us to rely on the promise of the Lord." (Joseph Fielding Smith, *CHMR* 1:344-45.)

84:87 *"reprove the world"*

" 'Reprove,' as stated (v. 76) is to 'convict.' God's messengers, as it were, are lawyers before the bar of God. It is their duty to 'convict' the world of sin, and to warn all men of the 'judgment which is to come.' They are not sent out to entertain the world with philosophical lectures, or ethical discourses, or flowery oratory, or amusing anecdotes. Their one duty is to secure conviction and, if possible, repentance and salvation." (Smith and Sjodahl, *DCC*, p. 518.)

84:92-96 *"cleanse your feet, even with water . . . and bear testimony"*

See *Feet* in Appendix A.

For information on the topic of casting off the dust of your feet, read the materials listed after 24:15.

84:98-102 *"sing this new song"*

"The new song which they shall sing at this great day will be concerning the redemption of Zion and the restoration of Israel. Even now there are those who have set to music these beautiful words (vs. 99-102), but we may believe that no music has yet been produced that will compare with the music for this song when Zion is redeemed." (Joseph Fielding Smith, *CHMR* 1:346.)

84:103 *Gifts to missionaries might be sent to their families*

"The Lord gave commandment that the families of those who go forth should be cared for. The missionaries were at liberty, if they received means beyond their needs, to send it to their families and for the printing of revelations and the establishment of Zion. They were told to take their old coat or suit, or whatever it might be, and give to the poor when some benevolent person supplied them with that which was new." (Joseph Fielding Smith, *CHMR* 2:110.)

84:110   *"the body hath need of every member"*

"The Apostle Paul . . . in his beautiful figure compared the Church of Christ to the body of a man. (1 Cor. 12:13-31.) I have asked myself, what is the greatest cause for the difference between the Church of Christ and the churches that have been established by men, for there are many forms of religions, some patterning closely after the one founded by our Lord and Master Jesus Christ. And I have thought, is it not because these different bodies have not the Spirit? . . . I thought to myself what a comparison there was between the true Church of God, with the Priesthood and Spirit to enliven it, and the dead forms of religion, as they have been instituted by man. We might carry this comparison a little farther, and take the skeleton of this body, the organization of the Church of Christ, animated by the Spirit and Priesthood of God, and in connection with this skeleton we have the sinews, the helps in government, the muscles, the nerve system and the circulation of the blood from the heart into all parts of the body. And just as it is impossible for a human body to exist without the spirit, so is it impossible for the Church of Christ to exist without the Priesthood of the Son of God. Just as it is impossible for a body to be complete without the brain, the heart and the other organs of the system so would it be impossible for the Church of Christ to exist in perfection without the Presidency, the Apostles, the Seventies, the High Priests, the Elders, the Priests, Teachers and Deacons. All of them have their special work to perform, just as the organs of the human system have their particular part to do. I compared the circulation of the blood in the body to the active Priesthood, which goes about the whole body of the Church imparting life and vigor and setting in order all of the parts that may be out of place. Whenever a member becomes injured, the blood assists in building it up. So with the workings of the Priesthood of the Son of God, in the great body which Christ has established." (Abraham O. Woodruff, *CR,* April 1900, pp. 37-38.)

84: 114-15   *Cities of New York, Albany, and Boston to be warned specifically*

"When we become ripe in iniquity, then the Lord will come. . . . The Lord threatened destruction to great cities if they in their iniquity rejected his truth. This destruction evidently is to come when their cup is full. Desolation awaited them and the hour of their judgment would come." (Joseph Fielding Smith, *CHMR* 2:110.)

84:117 *"desolation of abomination in the last days"*

See *Second coming* in Appendix A.

"The Lord is not going to wait for us to get righteous. When he gets ready to come, he is going to come—when the cup of iniquity is full—and if we are not righteous then, it will be just too bad for us, for we will be classed among the ungodly, and we will be as stubble, to be swept off the face of the earth, for the Lord says wickedness shall not stand.

"Do not think the Lord delays his coming, for he will come at the appointed time, not the time which I have heard some preach when the earth becomes righteous enough to receive him. . . . Christ will come in the day of wickedness, when the earth is ripe in iniquity and prepared for the cleansing, and as the cleanser and purifier he will come, and all the wicked will be as stubble and will be consumed." (Joseph Fielding Smith, *DS* 3:3.)

SECTION 85

Background information on section 85

"On the 27th day of November, 1832, the Prophet wrote [Kirtland, Ohio] to Elder William W. Phelps who was in Independence, Missouri, in charge of the printing and with authority to assist the bishop in matters concerning the establishing of their inheritances and expressed to him in words of tender fellowship, his love and confidence. Matters pertaining to the establishing and building up of Zion weighed heavily on the mind of the Prophet Joseph Smith. His anxiety was very great because of the strictness of the commandments the Lord had given, and because of the grave responsibilities which had been placed upon his brethren to see that the covenants pertaining to consecration were faithfully kept. Especially was he concerned over the duties and responsibilities of the bishop in Zion, for they were very great. It was the duty of the bishop, assisted by his brethren, to see that justice was done, as the Lord had pointed out in the revelations, in the matter of deciding and alloting inheritances in Zion. This history reveals that there were some things that had not been attended to in the Spirit and according to the instructions which had been declared essential in the revelations. These matters caused the Prophet some anxiety and therefore he wrote to Brother Phelps stating that there were some things that were 'lying with great weight' on his mind. By the Spirit of prophecy he uttered this prayer, as though it were a prayer in the heart of William Phelps.

" 'My God, great and mighty art Thou, therefore, show unto Thy servant what shall become to all those who are essaying to come up unto Zion, in order to keep the commandments of God, and yet receive not their inheritance by consecration, by order or deed from the Bishop, the man that God has appointed in a legal way, agreeably to the law given to organize and regulate the Church, and all the affairs of the same.

"Then the Prophet adds: 'Brother William, in the love of God, having the most implicit confidence in you as a man of God, having obtained this confidence by a vision of heaven, therefore, I will proceed to unfold to you some of the feelings of my heart, and to answer the questions.' Then what follows by the inspiration of the Spirit of the Lord has been accepted by the Church as a revelation. [Section 85.]" (Joseph Fielding Smith, *CHMR* 2:111-12.)

85:1 *"It is the duty of the . . . clerk . . . to keep a history, and a . . . record"*

See *Records* in Appendix A.

85:6 *"the still small voice"*

"When the 'still small voice' of the Lord speaks to men it is overwhelming. We have the story of Elijah, who withstood the great wind when the Lord passed by, that rent the mountains, likewise the earthquake which shook the earth, and then fire, but the Lord was not in the fire and then the Lord spoke by the 'still small voice.' Then Elijah wrapped his face in his mantle, for the fear of the Lord came upon him. [1 Kings 19:9-14.] When the Lord comes he will speak, and the rocks will be rent, the mountains will be laid low and the valleys exalted and men will try to hide themselves from his presence. They will not be able to stand the piercing of the 'still small voice,' unless the Spirit of the Lord is upon them. [Sec. 133:40-51.]" (Joseph Fielding Smith, *CHMR* 1:51-52.)

"The Lord gives to many of us the still, small voice of revelation. [Sec. 85:6.] It comes as vividly and strongly as though it were with a great sound. It comes to each man, according to his needs and faithfulness, for guidance in matters that pertain to his own life. For the Church as a whole it comes to those who have been ordained to speak for the Church as a whole." (Heber J. Grant, *CR,* April 1945, p. 9.)

85:7 *"one mighty and strong"*

The First Presidency of the Church in 1907 (Joseph F. Smith, John R. Winder, and Anthon H. Lund) published a thorough statement on the "one mighty and strong," which was published in the *Improvement Era,* October 1907, pp. 929-43. Following is a small portion:

Now, as to the "one mighty and strong," who shall be sent of

God, to "set in order the house of God, and to arrange by lot the inheritance of the Saints." Who is he? What position will he hold in the Church? In what manner will he come to his calling? We draw attention first of all to the fact that his whole letter to William W. Phelps, as well as the part afterwards accepted as the word of the Lord, related to the affairs of the Church in Zion, Independence, Jackson county, Missouri. And inasmuch as through his repentance and sacrifices and suffering, Bishop Edward Partridge undoubtedly obtained a mitigation of the threatened judgment against him of falling "by the shaft of death, like as a tree that is smitten by the vivid shaft of lightning," so the occasion for sending another to fill his station—"one mighty and strong to set in order the house of God, and to arrange by lot the inheritances of the Saints"—may also be considered as having passed away and the whole incident of the prophecy closed. . . .

If, however, there are those who will still insist that the prophecy concerning the coming of "one mighty and strong" is still to be regarded as relating to the future, let the Latter-day Saints know that he will be a future bishop of the Church who will be with the Saints in Zion, Jackson County, Missouri, when the Lord shall establish them in that land; and he will be so blessed with the spirit and power of his calling that he will be able to set in order the house of God, pertaining to the department of the work under his jurisdiction; and in righteousness and justice will "arrange by lot the inheritances of the Saints." He will hold the same high and exalted station that Edward Partridge held; for the latter was called to do just this kind of work—that is, to set in order the house of God as pertaining to settling the Saints upon their inheritances.

85:8 *Do not "steady the ark of God"*

See 1 Chronicles 13:9-12 for the story in the Old Testament pertaining to steadying the ark of God.

85:12 *"it shall be done unto them . . . as recorded" in Ezra 2:61-62*

"I will read now a few verses from Section 85 of the Book of Doctrine and Covenants, commencing at the 9th verse: [to v. 12, quoted.] I am going to turn now to Ezra (chapter 2) and see what is said there. We read: [Ezra 2:61-63 quoted.]

"This is the position the people will be in when they come to claim an inheritance in Zion, if their names are not found recorded in the book of the law of God. And I want to tell you that this refers directly to the law of tithing. . . .

"Some people may not care very much whether their names are recorded or not, but this comes from ignorance of the consequences. If their names are not recorded they will not only be cut off from the assistance which they would be entitled to from the Church if they needed it, but they will be cut off from the ordinances of the house of God; they will be cut asunder from their dead and from their fathers who have been faithful, or from those who shall come after them who shall be faithful, and they will be appointed their portion with the unbelievers, where there is weeping and gnashing of teeth. It means that you will be cut off from your fathers and mothers, from your husbands, your wives, your children, and that you shall have no portion or lot or inheritance in the kingdom of God, both in time and in eternity. It has a very serious and far reaching effect." (Joseph F. Smith, *CR*, October 1899, p. 42.)

"Look back to the time when Israel returned to Jerusalem from their captivity. How were they enabled to set in order the congregation, the singers, the priests in their courses, and the Levites? It was given to them by genealogy. The Lord had promised to Levi that the service of the Temple and the Sanctuary should belong to his tribe, his family, and especially that the Priesthood should go to the descendants of Aaron. [Num. 3:5-13.] But when they returned from their captivity in Babylon and wanted to be reinstated in their places to officiate at the altar and to eat of the holy bread, the records were searched and those whose names were not found were put away from the Priesthood as polluted, until a Priest should rise up having the Urim and Thummim, who could declare their genealogy, their right and title to this Holy Priesthood." (Franklin D. Richards, *MS* 57:644.)

SECTION 86

Background information on section 86

"In this revelation the Lord has given a more complete interpretation than he gave to his apostles as recorded by Matthew. The reason for this may be accounted for in the fact that it is to be in these last days that the harvest is gathered and the tares are to be burned. In Matthew's account the Lord declares that he is the sower of the good seed, and in the Doctrine and Covenants it is stated that the apostles were the sowers of the seed. There is no contradiction here. Christ is the author of our salvation and he it was who instructed the apostles, and under him they were sent to preach the Gospel unto all the world, or to sow the seed, and as the seed is his and it is sown under his command, he states but the fact in this revelation and also in the parable." (Joseph Fielding Smith, *CHMR* 1:353.)

86:1-11 *An explanation of the parable concerning the wheat and the tares*

See *Tares* and *Parables* in Appendix A.

"I want to ask this congregation a question: When I have the vision of the night opened continually before my eyes, and can see the mighty judgments that are about to be poured out upon the world, when I know these things are true and are at the door of Jew and Gentile; while I know I am holding this position before God and this world, can I withhold my voice from lifting up a warning to this people and to the nations of the earth? I may never meet with this people again; I cannot tell how that may be, but while I live and see these things continually before my eyes I shall raise my warning voice. . . .

"God has held the angels of destruction for many years, lest they should reap down the wheat with the tares. But I want to tell you now, that those angels have left the portals of heaven, and they stand over this people, and this nation now, and are hovering over the earth waiting to pour out judgments. And from this very day they shall be poured out. Calamities and troubles are increasing in the earth, and there is a meaning to these things." (Wilford Woodruff, *Young Women's Journal,* August 1894, 5:512-13.)

"In July (15th), 1894, President Woodruff repeated this prophecy [v. 5, above] and again declared that the angels had been sent forth to reap down the earth, while speaking at the Weber Stake Conference in Ogden, and again, October 4, 1896 at the general conference of the Church in Salt Lake City. On divers other occasions he also warned the Saints and told them that the gathering of the tares had commenced." (Joseph Fielding Smith, *CHMR* 2:120.)

86:3 *"Babylon"*

See *Babylon* in Appendix A.

86:3 *"drink of her cup"*

See material for 35:11 and 101:11.

86:3 *"Satan"*

See *Satan* in Appendix A.

86:8-11 *Priesthood members "are lawful heirs, according to the flesh"*

"It is in harmony with this promise to Abraham [Abr. 2:9-11] the Lord declared to these Elders of the Church that the Priesthood had continued through the lineage of their fathers, 'for ye are lawful heirs, according to the flesh, and have been hid from the world with Christ in God.' Moreover that this Priesthood must remain through them and their lineage until the restoration of all things. This saying does not mean that the Priesthood has come down from olden times by lineage from generation to generation, for there was a great apostasy intervening between the days of their fathers who held the Priesthood and these elders unto whom this revelation was given. But since they were of the House of Israel, and therefore descendants of Abraham, they were lawful heirs to the Priesthood according to the covenant made with Abraham, and the Priesthood which they held and came down to them from them of old who held it. Then, again, we discover in Section 84, verses 32-34, that all who are true to the Priesthood and the Church become the sons of Aaron and Moses and the seed of Abraham, and the

Church and the kingdom, and the elect of God. All souls coming into the Church become the seed of Abraham according to the promise, and there is a literal change which comes over them by which they are grafted into the House of Israel even if they are not literally of his lineage. Speaking of this change the Prophet Joseph Smith has said:

" 'The . . . Holy Ghost has no other effect than pure intelligence. It is more powerful in expanding the mind, enlightening the understanding, and storing the intellect with present knowledge, of man who is of the literal seed of Abraham, than one that is a Gentile, though it may not have half as much visible effect upon the body; for as the Holy Ghost upon one of the literal seed of Abraham, it is calm and serene; and his whole soul and body are only exercised by the spirit of intelligence; while the effect of the Holy Ghost upon a Gentile, is to purge out old blood, and make him actually of the seed of Abraham.' [*HC* 3:380.]" (Joseph Fielding Smith, *CHMR* 1:356-57.)

SECTION 87

Background information on section 87

"Appearances of troubles among the nations became more visible this season than they had previously been since the Church began her journey out of the wilderness. The ravages of the cholera were frightful in almost all the large cities on the globe. The plague broke out in India, while the United States, amid all her pomp and greatness, was threatened with immediate dissolution. The people of South Carolina, in convention assembled (in November), passed ordinances, declaring their state a free and independent nation; and appointed Thursday, the 31st day of January, 1833, as a day of humiliation and prayer, to implore Almighty God to vouchsafe His blessings, and restore liberty and happiness within their borders. President Jackson issued his proclamation against this rebellion, called out a force sufficient to quell it, and implored the blessings of God to assist the nation to extricate itself from the horrors of the approaching and solemn crisis.

"On Christmas day [1832], I received the following revelation and prophecy on war: [D&C 87.]" (Joseph Smith, *HC* 1:301.)

"This revelation [Section 87 on war] was made known at that time to the Saints and was a subject of constant remarks in the Church; in 1851 it was published to the world and obtained a somewhat wide circulation nearly twenty-nine years after its date; its wondrous fulfillment began when the first gun was fired at Fort Sumter, South Carolina. [Sec. 130:12-13.] Since that time wars and rumors of wars have prevailed throughout the world. Peace has fled, and in view of all the Lord has said, it is not too much to expect it has fled no more to return till the reign of righteousness shall begin. [Sec. 97:22-23.]

"It is strange that the solemn warning uttered by Joseph in 1832 should have gone unheeded. His prophecy was not without its purpose. The Lord inspired his mind with visions of the future and with power to view the paths by which the nation might escape the impending disasters, but, like other parts of his message of salvation to the human race, this warning also was rejected." (George Q. Cannon, *LJS,* pp. 126-27.)

"When I was a boy, I traveled extensively in the United States and the Canadas, preaching this restored Gospel. I had a manuscript copy of this revelation, which I carried in my pocket, and I was in the habit of reading it to the people among whom I traveled and preached. As a general thing the people regarded it as the height of nonsense, saying the Union was too strong to be broken; and I, they said, was led away, the victim of an impostor. I knew the prophecy was true, for the Lord had spoken to me and had given me revelation." (Orson Pratt, *JD* 18:224-25.)

"Scoffers have said it was nothing remarkable for Joseph Smith in 1832, to predict the outbreak of the Civil War and that others who did not claim to be inspired with prophetic vision had done the same. It has been said that Daniel Webster and William Lloyd Garrison in 1831 had predicted the dissolution of the Union. It is well known that senators and congressmen from the South had maintained that their section of the country had a right to withdraw from the Union, for it was a confederacy, and in 1832, war clouds were to be seen on the horizon. It was because of this fact that the Lord made known to Joseph Smith this revelation stating that wars would shortly come to pass, beginning with the rebellion of South Carolina, which would eventually terminate in war being poured out upon all nations and in the death and misery of many souls. It may have been an easy thing in 1832, or even 1831, for someone to predict that there would come a division of the Northern States and the Southern States, for even then there were rumblings, and South Carolina had shown the spirit of rebellion. It was not, however, within the power of man to predict in the detail which the Lord revealed to Joseph Smith, what was shortly to come to pass as an outgrowth of the Civil War and the pouring out of war upon all nations." (Joseph Fielding Smith, *CHMR* 1:358-59.)

87:1-8 *The prophecy on war*

"A remarkable prediction regarding national affairs was uttered by Joseph Smith, December 25, 1832; it was soon thereafter promulgated among the members of the Church and was preached by the elders, but did not appear in print until 1851. . . .

"Every student of United States history is acquainted with the facts establishing a complete fulfillment of this astounding prophecy. In 1861, more than twenty-eight years after the foregoing prediction was recorded, and ten years after its publication in England, the Civil War broke out, beginning in South Carolina. The ghastly records of that fratricidal strife sadly support the prediction concerning 'the death and misery of many souls,' though this constituted but a partial fulfillment. It is known that slaves deserted the South and were marshaled in the armies of the North, and that the Confederate States solicited aid of Great Britain. While no open alliance between the Southern States and the English government was effected, British influence gave indirect assistance and substantial encouragement to the South. . . .

"A careful study of the Revelation and Prophecy on War, given, as stated, through the Prophet Joseph Smith, December 25, 1832, makes plain that the conflict between North and South in America was to be, as now we know it to have been, but the beginning of a new era of strife and bloodshed. The Lord's words were definite in predicting wars 'beginning at the rebellion of South Carolina'; and declared further: 'And the time will come that war will be poured out upon all nations, beginning at this place.' The great World War, 1914-1918, embroiled, directly or indirectly, every nation of the earth. . . .

"The revelation cited, as given through Joseph Smith, contained other predictions, some of which are yet awaiting fulfillment. The evidence presented is sufficient to prove that Joseph Smith is prominent among men by reason of his instrumentality in fulfilling prophecies uttered by the Lord's representatives in former times, and that his own place as a prophet is abundantly vindicated." (James E. Talmage, *AF*, pp. 25-27.)

"Well, it seems as if the Lord our God is giving the nation a pretty thorough warning. He told this nation by revelation, twenty-eight years before it commenced, of the great American war. He told all about how the Southern States should be divided against the Northern States, and that in the course of the war many souls should be cut off. This has been fulfilled.

"I went forth before my beard was gray, before my hair began to turn white, when I was a youth of nineteen, now I am fifty-eight, and from that time on I published these tidings among the inhabitants of the earth. I carried forth the written revelation, foretelling this great contest, some twenty-eight years before the war commenced. This prophecy has been printed and circulated extensively in this and other nations and languages. It pointed out the place where it should commence in South Carolina. That which I declared over the New England States, New York, Pennsylvania, Ohio, and many other parts in the East, when but a boy, came to pass twenty-eight years after the revelation was given.

"When they were talking about a war commencing down here in Kansas, I told them that was not the place; I also told them that the revelation had designated South Carolina, 'and,' said I, 'you have no need to think that the Kansas war is going to be the war that is to be so terribly destructive in its character and nature. No, it must commence at the place the Lord has designated by revelation.'

"What did they have to say to me? They thought it was a Mormon humbug, and laughed me to scorn, and they looked upon that revelation as they do upon all others that God has given in these latter days—as without divine authority. But behold and lo! in process of time it came to pass, again establishing the divinity of this work, and giving another proof that God is in this work, and is performing that which He spoke by the mouths of the ancient prophets, as recorded in the Book of Mormon before any Church of Latter-day Saints was in existence." (Orson Pratt, *JD* 13:135.)

87:3 *"the southern states will call on . . . Great Britain"*

"Nearly thirty years before it occurred, Joseph Smith predicted the great civil war which should occur in our own country. Well, the unbeliever says, 'Any far-seeing man might have known that the Southern states would be divided against the Northern states and there would be war.' But the Prophet states more than that. He told us just where the war would begin. He told us just what the result would be, and has the sequel not proven that that war began just as this revelation said it would begin, in South Carolina? We might have some reason to doubt or to question the inspiration of this prophet of the Lord, if during that war the Southern states had not called upon Great Britain for assistance. There might be some reason to doubt if in a single detail there had been a mistake, but it chanced that the Southern states did call upon Great Britain, and we were very nearly at war with that nation because of her participation in behalf of the Confederacy in that struggle." (Anthony W. Ivins, *CR,* October 1913, pp. 94-95.)

87:3   *"and then war shall be poured out upon all nations"*

"The prophecy [Sec. 87] went on to say that 'the days will come that war will be poured out upon all nations.' World Wars I and II, three quarters of a century and more later were complete fulfillments of this part of the prophecy. This great and remarkable prophecy still stands as evidence of Joseph Smith's mighty prophetic power." (John A. Widtsoe, *JS,* p. 279.)

87:4   *"slaves shall rise up against their masters"*

"The rising up of slaves, it is thought by many, was fulfilled in the Civil War when many of the Negroes found their way into the armies of the North and fought against their former masters. Others think this is yet to come. The history of this American continent also gives evidence that the Lamanites have risen up in their anger and vexed the Gentiles. This warfare may not be over. It has been the fault of people in the United States to think that this prophetic saying has reference to the Indians in the United States, but we must remember that there are millions of the 'remnant' in Mexico, Central and South America. It was during our Civil War that the Indians in Mexico rose up and gained their freedom from the tyranny which Napoleon endeavored to inflict upon them contrary to the prediction of Jacob in the Book of Mormon, that there should be no kings among the Gentiles on this land. The independence of Mexico and other nations to the south has been accomplished by the uprising of the 'remnant' upon the land. However, let us not think that this prophecy has completely been fulfilled." (Joseph Fielding Smith, *CHMR* 1:363.)

87:6 *"until the consumption decreed hath made a full end of all nations"*

"The Lord made the earth and placed man upon it, and He owns it still and He will cut off wickedness, no matter where it exists, so that there will be room for the good fruit to grow. As true as the Lord lives, if we wish to exist upon the earth in these days, we must be righteous; if we expect to have a place, an inheritance, and dwell on the earth, we must keep the law of God, or we shall be cut off. This will apply to all, to Jew and Gentile, bond and free; this will apply to all men in every nation, and under all circumstances.

"It is the decree of the Almighty God, that the kingdom of heaven shall be established, and shall never again be overthrown, that judgments shall lay waste the nations, enough at least to give that kingdom room to grow, and spread, and prosper. This is the truth, and you will all find it so. Those judgments have begun, that will never leave the earth until it is swept as with the besom of destruction, until thrones are cast down and kingdoms overthrown, until each man draws his sword against his neighbor, and every nation and kingdom that exists will be at war with each other, except the inhabitants of Zion. The Lord has spoken it, and it will come to pass. [D&C 45:66-75.]" (Wilford Woodruff, *JD* 2:201.)

87:7 *"the Lord of Sabaoth"*

See *Sabaoth* in Appendix A.

87:8 *"stand ye in holy places"*

See *Stand ye in holy places* in Appendix A.

SECTION 88

Background information on section 88

"The 'Olive Leaf' is the name given by the Prophet to the wonderful revelation known as Sec. 88, in the Doctrine and Covenants. There are few, if any, revelations given to the Church—and to the world if the world will receive them— greater than this 'Olive Leaf, plucked from the Tree of Paradise.' In this letter to W. W. Phelps, one of the presiding brethren in Missouri, the Prophet raises a warning voice based upon the word of the Lord as revealed in the revelation and correspondence from Missouri.

Kirtland, January 14, 1833

"Brother William W. Phelps:

"I send you the 'olive leaf' which we have plucked from the Tree of Paradise, the Lord's message of peace to us; for though our brethren in Zion indulge in feelings towards us, which are not according to the requirements of the new covenant, yet, we have the satisfaction of knowing that the Lord approves of us, and has accepted us, and established His name in Kirtland for the salvation of the nations; for the Lord will have a place whence His word will go forth, in these last days, in purity; for if Zion will not purify herself, so as to be approved of in all things, in His sight, He will seek another people; for His work will go on until Israel is gathered, and they who will not hear His voice, must expect to feel His wrath. Let me say unto you, seek to purify yourselves, and also the inhabitants of Zion, lest the Lord's anger be kindled to fierceness." (Joseph Fielding Smith, *TPJS*, p. 18.)

88:2 *"Lord of Sabaoth"*

See *Sabaoth* in Appendix A.

88:2 *"book of the names of the sanctified"*

See *Book of Life* in Appendix A.

"We are not going to be saved in the kingdom of God just because our names are on the records of the Church. It will require more than that. We will have to have our names written in the Lamb's Book of Life, and if they are written in the Lamb's Book of Life then it is an evidence we have kept the commandments. Every soul who will not keep those commandments shall have his name blotted out of that book." (Joseph Fielding Smith, *CR*, September 1950, p. 10.)

88:3   *"another Comforter . . . the Holy Spirit of Promise"*

See *Holy Ghost* in Appendix A.

"The Holy Spirit of Promise is not the Second Comforter; the Holy Spirit of Promise is the Holy Ghost who places the stamp of approval upon every ordinance that is done righteously and when covenants are broken he removes the seal." (Joseph Fielding Smith, *DS* 1:55.)

88:4   *"eternal life"*

See *Eternal life* in Appendix A.

88:5   *"Church of the Firstborn"*

See same title in Appendix A.

88:7-13   *"light of Christ"*

See *Light* in Appendix A.

88:15   *"the spirit and the body are the soul of man"*

"It is peculiar to the theology of the Latter-day Saints that we regard the body as an essential part of the soul. Read your dictionaries, the lexicons, and encyclopedias, and you will find that nowhere, outside of the Church of Jesus Christ, is the solemn and eternal truth taught that the soul of man is the body and the spirit combined. It is quite the rule to regard the soul as that incorporeal part of man, that immortal part which existed before the body was framed and which shall continue to exist after that body has gone to decay; nevertheless, that is not the soul; that is only a part of the soul; that is the spirit-man, the form in which every individual of us, and every individual human being, existed before called to take tabernacle in the flesh. It has been declared in the solemn word of revelation, that the spirit and the body constitute the soul of man; and, therefore, we should look upon this body as something that shall endure in the resurrected state, beyond the grave, something to be kept pure and holy." (James E. Talmage, *CR*, October 1913, p. 117.)

"We do not look upon death as the end of our individual existence. [D&C 59:2; Alma 40:11-14.] On the contrary, knowing Him [Jesus] to be our prototype, we have the assurance that death is only temporary, and that there will come a time after death when we shall again receive these same bodies which we possess here upon the earth, and that the union of spirit and body shall never be dissolved. [D&C 93:33-34; Alma 11:45; 12:16-18.] The bodies we shall receive will be immortal, and the spirit and body reunited will constitute a living soul." (Anthon H. Lund, *CR*, April 1904, p. 7.)

88:16 *"the resurrection from the dead is the redemption of the soul"*

See *Resurrection* in Appendix A.

88:18 *"sanctified from all unrighteousness"*

See *Sanctify* in Appendix A.

88:19 *"it [the earth] shall be crowned with glory"*

See *Earth* in Appendix A.

88:22 *"Celestial kingdom . . . glory"*

See *Celestial* in Appendix A.

88:25-26 *"the earth abideth the law of a celestial kingdom"*

See *Earth* and *Celestial* in Appendix A.

88:28 *"natural body"*

See *Natural* in Appendix A.

88:32 *"they who remain shall also be quickened"*

See *Perdition* in Appendix A.

"A superficial reading of Sec. 76:38-39 might give the impression that the sons of perdition are not to be resurrected, but here it is expressly stated that they, too, will be quickened, and then return to 'their own place.' They were not willing to receive a degree of glory, by keeping the law pertaining to either of the glories; wherefore they were to remain under the dominion of him whom they had chosen to serve." (Smith and Sjodahl, *DCC*, p. 545.)

88:34-47 *"All kingdoms have a law given"*

See *Law* in Appendix A.

"Every law God has given us is of such a nature that, by keeping it, we are preserved, perfected and sanctified. If we keep the Word of Wisdom, our bodies will be kept pure. If we observe the law of tithing, we shall learn to be unselfish and honest. If we pray, we shall hold communion with the Holy Spirit. If we try to do our duty in everything, we shall come, day by day, nearer to perfection.

"On the other hand, those who refuse to be governed by law and are a law unto themselves cannot be sanctified. They are outside the pale of mercy and justice and judgment, as well as law, and must remain 'filthy still' (v. 35). It is only when we try to obey God's laws that we have claim upon His mercy. Justice will take into account, in the judgment, every honest effort to do the will of God." (Smith and Sjodahl, *DCC*, p. 546.)

88:45 *"the earth rolls upon her wings"*

See *Earth* in Appendix A.

88:49 *"The light shineth in darkness"*

See *Light* in Appendix A.

88:51-61 *An explanation of the parable concerning the man, his field, and his laborers*

"Do we not expect that the Lord will, by and by, come and visit us and stay a little while, about a thousand years. [Sec. 43:29-30.] Yes, and then we shall be made glad with the joy of the countenance of our Lord. He will be among us, and will be our King, and he will reign as a King of Kings and Lord of Lords. He will have a throne in Zion, and another in the Temple of Jerusalem, and he will have with him the twelve disciples who were with him during his ministry at Jerusalem; and all the people of this globe who are counted worthy to be called Zion, the pure in heart, will be made glad by the countenance of their Lord for a thousand years, during which the earth will rest. Then what? He withdraws. What for? To fulfill other purposes; for he has other worlds or creations and other sons and daughters, perhaps just as good as those dwelling on this planet, and they, as well as we, will be visited, and they will be made glad with the countenance of their Lord. Thus he will go, in the time and in the season thereof, from Kingdom or from world to world, causing the pure in heart, the Zion that is taken from these creations, to rejoice in his presence. [Moses 7:64.]

"But there is another thing I want you to understand. This will not be kept up to all eternity, it is merely a preparation for something still greater. And what is that? By and by, when each of these creations has fulfilled the measure and bounds set and the times given for its continuance in a temporal state, it and its inhabitants who are worthy will be made celestial and glorified together. Then, from that time henceforth and forever, there will be no intervening veil between God and his people who are sanctified and glorified, and he will not be under the necessity of withdrawing from one to go and visit another, because they will all be in his presence." (Orson Pratt, *JD* 17:331-32.)

88:63 *"Draw near unto me and I will draw near unto you"*

See *Prayer* in Appendix A.

"We learn in another revelation that was given to the Prophet Joseph Smith in 1832, something concerning the character of our Heavenly Father. In that revelation He says to His Church through the Prophet: [D&C 88:63-65, quoted.]

"Mark, how clear-cut are these words. There is no doubt, no dubiety. It does not say if and peradventure you call upon the Lord, He may be gone on a long journey and you cannot reach Him; or He is very busy; His attention is now attracted to the nations of the earth; probably He is busily engaged . . . and He cannot give you any attention, therefore you might as well cease praying. No. This revelation does not give forth any such ideas. . . . And yet—think of it! He says to you and to me: He says to this poor man and to this poor woman: He says to this rich man and to this rich woman: 'Draw near unto me and I will draw near unto you.' Yes, that poor widow down there, to whom nobody is paying attention, and who has very little influence,—to her the Lord says: 'Draw near unto me and I will draw near unto you.' 'My ear will be opened to hear your prayer and to answer it.' " (Rudger Clawson, *CR,* April 1904, pp. 43-44.)

88:65 *"ask"*

See *Prayer* in Appendix A.

88:68   *"become single to God"*

"The meaning of 'sanctification' is explained in the words that follow, 'That your minds become single to God.' Our Lord had regard only to the glory of the Father, when He undertook the salvation of man. To follow in His footsteps and to be able to say at all times, truthfully, 'Thine be the honor,' is to be sanctified; that is to be a Saint." (Smith and Sjodahl, *DCC,* p. 552.)

88:69   *"cast away your idle thoughts"*

See *Thoughts* in Appendix A.

88:70   *"call a solemn assembly"*

See *Solemn assembly* in Appendix A.

88:73   *"I will hasten my work"*

"There is an urgency in [the Lord's] work. Time is getting short. This sense of urgency in promoting the Lord's kingdom in these last days does not arise out of panic, but out of a desire to move swiftly and surely to establish and strengthen his kingdom among all people who are seeking the light and truth of the gospel, which is God's plan of life for all his children. God will hasten his work by opening the heavens and sending heavenly messengers to his prophets to warn his children to prepare themselves to receive their Lord at his second coming. The Christ has emphasized, 'It is the eleventh hour, and the last time that I shall call laborers into my vineyard.' (D&C 33:3.)" (Delbert L. Stapley, *Ensign,* November 1975, p. 49.)

88:76   *"prayer and fasting"*

See *Fasting* and *Prayer* in Appendix A.

"These are indispensable in the preparation for the ministry. Our Lord teaches us that there are evil spirits that cannot be overcome except by those whose spiritual life and faith are made strong by self-denial and communion with God. It is, therefore, of the utmost importance that the servants of the Lord should fast and pray. Through the fasting and prayer of the servants of the Lord, the mouth of Alma was opened, and his limbs strengthened (Mosiah 27:22-3). Through fasting and prayer the Nephites 'did wax stronger and stronger in their humility, and firmer and firmer in the faith of Christ' (Hel. 3:35)." (Smith and Sjodahl, *DCC,* p. 555.)

88:80   *Things in which to be instructed*

"Theology is not the only subject in which the Elders should be interested. They should study:

"Things both in heaven—Astronomy.

"And in the earth—Everything pertaining to the cultivation of the soil.

"And under the earth—Mineralogy, geology, etc.

"Things which have been—History, in all its branches.

"Things which must shortly come to pass—Prophecies.

"Things which are at home and abroad—Domestic and foreign politics.

"Wars—perplexities—judgment—The signs of the times by which the observer may know that the day of the Lord is at hand.

"A knowledge of countries and kingdoms—physical and political geography, languages, etc.

"These studies, the Lord considers necessary. [Sec. 88:80.] God does not require all His servants to become doctors, or professors, or even profound students of these subjects, but He expects them to know enough of these things to be able to magnify their callings as His ambassadors to the world." (John A. Widtsoe, *Priesthood and Church Government,* pp. 55-56.)

88:81   *"testify and warn"*

See *Missionary service* in Appendix A.

"Now this gives us two premises. On the one hand we are obligated and required to know the doctrines of the Church. We are to treasure up the words of eternal life. We are to reason as intelligently as we are able. We are to use every faculty and capacity with which we are endowed to proclaim the message of salvation and to make it intelligent to ourselves and to our Father's other children. But after we have done that, and also in the process of doing it, we are obligated to bear testimony—to let the world know and our associate members of the Church know—that in our hearts, by the revelation of the Holy Spirit to our souls, we know of the truth and divinity of the work and of the doctrines that we teach." (Bruce R. McConkie, *Ensign,* July 1973, p. 28.)

88:87-95   *Signs of the second coming of Christ*

See *Second coming* in Appendix A.

88:92 *"the Bridegroom cometh"*

See *Bridegroom* in Appendix A.

88:93 *"there shall appear a great sign in heaven"*

"Immediately after the testimony of these messengers a great sign will appear in heaven, which, like the sun, will be seen all round the world. Our Lord calls it the 'Sign of the Son of Man' (Matt. 24-30). What this sign is has not been revealed, but there will be no uncertainty about it, when it appears. In 1843 one Mr. Redding, of Ogle county, Ill., claimed to have seen the sign. The Prophet Joseph then wrote to the *Times and Seasons:*

" 'Notwithstanding Mr. Redding may have seen a wonderful appearance in the clouds one morning about sunrise [which is not very uncommon in the winter season], he has not seen the sign of the Son of Man, as foretold by Jesus; neither has any man, nor will any man, until after the sun shall have been darkened and the moon bathed in blood; for the Lord hath not shown me any such sign; and as the Prophet saith, so it must be—"Surely the Lord God will do nothing, but he revealeth his secret unto his servants the prophets" (Amos 3:7). Therefore, hear this, O Earth! The Lord will not come to reign over the righteous, in this world, in 1843, nor until everything for the Bridegroom is ready' (*HC* 5:291).

"It may be gathered from this that when the sign appears, God will make its meaning known to the Prophet, Seer and Revelator who at that time may be at the head of the Church, and through him to His people and the world in general." (Smith and Sjodahl, *DCC,* p. 560.)

"After the angels have sounded this in the ears of all living [D&C 88:92] we are informed that there will be a great sign in the heavens. It is not to be limited so that some few only of the human family can see it; but it is said, 'all people shall see it together!' At least, it is to be like our sun seen over one entire side of the globe, and then passing immediately round to the other, or else it will encircle the whole earth at the same time. But the bridegroom does not come then. These are only the preceding events to let the Latter-day Saints and the pure in heart know that these are the times that they may trim up their lamps and prepare for the triumphant appearing of their Lord." (Orson Pratt, *JD* 8:50.)

88:94 *"drink of the wine of the wrath of her fornication"*

See material for 35:11.

88:94 *"she is the tares of the earth"*

See *Tares* in Appendix A.

88:94-98 *"another angel shall sound his trump"*

"Here begins a series of world events, each signalized by the sounding of a trump by an angel—a divine messenger. There is some analogy between this vision and that recorded in Revelation 8:7—9:21, although they do not appear to cover the same events.

"When the first angel sounds his trump, the doom upon the apostate church is pronounced. 'She is ready to be burned.' Then there is silence in heaven for half an hour. The heavenly hosts are waiting, awestruck, for the execution of this judgment.

" 'Whether the half hour here spoken of is according to our reckoning—thirty minutes, or whether it be according to the reckoning of the Lord, we do not know. . . . During the period of silence all things are perfectly still; no angels flying during that half hour; no trumpets sounding; no noise in the heaven above; but immediately after this great silence the curtain of heaven shall be unfolded as a scroll is unfolded. . . . The face of the Lord will be unveiled, and those who are alive will be quickened, and they will be caught up; and the Saints who are in their graves will come forth and be caught up, together with those who are quickened, and they will be taken into the heavens into the midst of those celestial beings who will make their appearance at that time. These are the ones who are the first fruits at the time of His coming' (Orson Pratt, *JD* 16:328)." (Smith and Sjodahl, *DCC*, p. 560.)

88:95-116 *The order of the resurrection and judgment*

See *Resurrection* and *Judgment* in Appendix A.

88:98 *"they who shall descend with him first"*

See *Second coming* and *Millennium* in Appendix A.

88:104 *"every ear . . . knee . . . tongue"*

See *Knee* in Appendix A.

88:106 *"trodden the wine-press alone"*

See *Wine-press* in Appendix A.

88:110 *"there shall be time no longer"*

See *Time* in Appendix A.

88:110 *"Satan shall be bound"*

See *Satan* in Appendix A.

88:113 *"Michael and his armies"*

See *Adam* in Appendix A.

88:118 *"seek ye out of the best books"*

"Never become narrowly educated, but broadly so, feeding all sides of yourselves, reading and becoming acquainted with good books, with great minds and great men of the past; becoming acquainted with scripture and reading scripture itself. Do not be satisfied to read books about scripture or books about books, but to the prime and primary sources go. You do not catch much of the spirit of Shakespeare merely by reading commentaries on Shakespeare, and so it is in large measure with scripture. Keep balanced in your lives and starve no side of yourselves." (Richard L. Evans, *CR,* April 1961, p. 75.)

"You know that your children will read. They will read books and they will read magazines and newspapers. Cultivate within them a taste for the best. While they are very young, read to them the great stories which have become immortal because of the virtues they teach. Expose them to good books. Let there be a corner somewhere in your house, be it ever so small, where they will see at least a few books of the kind upon which great minds have been nourished.

"Let there be good magazines about the house, those which are produced by the Church and by others, which will stimulate their thoughts to ennobling concepts. Let them read a good family newspaper that they may know what is going on in the world without being exposed to the debasing advertising and writing so widely found." (Gordon B. Hinckley, *CR,* October 1975, pp. 57-58.)

88:118 *"seek learning, even by study and also by faith"*

"One might well ask: How does one get 'learning by

faith"? One prophet explains the process: First, one must arouse his faculties and experiment on the words of the Lord and desire to believe. Let this desire work in you until ye believe in a manner that you can give place even to a portion of the word of the Lord; then, like a planted seed, it must be cultivated and not resist the Spirit of the Lord, which is that which lighteneth everyone born into the world; you can then begin to feel within yourselves that it must be good, for it enlarges your soul and enlightens your understanding and, like the fruit of the tree in Lehi's vision, it becomes delicious to the taste. (See Alma 32.) . . .

"Let no one think that 'learning by faith' contemplates an easy or lazy way to gain knowledge and ripen it into wisdom.

"From heavenly instructions and added to which are the experiences of almost anyone who has sought diligently for heavenly guidance, one may readily understand that learning by faith requires the bending of the whole soul through worthy living to become attuned to the Holy Spirit of the Lord, the calling up from the depths of one's own mental searching, and the linking of our own efforts to receive the true witness of the Spirit." (Harold B. Lee, *Ensign,* June 1971, p. 10.)

88:124 *"cease to find fault one with another"*

"Now, when anyone offends us . . . let us remember the example given us, let us not take offense at every little thing that may appear offensive to us, for in the great majority of cases, when we investigate the matter, we find that no intentional offense was meant, but only thoughtlessness was the cause. Often, we do not try to examine it; we take it as an affront, and forget the advice given us that if we have ought against our brother, we should go to him and make it right. [D&C 64:6-11; Matt. 5:23-24.]" (Anthon H. Lund, *CR,* April 1912, p. 13.)

88:124 *"retire to thy bed early . . . arise early"*

"The blessings of food, sleep, and social enjoyment are ordained of God for His glory and our benefit, and it is for us to learn to use them and not abuse them, that his kingdom may advance on the earth, and we advance in it." (Brigham Young, *JD* 6:149.)

88:126   *"Pray always, that ye may not faint"*

"There is one admonition of our Savior that all the Saints of God should observe, but which I fear, we do not as we should, and that is, to pray always and faint not. I fear, as a people, we do not pray enough in faith. We should call upon the Lord in mighty prayer, and make all our wants known unto Him. For if He does not protect and deliver us, and save us, no other power will. Therefore our trust is entirely in Him. Therefore, our prayers should ascend into the ears of our Heavenly Father day and night." (Wilford Woodruff, *MS*, October 26, 1886, 48:5-6.)

88:127-141   *"the school of the prophets"*

"There were two schools conducted in Kirtland. One was a school of the Elders where they carried out some of the provisions of this revelation (Sec. 88) in seeking knowledge of countries and kingdoms and languages, all such information as may be gained in the regular daily school. . . .

"The other was the 'School of the Prophets,' and a very good description of this school and its purpose is given in this section of the Doctrine and Covenants (Sec. 88:117 to the end of the section). In a letter written by the Prophet Joseph to William W. Phelps in Zion, January 14, 1833, the following appears: 'You will see that the Lord commanded us, in Kirtland, to build a house of God, and establish a school for the prophets, this is the word of the Lord to us, and we must, yea, the Lord helping us, we will obey: as on conditions of our obedience he has promised us great things; yea, even a visit from the heavens to honor us with His own presence.' . . .

"The Prophet further writes: 'This winter (1832-3) was spent in translating the scriptures; in the School of the Prophets; and sitting in conferences. I had many glorious seasons of refreshing.' (*HC* 1:332.) This School of the Prophets and the schools where the ordinary branches were taught continued in Kirtland until the exodus from that place. It was for this school that the lectures on faith were prepared and which were delivered to the Elders. . . .

"The object for which this school was organized is plainly stated in the revelation. None could join except he was clean from the blood of this generation. The only way he could be clean was to be obedient to the covenants of the Gospel and labor in behalf of his fellows for the salvation of their souls. Thus the preaching of the Gospel was a requirement made of those who desired to join this school. The School of the Prophets continued in Utah for several years under the administration of President Brigham Young, but after that time it was discontinued." (Joseph Fielding Smith, *CHMR* 2:136-37.)

"The School of the Prophets was organized, according to the instructions in this Revelation, during the month of February, 1833, and was continued throughout the winter. At this time the Elders and the Saints had many manifestations of the presence of the Spirit of the Lord. The Prophet spoke to a Conference, held in January, that year, in a foreign tongue, and others followed. Says Brigham Young:

" 'The members of that school were but few at first, and the Prophet commenced to teach them in doctrine to prepare them to go out into the world to preach the gospel unto all people, and gather the select from the four quarters of the Earth, as the prophets anciently have spoken. While this instruction prepared the Elders to administer in word and doctrine, it did not supply the teachings necessary to govern their private, or temporal lives; it did not say whether they should be merchants, farmers, mechanics, or money-changers. The Prophet began to instruct them how to live, that they might be better prepared to perform the great work they were called to accomplish.'

"A School of the Prophets was also established in Zion. The Lord approved of this institution, although contention had arisen in it (see Sec. 95:10; 97:3), which called forth severe rebuke. A school of Elders—an extension of the School of the Prophets—was held in the early days of Utah, with President Brigham Young at its head. This was, practically, a theological department of the University of Utah, while that seat of learning was in its infancy." (Smith and Sjodahl, *DCC*, p. 567.)

88:139-141   *The ordinance of the washing of the feet*

See *Washing of feet* in Appendix A.

SECTION 89

"The only comment made by the Prophet Joseph Smith, February 27, 1833, when the revelation on the Word of Wisdom was received, is: 'I received the following revelation.' In those early days of the Church men had not been trained when they came into the Church that their bodies were tabernacles which should be kept sanctified and cleansed physically and morally, as well as spiritually. The use of liquor, tobacco and stimulants of various kinds, was very common. Tea and coffee were looked upon as foods, and the same to some extent was the attitude towards alcoholic beverages." (Joseph Fielding Smith, *CHMR* 1:382-83.)

"I think I am as well acquainted with the circumstances which led to the giving of the Word of Wisdom as any man in the Church, although I was not present at the time to witness them. The first school of the prophets was held in a small room situated over the Prophet Joseph's kitchen, in a house which belonged to Bishop Whitney, and which was attached to his store, which store probably might be about fifteen feet square. In the rear of this building was a kitchen, probably ten by fourteen feet, containing rooms and pantries. Over this kitchen was situated the room in which the Prophet received revelations and in which he instructed his brethren. The brethren came to that place for hundreds of miles to attend school in a little room probably no larger than eleven by fourteen. When they assembled together in this room after breakfast, the first they did was to light their pipes, and, while smoking, talk about the great things of the kingdom, and spit all over the room, and as soon as the pipe was out of their mouths a large chew of tobacco would then be taken. Often when the Prophet entered the room to give the school instructions he would find himself in a cloud of tobacco smoke. This, and the complaints of his wife at having to clean so filthy a floor, made the Prophet think upon the matter, and he inquired of the Lord relating to the conduct of the Elders in using tobacco, and the revelation known as the Word of Wisdom was the result of his inquiry." (Brigham Young, *JD* 12:158.)

"On the 27th day of February, 1833, [at Kirtland, Ohio] the Prophet received the revelation known as the Word of Wisdom, warning the people to abstain from impurities and grossness in their food and drink, and promising them rich blessings of physical strength and protection from the power of the adversary as a reward for their obedience. . . . Its delivery to Joseph marks another step in the divine plan for man's eventual elevation to divine acceptability." (George Q. Cannon, *LJS,* pp. 129-30.)

89:2 *"not by commandment or constraint, but by revelation"*

"The reason undoubtedly why the Word of Wisdom was given—as not by 'commandment or restraint' was that at that time, at least, if it had been given as a commandment it would have brought every man, addicted to the use of these noxious things, under condemnation; so the Lord was merciful and gave them a chance to overcome, before He brought them under the law. Later on, it was announced from this stand, by President Brigham Young [*JD* 12:118] that the Word of Wisdom was a revelation and a command of the Lord." (Joseph F. Smith, *CR,* October 1913, p. 14.)

"It is expressly stated that it is given 'not by commandment or constraint,' but as a Word of Wisdom—a word dictated by wisdom. It is a commandment that may be compared to that issued by the General Council at Jerusalem to the Gentiles, concerning the abstinence from meats offered to idols, from blood, from things strangled, and from fornication, of which the Apostles wrote, 'From which if ye keep yourselves, ye shall do well' (Acts 15:29)." (Smith and Sjodahl, *DCC,* p. 571.)

"The High Council of the Church over which the Prophet Joseph Smith presided declared in 1834 by unanimous vote after a full and free discussion on the subject, that, 'No official member of this Church is worthy to hold office after having the Word of Wisdom properly taught him; and he, the official member, neglecting to comply with or obey it.' " (Joseph Fielding Smith, *ECH,* p. 169.)

"The Word of Wisdom revelation was given on February 27, 1833, but its acceptance by many in the Church was gradual. On September 9, 1851, some eighteen years after the revelation was given, President Brigham Young proposed in a general conference that all Saints discontinue the use of tea, coffee, tobacco, and whiskey. The motion carried unanimously, and the principle known as the Word of Wisdom was accepted as a binding commandment for all members. ('General Minutes of Conference,' *Millennial Star* 14:35 [Feb. 1, 1852].) But the Saints were slow to remember their covenants. Repeated admonitions from the prophets to observe the Word of Wisdom met with varying degrees of obedience. As late as the October conference of 1942, the First Presidency (Heber J. Grant, J. Reuben Clark, Jr., and David O. McKay) urged the Saints to 'quit trifling with this law and so to live it that we may claim its promises.' " (First Presidency, *IE* 45:687, November 1942.)

"The Lord gave in a sacred revelation in 1833 what we have more recently learned through research: 'Hot drinks are not for the body.' This is tea and coffee. 'Tobacco is not for the body . . . and is not good for man. . . . Wine or strong drink . . . is not good, neither meet in the sight of your Father.' (See D&C 89:5-9.) The Lord knew when these things were discovered that constant smoking could lead to cancer; that constant drinking could lead to many accidents and diseases. It is now a command to all his members, and as we see some members using these prohibited things, we wonder how they reconcile such activities with the statement of the Lord Jesus Christ when he said: 'And why call ye me, Lord, Lord, and do not the things which I say?' (Luke 6:46.) We sincerely hope the members of the Church will give heed." (Spencer W. Kimball, *Ensign,* May 1975, p. 6.)

89:2 *"the temporal salvation of all saints"*

"Many parents, in so simple a thing as keeping the Word of Wisdom, excuse themselves sometimes on the basis of social exigency, sometimes on the basis of business exigency. There is only one basis for it and that is either a lack of belief or moral cowardice. No parent would deliberately subject his child to physical suffering. Any parent who would do that we would say is cruel, and yet it is just as much an act of cruelty and ultimately more damaging, to impale the child on the horns of a dilemma of conflicting loyalties. He cannot be fully loyal to a Church which teaches one doctrine and fully loyal to parents who decline to observe that doctrine. That conflict will be resolved either by the destruction of one or other or both of those loyalties." (Joseph F. Smith, *CR*, April 1944, p. 78.)

89:4 *"In consequence of evils and designs which do and will exist"*

"We, today, have before us abundant evidence of the evils and designs of wicked men. It is seen in the advertising of tobacco, tea, coffee, liquors and beers and wines. It is also seen in the advertising of prepared foods. So bad did this condition become some decades ago that the National Government had to take the matter in hand and Congress passed laws to control the evils which had arisen. These pure food laws have been very beneficial but even now there are ways by which the laws are evaded." (Joseph Fielding Smith, *CHMR* 1:384.)

"The revelation [Section 89], a warning against 'evils and designs' of 'conspiring men,' which may interfere with full human health, is prophetic. Throughout the ages the lust for gold has tempted men to place adulterated or dangerous foods upon the market. While pure food and drug laws now protect the people more than in the past, these 'evils and designs,' through excessive and misleading advertising, continue to appear in new and deceptive forms." (John A. Widtsoe, *ER* 3:154.)

"One of the most significant statements in the Doctrine and Covenants, one which carries with it evidence of the inspiration of the Prophet Joseph Smith, is found in the 89th Section of the Doctrine and Covenants: [D&C 89:4, quoted.]

"The purport of that impressed me in the twenties and the thirties of this century. I just ask you . . . to recall the methods employed by certain tobacco interests to induce women to smoke cigarettes.

"You remember how insidiously they launched their plan. First, by saying that it would reduce weight. They had a slogan: 'Take a cigarette instead of a sweet.'

"Later, some of us who like the theatre, noticed that they would have a young lady light the gentleman's cigarette. Following this a woman's hand would be shown on billboards lighting or taking a cigarette. A year or two passed and soon they were brazen enough to show the lady on the screen or on the billboard smoking the cigarette. . . .

"Now, it is common to see beautiful young ladies depicted on billboards, and in the popular journals advertising certain brands of cigarettes. . . .

"The radio has become one of the most successful means of advertising cigarettes. Attractive programs are presented, not for the purpose of entertaining the youth, but for the purpose of enticing and encouraging them to reach for a cigarette.

"Parents meekly submit to this and later deplore the fact when their children are hopeless cigarette addicts." (David O. McKay, *CR,* September 1949, pp. 185-86.)

89:5   *"Strong drink . . . is not good"*

"Over the earth, and it seems particularly in America, the demon drink is in control. Drunken with strong drink, men have lost their reason; their counsel has been destroyed; their judgment and vision are fled; they reel forward to destruction.

"Drink brings cruelty into the home; it walks arm in arm with poverty; its companions are disease and plague; it puts chastity to flight; and it knows neither honesty nor fair dealing; it is a total stranger to truth; it drowns conscience; it is the bodyguard of evil; it curses all who touch it.

"Drink has brought more woe and misery, broken more hearts, wrecked more homes, committed more crimes, filled more coffins, than all the wars the world has suffered. . . .

"But so great is the curse of drink that we should not be held guiltless did we not call upon all offending Saints to forsake it and banish it from their lives forever. . . .

"For more than half a century President [Heber J.] Grant has on every appropriate occasion admonished the Saints touching their obligation to keep the Word of Wisdom. He has told them what it means to them in matters of health, quoting the words of the Lord thereon. He has pointed out that treasures of knowledge, even hidden knowledge, would come to those who lived the law. He has, over and over again, shown what it would mean financially to every member who would keep the law, what it would mean financially to our people and what it would mean in ending human woe, misery, sorrow, disease, crime, and death. But his admonitions have not found a resting place in all our hearts.

"We the First Presidency of The Church of Jesus Christ of Latter-day Saints, now solemnly renew all these counsels, we repeat all these admonitions, so we reinvoke obedience to God's law of health given us by God himself." (Message of the First Presidency, Oct. 3, 1943.)

89:6 *"pure wine of the grape of the vine"*

"The use of 'pure wine' in the Sacrament is permitted. But what is 'pure wine' if not the pure juice of the grape, before it has been adulterated by the process of fermentation? No fewer than thirteen Hebrew and Greek terms are rendered in our Bible by the word 'wine.' There is the pure grape juice, and a kind of grape syrup, the thickness of which made it necessary to mingle water with it previously to drinking (Prov. 9:2, 5). There was a wine made strong and inebriating by the addition of drugs, such as myrrh, mandragora, and opiates (Prov. 23:30; Isa. 5:22). Of the pure wine which was diluted with water, or milk, Wisdom invites her friends to drink freely (Prov. 9:2, 5). There was also 'wine on the lees,' which is supposed to have been 'preserves' or 'jellies' (Isa. 25:6). The 'pure wine' is not an intoxicating, but a harmless liquid." (Smith and Sjodahl, *DCC*, p. 572.)

89:8 *"tobacco . . . is not good for man"*

"Tobacco is a nauseous, stinking, abominable thing, and I am surprised that any human being should think of using it. For an Elder especially to eat or smoke it is a disgrace—he is not fit for the office; he ought first to learn to keep the word of wisdom and then to teach others. God will not prosper the man who uses it." (Joseph Smith, *Times and Seasons* 3:799-801.)

"God has spoken to us by his latter-day prophets. He has given us modern-day revelation, declaring that tobacco is not good for man. That is the word and the will of the Lord to Latter-day Saints. Whenever we turn our back upon that principle, to that extent we turn our backs upon the Lord. . . .

"If you adopt the cigaret habit, it will, in large measure determine the kind of life you are going to live, the kind of friends you will have, the kind of person you are going to marry, even the kind of children you may have. Have you ever really considered what cigarets mean to a Latter-day Saint? You who smoke now, do not make the mistake of supposing that the Church is against you, because it is not. It only desires your welfare, and it hopes and prays for the day when you will declare your independence from the slavery of nicotine. And you who do not smoke, before you take that first cigaret ask yourself, 'Will it help me or hurt me?' " (Mark E. Petersen, *CR*, April 1948, pp. 152-56.)

89:9 *"hot drinks are not for the body or belly"*

"Again, hot drinks are not for the body or belly. There are many who wonder what this can mean, whether it refers to tea or coffee, or not. I say it does refer to tea and coffee." (Joseph Smith, *Times and Seasons* 3:799-801.)

" 'Hot drinks' means tea and coffee, as those two beverages were the only ones in common use among the members of the Church, and drunk at a high temperature, at the time when the Revelation was given. The reason why those beverages were condemned was because they contained a habit-forming drug, rather than because of the temperature at which they were swallowed; although liquids taken into the stomach at too high a temperature, frequently and in large quantities, would be hurtful. But the chief objection to tea and coffee is the drug they contain. It follows logically that any other beverage which contains a hurtful drug or element, is open to the same objection, regardless of the temperature at which it is taken." (Smith and Sjodahl, *DCC*, p. 573.)

"The Word of Wisdom does not mention tea and coffee, but does speak of hot drinks. Patriarch Hyrum Smith delivered an address to the Saints in Nauvoo, in 1842, in which he declared that hot drinks include tea and coffee, and this interpretation was accepted by the Church. However, all hot drinks, whether they are stimulants or not, are harmful to the body. This discourse, which was published in the *Times and Seasons*, Vol. 3:799-801, and in the *Era*, Vol. 4, should be read by all, for the timely instruction it contains." (Joseph Fielding Smith, *CHMR* 1:385.)

89:11 *"every fruit in the season thereof"*

"The phrase 'in the season thereof,' referring to fruits and vegetables, has raised much speculation. It indicates simply the superior value of fresh foods as demonstrated by modern science, but does not necessarily prohibit the use of fruits or vegetables out of season if preserved by proper methods." (John A. Widtsoe, *ER* 3:157.)

"Some have stumbled over the meaning of the expression 'in the season thereof,' and have argued that grains and fruits should only be used in the season of their growth and when they have ripened. This is not the intent, but any grain or fruit is out of season no matter what part of the year it may be, if it is unfit for use. The apple under the tree bruised and decaying is out of season while the good fruit is waiting to be plucked from the tree." (Joseph Fielding Smith, *CHMR* 1:385.)

89:11   *"with prudence and thanksgiving"*

"The Lord has given us all good herbs, fruits and grains. These are to be the main foods of men, beast, and fowls. But we should not overlook the fact that they are to be used with 'prudence and thanksgiving.' In another revelation (Sec. 59) we are told they are not to be used 'to excess, neither by extortion.' The difficulty with most of the human family, is eating too much, and failing to heed his counsel. There would be less disease and mankind would live longer if all would also heed the counsel of the Lord concerning the use of wholesome foods." (Joseph Fielding Smith, *CHMR* 1:385.)

89:12-13   *The Lord has ordained the use of flesh "to be used sparingly"*

"The Word of Wisdom is not a system of vegetarianism. Clearly, meat is permitted. Naturally, that includes animal products, less subject than meat to putrefactive and other disturbances, such as eggs, milk, and cheese. These products cannot be excluded simply because they are not mentioned specifically. By that token most of our foodstuffs could not be eaten.

"That man can live without meat is well known, and he may live well if his knowledge is such as to enable him to choose adequate vegetable protein. And, all have the right if they so choose to live without meat." (John A. Widtsoe, *ER* 3:155-57.)

89:18-20   *"all saints who remember to keep and do these sayings"*

"Among . . . questions received we find such as this: 'Why does not the Lord give us further revelation to cover the many other stimulants and drinks and the proper foods for the body?' The answer is because such revelation is unnecessary. The Word of Wisdom is a basic law. It points the way and gives us ample instruction in regard to both food and drink, good for the body and also detrimental. If we sincerely follow what is written with the aid of the Spirit of the Lord, we need no further counsel. . . .

"Thus by keeping the commandments we are promised inspiration and the guidance of the Spirit of the Lord through which we will know what is good and what is bad for the body, without the Lord presenting us with a detailed list separating the good things from the bad that we may be protected. We will learn by this faithful observance that the promises of the Lord are fulfilled." (Joseph Fielding Smith, *IE*, February 1956, 59:78-79.)

89:18 *"walking in obedience to the commandments"*

"When we first heard the revelation upon the Word of Wisdom many of us thought it consisted merely in our drinking tea and coffee, but it is not only using tea and coffee and our tobacco and whisky, but it is every other evil which is calculated to contaminate this people. The Word of Wisdom implies to cease from adultery, to cease from all manner of excesses, and from all kinds of wickedness and abomination that are common amongst this generation—it is, strictly speaking, keeping the commandments of God, and living by every word that proceedeth from His mouth." (Ezra T. Benson, *JD* 2:358.)

89:19 *"shall find . . . great treasures of knowledge, even hidden treasures"*

"No man who breaks the Word of Wisdom can gain the same amount of knowledge and intelligence in this world as the man who obeys that law. I don't care who he is or where he comes from, his mind will not be as clear, and he cannot advance as far and as rapidly and retain his power as much as he would if he obeyed the Word of Wisdom." (Heber J. Grant, *CR*, April 1925, p. 10.)

"Our spiritual senses are more delicately balanced than any of our physical senses. Like a fine radio receiver with a sensitive tuning mechanism, they can easily be thrown off channel or even jammed by corrosive influences introduced into our minds and bodies.

"You, my young friends, can be sensitive to inspiration and spiritual guidance. To do this you need the wisdom and treasures of knowledge—they constitute a spiritual confirmation, your testimony of the truth. To have this witness fulfils the promise of the Lord. To be denied it is the penalty." (Boyd K. Packer, *CR,* April 1963, p. 108.)

"Knowledge is not merely the equations of algebra, the theorems of geometry, or the miracles of space. It is hidden treasures of knowledge. . . .

"Knowledge is that power which raises one into new and higher worlds and elevates him into new spiritual realms.

"The treasures of both secular and spiritual knowledge are hidden ones—but hidden from those who do not properly search and strive to find them. The knowledge of the spiritual will not come to an individual without effort any more than will the secular knowledge or college degrees. Spiritual knowledge gives the power to live eternally and to rise and overcome and develop and finally to create.

"Hidden knowledge is not unfindable. It is available to all who really search. Christ said, '. . . seek and ye shall find. . . .' (Matt. 7:7.) Spiritual knowledge is not available merely for the asking; even prayers are not enough. It takes persistence and dedication of one's life. The knowledge of things in secular life are of time and are limited; the knowledge of the infinite truths are of time and eternity. . . .

"The Christ said: 'He that hath my commandments, and keepeth them, he it is that loveth me; and he that loveth me shall be loved of my Father, and I will love him, and will manifest myself unto him.' (John 14:21.) . . .

"And the Prophet Joseph Smith explained: 'And this means that the coming of the Father and the Son to a person is a reality—a personal appearance—and not merely dwelling in his heart.' (D&C 130:3 [paraphrased].)

"This personal witness, then, is the ultimate treasure." (Spencer W. Kimball, *CR,* October 1968, p. 129.)

89:21 *"I, the Lord, give unto them a promise"*

"A statement of the blessings that will follow the observance of the rules laid down in the Word of Wisdom: [D&C 89:18-21, quoted.] That is, the reward for keeping the

Word of Wisdom is four-fold. 1. Self-control is developed. That is implied in verse 3 of the revelation which states that the Word of Wisdom is 'adapted to the capacity of the weak and the weakest of all saints, who are or can be called saints.' 2. Strength of body, including resistance to contagion, is a result of wise living. 3. Clearness of mind is the gift of those whose bodies are in healthy condition. 4. Spiritual power comes to all who conquer their appetites, live normally and look upward to God." (John A. Widtsoe, *PC*, pp. 39-40.)

"Every commandment of God is spiritual in nature. There are no carnal commandments. We have learned this from modern revelation. [Section 29:34-35.] While the commandments have effect upon the body and temporal things they are all in essence spiritual. The Word of Wisdom is spiritual. It is true that it enjoins the use of deleterious substances and makes provision for the health of the body. But the largest measure of good derived from its observance is in increased faith and the development of more spiritual power and wisdom. Likewise, the most regrettable and damaging effects of its infractions are spiritual, also. Injury to the body may be comparatively trivial to the damage to the soul in the destruction of faith and the retardation of spiritual growth. So I say, every commandment involves a spiritual principle." (Stephen L Richards, *CR*, April 1949, p. 141.)

89:21 *"the destroying angel shall pass by them"*

"From this promise in the Word of Wisdom and other scriptures, it appears that there are destroying angels who have a work to do among the peoples of the earth in this last dispensation. [Sec. 86:4-7.] The Lord told the Prophet Joseph Smith that because all flesh was corrupted before him, and the powers of darkness prevailed upon the earth, these angels were 'waiting the great command to reap down the earth, to gather the tares that they may be burned.' (Sec. 38:11-12.) That was in 1831. In 1894, President Woodruff said: 'God has held the angels of destruction for many years lest they should reap down the wheat with the tares. But I want to tell you now, those angels have left the portals of heaven, and they stand over this people and this nation now, and are hovering over the earth waiting to pour out the judgments. And from this very day they shall be poured out. Calamities and troubles are increasing in the earth, and there is a meaning to these things.' (*IE* 17:1165.)

"Now . . . in view of this revealed knowledge and understanding which the Lord has given concerning what is transpiring about us, is it not a glorious thing to have the assurance that if we will clothe ourselves with bodies purified through observance of the Word of Wisdom, these destroying angels will pass us by, as they did the children of Israel, and not slay us? Well, this is one of the blessings to follow observance of the Word of Wisdom." (Marion G. Romney, *CR*, October 1952, pp. 32-33.)

"This does not say and this does not mean, that to keep the Word of Wisdom is to insure us against death, for death is in the eternal plan, co-equal with birth. This is the eternal decree. [1 Cor. 15:22; 2 Nephi 9:6.] But it does mean that the destroying angel, he who comes to punish the unrighteous for their sins, as he in olden time afflicted the corrupt Egyptians in their wickedness [Ex. 12:23, 29], shall pass by the Saints, 'who are walking in obedience to the commandments,' and who 'remember to keep and do these sayings.' These promises do mean that all those who qualify themselves to enjoy them will be permitted so to live out their lives that they may gain the full experiences and get the full knowledge which they need in order to progress to the highest exaltation in eternity, all these will live until their work is finished and God calls them back to their eternal home, as a reward." (J. Reuben Clark, Jr., *CR,* October 1940, pp. 17-18.)

SECTION 90

Background information on section 90

"No explanation is given why this revelation was received, but it is one containing information of the greatest importance and may have come through the prayers of the brethren as indicated in this divine message. It begins by saying that the sins of the Prophet are forgiven according to his petition, for 'thy prayers and the prayers of thy brethren have come up unto my ears.'" (Joseph Fielding Smith, *CHMR* 1:387.)

90:1-9 *The keys of the Church are with the President and his counselors*

See *Keys of priesthood* in Appendix A.

"When Joseph received the keys of the Priesthood, he alone on the earth held them; that is, he was the first, he stood at the head. It was promised that he should not lose them or be removed out of his place, so long as he was faithful. . . .

"If any man in that position should become unfaithful, God would remove him out of his place. I testify in the name of Israel's God that He will not suffer the head of the Church, him whom He has chosen to stand at the head, to transgress His laws and apostatize; the moment he should take a course that would in time lead to it, God would take him away. Why? Because to suffer a wicked man to occupy that position, would be to allow, as it were, the fountain to become corrupted, which is something He will never permit. And why will He not suffer it? Because it is not the work of Joseph Smith. . . . It is not the work of man but of God Almighty, and it is His business to see that the men who occupy this position are men after His own heart, men that will receive instructions from Him, and that will carry out the same according to the counsels of His will." (Joseph F. Smith, *JD* 24:192.)

"He [Joseph Smith] holds the keys of the kingdom of God on earth, and will hold them until the coming of the Son of Man, whether in this world or in the world to come. . . . The last speech that Joseph Smith ever made to the Quorum of the Apostles was in a building in Nauvoo, and it was such a speech as I never heard from mortal man before or since. He was clothed upon with the Spirit and power of God. His face was clear as amber. The room was filled as with consuming fire. He stood three hours upon his feet. Said he: 'You Apostles of the Lamb of God have been chosen to carry out the purposes of the Lord on the earth.' " (Wilford Woodruff, *CHMR* 2:151-52.)

90:4 *"oracles . . . unto the church"*

"The interpretation of the term 'oracles' as used in this revelation is given in the dictionary to be 'an infallible authority.' For the perpetuity of the Church that provision must be made for a successor to the president who holds the keys, when he shall pass away. The word of the Lord was fulfilled wherein he said that through Joseph Smith the oracles should be given to the Church, and by command of the Lord the Prophet, in Nauvoo a few months before his death, called the apostles together and said to them that the Lord had commanded him to confer upon them all the keys and authorities which he had had conferred upon him, so that the work could be 'rolled off' of his shoulders onto theirs. He thereupon conferred upon them this divine governing power, but this governing power could not be exercised by any one of the twelve while the Prophet was living. Upon his death the right to preside and set in order and to hold the keys of authority in the Priesthood and in the Church, rightfully belonged to President Brigham Young and by authority of the ordination he had received under the hands of Joseph Smith and by being sustained by his brethren and the Church, he was vested with the supreme power." (Joseph Fielding Smith, *CHMR* 1:388-89.)

90:6-11 *"Sidney Rigdon and Frederick G. Williams . . . are accounted as equal with thee"*

At this particular time, these two brethren were serving as counselors to Joseph Smith in the First Presidency. For biographical information on these brethren, see Appendix B.

"It is also recorded in this revelation [Section 90] that the sins of Sidney Rigdon and Frederick G. Williams are forgiven them, and they were to hold the keys of the kingdom with the Prophet in the First Presidency of the church, and in the school of the prophets. This school had been organized according to the Lord's instruction. These two men were told that through this divine call to the presidency they were to perfect themselves for their ministry for the salvation of Zion." (Joseph Fielding Smith, *CHMR* 1:390.)

"Joseph Smith was given two Counsellors, the three forming the first Presidency of the Church. (March 18, 1833.) This was preceded on March 8, 1833, by a revelation declaring that 'Through you [Joseph Smith] shall the oracles be given to another, even unto the Church.' The pre-eminence of the President of the Church was maintained. . . . The Counsellors do not possess the power of the President and cannot act in Church matters without direction and consent of the President.

"All this defined clearly the position and authority of the President of the Church." (John A. Widtsoe, *JS,* p. 303.)

"Elder Rigdon expressed a desire that himself and Brother Frederick G. Williams should be ordained to the offices to which they had been called, viz., those of the Presidents of the High Priesthood, and to be equal in holding the keys of the kingdom with Brother Joseph Smith, Jun., according to the revelation given on the 8th of March, 1833. Accordingly I laid my hands on Brothers Sidney and Frederick, and ordained them to take part with me in holding the keys of the last dispensation and to assist in the Presidency of the High Priesthood, as my Counsellors; after which I exhorted the brethren to faithfulness and diligence in the keeping the commandments of God, and gave much instruction for the benefit of the Saints, with a promise that the pure in heart should see a heavenly vision; and after remaining a short time in secret prayer, the promise was verified; for many present had the eyes of their understanding opened by the Spirit of God, so as to behold many things." (Joseph Smith, *HC* 1:334.)

90:8-9 *"unto the Gentiles first, and then . . . unto the Jews"*

See material for 29:30.

"The Gospel was . . . taken first to the Jews in the

Meridian Dispensation, and when the Jews rejected it, then
it was taken to the Gentiles. [Acts 11:18; 13:46.] The Lord
promised that the first should be last and last first in the final
dispensation. Therefore the Gospel was revealed and
declared to the Gentiles in this dispensation and then it must
go to the Jews." (Joseph Fielding Smith, *CHMR* 1:390.)

90:11 *"Every man shall hear the fulness of the gospel in his own
tongue"*

"It is the plan from the foundation of the earth that every
soul shall have the opportunity of hearing the Gospel. The
only way that this can be accomplished is by granting to the
dead who died without this privilege the right to hear it in
the spirit world. Therefore we are taught the doctrine of salvation for the dead. In order that the Gospel might be
declared among the nations and kindreds and tongues, the
Lord commanded that the elders should study languages and
with all good books be prepared to carry the message so that
people could hear it in their own tongue. This was one great
opportunity presented in the school of the prophets. It is a
remarkable fact that the elders of the Church going forth to
foreign lands have had the gift of tongues by which they
have learned to speak these foreign tongues within very brief
periods of time. Not only is this the case, but there are many
instances of record where the missionaries in conversation
and when preaching have been understood by others in their
native language. These cases have been similar with the gift
of tongues as it was made manifest on the day of Pentecost,
when Peter and the apostles stood up and spoke to the
assembled people from all countries who had come to
Jerusalem to the celebration of Pentecost. Elders who have
labored in foreign fields who have relied upon the Spirit of
the Lord and have been diligent in their labors can testify
from all parts of the Church that through the help of the
Spirit they were able to speak the languages of the people
among whom they were appointed to labor, and this beyond
their natural powers." (Joseph Fielding Smith, *CHMR*
1:390.)

90:11 *"the Comforter"*

See *Holy Ghost* in Appendix A.

90:18 *"set in order your houses"*

"Now . . . are you living so that you can go to the Lord with reasonable confidence that he will hear you? Can you go and ask him to heal your little ones? or yourselves? or your wife? If you can, when the time comes you will be happy and you will go to the Lord in faith, and the prayer of faith availeth much." (J. Reuben Clark, Jr., *CR,* October 1942, p. 84.)

90:25 *An explanation of "Let your families be small . . . as pertaining to those who do not belong to your families"*

Both the Prophet Joseph Smith and his father had provided food and lodging for many visitors and members of the Church as they came to meet the Smith family. Here the Lord cautions them to be wise in these things so that "those things that are provided for you . . . be not taken from you and given to those that are not worthy." (D&C 90:26.)

0:28-31 *Instructions pertaining to Sister Vienna Jaques*

"Vienna Jaques, a woman who had been kind to the Prophet and had cared for his wants when in need and had helped the elders, was now by revelation to be helped with means so that she could gather with the Saints in Zion." (Joseph Fielding Smith, *CHMR* 2:152.)

"A conference of high priests assembled April 30, 1833, in the schoolroom in Kirtland and took steps to raise means to pay the rent for the house where their meetings had been held during the past season. John P. Green was appointed to take charge of a branch of the Church in Parkman County. It was also decided that Sister Vienna Jaques should not proceed immediately on her way to Zion, but wait until William Hobart and others were ready, as it would be a matter of safety." (Joseph Fielding Smith, *CHMR* 1:403-4.)

90:30 *"meet in mine eyes"*

See *Meet* in Appendix A.

90:32 *"say unto your brethren in Zion"*

"From the time that Zion had been designated and many of the members of the Church had gone there to make permanent homes, it became necessary that they have an organization and a presidency was appointed. The Lord seeing the danger of a presidency in this place growing in authority to think that they were supreme in that place, the Lord declared that word should be sent to Zion and the elders presiding there that the Prophet was to say to them 'in love greeting, that I have called you also to preside over Zion in mine own due time.' " (Joseph Fielding Smith, *CHMR* 1:391.)

90:35   *"I am not well pleased with William E. McLellin, neither . . . Sidney Gilbert"*

For biographical information on these brethren, see Appendix B.

90:36-37   *"I . . . will chasten [Zion] until she overcomes"*

"I rejoice to know that, while some of us may falter and hesitate, this people shall not be rejected. The Lord said to Daniel that the work should not go to another people [Dan. 2:44]; and the Lord has indicated that in a revelation given to the Prophet Joseph Smith. You find it in the closing two verses of the ninetieth section of the Book of Doctrine and Covenants: [D&C 90:36-37, quoted.]

"That kind of promise entails the necessity of chastisement, when we need to be chastened and corrected and brought to a condition of repentance. I recognize that the Lord cannot fulfil his work nor accomplish his purposes without our willing obedience. He will not use this people unless we are willing to be used; but he has means of correcting, he has means of chastisement, which he will apply from time to time, and the only thing that impedes our progress today is our own lack of willingness to follow the counsel of those whom God has appointed to lead this people because of the imagination of our hearts that we are wiser than they are." (Melvin J. Ballard, *CR,* October 1921.)

SECTION 91

Background information on section 91

"On the 9th of March 1833, while the Prophet was busy considering the translation of the Scriptures, he inquired of the Lord regarding the Apocrypha of the Old Testament. He received the answer that it was not necessary for him to translate this record, for it contained many things that were not true having been interpreted by the hands of men. However, in the main it was correctly translated but its value was not of sufficient import for time to be taken to revise it." (Joseph Fielding Smith, *CHMR* 1:391.)

"The Apocrypha embrace a number of books of doubtful authenticity, though such have been at times highly esteemed. Thus, they were added to the Septuagint, and for a time were accorded recognition among the Alexandrine Jews. However, they have never been generally admitted, being of uncertain origin. They are not quoted in the New Testament. The designation *apocryphal,* meaning hidden, or secret, was first applied to the books by Jerome. The Roman Church professes to acknowledge them as scripture, action to this end having been taken by the Council of Trent (1546); though doubt as to the authenticity of the works seems still to exist even among Roman Catholic authorities. The Sixth article in the Liturgy of the Church of England defines the orthodox view of the church as to the meaning and intent of Holy Scripture and, after specifying the books of the Old Testament which are regarded as canonical, proceeds in this wise: 'And the other books (as Hierome [Jerome] saith) the church doth read for example of life and instruction of manners; but yet doth it not apply them to establish any doctrine; such are these following:—The Third Book of Esdras; The Fourth Book of Esdras; The Book of Tobias; The Book of Judith; The rest of the Book of Esther; The Book of Wisdom; Jesus, the Son of Sirach; Baruch the Prophet; The Song of the Three Children; The Story of Susanna; Of Bel and the Dragon; The Prayer of Manasses; The First Book of

Maccabees; The Second Book of Maccabees.' " (James E. Talmage, *AF,* pp. 244-45.)

91:1-6 *"the Apocrypha"*

"The word 'apocrypha' generally means 'secret' or 'hidden' or 'of dubious authenticity.' 'The Apocrypha' refers to fourteen books which were part of early Greek and Latin versions of the Bible but were not part of the Hebrew Bible.

"The apocrypha was included in the King James Version of 1611, but by 1629 some English Bibles began to appear without it, and since the early part of the 19th century it has been excluded from almost all protestant Bibles. The American Bible Society, founded in 1816, has never printed the Apocrypha in its Bibles, and the British and Foreign Bible Society has excluded it from all but some pulpit Bibles since 1827.

"From these dates it is apparent that controversy was still raging as to the value of the Apocrypha at the time the Prophet began his ministry. Accordingly, in 1833, while engaged in revising the King James Version by the spirit of revelation, the Prophet felt impelled to inquire of the Lord as to the authenticity of the Apocrypha." (Bruce R. McConkie, *MD,* p. 41.)

SECTION 92

Background information on section 92

"In the Revelation given on April 26th, 1832 (sec. 82), the Lord instructed the Prophet Joseph, Oliver Cowdery, Martin Harris, Sidney Rigdon, Newel K. Whitney, and a few others (v. 11) to unite their temporal interests under the rule of the Order of Enoch. In this Revelation the brethren in that organization are commanded to receive, as a member, Frederick G. Williams, whom the Lord had declared to be the equal of Joseph Smith and Sidney Rigdon in holding the keys of the kingdom (D&C 90:6)." (Smith and Sjodahl, *DCC,* pp. 586-87.)

92:1 *"I give unto you the united order"*

See *United Order* in Appendix A.

92:1-2 *"Shederlaomach"* [*Frederick G. Williams*]

For biographical information on Frederick G. Williams, see Appendix B. For explanation of "Shederlaomach," see background information for section 78.

SECTION 93

Background information on section 93

"On the 4th of May, 1833, a meeting of High Priests was held at Kirtland, for the purpose of considering ways and means for the building of a house in which to accommodate the School of the Prophets (Sec. 90:6-9). Hyrum Smith, Jared Carter, and Reynolds Cahoon were appointed a committee to obtain subscriptions for that purpose. The Saints were few and far from wealthy, and an undertaking of that kind must have seemed stupendous to them, but the leaders of the Church were men of God, and their faith was of the practical kind, by which mountains are removed. When this important step had been taken, two instructive Revelations were given on the same date." (Smith and Sjodahl, *DCC*, pp. 587-88.)

93:1-3 *"every soul who forsaketh his sins and cometh unto me . . . shall . . . know that I am"*

"Every Latter-day Saint is entitled to this witness and testimony. If we have not received this witness and testimony . . . I want you all to remember that the fault is ours, and not the Lord's; for every one is entitled to that witness through faith and repentance, forsaking all sin, baptism by immersion for the remission of sins, and the reception of the Holy Ghost through the laying on of hands. Now, if any of our brethren and sisters have lived for years without really knowing, being thoroughly satisfied and thoroughly convinced, just as positive as of anything in life, that this work is of God, if they have lacked that witness and testimony it is their fault, for it is not possible for a man to do the will of the Father and not know the doctrine." (Francis M. Lyman, *CR*, April 1910, pp. 29-30.)

"I consider this is a most precious promise. We who were raised in the world, were subject to priestcraft, and false doctrine, and evil influences, but the Lord, in His loving kindness and tender mercy, and in the wonderful dispensations of His providence, brought us into His Church. He drew us into the fold. . . .

"The Apostle Paul said 'the things of God knoweth no man, but the Spirit of God' [1 Cor. 2:11], showing that it is necessary for us to be taught of God by His Spirit. Jesus promised that whoso would do the will of the Father should know of the doctrine. [John 7:17.] He also said, 'Not every one that saith unto me Lord, Lord, shall enter into the kingdom of heaven; but he that doeth the will of my Father which is in heaven.' [Matt. 7:21.] The Latter-day Saints have received, and are continually receiving testimonies." (George Teasdale, *CR*, October 1903, pp. 48-50.)

93:3 *"the Father and I are one"*

See *Godhead* in Appendix A.

"The saying which appears in the Book of Mormon (Mosiah 15:1-5) and in some of the revelations including Section 93, that Jesus Christ is both the Father and the Son has been a mystery, if not a stumbling block, to some. The question has been asked how Joseph Smith could reconcile his Vision with these sayings. A careful reading of verses 3-4, Sec. 93, will give a clear explanation of this apparent mystery. Here the Savior says he is the Father because his Father gave him of his fulness, and he is the Son of the Father because he was born into the world. Jesus Christ is our Father because he gave us life—eternal life—through his sacrifice. He is the Father because of his everlasting and presiding power—the fulness which he holds as one of the Godhead. He never did say that he and his Father are the same personage, but always that his Father is greater than he. (See John 14:28 and 1 Cor. 15:27-28.)" (Joseph Fielding Smith, *CHMR* 1:399.)

93:3-5 *The titles "Father" and "Son" as they pertain to Jesus Christ*

See *Jesus Christ* in Appendix A.

93:12 *"he received not of the fulness at the first"*

"When Jesus lay in the manger, a helpless infant, He knew not that He was the Son of God, and that formerly He created the earth. When the edict of Herod was issued, He knew nothing of it; He had not power to save Himself; and His father and mother had to take Him and fly into Egypt to preserve Him from the effects of that edict. Well, He grew up into manhood, and during His progress it was revealed unto Him who He was, and for what purpose He was in the world. The glory and power He possessed before He came into the world was made known unto Him." (Lorenzo Snow, *CR*, April 1901, p. 3.)

93:18 *"you shall receive a fulness of the record of John"*

"Mormon says, concerning these three [Nephite disciples] that were to tarry, that great works shall be wrought by them before the great day of the Lord shall come. Then he says, that if you had all the Scriptures, you would know that these things would be fulfilled. We would know a great many things if we only had these Scriptures and revelations. [3 Nephi 28:33.] They are to be revealed to fill our earth with the knowledge of God, as the waters cover the great deep.

"Not only the records of the ancient inhabitants of the land are to come forth, but the records of those who slept on the eastern hemisphere. The records of John, him who baptized the lamb of God, are yet to be revealed. We are informed in the book of Doctrine and Covenants [93:18] that the fulness of the record of John is to be revealed to the Latter-day Saints." (Orson Pratt, *JD* 16:57-58.)

93:19 *"that you may . . . know how to worship, and . . . what you worship"*

See *Worship, God,* and *Jesus Christ* in Appendix A.

93:21 *"I . . . am the Firstborn"*

See *Firstborn* in Appendix A.

93:22 *"church of the Firstborn"*

See same title in Appendix A.

93:23 *"Ye were also in the beginning with the Father"*

See *Pre-earthly existence* in Appendix A.

93:24 *Definition of truth*

See *Truth* in Appendix A.

"This definition of truth was given by the Lord and is very comprehensive. For ages men have discussed this question and have pondered over the meaning, or definition, of truth. It is, as defined here, that which will always be, or that which is eternal. John Jaques, accepting the Lord's definition, has written a very beautiful hymn—'O Say What Is Truth,' and declares it is the 'sum of existence.' " (Joseph Fielding Smith, *CHMR* 1:401.)

93:26 *"Spirit of Truth"*

See *Truth* in Appendix A.

93:29 *"Intelligence"*

See *Intelligence* in Appendix A.

"In a revelation through Joseph Smith the prophet given in 1833, the character of Divine authority and power is thus summarized: 'The Glory of God is Intelligence.' [D&C 93:36.] The context of the passage shows that the intelligence therein referred to as an attribute of Deity is spiritual light and truth ; and that man may attain to a measure of this exalting light and truth is thus made certain: [D&C 93:28-30, quoted.] The intelligence that saves comprises knowing and doing what is required by the Gospel of Christ; and such intelligence with you will endure beyond death. [D&C 130:18-19.]" (James E. Talmage, *VM*, pp. 277-78.)

93:31 *"agency of man"*

See *Free agency* in Appendix A.

93:33 *"man is spirit"*

See *Pre-earthly existence* in Appendix A.

"Spirits are eternal. At the first organization in heaven we were all present, and saw the Savior chosen and appointed and the plan of salvation made, and we sanctioned it. [Moses 4:1-3.]

"We came to this earth that we might have a body and present it pure before God in the celestial kingdom. The great principle of happiness consists in having a body. The devil has no body, and herein is his punishment. He is pleased when he can obtain the tabernacle of man, and when cast out by the Savior he asked to go into the herd of swine, showing that he would prefer a swine's body to having none. [Luke 8:26-33.]" (Joseph Smith, *TPJS,* p. 181.)

93:33 *"elements are eternal"*

"The Lord has shown to us that the elements are eternal and that it requires the eternal union of spirit and element to obtain a fulness of joy. For the spirit part of man and the earthly or temporal part just now, shall be united together perpetually, eternally, the body and the spirit being made one again, only rejoined together after the power of an endless life, that without that union a fulness of joy cannot be obtained. That is very easy to understand in a degree, if we will reflect upon our nature and upon the position that we now occupy. The spirit having come from God who is the Father literally, the Father of the spirit, and the body formed from the earthly elements, through earthly parentage, without this body many things that will give joy, pleasure, power, increase, perpetuity, cannot be enjoyed. This is rational. The spirit reaches out to that which is spiritual, the body reaches down to that which is called temporal, that is, physical—the grosser materials of earth and air and all the surroundings that pertain thereunto. These are realities as much as those are spiritual." (Charles W. Penrose, *CR*, October 1914, pp. 35-36.)

93:33   *"spirit and element, inseparably connected"*

"The word of the Lord revealed in this dispensation is very emphatic in teaching that after the resurrection the spirit and the body become inseparably connected. (See Alma 11:40-45; 12:17-18; D&C 63:49-52.) The Lord also declared that he is 'the resurrection and the life,' and 'whosoever liveth and believeth in me shall never die.' (John 11:25-26.) The spirit and the body are welded so that they can never again be divided when the resurrection comes. And this resurrection is the redemption of the soul, no matter to which kingdom it is assigned. (D&C 88:16.)" (Joseph Fielding Smith, *CHMR* 1:402.)

93:36   *"the glory of God is intelligence, or, in other words, light and truth"*

"The glory of God is intelligence. On this President Joseph F. Smith has said: 'Christ inherited his intelligence from his Father. There is a difference between knowledge and pure intelligence. Satan possesses knowledge, far more than we have, but he has not intelligence, or he would render obedience to the principles of truth and light. . . . Pure intelligence comprises not only knowledge, but also the power to properly apply that knowledge.' (*The Way to Perfection*, p. 231.)

"The Lord has defined intelligence, which is the glory of

God, as light and truth, and says that 'Light and truth forsake that evil one.' Satan, of course, in his rebellion and hatred of all things righteous, desires to destroy the souls of men, therefore he tries to take from them light and truth that they may be left in spiritual darkness." (Joseph Fielding Smith, *CHMR* 1:402.)

"Among the many great truths revealed to the Prophet Joseph Smith, none is more beloved by the Church than 'The Glory of God is intelligence.' The word *intelligence*, as used in common speech, means readiness in learning, quickness of mind. Its higher Gospel meaning is more profound. The intelligent man is he who seeks knowledge and uses it in accordance with the plan of the Lord for human good. This is implied in the revelation from which the quotation is made, for the full sentence reads, 'The Glory of God is intelligence, or in other words, light and truth.' When men follow the light, their knowledge will always be well used.

"Intelligence, then, becomes but another name for wisdom. In the language of mathematics we may say that knowledge, plus the proper use of knowledge, equals intelligence, or wisdom. In this sense intelligence becomes the goal of the successful life." (John A. Widtsoe, *CR*, April 1938, p. 50.)

93:38 *"every spirit of man was innocent in the beginning"*

"Every spirit was innocent in the beginning. When Lucifer rebelled because of his agency, he persuaded others to follow him, then their innocence came to an end, for they were in rebellion before God and had to be cast out. [D&C 29:36-37.] It seems very reasonable that others were not valiant in that premortal state, and they may have led to the gradations upon the earth. However, the Lord declares that every spirit coming into this world is innocent. That is to say, so far as this life is concerned the spirit coming here is innocent. Nothing is to be laid to its charge; this is a correction of the false doctrine which prevails in some religious organizations, that children are born with the taint of 'original sin' upon them. Such false doctrine denies the mercies of Jesus Christ and declares ignorance of the atonement of our Lord. [Moroni 8:19-23.]" (Joseph Fielding Smith, *CHMR* 2:163.)

"Many rivers have their beginning from springs of pure, crystal-clear water gushing forth from a mountainside. As the water wends its way to the sea, there are side tributaries that join the main stream. Some of these tributaries are polluted and contaminate the main stream, which started pure at its source. By the time the river reaches the sea, pollution has occurred in the body of the stream.

"How much like life this symbolic representation is! The Lord has revealed that 'every spirit of man was innocent in the beginning; and God having redeemed man from the fall, men became again, in their infant state, innocent before God.' (D&C 93:38.) With this statement in mind, we can understand why the Savior said, 'Except ye be converted, and become as little children, ye shall not enter into the kingdom of heaven.' (Matt. 18:3.)

"When a child reaches the age of accountability, the Lord warned, 'And that wicked one cometh and taketh away light and truth, through disobedience, from the children of men. . . .' (D&C 93:39.)

"We learn from this revelation that in the beginning of mortal life all mankind is innocent before God and, therefore, is like the beginning river of water, pure and undefiled. As the polluted tributaries of water enter the main stream, our lives too become polluted when we allow tributaries of evil and wickedness to enter. It is these tributaries of evil we must be concerned about and fortify ourselves against." (Delbert L. Stapley, *Ensign*, December 1971, p. 97.)

93:41, 44, *For biographical information on the persons mentioned,*
47, 50 *see Appendix B.*

93:53 *"Hasten to translate my scripture"*

"On the second day of February, 1833, the Prophet completed, for the time being, his inspired translation of the New Testament. No endeavor was made at that time to print the work. It was sealed up with the expectation that it would be brought forth at a later day with other of the scriptures. Joseph did not live to give the world an authoritative publication of these translations. [Footnote: We have heard President Brigham Young state that the Prophet before his death had spoken to him about going through the translation of the scriptures again and perfecting it upon points of doctrine which the Lord had restrained him from giving in plainness and fullness at the time of which we write.] But the labor was its own reward, bringing in the performance a special blessing of broadened comprehension to the Prophet and a general blessing of enlightenment to the people through his subsequent teachings.

"The Lord revealed His purpose in this matter when He said to Joseph at a later time: [D&C 93:53, quoted.]" (George Q. Cannon, *LJS*, p. 129.)

SECTION 94

Background information on section 94

"A conference of high priests assembled April 30, 1833, in the school room in Kirtland and took steps to raise means to pay the rent for the house where their meetings had been held during the past season. John P. Green was appointed to take charge of a branch of the Church in Parkman County. It was also decided that Sister Vienna Jaques should not proceed immediately on her way to Zion, but wait until William Hobart and others were ready, as it would be a matter of safety. The next day the conference again convened and took into consideration the necessity of building a schoolhouse, for the accommodation of the elders, who were to come together to receive instruction preparatory to taking missions and continuing in the ministry according to the revelation of March 8, 1833. By unanimous voice of the conference, Hyrum Smith, Jared Carter and Reynolds Cahoon were appointed a committee to obtain subscriptions for the purpose of erecting such a building. Two days later the Lord gave a revelation with directions for the building of this house." (Joseph Fielding Smith, *CHMR* 1:403-4.)

94:1 *"commence [the] . . . foundation of the city of the stake of Zion in . . . Kirtland"*

"At a conference held March 23rd, 1833, a committee was appointed to purchase land in Kirtland, upon which to build up a Stake of Zion. Several large farms were bought, and among these was the French farm, so called after its owner. This had an excellent stone quarry and good material for brick-making. A city plat was surveyed, and the Saints gathered from surrounding States, until the Church in Kirtland numbered about 1,500 souls. The Lord, in this Revelation, instructed them to build the city of Kirtland Stake, beginning at His house. He also gave instructions for the consecration of a lot upon which to build a House of the Lord for the ministry of the First Presidency, 'in all things pertaining to the church and kingdom.' Further particulars about this house are given." (Smith and Sjodahl, *DCC*, p. 600.)

94:3-17 *Instructions on the building of houses*

"A lot was set apart for the building of a house for the use of the First Presidency and where revelation could be given and all matters pertaining to the progress of the Church could receive proper attention. . . . It was to be dedicated unto the Lord from the foundation thereof, according to the order of the Priesthood. There is no question that the First Presidency needed a place where they could attend to the matters of Church government. This was to be a sacred house; no unclean thing was to be permitted to enter it, and if the builders would remember this the presence of the Lord should be in the building.

"The second lot south of this building was to be dedicated for the building of another house where the printing for the Church could be done and the translation of the Scriptures, on which the Prophet had been working off and on for many months, could be published. . . . This house also was to be dedicated to the service of the Lord and set apart for the printing. [D&C 94:12, quoted.] The third lot was to be given to Hyrum Smith for his inheritance. Reynolds Cahoon and Jared Carter were also to receive inheritances. [D&C 94:15, quoted.] These two houses . . . were not to be built until he [the Lord] should give the commandment for the building of them." (Joseph Fielding Smith, *CHMR* 2:165.)

94:13-14 *For information on these brethren, see Appendix B.*

SECTION 95

"Great preparations were making to commence a house of the Lord; and notwithstanding the Church was poor, yet our unity, harmony and charity abounded to strengthen us to do the commandments of God. The building of the house of the Lord in Kirtland was a matter that continued to increase in its interest in the hearts of the brethren. . . . The same day [June 1, 1833] I received the following: [D&C 95.]" (Joseph Smith, *HC* 1:349-50.)

"On the 1st of June, 1833, Hyrum Smith, Reynolds Cahoon, and Jared Carter, the building committee (Sec. 94:14, 15), issued a circular to the Saints in which they urged them to exert themselves 'to bring about the fulfilment of the command of the Lord concerning the establishing, or preparing of a house, wherein the Elders who have been commanded of the Lord so to do, may gather themselves together, and prepare all things, and call a solemn assembly, and treasure up words of wisdom, that they may go forth to the Gentiles for the last time' (*HC* 1:349). This, then, was the object for which this Temple was to be built.

"Great interest in this undertaking was now aroused among the Saints, and this Revelation was received, in which the Lord (1) reproves His people for their neglect to begin building the temple (1-12); (2) commands them again to go to work (13-17)." (Smith and Sjodahl, *DCC,* p. 603.)

95:1 *"whom I love I also chasten"*

Our Heavenly Father loves us and wants us to keep his commandments so that we can receive the joy and happiness that would result from such obedience. When we do not keep his commandments, he chastens us so that hopefully we will repent. In much the same way, an earthly father may chasten his wayward child when the child is doing something that is not for the child's best welfare.

95:2 *"ye must needs be chastened"*

"At times I may to many of the brethren appear to be severe. I sometimes chasten them; but it is because I wish them to so live that the power of God, like a flame of fire, will dwell within them and be round about them. These are my feelings and desires." (Brigham Young, *JD* 8:62.)

95:3 *"ye have sinned . . . concerning the building of my house"*

"The same day, [June 1, 1833] the Lord gave another revelation (Sec. 95) in which he rebuked the elders of the Church for their delay in building another house which they had been commanded to build. This was the Kirtland Temple. . . .

"It was Dec. 27, 1832, that the Lord gave the command to the Church that his house should be built. . . . The elders of the Church, it would appear, had not taken this command seriously, presumably it had been overlooked in the consideration of so many wonderful things in that particular revelation. The month of May, in the following year, had arrived; the officers of the Church had met in solemn council to consider other matters, the building of other houses for which there was sore need, and the building of the more weighty and important building had been neglected. While the Lord approved the plan for the building of these other houses, and commended the brethren for their enthusiasm and energy in taking steps to erect them, yet he called attention to the grievous sins of the brethren in their neglect to build the more important structure. The Kirtland Temple was necessary before the apostles (who had not yet been called), and other elders of the Church could receive the endowment which the Lord had in store for them. The elders had been out preaching the Gospel and crying repentance ever since the Church was organized and many great men had heard and embraced the truth, nevertheless the elders could not go forth in the power and authority which the Lord intended them to possess until this Temple was built where he could restore keys and powers essential to the more complete preaching of the Gospel and the administering in its ordinances. . . .

"Four days after the Lord had rebuked the brethren for their neglect, without waiting for subscriptions, the brethren went to work on the Temple. Elder George A. Smith, a recent convert, hauled the first load of stone for the Temple. Hyrum Smith and Reynolds Cahoon commenced digging the trench for the walls, and they finished the same with their own hands." (Joseph Fielding Smith, *CHMR* 1:405-7.)

95:4 *"prune my vineyard"*

See *Vineyard* in Appendix A.

95:4 *"my strange act"*

See material for 101:95.

"The purpose of the Lord was to prepare His Apostles (that is to say, His messengers) for the labor in the vineyard, for the last time, and bring to pass His 'strange act' and pour out His Spirit on all flesh.

"The expression quoted is from the Prophet Isaiah (28:21), where it refers to the fact that God would fight against His own people, because of their apostate condition. 'Shall I not, as I have done to Samaria and her idols, so do to Jerusalem and her idols (Isa. 10:11)? That was in the estimation of the Jews, who did not realize their apostate condition, 'strange.' But in this dispensation our Lord was to perform an equally strange act, in revealing His marvelous plan of salvation and making war upon an apostate church which is boasting of its intimate relations with Deity. He was now waiting for the Saints to build that house, in which His messengers were to be prepared for that strange war and endowed with power from on High (v. 8). No wonder that He rebuked them for their tardiness!" (Smith and Sjodahl, *DCC,* p. 604.)

95:6 *"they are walking in darkness at noon-day"*

See *Darkness* and *Light* in Appendix A. Now that the light of the gospel had been restored, it was a "very grievous sin" for people to still be walking in the darkness of the apostasy, especially for those who had been ordained.

95:7 *"solemn assembly"*

See *Solemn assembly* in Appendix A.

95:8 *"endow"*

See *Endowment* in Appendix A.

95:10 *"school of the prophets"*

See material for 88:127, 136.

95:11 *"you should build a house"*

"This house was not to be built after the manner of the world, but after the manner which the Lord would show them. The saints also were not to live after the manner of the world, but after the manner which the Lord would show them. This building also was to be fifty-five by sixty-five feet in the inner court as the Lord had instructed in the buildings previously mentioned. [Sec. 94:4, 11.] The lower part of the inner court of this Temple was to be dedicated unto the Lord for the sacrament offerings and for the preaching, and for fasting and prayer, and the offering 'of your most holy desires unto me, saith your Lord.' (Sec. 95:16.) The upper floor, or court, was to be dedicated unto the Lord as 'the school of mine apostles' (Sec. 95:17), the Lord declared in closing his revelation. However, this building was to be erected for other and greater purposes than those made known at this time to the officers and members of the Church. The time had not come for the real purposes and the nature of the endowment to be revealed. The elders, much less the members, were not prepared in 1833 for the fulness of the revelation which the Lord declared would be bestowed upon them. The severe rebuke administered to the Church had its effect and the brethren forgot the need of other buildings and commenced to concentrate their efforts upon this house of the Lord." (Joseph Fielding Smith, *CHMR* 2:167.)

95:17 *"Son Ahman . . . Alphus . . . Omegus"*

See *Son Ahman* and *Alpha and Omega* in Appendix A.

SECTION 96

Background information on section 96

"On the 4th of June, 1833, the High Priests met in Conference, in the Translating Room, to consider what disposition to make of the French farm, which, together with other real estate, had been bought for the Church. The Conference was not able to agree on a manager, but all were willing to submit the question to the Lord, in prayer. In answer to their petitions, they received this Revelation, in which the Lord directed them (1) to give Bishop Newel K. Whitney charge of the farm (1-5); and (2) to accept John Johnson as a member of the United Order (6-9)." (Smith and Sjodahl, *DCC*, p. 606.)

96:1 *"this stake . . . should be made strong"*

See *Stake* in Appendix A.

96:2, 7 *"Newel K. Whitney . . . John Johnson"*

For biographical information on these brethren, see Appendix B. For an explanation and listing of the unusual names (Ahashdah, Zombre, etc.), see background information on section 78.

SECTION 97

"On the second day of August 1833, the Prophet received a revelation concerning Zion. While he was aware of the fact that trouble was brewing in Jackson County and the spirit of opposition was very great he did not know that the mob had risen and had destroyed property and violently handled some of the brethren. In this revelation the Lord said that he desired to make known his will concerning the brethren in Zion. Many of them had truly humbled themselves and were seeking wisdom. Because of their repentance they would be blessed, for the Lord was merciful to the meek, and all who will not humble themselves will be brought to judgment." (Joseph Fielding Smith, *CHMR* 1:430.)

"The revelation [Sec. 97] was not complied with by the leaders and Church in Missouri, as a whole; notwithstanding many were humble and faithful. Therefore, the threatened judgment was poured out to the uttermost, as the history of the five following years will show." (Parley P. Pratt, *APPP*, p. 96.)

97:1 *"the voice of my Spirit"*

See *Voice of the Lord* in Appendix A.

97:3-5 *"Parley P. Pratt . . . to preside over the school"*

For biographical information on Parley P. Pratt, see the material following his name in Appendix B.

"In the latter part of summer and in the autumn [1833], I devoted almost my entire time in ministering among the churches; holding meetings; visiting the sick; comforting the afflicted, and giving counsel. A school of Elders was also organized, over which I was called to preside. This class, to the number of about sixty, met for instruction once a week. The place of meeting was in the open air, under some tall trees, in a retired place in the wilderness, where we prayed, preached and prophesied and exercised ourselves in the gifts of the Holy Spirit. Here great blessings were poured out, and many great and marvelous things were manifested and taught. The Lord gave me great wisdom, and enabled me to teach and edify the Elders, and comfort and encourage them in their preparations for the great work which lay before us. I was also much edified and strengthened. To attend this school I had to travel on foot, and sometimes with bare feet at that, about six miles. This I did once a week, besides visiting and preaching in five or six branches a week." (Parley P. Pratt, *APPP*, pp. 93-94.)

97:10 *A temple to be built "in the land of Zion"*

For information on the temple to be built in the New Jerusalem, read the materials listed after 84:5.

97:10-14 *"a place of instruction . . . in all things"*

"Temple work, for example, gives a wonderful opportunity for keeping alive our spiritual knowledge and strength. The mighty perspective of eternity is unraveled before us in the holy temples; we see time from its infinite beginning to its endless end; and the dream of eternal life is unfolded before us. Then I see more clearly my place amidst the things of the universe, my place among the purposes of God; I am better able to place myself where I belong, and I am better able to value and to weigh, to separate and to organize the common, ordinary duties of my life, so that the little things shall not oppress me or take away my vision of the greater things that God has given us." (John A. Widtsoe, *CR*, April 1922, pp. 97-98.)

97:11 *"by the tithing of my people"*

See *Tithing* in Appendix A.

97:18-21 *"this is Zion—THE PURE IN HEART"*

See *Zion* in Appendix A.

"And what is Zion? In one sense Zion is the pure in heart. But is there a land that ever will be called Zion? Yes, brethren. What land is it? It is the land that the Lord gave to Jacob, who bequeathed it to his son Joseph, and his posterity, and they inhabit it, and that land is North and South America." (Brigham Young, *JD* 2:253.)

"It is the honest and pure in heart that will hearken to the everlasting covenant." (Hyrum Smith, *HC* 6:320.)

:25-28   *"Zion shall escape if . . ."*

"What a pity it is that we have not heeded this commandment: [D&C 97:25, quoted.] Heeding it is our safety, and while we may be preserved from many of the calamities, yet the promise is made that if we observe not to do the things the Lord has commanded us, Zion—who should be the pure in heart—shall be visited with sore afflictions, pestilence, plague, sword, vengeance and devouring fire. . . . While in a measure this revelation applied to the inhabitants of Zion in the early days, yet it applies to us today, to Zion the land and also her inhabitants." (Joseph Fielding Smith, *CHMR* 2:191.)

SECTION 98

Background information on section 98

"Seventeen days after the mobbing of the saints in Missouri [on Aug. 6, 1833], the Prophet received a revelation in which the Lord said that the prayers of saints were heard in heaven, and counsel was given them to be patient in their afflictions and not seek vengeance against their enemies. Oliver Cowdery did not leave Independence on his special mission until after the 23rd of July, and if he arrived in Kirtland before the 6th of August when this revelation was received, it certainly was a miraculous journey considering the distance and the means he had of transportation. Just when he arrived we do not know, but the Prophet had learned that difficulties of a serious nature had commenced in Jackson County. Naturally the members of the Church there were extremely aroused and it was only natural that in their hearts there should be some spirit of retaliation and revenge upon their enemies. Because of this the Lord gave this revelation." (Joseph Fielding Smith, *CHMR* 1:432-34.)

98:2 *"Lord of Sabaoth"*

See *Sabaoth* in Appendix A.

98:4-8 *Members of the Church commanded to uphold the constitutional law of the land*

See *Constitution* in Appendix A.

"I am the greatest advocate of the Constitution of the United States there is on the earth. In my feelings I am always ready to die for the protection of the weak and oppressed in their just rights." (Joseph Smith, *HC* 6:56-57.)

98:9 *"when the wicked rule the people mourn"*

"Laws which are enacted for the protection of society have no value except when they are administered in righteousness and justice, and they cannot be so administered in righteousness and justice, if dishonest men occupy administrative offices.

"The Lord says; 'When the wicked rule, the people mourn.' Wise men, good men, patriotic men are to be found in all communities, in all political parties, among all creeds. None but such men should be chosen. . . .

"Without beneficent laws, righteously administered, the foundations of civilization crumble, anarchy reigns, decay and dissolution follow." (First Presidency, *CR,* October 1928, p. 16.)

"I tell you one thing that I will do: I will support good men in every position. I care not what proposition may be submitted to me, I will sustain good men. For it is written, 'When the wicked rule, the people mourn.' When the righteous rule, the people rejoice.

". . . What do I care about party feeling! A lot of men meet together and get up names, among them some shyster that has foisted himself into the notice through some means or other of his own making, and they rush that upon me, and because I would not vote for such men two or three years ago, they said, 'You are a mugwump.' Well, I would rather be a know-nothing than to subscribe to conditions which will make me responsible for the actions of the wicked. I will not do it, I do not care who it cuts, nor what the consequences may be. I say it to the nation, I say it to the world: As God lives, I will never support a man that I know is a wicked man, for any office. The word of the Prophet of God has been given to me, as it has to you, and we have to take cognizance of these things." (Brigham Young, Jr., *CR,* October 1900, pp. 43-44.)

98:10 *"honest . . . and wise men should be sought for diligently"*

"The Church is telling its members to look upon the franchise as a sacred gift, to exercise it according to their very best judgment before the Lord, and the Church's ticket is the ticket of the best men, according to the best judgment of the people, to whichever party they belong." (James E. Talmage, *CR,* October 1920, p. 66.)

"Can man's knowledge and intellect supplant the revealed word of God? Do we really believe we can prosper by letting this land, established by the hand of God, be run by those who know not God and acknowledge not his hand in all things? There have always been ungodly men who fancied their wisdom superior to any other. Why should we, who have testimonies of the reality of God burning within us, submit ourselves to the wisdom of men, which has always been foolishness to God?

"The Lord has made plain that we have a solemn obligation to choose good and honest men to represent us in secular governmental service. It is obvious that a man's spiritual and moral qualifications should be considered before his academic record or his oratorical ability. It is a sobering thought that whatever laws the elected enact, we are obligated then to obey. The Lord said, 'And now, verily I say unto you concerning the laws of the land, it is my will that my people should observe to do all things whatsoever I command them.'" (Hartman Rector, Jr., *Ensign,* May 1975, p. 11.)

98:12   *"line upon line, precept upon precept"*

A loving, kind, merciful Heavenly Father will not give his children more or higher laws than they are willing to try and live. Otherwise, he brings them under greater condemnation, for "where much is given, much is required." (D&C 82:3.) He gives unto children "line upon line, precept upon precept, here a little and there a little." (2 Ne. 28:30.) Then as they learn the lesser laws and obey them, he "will give more." (2 Ne. 28:30.) However, if the people do not keep even the lesser laws, the greater things will "be withheld from them, unto their condemnation." (3 Ne. 26:10.)

98:16   *"renounce war and proclaim peace"*

"We stand in the world for peace among men and not war. We detest war; we love peace. Does the world love peace? No. Do they want peace? It is not apparent that they do. The devil reigns in the world, and he has stirred up the hearts of men to anger and to hatred and to bloodshed. . . . After this war [World War I] is over will there be peace? No, there will be no peace. [Sec. 1:35.] It will take generations to outlive the impressions of hatred and animosity that are now being made upon the hearts of the children against their fellow men. . . . Peace to be permanent must come from within as well as to be seen externally. Man must have peace in his heart and love in his heart both for God and man, else there will be no peace." (Hyrum M. Smith, *CR,* October 1916, pp. 44-45.)

"The Lord has revealed again in these latter days the

charge to His followers to—'Renounce war, and proclaim peace.' To endeavor in every proper way, through example and influence, to promote peace everywhere, that the way may be prepared so that 'nations shall not lift up the sword against nations' but be prepared for the coming of the reign of the Lord, that peace and good will toward men shall prevail everywhere. This, we are confident, will eventually occur." (Hugh B. Brown, *CR*, April 1940, p. 27.)

:16-17 *"seek diligently to turn . . . the hearts of the Jews unto the prophets, and the prophets unto the Jews"*

See *Elijah* in Appendix A.

"As I understand this command we the prophets must turn our hearts unto the Jews, and then we may hope that they will turn their hearts unto us because of the message that we shall bring unto them through the restoration of the gospel in this dispensation. The importance of this the Lord declared in these words: '. . . lest I come and smite the whole earth with a curse, and all flesh be consumed before me.' " (LeGrand Richards, *CR*, October 1956, p. 24.)

"It is the duty of the elders to endeavor to get the Jews to understand the prophets which they profess to believe, but do not understand; and to believe in Christ, of whom the prophets of old have spoken. Moreover, to prepare themselves for that which was yet to come when Elijah should come to restore his keys of sealing." (Joseph Fielding Smith, *CHMR* 2:193.)

98:18 *"in my Father's house are many mansions"*

See *Degrees of glory* in Appendix A.

98:22 *"the gates of hell shall not prevail against you"*

See *Hell* in Appendix A.

:23-32 *"if men . . . smite you . . . bear it patiently"*

"The Lord here states what may, perhaps, be called *the lex talionis* of the gospel. 'An eye for an eye and a tooth for a tooth,' was the highest ideal of justice to which the majority of the Children of Israel could rise under the Mosaic law. Our Lord enunciated a higher ideal, 'But I say unto you, that ye resist not evil; but whosoever shall smite thee on thy right cheek, turn to him the other also. And if any man will sue thee at the law, and take away thy coat, let him have thy cloak also' (Matt. 5:39-40). This principle is set forth in further detail in the paragraphs before us. If men will smite you, or your families, and ye will bear it patiently, and not seek revenge, ye shall be rewarded (v. 23). If the offense is repeated, and ye bear it patiently, your reward shall be a hundred fold (v. 25). If it is repeated again, and ye bear it patiently the reward shall be multiplied four times (v. 26), and the Lord will judge the offender (v. 27). If he still persists, he must be solemnly warned, and if he does not heed the warning, the victim is justified in 'rewarding him according to his works' (v. 31); but if the wronged party will spare the offender, the reward for his righteousness will surely come (v. 30).

"As the world is constituted at present, it is impossible to live in it without being wronged some time. What to do, when wronged, is one of the great problems of a Christian life. The world says, 'Get even!' The Master says, 'Forgive!' 'Absurd!' the world exclaims; 'what are laws and courts and jails for?' Christ bids us remember that our worst enemy is, after all, one of God's children whom Christ came to save, and that we ought to treat him as we would an erring brother. Very often Christian love in return for a wrong proves the salvation of the wrong-doer. It always has a wonderful effect upon those who practice it. It makes them strong, beautiful and God-like, whereas hatred and revenge stamp, upon the heart in which they dwell, the image of the devil." (Smith and Sjodahl, DCC, p. 623.)

98:23-48   *The law of the Lord concerning war and vengeance*

"Here is a law given that is of the utmost importance to the inhabitants of the earth as well as to us as a people. It is the law by which the inhabitants of the earth should be governed and we, as Latter-day Saints, especially should understand this law and be governed by it. . . . We should be a peaceful people, seeking peace, and endeavoring to escape all the horrors of war, and to avert them from the nations of the earth, particularly our own nation. The Lord says: [Sec. 98:34-38, quoted.]. . .

"I do not look for our nation to do this. It is scarcely to be expected, in the nature of things, that they would do it. But it is the true principle, and we as a people should use our influence for his purpose. Our prayers should ascend to God, our petitions should ascend to the government of our nation to do everything that honorable people can do to avert war. We have no fear of the effect of the combinations against us. . . . But the promise of God is that if we will do right as a nation, if we will serve Him, they shall not have power over us, or be able to bring us into bondage; and in the end we shall prevail. This is a glorious promise which is made to the inhabitants of the land. (2 Nephi 10:10-14.)" (George Q. Cannon, *CR*, April 1898, pp. 85-87.)

"In the 98th section the Lord gives the law that he gave in ancient times to his people when they were to go forth to battle. It is in substance: 'If thine enemy come against thee, thou shalt forgive him; if he come again the second time, thou shalt forgive him; and if he even come the third time and you forgive him, it will be reckoned unto you for glory, but if he come again, I, the Lord, justify you in going forth to battle and I will strengthen you and I will fight your battles.' Now the great distinction should be, and we should understand it, that circumstances may arise which will require a different precept from that given at one time when another time comes. In the 22nd chapter of Luke, you will read that Jesus, just before he was taken by the men that came out to bring him before the judgment seat, cried out to his apostles: 'When I sent you without purse and scrip and shoes, lacked ye anything?' And they said, 'Nothing.' Then said he, 'But now, he that hath a purse let him take it, and likewise his scrip: and he that hath no sword, let him sell his garment, and buy one.' (Verses 35, 36.) Well, some people will say perhaps, then, the Lord is a changeable being. Not at all. The Lord always is like that. From the eternities that are past down to the present, when circumstances change, he adapts his laws to the conditions and gives his people counsel and instructions suited to the times and circumstances." (Charles W. Penrose, *CR*, April 1917, pp. 20-22.)

"Perhaps Peter had met people who continued to trespass against him, and he asked: 'Lord, how oft shall my brother sin against me, and I forgive him?' (Matt. 18:21.) And the Lord said: 'I say not unto thee, Until seven times: but, Until seventy times seven.' (*Ibid.*, 18:22.) '. . . and as oft as thine enemy repenteth of the trespass wherewith he has trespassed against thee, thou shalt forgive him, until seventy times seven.' (D&C 98:40.) Until seventy times seven! That seems very difficult indeed for us mortals, and yet there are still harder things to do. When they have repented and come on their knees to ask forgiveness, most of us can forgive, but the Lord has required that we shall even forgive them if they do not repent nor ask forgiveness of us.

"In D&C Sec. 98:41-45, he said: [quoted.]

" 'And if he do this, thou shalt forgive him with all thine heart'; we must still forgive. The Lord will avenge us. 'Vengeance is mine; I will repay, saith the Lord' (Rom. 12:19) and man must not seek vengeance nor retaliate against those who have damaged him. Bitterness injures the one who carries it more than the one against whom it is directed." (Spencer W. Kimball, *CR,* September 1949, pp. 129-30.)

"There are, however, two conditions which may justify a truly Christian man to enter—mind you, I say *enter, not begin*—a war: (1) An attempt to dominate and to deprive another of his free agency, and, (2) Loyalty to his country. Possibly there is a third, viz., Defense of a weak nation that is being unjustly crushed by a strong, ruthless one.

"Paramount among these reasons, of course, is the defense of man's freedom. An attempt to rob man of his free agency caused dissension even in heaven. . . .

"To deprive an intelligent human being of his free agency is to commit the crime of the ages. . . .

"So fundamental in man's eternal progress is his inherent right to choose, that the Lord would defend it even at the price of war. Without freedom of thought, freedom of choice, freedom of action within lawful bounds, man cannot progress. . . .

"The greatest responsibility of the state is to guard the lives, and to protect the property and rights of its citizens; and if the state is obligated to protect its citizens from lawlessness within its boundaries, it is equally obligated to protect them from lawless encroachments from without— whether the attacking criminals be individuals or nations." (David O. McKay, *CR,* April 1942, pp. 72-73.)

"Does the Lord permit the shedding of blood and justify it? Yes, sometimes he does. Was not the war of independence of this country justifiable? Were not the rights and privileges of the people of this land trampled under foot, and did they not rise in their might and the God of Battles strengthen their arms and they went forth to victory and brought liberty, not only to themselves and their immediate families, but to hosts of people from down-trodden Europe who are rejoicing today under the Stars and Stripes with liberty of conscience and liberty of speech and liberty of action within proper guidance and direction of righteous law. . . .

". . . Now if a nation essays to go forth against another nation for the purpose of conquest, to gain territory, to grasp something that does not belong to that nation, then the nation thus assailed has the right to resist even to the shedding of blood, as it was in this land in the war for independence. But we have to be careful as to what spirit we are guided by. If we want to go out to battle, to encroach upon other people's liberties and rights, to gain their lands, to destroy their property without any right or reason, that is one thing; but if somebody comes against us to destroy us and our property and our homes and our rights and our privileges, either on land or sea, then we have the right under the divine law to rise for our own protection and take such steps as are necessary." (Charles W. Penrose, *CR,* April 1917, pp. 20-21.)

98:45 *"forgive him with all thine heart"*

"Remember that we must forgive even if our offender did not repent and ask forgiveness. . . .

"It frequently happens that offenses are committed when the offender is not aware of it. Something he has said or done is misconstrued or misunderstood. The offended one treasures in his heart the offense, adding to it such other things as might give fuel to the fire and justify his conclusions. Perhaps this is one of the reasons why the Lord requires that the offended one should make the overtures toward peace. . . .

"Do we follow that commandment or do we sulk, in our bitterness, waiting for our offender to learn of it and to kneel to us in remorse? And this reconciliation suggests also forgetting. Unless you forget, have you forgiven?

"The Lord forgets when he has forgiven, and certainly must we. He inspired Isaiah to say: 'I, even I, am he that blotted out thy transgressions for mine own sake, and will not remember thy sins.' (Isaiah 43:25.)

"And again in our dispensation, he said: 'Behold, he who has repented of his sins, the same is forgiven; and I, the Lord, remember them no more.' (D&C 58:42.)

"And we are instructed by him that: '. . . thou shalt forgive him with all thine heart. . . .' (D&C 98:45.)

"No bitterness of past frictions can be held in memory if we forgive with all our hearts." (Spencer W. Kimball, *CR*, September 1949, pp. 132-33.)

98:47 *"might, mind, and strength"*

See *Might, mind, and strength* in Appendix A.

SECTION 99

"This is a Revelation calling Elder John Murdock to go on a mission to the Eastern States. He was one of the men who received the gospel in Kirtland when Oliver Cowdery and companions passed through that city on the first western journey to the Lamanites, and together with Sidney Rigdon, Edward Partridge, Isaac Morley, Lyman Wight, and others, he was called to the ministry at that time. He held many important positions in the Church and discharged his duties faithfully. One of his children, Joseph S., died at the age of eleven months, as a result of exposure during the night of mob assault upon the Prophet at Hiram. Emma Smith, the Prophet's wife, had given birth to twins on the 30th of April, 1831. On the same date the home of the Murdocks had been blessed with twin children, Joseph S. and Julia. Sister Emma Smith's babies lived but three hours, and, when Sister Murdock passed away, Sister Emma took the motherless infants to rear. During the mob outrage, the infant boy contracted a cold that ended fatally, a few days later. . . .

". . . John Murdock was a member of Zion's camp, and made the journey to Zion in that choice company of men. In 1834, he was appointed a member of the High Council in Clay County, and in 1837, of the High Council in Far West. In 1838, he and George M. Hinckle, as trustees for the Church, purchased a townsite at De Witt, on the Missouri River, and in 1842, he was appointed Bishop of the Nauvoo Fifth Ward." (Smith and Sjodahl, *DCC*, p. 629.)

99:1 *"my servant John Murdock"*

See background information for this section.

99:4 *"whoso rejecteth you shall be rejected of my Father"*

"Who have rejected this gospel? The indifferent, those who would not take the trouble to investigate it, those who would not take the trouble to bow in submission before the

Lord and ask His testimony concerning it, those who thought it beneath them, those who have been too proud, or too rich or too well situated or who for some other reason, have failed to take any interest in this work; these are they who are not members of this Church and who have failed to obey this gospel when they heard it preached in its simplicity and its purity amongst the nations of the earth. . . . There will be a heavy condemnation fall upon this generation because of their inattention to these things. Judgments and calamities will be visited upon the inhabitants of the earth in consequence of neglecting the word of God written in the Scriptures, and also the word of God to His servants in these days." (George Q. Cannon, *JD* 20:248.)

99:4 *"cleanse your feet"*

See *Feet* in Appendix A.

99:8 *"continue proclaiming my gospel"*

See *Missionary service* in Appendix A.

SECTION 100

Background information on section 100

"The Prophet felt that the field of souls was white for the harvest and that it was incumbent upon him to thrust in his sickle and gather the honest-in-heart. On the 5th day of October, 1833, he departed from Kirtland upon a missionary journey to Canada, in company with Sidney Rigdon and Freeman A. Nickerson. At various places on the road, they stopped and proclaimed the word of the Lord unto the inhabitants. In some villages they found God-fearing men and women who were praying for light and were willing to obey when the simple gospel was presented before the eyes of their understanding. On the 12th day of October they had arrived at Perrysburg, New York, where they halted for a little time. Here the Prophet received a revelation [Sec. 100] in which the Lord instructed him that Zion must be chastened yet for a season, although she would finally be redeemed." (George Q. Cannon, *LJS*, p. 142.)

"It is a very striking fact that The Church of Jesus Christ of Latter-day Saints, ever since its organization, has proceeded on its onward course, no matter what the outward circumstances have been. There has been no turning back, no hesitation, no vacillation. As a mighty ship with its precious cargo, it has steered straight for the goal. The wind may have been adverse at times; the waves may have been breaking over it from stem to stern; it may have been assailed by hostile craft from above and from below, and from all sides. There may have been disaffection and even mutiny among the crew, but the command has always sounded clear and high above the storm and the din of conflict. 'Forward, full speed!'

"These reflections are suggested by the fact that while the enemies in Missouri were gathering their lawless forces for an assault upon the Church there, the Lord inspired the Prophet Joseph to go on a mission and proclaim the gospel message. He was not to mind the enemies. His calling was to testify to the world. And he went on this mission as far as Canada, as full of faith and hope as if there had been no storm-clouds in the sky. What a testimony to his divine commission!" (Smith and Sjodahl, *DCC,* p. 630.)

100:1-2   *"your families are well; they are in mine hands"*

"As regards the circumstances of their [missionaries'] families, it is proper and correct that men should have some feelings for those they have left at home. It is true there ought to be sympathy and some care for those with whom they have been immediately associated; yet their families as well as our families, and all of us and our affairs are in the hands of God, and, inasmuch as they go forth putting their trust in the living God all will be peace, and they will find peace and contentment from this time forth until they return, inasmuch as they will magnify their callings and lean upon their God." (John Taylor, *JD* 10:37.)

100:7   *"in solemnity of heart"*

One definition of *solemn* is "marked by grave sedateness and earnest serious sobriety." The eternal truths of the gospel of Jesus Christ should be spoken in reverence, dignity, earnestness, seriousness, with deep and sincere feeling—in solemnity of heart.

100:9   *"my servant Sidney, should be a spokesman unto this people"*

"He [Sidney Rigdon] was baptized in the town of Kirtland, and the foundation of a great work was laid there. God afterwards revealed that this man was to be a spokesman, and he became the spokesman to this people and to the world for the Prophet Joseph. Those who knew Sidney Rigdon, know how wonderfully God inspired him, and with what wonderful eloquence he declared the word of God to the people. He was a mighty man in the hands of God, as a spokesman, as long as the prophet lived, or up to a short time before his death. Thus you see that even this which many might look upon as a small matter, was predicted about 1,700 years before the birth of the Saviour, and was quoted by Lehi 600 years before the same event, and about 2,400 years before its fulfillment [2 Nephi 3:18], and was translated by the power of God, through his servant Joseph, as was predicted should be the case." (George Q. Cannon, *JD* 25:126-27.)

100:10 *Joseph Smith to be "mighty in testimony"*

"The Prophet Joseph was indeed 'mighty in testimony.' As one who had seen the heavens opened and heard the voice of God, the Father, and His Son, and had conversed with angels, he could 'testify,' and his words had the force of those of an eye witness. Parley P. Pratt says that 'even his most bitter enemies were overcome generally if he could once get their ears.' " (Smith and Sjodahl, *DCC*, p. 633.)

"In one of those tedious nights, [in a Richmond, Mo. jail] we had lain as if in sleep till the hour of midnight had passed, and our ears and hearts had been pained, while we had listened for hours to the obscene jests, the horrid oaths, the dreadful blasphemies and filthy language of our guards, Colonel Price at their head, as they recounted to each other their deeds of rapine, murder, robbery, etc., which they had committed among the 'Mormons' while at Far West and vicinity. They even boasted of defiling by force wives, daughters and virgins, and of shooting or dashing out the brains of men, women and children.

"I had listened till I became so disgusted, shocked, horrified, and so filled at the spirit of indignant justice that I could scarcely refrain from rising upon my feet and rebuking the guards: but had said nothing to Joseph [Smith], or any one else, although I lay next to him and knew he was awake. On a sudden he arose to his feet, and spoke in a voice of thunder, or as the roaring lion, uttering, as near as I can recollect, the following words:

" 'SILENCE, ye fiends of the infernal pit! In the name of Jesus Christ I rebuke you and command you to be still; I will not live another minute and hear such language. Cease such talk, or you or I die THIS INSTANT!'

"He ceased to speak. He stood erect in terrible majesty. Chained, and without a weapon; calm, unruffled and dignified as an angel, he looked upon the quailing guards, whose weapons were lowered or dropped to the ground; whose knees smote together and who, shrinking into a corner, or crouching at his feet, begged his pardon, and remained quiet till a change of guards.

"I have seen the ministers of justice, clothed in magisterial robes, and criminals arraigned before them, while life was suspended on a breath, in the Courts of England; I have witnessed a Congress in solemn session to give laws to nations; I have tried to conceive of kings, of royal courts, of thrones and crowns; and of emperors assembled to decide the fate of kingdoms; but dignity and majesty have I seen but once, as it stood in chains, at midnight, in a dungeon in an obscure village of Missouri." (Parley P. Pratt, *APPP*, pp. 210-11.)

100:14   *"my servants, Orson Hyde and John Gould, are in my hands"*

For biographical information on Orson Hyde, see Appendix B.

"About this time, Elders [Orson] Hyde and [John] Gould arrived in Zion, and the Church having made the necessary preparations, Elders W. W. Phelps and Orson Hyde were dispatched to the Governor of Missouri [Daniel Dunklin], residing at Jefferson City, the capital of the state, with the following: [Petition setting forth the outrages committed by mobs against the Saints]." (Joseph Smith, *HC* 1:410-15.)

100:15   *"to them that walk uprightly"*

"When you are in the line of your duty it is like standing in front of a line of posts, and every post is in line. But step one step aside, and every post looks as though it were not quite in line. The farther you get away from that straight line, the more crooked the posts will appear. It is the straight and narrow path of duty that will lead you and me back to the presence of God." (Heber J. Grant, *CR*, October 1935, p. 5.)

SECTION 101

Background information on section 101

"In Section 97 the Lord declares that if Zion will do his will she shall prosper, but if not then she shall be visited by sore affliction, pestilence, plague, sword, vengeance and devouring fire. When this was uttered the trouble between the Saints and the Missourians was on and some of the Saints had been driven from their homes." (Joseph Fielding Smith, *CHMR* 1:459.)

"In this letter to the scattered Saints in Missouri, dated December 10th, 1833, the Prophet stated that the spirit withheld from him definite knowledge of the reason why the calamity had fallen upon Zion. Here is another striking evidence of his sincerity. If he had been in the habit of writing revelations without divine inspiration, he could have done so at this time. But it is perfectly evident that he did not speak in the name of the Lord except when prompted to do so by the Spirit. On the 16th of December, however, this Revelation was received concerning the Saints in Zion." (Smith and Sjodahl, *DCC,* p. 637.)

"Thursday night, the 31st of October [1833], gave the Saints in Zion abundant proof that no pledge on the part of their enemies, written or verbal, was longer to be regarded; for on that night, between forty and fifty persons in number, many of whom were armed with guns, proceeded against a branch of the Church, west of the Big Blue, and unroofed and partly demolished ten dwelling houses; and amid the shrieks and screams of the women and children, whipped and beat in a savage and brutal manner, several of the men: while their horrid threats frightened women and children into the wilderness. . . . On Friday, the first of November, women and children sallied forth from their gloomy retreats, to contemplate with heartrending anguish the ravages of a ruthless mob, in the lacerated and bruised bodies of their husbands, and in the destruction of their houses, and their furniture. Houseless and unprotected by the arm of the civil law in Jackson county, the dreary month of November staring them in the face and loudly proclaiming an inclement season at hand; the continual threats of the mob that they would drive every 'Mormon' from the county; and the inability of many to move, because of their poverty, caused an anguish of heart indescribable.

"On Friday night, the 1st of November, a party of the mob proceeded to attack a branch of the Church settled on the prairie, about twelve or fourteen miles from the town of Independence. . . .

"The same night, (Friday), another party in Independence commenced stoning houses, breaking down doors and windows and destroying furniture. . . .

"Thursday, November 7th, the shores of the Missouri river began to be lined on both sides of the ferry, with men, women and children; goods, wagons, boxes, chests, and provisions; while the ferrymen were busily employed in crossing them over. When night again closed upon the Saints, the wilderness had much the appearance of a camp meeting. Hundreds of people were seen in every direction; some in tents, and some in the open air, around their fires, while the rain descended in torrents. Husbands were inquiring for their wives, and women for their husbands; parents for children, and children for parents. Some had the good fortune to escape with their families, household goods, and some provisions; while others knew not the fate of their friends, and had lost all their effects. The scene was indescribable, and would have melted the hearts of any people upon earth, except the blind oppressor, and the prejudiced and ignorant bigot. . . .

"The Saints who fled from Jackson county, took refuge in the neighboring counties, chiefly in Clay county, the inhabitants of which received them with some degree of kindness. Those who fled to the county of Van Buren were again driven, and compelled to flee, and these who fled to Lafayette county, were soon expelled, or the most of them, and had to move wherever they could find protection." (Joseph Smith, *HC* 1:426-27, 437-38.)

101:3 *"I shall come to make up my jewels"*

See material for D&C 60:4.

"This does not refer to the day of final judgment but to the day of the restoration of the Earth to its lawful Ruler and King, our Lord Jesus Christ. (See Malachi 3:16-18). On that day, the Lord will own them and value them as jewels." (Smith and Sjodahl, *DCC*, p. 637.)

101:4 *"must . . . be chastened and tried, even as Abraham"*

The story of Abraham and Isaac is recorded in Genesis 22:1-19.

"The sacrifice required of Abraham in the offering up of Isaac, shows that if a man would attain to the keys of the kingdom of an endless life, he must sacrifice all things. When God offers a blessing or knowledge to a man, and he refuses to receive it, he will be damned." (Joseph Smith, *HC* 5:555.)

"Here comes the command of God to this man [Abraham] who has been taught so scrupulously about the sinfulness of murder and human sacrifice, to do these very things. Now, why did the Lord ask such things of Abraham? Because, knowing what his future would be and that he would be the father of an innumerable posterity, he was determined to test him. God did not do this for His own sake; for He knew by His foreknowledge what Abraham would do [Abr. 1:22-23]; but the purpose was to impress upon Abraham a lesson, and to enable him to attain unto knowledge that he could not obtain in any other way. That is why God tries all of us. It is not for His own knowledge for He knows all things beforehand. He knows all your lives and everything you will do. But He tries us for our own good, that we may know ourselves, for it is most important that a man should know himself. He required Abraham to submit to this trial because he intended to give him glory, exaltation and honor; He intended to make him a king and a priest, to share with Himself the glory, power and dominion which He exercised." (George Q. Cannon, *CR*, April 1899, pp. 66-67.)

101:5 *"those who will not endure chastening, but deny me, cannot be sanctified."*

See *Adversity* and *Sanctify* in Appendix A.

101:6 *"they polluted their inheritances"*

"An attempt to rear the New Jerusalem was made in the

summer of 1831, a colony approximating fifteen hundred men, women and children, settling for that purpose in Jackson County, Missouri (Sec. 45:64-71), upon lands purchased from the Federal Government. Ground was consecrated, and a City laid out, including the site for a Temple. But a lack of the perfect unity necessary on the part of these selected for this sacred task, prevented its accomplishment at that time: [Sec. 101:6, quoted.] Forewarned by the Prophet of what would result if these evils were not corrected [Sec. 84:54-59], the colonists did not as a whole pay sufficient heed to the admonition, and the Lord permitted their enemies to come upon them and drive them from 'the goodly land.' " (Orson F. Whitney, SNT, pp. 181-82.)

101:10-12 *"the sword of mine indignation"*

See *Sword* in Appendix A.

"While there was punishment in the suffering the Saints had to endure and that because they were slow to hear the Lord, nevertheless the actions of their enemies were not justifiable; and therefore the Lord promised that he would let fall the sword of his indignation in behalf of his people. [Sec. 101:11-12, quoted.] The sword of indignation commenced to fall upon the enemies of the saints shortly after the saints were driven from Missouri, and from time to time it has fallen, both in this land, [and] in foreign lands." (Joseph Fielding Smith, *CHMR* 2:216.)

101:11 *"cup of their iniquity"*

When people disobey the commandments of God so long and so extensively that the law of justice requires payment, those people are "ripened in iniquity" (1 Ne. 17:35; Ether 2:9; 9:10), or the "cup of their iniquity" is full. Such people might also be referred to as "drunken with iniquity" (2 Ne. 27:1), "fully ripe in iniquity" (2 Ne. 28:16), and having "waxed strong in iniquity" (Alma 13:17); they are also in the "bonds of iniquity" (Alma 41:11).

101:18 *"They that . . . are pure in heart shall return"*

"We are going back to Jackson county, Missouri, one of these days. . . . The day will come when Latter-day Saints will be selected—all may not be called at once, but those who are worthy will be called." (George Q. Cannon, *CR,* April 1898, p. 14.)

"We talk about going back to build up the center (stake) of Zion; it is the burden of our daily prayers. The aspirations of thousands of the people ascend in the ears of the Lord of Saboath in behalf of the redemption of Zion, and that the purposes of God may be forwarded, and that the time may soon come when the center stake of Zion shall be built up and the people be prepared to go back and inhabit that land. Why do we wish this? Because we anticipate when that day shall come that we will be that much nearer the day of triumph, the day when Jesus will come and reign among his Saints. . . .

"The spot has been designated, and we look forward with peculiar feelings to repossessing that land. We expect when that day shall come that we will be a very different people to what we are today. . . . We expect that a society will be organized there that will be a pattern of heavenly society, that when Jesus and his heavenly beings who come with him are revealed in the clouds of heaven, their feelings will not be shocked by the change, for a society will be organized on the earth whose members will be prepared through the revelations of God to meet and associate with them, if not on terms of perfect equality, at least with some degree of equality." (George Q. Cannon, *JD* 11:336-37.)

101:21 *"Until . . . there is found no more room for them"*

"Zion will extend, eventually, all over this earth. There will be no nook or corner upon the earth but what will be a Zion. It will all be Zion." (Brigham Young, *JD* 9:138.)

101:22 *"stand in holy places"*

See *Stand ye in holy places* in Appendix A.

101: 23-31 *Conditions during the Millennium*

See *Millennium* in Appendix A.

101:23 *"all flesh shall see me together"*

"Jesus will come in a cloud, or as is expressed in the 40th chapter of Isaiah—'The glory of the Lord will be revealed and all flesh shall see it together.' It is also expressed in the revelations of St. John, that when he comes in a cloud every eye shall see him, and they also which pierced him. [Rev. 1:7.] It seems then that the second advent of the Son of God is to be something . . . accompanied with great power and glory, something that will not be done in a small portion of the earth like Palestine, and seen only by a few; but it will be an event that will be seen by all—all flesh shall see the glory of the Lord; when he reveals himself the second time, every eye, not only those living at that time in the flesh, in mortality on the earth, but also the very dead themselves." (Orson Pratt, *JD* 18:170.)

101:25 *"all things shall become new"*

See *New heaven and a new earth* in Appendix A.

101:26 *"enmity of all flesh shall cease"*

"The enmity of the beasts of the field as well as that of all flesh will cease; no more one beast of prey devouring and feasting upon another that is more harmless in its nature; no more will this enmity be found in the fish of the sea or in the birds of the air. This change will be wrought upon all flesh when Jesus comes; not a change to immortality, but a change sufficient to alter the ferocious nature of beasts, birds and fishes. In those days the lion will eat straw like the ox; he will no more be the terror of the forest, but will be perfectly harmless, and gentleness will characterize all the wild and ferocious animals, as well as the venomous serpents, so much so that the little child might lead them and play with them, and nothing shall hurt or destroy in all the holy mountain of the Lord, all things becoming, in some measure, as when they were first created." (Orson Pratt, *JD* 20:18.)

101:28 *"Satan shall not have power"*

See *Satan* and *Millennium* in Appendix A.

101:28-31 *"an infant shall not die until he is old"*

"The children that shall grow up unto the Lord shall not taste of death; that is, they shall not sleep in the earth, but they shall be changed in a moment, in the twinkling of an eye, and they shall be caught up, and their rest shall be glorious. I thus distinguish between them and us, because at that time they shall grow up with a more complete and perfect understanding of the laws of life and health, and they will observe them. And temptations and evils that surround us on every hand shall be removed from them. . . . Hence their tabernacles shall not be subject to pain and sickness like unto ours." (Erastus Snow, *JD* 7:355-56.)

101: *"the Lord . . . shall reveal all things"*
32-34

Evidently the present theories of man as to how the earth was created are not true, for when the Savior comes in power and glory he will reveal "hidden things which no man knew, things of the earth, by which it was made, and the purpose and the end thereof." (D&C 101:33.)

"There is an eternity before us, and it is full of matter; and if we but understand enough of the Lord and his ways, we would say that he took of this matter and organized this earth from it. How long it has been organized it is not for me to say, and I do not care anything about it . . . whether he made it in six days or in as many millions of years, is and will remain a matter of speculation in the minds of men unless he gives revelation on the subject." (Brigham Young, *JD* 14:116.)

101:37 *"care not for the body . . . but care for the soul"*

See material for D&C 88:15.

"Have I not told you often that the separation of body and spirit makes no difference in the moral and intellectual condition of the spirit? When a person who has always been good and faithful to his God, lays down his body in the dust, his spirit will remain the same in the spirit world. It is not the body that has control over the spirit, as to its disposition, but it is the spirit that controls the body. When the spirit leaves the body the body becomes lifeless, the spirit has not changed one single particle of itself by leaving the body." (Heber C. Kimball, *JD* 3:108.)

101:38 *"eternal life"*

See *Eternal life* in Appendix A.

101:39 *"salt of the earth and the savor of man"*

See *Salt and savor* in Appendix A.

101: *Parable of the nobleman, his servants, and his vineyard*
43-62

See *Parables* in Appendix A. This parable of the Lord concerned the situation then in Missouri, and the Lord said it was his "will concerning the redemption of Zion." (D&C 101:43.)

"In a revelation given December 16, 1833, the Lord in a parable spoke of the conditions in Missouri. A certain nobleman had a spot of land and he sent his servants in this choice land, and set watchmen round about and to build a tower for the protection of the land. While the workmen were yet building they questioned the need of the tower and said that the money required to build it could be put to better purpose. While they were at variance the enemy came by night and broke down the hedge and the servants were scattered. The Lord then commanded one of his servants to go and gather together the residue of his servants and go straightway to the land of his vineyard, for it was his; he had purchased it. They were to break down the walls of his enemies and possess the land." (Joseph Fielding Smith, *CHMR* 3:18.)

"The vineyard—in this Revelation, the vineyard is regarded as separate from the olive grove, for the nobleman planted olive trees in his vineyard, doubling its value.

"Build a tower—The safety of the settlement of the Saints depends on the Temple, or rather on the power of God manifest in His holy House.

"While they were at variance . . . slothful—This never fails. Strife always engenders slothfulness and neglect of duty.

"Watchmen upon the walls—Watchmen upon the tower or walls, has reference to those who are appointed to positions of responsibility. The watchman on the tower is the presiding officer in the stake, ward or community.

"Unto one of his servants—The Prophet Joseph (see Sec. 103:21).

"Redeem my vineyard—The Prophet Joseph is commanded to gather up a company of men, faithful and true, and proceed to Zion and scatter the enemies; but he was not to make war upon them, but redeem the land by purchase (see Sec. 103:23).

"After many days—The Prophet did as directed by Revelation, and in due time 'all things were fulfilled.' " (Smith and Sjodahl, *DCC*, p. 648.)

101:63-67   *The gathering of Israel is according to the parable of the wheat and the tares*

See *Parables* and *Tares* in Appendix A.

101:64   *"time of harvest is come"*

See *Harvest symbols* in Appendix A.

101:66   *"unquenchable fire"*

See *Everlasting fire* in Appendix A.

101:76, 81-95   *"continue to importune for redress . . . of those . . . in authority over you"*

"The Saints were also to carry their grievances to the proper tribunals and seek for redress of their wrongs. This was a very necessary step, and when the Saints did this and were denied their civil and religious rights, those officials were left without excuse and the judgments of the Almighty which later came upon them during the Civil War, were justified. . . .

"Since there is a just law of retribution, as fixed and eternal as are other laws of the Almighty [Sec. 6:33; 2 Cor. 9:6], the day must come when there shall be adjustments made before a Just Magistrate who will not be cowed by the threats of mobs." (Joseph Fielding Smith, *CHMR* 2:218, 224.)

101:80   *"I raised up [wise men] unto this very purpose"*

"We know the signers of the sacred Declaration of Independence and the Founding Fathers, with George Washington at their head, have made appearance in holy places. Apostle Wilford Woodruff was president of the St. George Temple at the time of their appearance and testified that the founders of our republic declared this to him: 'We laid the foundation of the government you now enjoy, and we never apostatized from it, but we remained true to it and were faithful to God.' (*Journal of Discourses,* 19:229.) . . .

"Yes, I thank God for the sacrifices and efforts made by these Founding Fathers, whose efforts have brought us the blessings of political liberty and economic prosperity we have today." (Ezra Taft Benson, *Ensign,* November 1976, p. 34.)

"I am going to bear my testimony to this assembly, if I never do it again in my life, that those men who laid the foundation of this American government and signed the Declaration of Independence were the best spirits the God of heaven could find on the face of the earth. They were choice spirits, not wicked men. General Washington and all the men that labored for the purpose were inspired of the Lord.

"Another thing I am going to say here, because I have a right to say it. Every one of those men that signed the Declaration of Independence, with General [George] Washington, called upon me, as an Apostle of the Lord Jesus Christ, in the Temple at St. George, two consecutive nights and demanded at my hands that I should go forth and attend to the ordinances of the House of God for them. Men are here, I believe, that know of this, Brother J. D. T. McAllister, David H. Cannon and James G. Bleak. Brother McAllister baptized me for all those men and I told those brethren that it was their duty to go into the Temple and labor until they had got endowments for all of them. They did it. Would those spirits have called upon me, as an Elder in Israel, to perform that work if they had not been noble spirits before God? They would not.

"I bear this testimony, because it is true. The Spirit of God bore record to myself and the brethren while we were laboring in that way." (Wilford Woodruff, *CR,* April 1898, pp. 89-90.)

101:77-80 *"I established the Constitution of this land"*

See *Constitution* in Appendix A.

"To me . . . that statement of the Lord, 'I have established the Constitution of this land,' puts the Constitution of the United States in the position in which it would be if it were written in the book of Doctrine and Covenants itself. This makes the Constitution the word of the Lord to us. That it was given, not by oral utterance, but by the operation of his mind and spirit upon the minds of men, inspiring them to the working out of this great document of human government, does not alter its authority." (J. Reuben Clark, Jr., *CR,* April 1935, pp. 93-94.)

"I regard as essential to the welfare of this country the things contained in the Constitution of our land. Of course it may be amended, but amending the Constitution and ripping it up the back and tearing out its vitals are two different things. We want to stand by the Constitution in its spirit and meaning and intent, and in the fundamental parts thereof." (Charles W. Penrose, *CR,* October 1912, pp. 67-68.)

101:77 *"for the rights and protection of all flesh"*

"In section 101 the Lord speaks about the constitution of this land. He says it was framed by wise men whom he raised up for that very purpose. What for? To maintain the rights and privileges '*of all flesh.*' Not alone the people of this land. The principles of that great instrument are to go forth to the nations, and the time will come when they will prevail, just as sure as the sun shines even when it appears to be in darkness and the clouds are over it." (Charles W. Penrose, *CR,* April 1917, p. 20.)

101: 81-85 *Parable of the woman and the unjust judge*

See *Parables* in Appendix A.

The Lord indicated that he would liken "the children of Zion" unto this parable. The widow in the parable is evidently representative of the children of Zion (members of the Church), while the unjust judge is representative of the various state and national leaders who had it in their power to redress the wrongs of the Saints (children of Zion), but refused to do so.

101:95 *"my act, my strange act, and . . . my work, my strange work"*

See material for D&C 95:4.

"The Lord has said by the mouth of the Prophet Isaiah, that he would proceed to do a marvelous work and a wonder [Isa. 29:14]; and when I look at the rise and progress of this Church, when I behold the great work the Lord has performed, it was a marvelous work and a wonder indeed. . . . This is certainly a strange work and a wonder. There has been every exertion made to stay it. Armies have been sent forth to destroy this people; but we have been upheld and sustained by the hand of the Lord until today." (Wilford Woodruff, *JD* 21:124-25.)

101:96 *"Sidney Gilbert"*

For biographical information on Sidney Gilbert, see Appendix B.

SECTION 102

Background information on section 102

"At a council of the High Priests and Elders, (Orson Hyde, clerk,) at my house in Kirtland, on the evening of the 12th of February, I remarked that I should endeavor to set before the council the dignity of the office which had been conferred on me by the ministering of the angel of God, by His own voice, and by the voice of this Church; that I had never set before any council in all the order in which it ought to be conducted, which, perhaps, has deprived the councils of some or many blessings.

"And I continued and said, no man is capable of judging a matter, in council, unless his own heart is pure; and that we are frequently so filled with prejudice, or have a beam in our own eye, that we are not capable of passing right decisions.

"Our acts are recorded, and at a future day they will be laid before us, and if we should fail to judge right and injure our fellow-beings, they may there, perhaps, condemn us; there they are of great consequence, and to me the consequence appears to be of force, beyond anything which I am able to express. Ask yourselves, brethren, how much you have exercised yourselves in prayer since you heard of this council; and if you are now prepared to sit in council upon the soul of your brother.

"On the 18th of January I reviewed and corrected the minutes of the organization of the High Council, and on the 19th of February, the Council assembled according to adjournment, from the 17th, (Oliver Cowdery and Orson Hyde, clerks,) when the revised minutes were presented and read to the Council. I urged the necessity of prayer, that the Spirit might be given, that the things of the Spirit might be judged thereby, because the carnal mind cannot discern the things of God. The minutes were read three times, and unanimously adopted and received for a form and constitution of the High Council of the Church of Christ hereafter; with this provision, that if the President should hereafter discover anything lacking in the same, he should be privileged to supply it." (Joseph Smith, *HC* 2:25-26, 31.)

"A few days before the organization of this High Council, the Prophet addressed a council of High Priests and Elders on the subject of the proper order in such gatherings. 'In ancient days,' he said, 'councils were conducted with such strict propriety, that no one was allowed to whisper, be weary, leave the room, or get uneasy in the least, until the voice of the Lord, by revelation, or the voice of the Council, by the Spirit, was obtained, which has not been observed in this Church to the present time' (*HC* 2:25)." (Smith and Sjodahl, *DCC*, p. 658.)

2:1-34   *Procedures governing "the high council of the church of Christ"*

"After giving . . . instruction the Prophet organized the first high council in the Church. There were twenty-four of the brethren present all of whom were high priests. The high council was appointed by revelation and the Lord pointed out the duties of such a council, which are to settle difficulties in the Church which could not be settled in a bishop's court. The First Presidency of the Church acted as the presidency of this high council which was given jurisdiction over the affairs in dispute, in all the Church. . . .

"It was voted that this council could not act without a majority of the members being present. Then if there were only seven they could appoint temporarily other priests (high priests) who were considered worthy to sit in the place of absent members. It was also voted that whenever any vacancy should occur by death or removal, the vacancy should be filled by the nomination of the president or presidents, and then sanctioned by the general council of high priests. The President of the Church was appointed by revelation to preside in this council, his counselors were chosen in like manner. In the absence of the president then the counselors had power to preside, both or either of them.

"The twelve councilors, when cases were brought before them, were to cast lots by numbers to ascertain which of the twelve should speak first, commencing with number one and so on in succession to number twelve. In simple cases only two would speak; if the cases were difficult then four would be appointed and in extreme cases six could speak, but never more than six. The accused was entitled to one-half of the council to watch his case to see that justice was given him, but every man was to speak according to equity and justice. The councilors who drew the even numbers were to stand in behalf of the accused. After the evidence was given the president would give his decision. A majority of the council was necessary to sustain a decision.

"When abroad a council of high priests could be called in difficult cases to sit in judgment. Written decisions by such councils were to be forwarded to the First Presidency of the Church. In case of a person being dissatisfied with a decision he had the right to appeal. When the twelve apostles sit as a high council no appeal can be taken from their decision, except it be in cases of transgression and then the matter is to be considered, if evidence warrants, by the general authorities of the Church.

"Immediately after the organization of this council there were several cases brought before it and decisions rendered. It might be considered in this day when we have a few high council trials, that many of the cases brought before this first high council were trivial in their nature. Today only major cases of transgression, seemingly, are considered by such bodies in the stakes of Zion." (Joseph Fielding Smith, *CHMR* 3:15-16.)

"Many high councils exist in the Church at the present time, there being one in every Stake of Zion. . . . The plan of settling disputes and preventing litigation among brethren, which the Prophet was then inspired to introduce [The high council, Nov. 17, 1834] has grown with the growth of the Church, and the high council has performed an important mission in the years which have followed. It has worked without fees; it has known no coercion; the honesty of its decisions have been beyond question; and often it has been appealed to by men not of the faith that their disputes might be settled with fairness and economy. It has never usurped the function of the criminal courts; it has never sought to enforce its judgment by any civil process. It has only decreed according to clear and unmistakable justice and has left the parties to accept the judgment, and if not complied with or appealed from, to have Church fellowship withdrawn from them. The rules which the Prophet established to control its proceedings under divine guidance were delivered to it at the time of organization, and they, speaking of all the high councils which have since been organized, are still governed by them." (George Q. Cannon, *LJS,* pp. 154-55.)

President Harold B. Lee has indicated some of the many duties of the present stake high councils throughout the Church:

"It is the most serious responsibility when they must sit as a court in judgment upon those who are living in defiance of the commandments. . . . But if this were the only thing that the high council had to do, they would not be too busy. I am sure they are not as busy as they ought to be in that field sometimes. . . . But most of their duties lie in . . . what we call 'semiadministrative' functions. . . . One of the most fundamental is to have, under the direction of the Presidency, the supervision of the Priesthood . . . to do for the Priesthood quorums supervising, training, doing all things necessary to strengthen the Priesthood. They are to look after the auxiliaries, to be advisors there, and then they have a responsibility between the presidency in the ward, and it is a very delicate relationship, and I have tried to word it carefully, they are to be 'contacts or intermediaries' to such extent as the presidency may direct. . . .

"They're to be home missionaries sent out once a month by the stake presidency to speak on subjects or to discuss matters that might be thought pertinent to the need at that time. This may be extended to any assignment that the Presidency wants to give. If we have a weak bishopric or weak branch presidency, the high council member may be assigned to actually live with that weak leader in the ward or branch to teach him his duties. He might go there as a watchman if it is understood that there are some doctrines being taught which are false. He might present himself at the Sacrament meeting, he might go to the gospel doctrine class or the Seventies class, wherever that may be reported, and he goes there to get the climate of the ward in order to be what the presidency has assigned him to be, a 'watchman on the tower' as it were.

"Now when you see the stake organization functioning that way, you see how important the work of the high council in today's organization becomes." (*CN,* Aug. 26, 1961, p. 11.)

SECTION 103

Background information on section 103

"In a previous Revelation (Section 101:55-60), it was made known to the Prophet that he would be required, at some future time, to lead 'the strength of mine house' to the land of Zion, in order to 'redeem' it. The Revelation in this Section was received four months and twelve days afterwards, directing him to begin to gather up the strength of the Church for a relief expedition. Elders Lyman Wight and Parley P. Pratt had just arrived in Kirtland, from Missouri, with a message from the Saints. A meeting of the High Council was called. The messengers from Zion told the Council that the scattered Saints had obtained food and clothing in exchange for labor, and that they were quite comfortable for the time being; but they were grief-stricken because they had been driven from their homes in Zion, and they earnestly desired to know, if possible, how and by what means Zion was to be redeemed. This Revelation, given before the meeting of the Council was held, is an answer to that very question. When the messengers had stated the case, the Prophet had the answer ready. He had prepared to announce that he was going to Zion and that he would call for volunteers to accompany him. The Council endorsed this, and between thirty and forty men volunteered to go, whereupon the Prophet Joseph was elected Commander-in-Chief of the expedition." (Smith and Sjodahl, *DCC,* pp. 659-60.)

"The high council of the Church met February 24, 1834, at the house of the Prophet for the purpose of receiving the message of Lyman Wight and Parley P. Pratt, delegates from the brethren in Missouri who came to Kirtland to report on conditions among the exiles driven from Jackson County. Hyrum Smith and Joseph Coe were appointed to act in the stead of John Smith and John P. Greene who were absent. When the council was called to order and prayer had been offered by the Prophet, these two brethren delivered their message in relation to the condition of the brethren in Clay

County, Missouri. They stated that the brethren there were anxious to know how and by what means Zion was to be redeemed. In Clay County they had been able to obtain food and raiment from the citizens in exchange for their labor, but the idea of being driven from their homes pained them, and they desired to know what the Lord would direct in the matter of reinstating them in their lands. None of them had broken their covenant by selling their lands, except William E. M'Lellin, who had sold into the hands of the enemy thirty acres, and he would have sold seven more acres if a brother had not come to the rescue and purchased them." (Joseph Fielding Smith, *CHMR* 1:481-82.)

"After making our escape into the county of Clay—being reduced to the lowest poverty—I made a living by day labor, jobbing, building, or wood cutting, till some time in the winter of 1834, when a general Conference was held at my house, in which it was decided that two of the Elders should be sent to Ohio, in order to counsel with President Smith and the Church at Kirtland, and take some measures for the relief or restoration of the people thus plundered and driven from their homes. The question was put to the Conference: 'Who would volunteer to perform so great a journey?'

"The poverty of all, and the inclement season of the year made all hesitate. At length Lyman Wight and myself offered our services, which were readily accepted. I was at this time entirely destitute of proper clothing for the journey; and I had neither horse, saddle, bridle, money nor provisions to take with me; or to leave with my wife, who lay sick and helpless most of the time.

"Under these circumstances I knew not what to do. Nearly all had been robbed and plundered, and all were poor. As we had to start without delay, I almost trembled at the undertaking; it seemed to be all but an impossibility; but 'to him that believeth all things are possible.'... We were soon ready, and on the first of February we mounted our horses, and started in good cheer to ride one thousand or fifteen hundred miles through a wilderness country. We had not one cent of money in our pockets on starting.

"We traveled every day, whether through storm or sunshine, mud, rain or snow; except when our public duties called us to tarry. We arrived in Kirtland early in the spring, all safe and sound; we had lacked for nothing on the road, and now had plenty of funds in hand. President Joseph Smith and the Church in Kirtland received us with a hospitality and joy unknown except among the Saints; and much interest was felt there, as well as elsewhere, on the subject of our persecution.

"The President inquired of the Lord concerning the matter, and a further mission was appointed us [Section 103]." (Parley P. Pratt, *APPP*, pp. 107-9.)

103:3 *"measure of their iniquities, that their cup might be full"*

See material for 101:11.

103:4 *"chastened for a little season"*

See *Season* in Appendix A.

"All this time the cry of the exiled Saints in Missouri was ascending to heaven for the redemption of their homes and for their own release from oppression. In a revelation given to the Prophet February 24, 1834, the Lord made known that the wicked had been permitted to fill up the measure of their iniquities that those who are called after His name might be chastened for a season; because in many things they had not hearkened unto His commandments." (George Q. Cannon, *LJS*, pp. 155-56.)

"The Lord here explains and describes to the Church very plainly the reasons why they were so grievously and severely chastened: [Sec. 103:5-10, quoted.]

"There cannot be a doubt in any faithful man's mind concerning the truth of this promise—the promise of victory and deliverance on the one hand, the promise of punishment, disaster and trouble on the other. The Latter-day Saints have in their experience proved fully the truth of these words. They have seen them fulfilled to the very letter. When they have been faithful in keeping the commandments of God they have prospered and they have had deliverance. When they have been unfaithful they have met with trouble and serious difficulty. It is necessary that the wicked should have the opportunity to exercise their agency in fighting the work of God. They have the privilege to do everything in their power to destroy it, and they will be permitted to do this until the cup of their iniquity is full." (George Q. Cannon, *CR*, October 1899, pp. 47-49.)

103:9 *"a light unto the world . . . saviors of men"*

See *Saviors* in Appendix A.

103:10 *"as salt that has lost its savor"*

See *Salt and savor* in Appendix A.

"The Latter-day Saints are called upon to obey the commandments of God. He has revealed Himself with power to them. He bears testimony to them all the time concerning His great work that He is seeking to establish in the earth. He wants to make us the saviors of men. He calls us the salt of the earth. We are the salt of the earth. We are not conceited in saying this, because the acts of the faithful Latter-day Saints are such as to bring salvation to those who are connected with them. I wish to illustrate this so that you can see it for yourselves. Look around you and see the men and the women who have proved themselves unworthy of the principles of the Gospel, and have departed from them. Are they not like salt that has lost its savor? We have had hundreds of them; they have got indifferent; they have lost their savor, and are good for nothing. The Saints are compared to salt that has its saving properties. [Sec. 101:39-40.] Wherever we go we should be saviors of men. We should seek for the salvation of the human family to the fullest extent in our power." (George Q. Cannon, *CR,* October 1899, pp. 47-49.)

103: 15-20 *"the redemption of Zion must needs come by power"*

"It appears from this declaration that the redemption of Zion was not to come immediately, but was to be postponed to some future day. Moreover, that day would not come until the members of the Church were willing to keep their covenants and walk unitedly, for until the members of the Church learn to walk in full accord and in obedience with all of the commandments, this day cannot come. It may be necessary in order to bring this to pass for the Lord to use drastic measures and cleanse the Church from everything that offends. This he has promised to do when he is ready to redeem Zion. (See Matt. 13:41.) Orson Pratt discoursing on the redemption of Zion said:

" 'When we go back to Jackson County, we are to go back with power. Do you suppose that God will reveal his power among an unsanctified people, who have no regard nor respect for his laws and institutions but who are filled with covetousness? No. When God shows forth his power among the Latter-day Saints, it will be because there is a union of feeling in regard to doctrine, and in regard to everything that God has placed in their hands; and not only a union, but a sanctification on their part, that there shall not be a spot or wrinkle as it were, but everything shall be as fair as the sun that shines in the heavens.' (JD 15:361.)" (Joseph Fielding Smith, *CHMR* 1:484.)

"I expect that when the Lord leads forth His people to build up the city of Zion, His presence will be visible. When we speak of the presence of the Lord we speak of an exhibition of power. . . . We shall go back to Jackson County. Not that all this people will leave these mountains, or all be gathered together in a camp, but when we go back there will be a very large organization consisting of thousands, and tens of thousands, and they will march forward, the glory of God overshadowing their camp by day in the form of a cloud, and a pillar of flaming fire by night, the Lord's voice being uttered forth before his army. Such a period will come in the history of this people . . . and his people will go forth and build up Zion according to celestial law." (Orson Pratt, *JD* 15:364.)

103:16 *"a man . . . like as Moses"*

"In modern revelation the President of the Church is frequently compared to Moses. Soon after the organization of the Church, the Lord said, 'No one shall be appointed to receive commandments and revelations in this Church excepting my servant, Joseph Smith, Jun., for he receiveth them even as Moses.' [D&C 28:2.] In one of the great revelations upon Priesthood, this is more specifically expressed: 'The duty of the President of the office of the High Priesthood is to preside over the whole church, and to be like unto Moses.' [D&C 107:91.] The discussion of this question among the Saints, led to the following statement in the Times and Seasons (6:922) by John Taylor, then the editor: 'The President (of the Church) stands in the Church as Moses did the children of Israel, according to the revelations.' The man like unto Moses in the Church is the President of the Church." (John A. Widtsoe, *ER*, p. 197.)

103:21 *"Joseph Smith is the man . . . in the parable"*

"In a revelation given December 16, 1833, the Lord in a parable spoke of the conditions in Missouri. . . . [Sec. 101:43-62.]

"In a revelation given February 24, 1834 [Sec. 103], the Lord referred to this former revelation and said that Joseph Smith (Baurak Ale) was the man to whom he likened the servant 'to whom the Lord of the vineyard spake in the parable which I have given unto you.' [Sec. 103:21.]" (Joseph Fielding Smith, *CHMR* 3:18.)

103:27 *"Let no man be afraid to lay down his life for my sake"*

"On the Sabbath day, February 8th, 1835, Joseph invited Brigham and Joseph Young to his home and listened to some of their sweetest hymns. . . . Joseph had seen in vision the brethren who had died of cholera in Missouri; and he related the vision to his visitors, saying: 'If I get a mansion as bright as theirs, I shall ask no more.' " (George Q. Cannon, *LJS*, p. 176.)

:29-30, 37-40 *For biographical information on persons mentioned in these verses, see Appendix B.*

:30-40 *Instructions pertaining to the organization of Zion's Camp*

"Parley P. Pratt and Lyman Wight, the messengers from the land of Zion, were commanded not to return until they had obtained companies to go up unto the land of their brethren. The companies were to be by tens, or by twenties, or by fifties, or by hundreds, until they had obtained the number of five hundred men. If they could not obtain five hundred they were to seek diligently to get three hundred, and if they could not obtain three hundred, then they were to obtain one hundred. They were not, however, to go up to the land of Zion until they had obtained at least one hundred. The Prophet Joseph was to go up with them and preside in their midst, for, [Sec. 103:36, quoted]. Parley P. Pratt was to go with Joseph Smith, the Prophet; Lyman Wight with Sidney Rigdon; Hyrum Smith with Frederick G. Williams; Orson Hyde with Orson Pratt, on this mission to raise funds and volunteers to undertake this journey to assist their exiled brethren in the land of Zion." (Joseph Fielding Smith, *CHMR* 3:20-21.)

SECTION 104

Background information on section 104

"April 23.—Assembled in Council with Elders Sidney Rigdon, Frederick G. Williams, Newel K. Whitney, John Johnson, and Oliver Cowdery; and united in asking the Lord to give Elder Zebedee Coltrin influence over Brother Jacob Myres, to obtain the money which he has gone to borrow for us, or cause him to come to this place and bring it himself. I also received the following: [D&C 104.]" (Joseph Smith, *HC* 2:54.)

"The Church being in dire distress financially, brethren had been sent out to see if they could not collect funds for its relief, both in Kirtland and for Zion. A strong appeal to Orson Hyde was issued April 7, 1834. (See *HC* 2:48.) In the minutes of the conference held at Norton, Medina County, Ohio, the deliverance of Zion was earnestly discussed. The Prophet Joseph Smith who was present said in the course of his remarks that 'if Zion is not delivered, the time is near when all of this Church, wherever they may be found, will be persecuted and destroyed in like manner'; that is in the manner in which the saints in Jackson County were destroyed. Destruction in this sense means to be persecuted, mobbed and scattered, their property being lost to them.

"On the 10th of April, a council of the United Order was held. It was there agreed that the Order, as it was then organized, be dissolved, and each member have his stewardship set off to him. Previously to this time, the United Order of Zion and of Kirtland stood as one unit. On April 23, 1834, the Prophet received an important revelation concerning the 'Order of the Church for the benefit of the poor.' (D&C 104.)" (Joseph Fielding Smith, *CHMR* 1:487.)

"Before the brethren of Zion's Camp were ready to begin the journey to Missouri, the Prophet received this Revelation concerning the property belonging to the United Order. This Order had been established by Revelation (See Sec. 82), and its temporal affairs were to be placed on a solid foundation, before the journey to Zion. The brethren were going to face the lion in his den. They did not know whether they would return. Heber C. Kimball says of the departure, on the 5th of May, 'Truly, this was a solemn morning to me. I took leave of my wife and children and friends, not knowing whether I would see them again in the flesh, as myself and brethren were threatened, both in that country and Missouri, by enemies, that they would destroy us and exterminate us from the land.' " (Smith and Sjodahl, *DCC*, p. 668.)

104:1   *"a united order, and an everlasting order for the benefit of my church"*

See *United Order* in Appendix A.

104:7   *"at my right hand"*

See *Right hand* in Appendix A.

04:9-10   *"buffetings of Satan"*

See *Satan* in Appendix A.

104: 11-12   *"stewardship"*

See *Steward* in Appendix A.

104:16   *"the poor shall be exalted"*

See *Poor* in Appendix A.

104:17   *"the earth is full, and there is enough and to spare"*

The Lord created the heavens and the earth and all things that are in them. (3 Ne. 9:15.) Also, God knows all things from the beginning of the earth to the end thereof. Thus, the Lord knows how many people are destined to live upon this earth, and he has provided resources whereby all their physical needs can be met if these resources are used properly.

104:20   *For information on the persons mentioned in this section, see Appendix B.*

For an explanation of the use of the unusual names and titles, see background information for section 78.

104: 20-42   *"stewards . . . stewardship"*

See *Steward* in Appendix A.

"Then, in the revelation the Lord assigns stewardships to many of the brethren. He commanded that there should be a separation of the United Order in Zion from the Order in Kirtland. Each was to act henceforth independently of the other. Distance was too great between these places for unity of purpose in all things. Each order was to be organized in the names of the brethren residing in each place, and to do business in their own names. This separation and dissolving of the former order came about also because of transgression and covetousness on the part of some. They were to understand that all the properties were the Lord's, otherwise their faith was vain, and therefore they were stewards before the Lord. All of this was to be done for the purpose of building up the Church and Kingdom of God on the earth, and to prepare the people for the time when the Lord should come to dwell upon the earth." (Joseph Fielding Smith, *CHMR* 1:489-90.)

104:31, 33-46   *"I will bless, and multiply blessings upon them"*

"Now some persons may begin to harrow up their feelings, and to cherish in their hearts murmurings because God in his providence and in his mercy and kindness, may begin to pour upon this man and upon that man blessings by which he accumulates wealth, and by which he is made comfortable and happy; they are envious and jealous. . . . If we envy those that are really beginning to participate a little in the inheritance of all things, is not this a strong presumptive evidence within ourselves that we are not heirs to all things, neither are we willing that our brethren should be.

"When a man of God is blessed from on high and shall begin to gather around him means sufficient to place him beyond the reach of immediate want, God hath done it—God hath blessed that person—and every Saint will feel thankful to see his brethren so prospered and blessed of the Lord, feeling encouraged that his time will come sometime if he continues faithful. . . .

"The Lord sees us all and knows what our feelings are— the very thoughts and intents of our hearts are laid bare before Him [Sec. 38:2], and when He sees that we are prepared to endure great earthly blessings, do you think that any trifling circumstance will cause him to delay and wait and put us off and make us wait for his blessings." (Orson Hyde, *JD* 10:263.)

104:43   *"Gazelam"*

For an explanation of this and other unusual names and titles, see background information on section 76. "He was also called Gazelam, being a person to whom the Lord had given the Urim and Thummim." (Orson Pratt, *JD* 16:156.)

104:66   *"the sacred treasury of the Lord"*

"As the plan developed the Lord provided for the establishment of a 'sacred treasury' [see Sec. 104:60-77] and 'another treasury' into which the general funds of the Church—the avails of the 'residues'—were to be paid and which were to be drawn upon for the immediate needs of the poor primarily and after that for the general needs of the Church. [D&C 104:67-69; 42:33-35.] It would seem that funds from the treasury for the improvement of the property of a stewardship might properly be granted under justifying circumstances. [D&C 104:62, 73; 58.]" (Albert E. Bowen, *Church Welfare Program*, pp. 9-10.)

"They were to prepare a treasury and a treasurer for the sacred things of the Church. One who was wise was to be appointed to this labor. Then again they were to have another treasury and treasurer to keep the moneys and properties of the Church. These men so appointed were to be trustworthy and fitted for their callings. A seal was to be placed upon each treasury. In the first, all the sacred documents, writings and all sacred things that should be preserved, should have a seal, which was to be placed upon them. In the second treasury should be placed the funds received from the people, which funds were to be used for holy and sacred purposes. [Sec. 104:60-69.]" (Joseph Fielding Smith, *CHMR* 3:25-26.)

104: 71-72   *"common consent of the order"*

See *Common consent* in Appendix A.

"All these things were to be done by common consent. There were to be no dictators in the management of the Lord's business. No part of the funds or property could be taken out of the treasury without the voice of the order. If any man among them should declare, I have need of this to help me in my stewardship, if it be five talents, or ten talents (dollars) or whatever the amount his claim might be it was to be investigated and if found to be worthy the request would be granted. This had to be, however, by the common consent." (Joseph Fielding Smith, *CHMR* 3:25-26.)

104:78 *"it is my will that you shall pay all your debts"*

"Joseph was doing business in Kirtland, and it seemed as though all creation was upon him, to hamper him in every way, and they drove him from his business, and it left him so that some of his debts had to be settled afterwards; and I am thankful to say that they are settled up; still further, we have sent East to New York, to Ohio, and to every place where I had any idea that Joseph had ever done business, and inquired if there was a man left to whom Joseph Smith, jun., the Prophet, owed a dollar, or a sixpence. If there was we would pay it. But I have not been able to find one. I have advertised this through every neighborhood and place where he formerly lived, consequently I have a right to conclude that all his debts were settled." (Brigham Young, *JD* 18:242.)

"It is a rule of our financial and economic life in all the world that interest is to be paid on borrowed money. May I say something about interest?

"Interest never sleeps nor sickens nor dies; it never goes to the hospital; it works on Sundays and holidays; it never takes a vacation; it never visits nor travels; it takes no pleasure; it is never laid off work nor discharged from employment; it never pays taxes; it buys no food; it wears no clothes; it is unhoused and without home and so has no washing, it has neither wife, children, father, mother, nor kinfolk to watch over and care for; it has no expense of living; it has neither weddings nor births nor deaths; it has no love, no sympathy; it is as hard and soulless as a granite cliff. Once in debt, interest is your companion every minute of the day and night; you cannot shun it or slip away from it; you cannot dismiss it; it yields neither to entreaties, demands, or orders; and whenever you get in its way or cross its course or fail to meet its demands, it crushes you.

"So much for the interest we pay. Whoever borrows should understand what interest is; it is with them every minute of the day and night." (J. Reuben Clark, Jr., *CR*, April 1938, pp. 102-3.)

SECTION 105

Background information on section 105

"Zion's Camp arrived at Fishing River on the 19th of June, 1834. On the 22nd, Sheriff Gillium, of Clay County, visited the Camp in order to find out the intention of the brethren. The Prophet addressed him and his companions and then issued a signed statement in which the following occurs, 'We are willing for twelve disinterested men, six to be chosen by each party, and these men shall say what the possessions of those men are worth who cannot live with us in the County: and they shall have their money in one year; and none of the "Mormons" shall enter that County to reside, until the money is paid. The damages that we have sustained in consequence of being driven away, shall also be left to the twelve men; or, they may all live in the County if they choose, and we will never molest them if they let us alone and permit us to enjoy our rights. We want to live in peace with all men; and equal rights is all we ask.' The opponents refused to listen to this fair proposition.

"The very day on which Sheriff Gillium visited the Camp, the Prophet received this Revelation." (Smith and Sjodahl, *DCC,* p. 679-680.)

"Cornelius Gillium, the sheriff of Clay county, came to our camp to hold consultation with us. I marched my company into a grove near by, and formed in a circle, with Gillium in the centre. Gillium commenced by saying that he had heard that Joseph Smith was in the camp, and if so he would like to see him. I arose and replied, 'I am the man.' This was the first time that I had been discovered or made known to my enemies since I left Kirtland. Gillium then gave us instruction concerning the manners, customs, and dispositions of the people, and what course we ought to pursue to secure their favor and protection, making certain inquiries, to which we replied, which were afterwards published, and will appear under date of publication.

"I received the following:—[D&C 105.]" (Joseph Smith, *HC* 2:108.)

105:8 *"there are many who will say: Where is their God?"*

"In that day when branches of the Church were called upon to assist their brethren they said, [Sec. 105:8, quoted]. There were many who refused to go with the Prophet in Zion's Camp or send money to help their afflicted brethren. Because of this lack of faith and obedience, instead of redeeming Zion at that time, the Lord declared that Zion should have to 'wait for a little season.' This waiting was for the purpose of preparing the members of the Church, through faith, obedience, experience in suffering if they would not repent, so that they would eventually be willing to be obedient." (Joseph Fielding Smith, *CHMR* 3:37-38.)

105:9-10 *"that my people may be taught more perfectly"*

"The Saints in Jackson County and other localities, refused to comply with the order of consecration, consequently they were allowed to be driven from their inheritances; and should not return until they were better prepared to keep the law of God, by being more perfectly taught in reference to their duties, and learn of obedience. And I think we are not justified in anticipating the privilege of returning to build the center stake of Zion, until we shall have shown obedience to the law of consecration. One thing, however, is certain, we shall not be permitted to enter the land from whence we were expelled, till our hearts are prepared to honor this law, and we become sanctified through the practice of the truth." (Lorenzo Snow, *JD* 16:276.)

105:11-12, 18, 33 *"endowed with power from on high"*

See *Endowment* in Appendix A.

"While thus encamped on Fishing River the Lord also in this revelation emphasized the fact that the Kirtland Temple was not to be delayed but built unto his name. He had promised the brethren an endowment, those who were faithful. This temple had to be built so that this endowment could be given. At the end of the journey of this Zion's Camp, the Lord named some of the faithful brethren whom he had appointed to receive this endowment." (Joseph Fielding Smith, *CHMR* 2:6.)

105:14 *"I will fight your battles"*

"As Zion's Camp approached Richmond and they were nearing Jackson County, the Prophet's anxiety for the camp increased, for they were in constant danger of attack from their enemies. On the 18th of June about fifty of the mob crossed the Lexington Ferry for the purpose of joining the Ray County mob preparatory to making an attack on the camp. Others had returned to Jackson County under the direction of Samuel C. Owen and James Campbell. This man Campbell swore that 'the eagles and turkey buzzards shall eat my flesh if I do not fix Joe Smith and his army so that their signs will not hold shucks, before two days have passed.' As these mobbers attempted to cross the Missouri River, 'the angel of God saw fit to sink the boat about the middle of the river, and seven out of twelve that attempted to cross, were drowned. Thus suddenly and justly, went they to their own place. Campbell was among the missing. His body floated down the river some four or five miles and lodged upon a pile of driftwood, where the eagles, buzzards, ravens, crows, and wild animals ate his flesh from his bones, to fulfill his own words and left him a horrible example of God's vengeance.' (*HC* 2:99-100.)

"On the morning of the 19th of June, the Prophet feeling that they were in an unsafe place commanded that the camp move forward without delay. They passed through Richmond, where a black woman called to Luke Johnson. He went to hear what she had to say and she said, 'There is a company of men lying in wait here, who are calculating to kill you this morning as you pass through.' The company halted for breakfast and were kindly treated and given milk by a farmer. After their breakfast they attempted to continue their journey, but had not gone far before a wagon broke down, the wheels ran off another, and many incidents occurred to hinder their progress. That night they had traveled only to an elevated piece of ground between Little and Big Fishing rivers. While they were making their camp five men with guns rode into the camp and told them they would 'see hell before morning.' This was said with accompanying oaths and blasphemy. They stated that armed men were gathering from Ray and Clay counties to join those from Jackson, and they had sworn the destruction of the camp. During that day about two hundred men from Jackson County made arrangements to cross the Missouri River near the mouth of Fishing River, and be ready to meet the Richmond mob near the Fishing River ford. After the first scow load of about forty had passed over the river the scow had great difficulty in returning and did not reach the Jackson side until dark. While this was going on and the five ruffians were in the camp swearing vengeance, wind and thunder and a rising cloud indicated an approaching storm. Shortly after, it began to rain and hail and the storm increased in intensity. An hour before sundown the mobbers commenced firing a cannon, but when the storm broke they sought shelter under their wagons, in hollow trees and wherever they could hide. Their ammunition became soaked, and when morning came they 'took the back track for Independence.' Very little hail fell in the camp. The brethren found shelter in an old meetinghouse while in the camp of the mobbers hailstones and lumps of ice cut down trees, and crops and trees were twisted out of shape. The water in Little Fishing River rose thirty feet in that many minutes. It was reported that one mobber was killed by lightning and another had his hand torn off when his horse drew his hand between logs of a corn crib. Some out of this wicked mob said if that was the way God fought for the Mormons, they might as well go about their business." (Joseph Fielding Smith, *CHMR* 2:1-3.)

105:25-27   *"I will soften the hearts of the people, as I did the heart of Pharoah"*

The dealings of the Lord with the Pharoah of Egypt are recorded in Exodus, chapters 5 through 15.

105:29   *"laws of consecration"*

See *Consecration* in Appendix A.

105:31   *"fair as the sun"*

See *Banners* in Appendix A.

SECTION 106

Background information on section 106

"It now being the last of the month, and the Elders beginning to come in, it was necessary to make preparations for the school for the Elders, wherein they might be more perfectly instructed in the great things of God, during the coming winter. A building for a printing office was nearly finished, and the lower story of this building was set apart for that purpose, (the school) when it was completed. So the Lord opened the way according to our faith and works, and blessed be His name.

"No month ever found me more busily engaged than November; but as my life consisted of activity and unyielding exertions, I made this my rule: *When the Lord commands, do it.* . . .

"I continued my labors daily, preparing for the school, and received the following: [D&C 106.]" (Joseph Smith, *HC* 2:169-70.)

"On his journey among the churches to gather up the strength of the Lord's House, the Prophet came to the City of Freedom, N. Y., where he was entertained by Warren A. Cowdery. He held several meetings there. One of the converts was Heman Hyde, and shortly after his baptism, March 11, 1834, his parents and thirty or forty others were baptized and organized into a Branch, from which nucleus the light spread and souls were gathered into the fold in all the regions round. In this Revelation, Warren A. Cowdery is called to the office of presiding High Priest over the Branch in Freedom and vicinity." (Smith and Sjodahl, *DCC,* pp. 689-90.)

106:1-8 *"Warren A. Cowdery . . . warn the people"*

See *Missionary service* in Appendix A. Warren Cowdery was an older brother of Oliver Cowdery; they were two of eight children born to William, Jr., and Rebecca Fuller Cowdery.

"Warren A. received a revelation November 25, 1834 calling him to the office of presiding High Priest in Freedom, New York. While residing here, he preferred charges against the Twelve Apostles for their alleged failure to teach the Saints while in Freedom, but he later made an apology. He no doubt left the Church at the same time as Oliver, but he remained in the East and did not join his brother when he (Oliver) was reunited with the Church." (*Oliver Cowdery—Second Elder and Scribe*, p. 17.)

106:4-5 *The second coming will overtake "the world as a thief in the night"*

See *Second coming* in Appendix A, and material for 45:19.

106:5 *"gird up your loins"*

See *Armor of God* in Appendix A.

106:6 *"scepter"*

See *Scepter* in Appendix A.

SECTION 107

Background information on section 107

"This evening [March 12, 1835] the Twelve assembled, and the Council was opened by President Joseph Smith, Jun., and he proposed we take our first mission through the Eastern States, to the Atlantic Ocean, and hold conferences in the vicinity of the several branches of the Church for the purpose of regulating all things necessary for their welfare.

"It was proposed that the Twelve leave Kirtland on the 4th day of May, which was unanimously agreed to. . . .

"This afternoon [March 28, 1835] the twelve met in council, and had a time of general confession. On reviewing our past course we are satisfied, and feel to confess also, that we have not realized the importance of our calling to that degree we ought; we have been light-minded and vain, and in many things have done wrong. For all these things we have asked the forgiveness of our heavenly Father; and wherein we have grieved or wounded the feelings of the Presidency, we ask their forgiveness. The time when we are about to separate is near; and when we shall meet again, God only knows; we therefore feel to ask of him whom we have acknowledged to be our Prophet and Seer, that he inquire of God for us, and obtain a revelation, (if consistent) that we may look upon it when we are separated, that our hearts may be comforted. Our worthiness has not inspired us to make this request, but our unworthiness. We have unitedly asked God our heavenly Father to grant unto us through His Seer, a revelation of His mind and will concerning our duty the coming season, even a great revelation, that will enlarge our hearts, comfort us in adversity, and brighten our hopes amidst the powers of darkness." (Joseph Smith, *HC* 2:209-10. Recorded by Orson Hyde and William E. M'Lellin, clerks of the high council.)

"One hundred years ago this spring great things happened in this Church; the greatest, as an evidence of God's guiding hand over his Church, occurred on March 28th, 1835, just a few days more than one hundred years ago. On that day The Church of Jesus Christ of Latter-day Saints received a revelation which is one of the most remarkable documents in the possession of man. It stands absolutely unique; there is none like it . . . it sets forth, in plainness and simplicity, the organization of the quorums of the priesthood; the mutual relations of the quorums to one another; the judicial system of the Church is foreshadowed and outlined; and there is a wonderful picture of the early history of the priesthood. I doubt whether any other such documents, of the same small extent, the same few number of words, lie at the foundation of any other great human institution. . . .

"It is so comprehensive in its brevity, so magnificent in its simplicity, that we have found no occasion, up to the present, to wish that it might have been more complete." (John A. Widtsoe, *CR,* April 1935, pp. 80-82.)

107:1 *The names of the priesthoods in the Church*

See *Aaronic Priesthood* and *Melchizedek Priesthood* in Appendix A.

107:2-12, 18-19, 22-40, 64-67, 89-98 *Explanation of, and offices in, the Melchizedek Priesthood*

See (1) *Melchizedek Priesthood,* (2) *Priesthood,* (3) *Priesthood offices,* and (4) *Church offices and presiding quorums* in Appendix A.

"*Melchizedek Priesthood*—So called after Melchizedek, king of Salem and Priest of the Most High God. In Psalm 110:4 it is foretold that the Messiah would be a 'Priest for ever after the order of Melchizedek.' Paul applies this prophecy to our Lord (Heb. 6:20), and the Jews generally regarded Melchizedek as a type of the royal Priesthood which the Messiah would hold." (Smith and Sjodahl, *DCC,* p. 696.)

107:5 *Offices are appendages to the priesthood*

"The Lord here definitely declares that all authorities or offices, are appendages to the Melchizedek Priesthood. Every man ordained receives the Priesthood, and the office which he receives grows out of the Priesthood. Commenting on this principle, President Joseph F. Smith has said:

" 'There is no office growing out of this Priesthood that is or can be greater than the Priesthood itself. It is from the Priesthood that the office derives its authority and power. No office gives authority to the Priesthood. But all offices in the Church derive their power, their virtue, their authority from the Priesthood. If our brethren would get this principle thoroughly established in their minds, there would be less misunderstanding in relation to the functions of government in the Church than there is.' (*Gospel Doctrine,* p. 184.)" (Joseph Fielding Smith, *CHMR* 2:19.)

7:13-17, *Explanation of, and offices in, the Aaronic Priesthood.*
▸, 68-75,
85-88   See (1) *Aaronic Priesthood,* (2) *Priesthood,* (3) *Priesthood offices,* and (4) *Church offices and presiding quorums* in Appendix A.

"*Aaronic Priesthood*—So called after Aaron, the brother of Moses, who was made the High Priest, or presiding officer, of the Old Testament Priesthood and the Tabernacle service, an office which he filled for nearly forty years. It is also called the Levitical Priesthood, because Aaron was a descendant of Levi, the third son of Jacob and Leah, whose descendants were all set apart and consecrated for the sacred service. They had charge of the Sanctuary and the furniture belonging thereto." (Smith and Sjodahl, *DCC,* p. 696.)

107:15 "*bishopric*"

See *Bishop* and *Church offices and presiding quorums* in Appendix A.

107:19 "*mysteries of the kingdom of heaven*"

See *Mysteries* in Appendix A.

7:22, 65- *Duties of the First Presidency*
7, 78-84,
91-92   See *First Presidency* and *Church offices and presiding quorums* in Appendix A.

7:23-24, *Duties of the Quorum of Twelve Apostles*
33, 35,
38-39   See *Council of the Twelve* and *Church offices and presiding quorums* in Appendix A.

7:25-26, *Duties of the First Quorum of the Seventy*
▸, 93-97   See *First Quorum of the Seventy* and *Church offices and presiding quorums* in Appendix A.

7:33-35, "*first unto the Gentiles and secondly unto the Jews*"
97   See material for 29:30.

107:39-57   *"Evangelical ministers," or patriarchs to be ordained by the Apostles*

See *Patriarch* and *Church offices and presiding quorums* in Appendix A.

107:48-50   *"Enoch . . . was translated"*

See *Enoch* in Appendix A.

107:53   *"Adam-ondi-Ahman"*

See *Adam-ondi-Ahman* in Appendix A.

107:54-56   *"Adam . . . Michael, the prince, the archangel"*

See *Adam* in Appendix A.

107:57   *"book of Enoch"*

See *Enoch* in Appendix A.

"The Book of Enoch—The account is from the Book so named, but not from any book of Enoch now known to scholars. There is an alleged Book of Enoch extant, but it is no older than the second century B.C. Some time the genuine Book of Enoch will be revealed, from which some chapters in the Pearl of Great Price are copied, through the Spirit of Revelation." (Smith and Sjodahl, *DCC*, p. 706.)

107:65-66   *Titles of the President of the Church*

See *First Presidency* in Appendix A.

107:76   *"a literal descendant of Aaron has a legal right to the presidency of this priesthood"*

See *Aaronic Priesthood* and *Bishop* in Appendix A.

107:82-83   *The President of the Church can be tried before a Church court*

"August 11, 1834, a number of high priests and elders assembled to investigate certain charges made by Elder Sylvester Smith against the Prophet Joseph Smith of 'criminal conduct' during the journey to and from Missouri. The Prophet called the meeting to order and spoke at length on the journey of Zion's Camp, and of the rebellious spirit of Sylvester Smith and others while on that journey. He said that he was called on at times to rebuke Sylvester Smith and others, and called on several of the brethren to testify in relation to these matters. After the Prophet had spoken Sylvester Smith arose and stated his case and made some confessions and asked forgiveness for some of his conduct. It appears from the minutes that this was a regular trial at which the Bishop of the Church, Newel K. Whitney, was called on to preside. After both the Prophet and Sylvester Smith had spoken, the members of the council which had been called spoke, on the invitation of Bishop Whitney, expressing their views as to the proper disposal of the case. After the brethren had spoken, Bishop Whitney, after a few remarks gave his decision, according to a motion previously made. The decision was to the effect 'that an article be published in the *Evening and Morning Star,* by the direction of the council, that the Church in Kirtland has investigated the conduct of President Joseph Smith, Jun., while journeying to the west, and returning; and that we find that he has acted in every respect in an honorable and proper manner with all monies and other properties entrusted to his charge, after which a vote was taken and carried to the above effect.' A committee was appointed to prepare an article for publication and Elder Sylvester Smith said he was willing to publish a confession in the *Star.*

"This is the first time in the history of the Church that a President of the Church had been brought to trial before the bishop and high priests on an accusation, according to the provision stated in the revelation. . . . From this account published in the history we see that the Prophet was perfectly willing to have a case, where accusations were brought against him, tried before the proper tribunal of the Church." (Joseph Fielding Smith, *CHMR* 2:9-10.)

107:85 *"duty of a president over the office of a deacon"*

See *Deacon* and *Priesthood offices* in Appendix A.

107:86 *"duty of the president over the office of the teachers"*

See *Teacher* and *Priesthood offices* in Appendix A.

7:87-88 *"duty of the president over the Priesthood of Aaron [which is] . . . to be a bishop"*

See *Priest, Bishop,* and *Priesthood offices* in Appendix A.

107:89 *"duty of the president over the office of elders"*

See *Elders* and *Priesthood offices* in Appendix A.

107:92 *"a seer, a revelator, a translator, and a prophet"*

See *Seer* and *Prophet* in Appendix A.

107:99 *"let every man learn his duty, and to act in the office in which he is appointed, in all diligence"*

"While the revelation is definite in outlining the responsibility, duty and authority of this [first] presidency, the Lord in his mercy, has made the duties and responsibilities and authority of every other man that holds the priesthood, just as clearly defined as for the presidency of the Church. Every man in this Church knows his calling, knows his place, knows his authority. There is no schism, no division, no misunderstanding, because the Lord, after he has outlined all of their duties, sends them forth to labor with this admonition: [Sec. 107:99, quoted.]" (Alonzo A. Hinckley, *CR*, April 1935, p. 73.)

SECTION 108

Background information on section 108

"Lyman Sherman was one of the little band that made the journey to Missouri in company with the Prophet, in 1834, and when the Seventy were organized, he was chosen one of the first Seven Presidents. The day after Christmas, 1835, he went to the home of the Prophet and expressed a desire to have the Word of the Lord through him. 'For,' said he, 'I have been wrought upon to make known to you my feelings and desires, and was promised that I should have a Revelation which should make known my duty.' (*HC* 2:345.) This Revelation was given the same day in answer to prayer." (Smith and Sjodahl, *DCC*, p. 713.)

108:4 *"solemn assembly"*

See *Solemn assembly* in Appendix A.

"Eventually the time arrived for the gathering of the solemn assembly. Tuesday, January 12, 1836, the Presidency of the Church met and arranged for a meeting on the morrow, to consider the subject of the solemn assembly. At the time appointed on the following day a council meeting was held at which the leading brethren were present. Some brethren were ordained. Vinson Knight was named as a counselor in the bishopric in Kirtland, he was then ordained to the office of high priest by Bishop Whitney and set apart as his counselor in the stead of Hyrum Smith who had been set apart in the presidency of the high council in Kirtland. Several brethren were set apart in the high council in Kirtland, filling vacancies created by some of the brethren being called to the apostleship and to other offices. The day was spent in testimony and blessing." (Joseph Fielding Smith, *CHMR* 2:34.)

"At early candle-light I met with the Presidency at the west school room, in the Temple [Kirtland], to attend to the ordinance of anointing our heads with holy oil; also the Councils of Kirtland and Zion met in the two adjoining rooms, and waited in prayer while we attended to the ordinance. . . .

"Many of my brethren who received the ordinance with me saw glorious visions also. Angels ministered unto them as well as to myself, and the power of the Highest rested upon us, the house was filled with the glory of God, and we shouted Hosanna to God and the Lamb. . . .

"Friday 22.—Attended at the school room at the usual hour, but instead of pursuing our studies, we spent the time in rehearsing to each other the glorious scenes that occurred on the preceding evening, while attending to the ordinance of holy anointing.

"In the evening we met at the same place, with the Council of the Twelve, and the Presidency of the Seventy, who were to receive this ordinance (of anointing and blessing). The High Councils of Kirtland and Zion were present also.

"After calling to order and organizing, the Presidency proceeded to consecrate the oil. . . .

"The Twelve then proceeded to anoint and bless the Presidency of the Seventy, and seal upon their heads power and authority to anoint their brethren." (Joseph Smith, *HC* 2:379, 381-83.)

SECTION 109

Background information on section 109

"Long before the doors of the [Kirtland] temple were opened on the morning of the dedication, March 27, 1836, the people had assembled. When the doors were opened the people were admitted as far as the capacity of the building would permit. The First Presidency acted as ushers in the seating, and each quorum of the Priesthood was seated in their order. When the building was filled to capacity the doors were closed and those who could not enter were forced to wait until another session. . . .

"The Prophet then arose and presented the prayer of dedication. This prayer was given previously by revelation and is found in the Doctrine and Covenants, Section 109. Naturally this is a comprehensive prayer that can be studied with great profit. It gives reference to the commandment that the temple should be built and speaks of the purpose for which it was built." (Joseph Fielding Smith, *CHMR* 2:43-44.)

"During the ceremonies of the dedication [Kirtland Temple] an angel appeared and sat near President Joseph Smith, Sen., and Frederick G. Williams, so that they had a fair view of his person. He was a very tall personage, black eyes, white hair, and stoop shouldered; his garment was whole, extending to near his ankles; on his feet he had sandals. He was sent as a messenger to accept of the dedication." (Heber C. Kimball, *LHCK*, p. 91.)

109:5 *"Son of Man"*

See *Son of man* in Appendix A.

109:7 *"seek ye out of the best books words of wisdom"*

See material for 88:118.

"Let me plead with you to give more attention to the standard works of the Church. There is so much literature that comes into our homes, I am sure, that we can hardly reach the standard works of the Church, yet the standard works should come first, and other literature afterwards. Of course, we must keep track of daily events, things that are going on in the world, but when it comes to reading books of interest and value, let us give preference to the Church works because they are more precious than any other books in the world." (Rudger Clawson, *CR*, October 1937, p. 113.)

109:7 *"seek learning even by study and also by faith"*

See material for 88:118.

109:10 *"solemn assembly"*

See *Solemn assembly* in Appendix A.

109:22 *"thine angels have charge over them"*

"Undoubtedly angels often guard us from accidents and harm, from temptation and sin. They may properly be spoken of as guardian angels. Many people have borne and may bear testimony to the guidance and protection that they have received from sources beyond their natural vision. Without the help that we receive from the constant presence of the Holy Spirit, and from possibly holy angels, the difficulties of life would be greatly multiplied. The common belief, however, that to every person born into the world is assigned a guardian angel to be with that person constantly, is not supported by available evidence. It is a very comforting thought, but at present without proof of its correctness. An angel may be a guardian angel though he come only as assigned to give us special help. In fact, the constant presence of the Holy Spirit would seem to make such a constant, angelic companionship unnecessary." (John A. Widtsoe, *GI*, pp. 28-29.)

109:34 *"Jehovah"*

See *Jehovah* and *Jesus Christ* in Appendix A.

"Who was it that gave the law to Moses? We are told it was Jehovah. Well, was Jesus Jehovah? Yes, according to the scriptures, both ancient and modern. . . . (D&C 110:3-4.)" (Charles W. Penrose, *CR*, April 1916, p. 18.)

109:36 *"as . . . on the day of Pentecost"*

"We read that Jesus, after his resurrection, breathed upon his disciples and said, 'Receive ye the Holy Ghost.' But we also read that he said, 'Behold, I send the promise of my Father upon you: but tarry ye in the city of Jerusalem, until ye be endued with power from on high.' (Luke 24:49.) We read further, 'For the Holy Ghost was not yet given; because that Jesus was not yet glorified.' (John 7:39.) Thus the promise was made, but the fulfillment came after, so that the Holy Ghost sent by Jesus from the Father did not come in person until the day of Pentecost, and the cloven tongues of fire were the sign of his coming. This manifestation was repeated in this dispensation at the endowment on the Kirtland Temple, in the month of April, 1836." (First Presidency, *IE*, 19:460-61, March 1916.)

"I left the meeting in the charge of the Twelve, and retired about nine o'clock in the evening. The brethren continued exhorting, prophesying, and speaking in tongues until five o'clock in the morning. The Savior made His appearance to some, while angels ministered to others, and it was a Pentecost and an endowment indeed, long to be remembered, for the sound shall go forth from this place into all the world, and the occurrences of this day shall be handed down upon the pages of sacred history, to all generations; as the day of Pentecost, so shall this day be numbered and celebrated as a year of jubilee, and time of rejoicing to the Saints of the Most High God." (Joseph Smith, *HC* 2:432-33.)

109:37 *"let thy house be filled as with a rushing mighty wind with thy glory"*

"Elder George A. Smith rose to prophesy, when a noise was heard like the sound of a rushing wind. All the congregation arose, and many began to speak in tongues and prophesy. And then people of the neighborhood came running together (hearing an unusual sound within and seeing a bright light like a pillar of fire resting upon the Temple), and were astonished at what was taking place. This continued until the meeting closed, at 11 P.M. (Smith and Sjodahl, *DCC*, p. 721.)

109:44 *"Help thy servants to say . . . Thy will be done, O Lord, and not ours"*

"When things come up that require an exertion on our part, we should bring our wills into subjection to the will of the Father, and feel to say, what is the will of our Father, whom we are here in the world to serve? Then every act that we perform will be a success. We may not see its success today or tomorrow, nevertheless it will result in success." (Lorenzo Snow, *CR*, October 1899, p. 2.)

109:50   *"Have mercy, O Lord, upon the wicked mob, who have driven thy people"*

This touching plea by the Prophet not only reflects his great mercy and spirit of forgiveness, but also reinforces the commandment of the Savior that we should love our enemies. This prayer was given by revelation from the Savior to Joseph Smith.

109:51   *"make bare thine arm"*

See *Arm of the Lord* in Appendix A.

109:52   *"root and branch"*

See *Root* in Appendix A.

109:54   *"the constitution of our land"*

See *Constitution* in Appendix A.

109:62   *"that Jerusalem, from this hour, may begin to be redeemed"*

"The Lord has made great promises both to Israel, and the Jews, and concerning Jerusalem and its temple. Jerusalem, when Christ comes, is to be a holy city again. Another temple will be built, and Israel will be cleansed from all his sins.

"Ezekiel prophesied of the gathering of Israel and the building of the temple in Jerusalem after Israel has been gathered and cleansed. In that day the Lord will make an everlasting covenant with them, 'And I will place them, and multiply them, and will set my sanctuary in the midst of them for evermore. My tabernacle also shall be with them: yea, I will be their God, and they shall be my people. And the heathen shall know that I the Lord do sanctify Israel, when my sanctuary shall be in the midst of them for evermore.' After giving the account of the great battle of Gog and Magog and the destruction of the wicked, he gives a detailed description of the glorious temple which shall be built as this sanctuary. For this description see Ezekiel, Chapters 40-45.

"In that day, when the Lord creates the 'new heavens and

a new earth' he will 'create Jerusalem a rejoicing, and her people a joy.' He further says: 'And I will rejoice in Jerusalem, and joy in my people; and the voice of weeping shall be no more heard in her, nor the voice of crying. There shall be no more thence an infant of days, nor an old man that hath not filled his days: for the child shall die an hundred years old; but the sinner being an hundred years old shall be accursed.' (Isa. 65:17-25.) In that day Jerusalem is redeemed and our Lord comes to reign, the Lord promised through Zechariah that Jerusalem shall be safely inhabited. (14:11.) Moreover, when Jerusalem becomes one of the two capitals for the King of kings, 'it shall come to pass that every one that is left of all the nations which came against Jerusalem shall even go up from year to year to worship the King, the Lord of hosts, and to keep the feast of tabernacles.' (Zech. 14:16.)" (Joseph Fielding Smith, *CHMR* 1:411.)

109:64 *"the children of Judah may begin to return"*

". . . the tribe of Judah will return to old Jerusalem. [Sec. 133:8, 13, 35.] . . . Judah shall obtain deliverance at Jerusalem. (See Joel 11:32; Isaiah 16:20 and 21; Jeremiah 34:12; Psalm 1:5; Ezekiel 34:11, 12 and 13.) These are testimonies that the Good Shepherd will put forth His own sheep, and lead them out from all nations where they have been scattered in a cloudy and dark day, to Zion, and to Jerusalem." (Joseph Smith, *HC* 1:315.)

"This great event . . . is one of the signs of the times, and is very important, it seems to me, particularly to all Christian people. It is transpiring in a small strip of country about one hundred and ten miles long and fifty to sixty miles wide, in an area about the size of the state of Vermont. . . .

"The number of Jews has multipled in recent years in this area in a rather remarkable manner. Plans are underway for the incorporation of about a million and a half more during the immediate months ahead, and projected plans call for an eventual population of some four million in this area. . . .

"This miracle of the return of the Jews was to be one of the events to precede Christ's second coming, and the scriptures are very clear with reference to this fact. [Isa. 11:11-12; Jer. 30:3; 33:7.] . . .

"The prophets of the Book of Mormon even more clearly predict the conditions under which they will gather. These prophets also foresaw the time when they would begin to believe Jesus Christ [2 Nephi 30:7], that the kings of the Gentiles would be as nursing fathers and their queens nursing mothers in helping to bring about their return. [2 Nephi 10:3-9.] These prophets make it clear that eventually the fulness of the gospel will be carried to Jerusalem and to the descendants of Judah. [3 Nephi 20:29-31.]" (Ezra Taft Benson, *CR*, April 1950, pp. 72, 74.)

109:68 *"[Joseph Smith] hath sincerely striven to do thy will"*

"Joseph Smith was an obedient man. Humility always breeds obedience. Moreover, the revelations he received from God made obedience to truth the main issue of a happy gospel life. . . . His life was an example of obedience. He was shown the Book of Mormon plates; he knew where they were; yet despite his natural eagerness to possess them, he obediently saw them for four years only once a year, as commanded. Obediently, as the Lord directed, he went from place to place, built temples in the midst of his people's poverty, subjected himself to trials and toils, accepted plural marriage in the face of his training for monogamy—and in every manner throughout his life showed obedience to the Lord's will. As did Abraham of old, his all could be laid on the altar of the Lord. By these tests, as by many others, Joseph Smith was a great man." (John A. Widtsoe, *JS*, p. 333.)

109:73 *"fair as the moon, clear as the sun, and terrible as an army with banners"*

See *Banners* in Appendix A.

109:74 *"mountains to flow down . . . valleys to be exalted"*

"In the resurrection which now approaches, and in connection with the glorious coming of Jesus Christ, the earth will undergo a change in its physical features, climate, soil, productions, and in its political, moral and spiritual government.

"Its mountains will be levelled, its valleys exalted, its swamps and sickly places will be drained and become healthy, while its burning deserts and its frigid polar regions will be redeemed and become temperate and fruitful. [Sec. 133:19-25.]" (Parley P. Pratt, *KT*, p. 132.)

09:75 *"we shall be caught up in the cloud to meet thee"*

"With Christ shall come those who have already been resurrected; and His approach shall be the means of inaugurating a general resurrection of the righteous dead, while the pure and just who are still in the flesh shall be instantaneously changed from the mortal to the immortal state and shall be caught up with the newly resurrected to meet the Lord and His Celestial company, and shall descend with Him. [Sec. 88:96-98.]" (James E. Talmage, *JC*, p. 787.)

09:77 *"everlasting to everlasting"*

See *Eternity to eternity* in Appendix A.

09:79 *"shining seraphs around thy throne"*

See material for 38:1.

SECTION 110

Background information on section 110

"After the dedication of the Kirtland Temple, council and spiritual meetings were held in the building almost daily. Sunday, April 3, 1836, was one of the most eventful days in the history of the Church. A general meeting was held in the Lord's House. In the forenoon Elders Thomas B. Marsh and David W. Patten spoke to an audience of about one thousand persons. In the afternoon the sacrament was administered by the Presidency and the apostles. After this ordinance the prophet and Oliver Cowdery retired to the pulpit, the veils were dropped, and these two men bowed before the pulpit in silent prayer, and the following vision was manifested before them." (Joseph Fielding Smith, *CHMR* 2:46.)

"There were two stands, one on the west end and one on the east end, each consisting of four pulpits, one rising above the other, like terraces. The pulpits on the west end were reserved for presiding officers of the Melchizedek Priesthood, and those on the east end for the Aaronic Priesthood. Each of these pulpits could be separated from the others by means of veils of painted canvas, which could be let down or rolled up at pleasure.

"On Sunday, April 3rd, 1836, in the afternoon, after the Sacrament, the Prophet Joseph and Oliver Cowdery retired to the pulpit in order to engage in silent prayer. The veils were dropped. When they rose from their devotion, the visions recorded in this Section were given to both." (Smith and Sjodahl, *DCC*, p. 724.)

110:1-10 *"We saw the Lord"*

"Oliver Cowdery, as well as Joseph Smith, saw this vision [Sec. 110:1-4]; they beheld this glorious personage, even the Son of God, when He accepted the Kirtland Temple after its dedication. These witnesses are also supplemented by hundreds of others who have beheld in vision and otherwise, glorious personages in these last days. There are men alive who have beheld the Son of God, who have heard His voice, and who have been ministered unto by Him in this our day and generation. In the face of these testimonies, which cannot be impeached successfully, is it any wonder that faith grows in the hearts of the people of God, the Latter-day Saints?" (George Q. Cannon, *JD* 25:158.)

10:9-10   *"tens of thousands shall greatly rejoice"*

"That which took place [in the Kirtland Temple] on the third day of April in the year 1836 has spread forth to all lands. Thousands and tens of thousands, even hundreds of thousands have been blessed because of what took place upon that occasion. Not only the thousands in The Church of Jesus Christ of Latter-day Saints, but thousands upon thousands who are not members of the Church have partaken of the blessings which came at that time and which have spread forth throughout the earth. And while they may not know it, they have been influenced, and have many of them performed a wonderful work because of the things that took place, and because of the fulfillment of this prediction [Sec. 110:7-10] made by the Son of God." (Joseph Fielding Smith, *CR*, April 1936, p. 73.)

110:11   *"Moses appeared"*

See *Gathering* in Appendix A.

"Once more the heavens were opened and Moses, the great lawgiver of Israel, stood before Joseph Smith and Oliver Cowdery and committed to them the keys of his dispensation, saying that 'these keys were committed to them for the gathering of Israel from the four parts of the earth, and the leading of the ten tribes from the land of the north.' This is also the dispensation of the gathering. In it is Israel to be re-established in the land given to Abraham. Moses predicted both the scattering and the gathering of Israel. . . . [Deut. 4 quoted.]

"All of the prophets in ancient days predicted the scattering; they also predicted the gathering again which was to take place in the latter days, and when the Jews had been sufficiently punished for their transgressions they were to return to Palestine. Moses held the keys of the gathering of Israel. He led Israel out of Egypt into the land of Canaan. It was his appointment in this dispensation to come and restore those keys for the modern gathering." (Joseph Fielding Smith, *CHMR* 2:48.)

"We call attention to the fact that because Moses brought the keys of the gathering of Israel back to earth, The Church of Jesus Christ of Latter-day Saints as previously indicated, has builded over six hundred cities in the western part of the United States, in the process of gathering the seed of Israel from among the gentile nations of the earth. These converts to the new faith have not been asked or persuaded to emigrate to America, but this unseen power rests upon them who have authority to bestow it. Of their own accord they desire to gather with the Saints of the Lord in His latter-day Zion." (LeGrand Richards, *MWW*, p. 189.)

110:12 *"Elias appeared"*

See *Elias* in Appendix A.

"After the departure of Moses, Elias who held the keys of the gospel in the days of Abraham appeared and conferred the keys of his dispensation, saying 'that in us and our seed all generations after us should be blessed.' By this expression, reference is not made to the 'seed' of Joseph Smith and Oliver Cowdery but to the 'seed' of all faithful members of the Church. We know that the Lord called Abraham and made some very important promises to him and his posterity. His descendants through Isaac and Jacob, constitute the house of Israel, the people to whom the Lord intrusted the covenants and delivered his word through prophets for the guidance of the whole world. What prophet this Elias is that was sent to restore these keys is not definitely known. The title 'Elias' has been given to several prophets who have been appointed to important work in different dispensations. The work of an 'Elias' is the work of a forerunner or one who goes before a greater to prepare the way. John the Baptist was an Elias, Noah was an Elias. (D&C 27:7.) The Lord has declared that Elias shall restore all things spoken of by all the holy prophets. (D&C 27:6.) This may have reference to all the prophets who were sent with keys of authority to Joseph Smith and Oliver Cowdery." (Joseph Fielding Smith, *CHMR* 2:49.)

"Elias came, after Moses had conferred his keys, and brought the gospel of the dispensation in which Abraham lived. *Everything that pertains to that dispensation, the bless-*

ings that were conferred upon Abraham, the promises that were given to his posterity, all had to be restored [Abr. 2:8-11], and Elias, who held the keys of that dispensation, came." (Joseph Fielding Smith, *Utah Genealogical and Historical Magazine* 27:100.)

:13-16   *"Elijah . . . stood before us"*

See *Elijah* in Appendix A, and material for section 2.

"Then came another glorious manifestation in fulfillment of the prediction made by the prophet Malachi some four hundred years before the birth of Christ. We read again: [Sec. 110:13-16, quoted.] Since the bestowal of these keys the work of salvation for the dead has been proclaimed, has taken hold of the hearts of the children of men, I say, both in the Church and out of it. [Sec. 2.] There are thousands who are working in the gathering of the records of the dead, and why they do it they do not know." (Joseph Fielding Smith, *CR,* April 1936, p. 74.)

"We have an abundance of evidence that this story is true. If Joseph Smith and Oliver Cowdery had lied, it would have been impossible for them to have turned the hearts of the children to their fathers. Surely, they would not have any power to do that. It is true that following the declaration by them that Elijah did come, the hearts of the children commenced to turn to their dead fathers. There is strong presumptive evidence that this was because these keys were restored. This is a demonstrative fact, that the hearts of children have turned to their fathers. . . . Before the days of the coming of Elijah in 1836, there was no endeavor of any import to search the records of the dead. What was done, here and there, was usually where some estate was involved. The people were not turning their hearts to their dead fathers. They were not searching the records. They were not compiling them. There were no organizations or societies on the face of the earth, as far as I can learn, gathering records of the dead, before the year 1836. In 1837, however, one year later, Great Britain passed laws providing for and compelling the preservation of records of the dead. In the year 1844, the New England Historical and Genealogical Society was organized in Boston, and I think this was the first organization of the kind in the world. In 1869, the New York Genealogical and Biographical Society in the city of New York was organized. Then following rapidly other societies up and down the Atlantic coast of the United States, from Maine to Georgia. . . . In Great Britain, genealogical societies have been organized in practically every country in that land and in Scotland. These records have been kept and filed also in other countries in Europe, the countries from which the Latter-day Saints have come. The Spirit has taken hold of the people, not only in the Church but also of many who are not of the Church, and they, too, are searching the records, and compiling them, of the dead. . . .

"In 1935, Mr. T. B. Thompson published *A Catalogue of British Family Histories.* It included the titles and years of publication of some two thousand seventy-one families and was supposed to be a complete list of all such published records up to that date. Here are his figures from the date of the invention of printing:

From 1450 to 1600, were published 2 family histories.

From 1600 to 1700, were published 18 family histories.

From 1700 to 1800, were published 72 family histories.

From 1800 to 1836, when Elijah came, were published 100 family histories.

From 1837 to 1935, were published 1,879 family histories.

"These were records in Europe, and since the year 1836, there have been published in Great Britain and the United States thousands of records of the dead." (Joseph Fielding Smith, *CR,* April 1948, p. 135.)

"I want to call your attention to an incident which I think is of some importance. I am going to read to you a statement from Alfred Edersheim in his work 'The Temple.' . . .

And so also in the last days it would be the Paschal night when the final judgment should come upon "Edom," and the glorious deliverance of Israel take place. Hence to this day, in every Jewish home, at a certain part of the Paschal service—the door is opened to admit Elijah the prophet as forerunner of the Messiah, while appropriate passages are at the same time read which foretell the destruction of all heathen nations. It is a remarkable coincidence that, in instituting his own Supper, the Lord Jesus connected the symbol, not of judgment, but of his dying love, with his "third cup."

"It was, I am informed, on the third day of April, 1836, that the Jews, in their homes at the Paschal feast, opened their doors for Elijah to enter. On that very day Elijah did enter—not in the home of the Jews to partake of the Passover with them, but he appeared in the House of the

Lord, erected to his name and received by the Lord in Kirtland, and there bestowed his keys to bring to pass the very things for which these Jews, assembled in their homes, were seeking." (Joseph Fielding Smith, *CR*, April 1936, p. 75.)

10:13 *"Elijah the prophet . . . was taken to heaven without tasting death"*

For the Biblical account of the translation of Elijah, see 2 Kings 2:1-11.

10:16 *"the keys of this dispensation are committed into your hands"*

"Elijah restored to this Church and, if they would receive it, to the world, the keys of the sealing power; and that sealing power puts the stamp of approval upon every ordinance that is done in this Church and more particularly those that are performed in the temples of the Lord. Through that restoration each of you . . . has the privilege, of going into this house or one of the other temples to have your wife sealed to you for time and all eternity, and your children sealed to you also, or better, have them born under that covenant. What a glorious privilege it is to know that the family organization will remain intact. It is not destroyed. . . . We may go into the house of the Lord and do these things and be baptized for our dead, those who have died, the scriptures say . . . who died without the knowledge of the gospel." (Joseph Fielding Smith, *CR*, April 1948, p. 135.)

10:16 *"the great and dreadful day of the Lord is near"*

See (1) *Great and dreadful day of the Lord;* (2) *Second coming;* and (3) *Quickly* in Appendix A.

SECTION 111

Background information on section 111

"On the 25th of July, 1836, the Prophet Joseph, in company with Sidney Rigdon, Hyrum Smith, and Oliver Cowdery, left Kirtland for a mission to the East. They passed through Albany, New York, Providence, Boston, and arrived, early in August, in Salem, Mass., where they hired a hall in which they held meetings for about a month, and visited sections of the surrounding country. While there, this Revelation was received." (Smith and Sjodahl, *DCC*, p. 728.)

"On Monday afternoon, July 25th, in company with Sidney Rigdon, Brother Hyrum Smith, and Oliver Cowdery, I left Kirtland . . . and the next evening, about ten o'clock we arrived at Buffalo, New York. . . . We took passages on a line boat for Utica, where we arrived about eight o'clock A.M. of the 29th, just in time to take the railroad car for Schenectady, the first passenger car on the new road. . . .

"On the 30th, at seven o'clock A.M., we went on board the steamer *John Mason,* which took us to the *Erie,* lying over the bar. . . .

"From New York we continued our journey to Providence, on board a steamer; from thence to Boston, by steam cars, and arrived in Salem, Massachusetts, early in August, where we hired a house, and occupied the same during the month, teaching the people from house to house, and preaching publicly, as opportunity presented; visiting occasionally, sections of the surrounding country, which are rich in the history of the Pilgrim Fathers of New England, in Indian warfare, religious superstition, bigotry, persecution, and learned ignorance. . . .

"I received the following: [Section 111, follows.]" (Joseph Smith, *HC* 2:463-65.)

"While the Prophet gives a somewhat circumstantial account of this journey to Salem and his return to Kirtland in September, he nowhere assigns an adequate cause for himself and company making it—the object of it is not stated. Ebenezer Robinson, for many years a faithful and prominent elder in the church, and at Nauvoo associated with Don Carlos Smith—brother of the Prophet—in editing and publishing the *Times and Seasons*, states that the journey to Salem arose from these circumstances. There came to Kirtland a brother by the name of Burgess who stated that he had knowledge of a large amount of money secreted in the cellar of a certain house in Salem, Massachusetts, which had belonged to a widow (then deceased), and thought he was the only person who had knowledge of it, or of the location of the house. The brethren accepting the representations of Burgess as true made the journey to Salem to secure, if possible, the treasure. Burgess, according to Robinson, met the brethren in Salem, but claimed that time had wrought such changes in the town that he could not for a certainty point out the house 'and soon left.' They hired a house and occupied it and spent their time as per the narrative of the Prophet already quoted. While in Salem the Prophet received a revelation in which the folly of this journey is sharply reproved." (B. H. Roberts, *CHC* 1:411.)

111:3 *"form acquaintance with men in this city"*

"I wish the Elders of Israel to understand mankind as they are—to go to the people and take them as they are." (Brigham Young, *JD* 9:121.)

11:11 *"be . . . as wise as serpents"*

This is essentially the same statement by the Savior as found in Matthew 10:16 ("Be ye therefore wise as serpents, and harmless as doves"). In his Inspired Version of the Bible, Joseph Smith changed the account ir Matthew to "Be ye therefore *wise servants*, and as harmless as doves." (Matt. 10:14; italics added.)

SECTION 112

Background information on section 112

"The same day that the Gospel was first preached in England I received the following: [Section 112, quoted.]" (Joseph Smith, *HC* 2:499.)

"At this time the spirit of speculation in lands and property of all kinds, which was so prevalent throughout the whole nation, was taking deep root in the Church. As the fruits of this spirit, evil surmisings, fault-finding, disunion, dissension, and apostasy followed in quick succession, and it seemed as though all the powers of earth and hell were combining their influence in an especial manner to overthrow the Church at once, and make a final end. Other banking institutions refused the 'Kirtland Safety Society's' notes. The enemy abroad, and apostates in our midst, united in their schemes, flour and provisions were turned towards other markets, and many became disaffected toward me as though I were the sole cause of those very evils I was most strenuously striving against, and which were actually brought upon us by the brethren not giving heed to my counsel.

"No quorum in the Church was entirely exempt from the influence of those false spirits who are striving against me for the mastery; even some of the Twelve were so far lost to their high and responsible calling, as to begin to take sides, secretly, with the enemy.

"In this state of things, and but a few weeks before the Twelve were expecting to meet in full quorum, (some of them having been absent for some time), God revealed to me that something new must be done for the salvation of His Church. And on or about the first of June, 1837, Heber C. Kimball, one of the Twelve, was set apart by the spirit of prophecy and revelation, prayer and laying on of hands, of the First Presidency, to preside over a mission to England, to be the first foreign mission of the Church of Christ in the last days." (Joseph Smith, *HC* 2:487-89.)

112:1 *"Thomas"*

For biographical information on Thomas B. Marsh, see Appendix B.

112:4 *Gentiles and Jews*

See *Gentiles* and *Jews* in Appendix A.

112:7 *"gird up your loins . . . Let thy feet be shod"*

See *Armor of God* in Appendix A.

112:10 *"the Lord thy God shall lead thee"*

"Some of the older brethren who remember the days of President Joseph F. Smith have told me that frequently when President Smith was introduced as the 'head of the Church,' he was always quick to reply, 'Oh, no. I'm but the President of the Church. Jesus Christ is its head.' " (Harold B. Lee, *CR*, October 1960, pp. 16-17.)

:12-13 *"Admonish them . . . and if they harden not their hearts . . . I will heal them"*

"Immediately after this time, on September 3rd [1837], at a conference held in Kirtland, . . . Objection being . . . made to three of the apostles, Luke Johnson, Lyman E. Johnson and John F. Boynton, they were by the voice of the Saints shorn of their apostolic rank and were disfellowshiped; however, as they subsequently made protestation of their repentance, they were received back into the Church and into their station. But their humility was either a mere pretense or was very volatile in its character; because not many weeks elapsed until they were once more engaged in an effort to ruin the Church and the Prophet." (George Q. Cannon, *LJS*, pp. 215-16.)

112:14 *"take up your cross"*

See *Cross* in Appendix A.

"Let me say to the Latter-day Saints, if they will take up their cross and follow the Lord Jesus Christ in the regeneration, any of them will receive more, know more, and have more of the spirit of revelation than they are aware of." (Brigham Young, *JD* 3:209.)

"This seems to have been a common expression in religious circles at this time. Newel Knight said that he 'would try and take up his cross and pray vocally during meeting' (*HC* 1:82). It is a Scriptural expression. Our Lord says, 'If any man will come after me, let him deny himself, and take up his cross daily, and follow me' (Luke 9:23). The performance of duty is a task that requires continual effort. If anybody should join the Church because the services are 'grand,' or the sermons 'beautiful,' he would be disappointed, but he who comes determined to do his duty, will find life eternal. Paul says, 'For thy sake we are killed all the day long' (Rom. 8:36); again, 'I die daily' (1 Cor. 15:31). The followers of Christ 'carry the cross.'" (Smith and Sjodahl, *DCC*, pp. 734-35.)

112:15   *"I am with him [Joseph] . . . and the keys . . . shall not be taken from him"*

"It was decreed in the counsels of eternity, long before the foundations of the earth were laid, that he [Joseph Smith] should be the man, in the last dispensation of this world, to bring forth the word of God to the people, and receive the fulness of the keys and power of the Priesthood of the Son of God. The Lord had his eye upon him, and upon his father, and upon his father's father, and upon their progenitors clear back to Abraham, and from Abraham to the flood, from the flood to Enoch, and from Enoch to Adam. He has watched that family and that blood as it has circulated from its fountain to the birth of that man. He was foreordained in eternity to preside over this last dispensation." (Brigham Young, *JD* 7:289-90.)

"At the time this revelation was given some of the members of the council of the apostles were in open rebellion and had displayed a very bitter spirit towards the Prophet. The Lord endeavored to impress upon them the fact that the Prophet was the one who held the keys of this dispensation and that he would hold them constantly until the Lord should come. In a former revelation (Sec. 43:4-7) the Lord had said that the keys were in the hands of Joseph Smith and that if he should transgress and lose them they would be given to another. At that day the Prophet had not been tested and proved by tribulation and suffering, but now in July 1837, the Prophet having shown his integrity in all kinds of difficulties and tribulation the Lord declared that the keys shall never be taken from him. The Lord wished to impress upon the apostles and others in the councils of the Church that he had not forsaken his prophet and would be with him to the end." (Joseph Fielding Smith, *CHMR* 2:72-73.)

112:16   *"Thomas, thou art the man whom I have chosen"*

See *Thomas B. Marsh* in Appendix A.

112:17   *"my servant Hyrum"*

"It will be noted here that the Lord names Hyrum Smith with Sidney Rigdon as a counselor in the First Presidency. The reason for this is that Frederick G. Williams had partaken of the evil spirit which prevailed among so many of the brethren, and had to be relieved of his place and presidency in that exalted quorum. Fortunately, however, at a later date he humbly returned repentant and was received back into full fellowship in the Church." (Joseph Fielding Smith, *CHMR* 2:73.)

112:20   *"The First Presidency . . . I have made counselors"*

"The First Presidency, the Lord said, were to be counselors to the twelve. By this is meant that the twelve should not go forth without the counsel and direction of the First Presidency." (Joseph Fielding Smith, *CHMR* 2:73.)

112:21   *"the Twelve . . . shall have power . . . whithersoever ye shall send them"*

"And then the Prophet Joseph concludes his remarkable call of missionaries: '. . . and don't let a single corner of the earth go without a mission.' And when we think of that, we cover a lot of territory. The earth is a big earth.

"We crossed the Iron Curtain. . . . But now we have come to know there is no Iron Curtain, no Bamboo Curtain, no Wood or Steel Curtain, or Desert, or Mountain, or Sea that can keep us out. For we will bridge the oceans with ships, the mountains and deserts with planes, and the curtains with the word of God in their own tongues. [D&C 32:3 quoted.]

"There are these four points: Jesus will accompany the missionaries; he will be in their midst; he will be the advocate with the Father; and nothing shall prevail, nothing.

"This is a divine promise we have waited for a long time." (Spencer W. Kimball, Talk at Regional Representatives Seminar, June 27, 1974.)

112:23   *"darkness covereth the earth, and gross darkness the minds of the people"*

See *Darkness* in Appendix A.

"It seems sometimes as if the darkness that surrounds us is all but impenetrable. I can see on all sides the signs of one great evil master mind working for the overturning of our civilization, the destruction of religion, the reduction of men to the status of animals. This mind is working here and there and everywhere. May we hope and pray that this is the darkness before the dawn, and that soon the light will come in the east, that the darkness will fade out, that a sun of righteousness will rise and touch the peaks and flow down and fill the valleys, fill our hearts and fill our lives, until we shall be the people which God wishes us to be." (J. Reuben Clark, *CR,* October 1935, p. 92.)

112:24   *"a day of burning, a day of desolation"*

See *Burning* and *Calamities* in Appendix A.

112:25   *"upon my house shall it begin"*

"Sometimes we hear someone refer to a division in the Church. In reality, the Church is not divided. It simply means that there are some who, for the time being at least, are members of the Church but not in harmony with it. These people have a temporary membership and influence in the Church; but unless they repent, they will be missing when the final membership records are recorded.

"It is well that our people understand this principle, so they will not be misled by those apostates within the Church who have not yet repented or been cut off. But there is a cleansing coming. The Lord says that his vengeance shall be poured out 'upon the inhabitants of the earth. . . . And upon my house shall it go forth, saith the Lord; First among those among you, saith the Lord, who have professed to know my name and have not known me. . . .' (D&C 112:24-26.) I look forward to that cleansing; its need within the Church is becoming increasingly apparent.

"The Lord strengthened the faith of the early apostles by pointing out Judas as a traitor, even before this apostle had completed his iniquitous work. So also in our day the Lord has told us of the tares within the wheat that will eventually be hewn down when they are fully ripe. But until they are hewn down, they will be with us, amongst us." (Ezra Taft Benson, *IE,* June 1969, p. 42.)

112:28 *"purify your hearts"*

" 'Hearts,' is a figure used frequently in the Scriptures and stands for 'affections,' 'understanding,' 'courage,' 'joy,' etc. 'Broken heart' means one that is humble and willing to be obedient to the will of the Lord. 'Stony heart,' means that the individual is unrepentant, unbelieving. These messengers who were to go forth were to purify their hearts so that the Spirit of the Lord might be their guide as they went forth into all the world." (Smith and Sjodahl, *DCC,* p. 736.)

112:30 *"the dispensation of the fulness of times"*

See *Dispensation* in Appendix A.

112:33 *"lest the blood of this generation be required at your hands"*

"I . . . wish to state to the Twelve and to the Seventies, and to the Elders, that they are not responsible for the reception or the rejection by the world of that word which God has given to them to communicate. . . . When they have performed their labors, and fulfilled their duties, their garments are free from the blood of this generation, and the people are then left in the hands of God their Heavenly Father. For the people . . . will be held responsible to God for their rejection of the Gospel, and not to us." (John Taylor, *JD* 24:289.)

112:34 *"I come quickly . . . I am Alpha and Omega"*

See *Quickly* and *Alpha and Omega* in Appendix A.

SECTION 113

Background information on section 113

"On the 14th of March, as we were about entering Far West [Missouri], many of the brethren came out to meet us, who also with open arms welcomed us to their bosoms. We were immediately received under the hospitable roof of Brother George W. Harris, who treated us with all possible kindness, and we refreshed ourselves with much satisfaction, after our long and tedious journey, the brethren bringing in such things as we had need of for our comfort and convenience.

"After being here two or three days, my brother Samuel arrived with his family.

"Shortly after his arrival, while walking with him and certain other brethren, the following sentiments occurred to my mind:

"The Political Motto of the Church of Latter-day Saints. . . . The Prophet's Answers to Questions on Scriptures. [D&C 113.]" (Joseph Smith, *HC* 3:8-9.)

113:2 *"It is Christ"*

"As made known to the prophet [Isaiah] and by him proclaimed, the coming Lord was the living Branch that should spring from the undying root typified in the family of Jesse. [Isa. 11:1 and 10; compare Rom. 15:12, Rev. 5:5, 22:16; see also Jer. 23:5, 6.]" (James E. Talmage, *JC*, p. 47.)

113:3 *"rod"*

"This means a 'shoot' or branch coming out of the 'stem' of Jesse—a descendant." (Smith and Sjodahl, *DCC*, p. 738.)

113:5 *"root"*

"A branch from the root. Jesse was the father of David." (Smith and Sjodahl, *DCC*, p. 738.)

SECTION 114

Background information on section 114

"On April 17, 1838, the Prophet received a revelation for David W. Patten who had for some time been located in Missouri and with Elder Thomas B. Marsh was maintaining a steady influence amidst the opposition of disaffected brethren, including the three who had been appointed to preside, David Whitmer, William W. Phelps and John Whitmer. The Lord called upon Elder Patten to settle up his business as soon as possible, make a disposition of his merchandise, and prepare to take a mission the following spring, in company with others to preach the Gospel to all the world. . . . Elder Patten obedient to this revelation took steps to meet this call which had come to him. Events were to develop, however, which would change the nature of his mission before the following spring could arrive." (Joseph Fielding Smith, *CHMR* 2:85.)

114:1 *"David . . . testify of my name and bear glad tidings unto all the world"*

For additional information on David Patten, see Appendix B.

"David W. Patten is instructed to settle up his affairs and be prepared to take a mission. He was born in the State of New York, about the year 1800, and was baptized June 15th, 1832, by his brother, John Patten. He performed several missions and gradually rose to prominence. On February 15th, 1835, he was ordained an Apostle. He was absolutely fearless. His testimony was powerful and through him God performed many mighty works. In 1838, the mobbings in Missouri commenced anew, and Patten was foremost in the defense of the Saints. He died as a result of a wound received on the 25th of October, 1838, in a conflict with a lawless rabble at a place called Crooked River. His mission was on the other side of the veil." (Smith and Sjodahl, *DCC*, p. 739.)

114:2 *"inasmuch as there are those among you who deny my name, others shall be planted in their stead"*

During the very month this revelation was received (April 1838), several of the leading brethren in the Church were excommunicated. Elder George Q. Cannon reviews the events of the first months of that year:

"While the Prophet had been journeying toward Missouri after escaping the Kirtland mob in January, 1838, a general assembly of the Saints in Far West was held on the 5th day of February, at which David Whitmer, John Whitmer and William W. Phelps were rejected as the local presidency; and a few days later Thomas B. Marsh and David W. Patten, of the Twelve, were selected to act as a presidency until the Prophet should arrive. Oliver Cowdery too had been suspended from his position. Persisting in unchristianlike conduct, W. W. Phelps and John Whitmer had been excommunicated by the high council in Far West, four days previous to the arrival of Joseph.

"This was the sad situation as the Prophet approached the dwelling place of the Saints in Missouri. Many of the people went out to meet him, and at a distance of one hundred and twenty miles from Far West they found him and tendered him teams and money to help him forward. The joy they had in his presence arose from an absolute knowledge of his power and authority as a Prophet of God. They were certain that many of their difficulties would end with his presence, because he would give the light of truth by which to guide their footsteps. . . .

"At the same conference [April 6, 1838] Brigham Young, David W. Patten and Thomas B. Marsh were chosen to preside over the Church in Missouri.

"On the 12th of April, 1838, Oliver Cowdery was found guilty of serious wrong-doing for which he had not made repentance, and he was excommunicated by the high council at Far West. Before the same tribunal on the day following David Whitmer was charged with persistent disobedience of the word of wisdom and with unchristianlike conduct, and he was also cut off. Luke Johnson, Lyman E. Johnson and John F. Boynton were excommunicated about the same time, and less than a month later a similar fate befell William E. McLellin.

"It was a sorrowful day for Joseph when he lost the companionship of these men who had been with him during many trials and who had participated with him in the glorious undertaking of heavenly things. But they were no longer anything but dead branches, harmful to the growing tree, and it was necessary for the pruner to lop them off." (George Q. Cannon, *LJS,* pp. 221-24.)

SECTION 115

Background information on section 115

"On the 26th of April the Prophet received a very important revelation of instruction for the First Presidency, the apostles, the bishop, and the members of the Church. It will be noted that the counselors named to serve with the Prophet were Sidney Rigdon and Hyrum Smith. In the fall of the year 1837, Frederick G. Williams lost his standing because he had become disaffected and Hyrum Smith was called and sustained in his stead. . . .

"The word of the Lord was also to Bishop Partridge and those of the high council who had remained true, that from this time forth they should call the Church by its right name—The Church of Jesus Christ of Latter-day Saints, 'for thus shall my church be called in the last days.' . . . Since the Lord felt it important to remind the councils of the Church of its correct name and inform them that by that name it should be known in the last days, we should endeavor to carry out this commandment more nearly than it is the custom for many of us to do." (Joseph Fielding Smith, *CHMR* 2:85-86.)

115:4 *"thus shall my church be called . . . The Church of Jesus Christ of Latter-day Saints"*

"It will be observed that in verses three and four of this revelation the Lord gives to the Church its official name, 'The Church of Jesus Christ of Latter-day Saints.' Previous to this the Church had been called 'The Church of Christ,' 'The Church of Jesus Christ,' 'The Church of God,' and by a conference of Elders held at Kirtland in May, 1834 [*HC* 2:62-63], it was given the name 'The Church of the Latter-day Saints.' All these names, however, were by this revelation brushed aside, and since then the official name given in this revelation has been recognized as the true title of the Church, though often spoken of as 'The Mormon Church,' the 'Church of Christ,' etc. The appropriateness of this title is self evident, and in it there is a beautiful recognition of the relationship both of the Lord Jesus Christ and of the Saints to the organization. It is 'The Church of Jesus Christ.' It is the Lord's; He owns it, He organized it. It is the Sacred Depository of His truth. It is His instrumentality for promulgating all those spiritual truths with which He would have mankind acquainted. It is also His instrumentality for the perfecting of the Saints, as well as for the work of the ministry. It is His in all these respects; but it is an institution which also belongs to the Saints. It is their refuge from the confusion and religious doubt of the world. It is their instructor in principle, doctrine, and righteousness. It is their guide in matters of faith and morals. They have a conjoint ownership in it with Jesus Christ, which ownership is beautifully recognized in the latter part of the title. 'The Church of Jesus Christ of Latter-day Saints,' is equivalent to 'The Church of Jesus Christ,' and 'The Church of the Latter-day Saints.' " (*HC* 3:23-24, footnote.)

"Now, the Lord not only directed Joseph to organize his church: he told him what to name it. It is a fact worth noting that of all the churches then claiming to represent Christ, not one of them bore his name. Joseph learned from the teachings of Jesus to the Nephites that no church could be Christ's church unless it did bear his name. When the Nephites raised the question about what to name his church, Jesus, as he ministered among them, said:

" '. . . how be it my church save it be called in my name? For if a church be called in Moses' name then it be Moses' church; or if it be called in the name of a man then it be the church of a man; but if it be called in my name then it is my church, if it so be that they are built upon my gospel.' (3 Ne. 27:8.)

"This statement gives us the twofold test: Christ's church (1) must bear his name, and (2) must be built upon his gospel. That there should be no uncertainty about the name in this last dispensation, the Lord said to Joseph Smith: '. . . thus shall my church be called in the last days, even *The Church of Jesus Christ of Latter-day Saints.*' (D&C 115:4. Italics added.) The phrase 'Mormon Church' is a nickname. The restored church thus meets the Savior's twofold test: it bears his name and it is built upon his gospel." (Marion G. Romney, *Ensign,* January 1973, p. 31.)

"Consider what the real name means—'The Church of Jesus Christ of Latter-day Saints.' We can understand, easily, what 'latter-day' means—modern day, this day; but what does the word 'Saint' mean? By derivation, by acceptation, and by the best authority in the language, it means directly, used as an adjective, 'holy,' and when used as a noun, 'a holy one,' and we, therefore, profess to be a body of holy men, holy women. We proclaim ourselves in the name of Jesus Christ to be the holy ones of the last days, a significant proclamation, blasphemous in the extreme if it be not justified. . . .

"What should it mean to you and me, to be thus called a holy man, a holy woman? As thus applied, the term does not mean that the one who bears it is necessarily without weakness or devoid of blemish. An authorized usage of the term 'holy' is that it shall apply for exclusive service in the cause of God, and such we profess to be, set apart amongst men and nations as the people of God." (James E. Talmage, *CR*, April 1922, p. 72.)

115:5 *"be a standard for the nations"*

"It is designed in the heavens that this people shall be at the head, and that the great men of the nation will come by and by to Zion for counsel and wisdom. Where are we going to get it? What are our opportunities above other people? Why, we commune with the heavens. There is where we are in advance of the world. We not only have the advantages of their learning, but we have divine inspiration, by which our minds are enlightened. The Presidency of the Church have the heavens opened to them by the Spirit, and power of God, and they will be able to counsel the wisest of the nations. This time will come; nor is it far off." (Marriner W. Merrill, *CR*, April 1901, p. 26.)

"Probably the thought that has come to me most often has been as to the place and purpose of the Church in this war-torn world, this world of strife and unhappiness. What is our mission to the world? I have turned to the scriptures to get the answer, and have found the answer, both in ancient and modern scriptures. It is that the Church of Christ at all times must be as a standard to the nations, a standard to which all nations, all people, all men may turn as they seek safety, peace, and happiness. . . .

"Let me say that the Church itself cannot be this standard. Since the Church is made up of individuals, it becomes an individual responsibility to make the church a standard for the nations. I must be a standard in my life. I must so conduct myself that I may be a standard worthy of being followed by those who seek the greater joy in life." (John A. Widtsoe, *CR*, April 1940, p. 35.)

115:6   *"the gathering ... may be for a defense"*

See *Gathering* in Appendix A.

115:8   *"build a house unto me" at Far West*

"It was also declared in this revelation that the city of Far West should be made holy by consecration: [Sec. 115:7, quoted.] They were commanded to build a house unto the Lord, and the saints were to commence the preparatory work the coming summer, the time being set as July 4, 1838, when this should begin, and from that time forth they were to labor diligently to build the house unto the name of the Lord. When this revelation was given there was no house, or temple, recognized by the Lord as his. He had promised to make holy the temple in Kirtland, but had declared also that if it should be defiled it should no longer be his house and his name would not be upon it. [Sec. 97:15-17.] April 3, 1836, he accepted that house, but in the summer of 1837, it had been polluted, and apostates, wicked in spirit, had taken possession of that temple, hence the Lord rejected it as a sacred spot, an holy temple to his name. [Sec. 124:28.] Now came the command to build another house on ground that was consecrated. This house was to be built according to the Lord's plan, for it was to be a temple to his name." (Joseph Fielding Smith, *CHMR* 3:115-16.)

115:18   *"other places should be appointed for stakes"*

See *Stakes* in Appendix A.

115:19   *"I will sanctify him"*

See *Sanctify* in Appendix A.

SECTION 116

"Friday, May 18, 1838, the Prophet Joseph Smith, accompanied by Sidney Rigdon, Thomas B. Marsh, David W. Patten, Bishop Edward Partridge, Elias Higbee, Simeon Carter, Alanson Ripley and many others, left Far West for the purpose of exploring the country north of Far West with the intention of preparing boundaries for stakes of Zion. On this trip they proposed to select locations and lay off claims to unoccupied lands preparatory to the gathering of the members of the Church from other parts, and for the benefit of the poor. They traveled to the mouth of Honey Creek, a tributary of Grand River, and camped for the night. They passed through a beautiful country, mostly a prairie which was thickly covered with grass and weeds. This territory they said was inhabited by wild turkeys, deer, prairie chickens and other game. They saw a wolf to which the Prophet's dog gave chase. The Prophet said they had nothing to fear except rattlesnakes that were occasionally found. Their horses were turned loose to feed on the prairie, and the next morning, after striking their tents, they crossed Grand River at the mouth of Honey Creek and at Nelson's Ferry. This stream they described as a large, beautiful, deep and rapid stream during high water in the spring, which would admit of navigation. They continued their course up the river through considerable timber, for about eighteen miles, and came to Lyman Wight's home. He lived at the foot of Tower Hill, as the Prophet called it, 'a name I gave the place in consequence of the remains of an old Nephite altar or tower that stood there, where we camped for the Sabbath.' In the afternoon after making camp, the Prophet, Sidney Rigdon, and George W. Robinson, his clerk, did a little exploring up Grand River about one half mile to Wight's Ferry, their object being to lay claim to a city plat near said ferry in Daviess County, township 60, ranges 27 and 28, and sections 25, 36, 31 and 30. The brethren called this place 'Spring Hill,' but the Prophet by the word of the Lord named it 'Adam-ondi-Ahman, because said the Lord, it is the place where Adam shall come to visit his people, or the Ancient of Days shall sit, as spoken of by Daniel the Prophet.' " (Joseph Fielding Smith, *CHMR* 2:88-89.)

"Adam-ondi-Ahman is located immediately on the north side of Grand River, in Daviess county, Missouri, about twenty-five miles north of Far West. It is situated on an elevated spot of ground, which renders the place as healthful as any part of the United States, and overlooking the river and the country round about, it is certainly a beautiful location." (Joseph Smith, *HC* 3:39.)

116:1 *"Adam-ondi-Ahman"*

See same title in Appendix A.

"One of the hymns sung at the dedication of the Kirtland Temple was by Elder William W. Phelps, known as 'Adam-ondi-Ahman.' The name, therefore, was well known before this visit to Tower Hill, and before the Prophet had pointed out this place as the one where Adam visited his posterity, and where he will come at the grand council. (See 'The Gathering at Adam-ondi-Ahman,' Chapter 40, *The Way to Perfection.*)" (Joseph Fielding Smith, *CHMR* 2:90.)

116:1 *"where Adam . . . the Ancient of Days"*

See *Adam* in Appendix A.

"Daniel in his seventh chapter speaks of the Ancient of Days; he means the oldest man, our Father Adam, Michael, he will call his children together and hold a council with them to prepare them for the coming of the Son of Man." (Joseph Smith, *HC* 3:386-87.)

"In the 107th Section, the Lord speaks of Adam as 'Michael, the Prince, the Archangel,' and says that he shall be a prince over the nations forever. We may with perfect propriety call him prince, the ancient of days, or even God in the meaning of the words of Christ, which I have just quoted [Sec. 78:16]; but we do not worship him, we worship the same God that he worshipped." (Anthon H. Lund, *CR*, October 1902, p. 81.)

SECTION 117

"July 8, 1838, the Lord gave the Prophet Joseph Smith a number of short, but very important revelations, including those on tithing, one to William Marks, and Oliver Granger, one to Bishop Whitney and one in relation to the apostles. These are sections 117, 118, 119 and 120 in the Doctrine and Covenants, but they are not arranged in the Doctrine and Covenants in the order in which they appear in the *Documentary History of the Church.* Then there was another revelation to William W. Phelps and Frederick G. Williams, which is not in the Doctrine and Covenants." (Joseph Fielding Smith, *CHMR* 2:95.)

"The departure of the Church leaders from Kirtland [Jan. 1838] had been the signal for a general migration of the Mormons from Ohio to Missouri. Far West was now their gathering place—not their Zion, but only a stake of Zion, as Kirtland had been before. All during the spring and summer of 1838 the exodus continued, until the Saints remaining at Kirtland were very few. Apostles [Heber C.] Kimball and [Orson] Hyde, arriving there from Europe in May, tarried only long enough to arrange their affairs and make suitable preparations for their journey to Missouri. About the 1st of July the two Apostles, accompanied by Erastus Snow, Winslow Farr and others, with their families, set out for Far West. Among those remaining at Kirtland were Bishop N. K. Whitney and Oliver Granger, who had charge of the Church property in Ohio." (Orson F. Whitney, *History of Utah,* 1:140-44.)

"The Lord had commanded the Saints to gather and build up Far West speedily (See Sec. 115:17). A company of 515 souls, known as the *Kirtland Camp,* left Kirtland on the 6th of July, 1838, for Zion. On the 14th of September, it appears only 260 members were left, the others having been scattered 'to the four winds.' The camp arrived in Adam-ondi-Ahman on the 4th of October. Neither Marks, Whitney, nor Granger were members of this company. Joseph Smith at Far West had no means of knowing, at that time, who had, or who had not, left for Zion; but the Lord knew. Hence this Revelation in which He (1) calls William Marks and Newel K. Whitney to come to Zion and instructs the Saints concerning the property in Kirtland. (*Commentary,* p. 744.)

"It is quite evident that these two brethren had fallen under the spell of speculation and temptation so rife in Kirtland in 1837, and which was the downfall of so many of the leading brethren of the Church. However, they had not lost their faith and when the Lord gave them this call, they proceeded to obey the command." (Joseph Fielding Smith, *CHMR* 2:96.)

17:1, 12   *William Marks, Newel K. Whitney, Oliver Granger*

For additional information on these brethren, see Appendix B.

"William Marks was born November 15, 1792, in Rutland, Rutland County, Vermont. This is the first mention of his name in the Prophet's narrative, and nothing can be learned of his career previous to this time." (Joseph Smith, *HC* 2:486.)

"Oliver Granger was a man of faith and business ability—two qualities which form a rare combination. He characterized the Kirtland Camp as the greatest undertaking since the organization of the Church, and he firmly believed that God would bless that endeavor. (*HC* 3:96.) When the Prophet fled from Kirtland, he appointed Granger his business agent, and so well did he perform this duty that he was commended by business men. At a conference held at Quincy, May 4th to 6th, 1839, he was appointed to return to Kirtland and take charge of the Temple and Church there. This makes the concluding verses of the Revelation perfectly clear. His name is to be held in remembrance for his faithful services as a man of business, having sanctified his talent to the service of the Lord." (Smith and Sjodahl, *DCC*, p. 746.)

117:4   *"what is property unto me? saith the Lord"*

The Lord has created the heavens and the earth "and all things that in them are." (3 Ne. 9:15.) He can create (organize) many other earths if necessary. Thus, one soul is much more important to the Lord than the whole earth: "For what is a man profited, if he shall gain the whole world, and lose his own soul?" (Matt. 16:26.)

117:6 *"Do I not hold the destinies of all the armies of the nations?"*

"Surely the Lord made the earth and he owns it. His government the nations of the earth rejected and in its stead set up governments of their own making, and this has been the condition from the beginning until now. Kings and potentates all down the ages, thought they, by their own acts, controlled the destinies of nations, and held dominion. Without the permission of the Almighty they never could have ruled and held dominion. All who have a correct insight into the history of nations must surely know that the Lord has always held a controlling hand over the nations of the world. When they have become corrupt he has relieved them of power. When they have entered on expeditions of conquest he has permitted them to go just so far, then as he said to Ezekiel concerning Gog and Magog, he puts hooks in their jaws, and defeats their purpose. Truly he holds the destinies of the armies of the nations of the earth; and not only the armies, but the destinies of nations, and when the time is ripe he will make an end of all nations that now rule in their arrogance and mistaken idea of might and power, and set up his own kingdom to endure forever." (Joseph Fielding Smith, *CHMR* 2:96-97.)

117:7 *"will I not make solitary places to bud and to blossom?"*

"He has promised to make the solitary places to bud and to blossom, and to bring forth in abundance. . . . From this we gather that these brethren still regretted leaving their possessions in Kirtland, and the Lord assures them that there is more in store for them in the land to which he has called them." (Joseph Fielding Smith, *CHMR* 2:97.)

117:8 *"the plains of Olaha Shinehah"*

"The plains of Olaha Shinehah, or the place where Adam dwelt, must be a part of, or in the vicinity of Adam-ondi-Ahman. This name Olaha Shinehah, may be, and in all probability is, from the language of Adam. We may without great controversy believe that this is the name which Adam gave to this place, at least we may venture this as a probable guess. Shinehah, according to the Book of Abraham, is the name given to the sun. (Abraham 3:13.) It is the name applied to Kirtland when the Lord desired in a revelation to hide its identity. (Sec. 82.) Elder Janne M. Sjodahl commenting on the name, Olaha Shinehah, has said: 'Shinehah means sun, and Olaha is possibly a variant of the word Olea, which is "the moon." (Abraham 3:13.) If so the plains of Olaha Shinehah would be the Plains of the Moon and the Sun, so called, perhaps because of astronomical observations there made.' We learn from the writings of Moses that the Lord revealed to the ancients great knowledge concerning the stars, and Abraham by revelations and through the Urim and Thummim received wonderful information concerning the heavens and the governing planets, or stars. It was also revealed by the Prophet Joseph Smith that Methuselah was acquainted with the stars as were others of the antediluvian prophets including Adam. So it may be reasonable that here in this valley important information was made known anciently in relation to the stars of our universe." (Joseph Fielding Smith, *CHMR* 2:97-98.)

117:11 *"Newel K. Whitney be ashamed of the Nicolaitane band"*

"Bishop Whitney was called on to forsake the abominations of those in Kirtland, whom the Lord designates as the 'Nicolaitane band.' He was to be ashamed of 'his littleness of soul,' and go to the land of Adam-ondi-Ahman and there serve as bishop." (Joseph Fielding Smith, *CHMR* 3:125.)

7:12-16 *Revelation pertaining to Oliver Granger*

"Oliver Granger, who had remained faithful, was commended by the Lord and also commanded to move to Far West. The Lord promised that his name should be had in 'sacred remembrance from generation to generation, forever and ever, saith the Lord.' Oliver Granger came as he was commanded and fulfilled his mission as a merchant in that place. In May, 1839, he was appointed to return to Kirtland and take charge of the temple and church property. He died while in this service, September 23, 1841." (Joseph Fielding Smith, *CHMR* 3:125-26.)

SECTION 118

Background information on section 118

See background information for section 117.

118:1 *"Let a conference be held immediately; let the Twelve be organized"*

"In answer to the supplication: 'Show us thy will, O Lord, concerning the twelve,' the Lord commanded that a conference be held immediately to fill the places vacated by those who had fallen. . . . The command was given that the apostles were to take their leave next spring and cross the 'great waters' and there take up the work commenced by Elders Kimball, Hyde and others in 1837. The Lord said: 'Let them take leave of my saints in the city of Far West, on the twenty-sixth day of April next, on the building-spot of my house, saith the Lord.' Men were selected to fill the vacancies caused by the excommunication of William E. M'Lellin, Luke S. Johnson, John F. Boynton, and Lyman E. Johnson. The men appointed by revelation were: John Taylor, John E. Page, Wilford Woodruff and Willard Richards, the latter serving as a counselor in the British Mission at the time. These four brethren were to be officially notified of their appointment.

"According to this commandment a council meeting was called and convened July 9, 1838." (Joseph Fielding Smith, *CHMR* 2:98.)

118:5 *"Let them take leave . . . of Far West, on the twenty-sixth day of April next"*

"The Lord knew, of course, that events would happen before April 26, 1839, by which the Latter-day Saints who remained true to the faith would be driven from Missouri by the exterminating order of Governor Boggs, but apostates would be permitted to remain and be nurtured by the mob. It appears that this call was made to try the faith of the brethren, to see if they would fulfill the commandment at the risk of their lives. Before the end of the year 1838 most of the saints had been driven from their homes. The few who remained were given orders to be gone by Friday, April 11, 1839, or forfeit their lives. The last to leave were the members of the committee on removal, who were told April 18th, to be gone within one hour or take the consequences. By the 26th of that month Far West was practically deserted, so far as members of the Church were concerned. That this prophecy might be fulfilled appeared to be impossible, for the members of the mob had declared that should one of the apostles return to Far West they would kill him on the spot." (Joseph Fielding Smith, *CHMR* 2:195.)

"Enemies of the Church threatened to make compliance with this command impossible, but when the day came, the Twelve and others met on the Temple ground at Far West, and Alpheus Cutler laid the foundation stone again, by rolling up a stone and placing it near the southeast corner, according to the Revelation (Section 115:11), whereupon the Twelve engaged in prayer. Then they sang, 'Adam-ondi-Ahman,' and, finally, took leave of the Saints. Then they were ready for their respective missions. When the enemies heard of the proceedings, they were very much chagrined because they had forgotten the *date.*" (Smith and Sjodahl, *DCC,* pp. 747-48.)

118:6 *For biographical information on the brethren mentioned, see Appendix B.*

SECTION 119

Background information on section 119

See background information for section 117.

"July 8, 1838, the Prophet prayed to the Lord saying: 'O Lord! Show unto thy servant how much thou requirest of the properties of thy people for a tithing,' and he received a revelation known as Section 119. The Lord had given to the Church the law of consecration and had called upon the members, principally the official members, to enter into a covenant that could not be broken and to be everlasting in which they were to consecrate their properties and receive stewardships, for this is the law of the celestial kingdom. Many of those who entered into this solemn covenant broke it and by so doing brought upon their heads, and the heads of their brethren and sisters, dire punishment and persecution. This celestial law of necessity was thereupon withdrawn for the time, or until the time of the redemption of Zion. While suffering intensely because of their debts and lack of means to meet their obligations, Joseph Smith and Oliver Cowdery, November 29, 1834, in solemn prayer promised the Lord that they would give one tenth of all that the Lord should give unto them, as an offering to be bestowed upon the poor; they also prayed that their children, and children's children after them should obey this law. (*HC* 2:174-5.) Now, however, it became necessary for the law to be given to the whole Church so the Prophet prayed for instruction. The answer [Section 119] they received [came] in the revelation." (Joseph Fielding Smith, *CHMR* 2:90-91.)

"The law of tithing, as now understood, had not been given to the Church previous to this Revelation. The term 'tithing' in the prayer quoted in the headlines, and in previous Revelations (64:23; 85:3; 97:11), is, therefore, synonymous with 'free-will offering,' or 'contribution' to the Church funds. The question presented in the petition to the Almighty was not how much a tenth part of the property of the people amounted to, but how much of that property He required for sacred purposes. The answer was this Revelation on the Law of Tithing." (Smith and Sjodahl, *DCC,* p. 749.)

119:1 *"I require all their surplus property to be put into the hands of the bishop"*

"Let us consider for a moment this word 'surplus.' What does it mean when applied to a man and his property? Surplus cannot mean that which is indispensably necessary for any given purpose, but what remains after supplying what is needed for that purpose. Is not the first and most necessary use of a man's property that he feed, clothe and provide a home for himself and family! . . . Was not 'surplus property,' that which was over and above a comfortable and necessary substance? In the light of what had transpired and of subsequent events, what else could it mean? Can we take any other view of it when we consider the circumstances under which it was given in Far West, in July, 1838?

"I have been unable in studying this subject to find any other definition of the term 'surplus,' as used in this revelation, than the one I have just given." (Franklin D. Richards, *JD* 23:313.)

"In more recent years the Church has not called upon the members to give all their surplus property to the Church, but it has been the requirement according to the covenant, that they pay the tenth." (Joseph Fielding Smith, *CHMR* 3:120.)

119:3 *"tithing"*

See *Tithing* in Appendix A.

"Tithe-paying is not a principle new to our dispensation. Whenever the Lord has had a people on the earth who were willing to observe his laws, and they were not practicing the law of consecration, they have been called upon to pay tithes and offerings. Abraham gave tithes of all to Melchizedek, keeper of the Lord's storehouse, and king of Salem. (Gen. 14:20.) Jacob made a covenant very similar to that of Joseph Smith and Oliver Cowdery. (Gen. 28:22.) This law was given through Moses to Israel. Malachi said the people in his day had robbed the Lord in withholding their tithes and offerings. The Savior commended those who paid an honest tithing, such as the widow and her mite. This law is one binding upon members of the Church. We call it a free-will offering, and so it is, for everything in the Gospel is by free will, but nevertheless it is a law of God which to us is everlasting." (Joseph Fielding Smith, *CHMR* 2:92.)

119:4 *"one-tenth of all their interest annually"*

"When you are in doubt as to just how you should calculate your tithes, reverse the terms as we sometimes do in solving complex mathematical problems, and suppose for the time being that the Lord had said this; let us postulate this is an assumed law given to the Church: 'In order to show my love for my people, the faithful members of my Church, it is my will, saith the Lord, that each one shall receive from my storehouse, the storehouse of my Church, at regular intervals during the year, an amount equal to one-tenth of his income.' Now my dear brother, sit down and calculate how much the Lord owes you under that kind of law, and then go pay it to your bishop." (James E. Talmage, *CR*, October 1928, p. 119.)

"I want to say to you . . . that the law of tithing is not a question of dollars and cents alone. I believe that the man who pays his honest tithing to God will not only be blessed by God himself, but that the nine-tenths will reach farther than the other ten-tenths would if he did not obey that law." (Reed Smoot, *CR*, October 1900, pp. 7-8.)

119:4 *"this shall be a standing law unto them forever, for my holy priesthood"*

"Do we not hope and expect to have an inheritance in the celestial kingdom, even upon this earth in its redeemed and sanctified state? [Sec. 88:25-26; 130:9.] What are the terms under which we may obtain that inheritance? The law of tithing is the law of inheritance. It leads to it. No man may hope or expect to have an inheritance on this celestial globe who has failed to pay his tithing. By the payment of his honest tithing he is establishing a right and a title to this inheritance, and he cannot secure it upon any other terms but by complying with this and other just requirements; and this is one of the very essential things." (Melvin J. Ballard, *CR*, October 1929, pp. 50-51.)

"There is a great deal of importance connected with this principle, for by it shall be known whether we are faithful or unfaithful. In this respect it is as essential as faith in God, as repentance of sin, as baptism for the remission of sin, or as the laying on of hands for the gift of the Holy Ghost. For if a man keep all the law save in one point, and he offend in that, he is a transgressor of the law, and he is not entitled to the fulness of the blessings of the Gospel of Jesus Christ. [Sec. 93:10; James 2:10.] But when a man keeps all the law that is revealed, according to his strength, his substance and his ability, though what he does may be little, it is just as acceptable in the sight of God as if he were able to do a thousand times more." (Joseph F. Smith, *CR*, April 1900, p. 47.)

119:6   *"by this law sanctify the land of Zion"*

"Do you know that the soil can be sanctified by the tithing of its products? The land can be sanctified. [Mal. 3:8-10.] There is a relationship between the elements and forces of nature and the actions of men." (James E. Talmage, *CR*, October 1929, p. 68.)

SECTION 120

See background information for section 117.

"This Revelation is dated July 18th, but from the *History of the Church* (Vol. III, p. 44) it appears that it was given on the 8th, the same day on which the Revelations contained in Sections 117, 118, and 119 were received. It is a promise that the Lord will guide His servants by His Spirit in the expenditure of the offerings of the Saints—a promise that, as the results prove, has been fulfilled." (Smith and Sjodahl, *DCC,* p. 750.)*

120:1 *The tithing "shall be disposed of by a council"*

"Pursuant to these revelations [Sections 119 and 120], and as explained at recent conferences, the church has a council on the Distribution of Tithes, made up of the First Presidency, the Council of the Twelve, and the Presiding Bishopric. This Council considers the proposed budget of the Church, which is itemized under general headings, and then approves and authorizes such expenditures as it deems proper.

"A subcommittee of this Council on the Distribution of Tithes then makes the detailed appropriations from the sums approved and authorized by the Council. This subcommittee is known as the Committee on Expenditures, and is made up of the First Presidency, three members of the Council of the Twelve, and the Presiding Bishopric." (J. Reuben Clark, Jr., *CR,* April 1948, pp. 116-17.)

---

*Note: From the above information, it would seem that the date of this revelation should be July 8, 1838, rather than July 18, 1838, which appears in the 1950 edition of the Doctrine and Covenants.

SECTION 121

Background information on section 121

"LIBERTY JAIL, CLAY COUNTY, MISSOURI,
"March 25, 1839.
"To the Church of Latter-day Saints at Quincy, Illinois, and Scattered Abroad, and to Bishop Partridge in Particular: Your humble servant, Joseph Smith, Jun., prisoner for the Lord Jesus Christ's sake, and for the Saints, taken and held by the power of mobocracy, under the exterminating reign of his excellency, the governor, Lilburn W. Boggs, in company with his fellow prisoners and beloved brethren, Caleb Baldwin, Lyman Wight, Hyrum Smith, and Alexander McRae, send unto you all greeting. May the grace of God the Father, and of our Lord and Savior Jesus Christ, rest upon you all, and abide with you forever. May knowledge be multiplied unto you by the mercy of God. And may faith and virtue, and knowledge and temperance, and patience and godliness, and brotherly kindness and charity be in you and abound, that you may not be barren in anything, nor unfruitful." (Joseph Smith, *HC* 3:289.)

"While the Prophet Joseph Smith and his companions, Hyrum Smith, Lyman Wight, Caleb Baldwin, Alexander McRae and part of the time, Sidney Rigdon, were confined in Liberty [Missouri] Jail awaiting trial on false charges, and suffering unspeakable abuse from the wicked and filthy guards who attended them, they were, notwithstanding all the abuse, permitted to see some of their friends occasionally. These friends who were permitted to come to the jail were also permitted at times to bring letters from the prisoners' families. They were also able to forward communications in this way to their friends. One of these communications from the Prophet to the Church at Quincy—for the Saints had been driven from Missouri—was written March 25, 1839, and was signed by all of his companions. This is one of the greatest letters that was ever penned by the hand of man. In fact it was the result of humble inspiration.

It [Section 121] is a prayer and a prophecy and an answer by revelation from the Lord. None other but a noble soul filled with the spirit of love of Christ could have written such a letter. Considering the fact that these prisoners had been confined several months; were fed on food at times not fit for a pig, and at times impregnated with poison and once being offered human flesh, evidently from the body of one of their brethren, it is no wonder that the Prophet cried out in the anguish of his soul for relief. Yet, in his earnest pleading, there breathed a spirit of tolerance and love for his fellow man." (Joseph Fielding Smith, *CHMR* 2:175-76.)

121:1 *"O God, where art thou?"*

"In his anguish the Savior cried unto his Father while on the cross. In his anguish yet pleading not so much for himself as for his afflicted brethren, the Prophet also cried in earnest pleading: 'O God, where art thou? And where is the pavilion that covereth thy hiding place?' Did he feel that he had been forsaken? This he alone can answer. Yet his trust was in the Lord, for all other help had failed him." (Joseph Fielding Smith, *CHMR* 2:176.)

121:4 *"O Lord God Almighty, maker of heaven, earth, and seas, and of all things that in them are"*

See *Creator, Jesus Christ,* and *God* in Appendix A.

121:4 *"thy pavilion . . . thy hiding place"*

"These are expressions used by the authors of the Bible. When David says, 'He made darkness his hiding-place, his pavilion round about him; darkness of waters, thick clouds of the skies' (Ps. 18:11), he considers the darkness of the thundercloud as a tent, or pavilion, in which Jehovah dwells in His majesty. The thunder-bolts, the hail, the wind, are His messengers. The Prophet Joseph, by using this grand, poetic conception, entreats the Lord to manifest Himself in His power for the salvation of the Saints from their enemies." (Smith and Sjodahl, *DCC,* p. 753.)

121:7 *"My son, . . . thine adversity and thine afflictions shall be but a small moment"*

See *Adversity* in Appendix A.

"The Lord said to Adam that for his sake the earth was cursed and that he should eat his food in sorrow all the days of his life. [Moses 4:23.] The scriptures say that man is born unto trouble as the sparks fly upward [Job 5:7], which means that it is in the design of God that we should have these adversities and experiences in the world. . . . The Prophet Joseph Smith one time said, when someone had remarked that somebody had affliction because of his sins, that it is an unhallowed statement to make, that afflictions come to all. . . .

"The Lord has expressed himself about these adversities that come, and I speak for example, of the Prophet Joseph Smith, who had adversity from the moment he delivered his glorious message of the vision in the grove. You will remember in Liberty Jail he cried out: [Sec. 121:1, 3, quoted.]

"What was the Lord's answer to this prayer? [Sec. 121:7-8, quoted.] Then the Lord held up before him other trials and difficulties that were to come, some even worse than he had had, but then said to him: '. . . know thou, my son, that all these things shall give thee experience, and shall be for thy good. The Son of Man hath descended below them all. Art thou greater than he?' [D&C 122:7-8.]

"So, in adversity we may have that which will exalt us, or we may have that which will degrade us. We may have that which, 'if we endure it well,' will ennoble us, and we may have that which, if we indulge in self-pity and bitterness, may destroy us. In all our adversities there are these two elements, and the determining factor is how shall we endure them? Shall we endure them well? If not, they may destroy us." (George Q. Morris, *CR*, October 1958, pp. 70-72.)

121:10   *"Thou art not yet as Job"*

The story of Job is found in the Old Testament book that carries his name, but the New Testament also refers to the "patience of Job." (See James 5:11.)

"I wonder if there are a few here within the sound of my voice, that have feelings of this kind [everything is going wrong], like old Job had, for instance. A poor man who wondered why his children were taken from him; why his herds were destroyed and why his houses, his dwellings, went up in flames, and why he was left without anything. . . . The Lord had a certain position in which He sought to place Job in the future at some future time when years and years had rolled away perhaps, and He wanted to try him. He wanted to educate him so that he would not complain, no matter how illy he thought himself treated by the Lord. That was a glorious trial of Job's. It has come down in history; his experience and his trials, and it has been a wonderful consolation to the people of the Lord to read the history of his experiences and his trials and how well he passed through them." (Lorenzo Snow, *CR*, October 1900, p. 4.)

121:11 *"their hope shall be blasted"*

"From the earliest days of the Church, malcontents, apostates, 'soreheads,' have railed out with slander, false-hood, derision, against those whom God called to lead the people. They so treated the Prophet, and Brother Brigham [Young], and to a lesser degree, every President who has followed. But the Lord has always prospered the Church as it followed their leadership. The detractors have gone down to the oblivion they deserved. So it will always be. The Prophet of the Lord has stood above and beyond the carpings of those unrighteous critics. He has always lived, as our leader lives today, in the kindly light of the Lord's approval, the recipient of the Lord's choicest blessings, manifested openly to those who will but look." (J. Reuben Clark, Jr., *CR*, April 1940, p. 22.)

121:12 *"God hath set his hand and seal to change the times and seasons"*

When read in context, it is quite evident that this statement is reinforcing the power and "marvelous workings" of God. Only the Lord has the power to change the times and seasons of this earth.

121:16 *"Cursed are all those . . . against mine anointed"*

"There are some who look upon the leaders of this Church and God's anointed as men who are possessed of selfish motives. By them the words of our leaders are always twisted to try to bring a snare to the work of the Lord. Mark well those who speak evil of the Lord's anointed for they speak from impure hearts. . . .

"I remember the prophetic pronouncement that was made from this stand by President George Albert Smith eighteen months ago when he said: 'Many have belittled Joseph Smith, and those who have will be forgotten in the remains of mother earth and the odor of their infamy will be ever with them, but honor, majesty, and fidelity to God attached to Joseph Smith's name and exemplified by him will never die.' I wish that statement could be heard to all the ends of the earth." (Harold B. Lee, *CR*, October 1947, pp. 66-67.)

:16-17   *"they have sinned"*

Several references in these two verses seem rather vague, but it is quite evident the correct meaning is indicated in the following words enclosed in brackets:

Cursed are all those that shall lift up the heel against mine anointed, saith the Lord, and cry they [mine anointed] have sinned when they have not sinned before me, saith the Lord, but have done that which was meet in mine eyes, and which I commanded them.

But those who cry transgression [on the part of mine anointed] do it because they [those who lift up the heel against mine anointed] are the servants of sin, and are the children of disobedience themselves.

121:23   *"Wo unto all those that discomfort my people"*

"Our enemies have never done anything that has injured this work of God, and they never will. I look around, I read, I reflect, and I ask questions, where are the men of influence, of power and prestige, who have worked against the Latter-day Saints? Where is the reputation for honor and courage, of the governors of Missouri and Illinois, the judges, and all others who have come here to Utah on special missions against the Latter-day Saints? Where are there people to do them honor? They cannot be found. . . . Where are the men who have assailed this work? Where is their influence? They have faded away like dew before the sun." (Heber J. Grant, *CR*, April 1909, p. 11.)

121:26   *"God shall give unto you knowledge"*

"The promise was made that knowledge by the Holy Spirit would be given to the Prophet, even the unspeakable gift of the Holy Ghost, and things would be made known that had not been revealed since the world was until now. . . . Much of this information was revealed to the Prophet in the following years in Nauvoo and pertained to the eternal salvation of mankind both living and dead. Much of it still awaits fulfillment, so far as the saints are concerned. How much the Lord revealed to Joseph Smith we do not know, but it was far more than he was permitted to reveal to his fellows." (Joseph Fielding Smith, *CHMR* 2:177.)

121:26 *"the unspeakable gift of the Holy Ghost"*

See *Holy Ghost* in Appendix A.

121:28 *"whether there be one God or many Gods"*

"I want to say this to all Israel: Cease troubling yourselves about who God is; who Adam is, who Christ is, who Jehovah is. Let these things alone. Why trouble yourselves about these things? God has revealed Himself, and when the 121st section of the Doctrine and Covenants is fulfilled, whether there be one God or many Gods they will be revealed to the children of men as well as thrones and dominions, principalities, and powers. Then why trouble yourselves about these things? God is God. Christ is Christ. The Holy Ghost is the Holy Ghost. That should be enough for you and me to know. If we want to know any more wait till we get where God is in person." (Wilford Woodruff, *MS* 57:355-56.)

121:31 *"all . . . shall be revealed in the days of the dispensation of the fulness of times"*

See *Dispensation* in Appendix A.

121:32 *"Council of the Eternal God . . . before this world was"*

See *Pre-earthly existence* in Appendix A.

121:34 *"there are many called"*

"Now who are those who are called? I take it that every man who is ordained to an office in the priesthood has been called." (Joseph Fielding Smith, *CR,* October 1945, p. 97.)

121:34 *"few are chosen"*

"There are many who are called to serve in the kingdom of God. The Priesthood has been conferred upon a multitude of brethren, but out of this multitude only those will be chosen who endure in faith to the end. The Lord has never promised to those who are unfaithful, who have received the call and appointment but have not endured, that they shall receive the blessing. While there are many who seemingly feel this to be the case, only those who serve and are faithful shall be chosen. The reason why so many fall away is explained to be, 'because their hearts are set . . . upon the things of this world, and aspire to the honors of men.' " (Joseph Fielding Smith, *CHMR* 2:177-78.)

21:35 *"their hearts are set so much upon the things of this world"*

"Some years ago, I read an editorial in the *Deseret News* entitled 'The Mechanical Rabbit.' I quote: 'Most of our readers must have smiled the other day when they read of the greyhounds in Britain *who don't know a rabbit when they see one.* So long had they chased a mechanical rabbit around the racetrack, that when a *real rabbit* bounded across the track, the dogs didn't give it a second look.

" 'Stupid, eh? But sad too, this perverting of the natural instincts. . . .

" 'We chase mechanical rabbits, too.

" 'We chase *paychecks,* and don't give a second look to the glint of the rising sun on a snow-topped peak.

" 'We chase our way through the *appointments* of a crowded desk calendar, and fail to take time to chat with the next-door neighbor or to drop in on a sick friend.

" 'We chase *social pleasures* on a glittering noisy treadmill—and ignore the privilege of a quiet hour telling bedtime stories to an innocent-eyed child.

" 'We chase *prestige* and *wealth,* and don't recognize the real opportunities for joy that cross our paths. . . .

" 'Race on, you poor, blind over-civilized hounds. You'll never catch your rabbit until you learn to recognize a genuine one.

" 'But, you'll have company in your race; the company of unnumbered men who'll never catch the joy they chase until they, too, learn to recognize a genuine one.' . . .

"In modern revelation the Lord said: 'Behold, there are many called, but few are chosen. And why are they not chosen? Because their hearts are set so much upon the things of this world, and aspire to the honors of men. . . .' (D&C 121:34-35.)

"Here is instruction to straighten out our values. . . . Have we sought 'so much' for material things while missing, even ignoring, the things of God?" (A. Theodore Tuttle, *Ensign,* December 1971, p. 90.)

21:38 *"he is left . . . to kick against the pricks"*

"Men begin to fall away. They first begin to 'kick against the pricks.' . . . These no doubt are the pricks of the gospel. I wonder, perhaps, if they are not those things President J.

Reuben Clark . . . called 'restraints,' the restraints of the word of wisdom, the restraints imposed in keeping the Sabbath day holy, injunctions against card playing, the restraints imposed by following out the welfare program. And so we might go on. These are the restraints against which some people seem to rebel and are kicking constantly against—the 'pricks' of the gospel. . . . These [persons] are the ones who next begin to 'persecute the Saints' and, finally, to fight against God." (Harold B. Lee, *CR,* October 1947, pp. 65-66.)

121:39 *"it is the nature and disposition of almost all men . . . to exercise unrighteous dominion"*

"Most men are inclined to abuse authority, especially those who wield it who are the least prepared to hold positions of trust. It has been the characteristic of men in power to use that power to gratify their own pride and vain ambitions. More misery has come to the inhabitants of this world through the exercise of authority by those who least deserved it, than from almost any other cause. Rulers of kingdoms in the past have oppressed their subjects, and where they had the power they have sought to increase their dominions. We have had some horrible examples of misplaced ambition which, in recent years, placed the very existence of humanity in peril. These conditions still prevail in high places bringing fear and consternation to the troubled world.

"There should not, however, be any of this unrighteous ambition within the Church, but everything should be done in the spirit of love and humility."(Joseph Fielding Smith, *CHMR* 2:178.)

"All men who hold position do not abuse its privileges, and the man who serves God humbly and faithfully never will, for the moment he yielded to the temptation so to do, that moment would he cease to serve the Lord; but there are many, alas, who sadly misuse the functions of their office, and prostitute every power and privilege to the gratification of self and the injury and embarrassment of their fellow men. It is dangerous to put some men into power. They swell up and become so distended with the ideas of their greatness and importance, that we are forcibly reminded of so many inflated toy balloons, which the slightest prick of a pin would burst and ruin forever. A very small office and a very little authority is sufficient to intoxicate some men and render them entirely unfit for duty." (Orson F. Whitney, *Scrapbook of Mormon Literature,* 2:510-13.)

121:43 *"Reproving betimes with sharpness"*

"I frequently rebuke and admonish my brethren, and that because I love them, not because I wish to incur their displeasure, or mar their happiness." (Joseph Smith, *HC* 2:478.)

"It is a kindness to reprove in the spirit of love. It is an unkindness to mitigate the gravity of offenses in those for whose guidance and direction we have responsibility. . . . Teach duty, require duty, if need be, in children to bless their lives with proper understanding and practices essential to their happiness." (Stephen L Richards, *CR,* April 1957, pp. 97-98.)

121:45 *"let virtue garnish thy thoughts unceasingly"*

"I know of no greater promise made by God to man than this promise made to those who let virtue garnish their thoughts unceasingly.

"Channing Pollock once remarked: 'A world in which everyone believed in the purity of women and the nobility of men, and acted accordingly, would be a very different world, but a grand place to live in.' (*Reader's Digest,* June 1960, p. 76.)

"I assure you, . . . that it would be a world of freedom in which the spirit of man might grow to undreamed-of glory, a world of peace, the peace of clear conscience, of unsullied love, of fidelity, of unfailing trust and loyalty. This may appear an unattainable dream for the world. But for each of you it can be a reality, and the world will become so much the richer and the stronger for the virtue of your individual lives." (Gordon B. Hinckley, *IE,* December 1970, p. 73.)

"How I wish that virtue garnished our thoughts unceasingly. How I wish that no man holding the Priesthood of the living God was ever guilty of allowing any words to fall from his lips that he could not repeat in the presence of his mother. Then he would be, to a very great extent, in that straight and narrow path that leads to life eternal." (Heber J. Grant, *CR,* April 1937, pp. 11-12.)

SECTION 122

See background information for section 121.

"The enemies of the work of God . . . imprisoned the Prophet in Liberty Jail [Missouri], where he received two very remarkable revelations. [March 25, 1839, *HC* 3:289-305.] They are known as Sections 121 and 122 of the Doctrine and Covenants, also a remarkable document which was published regarding the persecutions of the Saints. (Section 123.) The mob could not prevent the Prophet from receiving communications from God." (Heber J. Grant, *CR,* April 1937, p. 6.)

122:1 *"The ends of the earth shall inquire after thy name"*

"With comforting words to the Prophet during this time when all the world looked so dark and he lay in prison, the Lord informed him that the time would come when the ends of the earth should inquire after his name. Naturally this seemed impossible at that time, and only the Spirit of the Lord could have made it known. . . . We have lived to see all of this fulfilled, and yet it has only been fulfilled in part. However, through the preaching of the Gospel in most all parts of the earth, there have come out of the world, the righteous, the pure in heart and the noble to pay tribute to his name. They have sought after him and after his counsel. In the early days of the Church when the message of salvation was proclaimed in Great Britain, thousands accepted it and praised his name. They sought his counsel and the authority of the Priesthood. Many came out of this land, and later out of other European countries, seeking his fellowship, and his blessings under his hands. According to the promises of the Lord, this will continue, for it is the decree that the knowledge of the Gospel shall eventually cover the earth as the waters do the sea. When that day comes, Joseph Smith will receive from those on the earth who remain, their fellowship and they will praise his name, while those who reviled against him and held him in derision, shall be removed from the face of the earth." (Joseph Fielding Smith, *CHMR* 2:180-81.)

122:2 *"the pure in heart . . . shall seek counsel . . . under thy hand"*

"Here are the words of Deity, spoken to Joseph Smith, by which all men can judge the state of their own spiritual development: [Sec. 122:1-2, quoted.]

"All men may well ask themselves where they stand with reference to Joseph Smith and his divine mission. Do they inquire after his name and seek that salvation found only in the gospel of Christ as revealed to his latter-day prophet, or do they deride and despise the Lord's living oracles and say that God no longer speaks to men in the way he did anciently? The great question which all men in our day must answer—and that at the peril of their own salvation—is: Was Joseph Smith called of God?

"As for me and my house, we shall seek counsel and authority and blessing constantly from him and from those who now wear his prophetic mantle." (Bruce R. McConkie, *CR,* April 1976, p. 144.)

122:3 *Joseph, "thy people shall never be turned against thee by the testimony of traitors"*

"This is a significant truth that the enemies who turned away from the Church should have remembered. The Latter-day Saints who were acquainted with the Prophet personally, with very few exceptions, remained loyally true to him. There were some traitors in Nauvoo. One of the Prophet's counselors became his bitter enemy and sought his life. One other failed to give him loyal support. Others who had been his friends joined hands with the enemies of the Church and sought to bring him to his death, but the great majority of the people remained loyal and true.

"The influence of traitors caused him great trouble and cast him 'into bars and walls' and to his death, yet his voice speaks through his works and is more terrible and disconcerting to his enemies than the roaring of the fierce lion, and even in his death he was not forsaken by the Lord. His people remained true and the Lord has blessed them." (Joseph Fielding Smith, *CHMR* 2:181.)

"Speaking of the experience of the Prophet Joseph in the

early days, I want to say that though there were many who
turned from him, yet he had true and devoted friends, who
stood by his side and sustained him to the very last; and he
rolled upon their shoulders the cause of the kingdom, and
they have been true to that trust. This Church has been taken
care of from that time to this, and these men have walked in
the footsteps of their file leaders, in the footsteps of the
Prophet Joseph, and they have built upon the foundations
which he laid." (Francis M. Lyman, *CR,* October 1905, p.
11.)

122:4 *"thy voice shall be . . . terrible in the midst of thine
enemies"*

"In one of those tedious nights [Winter, 1838-39, Richmond, Mo. jail] we had lain as if in sleep, till the hour of
midnight had passed, and our ears and hearts had been
pained, while we had listened for hours to the obscene jests,
the horrid oaths, the dreadful blasphemies and filthy language of our guards, Colonel Price at their head, as they recounted to each other their deeds of rapine, murder, robbery, etc., which they had committed among the 'Mormons'
while at Far West and vicinity. They even boasted of defiling
by force wives, daughters, and virgins, and of shooting or
dashing out the brains of men, women and children.

"I had listened till I became so disgusted, shocked,
horrified, and so filled with the Spirit of indignant justice,
that I could scarcely refrain from rising upon my feet and
rebuking the guards, but I had said nothing to Joseph or
anyone else, although I lay next to him, and knew he was
awake. On a sudden he arose to his feet and spoke in a voice
of thunder, or as the roaring lion, uttering, as near as I can
recollect, the following words: *'Silence! Ye fiends of the infernal pit! In the name of Jesus Christ I rebuke you, and command you to be still; I will not live another minute and hear
such language. Cease such talk, or you or I die this instant!'*

"He ceased to speak. He stood erect in terrible majesty.
Chained, and without a weapon, calm, unruffled, and
dignified as an angel, he looked down upon his quailing
guards, whose knees smote together, and who, shrinking into
a corner, or crouching at his feet, begged his pardon, and
remained quiet until an exchange of guards.

"I have seen ministers of justice, clothed in ministerial

robes, and criminals arraigned before them, while life was suspended upon a breath in the courts of England; I have witnessed a congress in solemn session to give laws to nations; I have tried to conceive of kings, of royal courts, of thrones and crowns; and of emperors assembled to decide the fate of kingdoms; but dignity and majesty have I seen but once, as it stood in chains, at midnight, in a dungeon in an obscure village of Missouri." (Parley P. Pratt, *APPP*, pp. 210-11.)

122:6   *"if thine enemies fall upon thee"*

"Myself and fellow prisoners were taken to the town, [Far West, Mo.] into the public square, and before departure we, after much entreaty, were suffered to see our families, being attended all the while by a strong guard. I found my wife and children in tears, who feared we had been shot by those who had sworn to take our lives, and that they would see me no more. When I entered my house, they clung to my garments, their eyes streaming with tears while mingled emotions of joy and sorrow were manifested in their countenances. I requested to have a private interview with them a few minutes, but this privilege was denied me by the guard. I was then obliged to take my departure. . . .

"My partner wept, my children clung to me, until they were thrust from me by the swords of the guards. I felt overwhelmed while I witnessed the scene, and could only recommend them to care of that God whose kindness had followed me to the present time, and who alone could protect them, and deliver me from the hands of my enemies, and restore me to my family." (Joseph Smith, *HC* 3:193.)

122:7   *"all these things . . . shall be for thy good"*

"Few men have been called on to suffer more than did Joseph Smith. His entire life was spent in the midst of persecution by the hands of his enemies. No doubt he wondered many times why this had to be. In this revelation the Lord tells him. . . . There is great experience in tribulation that brings to pass much good. The person who goes through life without pain or sorrow, and who is not called upon to sacrifice comforts and partake of hardships, never receives the full value of life. We came here for experience, the benefits of which are not to be limited to this mortal life, but to be of value to those who receive the exaltation in the Kingdom of God." (Joseph Fielding Smith, *CHMR* 2:181.)

"It remained for the Prophet Joseph Smith to . . . set forth the why and wherefore of human suffering; and in revealing it he gave us a strength and power to endure that we did not before possess. For when men know why they suffer, and realize that it is for a good and wise purpose, they can bear it much better than they can in ignorance. . . .

"The fall of Adam and Eve was a great calamity, but it brought forth a wonderful blessing; it gave us our bodies, with endless opportunities to advance and achieve. It brought death into the world, but it also brought forth the human family. There was the compensation. 'Adam fell that men might be: and men are, that they might have joy.' [2 Nephi 2:25.] The crucifixion of Christ was a terrible calamity, but the atonement connected with it was the foreordained means of man's salvation. Israel's calamitous fate proved a blessing to the world in general. God's promises to Abraham had to be made good. 'In thee and in thy seed shall all the nations of the earth be blessed.' [Abr. 2:11.] This promise was fulfilled in Christ, but an important part of the fulfillment began when the children of Abraham, Isaac and Jacob were flung broadcast over the world, and the barren wastes of unbelief might be sprinkled with the blood that believes, and made fruitful of faith and righteousness.

"So it is with all our troubles and sorrows; there is a compensation for them. . . .

"When the sky darkens and the tempest threatens, where do we go for shelter? To the sagebrush or the willow? No, rather to some spreading oak that has withstood the storms of ages and become stronger because of the fierce winds that have swayed its branches and caused its roots to strike deeper and deeper into the soil. When we want counsel and comfort, we do not go to children, nor to those who know nothing but pleasure and self-gratification. We go to men and women who have suffered themselves and can give us the comfort that we need. Is not this God's purpose in causing his children to suffer? He wants them to become more like himself. God has suffered far more than man ever did or ever will, and is therefore the great source of sympathy and consolation. Who are these arrayed in white, nearest to the throne of God? asked John the Apostle, wrapt in his mighty vision. The answer was: 'These are they who have come up through great tribulation, and washed their robes and made them white in the blood of the Lamb.' [Rev. 7:13-14.]

"There is always a blessing in sorrow and humiliation. They who escape these things are not the fortunate ones. 'Whom God loveth he chasteneth.' [Heb. 12:6.] When he desires to make a great man he takes a little street waif, or a boy in the back-woods, such as Lincoln or Joseph Smith, and brings him up through hardship and privation to be the grand and successful leader of a people. Flowers shed most of their perfume when they are crushed. Men and women have to suffer just so much in order to bring out the best that is in them." (Orson F. Whitney, *IE,* November 1918, pp. 5-7.)

122:8 *"The Son of Man hath descended below them all. Art thou greater than he?"*

"It is not necessary, in the providence of God, that we should all be martyrs; it is not necessary that all should suffer death upon the cross, because it was the will of the Father that Jesus should so suffer, neither is it necessary that all the Saints of this last dispensation should perish because our prophet perished, but yet it may be necessary . . . that a sufficient number of faithful witnesses of God and of his Christ should suffer, and even perish by the hands of their enemies, to prove and show unto the world—the unbelieving and unthinking—that their testimony is true."(Erastus Snow, *JD* 21:26.)

"Do not let us be discouraged at difficulties and trials, for we are sent to this state of existence for the express purpose of descending below all things, that we may pass the ordeals and trials of this life and thereby prove our integrity and be prepared to rise above all things. And after all, we have not been called upon to endure to that extent that the Savior of the world was. But he was not subjected to the afflictions he had to endure without hope, neither are we. . . . If we can pass these tests and trials we shall prove to God and angels that we are worthy to receive the welcome plaudit, 'well done, thou good and faithful servant, enter thou into the joy of the Lord.' [Matt. 25:21-23.]" (Daniel H. Wells, *JD* 12:235.)

122:9 *"thy years shall not be numbered less"*

"I know what I say; I understand my mission and business. God Almighty is my shield; and what can man do if God is my friend? I shall not be sacrificed until my time comes; then I shall be offered freely." (Joseph Smith, *HC* 5:259.)

"Was there frustration in the martyrdom of Joseph Smith? Joseph was protected and his life saved in every instance of persecution until his work was finished and he had done his part in the restoration of the gospel and the priesthood and all other keys of the dispensation, and until the organization of the kingdom was effected. He could not be killed before that time, though all hell raged against him. He wanted to live. Life was sweet to him. It held promise of sweet associations with his family, his brethren and the satisfaction of seeing the work blossom into a full-blown flower. But his work was done; other strong leaders could now carry on; he was needed in other fields. Only in his thirties, a very young man, he died, and commenced his work in other realms." (Spencer W. Kimball, *CR,* April 1945, p. 59.)

SECTION 123

Background information on section 123

See background information on section 121.

"In prison [Liberty, Missouri, March 1839], Joseph was in constant communion with the heavens and he received revelation [Sections 121, 122 and 123; March 25, 1839, *HC* 3:289-305], without which he and his brethren must have been cast down and without hope. He also sent epistles full of instruction and hope to leading men among the Saints." (George Q. Cannon, *LJS*, p. 283.)

123:1 *Gather up "all the facts, and sufferings and abuses"*

"That records might be kept on earth as well as in heaven, the Lord commanded (Sec. 123) that there be gathered all the knowledge of all the acts, and sufferings and the abuses put upon the members of the Church by the State of Missouri. Also a record should be kept of all the property destroyed, the damages sustained, both to the character and the personal injuries and to the real property of the Saints. The names of those who were engaged in this wickedness and these murders and drivings were also to be gathered and preserved. A committee was appointed to gather this evidence that it might be on file. This information would be of value when presented before the Government of the United States when the Church should seek justice at the seat of government. If redress could not be obtained there, then the evidence would stand against those who were guilty, before the Eternal Tribunal which will try all men and all things." (Joseph Fielding Smith, *CHMR* 3:203-4.)

123:4 *"perhaps a committee can be appointed"*

"At a conference held near Quincy, Ill., May 4th-6th, 1839, Almon W. Babbitt, Erastus Snow, and Robert B. Thompson were appointed a committee to gather up the historical material required by this Revelation." (Smith and Sjodahl, *DCC*, p. 763.)

123:4   *"gather up the libelous publications"*

"This gathering of information was not to be confined to the deeds committed in Missouri, but should reach out to embrace the wickedness, falsehoods, and deeds of those who fought the truth throughout all time. Magazine articles, writings in encyclopedias, all libelous histories, and other writings . . . were to be gathered that they might be published to the world, sent to the heads of government. [Sec. 123:5, quoted.] . . .

"The work of gathering the libelous articles from magazines, books, newspapers, and all sources, still goes on. In the library of the Historian's Office, there are on file today upwards of 2,000 books, encyclopedias, magazines, histories, pamphlets, communications, etc., sent forth by Satan and his emissaries, and still this flood of wicked and malicious falsehood goes on and evidently will go on until the Lord comes to cleanse the earth of all its filthiness." (Joseph Fielding Smith, *CHMR* 3:203-4.)

"Now, what means are they using and what means have they been using, for years, against the Church? Ridicule, contumely, falsehood, slander, misrepresentation! Men that fight against The Church of Jesus Christ of Latter-day Saints build up 'men of straw' and slaughter them. They advance ideas that do not belong to us, that we have never held, that we do not advocate, that are no part of our doctrine or religion at all. They conjure up these propositions in their own minds, and then proceed, with all the eloquence and fervor of their souls, to tear in pieces and destroy the images of their own minds. They do not fight Mormonism—they can't, without they fight God and the truth! The moment that men attempt to fight this Church they fight God, they fight the principles of His gospel and His truth; they fight faith in God, faith in Jesus Christ, faith in righteousness, faith in the resurrection of the Lord Jesus Christ, faith in every principle that exalts and uplifts and ameliorates the condition of man in the world. If they undertake to fight us they fight these principles, because we have espoused these principles." (Joseph F. Smith, *CR,* October 1910, pp. 128-29.)

"It is impossible to take up all the misrepresentations given to the world by anti 'Mormon' preachers and writers. They have one merit. They stir up interest in what is called the 'Mormon' question. People are led thus to investigate and many of them find out the truth, and unite with the people who are so greatly maligned." (First Presidency, *CR*, April 1911, p. 130.)

123:5 *"concatenation . . . nefarious"*

Concatenate means "to link together in a series or chain."

Nefarious means "flagrantly wicked or impious." *Evil* and *vicious* are synonyms.

SECTION 124

Background information on section 124

"Almost as soon as the Prophet and his brethren arrived in Nauvoo from their imprisonment and persecutions in Missouri, the Lord gave instructions that a temple should be built in Nauvoo. By this time the fulness of the doctrine of salvation for the dead had been revealed and the importance of performing ordinances for the dead was impressed upon the mind of the Prophet and by him, in discourses and letter, upon the saints. No doubt Joseph Smith had been praying to the Lord on this subject, and this revelation (Sec. 124) is an answer to his pleadings." (Joseph Fielding Smith, *CHMR* 2:265-66.)

124:1 *"unto this end have I raised you up"*

"Joseph Smith was born of humble parentage in an obscure village. He never went to college nor attended high school, but he accomplished in the short period of his life of thirty-eight and one-half years more than any other mortal man of his time, if not of all time. . . .

"During the short life of the Prophet Joseph Smith he was instrumental in the hands of the Lord in the establishment of the Church and kingdom of God on earth as seen in vision by the Prophet Daniel. [Dan. 2.] Through him the everlasting gospel in its fulness was restored, with all its gifts, blessings, principles, and ordinances, and the power and authority of the priesthood to administer the ordinances of the gospel to the children of men, who, by repentance and obedience, are prepared to receive them.

"The works of Joseph Smith and the spirit that prompted them live on in the hearts and lives of his followers." (George F. Richards, *CR*, September 1949, p. 153.)

124:1 *"the weak things of the earth"*

See *Weak things of the world* in Appendix A.

24:2-7 *"make a solemn proclamation of my gospel . . . to all the kings of the world, . . . to the . . . president-elect, . . . the . . . governors . . . and to all the nations of the earth"*

"Toward the end of his mortal ministry, the Lord commanded the Prophet Joseph Smith as follows:

" 'Make a solemn proclamation of my gospel . . . to all the kings of the world, to the four corners thereof . . . and to all nations of the earth.' (D&C 124:2-3.) He was to invite them to come to the light of truth, and use their means to build up the kingdom of God on earth.

"In the spirit of this divine direction, on the sixth day of April 1845, and shortly after the Prophet Joseph Smith and his brother Hyrum had mingled their blood with that of the other martyrs of true religion, the Council of the Twelve made such a proclamation. They address it:

" '*To all the Kings of the World;*
To the President of the United States of America;
To the Governors of the several States;
And to the Rulers and People of all nations.' . . .

"It seems fitting and proper to me that we should reaffirm the great truths pronounced in this declaration and that we should proclaim them anew to the world." (Ezra Taft Benson, *Ensign,* November 1975, pp. 32-34.)

124:4 *"by the power of the Holy Ghost"*

See *Holy Ghost* in Appendix A.

124:10 *"the day of my visitation cometh speedily"*

See *Second coming* and *Quickly* in Appendix A.

124:12 *"Robert B. Thompson"*

"Elder Robert Blashel Thompson died at his residence in Nauvoo, in the 30th year of his age, in the full hope of a glorious resurrection. He was associate editor of the *Times and Seasons,* colonel in the Nauvoo Legion, and had done much writing for myself and the Church." (Joseph Smith, *HC* 4:411.)

124:15 *and following verses*

For additional information on persons mentioned in this section, see Appendix B.

124:15 *"Hyrum Smith . . . I, the Lord, love him"*

"No mortal man who ever lived in this Church desired more to do good than did Hyrum Smith, the patriarch. I have it from the lips of my own sainted mother, that of all the men she was acquainted with in her girlhood days in Nauvoo, she admired Hyrum Smith most for his absolute integrity and devotion to God, and his loyalty to the prophet of God." (Heber J. Grant, *CR,* October 1920, p. 84.)

124:19 *"David Patten"*

"I have thought it more than mere coincidence that one of the first martyrs in this dispensation, David W. Patten, a member of the Twelve Apostles, lost his life near the valley of Adam-ondi-Ahman, that same valley in which Adam had gathered his posterity, which the Lord had revealed to the Prophet Joseph Smith was near Wight's Ferry, at a place called Spring Hill, Daviess county, Missouri. [Section 116.]" (Harold B. Lee, *CR,* April 1948, p. 53.)

"And in speaking about David Patten, one of the twelve, it is written: [Sec. 124:130, quoted.] But his being dead made no difference in regard to his priesthood. He held it just the same in the heavens as on the earth. There is another man mentioned. Referring to the high council, it is stated: [Sec. 124:132, quoted.]" (John Taylor, *GK,* p. 184.)

124:19 *"Joseph Smith, Sr., who sitteth with Abraham"*

"Then there is something said concerning Joseph Smith, Sen., the father of the Prophet Joseph Smith, of whom it is said that he sitteth with Abraham, at his right hand. (See D&C 124:19.) Who was Abraham? A patriarch. Who was Father Joseph Smith? A patriarch. It is quite fitting, therefore, that he should associate with Abraham who was and is also a patriarch." (John Taylor, *GK,* p. 184.)

124:20-22, 62, 70 *"George Miller"*

"George Miller, as long as the Prophet Joseph lived, seemed to be a faithful Latter-day Saint. He was chosen to fill the important place of Bishop, left vacant by the death of Edward Partridge. He accompanied the Prophet on his journeys, on several occasions. He and Newel K. Whitney were appointed Trustees-in-trust of the Church, after the death of the Prophet. And when the Saints left Nauvoo, he was among the first to cross the river. But from now on he changed. In the Camp of Israel, slowly wending its way westward, he became disaffected. He always wanted to be ahead of the main body, and be a law unto himself. At Winter Quarters he expressed the view that Texas was the place to go to, and not the Rocky Mountains, and when Brigham Young refused to listen to him, knowing that the Prophet had pointed to the Great Basin as the gathering place of the Saints, he left the Camp with a few followers, and joined Lyman Wight in Texas. Shortly afterwards he disagreed with this schismatic and joined Strang, unable to find peace and rest anywhere. Here is another career, beginning in integrity and love of the gospel and ending in failure, because of lack of humility." (Smith and Sjodahl, *DCC,* p. 772.)

124:21 *"I seal upon his head [George Miller] the office of a bishopric"*

"I would here remark that Edward Partridge was the first Bishop of the Church, and that he was appointed at an early day to go to the land of Zion, and to preside over the Bishopric in that district of country. . . . In the same revelation that George Miller was called to occupy the place of Edward Partridge, and to hold the same kind of Bishopric that he held, we find that there was a Presiding Bishopric appointed." (John Taylor, *JD* 22:199.)

:22-23 *"build a house . . . for boarding"*

"The Spirit of Revelation directs the Saints to build a fine hotel for the entertainment of strangers. There is no greater inducement for travelers to visit a place than good hotel accommodations. This Revelation proves that the Lord wanted the tourists of the world to visit and become acquainted with the Saints. These were not to be surrounded by a wall of isolation. They had nothing to hide from the world.

"The erection of the hotel here referred to, generally known as the Nauvoo House, was commenced in the spring of 1841, and in 1846, when the Saints left Nauvoo, the walls were up above the windows of the second story. It fronted two streets, 120 feet on each. The estimated cost was $100,000. It was planned to be the most magnificent hotel in the West, at the time. When the Saints left the City, the unfinished building became the property of the Prophet's widow, and was subsequently claimed by her second husband, Mr. L. C. Bidamon. In 1872 he put part of it under roof and fitted it up as an hotel, known as the Bidamon House." (Smith and Sjodahl, *DCC*, pp. 772-73.)

". . . the Nauvoo House, [was] a place for the boarding of strangers. Joseph Smith, Sidney Rigdon, Hyrum Smith, and many others were called upon to 'pay stock' for themselves and their seed after them 'from generation to generation,' in this house. . . . Those who took stock were not to pay less than fifty dollars, and not more than fifteen thousand dollars for any one man." (Joseph Fielding Smith, *ECH*, p. 306.)

"October 21, 1841, the cornerstone of the 'Nauvoo House' was laid. However, this was never completed during the lifetime of the Prophet. August 31, 1843, he moved into the 'mansion house' in Nauvoo, a private dwelling, in which traveling guests could be entertained." (John A. Widtsoe, *JS*, p. 212.)

124:27 *"build a house to my name"*

"The importance of temples and the work in them has been a doctrine of the Church from the beginning. We have seen how the Lord rebuked the saints for not building the Kirtland Temple as soon as they should have done, after the call was given; also how the command was given to build a temple in Jackson County, which was prohibited by the enemies of the Church. Almost as soon as the Prophet and his brethren arrived in Nauvoo from their imprisonment and persecutions in Missouri, the Lord gave instructions that a temple should be built in Nauvoo." (Joseph Fielding Smith, *CHMR* 2:265.)

124:28 *"there is not a place . . . that he may come"*

"The Saints had to flee before mobocracy. And, by toil and daily labor, they found places in Missouri, where they laid the corner stones of Temples, in Zion and her Stakes, and then had to retreat to Illinois, to save the lives of those who could get away alive from Missouri. . . . But before all this had transpired, the Temple at Kirtland had fallen into the hands of wicked men, and by them been polluted, like the Temple at Jerusalem, and consequently it was disowned by the Father and the Son." (Brigham Young, *JD* 2:32.)

124:36 *"it is ordained that in Zion, and in her stakes, and in Jerusalem"*

A careful reading of this verse would seem to indicate that

Jerusalem will not be part of an organized stake of Zion at the time the temple is built there in the last days. Otherwise, the words "including Jerusalem" might have been used rather than "*and* in Jerusalem."

:37-39 *The tabernacle of Moses*

"The importance of the ordinances in the house of the Lord is shown in verses 37-39 [Section 124], where we are informed that Moses was commanded to build a portable temple, generally called tabernacle, which could be carried with them in the wilderness. This tabernacle, is the same temple where the boy Samuel heard the voice of the Lord. (1 Samuel 1-3.) This sacred building was later replaced by Solomon's Temple. The question is often asked, 'What was the nature of the ordinances performed in these edifices in ancient times?' The Lord explains this in the verses above cited. It is true that in ancient Israel they did not have the fulness of ordinances as we do today, and most, if not all, of which they were privileged to receive very likely pertained to the Aaronic Priesthood. (See D&C 84:21-26.) Neither did the ancients labor in their temples for the salvation of the dead. That work was reserved until after the Savior's visit to the spirit world where he unlocked the door to the prisons and had the gospel carried to the spirits who had been confined." (Joseph Fielding Smith, *CHMR* 4:82.)

127:38 *"that . . . ordinances might be revealed"*

"You have come from the nations abroad, to be instructed in the ways of the Lord, to be taught in the ordinances that pertain to the great and last dispensation of the fullness of times—ordinances that did not pertain to any former dispensation,—ordinances that were not made known to any former people, but ordinances and principles that pertain to the exaltation and glory of the world which we inhabit." (Orson Pratt, *JD* 21:205.)

124:41 *"I deign [condescend to give] to reveal . . . things . . . hid from before the foundation of the world"*

"Wednesday, May 4, 1842, the Prophet met with a number of brethren in the upper room of his store where he had his private office, where he kept his sacred writings, did his translating and received revelations and held council meetings. The special reason for the gathering was of the greatest moment to the Church and to this generation. It was the fulfillment of the promise the Lord made that he was about to reveal unto the Church 'things which have been kept hid from before the foundation of the world, things that pertain to the dispensation of the fulness of times.' These things were to be made known, and the blessings come from them to be given to the members of the Church, within the walls of temples built to the name of the Lord. The Lord said he would reveal unto his servant, Joseph Smith 'all things pertaining to his house, and the priesthood thereof, and the place whereon it shall be built.' (D&C 124:41-42.) Knowing that the Prophet would be taken in death before this house was finished, the Lord commanded him to make known to the trusted brethren the ordinances which later would be performed in the temple when it was finished. It was on this occasion, May 4, 1842, that the Prophet called some of these brethren to his upper room, and gave unto them instruction 'in the principles and order of the Priesthood, attending to washings, anointings, endowments and the communication of keys pertaining to the Aaronic Priesthood, and so on to the highest order of the Melchizedek Priesthood, setting forth the order pertaining to the Ancient of Days, and all those plans and principles by which any one is enabled to secure the fullness of those blessings which have been prepared for the Church of the Firstborn, and come up and abide in the presence of the Eloheim in the eternal worlds.' [*HC* 5:2.]" (Joseph Fielding Smith, *CHMR* 4:111-12.)

124:49-53 *"I [have] accepted the offerings"*

"If you will read carefully the revelations I speak of now [Sections 84 and 124], you will find that the Lord refers particularly to this very requirement in regard to Jackson county, Missouri, and he declares that the people there were commanded to build a house to him at that time, and on that spot. But their enemies came upon them and prevented them from doing that which the Lord commanded them, and therefore the Lord accepted their offering. The Lord lays down there a principle which it is well for us to understand. The Lord says that whenever he gives a commandment, no matter what it is about, to the children of man, and they go to with their might and endeavor to fulfil his commandment, and do that which is required of them, and they are prevented by their enemies, or by any other means, from accomplishing it, he does not require it any more at their hands. He accepts of their offering." (Charles W. Penrose, *CR*, April 1924, pp. 13-14.)

24:50 *"I will visit [iniquity] . . . unto the third and fourth generation"*

"You have an idea that the commandment [Exodus 20:5] means that when a man sins his children will be held responsible for his folly and be punished for it, for three or four generations. The commandment does not mean anything of this kind. The Lord never punishes a child for its parents' transgressions. He is just and merciful. The real meaning of this visiting of the iniquity is that when a man transgresses he teaches his children to transgress, and they follow his teachings. It is natural for children to follow in the practices of their fathers and by doing so suffer for the parents' iniquity which they have voluntarily brought upon themselves.

"There are numerous other passages of scripture showing the mercy and justice of the Lord and that they are not to be punished for the fathers' transgression. Here are a few: [Deut. 24:16; Kings 14:6; 2 Chron. 25:4; Jer. 31:29-30; Ezek. 18:20, quoted.]" (Joseph Fielding Smith, *IE*, June 1955, p. 383.)

78-79 *"Isaac Galland"*

"Most of the Saints expelled from the State of Missouri during the winter 1838-9, found their way into Illinois and Iowa. . . . Among the prominent citizens who, at this time, extended a helping hand to the Saints were Daniel H. Wells, a native of Trenton, New York, and Dr. Isaac Galland. Daniel H. Wells was the owner of a tract of land, which he divided into lots and which the exiles were offered, practically on their own terms. Dr. Galland, also, sold his land at a reasonable price and on the most favorable terms.

"The Prophet arrived at Quincy on the 22nd of April, 1839, and two days after, a Council was convened and resolutions were passed directing some of the Saints to go to Zion, and some to settle on Dr. Galland's land, near Commerce, Ill. This location soon became the central gathering place, and its name was changed to Nauvoo." (Smith and Sjodahl, *DCC*, p. 768.)

124:84   *"With Almon Babbitt . . . I am not pleased"*

"The Lord severely rebukes Almon. Babbitt. From these verses it may be gathered that his chief ambition was to make money, and that he advised the Saints to leave Nauvoo, contrary to the counsel of the Church leaders. Perhaps he was interested in the sale of land elsewhere. At all events, when the Saints left Nauvoo, he was appointed one of the real estate agents in whose hands the abandoned property was left, to be disposed of on the best terms obtainable. How he discharged this duty, we may infer from the following statement of Heber C. Kimball: 'My house was sold at $1,700, intended to be used to help to gather the Saints; but Almon W. Babbitt put it in his pocket, I suppose' (*JD* 8:350)." (Smith and Sjodahl, *DCC*, p. 784.)

124:89   *"the new translation"*

See *Inspired Version of the Bible* in Appendix A.

124:91   *"let my servant William be appointed . . . counselor"*

"William Law was called by revelation to act as second counselor in the First Presidency, in 1841, but when the doctrine of celestial marriage was revealed he turned away from the Church, and was one of the chief plotters against the Prophet and Patriarch and helped to bring them to martyrdom." (Joseph Fielding Smith, *CHMR* 4:83.)

124:91   *"my servant Hyrum may take the office of . . . Patriarch . . . by right"*

See *Patriarch* in Appendix A.

"From this [revelation] we learn, that Joseph Smith, Sen., inherited the Patriarchal Priesthood, by right from the fathers over the house of Israel in this dispensation. For this right to have descended to him, by lineage, he must of necessity be an Ephraimite, for Ephraim, by the right of appointment and ordination by his father Jacob, is the head of Israel. This fact is plainly stated in the scriptures. . . . By virtue of this adoption of Ephraim, as the head of the house of Israel, and Joseph Smith, Sen., being the oldest son of Ephraim, holding the Priesthood in this dispensation, he is Patriarch of the whole church by right. This right should be perpetuated in his family, as the oldest branch of the tribe of Ephraim." (Franklin D. Richards and James A. Little, *Compendium,* pp. 74-75.)

"Hyrum Smith served in the First Presidency as second counselor to his younger brother from the time of the release of Frederick G. Williams to January 19, 1841. At this time the Lord called Hyrum Smith to the office of patriarch by virtue of the law of primogeniture. It was his right, and so the Lord declared in this revelation. This office, as we have previously seen, descends from father to son through the chosen lineage. It was conferred upon Joseph Smith as the lawful heir to the blessings of Joseph and Ephraim, and descended to Hyrum Smith as a legal right. (See D&C 68:16-18, and 124:91.) This office belongs to the descendants of Hyrum Smith." (Joseph Fielding Smith, *CHMR* 2:269.)

"Hyrum Smith is pointed out as the legal successor of his father in the Patriarchal office; it is his 'by right' of lineage, no less than by Patriarchal blessing. The following is the blessing pronounced upon Hyrum Smith by his father: 'My son Hyrum, I seal upon your head your patriarchal blessing, which I placed upon your head before, for that shall be verified. In addition to this, I now give you my dying blessing. You shall have a season of peace, so that you shall have a sufficient rest to accomplish the work which God has given you to do. You shall be as firm as the pillars of heaven unto the end of your days. I now seal upon your head the patriarchal power, and you shall bless the people. This is my dying blessing upon your head in the name of Jesus. Amen.' " (Smith and Sjodahl, *DCC*, p. 786.)

91-95 *"a prophet . . . seer . . . revelator"*

See *Seer* in Appendix A.

" 'Can a number of men be Prophets, Seers, and Revelators and yet not interfere with the rights of him who stands at the head?" There is no reason why this should not be the case. By reference to Section 124, paragraphs 91-95; it will be seen that the Lord, by His own voice, appointed Hyrum Smith to 'be a prophet, seer and a revelator unto my church, as well as my servant Joseph.' " (George Q. Cannon, *JI*, Jan. 1, 1891, pp. 27-28.)

24:95 *"gifts . . . that once were upon . . . Oliver Cowdery"*

"This [D&C 124:94] was a special blessing given to Hyrum Smith and in accepting it he took the place of Oliver Cowdery, upon whom these keys had previously been bestowed. It should be remembered that whenever the Lord revealed Priesthood and the keys of Priesthood from the heavens, Oliver Cowdery stood with Joseph Smith in the presence of the heavenly messengers, and was a recipient, as well as Joseph Smith as the 'first' and Oliver Cowdery as the 'second' Elder of the Church. Thus the law pertaining to witnesses was fully established, for there were two witnesses standing with authority, keys and presidency, at the head of this the greatest of all dispensations. When through transgression Oliver Cowdery lost this wonderful and exalted blessing, Hyrum Smith was chosen by revelation of the Lord to take his place." (Joseph Fielding Smith, *Utah Genealogical and Historical Magazine,* April 1932, 5:51-52.)

124:103   *"Sidney"*

See *Sidney Rigdon* in Appendix B.

124:109   *"city of Nauvoo"*

"Shortly after the saints began to assemble at Commerce the name of the settlement was changed to Nauvoo. The Prophet declared that the word is of Hebrew origin, and 'signifies a beautiful situation, or place, carrying with it, also, the idea of rest.' It is about one hundred and ninety miles up the river from St. Louis and nearly the same distance west of Chicago." (Joseph Fielding Smith, *CHMR* 2:246-47.)

124: 111-14   *"Amos Davies"*

"From this Revelation it is evident that Amos Davies, notwithstanding his prominence, had some weaknesses. He was slow to obey counsel, and he shunned work. He is, therefore, commanded to 'labor with his own hands' and prove himself faithful in all things. It is to be feared that he heeded this commandment only in part, for on the 9th of March, 1842, he indulged in abusive language concerning the Prophet, whereupon the court bound him over, to keep the peace." (Smith and Sjodahl, *DCC,* p. 789.)

"In the evening attended trial at Brother Hyrum's office, the City of Nauvoo *versus* Amos Davis, for indecent and abusive language about me while at Mr. Davis' the day previous. The charges were clearly substantiated by the testimony of Dr. Foster, Mr. and Mrs. Hibbard, and others. Mr. Davis was found guilty by the jury, and by the municipal court, bound over to keep the peace six months, under $100 bond." (Joseph Smith, *HC* 4:549.)

24:115 *"Robert D. Foster"*

"Robert D. Foster was one of the men who fell from a high position of honor to the lowest depths of wickedness. The Prophet befriended him again and again, hoping that he would mend his ways. According to a statement made to Cyrus H. Wheelock, shortly before the tragedy at Carthage, he was one of a number of conspirators who were determined to take the life of the Prophet." (Smith and Sjodahl, *DCC,* p. 790.)

"So on the very day that the paper [Nauvoo *Expositor*] was to come forth burdened with lies, Robert D. Foster went to the mansion and demanded a private interview with Joseph. He asked the Prophet to go away with him alone, pretending that he wished to return to the Church and wanted to confer upon that subject. Joseph refused to talk except in the presence of witnesses, for this man Foster had often before misrepresented the Prophet's words. Joseph said to him that there was but one condition upon which he might return and that was to repent and to make restitution as far as possible.

"While they stood talking Joseph put his hand upon Foster's vest and said: 'What have you concealed there?'

"Foster stammered in reply: 'It's my pistol.'

"He would have lied, but under that piercing glance his bravado deserted him, and he was compelled to acknowledge the fact.

"The reason of this visit was soon made plain, and it was made plainer at a later time by the testimony of unimpeachable witnesses, Saints and strangers alike. He had not come to seek forgiveness and restoration of fellowship; he had not come to make amends. He had come to lure Joseph away to his death." (George Q. Cannon, *LJS,* 484-85.)

24:126 *"First Presidency"*

See *First Presidency* in Appendix A.

24:127 *"Twelve traveling council"*

See *Council of the Twelve* in Appendix A.

24:141 *"the bishopric"*

See *Bishop* in Appendix A.

24:143 *"above offices"*

See *Church offices and presiding quorums* in Appendix A.

124:144   *"at my general conference"*

"Reference to the Doctrine and Covenants will disclose the fact that there are four principal purposes of holding conferences of the Church: First, to transact current Church business. [Sec. 20:62.] Second, to hear reports and general Church statistics. [Sec. 73:2.] Third, to 'approve those names which I (the Lord) have appointed, or to disapprove of them.' [Sec. 124:144.] Fourth, to worship the Lord in sincerity and reverence, and to give and to receive encouragement, exhortation, and instruction. [Sec. 58:56; 72:7.]" (David O. McKay, *CR*, October 1938, pp. 130-31.)

SECTION 125

Background information on section 125

"When the Saints left Missouri, a large number of fugitives found their way into the Territory of Iowa. Large tracts of land were purchased, and several settlements were built up in the southeastern portion of that Territory. Before the arrival of the Saints, there were only 2,839 inhabitants in Lee County. In 1846 the population was estimated at 12,860. So rapidly did the County develop, when touched by the magic wand of 'Mormon' industry. Nauvoo was the central point of gathering at this time, and the question, stated in the first verse of this Revelation, arose. The answer follows." (Smith and Sjodahl, *DCC*, p. 795.)

"Mr. [Isaac] Galland in a communication to David W. Rogers [May 1839], suggested that the Saints locate in Iowa, which was a territory; for he thought they would be more likely to receive protection from mobs under the jurisdiction of the United States, than they would in a state of the Union, 'where murder, rapine and robbery are admirable (!) traits in the character of a demagogue; and where the greatest villains often reach the highest offices.' He also wrote to Governor Robert Lucas of Iowa, who had known the 'Mormon' people in Ohio, and who spoke very highly of them as good citizens." (Joseph Fielding Smith, *ECH,* p. 266.)

25:2-4   *"Zarahemla"*

The name *Zarahemla* was obviously taken from one of the major cities mentioned in the Book of Mormon. It has been suggested that the basic meaning of the word in Hebrew is "place of abundance"; thus, its meaning would be very similar to that of Bountiful, another Book of Mormon city. (*Ancient America and the Book of Mormon,* p. 152.)

"This settlement was founded by the Saints in 1839, on the uplands about a mile west of the Mississippi River, near

Montrose and opposite Nauvoo, Ill. The Church had bought an extensive tract of land here. At a conference held at Zarahemla, August 7th, 1841, seven hundred and fifty Church members were represented, of whom three hundred and twenty-six lived in Zarahemla. But when the Saints left for the Rocky Mountains, that city was lost sight of." (Smith and Sjodahl, *DCC,* p. 796.)

"Across the river [Mississippi at Nauvoo, Illinois] on the Iowa side, extensive holdings also were obtained. [1839.] The village of Nashville, in Lee County, with twenty thousand acres adjoining, were purchased; also other lands opposite Nauvoo. Here the Prophet instructed the Saints that a city should be built, to be called Zarahemla. A number of members of the Church had located here when the Saints were driven from Missouri, and it appeared to be a suitable location for a permanent settlement of the people. . . . The idea seemed to be that the Latter-day Saints should spread out over considerable territory, and form organizations in various parts of the country, but this plan was abandoned, and the Saints scattered abroad were commanded by revelation in January, 1841, to gather to Hancock County, Illinois, and to Lee County, Iowa, and to build up the settlements in these parts occupied by the members of the Church. This was, the presidency wrote, 'agreeable to the order of heaven.' Consequently the Saints began to immigrate to Nauvoo, and the city grew rapidly by such additions. About one year after the location of the site, Nauvoo had a population of over three thousand souls, and six years later, at the time of the great western exodus, about twenty thousand. The stake at Zarahemla was later discontinued, but John Smith remained there to preside over the Saints in Iowa. [1846.]" (Joseph Fielding Smith, *ECH,* pp. 268-69.)

SECTION 126

Background information on section 126

"In order to grasp fully the significance of this Revelation, an incident from the first meeting, in 1832, between the Prophet Joseph and his successor [to be] should be recalled. They had spent the evening in conversation on the gospel, and when the time for parting had come, Brigham Young was invited to lead in prayer. While he was praying, the Spirit of the Lord came upon him, and he spoke in tongues—the first instance of the bestowal of that gift upon anyone in this dispensation. Afterwards, it is asserted, the Prophet said, 'A time will come when Brother Brigham will preside over this Church.' (Whitney's *History of Utah* 1:112.)

"It should, further, be remembered that, at a Conference held at Nauvoo, August 16th, 1841, the Prophet Joseph, with this Revelation in mind, stated that, 'The time has come when the Twelve should be called upon to stand in their place *next to the First Presidency,* and attend to the settling of emigrants and the business of the Church at the Stakes, and to assist to bear off the kingdom victoriously to the nations.' (*HC* 4:403.) By this Revelation, therefore, Brigham Young, the President of the Twelve (D&C 124:127), was called to stand next to the First Presidency. Why? To take his place, whenever the Prophet should be called to another sphere of action. By this Revelation, the Spirit indicated that Brigham Young was to be the successor of Joseph Smith, as the Prophet had predicted in 1832." (Smith and Sjodahl, *DCC,* p. 797.)

"In the month of July, 1841, the Apostles began to return to Nauvoo from their missions to Europe, and their coming was a great comfort to the Prophet in his hour of affliction. At a special conference which was held at Nauvoo on the 16th of August, 1841, shortly after the return of the Twelve, Joseph stated to the people there assembled that the time had come when the Apostles must stand in their places next to the First Presidency. They had been faithful and had borne the burden and heat of the day, giving the gospel triumph in the nations of the earth, and it was right that they should now remain at home and perform the duty in Zion." (George Q. Cannon, *LJS*, p. 374.)

126:1 *"Dear and well-beloved brother, Brigham Young"*

See *Brigham Young* in Appendix B.

"Brigham Young was a man of undoubted genius,—a master mind, well balanced and powerful, thoroughly practical in thought and method, and of Napoleonic energy and intuition. . . . Brigham Young first saw the Book of Mormon in the spring of 1830, at the home of his brother Phineas in Mendon. It had been left there by Samuel H. Smith, brother to the Prophet. Two years later a party of Mormon Elders from Pennsylvania came preaching in that neighborhood. Being converted to the faith, Brigham was baptized by Eleazer Miller on the 14th of April, 1832. . . . Not long afterward Brigham . . . accompanied by Joseph Young, visited Kirtland and became acquainted with the Prophet. It was the summer or fall of 1832. This was the first meeting of Joseph Smith with the man who was destined to be his successor. It is said that Joseph predicted about this time that Brigham Young would yet preside over the Church." (Orson F. Whitney, *History of Utah,* p. 112.)

126:2 *"I have seen your labor and toil"*

"I came into this Church in the spring of 1832. Previous to my being baptized, I took a mission to Canada at my own expense; and from the time that I was baptized until the day of our sorrow and affliction, at the martyrdom of Joseph and Hyrum, no summer passed over my head but what I was traveling and preaching, and the only thing I ever received from the Church, during over twelve years, and the only means that were ever given me by the Prophet, that I now recollect, was in 1842, when brother Joseph sent me the half of a small pig that the brethren had brought to him. I did not ask him for it. . . .

"I have traveled and preached, and at the same time sustained my family by my labor and economy. . . . For me to travel and preach without purse or scrip was never hard. . . . In company with several of the Twelve I was sent to England in 1839. We started from home without purse or scrip, and most of the Twelve were sick. . . . I was not able to walk to the river, not so far as across this block, no, not more than half as far; I had to be helped to the river, in not even an overcoat; I took a small quilt from the trundle bed, and that served for my overcoat, while I was traveling to the State of New York, when I had a coarse sattinet overcoat given to me. Thus we went to England, to a strange land to sojourn among strangers. . . .

"I was there one year and sixteen days, with my brethren the Twelve and during that time I bought all my clothing, except one pair of pantaloons, which the sisters gave me in Liverpool soon after I arrived there and which I really needed. I told the brethren, in one of my discourses, that there was no need of their begging, for if they needed anything the sisters could understand that. The sisters took the hint, and the pantaloons were forthcoming. I paid three hundred and eighty dollars to get the work started in London, and when I arrived home, in Nauvoo, I owed no person one farthing." (Brigham Young, *JD* 4:34-35.)

"The career of Brigham Young was that of a missionary. Shortly after his baptism, he went to Canada, in company with his brother, Joseph, and as a result of their labors, several families joined the Church and went to Kirtland. Brigham Young labored at his trade and preached the gospel whenever an opportunity was found. He joined Zion's Camp when that organization was formed. He and his brother were the 'sweet singers' of the Camp, always cheerful and true. Brigham Young was chosen to be one of the Twelve Apostles, and early in May, 1835, he went to the Eastern States, as did the other Apostles, for the purpose of preaching the gospel, gathering the Saints, and collecting means to purchase land in Missouri. In 1836, after having attended the solemn assembly at Kirtland and received a promised endowment, he went on another mission to the Eastern States, traveling through New York, Vermont, Massachusetts, and Rhode Island, returning to Kirtland in the fall, where he became one of the chief supports of the Prophet, during the time of financial crash and apostasy. In 1840, Brigham Young, accompanied by Heber C. Kimball, Parley P. Pratt, Orson Pratt, George A. Smith, and Reuben Hedlock, left New York for a mission to Great Britain, where he labored with indomitable zeal and great success. On the 20th of

April, 1841, he set sail for New York on his return journey. While in the British mission field, he had been instrumental in performing a great work. He says 'Through the mercy of God we have gained many friends, established churches in almost every noted town and city of Great Britain, baptized between seven and eight thousand souls, printed 5,000 Books of Mormon, 3,000 hymn books, 2,500 volumes of the *Millennial Star,* and fifty thousand tracts.' It was shortly after the arrival of Brigham Young in Nauvoo, after his British mission, that this Revelation was received, in which the Lord expresses approval of his labors and commands him to leave his family no more, but to send His word abroad and provide for his family." (Smith and Sjodahl, *DCC,* pp. 796-97.)

SECTION 127

Background information on section 127

"During the summer and fall of 1842, the Prophet Joseph Smith was forced to go into hiding because of the attempt on the part of the Missouri mobocrats to get him in their clutches. He had been accused by ex-governor Boggs as being an accessory and Orrin Porter Rockwell as the principal in the shooting of Boggs, May 6, 1842. This was a conspiracy to get the Prophet back into the hands of the Missourian mobbers. Governor Carlin of Illinois, had joined in this conspiracy contrary to every principle of correct law, as it was later shown in the trial which was held in Springfield [Illinois]. . . . From his place of concealment the Prophet wrote these two letters (Sections 127 and 128 in the Doctrine and Covenants) by revelation to the Church." (Joseph Fielding Smith, *CHMR* 2:328.)

127:1 *"my enemies . . . pursue me without a cause"*

"I told them [members of the Church] it was likely I would have again to hide up in the woods, but they must not be discouraged, but build up the city, the Temple, etc. When my enemies take away my rights, I will bear it and keep out of the way; but if they take away your rights, I will fight for you. I blessed them and departed." (Joseph Smith, *HC* 5:181.)

127:2 *"unless I was ordained from before the foundation of the world"*

See *Foreordination* and *Pre-earthly existence* in Appendix A.

127:5 *"baptism for your dead"*

See *Dead* in Appendix A.

127:6 *"let there be a recorder . . . [an] eye witness"*

"I have one remark to make respecting the baptism for the dead to suffice for the time being, until I have opportunity to discuss the subject at greater length—all persons baptized for the dead must have a recorder present, that he may be an eyewitness to record and testify of the truth and validity of his record. It will be necessary, in the Grand Council, that these things be testified to by competent witnesses. Therefore let the recording and witnessing of baptisms for the dead be carefully attended to from this time forth. [D&C 128:2-5.] If there is any lack, it may be at the expense of our friends; they may not come forth." (Joseph Smith, *HC* 5:141.)

127:7   *"whatsoever you bind on earth, may be bound in heaven"*

See *Sealing power* in Appendix A.

"What is bound or sealed in the temples of the Lord, is also sealed in heaven. This is the great authority which Elijah restored. It also covers ordinances performed for the living as well as for the dead. The Prophet said that all of the ordinances for the living are required in behalf of all the dead who are entitled to the fulness of the exaltation. (See *HC* 6:183-184.)" (Joseph Fielding Smith, *CHMR* 2:329.)

127:11   *"the prince of this world cometh"*

See *Satan* in Appendix A.

SECTION 128

See background information on section 127.

"The important instructions contained in the foregoing letter made a deep and solemn impression on the minds of the Saints; and they manifested their intentions to obey the instructions to the letter." (Joseph Smith, *HC* 5:153.)

128:1 *"baptism for the dead"*

See *Dead* in Appendix A.

128:3 *"there can be a recorder appointed"*

See *Records* in Appendix A.

"In the early days of the Church some baptisms for the dead that were not properly witnessed and recorded, were rejected of the Lord, and the work had to be done over again. We know that great care and attention is given to this matter today in our Temples and that efficient help must be secured to do this. . . . Truly it is a great and marvelous work, and not the least important thing about it is that these ordinances are all carefully recorded in the books and are filed away in the archives of the Temple, to be brought forth in due time. From these records the people who have gone to that house will be judged. Nothing that is done in that Temple will be accepted of the Lord, except it is properly witnessed and recorded." (Rudger Clawson, *CR,* April 1900, pp. 43-44.)

128:5 *"prepared before the foundation of the world"*

See *Pre-earthly existence* in Appendix A.

128:5 *"for the . . . dead who . . . die without a knowledge of the gospel"*

"The heavens were opened upon us, and I beheld the celestial kingdom of God, and the glory thereof, whether in the body or out I cannot tell. I saw the transcendent beauty of the gate through which the heirs of that kingdom will enter, which was like unto circling flames of fire; also the blazing throne of God, whereon was seated the Father and the Son. I saw the beautiful streets of the kingdom, which had the appearance of being paved with gold. I saw Fathers Adam and Abraham, and my father and mother, my brother, Alvin, that has long since slept, and marvelled how it was that he had obtained an inheritance in that kingdom, seeing that he had departed this life before the Lord had set His hand to gather Israel the second time, and had not been baptized for the remission of sins.

"Thus came the voice of the Lord unto me, saying—

All who have died without a knowledge of this Gospel, who would have received it if they had been permitted to tarry, shall be heirs of the celestial kingdom of God; also all that shall die henceforth without a knowledge of it, who would have received it with all their hearts, shall be heirs of that kingdom, for I, the Lord, will judge all men according to their works, according to the desire of their hearts.

"And I also beheld that all children who die before they arrive at the years of accountability, are saved in the celestial kingdom of heaven." (Joseph Smith, *HC* 2:380-81.)

Note: This revelation is now in the Pearl of Great Price and is known as Joseph Smith—Vision of the Celestial Kingdom.

128:7   *"the book of life"*

See *Book of life* in Appendix A.

128:8   *"whatsoever you record on earth shall be recorded in heaven"*

See *Sealing power* in Appendix A.

128:8   *"God has prepared for their salvation from before the foundation of the world"*

See *Pre-earthly existence* in Appendix A.

"Malachi says promises of salvation, through aid rendered by the children, were made to the fathers. [Mal. 4:5-6; D&C 2.] When and how were such promises given? This promise was made even before the foundation of the earth was laid. It was part of the great plan and was understood before man was placed on the earth. Joseph Smith, by revelation, instructed the Saints and said that the Lord 'ordained and prepared' the means, 'before the foundation of the world, for the salvation of the dead who should die without a knowledge of the gospel.' [Sec. 128:5.]" (Joseph Fielding Smith, *WP*, p. 176.)

128:12 *"baptism . . . is in the likeness of the resurrection"*

See *Baptism* in Appendix A.

128:13 *"the baptismal font was instituted as a similitude of the grave"*

"The Lord has placed the baptismal font in our temples below the foundation, or the surface of the earth. This is symbolical, since the dead are in their graves, and we are working for the dead when we are baptized for them. Moreover, baptism is also symbolical of death and the resurrection, in fact, is virtually a resurrection from the life of sin, or from spiritual death, to the life of spiritual life. (See D&C 29:41-45.) Therefore when the dead have had this ordinance performed in their behalf they are considered to have been brought back into the presence of God, just as this doctrine is applied to the living. Other ordinances of the endowment and sealings therefore do not have to be performed below the surface of the earth as in the case of baptism." (Joseph Fielding Smith, *CHMR* 4:137-38.)

128:15 *"Paul"*

"He [the apostle Paul] is about five feet high; very dark hair; dark complexion; dark skin; large Roman nose; short face; small black eyes, penetrating as eternity; round shoulders; a whining voice, except when elevated, and then it almost resembled the roaring of a lion. He was a good orator, active and diligent, always employing himself in doing good to his fellow man." (Joseph Smith, *TPJS*, p. 180.)

128:17 *"for Malachi says . . . I will send you Elijah the prophet"*

See *Elijah* in Appendix A, and all the materials for section 2 and section 110, verses 13-16.

128:18 *"the earth will be smitten with a curse unless there is a welding link"*

"The dominant thought in the mind of the Prophet Joseph Smith during his last days on earth was expressed by him in the following forceful language: [Sec. 128:18, quoted.] . . . Why must the house of Israel be assembled? Why must the gospel dispensations—links of a mighty chain extending from the creation down to the end of time—be bound together in one? It is because God is coming down upon the earth, and the way must be prepared before him. Jesus Christ is coming to reign as King of Kings, to inaugurate the millennial era of universal freedom, righteousness and peace; and in order that his coming, which is designed as a blessing, may not prove a curse, a calamity, through the unpreparedness of His people and the world at large, he has set his hand in these days to perform the marvelous work and wonder that the Prophet Isaiah foretold. [Isa. 29:14.]" (Orson F. Whitney, *CR*, April 1918, p. 74.)

128:19   *"As the dews of Carmel"*

This has reference to the heavy dews that fall on Mount Carmel, which is located in the Holy Land alongside the Mediterranean Sea near the modern city of Haifa.

128:21   *"the voice of God in the chamber of old Father Whitmer"*

This was the house in which the Church was organized on April 6, 1830.

128:21   *"Michael . . . Gabriel . . . Raphael"*

"From the Revelations we know that Adam is Michael, and Noah, Gabriel; John the Baptist is called an angel (see Sec. 13). So is Moroni. Who Raphael was in the flesh is not revealed. In the Apocryphal book called Tobit (12-15) he is represented as saying, 'I am Raphael, one of the seven holy angels, which present the prayers of the Saints, and which go in and out before the glory of the Holy One.' " (Smith and Sjodahl, *DCC*, p. 810.)

128:22   *"Go forward and not backward"*

"We must go forward, not backward. I bear testimony to you . . . the whole spirit world is watching your labor and your works, and . . . if the veil was taken from off our eyes, we would see the responsibility of our acts and what would be the result of these things? We would labor diligently and do all we could for the rearing of these temples for the redemption of our dead." (Wilford Woodruff, *CR*, April 1880, p. 11.)

128:22   *"King Immanuel"*

See *Jesus Christ* in Appendix A.

128:24 *"the great day of the Lord is at hand"*

See *Great and dreadful day of the Lord* and *Second coming* in Appendix A.

128:24 *"he is like a refiner's fire"*

The art of refining precious metals such as gold and silver was known in ancient times. The ores were passed repeatedly through the furnace until their dross was taken away. It is believed that the refiner knew when the process was completed because he could see his image reflected in the purified metal.

The descriptive phrase "for he is like a refiner's fire" is found in the Old Testament (Malachi 3:2), the Book of Mormon (3 Ne. 24:2, which is a quotation from Malachi), and the Doctrine and Covenants (128:24). In each instance the occasion referred to is the second coming of the Savior, and the pronoun *he* refers to the Savior. Thus, when the Savior comes in power and great glory, he will be as a refiner's fire because all the wicked (dross) will be burned, and only those who have been refined (sanctified) will be able to endure his presence. Hopefully, his saints will then reflect in their lives the teachings of the Master Refiner.

128:24 *"he is like . . . fuller's soap"*

A *fuller* is "one who fulls or thickens cloth and who cleanses undressed cloth from oil or grease or who thoroughly cleanses soiled garments." (Bible dictionaries.) In order to whiten and cleanse the garments, they are washed in tubs with strong soap "where feet trod out the grime which has been loosened by the lye or soap."

The apt phrase "like fuller's soap" is used in the scriptures in connection with "refiner's fire" and with the second coming of the Savior. When he comes in great glory, he will be like the soap of the fuller, for he will cleanse people from their sins if they will but repent and follow him. (See Malachi 3:2; 3 Ne. 24:2; D&C 128:24.)

128:24 *"the sons of Levi . . . may offer unto the Lord an offering in righteousness"*

See material for 13:1.

"The 'offering in righteousness' is here identified with temple work for the salvation of the dead, which encompasses all the principles of the plan of salvation. When, therefore, the sons of Levi accept Christ and His gospel, subject themselves to the ordinances of the Church, and become active in gospel requirements, they will offer the offering in righteousness of which has been spoken." (John A. Widtsoe, *ER* 1:196.)

SECTION 129

Background information on section 129

"Spent most of the day in conversation with Parley P. Pratt and others. [Sec. 129, follows.]

"A man came to me in Kirtland, and told me he had seen an angel, and described his dress. I told him he had seen no angel, and that there was no such dress in heaven. He grew mad, and went into the street and commanded fire to come down out of heaven to consume me. I laughed at him, and said, You are one of Baal's prophets; your God does not hear you; jump up and cut yourself: and he commanded fire from heaven to consume my house." (Joseph Smith, *HC* 5:267-68.)

129:1 *"There are two kinds of beings in heaven"*

"He explained the difference between an angel and a ministering spirit; the one a resurrected or translated body, with its spirit ministering to embodied spirits—the other a disembodied spirit, visiting and ministering to disembodied spirits. Jesus Christ became a ministering spirit (while His body was lying in the sepulchre) to the spirits in prison, to fulfill an important part of His mission [1 Peter 3:18-20], without which He could not have perfected His work, or entered into His rest. After His resurrection He appeared as an angel to His disciples.

"Translated bodies cannot enter into rest until they have undergone a change equivalent to death. Translated bodies are designed for future missions." (Joseph Smith, *HC* 4:425.)

129:1 *"Angels"*

"The theme discoursed upon is the presence in heaven of two kinds or classes of beings, namely, first, resurrected beings and, second, spirits who are not resurrected. It is not asserted that there are no other kinds of persons in heaven than they, but the subject treated is of the two classes mentioned.

"Comparison with other texts of scripture, ancient and modern, makes clear the fact that there are other grades or classes of heavenly beings than the two spoken of in section 129. It is understood by ordinary students of modern religion that there are perfected beings called gods, who are higher than the angels (see D&C 132:16-39), and to whom the angels are servants. And even among the gods there are Presiding Personages, the Holy Trinity standing at the head. [D&C 121:32; 130:22-23.]

"There are angels of various appointments and stations. Michael is called an 'archangel.' (D&C 29:26; Dan. 10:13.) Some are resurrected beings like the angel that was sent to John the Revelator (Rev. 22:8, 9), and those already referred to in D&C, Section 132, while others are 'ministering spirits sent forth to minister unto them who shall be heirs of salvation.' (Heb. 1:14.) Some of these angels are described as 'the spirits of just men made perfect' and are 'not resurrected,' and others were made ministering spirits before entering into mortality, serving among their fellows in their pre-existent state. Christ was a ministering spirit before his birth into this world. [Ether 3:14-16.] He was 'anointed above his fellows.' The angel Gabriel was a ministering spirit after he had been a mortal man (Noah) and before his resurrection, for Jesus of Nazareth was . . . 'the firstfruits of them that slept.' (See Luke 1:11-30; Dan. 8:16; 9:21.)

"Angels are God's messengers, whether used in that capacity as unembodied spirits, selected according to their capacities for the work required, or as disembodied spirits, or as translated men, or as resurrected beings. . . .

"Angels high in authority have been clothed on special occasions with the right to represent Deity personally. They have appeared and have been recognized as God himself, just as royal ambassadors of earthly potentates have acted, as recorded in history. The angel spoken of in Exodus 23:20-22, was one of these. So also was the Angel already spoken of who ministered to John. . . .

"The popular notion that angels are winged beings, because it is stated by some scripture writers that they saw them 'flying through the heavens,' is a fallacy. Cherubim and Seraphim spoken of by Ezekiel [10:3] and Isaiah [6:2, 6] are not to be classed with the angels, for the angels are of the same race and descent as man, whether in body or in spirit, and do not need wings for locomotion, nor do they appear in birdlike form. They are of the family of Deity in different degrees of progression and are 'in the image and likeness' of the Most High.

"There are fallen angels, too, who were cast down for transgression, as mentioned by Jude (verse 6), chief among whom on this earth is Lucifer or Satan, who has sought on many occasions to appear as an 'angel of light' to deceive and lead astray, and who tempted the Son of God, but failed in his efforts as he did with Moses and with the Prophet Joseph Smith. (See Luke 4:1-13; Visions of Moses 1:12-22; D&C 128:20.) That great spiritual personage was an angel of God in his 'first estate,' and yet never had a body of flesh, but 'was in authority in the presence of God' as a spirit, before he rebelled and was 'thrust down.' (D&C 76:25-28.)

"Thus it will be seen that all angels are not resurrected beings, nor is it so declared." (Charles W. Penrose, *IE,* August 1912, pp. 949-52.)

129:4 *"When a messenger comes"*

"Most generally, when angels have come, or God has revealed himself, it has been to individuals in private, in their chamber, in the wilderness or fields, and that generally without noise or tumult. The angel delivered Peter out of prison in the dead of night [Acts 5:9]; came to Paul unobserved by the rest of the crew [Acts 27:23-24]; appeared to Mary and Elizabeth without the knowledge of others [Luke 1:28-30]; spoke to John the Baptist whilst the people around were ignorant of it [John 5:36-38]." (Joseph Smith, *HC* 5:31.)

129:8 *"If it be the devil as an angel"*

"There are bad spirits as well as good, and the vital question is: How can we know the difference between them? Let us at this stage consult an expert—for there are such—one who came in contact with spiritual forces to a marvelous extent, not only receiving messages from other worlds, but also interviewing the messengers. Joseph Smith knew the difference between good and evil communicants, and here is his testimony concerning them: [D&C 129:4-8, quoted.]

"In another place, the Prophet says:'Wicked spirits have their bounds, limits and laws, by which they are governed; and it is very evident that they possess a power that none but those who have the Priesthood can control.' (*HC* 4:576.) To his declaration that 'a man is saved no faster than he gets knowledge' [cf. 131:6], he adds that if men do not get knowledge including the knowledge of how to control evil spirits, the latter will have more power than the former, and thus be able to dominate them. This is precisely the condition of 'the spirits in prison.' They are dominated by a power which they cannot control. They are in Hell, and Satan sways the scepter over his own dominion. [D&C 76:81-85.]" (Orson F. Whitney, *SNT*, pp. 310-12.)

129:9   *"you may know"*

"It should be noted that this Revelation came about a year before so-called spirit-rapping had been discovered, or invented, by the Fox family at Hydeville, N. Y., in March, 1844, giving birth to Spiritism with all its delusions. By this Revelation the Saints were forewarned and therefore saved from being deceived by false pretensions or by evil spirits." (Smith and Sjodahl, *DCC,* p. 811.)

SECTION 130

Background information on section 130

"At ten a.m. went to meeting. Heard Orson Hyde preach.
. . . Alluding to the coming of the Savior, he said, 'When He shall appear, we shall be like Him, etc. He will appear on a white horse as a warrior, and maybe we shall have some of the same spirit. Our God is a warrior. (John 14:23.) It is our privilege to have the Father and Son dwelling in our hearts, etc.'

"We dined with my sister Sophronia McCleary, when I told Elder Hyde that I was going to offer some corrections to his sermon this morning. He replied, 'They shall be thankfully received.' [Section 130:1-16, follows.]

"At one p.m. attended meetings. . . .

"Then corrected Elder Hyde's remarks, the same as I had done to him privately. . . .

"At seven o'clock meeting. . . . [Sec. 130:17-23, follows.]" (Joseph Smith, *HC* 5:323-35.)

130:1 *"the Savior shall appear . . . he is a man"*

See *Second coming* in Appendix A.

130:2 *"sociality . . . will exist among us there"*

"A Saint who is one in deed and in truth, does not look for an immaterial heaven, but he expects a heaven with lands, houses, cities, vegetation, rivers, and animals; with thrones, temples, palaces, kings, princes, priests, and angels; with food, raiment, musical instruments, etc." (Orson Pratt, *JD* 14:40-41.)

130:3 *"the Father and the Son"*

See *Godhead* in Appendix A.

130:4 *"God's time . . . man's time"*

"Until our earth assumed its position among the planets, and began to perform its revolutions, and the earth was so far completed as to assume its position among the heavenly orbs, and perform its revolutions as now, present modes of reckoning time could not be appointed to man—either our days or months or our years, all of which are determined by the revolutions of the earth upon its axis, and the moon around the earth, and the earth in its orbit around the sun. But what is the rule or measure of time by which God reckons his labor and work? . . . There is, one saying of Apostle Peter which reads—'Be not ignorant of this one thing, that one day is with the Lord as a thousand years, and a thousand years as one day.' [2 Pet. 3:8.] But whether that has any reference to the days that Moses speaks of, in which the Lord was engaged in the formation of this earth, we are not told. [Gen. 1; Moses 2.]" (Erastus Snow, *JD* 19:324.)

130:5   *"angels who minister to this earth . . . belong to it"*

"We have no doubt of the correctness of the statement of the Prophet Joseph Smith that 'there are no angels that minister to this earth but those who do belong or have belonged to it'; but that does not necessarily imply that they took a mortal body. In our opinion they belonged to this earth from the time of its creation, when they covenanted to come and take the bodies thereon, at the time that the morning stars sang together and all the sons of God shouted for joy. [Job 38:4-7.] In just this same way was Jesus 'the Lamb slain from before the foundation of the world.' [Rev. 13:8.]

"We are taught to believe that Adam was the first man who took a body on this earth. [D&C 84:16; Moses 2:27; Abr. 4:27; 1 Ne. 5:11; 2 Ne. 2:22.] There was no death before he fell. Who, then, was the angel who taught him the law of sacrifice, or of faith and baptism? [Moses 4:31; 5:5-9; 6:51-53.] We cannot admit that the scriptures are false, and that these beings were not angels; neither can we admit that Adam was not the first man, and that the Savior was not the first fruits of the resurrection. Therefore, we are forced to the conclusion that the word 'angel' is used in the scriptures for any heavenly being bearing God's message or fulfilling His commands; and, further, that all beings who were created with the design that they should inhabit this earth, belong to it, and to no other planet." (George Q. Cannon, *JI,* Jan. 15, 1891, pp. 53-54.)

"When messengers are sent to minister to the inhabitants of this earth, they are not strangers, but from the ranks of our kindred, friends, and fellow-beings and fellow-servants. The ancient Prophets who died were those who came to visit their fellow creatures upon the earth. [D&C 129:3.] They came to Abraham, to Isaac, and to Jacob; it was such beings,—holy beings if you please,—that waited upon the Savior and administered to Him on the Mount. The angel that visited John when an exile, and unfolded to his vision future events in the history of man upon the earth, was one who had been here, and who had toiled and suffered in common with the people of God. . . . In like manner our fathers and mothers, brothers, sisters and friends who have passed away from this earth, having been faithful, and worthy to enjoy these rights and privileges, may have a mission given them to visit their relatives and friends upon the earth again, bringing from the divine presence messages of love, of warning, of reproof and instruction to those whom they have learned to love in the flesh." (Joseph F. Smith, *JD* 22:351.)

130:7   *"they reside in the presence of God"*

"Gods have an ascendancy over the angels [D&C 76:88; 132:16], who are ministering servants. In the resurrection, some are raised to be angels; others are raised to become Gods. [D&C 76:54-62; 132:17.]" (Joseph Smith, *HC* 5:426-27.)

:8, 10   *"Urim and Thummim"*

See *Urim and Thummim* in Appendix A.

130:9   *"This earth . . . will be a Urim and Thummim"*

See *Earth* and *Urim and Thummim* in Appendix A.

"Then will the earth receive its resurrection, for it, as well as man and all other living creatures, was redeemed by the atonement of Jesus Christ from the fallen state. When that day comes, the earth will become the sea of glass spoken of in John's Revelation. [Rev. 4:6; D&C 77:1.] This is a figure of speech typifying the earth in its celestial form. . . .

"Also speaking of this condition, President Brigham Young has said: 'When it (the Earth) becomes celestialized, it will be like the sun, and be prepared for the habitation of the saints, and be brought back into the presence of the Father and the Son. It will not then be an opaque body as it now is, but it will be like the stars of the firmament, full of light and glory; it will be a body of light. John compares it, in its celestial state to a sea of glass.' (*JD* 7:163.) He also said: 'When the earth is sanctified, cleansed, and purified by fire, and returns to its paradisiacal state, and becomes like a sea of glass, urim and thummim; . . . then and not till then, will the saints receive their everlasting inheritance.' " (Joseph Fielding Smith, *JD* 17:117.)

"This earth, when it becomes purified and sanctified, or celestialized, will become like a sea of glass; and a person, by looking into it, can know things past, present, and to come; though none but celestialized beings can enjoy this privilege. They will look into the earth, and the things they desire to know will be exhibited to them, the same as the face is seen by looking into a mirror." (Brigham Young, *JD* 9:87.)

130:13   *"It [the Civil War] may probably arise through the slave question"*

"It is a part of a prophet's work not only to foretell and warn of impending conflicts and calamities, but also to show the means of escape. Joseph Smith was a prophet—statesman. He predicted the war which would terminate in the death and misery of many souls [D&C 87:1]; but this great prophet had a peace offering to give to the people. He told them of ways and means to avoid war. . . .

"In 1844 the Prophet Joseph Smith gave the following counsel with respect to a coming event which was soon to cast its black shadow over the land, and which was of great and general concern. 'Pray Congress to pay every man a reasonable price for his slaves out of the surplus revenue arising from the sale of public lands, and from deduction of pay from the members of Congress, break off the shackles from the poor black man, and hire him to labor with other human beings, for an hour of virtuous liberty on earth is worth a whole eternity of bondage. . . .'

"Abraham Lincoln, the Great Emancipator, probably knew Joseph Smith very well. During a political campaign he wrote a letter in which 'he gives a long list of names to which he wants documents to be sent,' and in the same letter he tells a candidate 'that Joseph Smith is an admirer of his, and that a few documents had better be mailed to the Mormon people.' Abraham Lincoln was familiar with the prophetic message that Joseph Smith delivered and the means to escape that the Prophet opened up to the nation to save the people from the dreadful calamity which bathed the land in the blood of human bodies. . . .

"Lincoln wrote, in his own hand, the joint resolution to be presented to Congress, providing an appropriation of $400,000,000 to be paid to the owners of the slaves if war should cease immediately. He laid this proposition before his cabinet, but it was unanimously disapproved. The great and lonely Lincoln, the best friend the South had, turned away sadly. 'I see,' he said, 'you are all against me. The war is costing us $3,000,000 a day, and think of the lives being lost.' (*Abraham Lincoln, A History,* by John G. Nicolay and John Hay, 10:132-39.)

"Oh, if the words of Joseph Smith, the prophet-statesman, had been heeded, what an effusion of blood would have been prevented! Those young men buried in soldiers' graves would have walked the earth in the full vigor of youth and splendid manhood if the nation had accepted the means of escape which Joseph Smith pointed out to them." (Charles A. Callis, *CR,* October 1938, pp. 24-25.)

130:19 *"diligence and obedience"*

See *Obedience* in Appendix A.

"This scripture . . . is no doubt one of the most quoted in the Church. . . . [D&C 130:18-19, quoted.] Those words are most meaningful—and I have no fear of learning, of the pursuit of knowledge, for any of our young people, if they will keep in mind *diligence and obedience*—obedience to the commandments of God, diligence in keeping close to the Church, in keeping active, keeping prayerful, keeping clean, keeping circumspect in their conduct." (Richard L. Evans, *CR,* April 1956, pp. 43-44.)

:19-21 *"all blessings are predicated"* upon obedience to law

"This being true [D&C 130:19-21], then it would seem that we all should place the pursuit of light and truth, or intelligence, uppermost in our selection of goals, since we may have them eternally. We must seek after enlightenment. Since 'the glory of God is intelligence' (D&C 93:36), if we would be like our Heavenly Father, our course is fixed." (Hartman Rector, Jr., *Ensign,* June 1971, p. 79.)

0:22-23 *"the Father . . . Son . . . Holy Ghost"*

See *Godhead* in Appendix A.

SECTION 131

Background information on section 131

"Ramus, where this Revelation was received, was a settlement situated about 22 miles southeast of Nauvoo. The Prophet often visited this place and preached some powerful discourses there.

"On the 16th of May, 1843, a little company, consisting of Joseph Smith, George Miller, William Clayton, Eliza and Lydia Partridge, and J. M. Smith, went to Ramus. The Prophet and William Clayton stayed at Benjamin F. Johnson's over night. Before retiring, the little party of friends engaged in conversation on spiritual topics. The Prophet told them that 'except a man and his wife enter into an everlasting covenant and be married for eternity, while in this probation, by the power and authority of the holy Priesthood, they will cease to increase when they die; that is, they will not have any children after the resurrection.' Then he spoke of the unpardonable sin, explaining that it consists in shedding innocent blood, or being accessory thereto. 'All other sins,' he said, 'will be visited with judgment in the flesh, the spirit being delivered to the buffetings of Satan until the day of the Lord Jesus.' Then he spoke of the three heavens in the celestial glory, as recorded in the first four verses of this Revelation.

"On the 17th of May the Prophet preached a discourse on II. Pet. 1, and showed that knowledge is power. Among the truths announced at this time was that recorded in the 5th and 6th verses of this Revelation.

"In the evening the Prophet went to hear a Methodist preach. After the sermon he offered some corrections. On Gen. 2:7 he observed that it ought to read, 'God breathed into Adam his [that is, Adam's] spirit or breath of life'; but when the word *ruach* applies to Eve, it should be translated 'lives.'

"He added the truths recorded in the 7th and 8th verses of this Revelation." (Smith and Sjodahl, *DCC*, pp. 818-19.)

131:1 *"In the celestial glory there are three heavens or degrees"*

See *Celestial* and *Degrees of glory* in Appendix A.

131:2 *"the new and everlasting covenant of marriage"*

See *Marriage* and *Covenant* in Appendix A.

"The new and everlasting covenant is the fulness of the Gospel, in other words, the sum total of all the covenants, contracts, bonds, obligations, etc. that belong to the Gospel. Marriage for time and eternity is not *the* new and everlasting covenant, but one of the covenants which belong to the new and everlasting covenant." (Smith and Sjodahl, *DCC,* p. 818.)

"We believe in the eternal nature of the marriage relation, that man and woman are destined, as husband and wife, to dwell together eternally. We believe that we are organized as we are, with all these affections, with all this love for each other, for a definite purpose, something far more lasting than to be extinguished when death shall overtake us. We believe that when a man and woman are united as husband and wife, and they love each other, their hearts and feelings are one, that that love is as enduring as eternity itself, and that when death overtakes them it will neither extinguish nor cool that love, but that it will brighten and kindle it to a purer flame, and that it will endure through eternity; and that,if we have offspring they will be with us and our mutual associations will be one of the chief joys of the heaven to which we are hastening. . . . God has restored the everlasting priesthood, by which ties can be formed, consecrated and consummated, which shall be as enduring as we ourselves are enduring, that is, as our spiritual nature; and husbands and wives will be united together, and they and their children will dwell and associate together eternally, and this, as I have said, will constitute one of the chief joys of heaven; and we look forward to it with delightful anticipations." (George Q. Cannon, *JD* 14:320-21.)

131:4 *"an increase"*

"Except a man and his wife enter into an everlasting covenant and be married for eternity, while in this probation, by the power and authority of the Holy Priesthood, they will cease to increase when they die; that is, they will not have any children after the resurrection." (Joseph Smith, *HC* 5:391.)

"What do we mean by endless or eternal increase? We mean that through the righteousness and faithfulness of men and women who keep the commandments of God they will come forth with celestial bodies, fitted and prepared to enter into their great, high and eternal glory in the celestial kingdom of God; and unto them, through their preparation, there will come children, who will be spirit children. I don't think that is very difficult to comprehend and understand. The nature of the offspring is determined by the nature of the substance that flows in the veins of the being. When blood flows in the veins of the being, the offspring will be what blood produces, which is tangible flesh and bone, but when that which flows in the veins is spirit matter, a substance which is more refined and pure and glorious than blood, the offspring of such beings will be spirit children. By that I mean they will be in the image of the parents. They will have a spirit body and have a spark of the eternal or divine that always did exist in them." (Melvin J. Ballard, *SMJB,* pp. 239-40.)

131:5   *"sealed up unto eternal life"*

"After a person has faith in Christ, repents of his sins, and is baptized for the remission of his sins and receives the Holy Ghost (by the laying on of hands), which is the first Comforter, then let him continue to humble himself before God, hungering and thirsting after righteousness, and living by every word of God, and the Lord will soon say unto him, Son, thou shalt be exalted. When the Lord has thoroughly proved him, and finds that the man is determined to serve Him at all hazards, then the man will find his calling and his election made sure, then it will be his privilege to receive the other Comforter, which the Lord hath promised the Saints, as is recorded in the testimony of St. John, in the 14th chapter, from the 12th to the 27th verses. [D&C 88:3.]" (Joseph Smith, *HC* 3:380.)

131:6   *"It is impossible for a man to be saved in ignorance"*

See *Knowledge* in Appendix A.

"A man is saved no faster than he gets knowledge, for if he does not get knowledge, he will be brought into captivity by some evil power in the other world, as evil spirits will have more knowledge, and consequently more power than many men who are on the earth. Hence it needs revelation to assist us, and give us knowledge of the things of God." (Joseph Smith, *HC* 4:588.)

"Man can no more be saved in his ignorance than he can be saved in his sins. The gospel helps us to overcome both and here again it becomes the power unto our salvation, if we do our part." (Hugh B. Brown, *Eternal Quest,* p. 89.)

"Knowledge tested and tried is the beginning of faith. For that reason, 'it is impossible for a man to be saved in ignorance.' The extent of a person's faith depends in part on the amount of his knowledge. The more knowledge he gathers, the more extensive becomes his field of faith. The degree of faith possessed by any man depends not upon the extent of his knowledge, but upon the certainty of his knowledge, which leads to the proper use of his knowledge. Thus a man of great knowledge may have weak faith, while one of limited information may have strong faith. (Alma 32:34-41.)" (John A. Widtsoe, *JS,* p. 163.)

131:7   *"All spirit is matter"*

"The spirit of man is not a created being; it existed from eternity, and will exist to eternity. [D&C 93:29; Abr. 3:18.] Anything created cannot be eternal; and earth, water, etc., had their existence in an elementary state, from eternity." (Joseph Smith, *HC* 3:387.)

"The materials out of which this earth was formed, are just as eternal as the materials of the glorious personage of the Lord himself. . . . This Being, when he formed the earth, did not form it out of something that had no existence, but he formed it out of materials that had an existence from all eternity: they never had a beginning, neither will one particle of substance now in existence ever have an end. There are just as many particles now as there were at any previous period of duration, and will be while eternity lasts. Substance had no beginning; to say that laws had no beginning would be another thing; some laws might have been eternal, while others might have had a lawgiver. But the earth was formed out of eternal materials, and it was made to be inhabited and God peopled it with creatures of his own formation." (Orson Pratt, *JD* 19:286.)

131:8   *"We cannot see it"*

"The unseen world is much larger and greater and much more important than the world that is seen, the world in

which we live. The world in which we live is greatly
magnified by the fact that we can behold it with our mortal
eyes. The unseen world suffers in this respect, because we do
not see it with the mortal eye. Somebody may ask: 'Can it be
seen?' Yes, oh, yes, indeed, it can be seen. 'But how shall we
see it?' We must look at it through our spiritual eye, or in
other words, the eye of faith. There is no doubt that what it
exists, that greater world, and that it is very substantial. The
Prophet Joseph Smith has said this concerning it: [D&C
131:7-8, quoted.]" (Rudger Clawson, *CR*, April 1933, pp. 74-
75.)

SECTION 132

Background information on section 132

"This Revelation is dated the 12th of July, 1843. William Clayton, who was Temple Recorder and private clerk of the Prophet at that time, relates the following:

On the morning of the 12th of July, 1843, Joseph and Hyrum Smith came into the office in the upper story of the "brick store," on the bank of the Mississippi River. They were talking on the subject of plural marriage. Hyrum said to Joseph, "If you will write the revelation on celestial marriage, I will take and read it to Emma, and I believe I can convince her of its truth, and you will hereafter have peace." Joseph smiled and remarked, "You do not know Emma as well as I do." Hyrum repeated his opinion and further remarked, "The doctrine is so plain, I can convince any reasonable man or woman of its truth, purity or heavenly origin," or words to their effect. Joseph then said, "Well, I will write the revelation and we will see." He then requested me to get paper and prepare to write. Hyrum very urgently requested Joseph to write the revelation by means of the Urim and Thummim, but Joseph, in reply, said he did not need to, for he knew the revelation perfectly from beginning to end.

Joseph and Hyrum then sat down and Joseph commenced to dictate the revelation on celestial marriage, and I wrote it, sentence by sentence, as he dictated. After the whole was written, Joseph asked me to read it through, slowly and carefully, which I did, and he pronounced it correct. He then remarked that there was much more than he could write, on the same subject, but what was written was sufficient for the present. (*HR* 6:225-26.)

"This was not the first mention of the subject among the Saints. Sarah Ann Kimball and many others knew of it in 1842, and Joseph B. Noble heard of it in the fall of 1840. Orson Pratt says that the Prophet Joseph, in the forepart of 1832, while he was living at the house of Father Johnson at Hiram, Ohio, told Church members that he had enquired of the Lord concerning this doctrine, and received the answer that it was true, but that the time to practice it had not come (*Discourse by Orson Pratt*, Salt Lake City, October 7, 1869). Consequently, the Law of the Church remained as stated in

Doctrine and Covenants 42:22, and as it is to-day, 'Thou shalt love thy wife with all thy heart, and shall cleave unto her and none else.'

"The Revelation is divided into two parts. The first, comprising vv. 3-33, deals mainly with the principle of celestial marriage, or marriage for time and all eternity; the second, comprising the remaining verses, deals with plural marriage. The doctrine of celestial marriage remains in force; the practice of plural marriage was abandoned by the acceptancy by the Church, in Conference assembled October 6th, 1890, of the *Manifesto* of President Woodruff." (Smith and Sjodahl, *DCC,* pp. 820-21.)

"In [July 12] 1843, the law on celestial marriage was written [at Nauvoo, Illinois], but not published, and was known only to perhaps one or two hundred persons. It was written from the dictation of Joseph Smith, by Elder William Clayton, his private secretary, who is now in this city. [Salt Lake City, Utah.] This revelation was published in 1852, read to a general conference, and accepted as a portion of the faith of the Church. Elder Orson Pratt went to Washington and there published a work called the *Seer,* in which this revelation was printed, and a series of articles showing forth the law of God in relation to marriage." (George A. Smith, *JD* 14:213-14.)

132:1   *"thus saith the Lord unto you my servant Joseph"*

"He [President Lorenzo Snow] lived to bear his testimony to the world that Joseph Smith, the Prophet, taught him the doctrine of celestial marriage . . . that he knew positively that Joseph Smith did receive it by revelation and that that doctrine was true and of God." (Joseph F. Smith, *CR,* October 1902, p. 87.)

132:4   *"a new and everlasting covenant"*

See *Covenant* in Appendix A.

"Each ordinance of the Gospel is a covenant which is new and everlasting. It is new and everlasting because it is divine truth and never grows old. . . . This was said of baptism, and the Lord calls it 'a new and an everlasting covenant, even that which was from the beginning.' (D&C 22:1.) It is so with all the covenants and obligations in the Gospel which pertain to salvation and exaltation of man. . . .

"There are some members of the Church who seem to think that the new and everlasting covenant is the covenant of celestial marriage, or marriage for eternity, but this is not so. Marriage for eternity is an everlasting covenant, and like the Lord said of baptism, we may say of marriage, it is a new as well as an everlasting covenant because it was from the beginning. It will be, if properly performed according to the law of the Lord, eternal. In the opening verses of Section 132, the Lord draws a distinction between a new and everlasting covenant and *the* new and everlasting covenant. While the definition is given in the negative form, it is plainly discernible that the new and everlasting covenant is the fulness of the Gospel. [D&C 132:7, quoted.]" (Joseph Fielding Smith, *CHMR* 2:157-58.)

132:7   *"sealed by the Holy Spirit of Promise"*

See *Holy Ghost* in Appendix A.

"I will make an explanation of the expression, 'Sealed by the Holy Spirit of Promise.' This does not have reference to marriage for time and all eternity only, but to *every ordinance and blessing of the gospel.* Baptism into the Church is sealed by this Spirit, likewise confirmation, ordination, and all ordinances as well as marriage for time and all eternity.

"The meaning of this expression is this: Every covenant, contract, bond, obligation, oath, vow, and performance, that man receives through the covenants and blessings of the gospel, is sealed by the Holy Spirit with a promise. The promise is that the blessing will be obtained, if those who seek it are true and faithful to the end. If they are not faithful, then the Holy Spirit will withdraw the blessing, and the promise comes to an end. [D&C 76:50-54; 88:3-5; 124:124; 132:7; Moses 6:60.]" (Joseph Fielding Smith, *DS* 2:94.)

"The Lord . . . said that a man and wife who are sealed by the Holy Spirit of promise shall pass by the angels and gods that are set there to their exaltation and glory in all things, as has been sealed upon their heads. [132:19.]

"In an explanation of what it means to be sealed by the Holy Spirit of promise, one of our brethren said this: 'While we receive eternal blessings at the hands of the priesthood which has the right to seal on earth and it shall be sealed in the heavens, this revelation clearly states that it must be sealed by the Holy Spirit of promise also. A man and woman may by fraud and deception obtain admittance to the House of the Lord and may receive the pronouncement of the holy priesthood, giving to them so far as lies in their power these blessings. We may deceive men but we cannot deceive the Holy Ghost, and our blessings will not be eternal unless they are also sealed by the Holy Spirit of promise. The Holy Ghost is one who reads the thoughts and hearts of men, and gives his sealing approval to the blessings pronounced upon their heads. Then it is binding, efficacious, and of full force.' " (Harold B. Lee, *IE,* December 1970, p. 105.)

132:15 *"if . . . a man marry . . . her not by me . . . their covenant and marriage are not of force when they are dead"*

"The one officiating by authority of the law of the land pronounced you legally and lawfully husband and wife 'Until death do you part.' There they stand clearly before you—Death and Separation. You who are parties to a civil ceremony are to be married only during the period of your mortal lives. At death your marriage contract is to be dissolved and you are to be permanently separated or divorced from each other in the next life. Not only must this thought be a startling consideration, but if there be children and family life that too must end with death. According to the Lord's revelation, all manmade 'covenants, contracts, bonds, obligations, oaths, vows, performances, connections, associations, or expectations . . . are of no efficacy, virtue or force in and after the resurrection from the dead . . . and have an end when men are dead.' (D&C 132:7.)

"Even though the legal officer or minister had declared you to be husband and wife for 'time and all eternity,' unless he had the authority so to speak, then that promise or contract would 'not be valid, neither of force when they are out of the world.' (D&C 132:18.) The Master told Peter and the other apostles of a power beyond that of man which he called the 'keys to the kingdom of heaven,' and by this power he said, 'Whatsoever thou shalt bind on earth shall be bound in heaven.' (Matt. 16:19.) That power and authority, by which holy ordinances are administered, is known as the holy priesthood and is always to be found in the Church of Jesus Christ in every dispensation of the gospel upon the earth." (Harold B. Lee, *Youth and the Church,* pp. 125-26.)

·15-18 *"when they are out of the world they neither marry nor are given in marriage"*

"The following statement by Jesus has been very much misunderstood: [Matt. 22:23-30 quoted.]

"The late Dr. James E. Talmage of the Quorum of the Twelve Apostles, explained the Savior's answer to the question of the Sadducees, who deny there is any resurrection:

The Lord's meaning was clear, that in the resurrected state there can be no question among the seven brothers as to whose wife for eternity the woman shall be, since all except the first had married her for the duration of mortal life only, and primarily for the purpose of perpetuating in mortality the name and family of the brother who first died. Luke records the Lord's words as follows in part: "But they which shall be accounted worthy to obtain that world, and the resurrection from the dead, neither marry, nor are given in marriage: Neither can they die any more: for they are equal unto the angels: and are the children of God, being the children of the resurrection." In the resurrection there will be no marrying nor giving in marriage; for all questions of marital status must be settled before that time, under the authority of the Holy Priesthood, which holds the power to seal in marriage for both time and eternity. (James E. Talmage, *Jesus the Christ,* p. 548.)

"To this explanation add the Lord's own words in a revelation to the Prophet Joseph Smith at Nauvoo, Illinois, recorded July 12, 1843, relating to the new and everlasting covenant of marriage: [D&C 132:15-18, quoted.] Jesus must have had this very thought in mind when he answered the Sadducees who did not believe in the resurrection and whose marriage vows were for this world only." (LeGrand Richards, *MWW,* pp. 172-73.)

32:17 *"without exaltation, in their saved condition"*

See *Exaltation* and *Salvation* in Appendix A.

"From this revelation [D&C 132:4-6, 15-17, 19-20] it will be seen that men can become Gods and enjoy a 'fulness and a continuation of the seeds forever and ever,' only by observing the new and everlasting covenant of marriage, and that without marriage they can only become 'ministering servants, to minister for those who are worthy of a far more, and an exceeding, and an eternal weight of glory.'

"When the Lord said, referring to the new and everlasting

covenant of marriage, 'and if ye abide not that covenant, then are ye damned,' he does not use the term 'damned' in the sense that it is usually understood by the modern Christian world, for it will be noted he indicated they 'shall be appointed angels in heaven; which angels are ministering servants; to minister for those who are worthy of a far more and exceeding, and an eternal weight of glory.' In verse seventeen of the above quotation, the Lord stated that they shall 'remain separately and singly, without exaltation, in their saved condition.' Thus even they will be saved, but not exalted. The use of the word 'damned,' therefore, means that one's progress is stopped. (D&C 131:4.) 'They cannot be enlarged.' [D&C 132:17.]" (LeGrand Richards, *MWW*, p. 263.)

132:19 *"sealed . . . by the Holy Spirit of Promise"*

See material for 132:7.

132:19 *"in time, and through all eternity"*

See *Time* and *Eternity to eternity* in Appendix A.

"We sometimes speak of eternity in contradistinction to time; and often say, 'through time and into eternity;' and again 'from eternity to eternity,' which is simply another form of expressing the same idea, and 'pass through time into eternity.' In other words, time is a short period allotted to man in his probationary state—and we use the word time in contradistinction to the word eternity, merely for the accommodation of man in his finite sphere, that we may comprehend and learn to measure periods." (Erastus Snow, *JD* 21:23.)

132:20 *"Then shall they be gods"*

See *Godhood* and *Exaltation* in Appendix A.

"After men have got their exaltations and their crowns—have become Gods, even the sons of God—are made King of kings and Lord of Lords, they have the power then of propagating their species in spirit; and that is the first of their operations with regard to organizing a world. Power is then given to them to organize the elements, and then commence the organization of tabernacles." (Brigham Young, *JD* 6:275.)

132:22 *"strait is the gate . . . that leadeth unto . . . continuation of the lives"*

See *Strait* and *Eternal life* in Appendix A.

"The way to eternal lives is strait. That means that it is difficult of access, not easily attained. The expression 'continuation of the lives,' means the right and power of eternal increase, or posterity. 'Broad is the gate, and wide the way, that leadeth to the deaths, and many there are that go in thereat, because they receive me not, neither do they abide in my law.' The term 'deaths' mentioned here has reference to the cutting off of all those who reject this eternal covenant of marriage and therefore they are denied the power of exaltation and the continuation of posterity. To be denied posterity and the family organization, leads to the 'death,' or end of increase in the life to come." (Joseph Fielding Smith, *CHMR* 4:161-62.)

32:24   *"this is eternal lives"*

See *Eternal life* in Appendix A.

"He [Christ] will be King of Kings and Lord of Lords, and every man who has labored with him and for Him in this holy ministry will be crowned with glory and immortality and 'eternal lives.' That means more than life, more than mere existence, it means perpetual increase of posterity, worlds without end." (Charles W. Penrose, *CR,* October 1921, p. 22.)

32:24   *"to know ... God and Jesus Christ"*

"To *know* God and our Lord Jesus Christ is to be on the road to exaltation, and this includes eternal increase. But to *know* God is not merely to have heard of Him. It is 'to walk' with Him, as Enoch did; it is to 'believe,' or 'live by' Him, as Abraham did; it is to be familiar with Him, as a child with its father." (Smith and Sjodahl, *DCC*, p. 828.)

"No man can know the Father and the Son who does not dwell in their presence. Those who do dwell in their presence and have partaken of the fulness of the covenants and who have proved themselves worthy, shall be like God, for they are the sons and daughters of God, and numbered as the members of his grand family. The fulness of eternity is theirs." (Joseph Fielding Smith, *CHMR* 2:360-61.)

32:25   *"Broad is the gate ... that leadeth to the deaths"*

"The parallel passage, Matt. 7:13, has 'destruction' for 'deaths.' In this paragraph 'deaths' stands for the opposite of

'lives' in vv. 22 and 24. It is the end of eternal increase. Note
that there are only two gates and two roads. One gate is
broad and one is strait; one road is wide and one is narrow;
there is no middle road; few find the strait gate and the narrow way; many enter the broad gate and walk on the wide
way." (Smith and Sjodahl, *DCC,* p. 828.)

132:26-27 *"if . . . he or she shall commit any sin . . . and if they com-*
mit no murder . . . yet they shall come forth in the first
resurrection"

See *Resurrection* in Appendix A.

"Verse 26, in Section 132, is the most abused passage in
any scripture. The Lord has never promised any soul that he
may be taken into exaltation without the spirit of repentance.
While repentance is not stated in this passage, yet it is, and
must be, implied. It is strange to me that everyone knows
about verse 26, but it seems that they have never read or
heard of Matthew 12:31-32, where the Lord tells us the same
thing in substance as we find in verse 26, Section 132.

"It is wrong to take one passage of scripture and isolate it
from all other teachings dealing with the same subject. We
should bring together all that has been said by authority on
the question. . . . [3 Ne. 27:17-19.]

"So we must conclude that those spoken of in verse 26 are
those who, having sinned, have *fully repented* and are willing
to pay the price of their sinning, else the blessings of exaltation will not follow. Repentance is absolutely necessary for
the forgiveness, and the person having sinned must be
cleansed." (Joseph Fielding Smith, *DS* 2:94.)

132:26 *"buffetings of Satan"*

See *Satan* in Appendix A.

132:27 *"blasphemy against the Holy Ghost"*

See *Perdition* in Appendix A.

"A blasphemy is an indignity offered to God in words or
acts, and in the Scriptures it means also 'heresies.' " (Smith
and Sjodahl, *DCC,* p. 829.)

"The unpardonable sin is to shed innocent blood, or be
accessory thereto. All other sins will be visited with judgment
in the flesh, and the spirit being delivered to the buffetings of
Satan until the day of the Lord Jesus." (Joseph Smith, *HC*
5:391-92.)

"This unpardonable sin is explained to mean 'murder, wherein ye shed innocent blood, and assent unto my death, after ye have received my new and everlasting covenant.' Some of those who have been instrumental in shedding the blood of the martyrs, from Stephen, who was stoned in Jerusalem, to Joseph and Hyrum, who were slain at Carthage, may ultimately be found among those who come under this condemnation. God alone is their judge." (Smith and Sjodahl, *DCC*, p. 829.)

132:29 *"Abraham received all things . . . by revelation and commandment"*

"The next that we read of is that he [Abraham] had the Urim and Thummim, and thus he sought unto God for himself, and while searching unto him, God revealed himself unto Abraham. . . . Afterwards, the Lord revealed himself to him from time to time, communicated his will to him, and he was made acquainted with the designs of the Almighty. The Lord showed unto him the order of the creation of this earth on which we stand, and revealed unto him some of the greatest and most sublime truths that ever were made known to man. [Abr. 3.] He got these through revelation from God and through the medium of the Gospel of the Son of God." (John Taylor, *JD* 21:159-60.)

132:31 *"This promise is yours also, because ye are of Abraham"*

"If Abraham was to be a prince and a ruler, and his posterity become numerous, may we not, if faithful to our God and to our covenants, be as Abraham? Shall there be any end to our posterity? May they not be as numerous as the stars in the firmament, and as the sands upon the seashore? Abraham may be in advance of us; he lived in an earlier period; but we are following up in the same track." (Orson Hyde, *JD* 11:151-52.)

132:34 *"because this was the law"*

"Sarah gave Hagar to Abraham in accordance with law. It is known now that, according to the Code of Hammurabi, which, in many respects, resembles the later Mosaic law, if a man's wife was childless, he was allowed to take a concubine and bring her into his house, though he was not to place her upon an equal footing with his first wife, or the first wife might give her husband a maid-servant. This was the law in the country from which Abraham came. A concubine was a wife of inferior social rank." (Smith and Sjodahl, *DCC,* p. 831.)

132:37 *"they . . . are gods"*

See *Eternal life, Exaltation,* and *Godhood* in Appendix A.

132:39 *"Nathan . . . and others of the prophets . . . had the keys of this power"*

This statement clearly indicates that many of the prophets of ancient Israel held the sealing keys of the priesthood, even though the people as a whole did not hold the higher priesthood.

132:39 *"David's wives . . . he shall not inherit them"*

"A murderer, . . . one that sheds innocent blood, cannot have forgiveness. David sought repentance at the hand of God carefully with tears, for the murder of Uriah; but he could only get it through hell: He got a promise that his soul should not be left in hell.

"Although David was a king, he never did obtain the spirit and power of Elijah and the fulness of the Priesthood; and the Priesthood that he received, and the throne and kingdom of David is to be taken from him and given to another by the name of David in the last days, raised up out of his lineage." (Joseph Smith, *HC* 6:253.)

132:41 *"adultery"*

See *Adultery* and *Sex sins* in Appendix A.

132:46 *"whatsoever you seal on earth shall be sealed in heaven"*

See *Sealing power* and *Elijah* in Appendix A.

132:52 *"and let mine handmaid, Emma Smith, receive all those . . ."*

"Emma Smith, the widow of the Prophet, is said to have maintained to her dying moments that her husband had nothing to do with the patriarchal order of marriage, but that it was Brigham Young that got that up. I bear record before God, angels and men that Joseph Smith received that revelation, and I bear record that Emma Smith gave her husband in marriage to several women while he was living." (Wilford Woodruff, *JD* 23:131.)

32:55 *"crowns of eternal lives"*
See *Eternal life* in Appendix A.

32:57 *"Satan seeketh to destroy"*
See *Satan* in Appendix A.

32:65 *"law of Sarah"*
See material for 132:34.

32:66 *"Alpha and Omega"*
See *Alpha and Omega* in Appendix A.

SECTION 133

Background information on section 133

"Section 133, of the Doctrine and Covenants was received at the close of the conference of November 1, 1831, and two days after the Preface, or section one, was given. It was called 'The Appendix' because it was received after the revelation approving the selection of revelations to be published, and has occupied the position near the end of the volume in all editions and out of its chronological order. The tenor of this section is very similar to that of section one, in fact, is largely a continuation of the same theme." (Joseph Fielding Smith, *CHMR* 1:263.)

"It had been decided by the conference that Elder Oliver Cowdery should carry the commandments and revelations to Independence, Missouri, for printing, and that I should arrange and get them in readiness by the time that he left, which was to be by—or, if possible, before—the 15th of the month [November]. At this time there were many things which the Elders desired to know relative to preaching the Gospel to the inhabitants of the earth, and concerning the gathering; and in order to walk by the true light, and be instructed from on high, on the 3rd of November, 1831, I inquired of the Lord and received the following important revelation, which has since been added to the book of Doctrine and Covenants, and called the Appendix: [D&C 133.]" (Joseph Smith, *HC* 1:229.)

133:1 *"O ye people of my church"*

See *Church* in Appendix A.

133:2 *"The Lord who shall suddenly come to his temple"*

The tense of the verb indicates that this appearance of the Lord in his temple was still in the future as of November 1831.

"We read in the scriptures of divine truth that the Lord our God is to come to his temple in the last days . . . it is recorded in the 3rd chapter of Malachi that "the Lord whom ye seek shall suddenly come to his temple." This had no reference to the first coming of the Messiah, to the day when he appeared in the flesh; but it has reference to that glorious period termed the last days, when the Lord will again have a house, or a temple reared up on the earth to his holy name." (Orson Pratt, *JD* 14:274.)

133:2 *"the Lord who shall come down upon the world with a curse to judgment"*

"We are preparing for the second coming of the Lord Jesus Christ [by building temples], just as truly as the world is ripening in iniquity and preparing to receive His judgments when He does come." (Brigham Young, *JD* 25:192.)

133:3 *"he shall make bare his holy arm"*

See *Arm of the Lord* in Appendix A.

133:3 *"all the ends of the earth"*

See *Earth* in Appendix A.

133:4 *"sanctify yourselves"*

See *Sanctify* in Appendix A.

133:5 *"Go ye out from Babylon"*

See *Babylon* in Appendix A.

"The Lord commanded all the Saints, excepting those who were specially commanded to tarry for the preaching of the gospel and the warning of the nations, to gather on the land of Zion (v. 4). They were to go out of Babylon. This term the Lord, in a number of revelations, and also in John's Revelation, applied to the wicked world and the great and abominable church which rules a large portion of the earth (see sections 1:16; 35:11; 64:24; Rev. 16:19; 17:5; 18:2), and has made the nations drunken with her sins." (Smith and Sjodahl, *DCC*, p. 840.)

133:5 *"Be ye clean that bear the vessels of the Lord"*

See *Vessels of the Lord* in Appendix A.

133:6 *"Call your solemn assemblies"*

See *Solemn assembly* in Appendix A.

133:7 *"from one end of heaven to the other"*

The word *heaven* in this verse in regard to the gathering of the last days might refer to the gathering of the city of Enoch, the city of Melchizedek, etc. There are some who wonder if it might not also refer to the gathering of the lost tribes. For example, Wilford Woodruff made an entry in his record that indicates Brigham Young believed the lost tribes of Israel were off the earth and thus would be gathered from the heavens:

The leaders on their return from Provo made a visit to Logan. Here, President Young is quoted as saying that the ten tribes of Israel are on a portion of the earth—a portion separated from the main land. This view is also expressed in one of the . . . hymns written by Eliza R. Snow:

> And when the Lord saw fit to hide
> The ten lost tribes away,
> Thou, earth, was severed to provide
> The orb on which they stay.

(Matthias F. Cowley, *Wilford Woodruff*, p. 448.)

133:8 *"first upon the Gentiles, and then upon the Jews"*

See *Gentile* and *Jews* in Appendix A, and the material for 29:30.

133:10, 19 *"go forth to meet the Bridegroom"*

See *Bridegroom* in Appendix A.

133:13 *"let them who be of Judah flee unto Jerusalem"*

"In this great day of gathering, the Lord has commanded that those of the house of Israel who are scattered among the Gentiles should flee unto Zion, and those who are of the house of Judah should flee unto Jerusalem, 'unto the mountain of the Lord's house,' which is their gathering place. (D&C 133:12, 13.) . . .

"Jerusalem of old after the Jews have been cleansed and sanctified from all their sins, shall become a holy city where the Lord shall dwell and from whence he shall send forth his word unto all people. Likewise, on this continent, the city of Zion, New Jerusalem—shall be built, and from it the law of God shall also go forth. [D&C 45:66-67; 84:2.] There will be no conflict, for each city shall be headquarters for the Redeemer of the world, and from each he shall send forth his proclamations as occasion may require. Jerusalem shall be the gathering place of Judah and his fellows of the house of Israel, and Zion shall be the gathering place of Ephraim and his fellows, upon whose heads shall be conferred 'the richer blessings.' [D&C 133:34.]" (Joseph Fielding Smith, *IE,* July 1919, pp. 815-16.)

133:14 *"from Babylon, from the midst of wickedness"*

See *Babylon* in Appendix A.

"Now, we are here in obedience to a great command, a command given by the Almighty to his Saints to gather out from Babylon, lest they be partakers of her sins and receive of her plagues. But if we are going to partake of her sins and to nourish and cherish the wicked and ungodly, what better shall we be for gathering? Shall we escape her plagues by so doing? No, there is no promise to that effect, but if we practise the sins and iniquities of Babylon here in Zion, we may expect to receive of her plagues and be destroyed." (Daniel H. Wells, *JD* 18:98.)

133:18 *"the lamb shall stand upon Mount Zion . . . and upon the Mount of Olivet"*

See *Lamb* in Appendix A.

"Zion . . . will still remain upon the Western Hemisphere, and she will be crowned with glory as well as old Jerusalem, and, as the Psalmist David says, she will become the joy of the whole earth. . . .

"Zion will be caught up when Jesus comes, to meet him. Jesus will descend not only upon the Mount of Olives, but he will descend and stand upon Mount Zion. But before he stands upon it, it will be caught up to meet him in the air. Will the buildings of Zion be caught up? Yes. And its land? Yes. And Jesus will stand upon Mount Zion, according to the prediction of John the Revelator, and he will reign over his people during a thousand years; and his associates will be the resurrected righteous of all former dispensations." (Orson Pratt, *JD* 18:68-69.)

133:18 *"with him a hundred and forty-four thousand"*

See *Godhead* and *Godhood* in Appendix A.

"On that occasion he [John the Revelator] saw one hundred and forty-four thousand standing upon Mount Zion, singing a new and glorious song; the singers seemed to be among the most happy and glorious of those who were shown to John. They, the one hundred and forty-four thousand, had a peculiar inscription in their foreheads. [Rev.

14:1.] What was it? It was the Father's name. What is the Father's name? It is God—the being we worship. If, then, the one hundred and forty-four thousand are to have the name of God inscribed on their foreheads, will it be simply a plaything, a something that has no meaning? Or will it mean that which the inscriptions specify?—that they are indeed Gods—one with the Father and one with the Son; as the Father and Son are one, and both of them called Gods, so will all His children be one with the Father and the Son, and they will be one so far as carrying out the great purposes of Jehovah is concerned." (Orson Pratt, *JD* 14:242-43.)

133:23-24 *"the land of Jerusalem and the land of Zion shall be turned back"*

See *Second Coming* in Appendix A.

"There shall be famine, and pestilence, and earthquake in divers places; and the prophets have declared that the valleys should rise; that the mountains should be laid low [Isa. 40:4-5]; that a great earthquake should be, in which the sun should become black as sack-cloth of hair and the moon turn to blood; yea, the Eternal God hath declared that the great deep shall roll back into the north countries and that the land of Zion and the land of Jerusalem shall be joined together, as they were before they were divided in the days of Peleg. [Gen. 10:25.] No wonder the mind starts at the sound of the last days." (Joseph Smith, *Evening and Morning Star*, February 1835.)

133:26 *"they who are in the north countries"*

This has reference to the return of the lost ten tribes of Israel. They will come out of the north countries, but some have questioned whether or not this means they are now living in the north countries.

"[Concerning the] bringing forth of the Lost Tribes from their hiding place, which is known to God, but unknown to man. Nevertheless, I have found elders in Israel who would tell me that the predictions relating to the Lost Tribes are to be explained in this figurative manner—that the gathering of those tribes is already well advanced and that there is no hiding place whereto God has led them, from which they shall come forth, led by their prophets to receive their blessings here at the hands of gathered Ephraim, the gathered portions that have been scattered among the nations. Yea, let God be true, and doubt we not his word, though it makes the opinions of men appear to be lies. The tribes shall come; they are not lost unto the Lord; they shall be brought forth as hath been predicted." (James E. Talmage, *CR*, October 1916, p. 76.)

"It is understood that the ten tribes of Israel, after their liberation from the captivity of the Assyrians, departed into the land northward and eventually were lost to the knowledge of other nations. Just where they went and where they are we do not know more than what the Lord has revealed. We learn from the Book of Mormon (3 Nephi, 15th and 16th chapters) that the Savior visited them and taught them the gospel. They have their records, and prophets have been among them to teach them in part, at least, the gospel. . . .

At a conference of the Church held in June 1831, the Prophet said that John the Revelator was then among the ten tribes of Israel who had been led away by Shalmaneser, king of Assyria, to prepare them for their return from their long dispersion." (Smith and Sjodahl, *DCC*, pp. 843-44.)

"But hear it all Israel, after your sorrow and pain and distress and after the days of your tribulation, your great Eloheim will stretch out his hand and gather you from every nation wherever you are driven, and he will bring you home to your own land, and you shall rebuild, your temple and city, and you shall be delivered by Shiloh when he comes. That will be fulfilled; and all that God has said with regard to the ten tribes of Israel, strange as it may appear, will come to pass. They will, as has been said concerning them, smite the rock, and the mountains of ice will flow before them, and a great highway will be cast up, and their enemies will become a prey to them; and their records, and their choice treasures they will bring with them to Zion. These things are as true as God lives." (Wilford Woodruff, *JD* 21:301.)

133:32 *"and they shall . . . be crowned . . . by the hands of . . . the children of Ephraim"*

"Joseph, son of Jacob, was blessed by the Lord with the birthright in Israel, and stood first among the sons of Jacob. This blessing was also the inheritance of Ephraim, the second son of Joseph. We read in the fifth chapter of Chronicles the following: 'The sons of Reuben, the firstborn of Israel, (for he was the firstborn; but forasmuch as he defiled his father's bed, his birthright was given unto the sons of Joseph, the son of Israel: and the genealogy is not to be reckoned after the birthright. For Judah prevailed above his brethren, and of him came the chief ruler, but the birthright was Joseph's.)' The Lord confirmed this through Jeremiah when he said: 'I am the father of Israel, and Ephraim is my firstborn' (Jer. 31:9). Thus, holding the first place in Israel, it is the right of Ephraim among the tribes to take the place of honor and stand at the head to minister unto the others. The Lord has called him to this mission in this dispensation. As the Tribes departed on their northern journey, many of the people fell by the way and mingled with the inhabitants of the land through which they passed. It is quite evident that those of Ephraim mingled with the nations in this way more than the people of any other tribe, for we have learned through revelation to Joseph Smith, that most of those now being gathered from the nations where the gospel has been preached, are of the lineage of Ephraim. This information has been imparted to thousands by our Patriarchs as they have been inspired to make the prediction on the heads of those who have received blessings at their hands. The Lord scattered the children of Ephraim that he might gather them in the latter days, to prepare the way for the coming of the other tribes to Zion. As the firstborn among the tribes, the Ephraimites receive the richer blessings and will be prepared through the fulness of the Priesthood to crown the people from the north with greater power pertaining to the gospel and their salvation when they come." (Smith and Sjodahl, *DCC,* p. 845)

133:34   *"the richer blessing upon the head of Ephraim"*

"It is my testimony that 'today' is the day of Ephraim. It is the day which the Lord has set to fulfil his promises made in the times of the Ancient Patriarchs, when he said that he would scatter Israel to the four corners of the world, and that Ephraim should be scattered in all the nations, and then in the 'last days' be gathered out again. [Jer. 30:3; 1 Nephi 19:15-16; 3 Nephi 5:24.] Many are being gathered out by our missionaries, as 'one of a family and two of a city' [Jer. 3:14] and they are found here, gathered into a gathering place appointed of the Lord, and they are receiving his blessings. This is why so many of us are declared to be of Ephraim." (Hyrum G. Smith, *CR*, April 1929, pp. 122-23.)

133:35 *"they also of the tribe of Judah . . . shall be sanctified"*

"We have a great desire for their [Jews] welfare, and are looking for the time soon to come when they will gather to Jerusalem, build up the city and the land of Palestine, and prepare for the coming of the Messiah. . . .

"When the Savior visits Jerusalem, and the Jews look upon him, and see the wounds in his hands and in his side and in his feet, they will then know that they have persecuted and put to death the true Messiah, and then they will acknowledge him, but not till then. [D&C 45:47-53.] They have confounded his first and second coming, expecting his first coming to be as a mighty prince instead of as a servant. They will go back by and by to Jerusalem and own their Lord and Master. [D&C 109:62-64; 110:11.]" (Brigham Young, *JD* 11:279.)

3:36-39 *"I have sent forth mine angel flying through the midst of heaven"*

"Now, this is the remarkable thing to which John the Revelator calls our attention; he said: [Rev. 14:6-7 quoted.]

"Wonder of wonders and mystery of mysteries! Is it possible that in the latter days an angel should be seen flying through the midst of heaven, having the everlasting Gospel to preach to the enlightened Christian nations of the world? It is so recorded in the Bible. We believe and claim as a people, that that angel has come to the earth and appeared to Joseph Smith, in the person of Moroni, who delivered to the youthful Prophet a record familiarly known as the Book of Mormon, a record containing the fulness of the Gospel, with a message that said the Gospel must be preached in every nation under the heavens before the end should come. [D&C 20:6-12; 27:5.] Shortly after the visitation of this angel, following the organization of the Church, the Spirit fell upon the early elders, and they went forth unto the regions round about, proclaiming the word." (Rudger Clawson, *CR*, April 1909, pp. 91-92.)

"The restoration of gospel knowledge commenced in modern times in the spring of 1820. The promised angel began the process of revealing gospel truths and powers in September of 1823. By November of 1831 the restoration was sufficiently advanced for the Lord to say to the world through Joseph Smith: [D&C 133:36-37 quoted.]

"We are thus commanded to preach the restored gospel in all the world. We are to carry its saving truths to every nation, and kindred, and tongue, and people. We are to raise the warning voice and testify of the mighty things which God hath wrought in our day. We are to gather the lost sheep of Israel into the fold of their true Shepherd. We are to take the message of salvation to the ends of the earth." (Bruce R. McConkie, *IE,* June 1969, p. 112.)

133:37   *"this gospel shall be preached"*

See *Missionary service* in Appendix A.

133:38-74   *Events associated with the second coming*

See *Second coming* in Appendix A.

133:46-48   *"the Lord shall be red in his apparel"*

In ancient times in some parts of the world, people used to squeeze the juice out of the grapes by placing the grapes in a wine vat and then stomping on them. Naturally, the clothes of those persons who "treadeth in the wine-vat" were soon stained with the grape juice and became the same color. When the Savior appears in the last days, his garments will be red "like him that treadeth in the wine-vat" (D&C 133:48), and "his voice shall be heard: I have trodden in the wine-press alone" (D&C 133:50).

"Isaiah has pictured this great day when the Lord shall come with his garments, or apparel, red and glorious, to take vengeance on the ungodly. (Isa. 64:1-6.) This will be a day of mourning to the wicked, but a day of gladness to all who have kept his commandments. Do not let anyone think that this is merely figurative language, it is literal, and as surely as we live that day of wrath will come when the cup of iniquity is full. We have received a great many warnings. The great day of the Millennium will come in; the wicked will be consumed and peace and righteousness will dwell upon all the face of the earth for one thousand years." (Joseph Fielding Smith, *CHMR* 1:91-92.)

133:55 *"Moses . . . Elijah . . . John . . . were with Christ in his resurrection"*

"Not only did Christ rise from the dead at that time, but others were seen who had risen from their graves—righteous men and women who died before Christ, and who had the privilege of rising with him. I do not believe that the resurrection then was a general one; I believe it extended to those only who, while upon earth, had proved themselves willing to do all for the kingdom of God, and to whom neither property, honor, nor life itself had been too dear to keep them from carrying out the purposes of God." (Anthon H. Lund, *CR*, April 1904, p. 6.)

133:56 *"the graves of the saints shall be opened"*

"It is expressly asserted that many graves shall yield up their dead at the time of Christ's advent in glory, and the just who have slept, together with many who have not died, will be caught up to meet the Lord. [1 Thes. 4:14-16.]" (James E. Talmage, *AF*, p. 388.)

133:59 *"the weak things of the earth"*

See *Weak things of the world* in Appendix A.

133:59 *"the Lord shall thrash the nations by the power of his Spirit"*

See material for 35:13.

133:62 *"unto him that . . . sanctifieth himself . . . shall be given eternal life"*

See *Sanctify* and *Eternal life* in Appendix A.

133:64 *"that which was written by the prophet Malachi"*

See material for section 2.

133:64 *"it shall leave them neither root nor branch"*

See *Root* in Appendix A.

:65-74 *The words of the Lord concerning his second coming*

"When Christ comes in his glory as conqueror and deliverer and to take vengeance upon the ungodly, he shall come as one who has trodden the winepress alone. It shall be the time of vengeance which is in his heart and all nations shall tremble at his presence. [D&C 45:74-75.] In that day he who has sanctified himself shall be saved, but he who has not shall be cut off from among the people. Then the words of Malachi (chaps. 3-4) shall be fulfilled. The wicked shall be as stubble and shall be consumed, but the righteous shall be spared, and their children grow up as 'calves of the stall' without sin unto salvation. The thousand years of peace shall be ushered in and Christ shall reign as King of Kings and Lord of Lords. In that day when the unrighteous question his coming and the authority of his punishment the Lord shall answer them: [D&C 133:65-74 quoted.]" (Joseph Fielding Smith, *CHMR* 2:266.)

133:67   *"my arm was not shortened"*

See *Arm of the Lord* in Appendix A.

133:72   *"they sealed up the testimony and bound up the law"*

See material for 109:46.

133:73   *"outer darkness"*

See *Darkness* in Appendix A.

SECTION 134

Background information on section 134

"At a general assembly held in Kirtland on August 16, 1835, the Saints adopted a series of statements regarding human government. [Section 134.] They are wise and as far-reaching as the Articles of Faith themselves. . . . They were given after the mobbings, plunderings, the assassinations of and part of our experiences in Missouri. They were uttered by a people, who, judged by human standards, had every reason to feel that their government had failed, and that they might not hopefully and successfully look thereto for their protection." (J. Reuben Clark, Jr., *CR,* April 1935, p. 90.)

"The reason for the article on 'Government and Laws in General,' is explained in the fact that the Latter-day Saints had been accused by their bitter enemies, both in Missouri and in other places, as being opposed to law and order. They had been portrayed as setting up laws in conflict with the laws of the country. This bitterness went so far that an accusation was brought against them, on one occasion in a Missouri court, of disloyalty because they believed that at some future time the Lord would set up his own kingdom which would supersede the government of the United States, and so believing that the time would come when such a kingdom would be established, they were disloyal to the United States. Every pretext that could be imagined against the Saints to try to show them disloyal and rebellious against established government, was brought into use." (Joseph Smith, *CHMR* 2:30-31.)

"This 'Declaration of Belief Regarding Governments and Laws in General,' is not a revelation. It was not written by the Prophet Joseph Smith, but was prepared by Oliver Cowdery and was read at the General Assembly of the Church, August 17, 1835, at the time the revelations, which had been prepared for publication, were submitted for the vote of approval by the elders of the Church. At the time this conference, or General Assembly, was held, the Prophet

Joseph Smith and his second counselor, Frederick G. Williams, were in Canada on a missionary journey, and the Prophet did not return to Kirtland until Sunday, August 23rd, one week after the Assembly had been held. Since the Assembly had voted to have this article on government and one on marriage, also prepared by Oliver Cowdery, published in the Doctrine and Covenants, the Prophet accepted the decision and permitted this to be done.

"It should be noted that in the minutes, and also in the introduction to this article on government, the brethren were careful to state that this declaration was accepted as the belief, or 'opinion' of the officers of the Church, and not as a revelation, and therefore does not hold the same place in the doctrines of the Church as do the revelations." (Smith and Sjodahl, *DCC*, p. 852.)

"A general assembly of the Church of Latter-day Saints was held at Kirtland on the 17th of August, 1835, to take into consideration the labors of a committee appointed by a general assembly of the Church on the 24th of September, 1834, for the purpose of arranging the items of the doctrine of Jesus Christ for the government of the Church. The names of the committee were: Joseph Smith, Jun., Sidney Rigdon, Oliver Cowdery, and Frederick G. Williams, who, having finished said book according to the instructions given them, deem it necessary to call a general assembly of the Church to see whether the book be approved or not by the authorities of the Church: that it may, if approved, become a law and a rule of faith and practice to the Church. . . .

"President Oliver Cowdery then read the following article on 'Governments and Laws in General,' which was accepted and adopted and ordered to be printed in said book, by a unanimous vote: [Beginning of article.] 'That our belief with regard to earthly governments and laws in general may not be misinterpreted nor misunderstood, we have thought proper to present, at the close of this volume, our opinion concerning the same.' [Section 134, follows.]" (Joseph Smith, *HC* 2:243, 247.)

134:1 *"governments were instituted of God for the benefit of man"*

"The Apostle Paul says truly: 'For there is no power but of God: the powers that be are ordained of God.' [Rom.

13:1.] At first this is a startling statement. . . . 'The powers are ordained of God,' not that they are always the best forms of government for the people, or that they afford liberty and freedom to mankind." (Erastus Snow, *JD* 22:151.)

"All governments are more or less under the control of the Almighty, and, in their forms, have sprung from the laws that he has from time to time given to man. Those laws, in passing from generation to generation, have been more or less adulterated, and the result has been the various forms of government now in force among the nations; for, as the Prophet says of Israel, 'They have transgressed the laws, changed the ordinances, and broken the everlasting covenant.' [Isa. 24:5.]" (Brigham Young, *JD* 6:342.)

"Taking this article [Section 134] in its entirety we are willing to accept it, for it contains sound principles that are acceptable today, and will be approved by the Church until that day comes when the Rightful Ruler of the earth shall come to set up his perfect government. [D&C 38:21-22.] One statement in this article, we could modify and give a better meaning. 'We believe that governments were instituted of God for the benefit of man,' might be more nearly correct if stated: 'A perfect government was instituted of God for the benefit of man.' The statement that governments, if this is interpreted to mean all governments, were instituted of God, may be questioned. Yet it is true that he holds men accountable for their acts in relation to the governments which man has set up, and which are not approved of God." (Joseph Fielding Smith, *CHMR* 2:63-64.)

134:1 *"he holds men accountable for their acts in relation to . . . laws"*

"This is the attitude of the Church in regard to law observance. We agree with the author of the following statement: 'In reality the man who defies or flouts the law is like the proverbial fool who saws away the plank on which he sits, and a disrespect or disregard for law is always the first sign of a disintegrating society. Respect for law is the most fundamental of all social virtues, for the alternative to the rule of law is that of violence and anarchy.' (*Case and Comment*, March/April 1965, p. 20.)

"There is no reason or justification for men to disregard or break the law or try to take it into their own hands. Christ gave us the great example of a law-abiding citizen when the

Pharisees, trying to entangle him, as the scriptures say, asked him if it were lawful to give tribute money unto Caesar. After asking whose inscription was on the tribute money, and their acknowledgment that it was Caesar's, he said: 'Render therefore unto Caesar the things which are Caesar's; and unto God the things that are God's.' (Matt. 22:21.)

"It is the duty of citizens of any country to remember that they have individual responsibilities, and that they must operate within the law of the country in which they have chosen to live." (N. Eldon Tanner, *Ensign,* November 1975, p. 83.)

"The Great Jehovah will award judgment or mercy to all nations according to their several deserts, their means of obtaining intelligence, the laws by which they are governed, the facilities afforded them of obtaining correct information, and His inscrutable designs in relation to the human family." (Joseph Smith, *HC* 4:596.)

134:4   *"human law has [no] right to interfere in prescribing rules of worship"*

"One of the fundamental articles of faith promulgated by the Prophet Joseph Smith was: 'We claim the privilege of worshiping Almighty God according to the dictates of our own conscience; and allow all men the same privilege, let them worship how, where, or what they may.' But we claim absolutely no right, no prerogative whatever, to interfere with any other people." (Heber J. Grant, *CR,* April 1921, p. 203.)

"A good government must secure for every citizen the free exercise of conscience. Matters of belief or religious practice should not be interfered with, unless they oppose laws formulated for the common good. There should be no mingling of religious influence with trespassing upon each others' field." (John A. Widtsoe, *JS,* p. 215.)

"When a man uses this God-given right to encroach upon the rights of another, he commits a wrong. Liberty becomes license, and the man a transgressor. It is the function of the state to curtail the violator and to protect the violated." (David O. McKay, *CR,* April 1940, p. 118.)

134:4   *"religion is instituted of God"*

"If . . . we admit that God is the source of all wisdom and

understanding, we must admit that by His direct inspiration He has taught man that law is necessary in order to govern and regulate His own immediate interest and welfare; for this reason, that law is beneficial to promote peace and happiness among men. . . . God is the source from whence proceeds all good; and if man is benefited by law, then certainly, law is good; and if law is good, then law, or the principle of it emanated from God; for God is the source of all good; consequently, then, he was the first Author of law, or the principle of it, to mankind. [Alma 5:40.]" (Joseph Smith, *HC* 2:12-13.)

134:5 *"sustain . . . governments"*

"We believe in being subject to kings, presidents, rulers, and magistrates, in obeying, honoring, and sustaining the law. [Article of Faith 12.]

"The three significant words used in the 12th Article of Faith express the proper attitude of the membership of the Church toward law. These words are—obey, honor, and sustain. The Article does not say we believe in submission to the law. Obedience implies a higher attitude then mere submission, for obedience has its root in good intent; submission may spring from selfishness or meanness of spirit. Though obedience and submission both imply restraint on one's own will, we are obedient only from a sense of right; submissive from a sense of necessity.

"Honor expresses an act or attitude of an inferior towards a superior. When applied to things it is taken in the sense of holding in honor. Thus, in honoring the law, we look upon it as something which is above selfish desires or indulgences.

"To sustain signifies to hold up; to keep from falling. To sustain the law, therefore, is to refrain from saying or doing anything which will weaken it or make it ineffective.

"We obey law from a sense of right. We honor law because of its necessity and strength to society. We sustain law by keeping it in good repute." (David O. McKay, *CR,* April 1937, p. 28.)

134:5 *"men are bound to . . . uphold . . . governments . . . while protected in their . . . rights"*

"A question has many times been asked of the Church and of its individual members, to this effect: In the case of a conflict between the requirements made by the revealed word of God, and those imposed by the secular law, which of these authorities would the members of the Church be bound to obey? In answer, the words of Christ may be applied—it is the duty of the people to render unto Caesar the things that are Caesar's, and unto God the things that are God's. [D&C 63:26; Matt. 22:21.] . . .

"Pending the overruling by Providence in favor of religious liberty, it is the duty of the saints to submit themselves to the laws of their country. Nevertheless, they should use every proper method, as citizens or subjects of their several governments, to secure for themselves and for all men the boon of freedom in religious service. It is not required of them to suffer without protest imposition by lawless persecutors, or through the operation of unjust laws; but their protests should be offered in legal and proper order. The saints have practically demonstrated their acceptance of the doctrine that it is better to suffer evil than to do wrong by purely human opposition to unjust authority. And if by thus submitting themselves to the laws of the land, in the event of such laws being unjust and subversive of human freedom, the people be prevented from doing the work appointed them of God, they are not to be held accountable for the failure to act under the higher law. [D&C 124:49-50.]" (James E. Talmage, *AF,* pp. 422-23.)

"Sustain the government of the nation wherever you are, and speak well of it, for this is right, and the government has a right to expect it of you so long as that government sustains you in your civil and religious liberty, in those rights which inherently belong to every person born on the earth." (First Presidency, *MS* 14:321-26.)

"It is most important that all citizens be informed in matters of government; that they know and understand the laws of the land; and that they take an active part wherever possible in choosing and electing honest and wise men to administer the affairs of government. There are many who question the constitutionality of certain acts passed by their respective governments, even though such laws have been established by the highest courts in the land as being constitutional, and they feel to defy and disobey the law. Abraham Lincoln once observed: 'Bad laws, if they exist, should be repealed as soon as possible; still, while they continue in force, they should be religiously observed.' " (N. Eldon Tanner, *Ensign*, November 1975, p. 83.)

134:5 *"governments have a right to enact . . . laws"*

"Not only should we seek humble, worthy, courageous leadership, but we should measure all proposals having to do with our national or local welfare by four standards: First, is the proposal, the policy or the idea being promoted, right as measured by the Gospel of Jesus Christ? . . . Second, is it right as measured by the Lord's standard of constitutional government, . . . the Lord's standard is a safe guide. Third, . . . Is it right as measured by the counsel of the living oracles of God? . . . Fourth, what will be the effect upon the morale and the character of the people if this or that policy is adopted?" (Ezra T. Benson, *Our Prophets and Principles*, pp. 69-70.)

134:8 *"step forward . . . in bringing offenders . . . to punishment"*

"Now, the Lord has provided that those in his Church shall live according to the law, and he makes a distinction between the law pertaining to the Church and what we call the secular law, or the law of the land, but he requires obedience to each. My love for my brother in this Church does not mean that I am to stand between him and righteous judgment. This Church is no organization like that of the secret combinations of old, which the Lord hath said he hates, the members of which were pledged, and bound by oath that they would cover up one another's crimes, that they would justify one another in theft and murder and in all things that were unclean. [Ether 8:13-19.] It is no such organization at all. It would not be of God if it were." (James E. Talmage, *CR*, October 1920, p. 63.)

134:9 *"We do not believe it just to mingle religious influence with civil government"*

"The Church of Jesus Christ of Latter-day Saints holds to the doctrine of the separation of church and state; the non-interference of church authority in political matters; and the absolute freedom and independence of the individual in the performance of his political duties. . . . We declare that from principle and policy, we favor: the absolute separation of church and state; no domination of the state by the church;

no church interference with the functions of the state; no state interference with the functions of the church, or with the free exercise of religion; the absolute freedom of the individual from the domination of ecclesiastical authority in political affairs; the equality of all churches before the law." (First Presidency, *CR,* April 1907, p. 14.)

134:10   *"all religious societies have a right to deal with their members"*

See *Excommunication* in Appendix A.

"There are really only three kinds of offenses of which the Church takes cognizance. First and most serious is the breaking of the moral law in any of its divisions. Second, deliberate disobedience to the regulations of the Church, which tenders a person liable to such punishment as the Church can properly mete out to its members. Third, the incorrect interpretation of doctrine, coupled with an unwillingness to accept the correct view after proper explanations of the doctrine have been made. The first two types of violation are of conduct, the third of belief. All imply non-conformity to the practices or non-acceptance of teachings of the Church." (John A. Widtsoe, *PC,* p. 164.)

134:11   *"men should appeal . . . for redress of . . . wrongs"*

"We shall abide all constitutional law, as we always have done; but while we are God-fearing and law-abiding, and respect all honorable men and officers . . . we will contend inch by inch, legally and constitutionally, for our rights as American citizens." (John Taylor, in B. H. Roberts, *Life of John Taylor,* p. 363.)

134:12   *"we do not believe it right to interfere with bond servants"*

"It should be the duty of an Elder, when he enters into a house, to salute the master of that house, and if he gain his consent, then he may preach to all that are in that house; but if he gain not his consent, let him not go unto his slaves, or servants, but let the responsibility be upon the head of the master of that house, and the consequences thereof." (Joseph Smith, *HC* 2:263-64.)

"All men are to be taught to repent; but we have no right to interfere with slaves, contrary to the mind and will of their masters. In fact, it would be much better, and more prudent, not to preach at all to slaves, until after their masters are converted, and then teach the masters to use them with kindness; remembering that they are accountable to God." (Joseph Smith, *HC* 2:440.)

SECTION 135

"This article on the Martyrdom of the Prophet Joseph Smith and his brother Hyrum, the Patriarch, touches the heart of every sincere believer in the Gospel of Jesus Christ and the restoration of the Church. This article was written by Elder John Taylor who offered his life with his beloved brethren in this tragedy in Carthage, Illinois. President Taylor was severely wounded and carried the balls with which he was wounded to his grave. His devotion and willingness and that of his companion, Willard Richards, bear a strong testimony of their conviction and integrity to the truth of the mission of the Prophet Joseph Smith." (Smith and Sjodahl, *DCC*, p. 855.)

"I have understood that this splendid account [Section 135] of the martyrdom of Joseph and Hyrum Smith was written by President John Taylor, known as the 'Champion of Liberty' who received four shots in his body and who lived carrying some of those bullets to his grave, and who, years after the martyrdom, stood before the people in this stand as the President, Prophet, Seer and Revelator of the Church of Jesus Christ." (Heber J. Grant, *CR*, October 1933, p. 7.)

135:3 *"Joseph Smith . . . has done more, save Jesus only, for the salvation of men in this world"*

"We are living in this dispensation, which is pregnant with greater events than any other dispensation that has ever existed on the earth, because in it is embraced all that ever existed any where among any people of the earth. [D&C 128:19-22; Acts 3:19-21.] Hence why we look upon Joseph Smith as so great and important a character in the world's history. I think he was one of the greatest Prophets that ever lived, Jesus himself excepted." (John Taylor, *JD* 18:326-27.)

"I spoke to the theme of Joseph Smith, the Prophet, indicating that, aside from Jesus Christ, I looked upon him as second in greatness to no other religious teacher that ever lived. And judged by the same standard used in judging greatness in men—by his works—as with Shakespeare, Washington, Lincoln, Einstein, etc.—I still believe my view of him is correct and that he is the greatest man America ever produced. Hence I am convinced that he is deserving of a careful, thorough, and honest study by every person interested in his personal well-being." (Joseph F. Merrill, *CR*, April 1948, p. 70.)

135:3 *"for the salvation of men"*

"Why did he [the Lord] call him [Joseph Smith] into the spirit world? Because he held the keys of this dispensation, not only before he came to this world and while he was in the flesh, but he would hold them throughout the endless ages of eternity. [D&C 90:3.] He held the keys of past generations—of the millions of people who dwelt on the earth in the fifty generations that had passed and gone who had not the law of the gospel. . . . He went to unlock the prison doors of these people, as far as they would receive his testimony, and the Saints of God who dwell in the flesh will build temples and perform certain ordinances for the redemption of the dead. This was the work of Joseph the prophet in the spirit world." (Wilford Woodruff, *CR*, April 1880, pp. 8-9.)

135:3 *"he has brought forth the Book of Mormon"*

"The Prophet Joseph Smith translated a record which was placed in his hands by an angel from God. It's a book of about 600 pages. He translated it in just under two months. . . . I'd like to ask you if you would undertake to write a history of the ancient inhabitants of America and limit your source material to that which was available in 1829? . . . You must write 329 chapters—54 chapters to deal with wars; 21 historical chapters, 55 chapters on visions and prophecies and 71 chapters on doctrines and exhortations; 17 chapters on missionary work and 21 on the ministry of Christ, and remember that every word you write must be in meticulous agreement with the Holy Bible. Therefore you must become so well acquainted with the Bible that you can, with confidence, write your book with no inaccuracies or contradictions." (Hugh B. Brown, *Joseph Smith among the Prophets*, p. 11.)

135:3 *"he has brought forth . . . many other wise documents"*

"The Pearl of Great Price contains the Book of Moses as revealed to the Prophet in 1830 shortly after the organization of the Church. . . .

"The Book of Abraham came out of the translation of some Egyptian papyri from the catacombs of Egypt which fell into the hands of the Prophet. . . . It [Pearl of Great Price] also includes a revision of chapter twenty-four of the Gospel of Matthew. The changes made are revealing to all students of sacred history. The Pearl of Great Price further contains extracts from the early history of the Prophet, recounting especially the events connected with the First Vision and the visitation of Moroni. The compilation closes with the Articles of Faith of the Church. These articles originally formed a part of a letter to Mr. John Wentworth, newspaper editor of Chicago. . . .

"The *History of the Church* is another of the literary efforts of the Prophet Joseph Smith." (John A. Widtsoe, *JS,* pp. 254-56.)

135:3 *"he . . . gathered many thousands of the Latter-day Saints"*

"He [Joseph Smith] undertook to carry the gospel message to all parts of the world, and the success of that project is miraculous. He undertook to weld men from practically all parts of the world into a brotherhood. . . . These people, despite national antagonisms, were bound together in a brotherhood such as is not known anywhere else in the world. That's a superhuman undertaking for a young man without education and with only thirty-nine years of life." (Hugh B. Brown, *Joseph Smith among the Prophets,* p. 11.)

135:3 *"He lived great"*

"You may be interested to hear what a nationally-known writer and publicist and once mayor of Boston, Josiah Quincy, wrote about Joseph Smith. In May 1844, Mr. Quincy and his cultured friend, Charles Francis Adams, son and grandson, respectively, of two United States Presidents, happened to make a two-day visit to Nauvoo. Being well-known, prominent men they were entertained at the Mansion House, Joseph Smith's residence. An account of this visit is given by Mr. Quincy, in the last chapter of his book entitled *Figures of the Past,* published in 1880. I quote the following from this twenty-four page chapter:

It is by no means improbable that some future textbook for the use of generations yet unborn, will contain a question something like this: What historical American of the nineteenth century has exerted the most powerful influence upon the destinies of his countrymen? And it is by no means impossible that the answer to that interrogatory may be thus written: Joseph Smith, the Mormon Prophet. And the reply, absurd as it doubtless seems to most men now living, may be an obvious commonplace to their descendants. History deals in surprises and paradoxes quite as startling as this. The man who established a religion in this age of free debate, who was and is today accepted by hundreds of thousands as a direct emissary from the Most High,—such a rare human being is not to be disposed of by pelting his memory with unsavory epithets. . . .

Born in the lowest ranks of poverty, without book-learning, and with the homeliest of all human names, he had made himself at the age of thirty-nine a power upon earth. Of the multitudinous family of Smith . . . none had won human hearts and shaped human lives as this Joseph. His influence, whether for good or evil, is potent to-day, and the end is not yet. . . .

"Mr. Quincy concludes his chapter with these words:

" 'I have endeavored to give the details of my visit to the Mormon prophet with absolute accuracy. If the reader does not know just what to make of Joseph Smith, I cannot help him out of the difficulty. I myself stand helpless before the puzzle.' " (Joseph F. Merrill, *CR,* April 1947, pp. 134-35.)

135:4 *"he was murdered in cold blood"*

"I told Stephen Markham that if I and Hyrum were ever taken again we should be massacred, or I was not a prophet of God. I want Hyrum to live to avenge my blood, but he is determined not to leave me. (*HC* 6:546, June 22, 1844.)

"It is thought by some that our enemies would be satisfied with my destruction; but I tell you that as soon as they have shed my blood they will thirst for the blood of every man in whose heart dwells a single spark of the spirit of the fullness of the Gospel. The opposition of these men is moved by the spirit of the adversary of all righteousness. It is not only to destroy me, but every man and woman who dares believe the doctrines that God hath inspired me to teach to this generation." (Joseph Smith, *HC* 6:498.)

135:6 *"Hyrum . . . and Joseph Smith . . . will be classed among the martyrs"*

"It was necessary for Hyrum Smith, as well as Joseph Smith, to lay down his life as a witness, for . . . the Lord had honored him with the responsibility of holding the keys of authority in this dispensation jointly with his younger brother. 'It is also written in your law,' said Jesus to the Jews, 'that the testimony of two men is true.' [John 8:17.] And this law was binding upon Joseph and Hyrum Smith. The shedding of their blood also bound that testimony upon an unbelieving world and this testimony will stand at the judgment seat as a witness against all men who have rejected their words of eternal life." (Joseph Fielding Smith, *IE,* June 1944, p. 364.)

135:6 *"their names shall go down to posterity as gems"*

"I would not have you indulge in man worship. God forbid. To Him be the glory always. We cannot glorify Joseph [Smith] without glorifying our Father in heaven. We must glorify our Lord Jesus Christ. We cannot indulge in any worship that will detract from or lessen our worship of our Great and Eternal Father and His Son Jesus Christ. But we can reverence the man of God; we can love him; we can emulate his example; we can cherish his memory; we can perpetuate this in our children; and we can seek to comprehend the truths that he taught, so that by comprehending and by practicing them we may be prepared to dwell with him, and dwell with our Father and our Lord Jesus Christ in eternity. This we can do." (George Q. Cannon, *MS* 57:326.)

135:7 *"They were innocent of any crime"*

"Joseph Smith was loved by his people, held in contempt by others, and misunderstood by the majority of men. Often he was hunted as if he were an animal. Arrest, imprisonment, trial followed one another until his death. It is said that about fifty times charges were made against him in the courts, yet, so the records prove, he was never found guilty of a violation of the law." (John A. Widtsoe, *JS,* p. 33.)

"I knew him [Joseph Smith] when at his mother's breast, I watched and counselled his youth, but when God spoke and taught him, I bowed to his superior knowledge, and although he was a boy and I an old man, and his uncle, yet I was not ashamed to learn true principles from him, and . . . drank in the truths which flowed from the prophet's lips. I was in jail with him and his brother Hyrum a few hours before they were killed, and I can testify before God, that they died innocent of any crime, and that they sealed their testimony with their blood." (John Smith, as quoted in George Albert Smith, *CR,* April 1927, p. 85.)

135:7 *"the martyrs under the altar that John saw"*

"But he [John the Revelator], under the inspiration of the Almighty, and filled with the light and intelligence of heaven, could gaze upon the position of things in the eternal worlds, and saw the souls of those who had been slain for the testimony of Jesus, and the word of God, etc. They were told that they should rest yet for a little season, until their fellow servants also and their brethren that should be killed as they were, should be fulfilled. [Rev. 6:9-11.] . . . His servants who have been called to lay down their lives, will come forth with crowns upon their heads and reign upon the earth." (John Taylor, *JD* 25:285.)

SECTION 136

Background information on section 136

"The Saints were driven from their homes in Nauvoo under the most trying circumstances and in poverty and destitution in large measure, for they had been robbed by their enemies. Therefore it was extremely needful for a revelation from the Lord for their guidance in their journeyings to the Rocky Mountains. The Lord did not fail them in this hour of distress and gave this revelation to President Brigham Young to guide them in their journeyings and admonishing them to keep His commandments. All the members of the Church were to be organized in companies and were required to keep the commandments faithfully that they might have the guidance of His Spirit with them in all their trying circumstances. These companies were to be on the order followed by Zion's Camp in their remarkable march from Kirtland to Missouri, with captains, over hundreds, fifties and tens and all under the direction of the council of Apostles." (Smith and Sjodahl, *DCC,* p. 857.)

"At length, all being ready for a start, on the 4th of February, 1846, the exodus of the Mormons from Illinois began. . . . By the middle of February a thousand souls, with their wagons, teams and effects had been landed on the Iowa shore.

"Sugar Creek, nine miles westward, was made the rendezvous and starting point of the great overland pilgrimage. Here the advance companies pitched their tents, and awaited the coming of their leaders. The weather was bitter cold, the ground snow-covered and desolate as to have dismayed souls less trustful in Providence, less inured to hardship and suffering than they. It was February 5th that the first camp formed on Sugar Creek. That night—a bitter night, nine wives became mothers; nine children were born in tents and wagons in that wintry camp. How these tender babes, these sick and delicate women were cared for under such conditions, is left to the imagination of the sensitive reader. How these Mormon exiles, outcasts of civilization, carrying their aged, infirm and helpless across the desolate plains and prairies, were tracked and trailed thereafter by the nameless graves of their dead, is a tale which though often attempted, has never been and never will be fully told. . . .

"At various points between the Mississippi and the Missouri the Mormons founded temporary settlements, or, as they called them, 'traveling stakes of Zion,' fencing the land, building log cabins, and putting in crops for their own use or for the benefit of their people who came after them. Two of these 'stakes' were named Garden Grove and Mount Pisgah; the former on the east fork of Grand River, one hundred and forty-five miles from Nauvoo, and the latter near the middle fork of the Grand, twenty-seven miles farther west. Mount Pisgah was on the Pottawatomie Indian lands.

"A thousand west-bound wagons of the Saints were now rolling over the prairies of Iowa. . . . Some of the Mormons had early crossed to the west side of the [Missouri] river, constructing a ferry-boat for that purpose, and settled, by permission of the Indians—Omahas—upon the lands set apart for their use by the Federal Government. . . .

"As the season advanced the settlers on the west side were instructed to congregate in one place, and a site being chosen for that purpose they there founded their celebrated Winter Quarters. This place is now Florence, Nebraska, five miles above the city of Omaha. . . . Garden Grove and Mount Pisgah were still inhabited; their numbers now swelled by the refugees from Nauvoo. Here in these humble prairie settlements, surrounded by Indians, hopeful and even happy, though enduring much sickness and privation, which resulted in many deaths, the pilgrim Mormons passed the winter of 1846-7. . . . 'The word and will of the Lord concerning the Camp of Israel in their journeyings to the West,' was issued by President Young at Winter Quarters [Iowa] on the 14th of January 1847. A few paragraphs of this manifesto—the first of its kind, penned by the Prophet's successor—will convey some idea of the nature of the preparations for the continued exodus: [D&C 136:2-11, 20-31, quoted.]

"Agreeable to these instructions the Saints went to work with a will, and as spring opened all was life, bustle and stir at their camps on the Missouri, and at their other settlements on the prairies of Iowa." (Orson F. Whitney, *HU* 1:233 ff.)

136:1-15 *"The Word and Will of the Lord concerning the Camp of Israel"*

For additional information on each of the persons mentioned in this section, see Appendix B.

"In 1847 the Latter-day Saints, under the leadership of President Brigham Young began to fulfill the prediction of the Prophet Joseph who had declared, two years before his death, that the Saints would 'become a mighty people in the midst of the Rocky Mountains.' In the book of Doctrine and Covenants there is a revelation entitled 'The Word and Will of the Lord,' to a people encamped upon the Missouri river, who had left civilization behind, who had been driven from their homes and were making preparation to cross the great plains and mountains and settle in this then empty and desolate land. That 'Word and Will of the Lord' commanded the people of The Church of Jesus Christ of Latter-day Saints to organize themselves . . . preparatory to the long and wearisome ox-team journey to Salt Lake Valley." (Orson F. Whitney, *CR,* October 1916, pp. 54-55.)

136:18 *"Zion shall be redeemed in mine own due time"*

See *Zion* in Appendix A.

136:22 *"I am he who led the children of Israel out of the land of Egypt"*

See *Israel, Gathering of Israel,* and *Jehovah* in Appendix A. Jesus Christ of the New Testament and the Doctrine and Covenants is the Jehovah of the Old Testament.

136:28 *"If thou art merry, praise the Lord"*

"The 'Mormon' Church has always encouraged legitimate amusements. . . . Away back in the days of Nauvoo we find the drama introduced by the Prophet Joseph. . . . Why, even on the plains, after a day's march, the wagons were drawn up in a circle, a man with the violin would take his place by the campfire, and there on the prairie the sturdy pioneers would join hands in a dance, opening it by prayer, and participate in amusement that fostered the spirit of the gospel. Two years had not passed after their entrance into the 'Valley' before they built the 'bowery,' and there presented, undoubtedly, the first drama that was ever given in the West. Later they built the Social Hall. . . . President Brigham Young . . . once said, in substance: 'The atmosphere of the dance should be such that if any elder be called from the party to go to administer to a sick person, he could leave with the same spirit that he would go from his elder's quorum meeting.' " (David O. McKay, *CR,* April 1920, pp. 116-17.)

136:30 *"Fear not thine enemies, for they are in mind hands"*

"Dear Brethren, we are sensible that the account of the death of the Prophet and Patriarch of the Church will be painful to your hearts; it is to ours. We feel and mourn their loss, but they have sealed their testimony with their blood; they have not counted their lives as dear unto themselves as the lives of the Church; they have died in the Lord and their works will follow them.

"The eyes of the Lord are upon those who have shed the blood of the Lord's anointed, and he will judge them with a righteous judgment. Let the Saints cultivate a meek and quiet spirit, and all things shall in the end work together for your good." (Brigham Young, *MS* 25:86.)

136:31 *"My people must be tried in all things"*

See *Adversity* in Appendix A.

"Suffering and trials are essential to the eternal welfare of man. Those who seek a place in the celestial kingdom in exaltation may be called upon to pass through tribulation. At an earlier day the Lord had declared that it would be after much tribulation that the blessings would come. [58:2-3 quoted.]" (Smith and Sjodahl, *DCC,* p. 861.)

136: 36-38 *"Which foundation he [Joseph Smith] did lay, and was faithful"*

"The details of the life of Joseph Smith are familiar to us. He announced at once his glorious vision of the Father and the Son and was immediately oppressed and persecuted. Modern scribes and Pharisees have published libelous books and articles by the hundreds, imprisoned him some forty-odd times, tarred and feathered him, shot at him, and did everything in their power to destroy him. In spite of their every effort to take his life, he survived through more than a score of years of bitter and violent persecution to fill his mission, until his hour should come.

"Twenty-four years of hell he suffered but also twenty-four years of ecstasy he enjoyed in converse with Gods and other immortals! His mission was finished—heaven and earth were linked again. . . . And his hour had come to seal with his blood his testimony, so often borne to multitudes of friends and foes. His Judas came from his own circle— Governor Ford was his Pontius Pilate, Nauvoo was his Gethsemane, and Carthage his Calvary. There were also modern Pharisees to goad the mobs and another martyr testified. . . . The shots rang out! And freely flowed the blood of martyrs, for Hyrum, his older brother, had chosen to remain with him. This precious blood soaked into the earth, sealing an undying and unanswerable testimony which continued to ring in minds and hearts. . . .

"His work was not lost. His testimony goes steadily forward on to infinity. As Alma had carried the torch for Abinadi, the apostles for the Savior, now came Brigham Young and the Twelve to continue the work of restoration.

"Men do not give their lives to perpetuate falsehoods. Martyrdom dissipates all questions as to the sincerity of the martyr. Personalities do not survive the ages. They rise like a shooting star, shine brilliantly for a moment and disappear from view, but a martyr for a living cause, like the sun, shines on forever. . . .

"Today a great people hailed for their education, practicability, and virtue, stand to bear witness that the martyrdom of Joseph Smith, like that of the martyrs before him, is another of the infallible proofs of the divinity of the gospel of Jesus Christ, restored in its fulness through that humble prophet." (Spencer W. Kimball, *CR,* April 1946, pp. 45, 50.)

"Under the Lord's direction, he [Joseph Smith] organized the Church of Christ, with apostles, prophets, pastors, teachers, evangelists, etc., as the Church should be organized, to continue thus until all should come to a unity of the faith. He ministered unto the people, he healed the sick; he loved the souls of the children of men. But, as had been the case with prophets whom the Lord had raised up before, it seemed necessary in this case that the testimony of His servant should be sealed with his life's blood. . . . He had given the keys for the gifts and blessings of God unto the people, and the Father had continued to bless him; finally he realized that his labor was about done." (George Albert Smith, *CR,* April 1904, p. 63.)

136:39 *"it was needful that he should seal his testimony with his blood"*

"Deep down, fundamentally, what was it that brought about the death of the Apostle Paul and the death of the Prophet Joseph? The fundamental reason was this: They were servants of God, and Satan wanted them out of the way. They stood as 'lions in the path,' and were building up God's kingdom in His own appointed way. Both these men had looked upon the face of Deity. Paul had been 'caught up to the third heaven' [2 Cor. 12:2-5], Joseph to the 'seventh heaven' and there 'heard things unlawful to be uttered.' [D&C 76:115.] Each was a divinely commissioned preacher of the gospel at the opening of a new dispensation." (Orson F. Whitney, *CR,* October 1912, p. 70.)

136:39 *"that he might be honored and the wicked might be condemned"*

"The Lord has suffered some of our Prophets and Apostles to be martyred; and what for? That the cup of the iniquity of the nations might be full and that his servants might be crowned heirs of God and joint heirs with Jesus Christ to a martyr's crown." (Wilford Woodruff, *JD* 5:269.)

136:40 *"Have I not delivered you from your enemies . . . ?"*

"The blood of innocence has stained the soil of free America—the blood of a Prophet, of a Patriarch, and of other righteous men and women who have suffered for their religion. . . . They were cruelly murdered, and we as a people were driven out by violence, driven out from the midst of civilization, driven out from our homes and our hard-earned possessions, and our track is marked with the blood and with the graves of our own people from the borders of civilization till we reached these Rocky Mountains, and for no other cause for which we could be punished legally. . . .

"But prejudice was created; men became excited; mobs were formed, and extermination was decided upon, and there was no alternative presented to us but this: either to submit to be killed off, men, women and children, from the face of the earth, or to take our flight as best we could in our poverty to some remote land where we could worship God according to the dictates of our own conscience in peace and in quietness. We chose the latter alternative. We preferred to come out among tribes of Indians of which we knew nothing, and live in their midst and trust to their mercies, savages though they were, than to remain among civilized men, men who called themselves Christians." (George Q. Cannon, *JD* 26:285.)

136:42   *"Be diligent . . . lest . . . your faith fail you"*

"Be faithful . . . be humble. Do not neglect any duty that devolves upon you. Whenever you neglect your prayers, you are on dangerous ground. Whenever you neglect to worship the Lord, and break the Sabbath day, you are on dangerous ground. Whenever you neglect to deal righteously and honestly by any person in the world, you are on dangerous ground and in danger of falling into the grasp of Satan. You cannot afford to do it. Satan has great power in the world, and he is more anxious about this little body of people gathered in these mountains than about any nation on this earth. Why? Because these people have the Priesthood of God; they have the ordinances of the Gospel; they have the power of God for salvation to the world. Hence he is agitated, and he agitates others and stirs them up with prejudice and evil thoughts against the Latter-day Saints. . . . The Lord has chosen spirits that have been sent here for the very work that has to be accomplished. Let us . . . develop the fact in our lives that we are among those that the Lord has selected to come here and perform His work." (Francis M. Lyman, *MS* 56:149.)

OFFICIAL DECLARATION

Background information on the Official Declaration (the Manifesto)

"The doctrine of plural marriage was made known to the Prophet in 1831, or 1832, although the Revelation on the subject was not committed to writing until the year 1843. It should be noted that even then it was not given to the *Church*. This step was taken on the 29th of August, 1852, when the Revelation was read to a General Conference in the 'Old Tabernacle,' Salt Lake City, and accepted by the assembly as a revelation from God and part of the law of the Church. In voting for the Revelation, the Saints firmly believed that they were only exercising their legal right as American citizens. They believed that, as a majority, they had the indisputable constitutional right to regulate their domestic affairs, within the boundaries of their own territory, and that the Supreme Court of the United States would uphold this view, even if Congress should be of a different opinion. And they were strengthened in their position by the fact that not until ten years after the action taken by the Church in 1852 was any effort made by Congress to stamp plural marriage as illegal.

"The first Congressional enactment against plural marriage, passed in 1862, remained a dead letter for twenty years. By that time, the anti-Mormons had evidence that the Supreme Court would uphold legislation of that kind, and the laws more drastic than the first were passed by Congress. The Church leaders appealed to the Supreme Court, as was their prerogative. For years there was a legal conflict. At last, when the Supreme Court had declared the anti-polygamy laws constitutional and there was no prospect that there would be a reversal of this decision, the Church loyally and gracefully accepted it. President Wilford Woodruff issued his Manifesto against the practice of plural marriage, and this was accepted by a unanimous vote of the General Conference assembled in Salt Lake City, Oct. 6th, 1890. This was done by divine revelation to President Wilford Woodruff. [Full text of the Manifesto is found on pages 256-57 of the Doctrine and Covenants.]

"After the Manifesto had been read to the Conference, President Lorenzo Snow offered the following: [This statement is given in full on page 257 of the Doctrine and Covenants.]

"The vote to sustain the . . . motion was unanimous.

"By this action the Church voted to conform to the laws of the land as interpreted by the highest tribunal, and to leave the issue with God. Since that conference, and, in fact, for some time previous to the acceptance of the Manifesto, no plural marriage has been performed anywhere with the sanction of the Church, or the approbation of the First Presidency, or anyone representing them, as was fully proved during the so-called Smoot investigation in the United States Senate, which commenced January 16, 1904.

" 'I want to say to this congregation, and to the world, that never at any time since my presidency in the Church of Jesus Christ of Latter-day Saints have I authorized any man to perform plural marriage, and never since my presidency of the Church has any plural marriage been performed with my sanction or knowledge, or with the consent of the Church of Jesus Christ of Latter-day Saints; and therefore such unions as have been formed unlawfully, contrary to the order of the Church, are null and void in the sight of God, and are not marriages.' (President Joseph F. Smith, at the General Conference of the Church, Oct. 4th, 1918.)" (Smith and Sjodahl, *DCC*, pp. 836-37.)

President Wilford Woodruff made the following statements in a talk at the Cache Stake quarterly conference in Logan, Utah, November 1, 1891:

I have had some revelations of late, and very important ones to me, and I will tell you what the Lord has said to me. Let me bring your minds to what is termed the Manifesto. The Lord has told me by revelation that there are many members of the Church throughout Zion who are sorely tried in their hearts because of that Manifesto. And also because of the testimony of the Presidency of the Church and the Apostles before the Master in Chancery. Since I received that revelation I have heard of many who are tried in these things, though I had not heard of any before that particularly. Now, the Lord has commanded me to do one thing, and I fulfilled that commandment at the conference at Brigham City last Sunday, and I will do the same here today. The Lord has told me to ask the Latter-day Saints a question, and He also told me that if they would listen to what I said to them and answer the question put to them, by the spirit and power of God, they would all answer alike, and they would all believe alike with regard to this matter. The question is this: "Which is the wisest course for the Latter-day Saints to pursue—to continue to attempt to practice plural marriage, with the laws of the nation against it and the opposition of sixty millions of people, and at the cost of the confiscation and loss of all the Temples, and the stopping of all the ordinances therein, both for the living and the dead, and the imprisonment of the First Presidency and the Twelve and the heads of families in the Church, and the confiscation of personal property of the people (all of which of themselves would stop the practice), or after going and suffering what we have through our adherence to this principle to cease the practice and submit to the law and through doing so leave the Prophets, Apostles, and fathers at home, so that they can instruct the people and attend to the duties of the Church, and also leave the temples in the hands of the Saints, so that they can attend to the ordinances of the Gospel, both for the living and the dead?"

The Lord showed me by vision and revelation exactly what would take place if we did not stop this practice. If we had not stopped it would have had no use for Brother Merrill, for Brother Adlefson, for Brother Roskelley, for Brother Leishman, or for any of the men in this temple at Logan; for all ordinances would be stopped through the land of Zion. Confusion would reign throughout Israel, and many men would be made prisoners. This trouble would have come upon the whole Church, and we would have been compelled to stop the practice. Now, the question is, whether it should be stopped in this manner, or in the way the Lord has manifested to us, and leave our Prophets and Apostles and fathers free men, and the temples in the hands of the people, so that the dead may be redeemed. A large number has already been delivered from the prison house in the spirit world, by this people, and shall the work go on or stop? This is the question I lay before the Latter-day Saints. You have to judge for yourselves. I want you to answer it for yourselves. I shall not answer it; but I say to you that is exactly the condition we as a people would have been in had we not taken the course we have.

I know there are a good many men and probably some leading men, in this Church who have been tried and felt as though President Woodruff had lost the spirit of God and was about to apostatize. Now, I want you to understand that he has not lost the Spirit, nor is he about to apostatize. The Lord is with him, and with this people. He has told me exactly what to do, and what the result would be if we did not do it. I have been called upon by friends outside of the Church and urged to take some steps with regard to this matter. They knew the course which the Government was determined to take. This feeling has also been manifested more or less by the members of the Church. I saw exactly what would come to pass if there was not something done. I have had this spirit upon me for a long time. But I want to say this: I should have let all the temples go out of our hands; I should have gone to prison myself, and let every other man go there, had not the God of Heaven commanded me to do what I did do, and when the hour came that I was commanded to do that, it was all clear to me. I went before the Lord, and wrote what the Lord told me to write. I laid it before my brethren—such strong men as Brother George Q. Cannon, Brother Jos. F. Smith, and the Twelve Apostles. I might as well undertake to turn an army with banners out of its course as to turn them out of a course that they considered to be right. These men agreed with me, and ten thousand Latter-day Saints also agreed with me. Why? Because they were moved upon by the Spirit of God and by the revelations of Jesus Christ to do it. (Quoted in *Historical Vignettes*, pp. 147-49, published by the Church Educational System.)

INDEX

Church of the devil, 135-36, 197
Church of the Firstborn. *See* Appendix A
Church offices and presiding quorums.
  See Appendix A
Churches: have form of godliness, 50;
  Saints should not contend with other,
  135; should be separate from state,
  687-88
Cigarettes, 466-67
Cincinnati, 328
Cities, great, destruction of, 435-36
Civil War, 444-48, 652-53
Cleansing: of earth, 46-47, 400; of
  Church, 576
Cloud, God manifested himself in, 423
Coe, Joseph. *See* Appendix B
Coffee, 469
Colesville, 172-73; Saints from,
  transgressed, 299-300; reunion with
  Saints from, 419
Coltrin, Zebedee, 295
Comforter, 247; the second, 656
Commandments: Saints should search
  and obey, 48, 52; God gives men
  power to obey, 96, 346; are all
  spiritual, 200, 473; ten, are still in
  force, 247; must all be kept, 253; God
  may revoke, out of mercy, 304, 624-
  25; first and second great, 319
Common consent, 183-84, 541. *See also*
  Appendix A
Communication, God's methods of, 22
Concatenate, 617
Condemnation, 236, 511
Conference, 159; God's power
  manifested at, in Kirtland, 294; vote
  of, to accept revelations of D&C, 369;
  Joseph Smith sustained at, 412; four
  reasons for holding, 630
Confession, 314, 549. *See also* Appendix
  A
Conscience, 108
Consecration: law of, to govern Zion,
  249, 375-76, 412-13, 544; training in
  principle of, 292; law of, Saints failed
  to keep, 304, 336, 417; tithing is
  preparation for, 345; withdrawal of
  law of, 594
Constitution of the United States, 502,
  526-27
Contention, 135, 146
Conversion: miracles do not produce, 71,
  175; is greater than conviction, 71;
  produces action, 236-37. *See also*
  Appendix A
Conviction, 433, 434
Copley, Leman, 279, 280, 299-300
Corinth, 379

Corrill, John, 290. *See also* Appendix B
Corrupt, definition of, 211-12
Council of the Twelve. *See* Appendix A
Courage, 81
Covenants: definition of, 33; new and
  everlasting, 168, 655, 660-61; must be
  kept to receive blessings, 313, 415;
  reaping blessings of, 406;
  consequences of breaking, 417, 429.
  See also Appendix A
Covet. *See* Appendix A
Covill, James, 234, 236
Cowdery, Oliver: meets Joseph Smith,
  75; had gift of Aaron, 78, 91; God
  knew thoughts of, 79; desired to
  translate, 79, 89; added his testimony
  to Joseph Smith's, 80; possessed gift
  of revelation, 90; failed in translating,
  92-93, 94; describes events
  surrounding his baptism, 115-16;
  received spiritual witness to Book of
  Mormon, 133; objected to one phrase
  of revelation, 158; pride of, 170; had
  no authority to receive
  commandments for Church, 191;
  letter from, concerning persecution,
  209; to take revelations to Missouri
  for printing, 367-68, 670; vision of, in
  Kirtland Temple, 564;
  excommunication of, 580; blessings
  of, given to Hyrum Smith, 627-28. *See
  also* Appendix B
Cowdery, Warren A., 547-48
Creation, spiritual and temporal, 199-200,
  394
Creator. *See* Appendix A
Crooked River battle, 383, 579
Cross, 573-74. *See also* Appendix A
Cumorah. *See* Hill Cumorah

Damned, 313. *See also* Appendix A
Daniel, 347
Dark Ages, 49
Darkness, 78, 413, 496, 576. *See also*
  Appendix A
David, 668
Davies, Amos, 628
Deacon. *See* Priesthood offices in
  Appendix A
Dead: seeking after our, 56; salvation for,
  640-41. *See also* Appendix A
Death: destroying of, 141; spiritual, 201;
  sweetness of, to righteous, 250, 251;
  comes upon all, 337; is temporary,
  452. *See also* Appendix A
Debating, 135, 146, 257
Debt, 346, 542
Decalogue, 247

Indolence, beware of, 297
Inheritances, assigning of, in Ohio, 292
Iniquity, ripeness of, 436, 520
Innocence, 489-90
Inspired Version of the Bible, 240, 269, 339, 477, 490-91. *See also* Appendix A
Intelligence, 487, 488-89, 653. *See also* Appendix A
Interest on debts, 542
Isaac, 519
Israel: gathering of, 104; rejected fulness of gospel, 426. *See also* Appendix A

Jackson County, Missouri, 269-70; Joseph Smith's journey to, 308; first sabbath in, 310; mob action in, 499, 502, 517-18; pure in heart shall return to, 520-21, 535-36
Jaques, Vienna, 479
Jehovah, 558. *See also* Appendix A
Jerusalem, 243, 623, 672; siege of, 263-64; two prophets in, 401-2; redemption of, 560-61
Jesse, 578
Jesus Christ: gave revelations of D&C, 20; church of, restored, 49; created heavens and earth, 122; salvation comes only through, 136; name of, 136-37; scriptures are words of, 138-39; various titles of, 140-41; suffering of, for man's sins, 143-44; pinpointing time of birth of, 148-51; justification through, 155; will partake of sacrament with Saints, 186; speaks sometimes in the Father's name, 193-94; role of, in judgment, 196; is head of Church, 239, 573; Jews shall recognize, 267-68, 677; knowledge of divinity of, 273; all things are to be done in name of, 275; testimony of, borne by Joseph and Sidney, 386; must visit all his creations, 453-54; as Father and Son, 485; did not receive fulness at first, 485-86; is Jehovah, 558; shall be red in his apparel, 678. *See also* Appendix A
Jethro, 423
Jewels of God, 324, 519
Jews: return of, to Palestine, 264, 561-62; shall recognize Christ, 267-68, 677; turning hearts to, 505. *See also* Appendix A
Job, 601-2
John the Baptist, 114. *See also* Appendix A
John the Beloved, 82-83; had power over death, 84, 85; mission of, among Ten

Tribes, 86, 401; words of, not to be added to, 156; little book eaten by, 401; saw martyrs in vision, 695. *See also* Appendix A
Johnson, John. *See* Appendix B
Johnson, Luke. *See* Appendix B
Johnson, Lyman. *See* Appendix B
Johnson, Mrs., healing of, 274-75, 342-43
Joseph, significance of name of, 133
Joy: in saving souls, 134; in reading and pondering scriptures, 147; God wants men to have, 322-23
Judge, unjust, parable of woman and, 527
Judgment: preparing for, 45; according to Golden Rule, 46; by Christ and apostles, 196; terror of, for wicked, 270; criteria for, 306; is not men's prerogative, 341; by bishops, 366; by men in council, 528. *See also* Appendix A
Justice, mercy cannot rob, 198
Justification, 155

Keys of priesthood: to remain with Joseph Smith, 340, 475-76, 574; were held by Peter, James, and John, 410-11; revealing of, is by Adam's authority, 424; restoration of, in Kirtland Temple, 564-69. *See also* Appendix A
Kicking against the pricks, 605-6
Killing. *See* Appendix A
Kimball, Heber C., 275. *See also* Appendix B
Kingdom of God: absence of competition in, 231; compared with kingdom of heaven, 350-51. *See also* Appendix A
Kingdom of heaven, animal life in, 395
Kirtland, Ohio, 226-27; Joseph Smith's arrival in, 238; general conference in, 260; obtaining lands in, 278; Saints to maintain strong hold upon, 343-44; bishop called in, 374; duties of bishop in, 375; stake to be built in, 492
Kirtland Temple: spiritual manifestations at dedication of, 355; Saints admonished to build, 494; neglect of Saints in building, 495; instructions for building of, 497; anointing of brethren in, 555-56; dedicatory prayer of, 557; restoration of keys in, 564-69; polluting of, 585
Knee, every, shall bow, 391-92. *See also* Appendix A
Knight, Joseph, Sen., 112, 171. *See also* Appendix B
Knight, Newel, 300. *See also* Appendix B

Treasury, sacred, 541
Tribulation. *See* Adversity
Trump, sounding of, 458. *See also*
    Appendix A
Truth: finding, 76; is God's mightiest
    weapon, 80; cleaves to truth, 194;
    eternal, pondering of, 259; will not
    conflict with revelation, 288; few rich
    men embrace, 305; definition of,
    486-87. *See also* Appendix A
Twelve apostles: testimony of, concerning
    D&C, 37-38; calling of, 132, 137-38;
    Joseph Smith conferred all authority
    upon, 476; authority of, is next to First
    Presidency, 633; return of,|from
    Europe, 633-34
Twinkling of an eye. *See* Appendix A
Twins, Emma Smith took, to raise, 511

Unbelief, sin of, 311-12
United Order, 403, 483; dissolving of,
    538, 539-40. *See also* Appendix A
United States, birth of, 150-51
Unity, 231
Unpardonable sin, 654, 666-67
Untoward generation, 223
Upbraid, definition of, 433
Urim and Thummim, 22-23, 59, 97,
    127-29; sanctified earth likened to,
    393-94. *See also* Appendix A

Valiance, 390
Vengeance is the Lord's, 508
Vespasian, 263
Vessels of the Lord. *See* Appendix A
Vineyard: corruption of, 211;
    of nobleman, parable of,
    523-24. *See also* Appendix A
Virgins. *See* Appendix A
Virtue, 607
Visions: interpretation of, 272; true,
    require Holy Ghost, 386;
    accompanying anointing in Kirtland
    Temple, 556. *See also* Appendix A
Voice of the Lord. *See* Appendix A
Voting, 503-4

Wakefield, Joseph, 296
War, 336-37; revelation and prophecy on,
    444-48; Saints should renounce, 504-5,
    506-7; justification for entering into,
    508-9
Ward. *See* Appendix A
Warning: God will give, 47-48, 72-73;
    men tend to ignore, 262; failure to
    give, brings sin on Saints' heads, 382

Washing of feet. *See* Appendix A
Watchmen. *See* Appendix A
Waters, dangers upon, 326-28
Weak things of the world. *See*
    Appendix A
Wealth: cannot of itself produce
    happiness, 77; chokes men with pride,
    305; should not be envied, 540
Welfare. *See* Appendix A
Wells, Daniel H., 625
Wheat and tares, parable of, 212, 441
Whitmer, David, 75, 120-21, 203. *See also*
    Appendix B
Whitmer family, 120
Whitmer, John, 123-24, 204,
    276-77, 367-68. *See also* Appendix B
Whitmer, Peter, Jr., 125, 204. *See also*
    Appendix B
Whitney, Newel K., 553, 591. *See also*
    Appendix B
Wicked: congregations of, 325; will be
    swept away, 436; when ruled by,
    people mourn, 503; were permitted to
    fill measure of iniquities, 534
Widows, 419-20
Wight, Lyman. *See* Appendix B
Will of God, men should seek to do,
    559-60
Williams, Frederick G., 410, 477. *See also*
    Appendix B
Wind, sound of rushing, 559
Wine: sacramental, 185-86; of the wrath
    of fornication, 219; pure, 468
Wine-press. *See* Appendix A
Wisdom, 274
Witnesses: the Lord always sends, 70;
    calling of three, 71-72, 126; three
    special, were shown five objects,
    127-30; reasons for calling, 130;
    apostles to act as special, 138; must be
    present at baptisms for dead, 637-38.
    See also Appendix A
Woman and unjust judge, parable of, 527
Women. *See* Appendix A
Woodruff, Wilford, on Manifesto, 704-6.
    See also Appendix B
Word of God, power of, 76
Word of Wisdom: giving of, 463-64; is
    now binding, 464-65; is not vegetarian
    system, 470; implies ceasing from
    every evil, 471; blessings
    accompanying observance of, 472-74
Words, idle, 248
Work, 249. *See also* Appendix A
Works, good or evil, follow men into
    spirit world, 318
World: entire, D&C is intended for,

12-13, 44; darkness of, 78;
overcoming, 339-40; unseen, 657-58.
See also Appendix A
Worship: law should not interfere with,
684; of men, 694. *See also*
Appendix A
Wrath of God, 46-47
Wresting of scriptures, 105

Young, Brigham, 634-36; defended living
oracles over written revelation, 8-9;
was chosen to succeed Joseph Smith,
633; conversion of, 634. *See also*
Appendix B

Zarahemla, 631-32
Zion: seeking to establish, 76-77; of
Enoch, return of, 229, 267; laws
governing, 242, 312, 412-13; location
of, revealed, 309; glory of, reserved
for future, 311, 315, 535; description
of land of, 314; dedication of temple
lot in, 315-16; instructions for
gathering to, 330-31, 334; land of, was
to be purchased, 335-36; was to be
built up by consecration, 375-76, 412,
544; enlarging and strengthening of,
415-16; responsibilities of bishop in,
437; must purify herself, 450;
presidency in, 479-80; is pure in heart,
500; afflictions of, 501, 517; Saints to
return to, 520-21, 535-36; redemption
of, 532-33, 535; shall be gathering
place for Ephraim's seed, 672-73; will
be caught up to meet Christ, 673. *See
also* Appendix A
Zion's Camp, 532; organizing of, 537;
Sheriff Gillium visited, 543; refusal of
many to join, 544; mobbers' threats to,
544-46